International Handbooks of Population

Volume 12

Series Editor

Dudley L. Poston, Jr., Dept. Sociology, Texas A & M University, College Station, TX, USA

The *International Handbooks of Population* offer up-to-date scholarly summaries and sources of information on the major subject areas and issues of demography and population. Each handbook examines its particular subject area in depth, providing timely, accessible coverage of its full scale and scope, discusses substantive contributions for deeper understanding, and provides reliable guidance on the direction of future developments.

Voumes will explore topics of vital interest such as: Population Ageing, Mortality, Rural Demography, Poverty, Family Demography, Gender and Demography, Applied Demography, Migration, Demography of Sexuality, Race and Ethnic Demography. Each volume will provide a state-of-the-art treatment of its respective area. The series will quickly prove useful to a broad audience including demographers, practitioners and scholars across a range of disciplines.

Ginny Garcia-Alexander
Dudley L. Poston, Jr.
Editors

International Handbook of the Demography of Obesity

Springer

Editors
Ginny Garcia-Alexander
Department of Sociology
University of Texas at San Antonio
San Antonio, TX, USA

Dudley L. Poston, Jr.
Department of Sociology
Texas A & M University
College Station, TX, USA

ISSN 1877-9204 ISSN 2215-1877 (electronic)
International Handbooks of Population
ISBN 978-3-031-10935-5 ISBN 978-3-031-10936-2 (eBook)
https://doi.org/10.1007/978-3-031-10936-2

This Springer imprint is published by the registered company Springer Nature Switzerland AG
The registered company address is: Gewerbestrasse 11, 6330 Cham, Switzerland

Preface

We are very grateful to a number of people who made this *Handbook* possible. First and foremost, we would like to thank all of our contributors for providing such thorough, thoughtful, and compelling chapters. We are thrilled to have overseen this collection. We are also grateful to Evelien Bakker, our editor at Springer, who helped to ensure the creation of this *Handbook* and provided us with assistance throughout its development.

The *International Handbook of the Demography of Obesity* will be the 12th handbook in the series International Handbooks of Population published by Springer. Ginny Garcia-Alexander wrote the chapter "The Demography of Obesity" in the second edition of the *Handbook of Population*, published in 2019. Upon completion of her chapter, editor Dudley Poston realized there was enough research in this area to constitute a standalone handbook and invited her to collaborate with him on a handbook focusing on the demography of obesity.

We modeled this *Handbook* on the *Handbook of Population* and also took into account the contributions of demographers to this field to develop our list of authors and chapter topics. We endeavored to include a sampling of works from authors who are active contributors to the discipline.

To develop this *Handbook*, we read and edited each of the *Handbook*'s chapters and sent them back to the authors for review. We very much appreciate their timely responses to our feedback. Chapters were copy edited at the University of Texas at San Antonio by Amethyst Marroquin Morgan; we are grateful for her assistance.

San Antonio, TX, USA — Ginny Garcia-Alexander

College Station, TX, USA — Dudley L. Poston, Jr.

Contents

Contributors

Kathryn Freeman Anderson Department of Sociology, University of Houston, Houston, TX, USA

Sharon Baker-Hughes Blinn College-Bryan Campus, Bryan, TX, USA

Shawna F. Bayerman University of Colorado Denver, Denver, CO, USA

James Bentham School of Mathematics, Statistics and Actuarial Science, University of Kent, Canterbury, UK

Petri Böckerman Labour Institute for Economic Research LABORE, Helsinki, Finland
IZA Institute of Labor Economics, Bonn, Germany

Amy M. Burdette Professor of Sociology and an Associate of the Pepper Institute on Aging and Public Policy, Florida State University, Tallahassee, FL, USA

Yağmur Çağatay Department of Sociology, Boğazici University, Istanbul, Turkey

Keri Carvalho Department of Community Health, Tufts University, Medford, MA, USA

D'Lane Compton University of New Orleans, New Orleans, LA, USA

Adolfo G. Cuevas NYU School of Global Public Health, New York, NY, USA

Mary Ann Davis Department of Sociology, University of New Orleans, New Orleans, LA, USA

Mariachiara Di Cesare Institute of Public Health and Wellbeing, University of Essex, Colchester, UK

Natalie Eckert Department of Community Health, Tufts University, Medford, MA, USA

Ceylan Engin Boğazici University, Istanbul, Turkey

Toni Falbo Department of Educational Psychology, University of Texas at Austin, Austin, TX, USA

Nicole Farris Department of Sociology and Criminal Justice, Texas A&M University-Commerce, Commerce, TX, USA

Michelle L. Frisco Department of Sociology & Criminology, The Pennsylvania State University, University Park, PA, USA

Qiang Fu Department of Sociology, University of British Columbia, Vancouver, BC, Canada

Samantha M. Galindo Department of Sociology, The University of Texas at San Antonio, San Antonio, TX, USA

Ginny Garcia-Alexander Department of Sociology, University of Texas at San Antonio, San Antonio, TX, USA

Jiaxin Gu Department of Sociology, University of British Columbia, Vancouver, BC, Canada

Terrence D. Hill Department of Sociology, The University of Texas at San Antonio, San Antonio, TX, USA

Robert A. Hummer Department of Sociology, University of North Carolina at Chapel Hill, Chapel Hill, NC, USA

Fanny Janssen Population Research Centre, Faculty of Spatial Sciences, University of Groningen, Groningen, The Netherlands
Netherlands Interdisciplinary Demographic Institute – KNAW/University of Groningen, The Hague, The Netherlands

Jamie Kennel Emergency Medical Services, Oregon Institute of Technology, Wilsonville, OR, USA

Patrick M. Krueger Department of Health & Behavioral Sciences, University of Colorado Denver, Denver, CO, USA
University of Colorado Population Center, Boulder, CO, USA

Kenneth C. Land Social Science Research Institute, Duke University, Durham, NC, USA

Shengjie Lin Yale Center for Emotional Intelligence, Yale University, New Haven, CT, USA

Angelica Lopez T. Denny Sanford School of Social and Family Dynamics, Arizona State University, Tempe, AZ, USA

Amethyst Morgan Marroquin Department of Sociology, University of Texas at San Antonio, San Antonio, TX, USA

Neil K. Mehta School of Public and Population Health, University of Texas Medical Branch, Galveston, TX, USA

Jaakko Pehkonen University of Jyväskylä, Jyväskylä, Finland

Dudley L. Poston, Jr. Department of Sociology, Texas A & M University, College Station, TX, USA

Eric N. Reither University of Colorado Denver, Denver, CO, USA

Kelsey Shaulis Department of Sociology & Criminology, The Pennsylviania State University, University Park, PA, USA

Sergi Trias-Llimós Center for Demographic Studies (CED-CERCA), Autonomous University of Barcelona, Barcelona, Spain

Jennifer Van Hook Department of Sociology & Criminology, The Pennsylvania State University, University Park, PA, USA

Nikoletta Vidra Department for Health Evidence, Radboud University Medical Center, Nijmegen, The Netherlands

Jutta Viinikainen University of Jyväskylä, Jyväskylä, Finland

Carol S. Walther Department of Sociology, Northern Illinois University, DeKalb, IL, USA

Hyeyoung Woo Sociology, Institute for Asian Studies, Portland State University, Portland, OR, USA

Yue Yuan School of Public Policy and Administration, Xi'an Jiaotong University, Xi'an, Shaanxi, China

Part I

Global Obesity Patterns and Implications

Chapter 1 opens this section with a broad overview of the demographic study of obesity. It describes the development of the field, key areas of study, and methodological approaches. Bentham and colleagues (Chap. 2) provide an expansive overview of global trends in obesity. Their chapter highlights several key countries that are representative of all major global regions, they detail differences in prevalence over time in these areas, and they suggest ways to engage in more effective surveillance of obesity. They offer a broad overview of the factors associated with obesity as well as the comorbidities that have been shown to be more prevalent in those with obesity or overweight. In addition, they describe the link between COVID-19 and obesity and provide evidence from numerous countries documenting higher rates of hospitalization, ICU admission, and death in those with obesity. Though it is unclear what leads to poorer outcomes in this group, it has been proposed that low-grade inflammation may account for this association. This presents an important area for continued study. Furthermore, they call attention to the fact that obesity rates appear to have been accelerated as a result of changing lifestyles prompted by pandemic responses and lockdowns.

Both Viinikainen and colleagues (Chap. 3) and Vidra and colleagues (Chap. 4) examine the implications of obesity in Europe. Chapter 3 focuses on the indirect costs, including losses to productivity and employment losses, associated with obesity. Viinikainen and colleagues review the literature on this topic, the results of which suggest that the indirect costs of obesity represent a significant burden to society. Vidra and colleagues describe the variations in obesity prevalence across Europe and focus on what its impacts are on life expectancy trends. This is especially important as life expectancy trends have been rather variable in different regions of Europe. For example, in Western Europe life expectancy has risen steadily since 1970; whereas in Eastern European countries stagnation and/or declines to life expectancy have been observed. These authors examine the impacts of obesity across a wide range of European countries as well as the United States.

Finally, Gu and colleagues provide us in Chap. 5 with an examination of trends and patterns in overweight and obesity in China. Public health officials have increasingly called attention to increasing levels of obesity prevalence as well as the implications of such a shift. Their chapter reviews the relevant societal changes that have contributed to increasing overweight and obesity. In addition, the authors describe available data sources and the implications of increasing obesity prevalence in global context.

1 Global Obesity Patterns, an Introduction

Ginny Garcia-Alexander and Dudley L. Poston, Jr.

Globally, obesity rates have been increasing since the 1970s, with recent estimates indicating that approximately 650 million adults, or 13%, were obese in 2016 (WHO, 2021). Among children, nearly 40 million under the age of 5, and more than 340 million aged 5–19, were overweight or obese in 2020 (WHO, 2021). While there are noticeable variations across countries, the overall trends suggest that since 1980 overweight and obesity have increased in all regions of the world. For a detailed discussion of global variations in trends see Chap. 2 in this *Handbook*.

As these trends continue on their upward trajectory, researchers from a diverse range of fields including demography, economics, sociology, psychology, epidemiology, and geography have attempted to characterize and explain these patterns. The World Health Organization (WHO) has highlighted two primary causes of increased obesity prevalence: increased consumption of energy-dense, i.e. high-fat or sugar-sweetened food items, and changing lifestyles that encourage more sedentary activity (2021). However, the body of work in this area reveals its complexity; an array of social, environmental, genetic, and political factors are relevant for its analysis.

Demographers have and will continue to contribute a great deal to our understanding of obesity and its associated mechanisms via formal demographic analyses and population studies. Health demographers have provided the bulk of information on trends in obesity as well as projections of future trends. For example, the National Centers for Health Statistics regularly publish trend data on obesity and overweight in the United States, and the World Health Organization (WHO) makes this information available at the global level. Similarly, projections and obesity forecasts are made available by the Centers for Disease Control (CDC) and the Organization for Economic Cooperation and Development (OECD). Demographic research further informs our knowledge of the impacts of obesity in various subgroups. Accordingly, demographers have undertaken numerous investigations of how obesity levels vary by such demographic characteristics as race/ethnicity, nativity, socioeconomic status, and gender. A number of the chapters in this *Handbook* offer thorough reviews of the literature in these areas along with recommendations for needed research. Demographers have also been instrumental in identifying mechanisms that might account for disparate patterns of obesity in certain subgroups. For example, they have undertaken investigations to explore the role of stress, discrimination, and genetic effects, among others, on obesity.

G. Garcia-Alexander (✉)
Department of Sociology, University of Texas at San Antonio, San Antonio, TX, USA
e-mail: ginny.garcia@utsa.edu

D. L. Poston, Jr.
Department of Sociology, Texas A & M University, College Station, TX, USA

G. Garcia-Alexander, D. L. Poston, Jr. (eds.), *International Handbook of the Demography of Obesity*, International Handbooks of Population 12, https://doi.org/10.1007/978-3-031-10936-2_1

Additionally, a review of some of the most widely-cited works on this topic suggests that health demographers have played a very important role in studying and establishing obesity's link to excess mortality risk (e.g. Calle et al., 2003; Flegal et al., 2005; Mokdad et al., 2004, 2005; Olshansky et al., 2005; Peeters et al., 2003). Ongoing work in this area continues to refine the approaches used to investigate this association and provides convincing evidence of the negative consequences of obesity on mortality. Chapter 6 in this *Handbook* offers a thorough review of the work on this topic and addresses the ways in which prior methodological challenges can be addressed in future work. Others have examined this issue via analyses that quantify its impacts on life expectancy. In Chap. 4 of this *Handbook*, Vidra and colleagues provide an analysis of obesity's impacts on life expectancy in a number of European countries. Demographers have further studied the implications of rising levels of obesity (see for example, Chap. 3, which examines the impacts of obesity on economic costs in Europe). However, formal efforts to articulate the demography of obesity have been limited. As such, this volume is meant to establish the importance of the field of demography for our understanding of obesity – its prevalence as well as its causes and consequences.

Development of the Demographic Study of Obesity

Demographers who study health are largely comprised of scholars from fields such as economics, sociology, anthropology, epidemiology, and geography, who apply demographic concepts to the study of health (Kawachi & Subramian, 2005). This area of study evolved in response to changing morbidity and mortality patterns, accompanying the demographic and closely related epidemiologic transitions. Subsequent increases in life expectancy resulted in a change in scholarly focus from quantity of life to quality of life, and a concordant expansion of population health to include additional measures of morbidity (Lamb & Siegel, 2004). Obesity is thus of interest to demographers because of its association with mortality, with various chronic health conditions, and with other quality of life-related concerns (Himes, 2011).

Demographers who study obesity often examine its prevalence in various populations, its morbidity and mortality risks, variations across sub-groups, and impacts on quality of life. They have produced a large body of cross-disciplinary literature in these areas, and commonly study the environmental and social contexts that might explain varying patterns of overweight and obesity. As with other health issues, rising obesity rates are thought to be the result of a combination of individual, social, economic, institutional, and environmental factors, and its sources are complex and remain unexplained. Many of these factors are explored and described in the chapters in this *Handbook*.

Historically, several important developments have contributed to the advancement of this area of study. The earliest demographic studies of obesity were conducted in the 1940s by Louis Dublin, a statistician with the Metropolitan Life Insurance Company, who prepared life tables using a height-to-weight index (based on Quetelet's[1] index, which is now known as the body mass index, or BMI). His findings suggested that there was an ideal weight at which life expectancy was maximized (Jarrett, 1986; Oliver, 2005). This practice, used primarily within the insurance industry, laid the groundwork for the identification of overweight and obese persons as well as its link to population health (Visscher & Seidell, 2001). Indeed, these tables were adopted by the government as the standard by the 1950s and remained in use through the 1970s.

Beginning in the 1980s, rates of obesity began to accelerate rapidly. This was most evident in the

[1] Lambert Adolphe Jacques Quetelet (1796–1874) was an astronomer, mathematician, statistician, and sociologist. He is credited with the development of the science of anthropometry, or the measurement of the human individual, and the influential construction of life tables (Siegel & Swanson, 2004). The Quetelet Index was first described in 1832, and was later coined as the Body Mass Index in 1972 by Ancel Keys (Eknoyan, 2008).

United States, but was also noticeable in other high-income countries (Cawley, 2015). Owing to increased levels of obesity, much of the published work in this area has occurred in the 1990s and later. This is tied to several key developments. First, obesity was initially described as an epidemic in nature beginning in the late 1980s and 1990s (Boero, 2007; Grol-Prokopczyk, 2010). The National Institutes of Health (NIH) identified obesity as a public health crisis and chose this topic for a consensus conference in 1985 (Sobal, 1995). The World Health Organization (WHO) made a similar call to action in the 1990s (WHO, 2018). Also, obesity was given a disease designation in the *International Classification of Diseases* in 1990 (Sobal, 1995).

Much of the increased attention to obesity was facilitated by the development of common standards for categorizing obesity, based on body mass index (BMI), which originally emerged from the 1985 consensus statement on obesity by the NIH (1985). Initial designations were slightly different from today's categories, which are as follows: BMIs less than or equal to 18.5 kg/m^2 are considered underweight, 18.5–24.9 kg/m^2 are defined as normal, 25.0–29.9 kg/m^2 are overweight, and a BMI of 30.00 kg/m^2 or higher reflects obesity (see Fig. 1.1). Following the application of these designations, 37 million Americans were classified as overweight (Oliver, 2005).

To date, BMI remains the standard method for classifying overweight and obesity in population-based studies of obesity. The CDC further identifies subcategories within the obesity category: BMI of 30–34.99 reflects Class I, Class II is 35–39.99, and Class III is 40.00 or higher (CDC, 2022). It is worth noting that BMI is regularly criticized as a measure of obesity given that it does not differentiate fat from other body mass (Burkhauser & Cawley, 2008). For example, individuals with greater musculature may be misidentified as obese. In addition, it has been argued that alternate measures, e.g. adiposity, waist-to-hip ratio, skinfold thickness, are more closely linked with health outcomes. However, BMI has been shown to be closely correlated with other measures of adiposity (Flegal & Graubard, 2009). Furthermore, it is readily available across multiple datasets, accepted by the global community of scholars, and may be applied across sex and age groups (excluding children). Thus, it remains the standard measure for identifying overweight and obesity.

A final development leading to increased population-based studies of obesity has been the growing availability of national health information systems and nationally representative surveys containing relevant measures (Grol-Prokopczyk, 2010). In the United States, efforts to collect these data date back to the 1950s, and there are numerous sources of data that can be readily accessed.[2] Another factor contributing to the awareness of rapidly rising obesity in the US was the compilation of maps that were made publicly available. These maps, prepared by researchers in the Center for Chronic Disease Prevention, used data from the Behavioral Risk Factor Surveillance System (BRFSS), to effectively illustrate the prevalence of obesity and its dramatic increases since 1985 (Oliver, 2005). In fact, these "Adult Obesity Prevalence Maps," prepared using BRFSS data, can still be found on the CDC's "Overweight and Obesity" webpage (CDC, 2022). Globally, obesity surveillance has varied from region to region, with less coverage of low-income countries until relatively recently. However, large-scale efforts such as the NCD Risk Factor Collaboration (2022) to increase coverage have resulted in much greater availability of high-quality data in nearly all regions. Bentham and Di Cesare describe global data on obesity in Chap. 2 of this *Handbook*.

As a result of the above-described changes and developments, the pace of scientific research on obesity has increased remarkably. While early demographic studies of obesity were largely undertaken by the insurance industry, scholarly attention to obesity and its implications, particularly those that are health-related, has increased

[2] Nationally representative datasets on obesity include: the Behavioral Risk Factor Surveillance System (BRFSS), the National Health and Nutrition Examination Survey (NHANES), the Youth Risk Behavior Surveillance System (YRBSS), and the National Health Interview Survey (NHIS). The National Collaborative on Childhood Obesity also maintains information on publicly available data sets (Catalogue of Surveillance Systems, 2022).

Weight Designation	BMI Range (Adults)	BMI Percentile Range (2-19 years)
Underweight	<18.5 kg/m^2	<5th percentile (-2 z-scores)
Normal Weight	18.5 to 24.9 kg/m^2	5th – 85th percentile
Overweight	25.0 to 29.9 kg/m^2	85th – 95th percentile
Obese (Class I)	≥30.0 kg/m^2	≥95th percentile (+1 z score)
Obese (Class II)/Severe	35.0 to 39.9 kg/m^2	≥97.7th percentile (+2 z-scores)
Obese (Class III)/Severe	≥40.0 kg/m^2	

Fig. 1.1 Example BMI levels and associated weight ranges. Note. For children, BMI is compared to the distribution of BMIs from a reference population to yield percentiles based on age and gender. (Sources: Centers for Disease Control and Prevention (CDC), 2022; World Health Organization, 2021)

steadily throughout the latter half of the twentieth century (Eknoyan, 2008). By the early 2000s, entire sessions on obesity began appearing on programs at national and international demography meetings. Similarly, the number of articles published on this topic in demographic outlets increased dramatically following its identification as a global pandemic. More recently, obesity has been identified as a risk factor for COVID-19 and has been linked to increased severity of illness (Gao et al., 2021), which has garnered a great deal of scholarly attention, and will likely continue to do so for some time.

Overall Trends in Obesity

As mentioned previously, obesity has been increasing in nearly all regions of the globe. Demographers have consistently broadened our understanding of the trajectories of these rates, and they have identified areas of needed investigation. Briefly, North America has long had the highest levels of overweight and obesity, with about 72% of all Americans identified as having overweight or obesity in 2017–2018 (NIDDK, 2021). Similarly, 63% of Canadians have overweight or obesity (Statistics Canada, 2019). In North America and Europe, rates appear to be plateauing at these high levels (World Obesity Federation, 2021). At present, the fastest gains in obesity appear to be in low-income countries (World Obesity Federation, 2021).

As more data have become available, information on the Middle East suggests rather high levels of obesity and overweight, particularly in the Gulf states of Bahrain, Oman, Qatar, Saudi Arabia, and the United Arab Emirates (Ng et al., 2011). In the countries of Europe, rates of obesity vary considerably, with the highest levels observed in the United Kingdom and Turkey (about 37% and 50%, respectively), and much lower levels in Denmark and Switzerland (World Obesity Federation, 2021). In the African region, data are limited, but obesity has become a growing concern with evidence showing that rates are on the rise. Obesity prevalence is highest in some of the Pacific Islands (American Samoa, Cook Islands, Nauru). Finally, rates are generally low in South, Southeast, and East Asia (World Obesity Federation, 2021). However, recent increases in average BMI in China and India have garnered interest and concern (HSPH, 2018). See Chap. 2 of this *Handbook* for a full description of the most up-to-date patterns of obesity and its implications in all major regions of the globe; and see Chap. 5 for details on obesity prevalence and correlates in China.

Demographic Analyses of Obesity

Obesity may be conceived of as both a cause and a consequence of shifts in population. Given that obesity rates are on the rise across the globe, researchers have focused on the potential implications of such a profound change. Population-based studies of obesity have investigated its impacts on population health as well as changes in population patterns that have accompanied its rise in prevalence.

Consequences of Rising Obesity

There is much agreement in the scientific community that obesity poses significant health, economic, and social risks. A great deal of work has concentrated on its link to excess mortality. In fact, population-based studies linking obesity to excess mortality risk are among the most widely cited and impactful. Moreover, there is widespread acceptance that excess mortality risk is associated with increasing levels of obesity.

This body of literature, spanning several decades, has concentrated on describing and understanding the link between excess body weight and mortality. Numerous contributions in this area have led to some disagreement in findings. Accordingly, studies have varied in their estimates of risk, and a few have reported an inverse association (Troiano et al., 1996). But many studies have failed to adequately account for confounding factors, such as smoking, they were not statistically representative of the general population, and/or they used inconsistent standards for the designation of obesity (Flegal et al., 2013). High-quality and long-term cohort studies, and representative data, have largely addressed these issues, with the consensus view suggesting that obesity is associated with an increased risk of mortality. See Chap. 8 in this volume, "Obesity and Mortality" by Neil Mehta, for a full discussion of this issue.

Multiple studies confirm a U-shaped association between body mass index (BMI) and mortality, with those at the high and low ends of the distribution experiencing greater risk (Mehta & Chang, 2009; Prospective Studies Collaboration, 2009). Specifically, those who are in the underweight category (BMI $\leq$ 18.5 kg/m^2) have an increased risk of mortality as do those who are in the obese category (BMI $\geq$ 30.00 kg/m^2), in comparison to those who are in the normal weight range (Flegal et al., 2005). Furthermore, a review of studies has revealed an increased risk of all-cause mortality for those in severe categories of obesity (Class II and Class III obesity, designated with BMIs of 35.00 and 40.00 kg/m^2, respectively) (Flegal et al., 2013). Another study indicated that the risk of death due to cancer was higher for those with BMIs of 40.00 or more (Calle et al., 2003). Recently, demographers have argued that existing research has likely underestimated the risk of mortality due to obesity as a result of bias and mismeasurement (Masters, 2018).

It has been suggested that gains to life expectancy, which have been observed for many decades, might be reversed due to increasing obesity (e.g. Stewart et al., 2009). Olshansky et al. (2005) used obesity-adjusted conditional probabilities of death to create life tables, which indicated that obesity reduces life expectancy by one-third to three-fourths of a year. However, projections developed over the period from 2010 to 2040 by Preston and his colleagues (2014) suggest that reductions in smoking will produce improvements that outweigh the ill-effects of obesity on life expectancy. Accordingly, while obesity exerts a negative effect, the combined effect results in small life expectancy gains, which are somewhat smaller for women. Ongoing work will need to continue to monitor these impacts over time. Demographic contributions to the study of obesity have also focused on its link to excess morbidity risk, and a large body of evidence indicates that obesity increases the risk of diabetes, heart disease, certain cancers, stroke, and depression, among others (NIH, 2018).

Many population-based studies have focused on the economic and/or societal burden generated by rising levels of overweight and obesity. Research in this area has considered both the economic costs to society as well as whether workers with obesity have reduced levels of productivity, higher levels of illness, or receive penalties in the form of lower wages. With respect to direct costs (medical costs related to the prevention, diagnosis, and treatment of obesity), severe obesity has been consistently linked with higher costs (Cawley, 2015). It has been estimated that the United States spent $173 billion in 2019 on direct costs (CDC, 2022). Globally, a recent study of the economic impacts of obesity on eight countries revealed losses ranging from 0.8% to 2.4% of annual GDP and projected impacts of up to 4.8% by 2060 (World Obesity Federation, 2021). Research in this area also finds evidence of sizable indirect costs (losses to productivity or absenteeism) of obesity (Trogdon et al., 2008). See Chap. 3 in this *Handbook* for a review of this literature and an examination of indirect costs in European countries.

Much of this work has focused on wealthy nations; however, the economic and social burdens associated with obesity are expected to rise across all levels of wealth and development. Accordingly, there has been growing concern about its potential consequences on the development of nations (De Onis et al., 2010).

Population-Based Perspectives on Rising Overweight and Obesity

Many factors have been implicated in rising levels of overweight and obesity. These include increasingly sedentary lifestyles, a toxic food environment that promotes the consumption of energy-dense foods high in fat and sugar, and an increasingly global food supply chain, among others. However, the exact causes of obesity remain unclear. An important contribution to our understanding of how shifts in diets and lifestyles lead to increasing overweight and obesity is the Global Nutrition Transition (Popkin, 2006). This perspective outlines the global nutritional shifts whereby societies transition from traditional to Western diets as a result of urbanization and globalization. Importantly, this shift entails increased consumption of processed, energy-dense (high-fat and high-sugar) foods and less active lifestyles, which tends to promote increased obesity prevalence. The United States is thought to have entered the fifth and final stage (Behavioral Change) of this transition in which certain individuals adopt healthier lifestyles and experience reduced obesity. However, many countries are thought to be transitioning toward obesity-promoting lifestyles (Popkin et al., 2012). Correspondingly, researchers have shown that economic and social development is often associated with increased obesity prevalence and wider socioeconomic disparities in obesity (Pampel et al., 2012).

Obesity has become increasingly problematic among middle- and low-income countries (Prentice, 2006). Yet, many of these countries have not experienced the economic expansion that previously accompanied modernization and development. This has led to a great deal of interest in the double burden of malnutrition, which refers to the burden faced by developing nations that must contend with issues related to hunger and malnutrition, while increasingly contending with health risks linked to obesity (World Obesity Federation, 2022). This now affects most middle and low-income countries (Popkin et al., 2020). A recent study observed that global obesity prevalence surpassed the prevalence of underweight in 2004 for women and 2011 for men; yet, underweight continues to represent a significant challenge in the world's poorest regions, particularly south Asia (NCD Risk Factor Collaboration, 2016). This paradoxical burden will continue to pose significant challenges for numerous countries, and the use of population-based perspectives has helped to shed light on the structural forces that have led to increased obesity prevalence. Further, this type of perspective will be especially important to the development of meaningful interventions and policies to reduce the spread of obesity.

Another topic of major importance to demographers is the aging of the world's population. This has largely been a consequence of fertility declines and mortality reductions and brings with it a number of implications. Given that widespread obesity is a relatively new phenomenon, demographers have yet to fully explore the long-term implications of increasing obesity in the context of an aging society. Applying a life course perspective has allowed demographers to consider the effects of rising obesity prevalence on quality of life. Accordingly, recent findings have indicated that disability may be more likely as years of exposure to obesity increase (Chang et al., 2015). Associations with activity limitation at older ages have also been observed, such that increasing levels of obesity pose an increasing risk to functional mobility (Himes, 2000). Other scholars have reported that obesity is expected to negatively impact both survival rates and disability (Cao, 2016). Demographers have also studied how changing family structures may contribute to obesity. For example, some have speculated that China may have to contend with rising rates of obesity as a result of its one-child policy and subsequently large number of single-child families, which are argued to be at greater risk of obesity (Tian & von Cramon-Taubadel, 2020). Falbo and Lin explore the role of sibling effects on obesity in Chap. 10 of this *Handbook*.

Demographers have made significant contributions to the examination of disparities in obesity prevalence. Factors that have drawn attention from demographers include socioeconomic status, race, ethnicity, nativity status, gender, and level of education. Particularly in high-income countries, socioeconomic disparities in obesity have been documented consistently with the highest rates affecting those at the lower end of the socioeconomic spectrum. Similarly, education appears to have an inverse relationship with obesity in developed countries, with some gender differences (Cohen et al., 2013). Krueger and colleagues review the role of socioeconomic status in addition to race and ethnicity in Chap. 9 of this volume. A large and growing body of work has documented racial and ethnic disparities in overweight and obesity. Accordingly, Black and Hispanic women have higher rates of obesity compared to both White and Asian women (Hales et al., 2020). Demographic investigations have yielded valuable insights into the factors that shape the risks of obesity for these groups. Frisco and colleagues describe this body of research along with relevant theoretical perspectives in Chap. 8.

Demographers have also examined the rising obesity prevalence among immigrants to the United States (Frank & Akresh, 2013). A great deal of scholarly effort has focused on the erosion of health status with more time spent in the United States. Relatedly, demographers have undertaken analyses to determine whether additional time spent in the U.S. is associated with higher BMI levels. The work in this area suggests that immigrants appear to arrive with healthier body weights, and they gain weight with additional time spent in the United States (Cunningham et al., 2008; Van Hook et al., 2012). One study observed that female immigrants converge to American BMIs within 10 years of arrival, while men converge within 15 years (Antecol & Bedard, 2006). The mechanisms underlying the appearance of weight gain are not fully understood. For example, a recent investigation found that immigrant vulnerability to childhood obesity largely depends on a combination of factors including generational status, gender, and age (Frisco et al., 2016). Demographers have investigated the extent to which factors such as acculturation, discrimination and stress, and concentrated poverty might play in weight-related outcomes in immigrants, but the complexity of these findings suggests the need for further investigation. See Chaps. 7 and 8 of this *Handbook* for an extended discussion of these issues.

Demographers are uniquely positioned to investigate the sources of obesity, and they have contributed to our understanding of the mechanisms that may explain disparate rates. For example, discrimination and stress have been posited as important pathways through which various minority groups experience heightened risk of overweight or obesity. This is explored in Chap. 12 (Cuevas et al.) in this *Handbook*. Religion has been consistently linked to health behaviors and outcomes with a large body of literature suggesting a beneficial association, yet its connection to body mass index has been understudied. In Chap. 11, Hill and colleagues examine the literature linking religion and body weight and describe the ways in which this literature should be developed to advance this area of study.

Demographers have also helped to establish the importance of the neighborhood environment for health. For example, individuals who are socially disadvantaged tend to experience greater exposure to features of the environment that increase the risk of obesity. Along these lines, Lopez and Anderson (Chap. 13) describe the linkages between obesity and the neighborhood environment. Another interesting area of study is weight bias, which may have important health-related implications. This is considered in Chap. 14, which examines patient outcomes in emergency medical service (EMS). Finally, a growing awareness of the need for high-quality investigations of health outcomes in sexual minority populations has been identified. To address this gap, Chaps. 15 through 19 of this volume examine overweight and obesity prevalence in various sexual minority populations.

Tools and Methods Employed by Demographers

Demographers utilize a variety of tools and perspectives to analyze and understand obesity including ecological analysis, age-period-cohort analysis, multivariate regression models, life tables, and population projections. Population-based studies have generally made use of data from national surveillance systems which are increasingly available for a growing number of countries. The application of demographic techniques has been fundamental to the advancement of the study of obesity. Yet, some challenges remain and will need to be addressed in future research efforts.

Ecological analysis is an important tool that is used to demonstrate the relationship between health outcomes and explanatory factors (Lamb & Siegel, 2004). In studies of obesity, many researchers have utilized place-based methodology to describe the importance of factors such as concentrated poverty and segregation. This approach has been important to the development of the field as state-level estimates of obesity used by the CDC to underscore the extent of the obesity crisis and contributed a great deal to scholarly interest. Furthermore, a population-based approach acknowledges the contribution of an obesogenic environment and the extent to which socially disadvantaged individuals experience greater exposure to risk. Future work will need to increasingly take this approach in order to fully describe the factors that promote poorer outcomes and to shift prevention efforts away from individuals.

Epidemiologic studies examine quantitatively the associations between body weight and general or cause-specific morbidity or mortality. Such studies establish trends and linkages and have been foundational to the advancement of the discipline. National and global surveillance systems are of vital importance to these efforts. Much emphasis has been placed on the coordination of efforts to generate high-quality data for all regions. However, gaps still remain, and additional work is needed to ensure that data is available for all countries. In addition, these studies have commonly relied on BMI as a measure of obesity. The shortcomings of this measure have been noted and data that includes alternate measures of adiposity are needed along with historical trends in obesity.

Many studies have relied on cross-sectional analyses as this form of data has been more readily available. Accordingly, there is a greater need for longitudinal analysis that can examine how changes over the life course contribute to obesity risk. Cohort analysis has shown that more recent cohorts have experienced greater exposure to obesity over the life course (Lee et al., 2010). This approach is especially useful to the study of obesity as it can effectively capture the role of current and past behaviors. In addition, it allows for the reduction of bias from various sources in the study of obesity and allows us to determine whether increases in the prevalence of overweight and obesity are specific to birth cohorts or racial and ethnic groups. Cohort analysis has also established the importance of the history of obesity for mortality risk (Preston et al., 2013, 2014; Abdullah et al., 2011; also see Chap. 6 in this *Handbook*).

Life tables are another tool used by demographers to estimate morbidity and mortality risk associated with obesity (e.g. Cao, 2016; Olshansky et al., 2005; Peeters et al., 2003; Preston et al., 2014; Stewart et al., 2009). Some findings in this area have suggested a lessening of mortality risk associated with obesity over time (Flegal et al., 2005; Mehta et al., 2014), yet there is convincing evidence of an increasing overall health burden (Peeters & Backholer, 2012).

Ongoing work is needed to understand the morbidity and mortality risks associated with obesity and how they may change over time. The development of future obesity scenarios has been very important in underscoring the severity of obesity and its related health, social, and economic implications. Furthermore, generating this type of evidence will continue to be an important task as it motivates support for action, highlights disproportionate burdens on vulnerable populations, and identifies areas of needed intervention (Swinburn et al., 2019).

In sum, demographers have made countless contributions to the study of obesity. Researchers from a variety of disciplines have applied the tools and methods of demography to effectively establish its prevalence, describe the health and economic implications of rising obesity, understand the factors that contribute to increasing obesity, examine how it varies in subpopulations, and develop scenarios for future impacts. In the chapters that follow, contributors explore an array of active areas of demographic research on obesity.

References

Abdullah, A., Wolfe, R., Stoelwinder, J. U., De Courten, M., Stevenson, C., Walls, H. L., & Peeters, A. (2011). The number of years lived with obesity and the risk of all-cause and cause-specific mortality. *International Journal of Epidemiology, 40*(4), 985–996.

Antecol, H., & Bedard, K. (2006). Unhealthy assimilation: Why do immigrants converge to American health status levels? *Demography, 43*(2), 337–360.

Boero, N. (2007). All the news that's fat to print: The American "obesity epidemic" and the media. *Qualitative Sociology, 30*(1), 41–60.

Burkhauser, R. V., & Cawley, J. (2008). Beyond BMI: The value of more accurate measures of fatness and obesity in social science research. *Journal of Health Economics, 27*(2), 519–529.

Calle, E. E., Rodriguez, C., Walker-Thurmond, K., & Thun, M. J. (2003). Overweight, obesity, and mortality from cancer in a prospectively studied cohort of US adults. *New England Journal of Medicine, 348*(17), 1625–1638.

Cao, B. (2016). Future healthy life expectancy among older adults in the US: A forecast based on cohort smoking and obesity history. *Population Health Metrics, 14*(1). https://doi.org/10.1186/s12963-016-0092-2

Catalogue of Surveillance Systems. (2022). *National Collaborative on Childhood Obesity Research*. Retrieved 1 June 2022 from https://www.nccor.org/nccor-tools/catalogue/

Cawley, J. (2015). An economy of scales: A selective review of obesity's economic causes, consequences, and solutions. *Journal of Health Economics, 43*, 244–268. https://doi.org/10.1016/j.jhealeco.2015.03.001

Centers for Disease Control (CDC). (2022). *Overweight & obesity*. Retrieved 1 June 2022 from https://www.cdc.gov/obesity/index.html

Chang, V. W., Alley, D. E., & Dowd, J. B. (2015). *Is obesity becoming more disabling over time? Evidence from the NHANES 1988–2012*. Population Association of America, 2015 Annual Meetings, San Diego, CA.

Cohen, R. M., Rehkopf, D. H., & Abrams, B. (2013). Educational attainment and obesity: A systematic review: Educational attainment and obesity. *Obesity Reviews, 14*(12), 989–1005. https://doi.org/10.1111/obr.12062

Cunningham, S. A., Ruben, J. D., & Venkat Narayan, K. M. (2008). Health of foreign-born people in the United States: A review. *Health & Place, 14*(4), 623–635. https://doi.org/10.1016/j.healthplace.2007.12.002

De Onis, M., Blössner, M., & Borghi, E. (2010). Global prevalence and trends of overweight and obesity among preschool children. *The American Journal of Clinical Nutrition, 92*(5), 1257–1264.

Eknoyan, G. (2008). Adolphe Quetelet (1796–1874) – The average man and indices of obesity. *Nephrology, Dialysis, Transplantation, 23*(1), 47–51. https://doi.org/10.1093/ndt/gfm517

Flegal, K. M., & Graubard, B. I. (2009). Estimates of excess deaths associated with body mass index and other anthropometric variables. *American Journal of Clinical Nutrition, 89*(4), 1213–1219.

Flegal, K. M., Graubard, B. I., Williamson, D. F., & Gail, M. H. (2005). Excess deaths associated with underweight, overweight, and obesity. *JAMA, 293*(15), 1861–1867.

Flegal, K. M., Kit, B. K., Orpana, H., & Graubard, B. I. (2013). Association of all-cause mortality with overweight and obesity using standard body mass index categories: A systematic review and meta-analysis. *Journal of the American Medical Association, 309*(1), 71–82.

Frank, R., & Akresh, I. R. (2013). Social patterning in body mass index (BMI) among contemporary immigrant groups: The emergence of a gradient. *Demography, 50*(3), 993–1012.

Frisco, M. L., Quiros, S., & Van Hook, J. (2016). One size may not fit all: How obesity among Mexican-origin youth varies by generation, gender, and age. *Demography, 53*(6), 2031–2043.

Gao, M., Piernas, C., Astbury, N. M., Hippisley-Cox, J., O'Rahilly, S., Aveyard, P., & Jebb, S. A. (2021). Associations between body-mass index and COVID-19 severity in 6.9 million people in England: A prospective, community-based, cohort study. *The Lancet Diabetes and Endocrinology, 9*(6), 350–359. https://doi.org/10.1016/S2213-8587(21)00089-9

Grol-Prokopczyk, H. (2010). Who says obesity is an epidemic? How excess weight became an American health crisis. In *Understanding emerging epidemics: Social and political approaches* (pp. 343–358). Emerald Group Publishing Limited.

Hales, C. M., Carroll, M. D., Fryar, C. D., & Ogden, C. L. (2020). *Prevalence of obesity and severe obesity among adults: United States, 2017–2018*. National Center for Health Statistics.

Harvard School of Public Health (HSPH). (2018). *Obesity prevention source*. Retrieved July 2018 from https://www.hsph.harvard.edu/obesity-prevention-source/

Health Implications of Obesity. (1985). *NIH Consensus Statement Online, 5*(9), 1–7. Retrieved 27 August 2018 from https://consensus.nih.gov/1985/1985Obesity049html.htm

Himes, C. L. (2000). Obesity, disease, and functional limitation in later life. *Demography, 37*(1), 73–82.

Himes, C. L. (2011). The demography of obesity. In J. Cawley (Ed.), *The Oxford handbook of the social science of obesity* (pp. 35–47). Oxford University Press.

Jarrett, R. J. (1986). Is there an ideal body weight? *British Medical Journal (Clinical Research Ed.), 293*(6545), 493–495.

Kawachi, I., & Subramian, S. V. (2005). Health demography. In D. L. Poston Jr. & M. Micklin (Eds.), *Handbook of population* (pp. 787–808). Kluwer Academic/Plenum Publisher.

Lamb, V. L., & Siegel, J. S. (2004). Health demography. In J. S. Siegel & D. S. Swanson (Eds.), *The methods and materials of demography* (pp. 341–370). Elsevier/Academic.

Lee, J. M., Pilli, S., Gebremariam, A., Keirns, C. C., Davis, M. M., Vijan, S., et al. (2010). Getting heavier, younger: Trajectories of obesity over the life course. *International Journal of Obesity, 34*, 614. Retrieved from https://link-gale-com.libweb.lib.utsa.edu/apps/doc/A224334948/HRCA?u=txshracd2604&sid=bookmark-HRCA&xid=b91a68dd

Masters, R. (2018). *Estimating mortality risks associated with overweight and obesity in the U.S. adult population*. Population Association of America 2018 Annual Meetings, Denver, CO.

Mehta, N. K., & Chang, V. W. (2009). Mortality attributable to obesity among middle-aged adults in the United States. *Demography, 46*(4), 851–872.

Mehta, T., Fontaine, K. R., Keith, S. W., Bangalore, S. S., de los Campos, G., Bartolucci, A., et al. (2014). Obesity and mortality: Are the risks declining? Evidence from multiple prospective studies in the United States. *Obesity Reviews, 15*(8), 619–629. https://doi.org/10.1111/obr.12191

Mokdad, A. H., Marks, J. S., Stroup, D. F., & Gerberding, J. L. (2004). Actual causes of death in the United States, 2000. *Journal of the American Medical Association, 291*(10), 1238–1245. https://doi.org/10.1001/jama.291.10.1238

Mokdad, A. H., Marks, J. S., Stroup, D. F., & Gerberding, J. L. (2005). Correction: Actual causes of death in the United States, 2000. *Journal of the American Medical Association, 291*, 293–294. https://doi.org/10.1001/jama.291.10.1238

National Institute of Diabetes and Digestive and Kidney Diseases (NIDDK). (2021). *Overweight and obesity statistics*. Retrieved 1 June 2022 from https://www.niddk.nih.gov/health-information/health-statistics/overweight-obesity

National Institutes of Health (NIH). (2018). *Obesity*. Retrieved 1 June 2022 from https://medlineplus.gov/obesity.html

NCD Risk Factor Collaboration (NCD-RisC). (2022). *National Adult Body-Mass Index*. Retrieved 1 June 2022 from https://ncdrisc.org/data-downloads-adiposity.html

NCD Risk Factor Collaboration NCD. (2016). Trends in adult body-mass index in 200 countries from 1975 to 2014: A pooled analysis of 1698 population-based measurement studies with 19.2 million participants. *Lancet, 387*(10026), 1377–1396.

Ng, S. W., Zaghloul, S., Ali, H. I., Harrison, G., & Popkin, B. M. (2011). The prevalence and trends of overweight, obesity and nutrition-related non-communicable diseases in the Arabian Gulf States. *Obesity Reviews, 12*(1), 1–13. https://doi.org/10.1111/j.1467-789X.2010.00750.x

Oliver, J. E. (2005). *Fat politics: The real story behind America's obesity epidemic*. Oxford University Press.

Olshansky, S. J., Passaro, D. J., Hershow, R. C., Layden, J., Carnes, B. A., Brody, J., et al. (2005). A potential decline in life expectancy in the United States in the 21st century. *New England Journal of Medicine, 352*(11), 1138–1145.

Pampel, F. C., Denney, J. T., & Krueger, P. M. (2012). Obesity, SES, and economic development: A test of the reversal hypothesis. *Social Science & Medicine, 74*(7), 1073–1081.

Peeters, A., & Backholer, K. (2012). Is the health burden associated with obesity changing? *American Journal of Epidemiology, 176*(10), 840–845. https://doi.org/10.1093/aje/kws328

Peeters, A., Barendregt, J. J., Willekens, F., Mackenbach, J. P., Al Mamun, A., & Bonneux, L. (2003). Obesity in adulthood and its consequences for life expectancy: A life-table analysis. *Annals of Internal Medicine, 138*(1), 24–32.

Popkin, B. M. (2006). Global nutrition dynamics: The world is shifting rapidly toward a diet linked with noncommunicable diseases. *The American Journal of Clinical Nutrition, 84*(2), 289–298. https://doi.org/10.1093/ajcn/84.2.289

Popkin, B. M., Adair, L. S., & Ng, S. W. (2012). Global nutrition transition and the pandemic of obesity in developing countries. *Nutrition Reviews, 70*(1), 3–21. https://doi.org/10.1111/j.1753-4887.2011.00456.x

Popkin, B. M., Corvalan, C., & Grummer-Strawn, L. (2020). Dynamics of the double burden of malnutrition and the changing nutrition reality. *The Lancet, 395*(10217), 65–74. https://doi.org/10.1016/S0140-6736(19)32497-3

Prentice, A. M. (2006). The emerging epidemic of obesity in developing countries. *International Journal of Epidemiology, 35*(1), 93–99.

Preston, S., Mehta, N., & Stokes, A. (2013). Modeling obesity histories in cohort analyses of health and mortality. *Epidemiology, 24*, 1–9. https://doi.org/10.1097/EDE.0b013e3182770217

Preston, S. H., Stokes, A., Mehta, N. K., & Cao, B. (2014). Projecting the effect of changes in smoking and obesity on future life expectancy in the United States. *Demography, 51*(1), 27–49.

Prospective Studies Collaboration. (2009). Body-mass index and cause-specific mortality in 900,000 adults: Collaborative analyses of 57 prospective studies. *Lancet, 373*, 1083–1096. https://doi.org/10.1016/S0140-6736(09)60318-4

Siegel, J. S., & Swanson, D. S. (2004). *The methods and materials of demography*. Elsevier/Academic.

Sobal, J. (1995). The medicalization and demedicalization of obesity. In D. Maurer & J. Sobal (Eds.), *Eating agendas: Food and nutrition as social problems* (pp. 67–90). Aldine de Gruyter.

Statistics Canada. (2019). *Overweight and obese adults, 2018*. Retrieved 1 June 2022 from https://www150.statcan.gc.ca/n1/pub/82-625-x/2019001/article/00005-eng.htm

Stewart, S. T., Cutler, D. M., & Rosen, A. B. (2009). Forecasting the effects of obesity and smoking on US life expectancy. *New England Journal of Medicine, 361*(23), 2252–2260.

Swinburn, B. A., Kraak, V. I., Allender, S., Atkins, V. J., Baker, P. I., Bogard, J. R., et al. (2019). The global syndemic of obesity, undernutrition, and climate change: The Lancet Commission report. *The Lancet, 393*(10173), 791–846. https://doi.org/10.1016/S0140-6736(18)32822-8

Tian, X., & von Cramon-Taubadel, S. (2020). Are only children in China more likely to be obese/overweight than their counterparts with siblings? *Economics and Human Biology, 37*, 100847.

Trogdon, J. G., Finkelstein, E. A., Hylands, T., Dellea, P. S., & Kamal-Bahl, S. J. (2008). Indirect costs of obesity: A review of the current literature. *Obesity Reviews, 9*(5), 489–500.

Troiano, R. P., Frongillo, J. E., Sobal, J., & Levitsky, D. A. (1996). The relationship between body weight and mortality: A quantitative analysis of combined information from existing studies. *International Journal of Obesity and Related Disorders, 20*(1), 63–75.

Van Hook, J., Baker, E., Altman, C. E., & Frisco, M. L. (2012). Canaries in a coalmine: Immigration and overweight among Mexican-origin children in the US and Mexico. *Social Science & Medicine (1982), 74*(2), 125–134. https://doi.org/10.1016/j.socscimed.2011.10.007

Visscher, T. L., & Seidell, J. C. (2001). The public health impact of obesity. *Annual Review of Public Health, 22*(1), 355–375.

World Health Organization (WHO). (2018). *Controlling the global obesity epidemic*. Retrieved from http://www.who.int/nutrition/topics/obesity/en/

World Health Organization (WHO). (2021). *Obesity and overweight fact sheet*. Retrieved 1 June 2022 from http://www.who.int/en/news-room/fact-sheets/detail/obesity-and-overweight

World Obesity Federation. (2021). *The economic impact of overweight & obesity in 8 countries*. Summary report. Retrieved from https://data.worldobesity.org/publications/

World Obesity Federation. (2022). *World Obesity Atlas 2022*. Retrieved from https://data.worldobesity.org/publications/World-Obesity-Atlas-2022.pdf

Obesity: A Long-Term Global Challenge 2

James Bentham and Mariachiara Di Cesare

Obesity is common across much of the world, reducing quality of life and causing chronic disease and premature mortality. Increases in prevalence, firstly in Oceania and western countries, then in regions including Latin America, the Middle East and northern and southern Africa, and now beyond, have been among the most important and harmful developments in global health in the late twentieth and early twenty-first centuries (NCD Risk Factor Collaboration (NCD-RisC), 2017). In the past 50 years, body-mass index (BMI) and obesity prevalence have increased dramatically worldwide (NCD Risk Factor Collaboration (NCD-RisC), 2016a, 2017; Finucane et al., 2011; Stevens et al., 2012); more than 772 million adults were living with obesity in 2019, while 39 million children were overweight in the same year (NCD Risk Factor Collaboration (NCD-RisC), 2017; 2021 Global Nutrition Report, 2022). The negative consequences of these trends will take decades to unfold, particularly given the difficulties encountered to date in combating excess weight at the population level.

In this chapter, we emphasise the worldwide extent of the epidemic and provide detailed information on obesity trends, focusing on countries of particular importance; either because they have large populations, distinctive trends, or because they are representative of global regions. Finally, we suggest ways to monitor obesity effectively in the medium to long term, which would help to guide efforts to reduce excess weight in the global population.

Obesity and Health Over the Life Course

Obesity is a largely preventable condition involving excessive accumulation of body fat. The World Health Organization (WHO) defines obesity in adults as BMI of 30 kg/m^2 or more, while thresholds for children and adolescents vary by age and sex (de Onis et al., 2004). Obesity has serious health-related consequences (Rito et al., 2019). It is strongly associated with premature mortality (Di Cesare et al., 2019), and with the risk of developing chronic conditions such as cardiovascular diseases (CVDs) (Umer et al., 2017), hypertension (Kumar, 2019), type 2 diabetes mellitus (T2DM) (Kawasaki et al., 2018), and some types of cancer, including endometrial and colon cancers, and breast cancer in postmenopausal women (Hidayat et al., 2018). Other medical conditions associated with obesity include gastrointestinal disease (John et al., 2006), sleep apnoea (Dong et al., 2020), respiratory problems (Ali & Ulrik, 2013), osteoarthritis (Silverwood

J. Bentham (✉)
School of Mathematics, Statistics and Actuarial Science, University of Kent, Canterbury, UK
e-mail: j.bentham@kent.ac.uk

M. Di Cesare
Institute of Public Health and Wellbeing, University of Essex, Colchester, UK

G. Garcia-Alexander, D. L. Poston, Jr. (eds.), *International Handbook of the Demography of Obesity*, International Handbooks of Population 12, https://doi.org/10.1007/978-3-031-10936-2_2

et al., 2015), musculoskeletal problems (Paulis et al., 2014), reproductive hormone abnormalities (Rosenblatt et al., 2015), and various psychological consequences such as poor self-esteem (Weinberger et al., 2016), body dissatisfaction (Weinberger et al., 2016), depression (Luppino et al., 2010), and psychological discomfort (Corica et al., 2008).

The obesity epidemic is not limited to adults, and over recent decades the prevalence of obesity in children has increased rapidly (NCD Risk Factor Collaboration (NCD-RisC), 2017; Di Cesare et al., 2019). In the short term, childhood obesity is associated with poor mental health outcomes, asthma, low-grade systemic inflammation, liver complications, and musculoskeletal problems (Di Cesare et al., 2019). In addition, children with obesity have a higher prevalence of cardiovascular risk factors, including dyslipidemia, high blood pressure, and T2DM (Bridger, 2009). These risks persist over time, increasing the likelihood of developing CVDs (Nadeau et al., 2011), T2DM (Hannon et al., 2005), and some cancers (Weihrauch-Blüher et al., 2019; Weihe et al., 2020) in adulthood, leading to higher levels of both morbidity and premature death in individuals with obesity (Must et al., 1992; Lindberg et al., 2017; Franks et al., 2010; Park et al., 2012).

Health Conditions Associated with Obesity in Adults and Children

Cardiometabolic Conditions

Metabolic syndrome is defined as the co-presence of multiple risk factors for CVDs and T2DM, which include abdominal obesity, dyslipidemia, hypertension, and insulin resistance (Huang, 2009). Over recent decades, the prevalence of metabolic syndrome has increased, partly owing to increasingly sedentary lifestyles and poor diet (Eckel et al., 2005; Saklayen, 2018). In 2016, the prevalence of metabolic syndrome in adults in the USA was 35%, but with substantial age effects: prevalence was less than 20% in ages 20–39 years but approximately 50% in those aged 60 or more years (Hirode & Wong, 2020). This contrasts with a meta-analysis of data from 17 countries, which estimated a prevalence of 5–7% in adults aged from 18 to 30 years (Nolan et al., 2017). The Cardiovascular Risk in Young Finns Study has shown substantial increases in metabolic syndrome in healthy adults of ages 24–39 years, driven mostly by increases in obesity prevalence (Raitoharju et al., 2014). Similarly, higher levels of metabolic syndrome are observed in children with obesity, with prevalence reaching up to 50% in those who have severe obesity (Weiss et al., 2004). A systematic review of 85 papers found that the median prevalence of metabolic syndrome in children was 3% in all individuals, 12% in overweight children and 29% in children with obesity (Friend et al., 2013); these effects occur regardless of age or sex (Juárez-López et al., 2010).

Chronic inflammation associated with obesity contributes to atherosclerosis in adults, causing more than three million deaths every year in the USA (Henning, 2021; Beauloye et al., 2007); meanwhile, the obesity epidemic is also associated strongly with rising incidence of T2DM in children and adults (Algoblan et al., 2014). The prevalence of diabetes in adults increased globally from 4.3% in 1980 to 9.0% in 2014 in men, and from 5.0% to 7.9% in women, with the number of adults with diabetes in the world increasing from 108 million in 1980 to 422 million in 2014 (NCD Risk Factor Collaboration (NCD-RisC), 2016b). Data from the 2009 to 2010 National Diabetes Audit in England showed that 90% of adults aged 16–54 years old with T2DM were overweight or obese (NHS Digital, 2022), while data from the 2018 Health Survey for England showed that 14% of men and 10% of women with high levels of central adiposity had diabetes, compared to 5% and 4% respectively in those with desirable waist circumference (NHS Digital, 2022). While data for children and adolescents are sparse, estimates from the UK suggest that children with obesity have an approximately four-fold greater risk of developing T2DM than those of normal weight (Abbasi et al., 2017).

Respiratory Conditions

Obesity is associated with asthma prevalence, incidence and morbidity (Baffi et al., 2015); adults with obesity are more likely to have multiple symptoms, more frequent and severe exacerbations, reduced efficacy of medication, and decreased quality of life (Peters et al., 2018). There is a positive association between abdominal obesity and asthma, including a clear dose-response relationship (Jiang et al., 2019). Associations between asthma and obesity have also been found in children. A meta-analysis of prospective studies has found increased incidence in overweight children, and a larger effect in boys with obesity than in girls (Chen et al., 2013).

Other Physical Consequences of Obesity

Obesity is associated with musculoskeletal disorders (Viester et al., 2013), with a meta-analysis of 33 studies showing associations between obesity and low back pain, seeking medical attention for low back pain, and chronic low back pain (Shiri et al., 2010). Children and adolescents with obesity are more likely to develop musculoskeletal issues, problems with movement, and orthopaedic conditions than those with normal weight (Manoff et al., 2005; Dietz Jr et al., 1982).

Weight gain in women is associated with increased risk of polycystic ovary syndrome (Barber et al., 2019), while a prospective population-based cohort study has shown that early adiposity rebound is associated with polycystic ovary syndrome diagnosis and higher levels of adult BMI (Koivuaho et al., 2019). Childhood obesity has also been associated with higher risk of menstrual irregularities, leading to higher prevalence of polycystic ovary syndrome in adulthood (He et al., 2020).

Short- and Long-Term Psychological Outcomes

There is strong interest in relationships between obesity and social factors including stigma (Puhl & Latner, 2007) and victimisation (Smith et al., 2013), and psychological factors including depression and self-esteem (Atlantis & Baker, 2008; Carpiniello et al., 2009), with studies also highlighting discrimination against people with obesity (Puhl et al., 2008; Jackson et al., 2015). A study of the association between obesity and psychosocial burden in adults suggests that up to 60% of individuals with obesity experience mental illnesses that impact their mood, self-esteem, self-image, and quality of life (Sarwer & Polonsky, 2016). There is also a growing body of literature on children (Puhl & Latner, 2007; Adams & Bukowski, 2008; Wardle & Cooke, 2005), which suggests that those with overweight and obesity also experience stigmatisation and negative stereotypes (Latner et al., 2008; Greenleaf et al., 2006), and that the association between obesity and poor body image is stronger in girls than boys (Schwartz & Brownell, 2004). A recent narrative review has examined the burden of paediatric obesity stigma in children and adolescents and their parents and caregivers, finding that it contributes to psychosocial impairments, unhealthy eating behaviours, and negative impacts on weight control (Haqq et al., 2021). A further review of 53 studies confirmed an association between overweight and obesity in children and a series of psychological comorbidities including depression, lower quality of life, emotional and behavioural disorders, and self-esteem, exacerbated by stigma, teasing and bullying (Rankin et al., 2016); however, the same study highlighted an absence of conclusive evidence on the association between obesity and attention-deficit or hyperactivity disorders (Rankin et al., 2016). A study of children aged 11–17 years old with overweight and obesity in Germany showed that these conditions were associated with lower physical wellbeing when compared to normal weight, with lower levels of psychological and parent-related wellbeing among boys with obesity (Meixner et al., 2020). Finally, a meta-analysis of children with overweight and obesity has shown a two-fold greater level of school absenteeism compared to their peers (Meixner et al., 2020; An et al., 2017).

COVID-19 Pandemic

COVID-19 has been defined as a *fast on slow pandemic*, in which the rapid and devastating viral pandemic is superimposed on the slow global obesity pandemic (2021 Global Nutrition Report, 2022). Obesity is a strong risk factor for severe disease from COVID-19 (Mohammad et al., 2021), with a meta-analysis of 30 studies confirming that presence of obesity in patients with COVID-19 increases the risks of hospitalisation, ICU admission, the need for invasive mechanical ventilation, and death (Huang et al., 2020), and that these findings are consistent across age groups. In the UK, a study of almost 7 million people has shown that a unit increase in BMI increases risk of hospital admission by 5%, ICU admission by 10%, and death by 4% (Gao et al., 2021). The mechanisms that cause these severe COVID-19 outcomes are not clear, but the evidence suggests that they are partly explained by chronic low-grade inflammation in people with obesity, which is amplified by the acute inflammation associated with COVID-19; this leads to increased disease severity and poorer outcomes (Mohammad et al., 2021).

Emerging evidence has shown how the COVID-19 pandemic has affected the obesity pandemic, with increases in BMI and overweight and obesity prevalence seen across age groups (Mulugeta et al., 2021; Senthilingam, 2021; Woolford et al., 2021). A study of more than 6000 adolescents in Shanghai found that 12 months after the start of the COVID-19 pandemic, BMI and obesity prevalence had increased and physical activity (PA) had decreased (Yang et al., 2019). Data from the National Child Measurement Programme in England for the 2020–2021 school year showed an increase in obesity prevalence from 10% to 14% in just 1 year among children aged 4–5 years and from 21% to 26% in children aged 10–11 years, with an increase in disparities between children living in the most deprived areas and those living in the least deprived (National Child Measurement Programme, 2022).

Lifestyle Factors, and Social and Environmental Determinants of Obesity

While understanding the physical pathways and mechanisms linking overweight and obesity to ill health is necessary to ensure appropriate clinical interventions, understanding the underlying causes of obesity is essential for public health prevention purposes, and these are undoubtedly complex. Changes in diet and PA are important factors; in much of the world, sedentary behaviours linked with leisure or screen time, motorised transportation, and sedentary work have contributed to a dramatic decrease in PA and energy expenditure (Choi et al., 2010; Liou et al., 2010; Heinonen et al., 2013; Bell et al., 2002; Hill et al., 2003; Pratt et al., 2012). On the other hand, increased energy intake is associated with greater availability and consumption of energy-dense and ultra-processed foods (Poti et al., 2017), leading to energy imbalances. However, while the input-output model is relevant for individual-level interventions, it is increasingly recognised that other social and environmental factors play a key role in the current obesity epidemic and in the success of individual-level interventions (Leeman et al., 2012).

Individual socio-economic status is strongly associated with obesity, but the association also varies depending on national income, with higher levels of obesity among the poorer in high-income countries, and higher levels of obesity among the wealthier in low-income countries (Jaacks et al., 2019; Di Cesare et al., 2013). Environmental factors such as neighbourhood deprivation, vulnerability, and crime are also associated with higher levels of obesity, mostly caused by a decrease in PA, especially among women (Yu & Lippert, 2016). The food environment of the neighbourhood is also associated with obesity, with both food swamps—areas with concentrations of establishments selling high-calorie fast food and junk food—and food deserts—areas with limited access to affordable and healthy foods—associated with obesity

(Cooksey-Stowers et al., 2017). One study has shown that presence of fast food within 0.5 miles of a residence is associated with a 1.6% increase in the probability of gaining over 20 kg in weight (Currie et al., 2009). While the cultural dimensions of obesity have not been explored in depth, a recent study has estimated that national cultural dimensions, particularly individualism and uncertainty avoidance, explained over 50% of the variance in BMI across countries (Wallace et al., 2019).

Obesity Trend Estimation

Definition of Obesity

Despite discussions on the suitability of BMI as a measure of adiposity, these metrics are strongly correlated (Revicki & Israel, 1986), BMI is inexpensive and straightforward to measure (Centers for Disease Control and Prevention, 2022), and it effectively describes changes in adiposity in children as they grow (Cole et al., 2005).

While there have been debates on adopting different cutoffs for adults from particular population groups (Misra, 2003; Stevens, 2003), WHO has adopted a single value. Defining obesity is more difficult during childhood, as healthy proportions of body fat vary by factors such as sex, age and ethnicity; this means that it is difficult to define physiological norms (Griffiths et al., 2011). The most common measures of obesity in childhood are based on relative BMI in a reference population for age-sex combinations although no single reference exists (de Onis et al., 2007; Cole & Lobstein, 2012; Monasta et al., 2011). The WHO growth reference for ages 5–19 years is based mainly on data from the USA, and defines overweight and obesity using cut-offs of 1 and 2 standard deviations, equivalent to 25 kg/m^2 and 30 kg/m^2 respectively at 19 years of age (de Onis et al., 2007). An alternative reference for ages 2–18 years has been published by the International Obesity Task Force, and is based on BMI in six countries and territories (Brazil, Hong Kong, Netherlands, Singapore, UK, USA), with cut-offs corresponding to 25 kg/m^2 and 30 kg/m^2 at 18 years (Cole & Lobstein, 2012).

Global Obesity Estimation

Although obesity was identified as a public health concern in the USA in the 1950s, global data are sparse before the 1970s. Surveys in that decade were mostly in high-income countries, although studies were also carried out in Polynesia and Micronesia, which were already experiencing high levels of obesity, as well as in India (NCD Risk Factor Collaboration (NCD-RisC), 2017). From the 1980s, geographical coverage increased, particularly in adults; for example, by 2017, the Non-Communicable Disease Risk Factor Collaboration (NCD-RisC) had collated data for the 1980s from 62 countries for adults and 23 countries for children and adolescents aged from 5 to 19 years (NCD Risk Factor Collaboration (NCD-RisC), 2017).

To develop effective interventions, we require obesity estimates by country, year, sex, age group, urban or rural place of residence, income level, and other factors such as education and ethnicity. However, in the past decade, extensive data collation efforts and sophisticated statistical modelling have been required simply to make globally comparable estimates for country-year-sex-age combinations. In 2011, estimates of mean BMI at national level in adults were published by the Global Burden of Metabolic Risk Factors of Chronic Diseases Collaborating Group (Finucane et al., 2011), based on 960 country-years of data comprising measurements for nine million individuals; this was followed by estimates of overweight and obesity in adults based on those mean BMI estimates (Stevens et al., 2012). The Global Burden of Disease study has also published estimates of overweight and obesity. The first estimates were for the period 1980–2013, based on 1769 studies and 19,244 data points (Ng et al., 2014). This was followed by quantification of the disease burden related to high BMI between 1990 and 2015, which included estimates of the numbers of children and adults with obesity (Ng et al., 2014; GBD

2015 Obesity Collaborators, 2017). Finally, updated estimates for 195 countries and territories were published in 2020 (Dai et al., 2020). In parallel, NCD-RisC has also published estimates of adiposity at national level, starting with BMI in adults for 200 countries and territories based on almost 1700 studies and 19 million participants (NCD Risk Factor Collaboration (NCD-RisC), 2016a). This was followed by estimates of BMI, obesity and other metrics such as underweight, in both adults and children, based on a larger dataset of more than 2400 studies and 129 million individuals (Fig. 2.1) (NCD Risk Factor Collaboration (NCD-RisC), 2017). Other published estimates include those stratified by urban or rural place of residence (NCD Risk Factor Collaboration (NCD-RisC), 2019), BMI trajectories in school-aged children and adolescents (NCD Risk Factor Collaboration (NCD-RisC), 2020), and on effects of changes in BMI distributions on obesity (NCD Risk Factor Collaboration (NCD-RisC), 2021).

Obesity Trends

Overview

Obesity trends have been estimated using various statistical models, and the cut-offs used for children and adolescents are not standardised. We have therefore selected a single source of estimates to illustrate global obesity trends, the NCD-RisC estimates that we contributed to, which are based on WHO definitions of obesity (NCD Risk Factor Collaboration (NCD-RisC), 2017). However, all estimation efforts give the same broad picture of the epidemic.

There are wide variations in obesity prevalence across the world. In 2016, almost two-thirds of females (65% [95% uncertainty interval, 58–72%]) in American Samoa had obesity, while this was the case for only 3% (2–4%) of females in Viet Nam. There were similar patterns for males, with the highest levels of obesity seen in Nauru at 60% (52–68%) and the lowest in Viet Nam at 2% (1–3%). Regionally, obesity levels were highest in Polynesia and Micronesia, followed by the Middle East and North Africa, North America and southern Africa; the lowest levels were in South, Southeast and East Asia, and in the rest of sub-Saharan Africa. Between 1975 and 2016, the largest absolute increases in obesity prevalence were in Polynesia and Micronesia in both sexes, and in parts of the Middle East in females. No country saw a decrease in obesity between 1975 and 2016, with the smallest increases occurring in Singapore in females and Viet Nam in males.

Severe and morbid obesity are now common in adults in many countries, and follow broadly similar patterns to obesity. The highest levels of severe obesity (>35 kg/m^2) in adults in 2016 were in American Samoa, at 40% (30–49%) and 32% (23–42%) for females and males respectively. This contrasts with estimates for Viet Nam, where severe obesity prevalence was only 0.3% (0.1–0.6%) in females and 0.1% (0.0–0.2%) in males. Morbid obesity (>40 kg/m^2) prevalence had reached 20% (12–29%) in females in Nauru in 2016 and 14% (7–22%) in males, while prevalence estimates in Japan were near zero. Global patterns are shown in more detail in Figs. 2.2, 2.3, and 2.4.

Approximately one-third of children aged 5 years had obesity in parts of Polynesia in 2016. The highest prevalence in females was in Nauru at 34% (14–52%), while for males, the highest prevalence was in Cook Islands at 33% (16–49%). This contrasts with extremely low values in parts of sub-Saharan Africa, with prevalence lowest in Burkina Faso for females at 1.3% (0.1–5.0%) and in Uganda for males at 0.7% (0.0–3.6%). Prevalence rose in every country, with the largest increases occurring in Polynesia and Micronesia for both sexes. Obesity is shown by country in Fig. 2.5.

In summary, in recent decades the obesity epidemic has spread beyond Pacific islands and high-income western countries, and is now of substantial concern in various middle-income regions and increasingly in low-income countries, where there is a dual burden of obesity and underweight (NCD Risk Factor Collaboration (NCD-RisC), 2017).

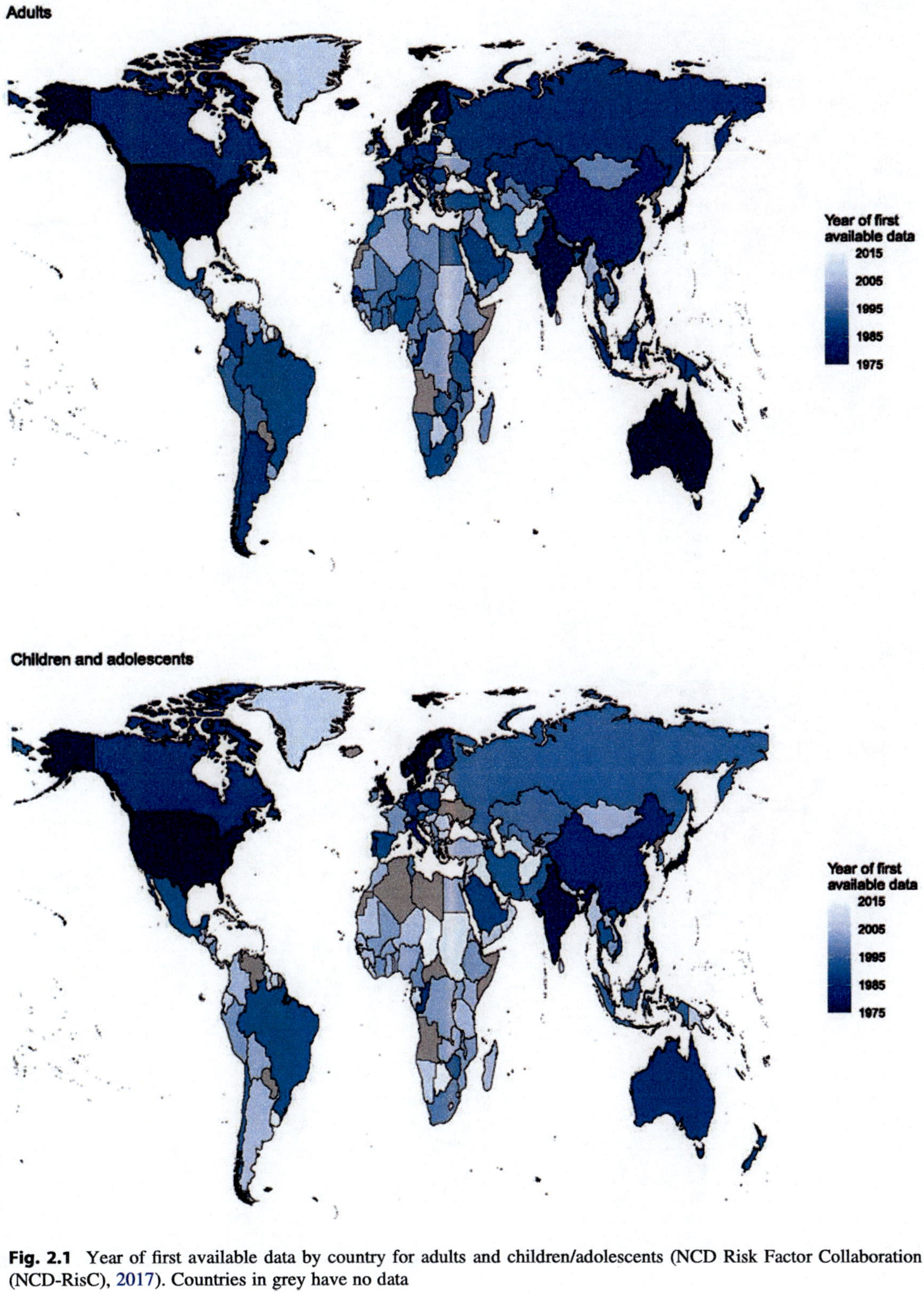

Fig. 2.1 Year of first available data by country for adults and children/adolescents (NCD Risk Factor Collaboration (NCD-RisC), 2017). Countries in grey have no data

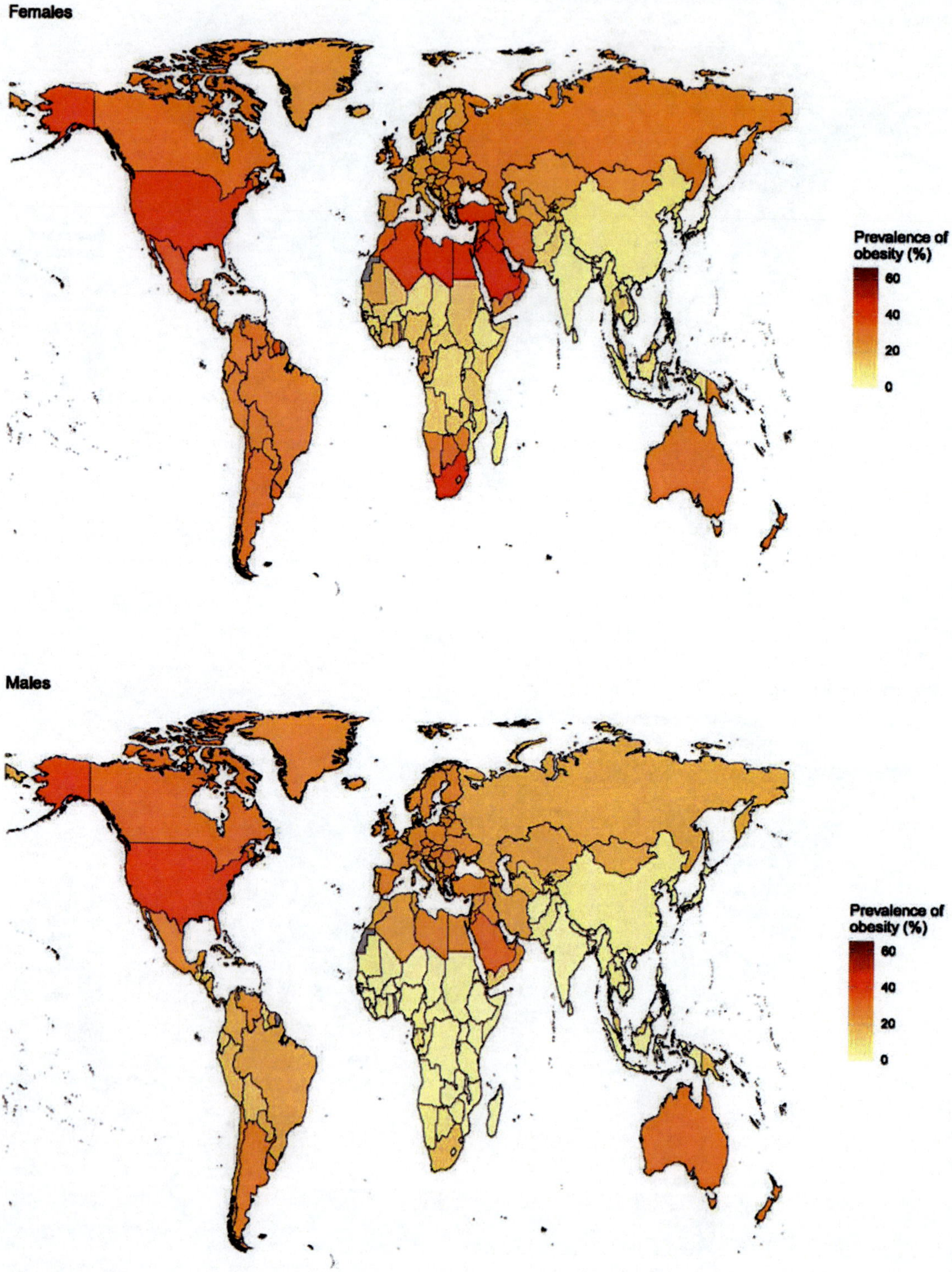

Fig. 2.2 Obesity by country in adults in 2016 (NCD Risk Factor Collaboration (NCD-RisC), 2017). Countries in grey have no estimates

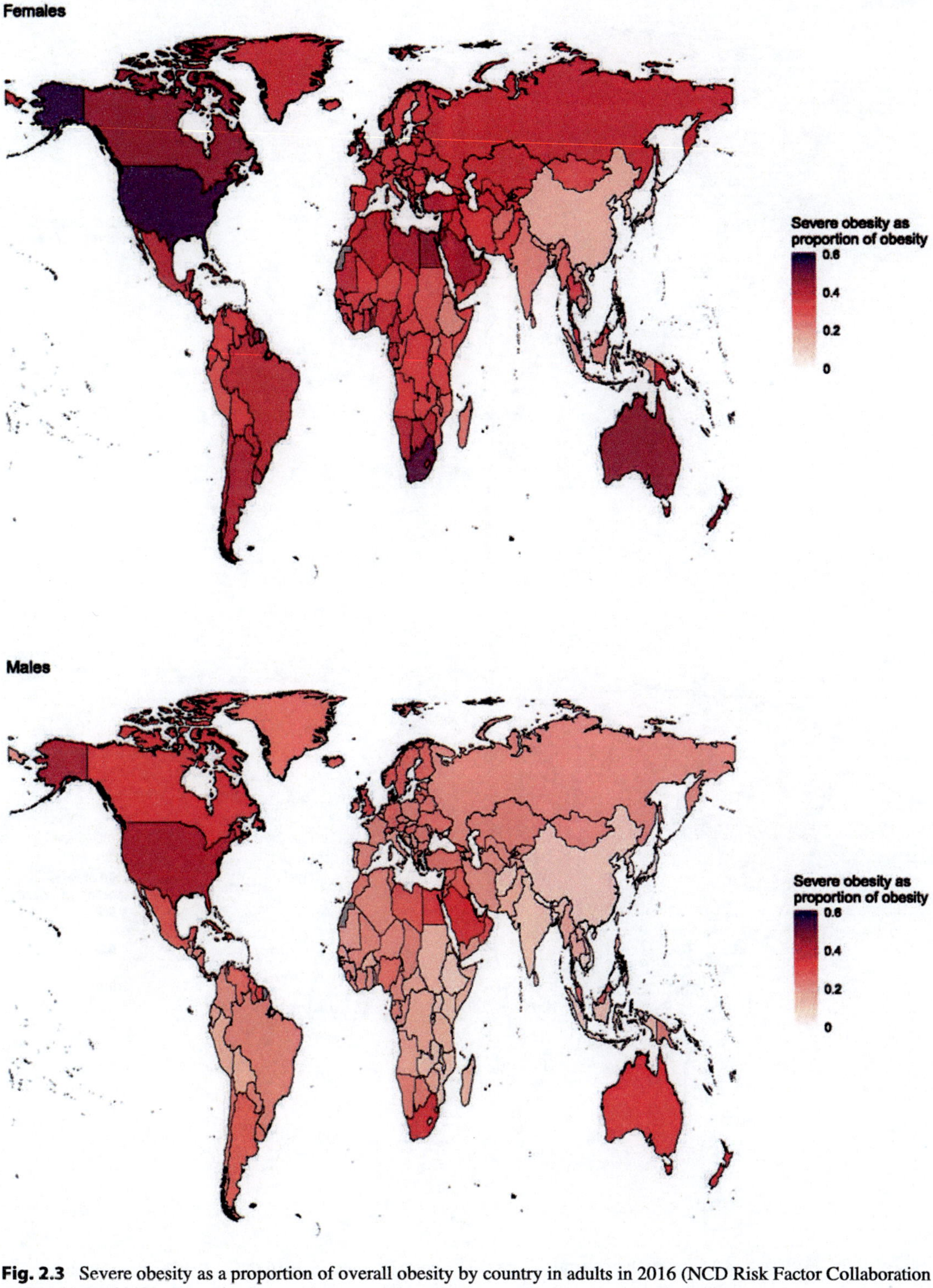

Fig. 2.3 Severe obesity as a proportion of overall obesity by country in adults in 2016 (NCD Risk Factor Collaboration (NCD-RisC), 2017). Countries in grey have no estimates

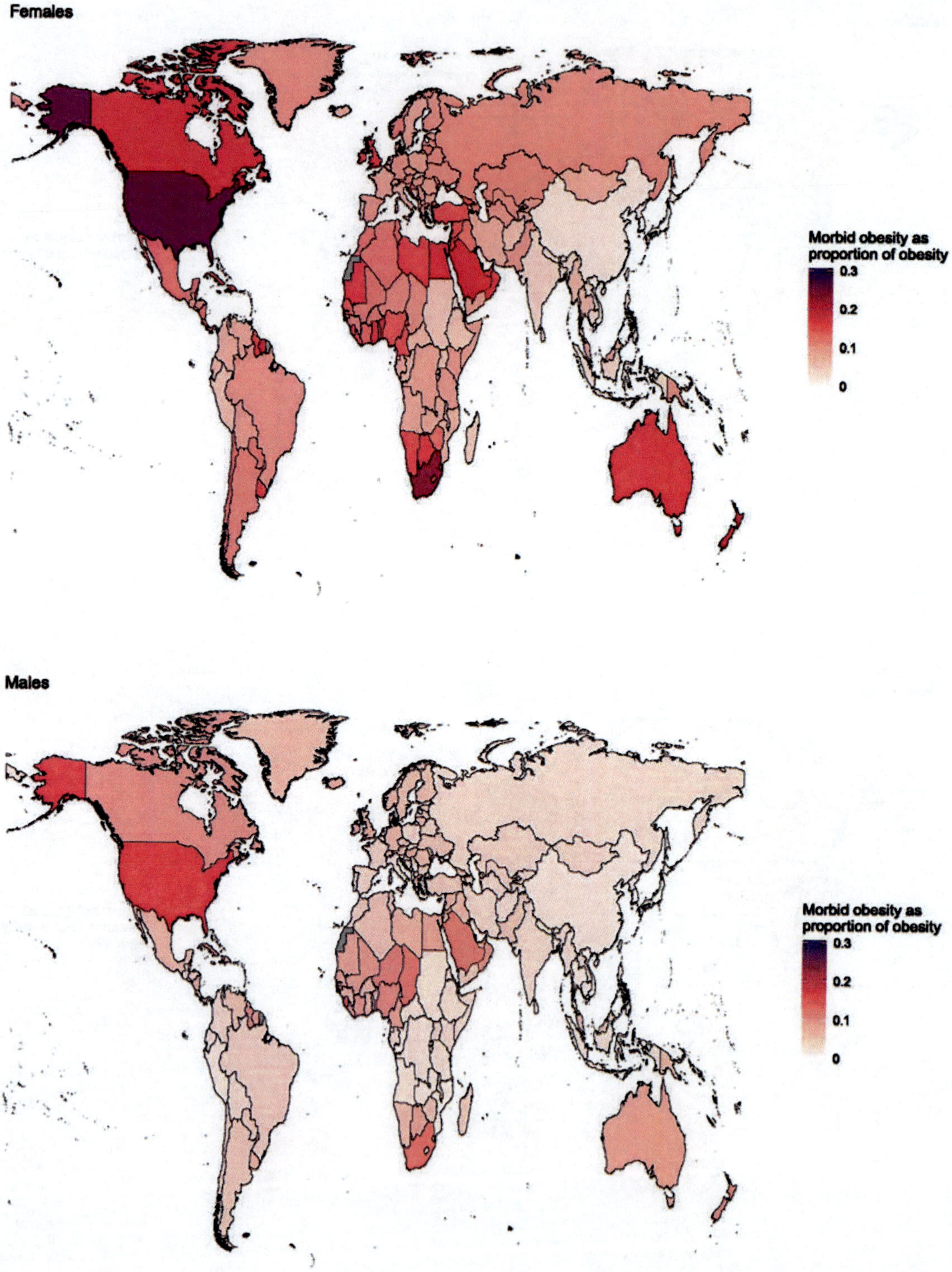

Fig. 2.4 Morbid obesity as a proportion of overall obesity by country in adults in 2016 (NCD Risk Factor Collaboration (NCD-RisC), 2017). Countries in grey have no estimates

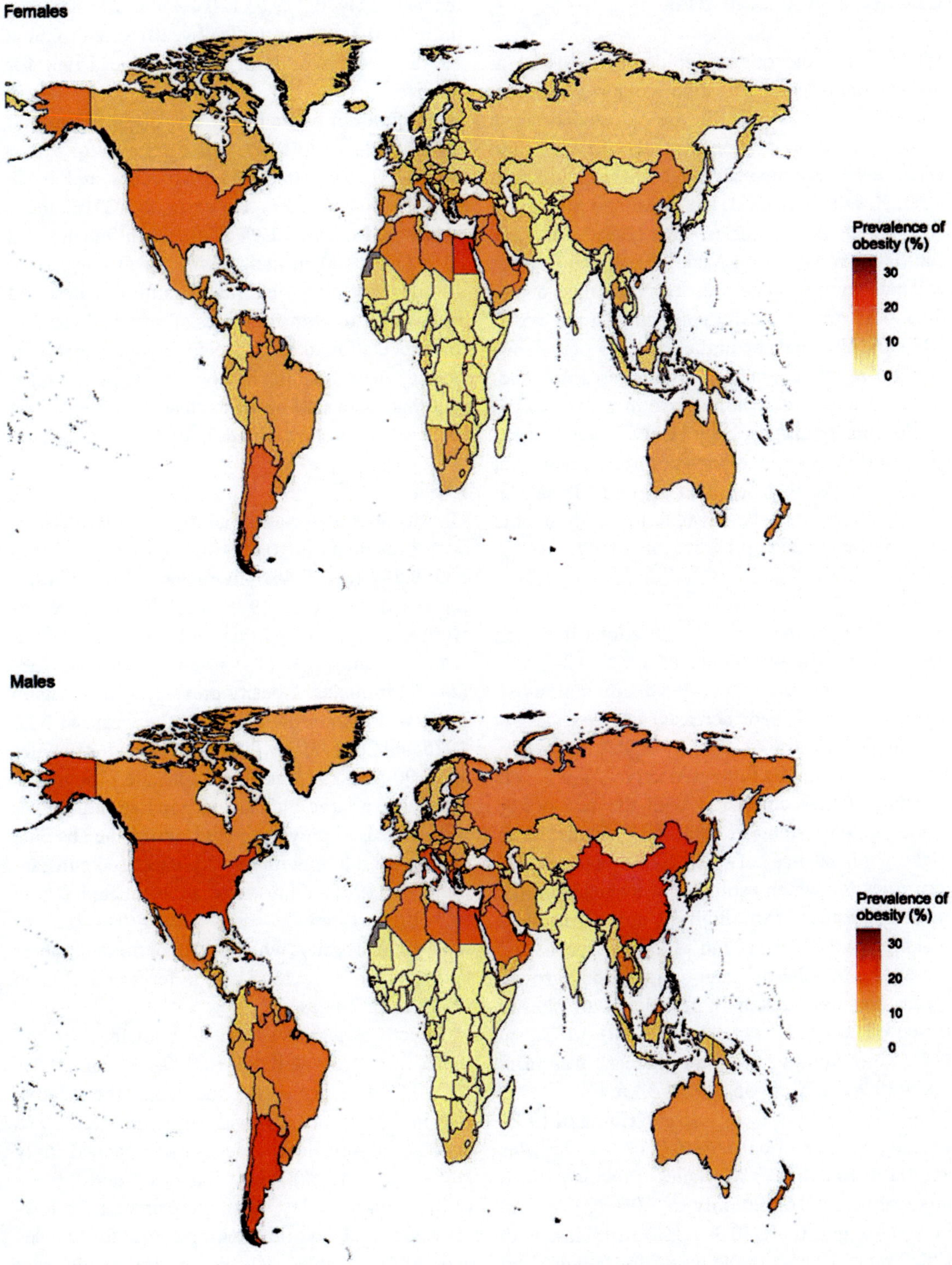

Fig. 2.5 Obesity by country in children aged 5 years in 2016 (NCD Risk Factor Collaboration (NCD-RisC), 2017). Countries in grey have no estimates

Obesity in Key Countries

We describe the obesity epidemic in detail at the national level for nine countries of key interest. **China** and **India** are selected because of their large population sizes, dense data, and because they are representative of East and South Asia. **Brazil**, **South Africa**, **Iran** and **Germany** are populous countries in Latin America, sub-Saharan Africa, the Middle East, and Europe, and have multiple data sources. **Nauru** has one of the most extreme obesity epidemics in the world, while the **USA** has the highest obesity prevalence in high-income countries; in both cases, the obesity epidemic started earlier than in the rest of the world. Finally, **Japan** has obesity trends that are quite different from other countries, given that they are lower than in other regions. Trends in obesity metrics and data availability in these nine countries are shown in Figs. 2.6 and 2.7.

China

In 1975, fewer than one in 100 adults in China had obesity, with prevalence of 0.8% (0.3–1.5%) in females and 0.2% (0.1–0.5%) in males. By 2016, prevalence had increased to 7% (5–10%) for females and 6% (4–9%) for males. However, China has continued to have relatively low levels of adult obesity compared with the rest of the world. In 1975, females in China had the 190th highest prevalence of the 200 countries and territories for which estimates were made, while males had the 178th highest; in 2016, these rankings were 191st and 145th respectively. Increases in obesity and population growth meant that the number of females with obesity increased from 1.6 m (0.7–3.3 m) to 38 m (24–57 m), and in males, the increase was from 0.6 m (0.2–1.2 m) to 35 m (21–53 m).

Severe obesity was very rare in China in 1975, with an estimate of 0.0% (0.0–0.1%) for females and 0.0% (0.0–0.0%) for males. Prevalence had increased by 2016, but only to 1.0% (0.6–1.6%) in females and 0.6% (0.3–1.1%) in males, with China ranked 195th in the world for females and 170th for males. Similarly, morbid obesity prevalence in China in 1975 was close to zero, and had reached only 0.2% (0.1–0.4%) in females and 0.2% (0.0–0.4%) in males by 2016, with China 195th in the world for females and 169th for males.

In children and adolescents, obesity also had low prevalence in 1975, with estimates for 5 year olds of 0.2% (0.0–0.7%) in females and 0.4% (0.0–1.4%) in males. However, by 2016, these values had reached 12% (7–19%) in females and 21% (14–29%) in males, with an increase from 144th to 60th in global rankings for females, and from 131st to 16th for males. There is, therefore, an expectation that the relatively low levels of obesity seen in adults in China will not continue, and that there will be an explosion in prevalence as these children reach adulthood.

India

Obesity was also rare in adults in India in 1975, with prevalence of 0.6% (0.2–1.1%) in females and 0.2% (0.1–0.4%) in males. While obesity increased between 1975 and 2016, increases were less pronounced than in China, with prevalence reaching 5% (4–7%) in females and 3% (2–4%) in males. Obesity prevalence in adults in India was among the lowest in the world in both 1975 and 2016, at 194th in both years for females and 190th in 1975 and 187th in 2016 for males. However, a large increase in population together with increased prevalence meant that the absolute number of adults with obesity increased substantially. In 1975, there were an estimated 0.8 m (0.3–1.6 m) females and 0.3 m (0.1–0.6 m) males with obesity, while by 2016, these numbers had reached 21 m (13–31 m) in females and 12 m (7–19 m) in males.

Severe obesity was rare in both females and males in 1975, at 0.0% (0.0–0.1%) and 0.0% (0.0–0.0%) respectively, and while the relative rise in severe obesity was large between 1975 and 2016, absolute values had reached only 1.1% (0.7–1.7%) in females and 0.3% (0.2–0.6%) in males; these were among the lowest values in the world, ranking 192nd for females and 188th for males. Morbid obesity remains rare in adults in India, reaching a prevalence of 0.2% (0.1–0.5%) in females and 0.1% (0.0–0.2%) in

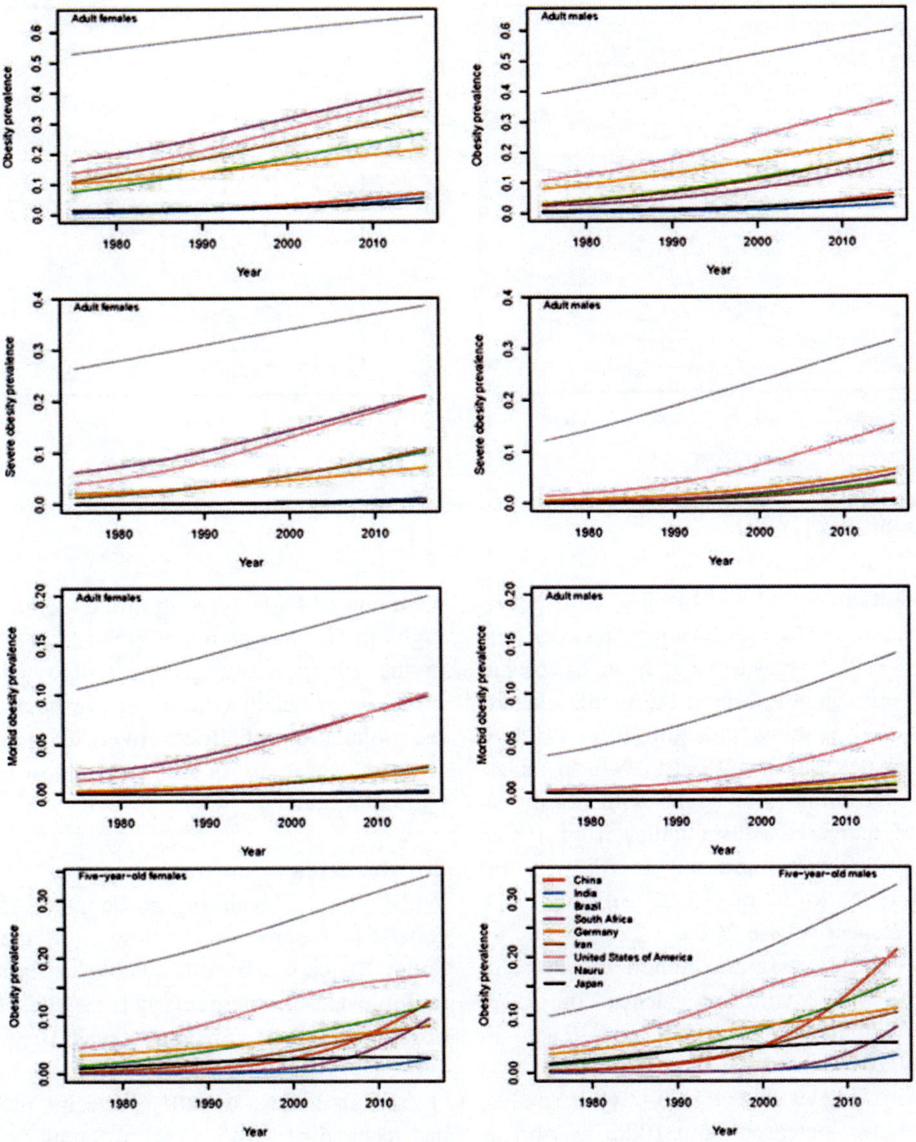

Fig. 2.6 Trends in obesity metrics in key countries between 1975 and 2016. (NCD Risk Factor Collaboration (NCD-RisC), 2017)

males in 2016, ranking 191st and 183rd in the world.

Obesity remains uncommon in children in India. In 1975, obesity in 5-year-olds was 0.0% (0.0–0.1%) in females and 0.1% (0.0–0.3%) in males. In contrast with China, increases by 2016 were modest, with prevalence reaching 2.5% (0.9–5.2%) in females and 3.1% (1.1–6.6%) in males; rankings remained the same between 1975 and 2016, at 194th for females and 158th for males. These results suggest that there will be contrasting trends in obesity in the world's two most populous countries in the coming decades.

Brazil

While obesity trends vary across Latin America, Brazil is representative of broad patterns in the region. In adults, obesity was already common in 1975, with prevalence of 8% (4–13%) in females and 3% (1–6%) in males. By 2016, more than one

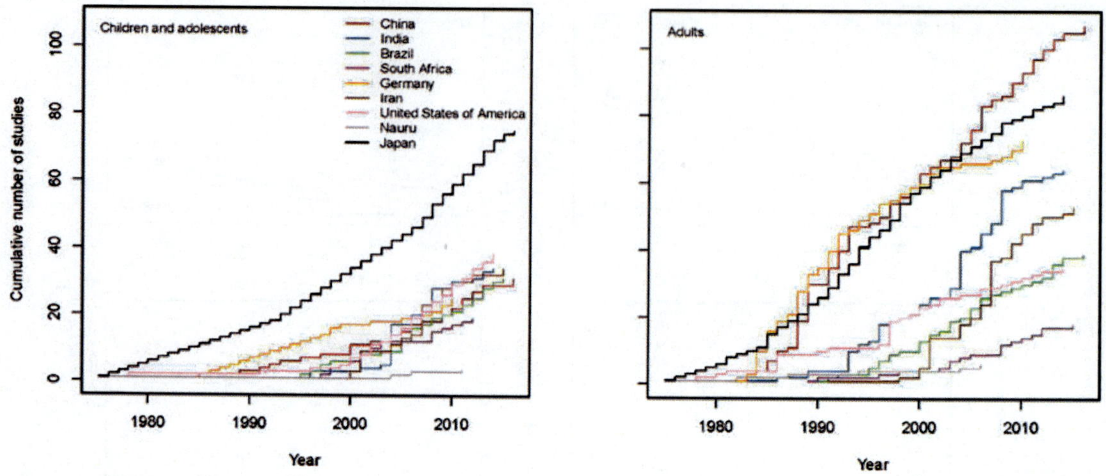

Fig. 2.7 Cumulative number of obesity studies in key countries between 1975 and 2016. (NCD Risk Factor Collaboration (NCD-RisC), 2017)

in five adults in Brazil had obesity, with prevalence reaching 26% (21–32%) in females and 19% (15–24%) in males. Obesity in Brazil has remained consistently around the median across countries, with rankings changing from 110th to 86th in females and from 99th to 94th in males. However, the number of adults with obesity in Brazil has increased substantially, from 1.8 m (0.8–3.4 m) females and 0.8 m (0.3–1.5 m) males in 1975, to 20 m (13–27 m) and 13 m (9–19 m) respectively in 2016.

Severe obesity was uncommon in adults in Brazil in 1975, with prevalence of 1.2% (0.4–2.7%) in females and 0.1% (0.0–0.4%) in males. By 2016, these values had reached 10% (7–14%) in females and 4% (3–7%) in males, while rankings increased from 108th to 74th in females, and from 104th to 93rd in males. Morbid obesity prevalence had reached 2.6% (1.3–4.6%) in females and 0.9% (0.3–1.9%) in males, with Brazil again around the median across countries, being ranked 92nd for females and 100th for males.

As in much of the world, there have been worrying increases in obesity in children and adolescents in Brazil over recent decades. In 1975, only 1.4% (0.1–5.3%) of females and 1.3% (0.1–5.4%) of males aged 5 years had obesity. By 2016, these values had reached 12% (5–21%) and 16% (8–26%), respectively, which were ranked 65th and 47th in the world. Accordingly, there is concern that high levels of obesity in the youngest age groups will translate into a long-term health issue affecting large parts of the population of Brazil over many decades, with increases in obesity in males being of particular note.

South Africa

While obesity levels in sub-Saharan Africa are consistently some of the lowest in the world, South Africa has been a notable exception over multiple decades, particularly in females. In 1975, obesity prevalence in adults was already 18% (11–26%) in females, while it was only 2% (1–5%) in males; by 2016, obesity prevalence had reached 41% (35–47%) in females and 16% (12–21%) in males. In females, these were some of the highest levels in the world outside Polynesia and Micronesia, ranking 28th and 23rd in 1975 and 2016, respectively. However, males had obesity prevalence below the median across countries in both years, ranking 119th and 112th in 1975 and 2016.

Severe obesity prevalence was 6% (3–12%) in females in 1975; this was substantially higher than in the USA, for example. However, the corresponding prevalence in males was only 0.3% (0.1–0.7%). There had been sharp increases by 2016, with severe obesity prevalence in females reaching 21% (16–27%), while in males it was 6% (3–9%), and again the rankings were quite different by sex. For females, South Africa was ranked 16th in both 1975 and 2016, while the ranking increased from 83rd to 65th for males. There were similar patterns for morbid obesity, with prevalence of 10% (6–14%) in females in 2016, and 2% (1–4%) in males. However, the rankings were more similar between the sexes, at 15th and 33rd respectively.

In children and adolescents in 2016, prevalence of obesity was more similar across the sexes in 5-year-olds than in adults, at 10% (3–20%) for females and 8% (3–17%) for males. Rankings had increased since 1975, from 148th to 91st in females, and from 140th to 128th in males. Together, these results illustrate the complex patterns present in obesity trends in South Africa across age groups and by severity of obesity.

Germany

As in much of Europe, obesity in adults was already common in Germany in 1975, with a prevalence of 10% (7–14%) in females and 8% (5–12%) in males. By 2016, more than one in five adults in Germany had obesity, with prevalences of 21% (17–26%) in females and 25% (20–31%) in males. However, despite these increases, global rankings for Germany dropped from 78th to 122nd for females and from 33rd to 48th for males, as the obesity epidemic spread even more quickly elsewhere in the world.

Severe obesity had low prevalence in Germany in 1975, at 2% (1–3%) in females and 0.5% (0.2–1.0%) in males; these values had increased to 7% (4–10%) in both sexes by 2016. Again, the ranking in females dropped below the median across countries, moving from 74th to 120th, while the ranking for males changed only slightly, from 47th to 46th. The prevalence of morbid obesity reached 2% (1–4%) in females and 2% (1–3%) in males, and similar patterns in rankings were observed: Germany moved from 87th to 117th in the world for females and from 59th to 54th for males between 1975 and 2016.

Obesity in children aged 5 years was not common in Germany in 1975, at 3% (0–10%) for both sexes. However, given the very low prevalence at that time in much of the world, Germany was ranked 30th for females and 29th for males. By 2016, obesity prevalence had increased to 8% (2–18%) in females and 11% (3–23%) in males. However, increases elsewhere in the world meant that in 2016, Germany was ranked 102nd in the world for 5-year-old females and 95th in the world for males. These results suggest that the earlier imbalance between obesity in females and males in Germany has reduced, with obesity levels relative to the rest of the world that are similar in both sexes.

Iran

Obesity trends in Iran are representative of the Middle East as a whole, which has some of the highest levels in the world. In adults in 1975, obesity was already common in females, with prevalence of 11% (6–18%), but less common in males, with prevalence of 3% (1–6%). Prevalence had increased substantially by 2016, but with persistent differences between the two sexes, as obesity prevalence was 34% (28–39%) in females and 20% (16–25%) in males. The increase in obesity in Iran occurred more quickly than in the rest of the world: female rankings increased from 69th to 41st, and male rankings from 108th to 87th. However, within the Middle East and North Africa region, Iran was below the median value by country in both 1975 and 2016.

Severe obesity was rare in females in Iran in 1975, with a prevalence of 1% (1–3%), while the corresponding value in males was 0.1% (0.0–0.4%). However, there had been large increases by 2016, with a prevalence of 11% (8–14%) in females and 4% (2–6%) in males; rankings increased from 99th to 68th in females and from 119th to 104th in males. Morbid obesity reached 3% (1–4%) in females in 2016 and 1% (0–2%) in males, ranking 86th and 116th respectively. Again, Iran was below the median for the Middle East and North Africa region for both severe and morbid obesity.

Obesity was rare in children aged 5 years in Iran in 1975, with prevalence estimates of 0.4% (0.0–1.7%) in both females and males, corresponding to rankings of 126th and 132nd respectively. There had been large increases in prevalence by 2016, with values of 8% (4–15%) in females and 10% (5–17%) in males; rankings increased to 99th in females and 106th in males. Iran therefore has high levels of obesity prevalence, but the epidemic is slightly less severe than in some other countries in the Middle East.

USA

Obesity was already common in adults in the USA in 1975, with a prevalence of 14% (10–18%) in females and 11% (7–15%) in males. By 2016, these values had increased substantially; almost 4 in 10 adults had obesity, with a prevalence of 38% (33–44%) in females and 37% (31–42%) in males. However, while the USA had the highest ranking among high-income western countries in 2016 for both sexes, the obesity epidemic was even more severe elsewhere in the world. The USA had only the 45th highest levels for females in 1975 and the 30th highest in 2016; for males, the corresponding rankings were 18th and 14th.

In 1975, severe obesity prevalence in adults in the USA was 4% (2–6%) and 1.4% (0.7–2.4%) in females and males respectively; by 2016, it had reached 21% (16–26%) in females and 15% (11–20%) in males. Global rankings were 33rd in 1975 and 17th in 2016 for females; for males, the corresponding rankings were 17th and 14th. Morbid obesity was rare in 1975, with prevalence of 1.3% (0.5–2.5%) in females and 0.2% (0.1–0.6%) in males. In contrast, by 2016, morbid obesity affected around one in twelve adults in the USA, with a prevalence of 10% (6–15%) in females and 6% (3–10%) in males. Rankings were 18th in 1975 and 14th in 2016 for females, while for males the corresponding values were 14th and 13th. There has, therefore, been a particularly concerning increase in extreme obesity in adults in the USA.

In children aged 5 years, obesity was uncommon in 1975, with prevalence of 4% (2–9%) in females and 4% (1–9%) in males. By 2016, these values had reached 17% (10–25%) in females and 20% (12–29%) in males. However, many other countries have experienced even worse childhood obesity epidemics, particularly in Polynesia and Micronesia, with the USA ranked 23rd and 22nd globally for females in 1975 and 2016, and 18th and 20th for males.

Nauru

Nauru is experiencing one of the most extreme obesity epidemics in the world. In 1975, obesity prevalence in adults had already reached 53% (43–62%) in females and 39% (30–49%) in males. By 2016, these values had increased even further, to 65% (57–72%) in females and 60% (52–68%) in males. Nauru was ranked first in the world for both sexes in 1975, and first for males but second for females in 2016, as American Samoa had slightly higher obesity prevalence.

Severe obesity was also common in Nauru in 1975, affecting one in four females, with a prevalence of 26% (18–36%); in males, prevalence was 12% (7–20%). By 2016, more than one in three adults in Nauru had severe obesity, with prevalence of 39% (29–48%) in females and 32% (22–41%) in males. While Nauru ranked first in both sexes in 1975, American Samoa had slightly greater prevalence in 2016. Morbid obesity was also common in females in Nauru in 1975, with prevalence of 11% (5–19%); in males, prevalence was 4% (1–9%). By 2016, one in six adults in Nauru had morbid obesity, with prevalence of 20% (12–29%) in females and 14% (7–22%) in males. Nauru had the most morbid obesity in the world in both sexes in 1975 and 2016.

Nauru also has an extreme childhood obesity epidemic. In 5-year-old children, obesity prevalence in 1975 was 17% (4–35%) in females and 10% (1–26%) in males, and by 2016, these values had reached 34% (14–52%) in females and 32% (14–49%) in males. Nauru had the highest levels of obesity in females aged 5 years in both 1975 and 2016, while it was ranked second and third for males in 1975 and 2016 respectively; in the latter year, Cook Islands and Palau had slightly higher prevalence. The obesity epidemic has therefore already affected Nauru for more than 50 years, and current childhood obesity will lead to severe health problems that will persist for the rest of this century.

Japan

Japan has experienced quite different obesity trends from most of the rest of the world. In adults, obesity was uncommon in 1975, with prevalence of 1.5% (0.9–2.3%) in females and 0.6% (0.4–1.0%) in males. However, in contrast to many other countries, prevalence has increased only modestly; in 2016, it was only 4% (3–6%) in females and 5% (3–7%) in males. While in 1975, numerous countries had lower obesity prevalence than Japan, which was ranked 168th for females and 138th for males, by 2016, obesity prevalence in females was only lower in Viet Nam, while Japan was ranked 157th for males.

More extreme forms of obesity remain very rare in Japan. The prevalence of severe obesity was 0.1% (0.0–0.1%) in females and 0.0% (0.0–0.0%) in males in 1975, and had risen only to 0.5% (0.3–0.9%) in females and 0.4% (0.2–0.7%) in males by 2016. Again, Japan's rankings fell as other countries experienced greater increases in obesity. For females, the ranking fell from 178th to 199th, with only Viet Nam having lower prevalence, while for males the ranking fell from 177th to 186th. Morbid obesity is very uncommon in Japan, with a prevalence of 0.0% (0.0–0.1%) in females and males in 2016. Japan had the lowest estimated prevalence of morbid obesity in any country or territory in both females and males in that year.

Obesity is also rare in children in Japan. In 1975, prevalence was 1.0% (0.4–1.8%) in females aged 5 years and 1.6% (0.8–2.9%) in their male counterparts. By 2016, these values had reached only 3% (2–4%) in females and 5% (3–8%) in males. Japan's ranking fell from 85th to 189th in females aged 5 years and from 55th to 146th in males. Japan is therefore an example of what can be achieved in the long-term fight against the obesity epidemic in a high-income society.

Future Obesity Monitoring

Given the spread of the obesity epidemic across most of the world, including high prevalence even in young children in many countries, it is likely that monitoring will be required across the world over several decades at least, and potentially for the rest of the century and beyond. Current interventions appear to have limited effects; to design more effective tools and policies, and to answer all of the research questions of interest to the global health community, we require long-term coordinated data collection efforts in as many countries as possible.

In this section, we make suggestions for how this data collection and modelling could proceed, based on our experiences of a large-scale data collation and modelling effort. These are personal perspectives, and we would expect other researchers to have different opinions; our aim is to contribute to a conversation on the data collection that is desirable and achievable in coming years. These discussions should include not only NGOs, governments, epidemiologists and global health experts, but also technical experts, particularly statisticians and computer scientists, who can maximise the efficacy and impact of data collection and analysis.

We suggest that a systematic data collection effort that starts around 2030 and continues indefinitely is needed. The types of data required are relatively inexpensive and straightforward to gather, and collection of measured data (rather than self-reported data) is feasible in most countries in the world. This effort would provide detailed longitudinal data in as many countries and territories in the world as possible, removing most of the requirements for considering countries as being representative of one another. There should be detailed planning during the rest of this decade; while this is a lengthy period, we need data that are measured using internationally agreed metrics and standard equipment. This will avoid future analysts having to carry out complex and time-consuming work to make data comparable and ready for analysis. This means that international agreement is required now on what should be measured and how.

If large cohorts can be recruited and then followed over the life course, perhaps at zero, 30 and 60 years of age in 2030, this would allow for more powerful statistical analyses than are possible at present. Current analyses rely on cross-sectional data, with many results simply describing associations at population level. Longitudinal data at individual level, including covariates at various time points, would allow more flexibility in statistical modelling, such as the option of applying survival analysis techniques, and perhaps recent developments on causality. Bayesian hierarchical models might still be used, but rather than borrowing strength between similar countries, they might be used to allow for data sparsity in a large range of variables, such as ethnicity or income levels.

Data on obesity need to be objective and measured, and we believe that discussions with computer scientists and technology experts before data collection starts would be fruitful. Our suggestions are speculative, but it appears possible that simple, robust, low-cost equipment for measuring both height and weight could be developed, and then provided to individuals in the study, rather than relying on measurements by researchers. This equipment could use technology such as Bluetooth and mobile telephones to connect to a cloud-based data repository (or a future equivalent); this technology would also make it easier to maintain contact with participants over time. These types of measurement could be carried out now with scales to measure weight, and laser-based devices are available for height (Mayol-Kreiser et al., 2015). Covariates could be updated using surveys accessible from mobile telephones, while individuals would only need to provide blood samples once in a lifetime for genotype data to be collected. Recruitment of large cohorts might also allow subsequent randomised clinical trials to be carried out to assess interventions, providing higher quality data on their efficacy than is often available at present.

To monitor the effect of interventions, we require large-scale objective measurement of PA and diet. This is currently difficult to do objectively; wearable technology for measuring PA is available, although it is still relatively expensive. However, we expect this technology to become cheaper, more reliable and robust, meaning that PA data should improve substantially in the near future. Dietary intake appears more difficult to measure objectively, and this gap should be a key focus of global research. It is possible to measure nutrition-related biomarkers in urine (Picó et al., 2019), and we speculate that it might be feasible to refine these techniques to measure some key aspects of household diet using wastewater.

There also needs to be careful consideration of future global targets. Many of the targets set around 10 years ago have proved to be unrealistic; if all or almost all countries fail to meet these targets, it reduces the effectiveness of the exercise, and makes it much harder for researchers to explain results to the public via the media. These difficulties in communication are exacerbated when targets are met because of wars or repressive governments. We suggest a system with various levels, perhaps one to five stars; one star would be made extremely easy to meet, although with some possibility of failure, while five stars would be reached only in a scenario that was close to ideal, such as morbid obesity prevalence in Japan.

Finally, we suggest that there also needs to be more discussion between more technically minded statisticians and global health researchers on the types of methodology that could potentially be applicable. We give one example here of cutting-edge statistical methodology that might be relevant, but which we believe is not well known beyond academic statisticians. These are Bayesian nonparametric methods, which can be used to estimate whole distributions of variables using data on individuals. Estimates made using these methods would provide a much richer understanding of trends than estimating means and prevalences based on cutoffs, potentially allowing earlier and more effective interventions to be made. Moreover, recent technical developments allow estimates of these distributions to vary based on covariates, providing richer information still.

Conclusions

Obesity is a long-term global health crisis, which we currently have few effective tools to tackle. We have shown how seriously obesity, and particularly more extreme forms of obesity, can affect health. We have described the monitoring efforts carried out to date, which have become more systematic over the past decade, and which we suggest need to be extended to the medium to long term. We have also shown that obesity levels are quite different across the world, but with few countries successfully containing the epidemic. In conclusion, the information we present is a call to further action to improve hundreds of millions of lives around the world.

References

2021 Global Nutrition Report. [cited 13 Apr 2022]. Available https://globalnutritionreport.org/reports/2021-global-nutrition-report/

Abbasi, A., Juszczyk, D., van Jaarsveld, C. H. M., & Gulliford, M. C. (2017). Body mass index and incident type 1 and type 2 diabetes in children and young adults: A retrospective cohort study. *Journal of the Endocrine Society, 1*, 524–537.

Adams, R. E., & Bukowski, W. M. (2008). Peer victimization as a predictor of depression and body mass index in obese and non-obese adolescents. *Journal of Child Psychology and Psychiatry, 49*, 858–866.

Adult overweight and obesity. In *NHS digital* [Internet]. [cited 13 Apr 2022]. Available https://digital.nhs.uk/data-and-information/publications/statistical/statistics-on-obesity-physical-activity-and-diet/england-2020/part-3-adult-obesity-copy

Algoblan, A., Alalfi, M., & Khan, M. (2014). Mechanism linking diabetes mellitus and obesity. *Diabetes, Metabolic Syndrome and Obesity: Targets and Therapy, 7*, 587.

Ali, Z., & Ulrik, C. S. (2013). Obesity and asthma: A coincidence or a causal relationship? A systematic review. *Respiratory Medicine, 107*, 1287–1300.

An, R., Yan, H., Shi, X., & Yang, Y. (2017). Childhood obesity and school absenteeism: A systematic review and meta-analysis. *Obesity Reviews, 18*, 1412–1424.

Atlantis, E., & Baker, M. (2008). Obesity effects on depression: Systematic review of epidemiological studies. *International Journal of Obesity, 32*, 881–891.

Baffi, C. W., Winnica, D. E., & Holguin, F. (2015). Asthma and obesity: Mechanisms and clinical implications. *Asthma Research and Practice, 1*, 1.

Barber, T. M., Hanson, P., Weickert, M. O., & Franks, S. (2019). Obesity and polycystic ovary syndrome: Implications for pathogenesis and novel management strategies. *Clinical Medicine Insights: Reproductive Health, 13*, 1179558119874042.

Beauloye, V., Zech, F., Tran, H. T. M., Clapuyt, P., Maes, M., & Brichard, S. M. (2007). Determinants of early atherosclerosis in obese children and adolescents. *The Journal of Clinical Endocrinology and Metabolism, 92*, 3025–3032.

Bell, A. C., Ge, K., & Popkin, B. M. (2002). The road to obesity or the path to prevention: Motorized transportation and obesity in China. *Obesity Research, 10*, 277–283.

Centers for Disease Control and Prevention. Body mass index measurement in schools. [cited 13 Apr 2022]. Available https://www.cdc.gov/healthyschools/obesity/bmi/pdf/BMI_execsumm.pdf

Bridger, T. (2009). Childhood obesity and cardiovascular disease. *Paediatrics & Child Health, 14*, 177–182.

Carpiniello, B., Pinna, F., Pillai, G., Nonnoi, V., Pisano, E., Corrias, S., et al. (2009). Obesity and psychopathology. A study of psychiatric comorbidity among patients attending a specialist obesity unit. *Epidemiologia e Psichiatria Sociale, 18*, 119–127.

Chen, Y. C., Dong, G. H., Lin, K. C., & Lee, Y. L. (2013). Gender difference of childhood overweight and obesity in predicting the risk of incident asthma: A systematic review and meta-analysis. *Obesity Reviews, 14*, 222–231.

Choi, B., Schnall, P. L., Yang, H., Dobson, M., Landsbergis, P., Israel, L., et al. (2010). Sedentary work, low physical job demand, and obesity in US workers. *American Journal of Industrial Medicine, 53*, 1088–1101.

Cole, T. J., & Lobstein, T. (2012). Extended international (IOTF) body mass index cut-offs for thinness, overweight and obesity. *Pediatric Obesity, 7*, 284–294.

Cole, T. J., Faith, M. S., Pietrobelli, A., & Heo, M. (2005). What is the best measure of adiposity change in growing children: BMI, BMI %, BMI z-score or BMI centile? *European Journal of Clinical Nutrition, 59*, 419–425.

Cooksey-Stowers, K., Schwartz, M. B., & Brownell, K. D. (2017). Food swamps predict obesity rates better than food deserts in the United States. *International Journal of Environmental Research and Public Health, 14*, 1366.

Corica, F., Corsonello, A., Apolone, G., Mannucci, E., Lucchetti, M., Bonfiglio, C., et al. (2008). Metabolic syndrome, psychological status and quality of life in obesity: The QUOVADIS study. *International Journal of Obesity, 32*, 185–191.

Currie, J., DellaVigna, S., Moretti, E., & Pathania, V. (2009). The effect of fast food restaurants on obesity and weight gain. *American Economic Journal: Economic Policy, 2*, 32–63.

Dai, H., Alsalhe, T. A., Chalghaf, N., Riccò, M., Bragazzi, N. L., & Wu, J. (2020). The global burden of disease attributable to high body mass index in 195 countries and territories, 1990-2017: An analysis of the Global Burden of Disease Study. *PLoS Medicine, 17*, e1003198.

de Onis, M., Garza, C., Victora, C. G., Onyango, A. W., Frongillo, E. A., & Martines, J. (2004). The WHO Multicentre Growth Reference Study: Planning, study

design, and methodology. *Food and Nutrition Bulletin, 25*, S15–S26.
de Onis, M., Onyango, A. W., Borghi, E., Siyam, A., Nishida, C., & Siekmann, J. (2007). Development of a WHO growth reference for school-aged children and adolescents. *Bulletin of the World Health Organization, 85*, 660–667.
Di Cesare, M., Khang, Y.-H., Asaria, P., Blakely, T., Cowan, M. J., Farzadfar, F., et al. (2013). Inequalities in non-communicable diseases and effective responses. *Lancet, 381*, 585–597.
Di Cesare, M., Sorić, M., Bovet, P., Miranda, J. J., Bhutta, Z., Stevens, G. A., et al. (2019). The epidemiological burden of obesity in childhood: A worldwide epidemic requiring urgent action. *BMC Medicine, 17*, 212.
Dietz, W. H., Jr., Gross, W. L., & Kirkpatrick, J. A., Jr. (1982). Blount disease (tibia vara): Another skeletal disorder associated with childhood obesity. *The Journal of Pediatrics, 101*, 735–737.
Dong, Z., Xu, X., Wang, C., Cartledge, S., Maddison, R., & Shariful Islam, S. M. (2020). Association of overweight and obesity with obstructive sleep apnoea: A systematic review and meta-analysis. *Obesity Medicine, 17*, 100185.
Eckel, R. H., Grundy, S. M., & Zimmet, P. Z. (2005). The metabolic syndrome. *Lancet, 365*, 1415–1428.
Finucane, M. M., Stevens, G. A., Cowan, M. J., Danaei, G., Lin, J. K., Paciorek, C. J., et al. (2011). National, regional, and global trends in body-mass index since 1980: Systematic analysis of health examination surveys and epidemiological studies with 960 country-years and 9·1 million participants. *Lancet, 377*, 557–567.
Franks, P. W., Hanson, R. L., Knowler, W. C., Sievers, M. L., Bennett, P. H., & Looker, H. C. (2010). Childhood obesity, other cardiovascular risk factors, and premature death. *The New England Journal of Medicine, 362*, 485–493.
Friend, A., Craig, L., & Turner, S. (2013). The prevalence of metabolic syndrome in children: A systematic review of the literature. *Metabolic Syndrome and Related Disorders, 11*, 71–80.
Gao, M., Piernas, C., Astbury, N. M., Hippisley-Cox, J., O'Rahilly, S., Aveyard, P., et al. (2021). Associations between body-mass index and COVID-19 severity in 6·9 million people in England: A prospective, community-based, cohort study. *The Lancet Diabetes and Endocrinology, 9*, 350–359.
GBD 2015 Obesity Collaborators. (2017). Health effects of overweight and obesity in 195 countries over 25 years. *The New England Journal of Medicine, 377*, 13–27.
Greenleaf, C., Chambliss, H., Rhea, D. J., Martin, S. B., & Morrow, J. R., Jr. (2006). Weight stereotypes and behavioral intentions toward thin and fat peers among White and Hispanic adolescents. *The Journal of Adolescent Health, 39*, 546–552.
Griffiths, L. J., Dezateux, C., & Cole, T. J. (2011). Sex and ethnic differences in the waist circumference of 5-year-old children: Findings from the Millennium Cohort Study. *International Journal of Pediatric Obesity, 6*, e196–e198.
Hannon, T. S., Rao, G., & Arslanian, S. A. (2005). Childhood obesity and type 2 diabetes mellitus. *Pediatrics, 116*, 473–480.
Haqq, A. M., Kebbe, M., Tan, Q., Manco, M., & Salas, X. R. (2021). Complexity and stigma of pediatric obesity. *Childhood Obesity, 17*, 229–240.
He, Y., Tian, J., Blizzard, L., Oddy, W. H., Dwyer, T., Bazzano, L. A., et al. (2020). Associations of childhood adiposity with menstrual irregularity and polycystic ovary syndrome in adulthood: The Childhood Determinants of Adult Health Study and the Bogalusa Heart Study. *Human Reproduction, 35*, 1185–1198.
Health Survey for England 2018. In *NHS digital* [Internet]. [cited 13 Apr 2022]. Available https://digital.nhs.uk/data-and-information/publications/statistical/health-survey-for-england/2018
Heinonen, I., Helajärvi, H., Pahkala, K., Heinonen, O. J., Hirvensalo, M., Pälve, K., et al. (2013). Sedentary behaviours and obesity in adults: The Cardiovascular Risk in Young Finns Study. *BMJ Open, 3*, e002901.
Henning, R. J. (2021). Obesity and obesity-induced inflammatory disease contribute to atherosclerosis: A review of the pathophysiology and treatment of obesity. *American Journal of Cardiovascular Disease, 11*, 504–529.
Hidayat, K., Du, X., & Shi, B.-M. (2018). Body fatness at a young age and risks of eight types of cancer: Systematic review and meta-analysis of observational studies. *Obesity Reviews, 19*, 1385–1394.
Hill, J. O., Wyatt, H. R., Reed, G. W., & Peters, J. C. (2003). Obesity and the environment: Where do we go from here? *Science, 299*, 853–855.
Hirode, G., & Wong, R. J. (2020). Trends in the prevalence of metabolic syndrome in the United States, 2011-2016. *Journal of the American Medical Association, 323*, 2526–2528.
Huang, P. L. (2009). A comprehensive definition for metabolic syndrome. *Disease Models & Mechanisms, 2*, 231–237.
Huang, Y., Lu, Y., Huang, Y.-M., Wang, M., Ling, W., Sui, Y., et al. (2020). Obesity in patients with COVID-19: A systematic review and meta-analysis. *Metabolism, 113*, 154378.
Jaacks, L. M., Vandevijvere, S., Pan, A., McGowan, C. J., Wallace, C., Imamura, F., et al. (2019). The obesity transition: Stages of the global epidemic. *The Lancet Diabetes and Endocrinology, 7*, 231–240.
Jackson, S. E., Steptoe, A., Beeken, R. J., Croker, H., & Wardle, J. (2015). Perceived weight discrimination in England: A population-based study of adults aged ≥50 years. *International Journal of Obesity, 39*, 858–864.
Jiang, D., Wang, L., Bai, C., & Chen, O. (2019). Association between abdominal obesity and asthma: A meta-analysis. *Allergy, Asthma and Clinical Immunology, 15*, 16.
John, B. J., Irukulla, S., Abulafi, A. M., Kumar, D., & Mendall, M. A. (2006). Systematic review: Adipose

tissue, obesity and gastrointestinal diseases. *Alimentary Pharmacology & Therapeutics, 23*, 1511–1523.
Juárez-López, C., Klünder-Klünder, M., Medina-Bravo, P., Madrigal-Azcárate, A., Mass-Díaz, E., & Flores-Huerta, S. (2010). Insulin resistance and its association with the components of the metabolic syndrome among obese children and adolescents. *BMC Public Health, 10*, 318.
Kawasaki, M., Arata, N., Miyazaki, C., Mori, R., Kikuchi, T., Ogawa, Y., et al. (2018). Obesity and abnormal glucose tolerance in offspring of diabetic mothers: A systematic review and meta-analysis. *PLoS One, 13*, e0190676.
Koivuaho, E., Laru, J., Ojaniemi, M., Puukka, K., Kettunen, J., Tapanainen, J. S., et al. (2019). Age at adiposity rebound in childhood is associated with PCOS diagnosis and obesity in adulthood—Longitudinal analysis of BMI data from birth to age 46 in cases of PCOS. *International Journal of Obesity, 43*, 1370–1379.
Kumar, A. (2019). The impact of obesity on cardiovascular disease risk factor. *Asian Journal of Medical Sciences, 10*, 1–12.
Latner, J. D., O'Brien, K. S., Durso, L. E., Brinkman, L. A., & MacDonald, T. (2008). Weighing obesity stigma: The relative strength of different forms of bias. *International Journal of Obesity, 32*, 1145–1152.
Leeman, J., Sommers, J., Vu, M., Jernigan, J., Payne, G., Thompson, D., et al. (2012). An evaluation framework for obesity prevention policy interventions. *Preventing Chronic Disease, 9*, E120.
Lindberg, L., Danielsson, P., Persson, M., Hagman, E., & Marcus, C. (2017). Childhood obesity increases risk of premature death in young adulthood—A prospective cohort study. *European Journal of Public Health, 27*, ckx189.254.
Liou, Y. M., Liou, T.-H., & Chang, L.-C. (2010). Obesity among adolescents: Sedentary leisure time and sleeping as determinants. *Journal of Advanced Nursing, 66*, 1246–1256.
Luppino, F. S., de Wit, L. M., Bouvy, P. F., Stijnen, T., Cuijpers, P., Penninx, B. W. J. H., et al. (2010). Overweight, obesity, and depression: A systematic review and meta-analysis of longitudinal studies. *Archives of General Psychiatry, 67*, 220–229.
Manoff, E. M., Banffy, M. B., & Winell, J. J. (2005). Relationship between body mass index and slipped capital femoral epiphysis. *Journal of Pediatric Orthopedics, 25*, 744–746.
Mayol-Kreiser, S. N., Garcia-Turner, V. M., & Johnston, C. S. (2015). Examining the utility of a laser device for measuring height in free-living adults and children. *Nutrition Journal, 14*, 93.
Meixner, L., Cohrdes, C., Schienkiewitz, A., & Mensink, G. B. M. (2020). Health-related quality of life in children and adolescents with overweight and obesity: Results from the German KIGGS survey. *BMC Public Health, 20*, 1722.
Misra, A. (2003). Revisions of cutoffs of body mass index to define overweight and obesity are needed for the Asian-ethnic groups. *International Journal of Obesity, 27*, 1294–1296.
Mohammad, S., Aziz, R., Al Mahri, S., Malik, S. S., Haji, E., Khan, A. H., et al. (2021). Obesity and COVID-19: What makes obese host so vulnerable? *Immunity & Ageing, 18*, 1.
Monasta, L., Lobstein, T., Cole, T. J., Vignerová, J., & Cattaneo, A. (2011). Defining overweight and obesity in pre-school children: IOTF reference or WHO standard? *Obesity Reviews, 12*, 295–300.
Mulugeta, W., Desalegn, H., & Solomon, S. (2021). Impact of the COVID-19 pandemic lockdown on weight status and factors associated with weight gain among adults in Massachusetts. *Clinical Obesity, 11*, e12453.
Must, A., Jacques, P. F., Dallal, G. E., Bajema, C. J., & Dietz, W. H. (1992). Long-term morbidity and mortality of overweight adolescents. *The New England Journal of Medicine, 327*, 1350–1355.
Nadeau, K. J., Maahs, D. M., Daniels, S. R., & Eckel, R. H. (2011). Childhood obesity and cardiovascular disease: Links and prevention strategies. *Nature Reviews. Cardiology, 8*, 513–525.
National Child Measurement Programme, England 2020/21 School Year. In *NHS digital* [Internet]. [cited 13 Apr 2022]. Available https://digital.nhs.uk/data-and-information/publications/statistical/national-child-measurement-programme/2020-21-school-year
NCD Risk Factor Collaboration (NCD-RisC). (2016a). Trends in adult body-mass index in 200 countries from 1975 to 2014: A pooled analysis of 1698 population-based measurement studies with 19·2 million participants. *Lancet, 387*, 1377–1396.
NCD Risk Factor Collaboration (NCD-RisC). (2016b). Worldwide trends in diabetes since 1980: A pooled analysis of 751 population-based studies with 4·4 million participants. *Lancet, 387*, 1513–1530.
NCD Risk Factor Collaboration (NCD-RisC). (2017). Worldwide trends in body-mass index, underweight, overweight, and obesity from 1975 to 2016: A pooled analysis of 2416 population-based measurement studies in 128·9 million children, adolescents, and adults. *Lancet, 390*, 2627–2642.
NCD Risk Factor Collaboration (NCD-RisC). (2019). Rising rural body-mass index is the main driver of the global obesity epidemic in adults. *Nature, 569*, 260–264.
NCD Risk Factor Collaboration (NCD-RisC). (2020). Height and body-mass index trajectories of school-aged children and adolescents from 1985 to 2019 in 200 countries and territories: A pooled analysis of 2181 population-based studies with 65 million participants. *Lancet, 396*, 1511–1524.
NCD Risk Factor Collaboration (NCD-RisC). (2021). Heterogeneous contributions of change in population

distribution of body mass index to change in obesity and underweight. *eLife, 10*, e60060.

Ng, M., Fleming, T., Robinson, M., Thomson, B., Graetz, N., Margono, C., et al. (2014). Global, regional, and national prevalence of overweight and obesity in children and adults during 1980-2013: A systematic analysis for the Global Burden of Disease Study 2013. *Lancet, 384*, 766–781.

Nolan, P. B., Carrick-Ranson, G., Stinear, J. W., Reading, S. A., & Dalleck, L. C. (2017). Prevalence of metabolic syndrome and metabolic syndrome components in young adults: A pooled analysis. *Preventive Medical Reports, 7*, 211–215.

Park, M. H., Falconer, C., Viner, R. M., & Kinra, S. (2012). The impact of childhood obesity on morbidity and mortality in adulthood: A systematic review. *Obesity Reviews, 13*, 985–1000.

Paulis, W. D., Silva, S., Koes, B. W., & van Middelkoop, M. (2014). Overweight and obesity are associated with musculoskeletal complaints as early as childhood: A systematic review. *Obesity Reviews, 15*, 52–67.

Peters, U., Dixon, A. E., & Forno, E. (2018). Obesity and asthma. *The Journal of Allergy and Clinical Immunology, 141*, 1169–1179.

Picó, C., Serra, F., Rodríguez, A. M., Keijer, J., & Palou, A. (2019). Biomarkers of nutrition and health: New tools for new approaches. *Nutrients, 11*, 1092.

Poti, J. M., Braga, B., & Qin, B. (2017). Ultra-processed food intake and obesity: What really matters for health-processing or nutrient content? *Current Obesity Reports, 6*, 420–431.

Pratt, M., Sarmiento, O. L., Montes, F., Ogilvie, D., Marcus, B. H., Perez, L. G., et al. (2012). The implications of megatrends in information and communication technology and transportation for changes in global physical activity. *Lancet, 380*, 282–293.

Puhl, R. M., & Latner, J. D. (2007). Stigma, obesity, and the health of the nation's children. *Psychological Bulletin, 133*, 557–580.

Puhl, R. M., Andreyeva, T., & Brownell, K. D. (2008). Perceptions of weight discrimination: Prevalence and comparison to race and gender discrimination in America. *International Journal of Obesity, 32*, 992–1000.

Raitoharju, E., Seppälä, I., Oksala, N., Lyytikäinen, L.-P., Raitakari, O., Viikari, J., et al. (2014). Blood microRNA profile associates with the levels of serum lipids and metabolites associated with glucose metabolism and insulin resistance and pinpoints pathways underlying metabolic syndrome: The cardiovascular risk in Young Finns Study. *Molecular and Cellular Endocrinology, 391*, 41–49.

Rankin, J., Matthews, L., Cobley, S., Han, A., Sanders, R., Wiltshire, H. D., et al. (2016). Psychological consequences of childhood obesity: Psychiatric comorbidity and prevention. *Adolescent Health, Medicine and Therapeutics, 7*, 125.

Revicki, D. A., & Israel, R. G. (1986). Relationship between body mass indices and measures of body adiposity. *American Journal of Public Health, 76*, 992–994.

Rito, A. I., Buoncristiano, M., Spinelli, A., Salanave, B., Kunešová, M., Hejgaard, T., et al. (2019). Association between characteristics at birth, breastfeeding and obesity in 22 countries: The WHO European Childhood Obesity Surveillance Initiative—COSI 2015/2017. *Obesity Facts, 12*, 226–243.

Rosenblatt, A., Faintuch, J., & Cecconello, I. (2015). Abnormalities of reproductive function in male obesity before and after bariatric surgery—A comprehensive review. *Obesity Surgery, 25*, 1281–1292.

Saklayen, M. G. (2018). The global epidemic of the metabolic syndrome. *Current Hypertension Reports, 20*, 12.

Sarwer, D. B., & Polonsky, H. M. (2016). The psychosocial burden of obesity. *Endocrinology and Metabolism Clinics of North America, 45*, 677–688.

Schwartz, M. B., & Brownell, K. D. (2004). Obesity and body image. *Body Image, 1*, 43–56.

Senthilingam, M. (2021). Covid-19 has made the obesity epidemic worse, but failed to ignite enough action. *BMJ, 372*, n411.

Shiri, R., Karppinen, J., Leino-Arjas, P., Solovieva, S., & Viikari-Juntura, E. (2010). The association between obesity and low back pain: A meta-analysis. *American Journal of Epidemiology, 171*, 135–154.

Silverwood, V., Blagojevic-Bucknall, M., Jinks, C., Jordan, J. L., Protheroe, J., & Jordan, K. P. (2015). Current evidence on risk factors for knee osteoarthritis in older adults: A systematic review and meta-analysis. *Osteoarthritis and Cartilage, 23*, 507–515.

Smith, E., Sweeting, H., & Wright, C. (2013). "Do I care?" Young adults' recalled experiences of early adolescent overweight and obesity: A qualitative study. *International Journal of Obesity, 37*, 303–308.

Stevens, J. (2003). Ethnic-specific revisions of body mass index cutoffs to define overweight and obesity in Asians are not warranted. *International Journal of Obesity, 27*, 1297–1299.

Stevens, G. A., Singh, G. M., Lu, Y., Danaei, G., Lin, J. K., Finucane, M. M., et al. (2012). National, regional, and global trends in adult overweight and obesity prevalences. *Population Health Metrics, 10*, 22.

Umer, A., Kelley, G. A., Cottrell, L. E., Giacobbi, P., Jr., Innes, K. E., & Lilly, C. L. (2017). Childhood obesity and adult cardiovascular disease risk factors: A systematic review with meta-analysis. *BMC Public Health, 17*, 683.

Viester, L., Verhagen, E. A., Hengel, K. M. O., Koppes, L. L. J., van der Beek, A. J., & Bongers, P. M. (2013). The relation between body mass index and musculoskeletal symptoms in the working population. *BMC Musculoskeletal Disorders, 14*, 1–9.

Wallace, C., Vandevijvere, S., Lee, A., Jaacks, L. M., Schachner, M., & Swinburn, B. (2019). Dimensions of national culture associated with different trajectories of male and female mean body mass index in countries over 25 years. *Obesity Reviews, 20*(Suppl 2), 20–29.

Wardle, J., & Cooke, L. (2005). The impact of obesity on psychological well-being. *Best Practice & Research. Clinical Endocrinology & Metabolism, 19*, 421–440.

Weihe, P., Spielmann, J., Kielstein, H., Henning-Klusmann, J., & Weihrauch-Blüher, S. (2020). Childhood obesity and cancer risk in adulthood. *Current Obesity Reports, 9*, 204–212.

Weihrauch-Blüher, S., Schwarz, P., & Klusmann, J.-H. (2019). Childhood obesity: Increased risk for cardiometabolic disease and cancer in adulthood. *Metabolism, 92*, 147–152.

Weinberger, N.-A., Kersting, A., Riedel-Heller, S. G., & Luck-Sikorski, C. (2016). Body dissatisfaction in individuals with obesity compared to normal-weight individuals: A systematic review and meta-analysis. *Obesity Facts, 9*, 424–441.

Weiss, R., Dziura, J., Burgert, T. S., Tamborlane, W. V., Taksali, S. E., Yeckel, C. W., et al. (2004). Obesity and the metabolic syndrome in children and adolescents. *The New England Journal of Medicine, 350*, 2362–2374.

Woolford, S. J., Sidell, M., Li, X., Else, V., Young, D. R., Resnicow, K., et al. (2021). Changes in body mass index among children and adolescents during the COVID-19 pandemic. *Journal of the American Medical Association, 326*, 1434–1436.

Yang, D., Luo, C., Feng, X., Qi, W., Qu, S., Zhou, Y., et al. (2021). Changes in obesity and lifestyle behaviours during the COVID-19 pandemic in Chinese adolescents: A longitudinal analysis from 2019 to 2020. *Pediatric Obesity, 2021*, e12874.

Yu, E., & Lippert, A. M. (2016). Neighborhood crime rate, weight-related behaviors, and obesity: A systematic review of the literature. *Sociology Compass, 10*, 187–207.

3 Economic Costs of Obesity in Europe

Jutta Viinikainen, Petri Böckerman, and Jaakko Pehkonen

Introduction

Obesity is a critical health metric. The increasing prevalence of obesity has been one of the most striking global health trends in the past few decades. Population-level evidence using nationally representative data shows that the prevalence of obesity has nearly tripled since 1975 worldwide. In 2016, 39% adults were overweight (Body Mass Index, BMI $\geq$ 25 kg/m^2) and 13% were obese (BMI $\geq$ 30 kg/m^2) (WHO, 2020a, b). Reflecting the global trend, most European countries have experienced a steady increase in obesity prevalence rates, even though there is also notable cross-country variation in the severity of obesity in Europe. In EU-28 countries, the prevalence of adult obesity grew by 46.7% over the period 1996–2016 and over one in five adults was found to be obese in 2016 (OECD, 2019a). EU-28 countries with the lowest obesity rates in 2016 were Denmark (19.7%), Italy (19.9%) and Austria (20.1%) while the highest obesity rates were found in Malta (28.9%), United Kingdom (27.8%) and Hungary (26.4%) (WHO, 2020c). The prevalence of obesity has increased among both men and women but it is notably more common among lower socioeconomic groups (e.g. low-educated individuals) (Pampel et al., 2012; OECD, 2019b). It has been projected, that by the year 2025, obesity will increase in 44 out of 53 countries in the WHO European region (Pineda et al., 2018).

Medical evidence shows that obesity is closely linked to increased morbidity and mortality. Obesity has been identified as a major driver of the development of non-communicable diseases such as cardiovascular diseases, type 2 diabetes, musculoskeletal disorders and some type of cancers (Dixon, 2010). The rising prevalence of obesity also causes a major financial burden to the public health systems. It has been projected that over the period of 2020–2050, EU-28 countries will spend 8% of their entire health budget on average on treating the consequences of overweight (OECD, 2019a), covering an increasing share of total health care costs.

Besides direct medical costs to the health care system, overweight and obesity are accompanied by significant indirect costs that result from productivity and employment losses in the labour market. Obesity has been connected to weaker labour market outcomes both at the extensive margin (employment, absenteeism, sick leaves and early retirement) as well as at the intensive

We are grateful for Juha Saarinen for excellent research assistance and Ginny Garcia-Alexander for very useful comments.

J. Viinikainen · J. Pehkonen
University of Jyväskylä, Jyväskylä, Finland
e-mail: jutta.i.viinikainen@jyu.fi; jaakko.k.pehkonen@jyu.fi

P. Böckerman (✉)
Labour Institute for Economic Research LABORE, Helsinki, Finland

IZA Institute of Labor Economics, Bonn, Germany
e-mail: petri.bockerman@labore.fi

G. Garcia-Alexander, D. L. Poston, Jr. (eds.), *International Handbook of the Demography of Obesity*, International Handbooks of Population 12, https://doi.org/10.1007/978-3-031-10936-2_3

margin i.e. conditional being employed (earnings/ wages). Existing literature shows that the indirect costs of obesity are substantial and may even exceed the direct medical costs of obesity (e.g. Goettler et al., 2017; Kjellberg et al., 2017).

This chapter summarizes the evidence on the indirect costs of obesity that result from adverse labour market outcomes (earnings and employment losses) at the individual level. We focus on empirical evidence covering European countries emphasizing the most recent studies in this field. The earlier review articles have mostly focused on the U.S. evidence (Cawley, 2015). Because both the prevalence of obesity and the labour market institutions differ substantially between the U.S. and Europe, the U.S. evidence may not be directly applicable to the European context. Accordingly, we offer an overview of the relevant measures for assessing the links between overweight and the labour market in the European context. Further, we provide insights on approaches that may be applied to overcome some of the challenges highlighted in earlier studies. We conclude with a discussion of promising avenues for future research in this area.

Empirical Approaches to Studying Obesity and Labour Market Outcomes

Methodological Approaches

The relationship between obesity and labour market outcomes at the individual level are most commonly evaluated using a simple regression framework with the following structure:

$$Y_i = \alpha + W_i\beta + X_i\gamma + \varepsilon_i$$

The model estimates the effects for labor market outcomes *Y* (earnings and employment) for an individual *i.* The variable of interest is body weight *W.* The vector of controls *X,* which includes variables such as educational attainment, are important drivers of labour market success.

Most studies documenting the links between body weight and labour market outcomes use body mass index (BMI; weight in kilograms divided by the square of height in meters) as the measure for excess weight. This is because BMI is available in almost all widely used survey data sets. The most common sources of data that have been used to explore the relationship between obesity and labour market outcomes in the European Union (EU) area are the German Socio-economic Panel and the Health Survey for England. Both of these data are publicly available for research purposes.

Identifying Obesity-Related Penalties

The economic costs of obesity include both direct and indirect costs both of which constitute a major financial burden for society. The direct costs of obesity include costs such as from physician visits, hospital stays, rehabilitation and medicine use linked to excess weight. Indirect costs are related to productivity losses due to obesity which results from lower earnings, reduced employment, sick absences, and early retirement. Indirect costs may also originate from a higher need for social income transfers although this dimension of indirect costs have received very little attention in previous literature (Böckerman et al., 2019).

Although obesity-related direct costs to the public health system are significant, it has been estimated that the indirect cost of obesity, resulting from weaker labour market outcomes, are comparable or may even exceed the direct medical costs caused by obesity. For example, Neovious et al. (2012) approximate that obesity-related lifetime productivity losses to the society – caused by sick leaves, disability pensions, and premature death – are almost twice as high as the productivity losses of normal-weight men due to the same reasons in Sweden. Significant direct and indirect costs of obesity have also been documented in other European countries such as Germany (Yates et al., 2016), Denmark (Kjellberg et al., 2017) and Ireland (Dee et al., 2015). Emphasizing the role of indirect costs, Kjellberg et al. (2017) conclude that it is the negative impact of obesity on labour market outcomes that accounts for most of the socio-economic burden of obesity.

This review focuses on the indirect costs of obesity. Since most of the previous studies have examined penalties resulting from earnings and employment, our review also focuses on these two central labour market outcomes.

There are two important points worth noting in the identification of obesity-related penalty. To begin with, there are two sources of biases that are important to consider in empirical studies assessing the links between obesity and labour market outcomes: First, there may be confounding factors that influence both obesity and labour market outcomes. Second, reverse causality may explain the observed associations between the variables of interest because low earnings as an indicator of low socioeconomic status may lead to obesity. Unless these two potential sources of bias are taken into account, empirical results may lead to faulty inferences. Another important point is that labour market institutions differ substantially between European countries, which may affect the observed links between obesity and labour market outcomes.

Review of the Empirical Literature

Obesity and Earnings

A large part of empirical literature shows that obesity is significantly associated with weaker labour market performance. Thus, earnings are used as a measure of productivity at the individual level. Most such studies use annual earnings as the outcome variable, because the data sets do not usually contain reliable information on working hours. The literature based on the U.S. data reveals notable differences in the links between obesity and earnings between demographic groups. In particular, heavier white women tend to earn much less compared to their healthy weight counterparts (Cawley, 2004, 2007).

Moreover, empirical studies using European data sets have found negative associations between obesity and earnings. However, there seems to be heterogeneity in the magnitude of the effect by country in Europe and compared to the results from the U.S., the gender difference in the wage penalty is less consistent in Europe. In what follows, we summarise the key empirical findings from recent European research published on this topic. The main findings and the relevant background characteristic of studies are presented in Table 3.1.

Substantial gender heterogeneity in the obesity-earnings relationship across European countries has been observed, but studies have shown that the wage penalty in many EU countries is greater for women. Using the European Community Household Panel (ECHP) data, Atella et al. (2008) found that women in Finland, Denmark, Ireland, Portugal, and Spain suffered a larger obesity-related wage penalty than men. Their study is especially important for comparative purposes in Europe as it uses an identical method for several countries, using nationally representative survey data that are harmonised across countries. Subsequent findings from Finland (Böckerman et al., 2019), Germany (Bozoyan & Wolbring, 2011; Caliendo & Gehrsitz, 2016; Caliendo & Lee, 2013), Denmark (Greve, 2008) as well as England, Scotland and Wales (Sargent & Blanchflower, 1994; Tyrrell et al., 2016) support the conclusion that compared to men, women are more likely to suffer from high BMI in terms of lower wages. However, the findings from Sweden (Dackehag et al., 2015) show a significant obesity penalty only for men.

Brunello and D'Hombres (2007) also used ECHP data to investigate the links between BMI and wages in nine European countries. While the findings by Atella et al. (2008) were based on OLS, Brunello and D'Hombres (2007) used the BMI of a biological relative as an instrument for BMI. They found that a 10% increase in the mean BMI reduced the wages of women and men by 3.49% and 5.29%, respectively. However, there is substantial and policy-relevant heterogeneity in the gender-segregated results by country. In Italy, Spain, Austria and Ireland, men are more likely to have obesity-related wage reductions; while in Portugal and Finland women, experience a higher wage penalty.

Further, the relationship between weight and earnings may also depend on the sector in which

Table 3.1 Studies of the association between excess body weight and wages

Author & country	Data and main characteristics (%) by gender (m/f)	Outcome Mean (%) by gender (m/f)	Measure of body weight	Method & Sample	Estimate by gender (m/f)	Notes/remarks
Atella et al. (2008) Nine European countries (Austria, Belgium, Denmark, Finland, Ireland, Greece, Italy, Portugal, Spain)	European Community Household Panel (1998–2001) N = 47,374/30,313 Obese, %: 10/7 Age: 39/40	Net hourly real wage at PPP W = 1.99/1.85 (log)	BMI > 30	OLS, pooled *average *15% wage quantile *50% wage quantile *85% wage quantile	0.00/ −0.05*** −0.02***/ −0.04** 0.02**/ −0.05** 0.01/ −0.04**	Detects differences between countries in the relation of obesity and wages in different parts of wage distribution, particularly for men. OLS analyses control for health status. IV results are not robust.
Brunello and D'Hombres (2007) Nine European countries (Beer belt: Austria, Belgium, Denmark, Finland, Ireland; Olive belt: Greece, Italy, Portugal, Spain)	European Community Household Panel (1998–2001) N = 25,101/17,767 Obese, %: 7/4 Age: 38/40	Net hourly real wage at PPP W = 8,6/7,7	BMI	IV *Pooled *Olive belt *Beer belt	−0.013***/ −0.008** −0.025***/ −0.014** −0.002/ −0.048	Association between BMI and wages is stronger in Southern Europe than in North European countries. 10-% increase in BMI reduces wages of men and woman approximately by 3.2 and 1.8 per cent. Use BMI of biological relative as instrument. Controls for health situation.
Bozoyan and Wolbring (2011) Germany	German Socio-Economic Panel (2002, 2004, 2006, 2008), N = 1592/1169 Obese, %: 14/17 Age: 43/43	Net hourly wage W = 13.0/9.86	BMI FFM BF	OLS FE OLS FE OLS FE	0.0013/ −0.003 0.0005/0.001 .0441*/ 0.0082* −0.0006/ −0.0054 −0.0023*/ −0.0047* 0.0007/ 0.0034	The study finds no significant correlation between BMI and wages. Using lagged BF and FFM measures make the associations stronger in women but weaker in men. Controls for self-reported health.

Böckerman et al. (2019) Finland	Cardiovascular Risk in Young Finns Study, Official Registers N = 1673 Obese, %: 12 Age: NA	Average annual earnings 2001–2012	BMI	OLS *Pooled IV *Pooled	−0.007 −0.071**	The analysis uses a genetic risk score as instrument for BMI (32 SNPs). The study shows that a one-unit increase in BMI is associated with 7-% lower wages.
Caliendo and Gehrsitz (2016) Germany	German Socio-Economic Panel (2002, 2004, 2006, 2008) N = 5373/4117 Obese. %: 14/12 Age: 41/41	Real hourly wage W = 14,22/11,29	BMI	OLS *Pooled *White collar *Blue collar	−0.001/ −0.007*** −0.020/ −0.006*** 0.001/ −0.007**	Non-linear models show that wages of woman (men) rise until BMI equals 21.5 (23.0). Men's wages decline after BMI is 30. Obese woman have lower wages. Controls for self-reported health.
Caliendo and Lee (2013) Germany	IZA Evaluation and Administrative records (2007–2008) N = 500/514 Obese, %: 14/13 Age: 36/38	Hourly wages W = 2,15/2,11	BMI > 30	OLS OLS^ Matching	−0.044/ −0.102* −0.061/ −0.092* −0.111/ −0.128*	The analysis is based on newly unemployed job applicants. Obese woman who found a job had lower wages than normal weight woman. Includes measures that control for self-reported health.
Dackehag et al. (2015) Sweden	Statistics Sweden, Survey of Living Conditions N = 2415/2184 Obese, %: 8/7 Age: 42/43	Annual labor income W = 2832/2050	BMI > 30	OLS OLS^ FE FE^	−0.059*/ −0.0126 −0.037/ 0.0045 −0.0956***/ −0.0238 −0.0916***/ −0.0173	Detects a considerable obesity penalty for men. Suggests that the penalty relates to discrimination rather than lower productivity due to bad health.
Greve (2008) Denmark	Danish Work Environment Cohort Study (2000) N = 2777/2545 Obese, %: 10/7 Age: 38/39	Annual wages W = 12,46 /12,13	BMI BMI*2	OLS *private sector *public sector	0.049*/ −0.068** −0.086*/ 0.121* 0.041/0.008 −0.076/ −0.009	In the private sector, BMI has a negative effect on wages for woman and an inverted U-shaped effect on wages for men. Controls for self-reported health and mental health.

(continued)

Table 3.1 (continued)

Author & country	Data and main characteristics (%) by gender (m/f)	Outcome Mean (%) by gender (m/f)	Measure of body weight	Method & Sample	Estimate by gender (m/f)	Notes/remarks
Johansson et al. (2009) Finland	Health 2000 (2000–01); National registers N = 1163/1170 Obese, %: 17/16 Age: 42/42	Hourly wage W = 8,58/7,39	BMI > 30 FFM > 30 WC > 88	OLS OLS^ OLS OLS^ OLS OLS^	−0.007/ 0.017 −0.013/ −0.008 −0.056*/ −0.017 −0.047/ −0.013 −0.030/ −0.027* −0.017/ 0.022	Obesity measures are not significant in linear wage models for men. Waist circumference has a negative association with wages for woman. Controls for self-reported health.
Lundborg et al. (2014) Sweden	Data on Swedish conscripts (1984–1993/94), National registers N = 448,667 (OLS) N = 145,193 (FE) Obese, %: 3 Age: 33	Annual earnings W = 12,36 (log)	BMI > 30	OLS FE FE^	−0.175*** −0.047*** −0.029	Provides results on adult male labor market penalty for being obese as a teenager. Controlling of sibling and occupational fixed effects reduces the penalty substantially.
Tyrrell et al. (2016)	UK Biobank N = 56,652/63,017 Obese, %: NA Age: 57/56	Annual household income, (survey, by categories)	BMI	OLS IV	−0.01***/ −0.09*** 0.06/ −0.14***	The study uses a genetic risk score as instrument for BMI (69 SNPs). 1DS higher BMI (4.6 kg/m2) lowers income by 2940£ in women.

Notes: ^ the model controls for health status, *BF* bodyfat, *FFM* fat-free mass, *WC* waist circumference, *** significant at 1% level, ** significant at 5% level, * significant at 10% level an individual works. For example, a study conducted in the private sector, using Danish data, revealed that higher BMI is associated with lower earnings among women, while for men the relationship follows an inverted U-shape form (i.e. moderate overweight is associated with higher wages for men) (Greve, 2008). In contrast, in the public sector, no statistically significant effect was found between BMI and wages for women or men. Using ECHP data (covering nine countries), Garcia and Quintana-Domeque (2006) concluded that there is weak evidence that individuals with obesity are more likely to be self-employed compared to non-obese ones. Therefore, it has been posited that these sectoral differences may stem from the pattern of obesity-related discrimination being more prevalent in the private sector.

Studies documenting the association between obesity and wages have revealed substantial heterogeneity in this relationship across European countries. For example, Brunello and D'Hombres (2007) found that the association between BMI and wages is stronger in Southern Europe as compared to Northern European countries. In the "olive belt" (Greece, Italy, Portugal and Spain) a one-unit increase in BMI was associated with 1.5% lower wages among women and 2.2% lower wages among men. Moreover, in the "beer belt" (Austria, Belgium, Denmark, Finland, and Ireland) the coefficients for BMI were close to zero and statistically insignificant. Other studies have used different classifications for European countries. Based on their empirical findings Atella et al. (2008) identified three clusters in Europe: (1) Belgium, Denmark, Finland, Ireland, Portugal, and Spain showed no statistically significant association between obesity and wages; (2) Greece and Italy showed a wage penalty; and (3) Austria recorded a wage premium.

European countries are notably heterogeneous in terms of culture, society, labour market institutions (union density, collective labour bargaining, and wage compression) and the prevalence of obesity, all of which may contribute to the varying associations between obesity in wages in different European countries. For example, high union density and binding collective agreements may mitigate the effects of discrimination against obese workers as unions may provide support and reduce the likelihood of obesity-based discrimination (discussed in more detail in the section below "Modifying role of culture and labour market institutions").

Obesity and Employment

Besides earnings, obesity may also affect labour supply at the extensive margin, i.e. labour force participation, which is usually an annual measure. Table 3.2 summarises the most important results from the recent European studies that have examined links between weight and employment outcomes. Generally, findings from European studies suggest that higher BMI and obesity lead to weaker labour market attachment.

Based on data from England (Kinge, 2017; Morris, 2007), Finland (Böckerman et al., 2019), Germany (Caliendo & Lee, 2013), Italy (Radice et al., 2013), Ireland (Mosca, 2013), and pooled results from 10 European countries (Lundborg et al., 2007), it can be seen that obesity is significantly related to a lower probability of employment. Likewise, Danish and French evidence links obesity or higher BMI to increased risk of unemployment and lower changes of employment (Bramming et al., 2019; Paraponaris et al., 2005).

Several studies (Böckerman et al., 2019; Kinge, 2017; Morris, 2007; Radice et al., 2013) have attempted to identify causal effects using instrumental variable approach, with varying instruments for BMI. The results of these studies combined suggest that obesity has an adverse effect on employment; although in some cases, no significant effect was found. To identify causal effects, Morris (2007) used the propensity of obesity in the area of residence, Radice et al. (2013) used an indicator for regular physical activity, Böckerman et al. (2019) used a genetic risk score for high BMI and Kinge (2017) used the BMI of the oldest biological child as an instrument for BMI. Lindeboom et al. (2010) also found, using data from the British National Child Development Study, a negative association

Table 3.2 Studies of the association between excess body weight and employment

Author & country	Data and mean characteristics by gender (m/f)	Outcome Mean (%) by gender (m/f)	Main measure	Method	Estimates by gender (m/f)	Remarks
Asgeirsdottir (2011) Iceland	Survey data collected by Gallup Iceland N = 368/385 Obese, %: 17/13 Age: 43/41	Employee or self-employed Employed, %: 89/78	BMI > 30	Probit Probit^	0.0195/ −0.0874 0.0202/ −0.0814	Detects a negative relationship between weight and the employment rate of women and a slightly positive relationship for men.
Böckerman et al. (2019) Finland	Cardiovascular Risk in Young Finns Study N = 1673 Obese, %: 12 Age: 42	Share of years employed Employed, %: NA	BMI	OLS *pooled IV *pooled	−0.002 −0.018**	Uses a genetic risk score as instrument for BMI. A one-unit increase in BMI is associated with 1,8-% fewer years employed. No controls for health status.
Caliendo and Gehrsitz (2016) Germany	German Socio-Economic Panel (2002, 2004, 2006, 2008) N = 9621/10022 Obese, %: 14/12 Age: 41/41	Employment Employed, %: app. 81/69	BMI BMI^2	Probit	0.019***/ 0.022*** −0.004***/ −0.004***	The relationship between weight and employment is poorly described by linear or non-linear models. The slimness premium for women is prevalent in white-collar occupations. No controls for health status.
Caliendo and Lee (2013) Germany	IZA Evaluation; Administrative records (2007–2008) N = 500/514 Obese, %: 14/13 Age: 36/38	Employment Employed, %: app. 64/58	BMI > 30	OLS OLS^ Matching	−0.118*/ −0.145** −0.078/ −0.097 −0.075/ −0.106	Obese women have worse employment outcomes than normal weight women. Analysis controls for health status.
Greve (2008) Denmark	Danish Work Environment Cohort Study (1995, 2000) N = 3618/3666 (Probit) N = 768/1254 (FE) Obese, %: 10/7 Age: 38/39	Employment Employed, %: app. 90/66	BMI > 30 BMI BMI^2 BMI	Probit Probit FE	−0.028/ −0.085** 0.039***/ −0.004 −0.069***/ 0.000 0.01/ −0.06**	A negative effect of BMI on employment for woman and an inverted U-shaped effect for men. Wald test suggests that BMI is exogenously related to employment. Models control for health status.

Kinge (2017) England	Health Survey for England (1998–99; 2001–13) N = 19,119/23,534 (Probit) N = 3410/5981(IV) Obese, %: 24 Age: 42	Employment Employed, %: app. 80	BMI > 30 WC > 102/ 88	Probit IV Probit IV	−0.026**/ −0.053** −0.159**/ −0.113 −0.024**/ −0.045** −0.145**/ −0.039	Impact of fat mass on employment do not depend on the measure. Analysis uses the BMI/WC of the oldest biological child as instrument. No controls for health.
Kinge (2016) England	Health Survey for England (1998–2013) N = 21,678/26,619 (OLS) N = 4818/9337(IV) Obese, %: 23 Age: 39	Not working % (due to disability): NA Employed, %: NA	BMI > 30	M-logit M-logit^ IV IV^	0.016***/ 0.017*** 0.002/0.002 0.057*/ 0.022* 0.022/0.006	Obesity increases the probability of "not working" due to disability. Obesity affects employment through its effect on health. Analysis uses the BMI of the oldest biological child as instrument.
Lindeboom et al. (2010) UK	National Child Development Study (cross-sections, 1958–2000) N = 4486/3898 Obese, %: 16/17 Age: 42/42	Employment Employed, %: app. 91/80	BMI > 30 (at age 42) BMI > 30 (at age 33) ΔBMI	OLS OLS^ IV OLS OLS^ IV FE	−0.023*/ −0.049*** −0.013/ −0.038** 0.113/0.014 −0.045***/ −0.061*** −0.027*/ −0.046** 0.149/0.082 0.026*/ −0.033	The IV results imply that the association between obesity and employment is not causal. Obesity status of own biological parents is used as instrument.
Morris (2007) England	Health Survey for England (1997–1998 N = 8324/8643 Obese, %: 19/17 Age: NA	Employment Employed, %: app. 77/65	BMI > 30	Probit Matching IV	−0.021*/ 0.004 −0.034*/ −0.013 −0.084*/ −0.213**	IV results show that obesity has a significant negative effect on employment. Propensity of obesity in the area of residence is used as instrument.

(continued)

Table 3.2 (continued)

Author & country	Data and mean characteristics by gender (m/f)	Outcome Mean (%) by gender (m/f)	Main measure	Method	Estimates by gender (m/f)	Remarks
Mosca (2013) Ireland	The Irish Longitudinal Study on Ageing (2009–2011) N = 1471/1732 Obese, %: 38/31 Age: 56/56	Employment Employed, %: app. 65/50	BMI > 30 WC > 118/109	Probit Probit^ Probit Probit^	−0.046**/ −0.072*** −0.019/ −0.052** −0.042/ −0.078*** −0.009/ −0.051*	All measures of fatness are negatively associated with employment probability for women. Controls for mental and behavioral health.
Radice et al. (2013) Italy	ISTAT; Aspects of Daily Life Survey (2009) N = 11221/12217 Obese, %: 10/7 Age: 16–65	Employment, self-employed Employed, %: 90/92	BMI > 30	Probit IV	−0.03**/ −0.04** −0.12**/ −0.06**	Instrument: individual practices physical activity. Controls for health status. Not accounting for confounding underestimates the effect of obesity on employment.
Reichert (2015) Germany	Data from field experiment (2010–12) N = 468/222 Obese, %: NA Age:48/48	Employment Employed, %: 85/75	ΔBMI	OLS OLS^ IV IV^	−0.005/ −0.001 −0.005/ −0.002 −0.012/ −0.026** −0.010/ −0.026**	Intervention based on monetary rewards provides evidence that weight loss positively affects the employment prospects of obese women but not of obese men.

Notes: ^ the model controls for health status, *WC* waist circumference, *** significant at 1% level, ** significant at 5% level, * significant at 10% level between obesity and the probability of employment. However, the instrumental variable results, which use the obesity status of an individual's own biological parent as an instrument for BMI, suggest that the observed association may not be causal. Andersen et al. (2015) explored the employment prospects after a significant weight loss using data on Norwegian patients, who went through an obesity surgery. Though they did not find changes in the employment rate, the number of sick days significantly reduced in the 5 years after the surgery. Also, no improvements in the employment rate were found in French data consisting of patients who underwent a bariatric surgery (Durand-Moreau et al., 2015). However, findings from the UK (Courtney et al., 2018; Hawkings et al., 2007) indicated the opposite: weight loss surgery seemed to improve employment prospects of previously obese individuals.

Notably, similar to wages, previous research suggests that the effect of weight on employment varies considerably between genders, with women experiencing more negative outcomes. Findings from Germany (Caliendo & Lee, 2013) and Ireland (Mosca, 2013) show that compared to men, women suffer more from obesity in terms of lower employment. Similarly, a study using data from 16 European countries, also found that the penalty from being obese was higher for women as compared to men (Feigl et al., 2019).

While women seem to suffer from obesity in terms of lower employment, for men, the link between obesity and employment tends to be positive, as shown by results from Iceland (Asgeirsdottir, 2011). Garcia and Quintana-Domeque (2006) also found weak evidence that obesity increases the risk of unemployment among women. The opposite relationship was found in Finland, Greece, Ireland, Italy, Portugal and Spain for men. Furthermore, the results based on Danish data (Greve, 2008) show a negative association between BMI and employment for women and an inverted U-shape association for men. Thus, the gender difference in obesity-related employment penalty seems to vary across countries (also see Lundborg et al., 2007). Studies (Kinge, 2017; Morris, 2007) that use methods that explicitly attempt to account for reverse causality and confounders reach slightly different conclusions about gender differences in obesity-employment relationship. Based on these findings, men suffer more from obesity in terms of lower employment – a finding that is worth investigating in future work.

Reichert (2015) provides a rare example of a field experiment that was conducted in Germany to study the impact of obesity on employment prospects. Individuals in a weight-loss intervention programme were randomly assigned to treatment and control groups. Individuals in the treatment group received monetary rewards from weight loss. The findings of this experiment showed that weight loss improved the employment prospects of obese women but had no significant effect on men.

Potential Mediators

Obesity can lead to weaker labour market performance for multiple reasons. A crucial issue for the interpretation of the negative association between weight and labour market success is that obesity is significantly related to weaker health status and chronic obesity-related illnesses such as type 2 diabetes, high blood pressure, high cholesterol, and atherosclerosis (Hu, 2008) and therefore with lower productivity and performance at work. The notion that poor health at least partly mediates the link between obesity and weaker labour market outcomes has received support from several studies that focus on links between obesity, sick leaves, and disability pensions. These studies have found that individuals who suffer from obesity are more likely to enter sick leave (Amiri & Behnezhad, 2019; van Duijvenbode et al., 2009; Jans et al., 2007; Lehnert et al., 2014; Neovious et al., 2009; Sanz-de-Galdeano, 2007) and exit from paid employment through disability pension (Robroek et al., 2013).

The second potential pathway through which obesity may affect labour market outcomes negatively is discrimination. Rooth (2009) conducted a field experiment to examine employers' perceptions towards obese job applicants in Sweden. Fictitious applications with manipulated facial photos were sent in pairs to real job openings. The paired applications were made as identical as possible, in terms of job-related qualifications, except that one photo out of the two was manipulated to make the applicant appear obese. Rooth (2009) found that the weight-manipulated applicants were significantly less likely to receive a call-back for an interview and that the call-back rate was significantly lower for weight-manipulated women than for men. This was consistent with findings in the U.S., which suggest that those who are obese but with otherwise identical qualifications are less likely to be hired than thin individuals (Roehling, 1999).

Moreover, there are other studies that have linked discrimination with labour market outcomes. A study based on German Socioeconomic Panel indirectly concludes that discrimination based on physical appearance rather than health problems is likely to explain the weaker labour market outcomes of women with high BMI (Caliendo & Gehrsitz, 2016). This conclusion was based on the finding that women's wages peak at the BMI level that is markedly below the overweight boundary value. Thus, women's wages seem to decline also at the levels of BMI that cannot reflect health concerns. Caliendo and Gehrsitz (2016) also found that women whose BMI matched well with societal standards earned the highest wages. Among men, such discrimination was not apparent. Further, support for weight-based discrimination in the labour market was also found in a meta-analytical study by Roehling et al. (2013), documenting that being overweight was associated with lower ratings in job-related outcomes, such as desirability as a co-worker and predicted job success.

Modifying Role of Culture and Labour Market Institutions

Notable heterogeneity in the culture and labour market institutions across European countries may explain the varying links between obesity and labour market outcomes. According to Sanz-de-Galdeano (2007), in countries with more stringent employment protection and generous unemployment benefit systems, links between obesity and work absenteeism were more pronounced, especially among women. Furthermore, an explorative analysis using ECHP data found that in countries with higher collective bargaining coverage, obese women were more likely to be unemployed, but the wage penalty was lower (Garcia & Quintana-Domeque, 2006). This result suggests that collective bargaining reduces obesity-based wage penalty but shifts discrimination to the extensive margin of labour adjustment. However, in countries where the prevalence of obesity is higher, the probability of unemployment among obese individuals is lower. This pattern may emerge, because in areas with higher obesity prevalence, excess weight is more socially acceptable and this translates into better labour market outcomes. Taken together, these results imply that labour market institutions and culture may modify the links between obesity and labour market outcomes. However, the identification of the role of labour market institutions and culture is challenging in empirical research as the relevant variation is (mostly) limited to the country level.

Methodological Challenges and Future Studies

The role of obesity as a potential driver of labour market success has received substantial interest among scholars in social sciences. However, there are still under-researched topics in the field, which must be addressed by future research. Next, we describe in brief the challenges related to methods, data improvements, novel outcome variables, and determination of moderators and mediators, which may shed new light on the links between excess weight and labour market outcomes.

Methodological Advancements

Due to potential unobserved confounders and reverse causality it is crucial to use identification strategies which take these considerations fully into account. Because randomised controlled trials, often referred as "the gold standard" for causal inference in science, are typically not feasible in social sciences, previous studies used different statistical methods and datasets to alleviate the aforementioned problems.

The existing literature has also used, for example, data on (identical) twins to account for shared family and genetic background which otherwise might confound the observed associations (Böckerman & Vainiomäki, 2013). However, as such, twin data do not take into account other potential confounders or reverse causality. Also, the fixed effects panel estimation method can be used to account for unobserved confounders as far as they are time invariant, but reverse causality and time-varying factors still remain a potential source of bias that makes it difficult to establish causal links.

Given that there is a suitable variable that correlates with obesity but is not significantly associated with the outcome variable conditional on the other covariates in the model under consideration, the instrumental variables (IV) method can be used to identify causal relationships between obesity and labour market outcomes. The challenge in the use of the IV method is to find a suitable variable (i.e. instrumental variable) which satisfies the strong instrument and exclusion restriction assumptions.

Previous studies have most commonly used the weight of a biological relative as an instrument for excess weight of an individual under consideration (e.g. Brunello & D'Hombres, 2007; Cawley, 2004; Kinge, 2016, 2017; Kline & Tobias, 2008; Lindeboom et al., 2010). The rationale for this is based on the finding that there is a significant inherited component in weight (e.g. Cawley, 2004; Locke et al., 2015). Thus, weights of biological family members are strongly positively correlated, which supports the strong instrument assumption. Since genes are randomly assigned before birth, variation in genetic predisposition towards obesity can be considered as a natural experiment, which can be used to identify causal effects (Cawley, 2007).

A caveat concerning the use of a biological relative's weight as an instrument is that it may suffer from the very same endogeneity problem as the original predicting variable; i.e. there may be an unaccounted unobserved variable correlated with the weight of both the individual under study and his/her biological relative, which could also be associated with labour market outcomes.

The drastic decline in DNA sequencing costs in the past decade has led to an increase in genome-wide association studies (GWAS), which attempt to find relationships between genetic variants and expressed phenotypes. Based on GWAS, recent genetic research has constructed the so-called genetic risk scores (GRS), describing the genetic risk of developing phenotypes such as high BMI (Locke et al., 2015). This has opened promising new avenues for empirical research in terms of statistical methods that have rarely been used in the field thus far.

A central method called Mendelian Randomisation (MR) exploits individual genetic variants (SNP) or GRS, which consist of multiple SNPs, as instruments for BMI in the instrumental variable models for identifying causal effects. Under certain conditions, MR estimator avoids biases related to the OLS results (see e.g. von Hinke et al., 2016). Besides, as an instrument in instrumental variable analyses, GRS information can also be exploited in reduced-form models to explore how genetic risk toward excess weight is associated with adult outcomes (Böckerman et al., 2019). GRS information also allows the estimation of gene-environment interactions to describe whether the socio-economic environment or health behaviour modify the effects of genetic endowments on adult outcomes (Amin et al., 2017; Pehkonen et al., 2017). Furthermore, the so-called "two-step MR" can be used to provide causal evidence in the mediation analysis framework (Burgess et al., 2015; Zheng et al., 2017).

An important feature concerning the IV method is that the local average treatment effect (LATE) identified by IV estimation captures the average effect of weight on labour market outcomes among compliers (Swanson & Hernán, 2013) i.e. among individuals whose weight is raised via the impact of genetic variation. Variation in weight originating from sources other than genetics may have a different impact on labour market outcomes.

Data Improvements

Most empirical research carried out is based on survey data, which relies on self-reported information on weight and labour market outcomes. This is problematic because self-reported measures, such as for height and weight, are prone to measurement errors (Stommel & Schoenborn, 2009). The best way to overcome the problems related to self-reported measures would be by using linked data which combines register-based information on labour market outcomes with weight measures that were based on measurements made by health care professionals.

Moreover, future research could also focus on novel ways to assess obesity since a potential shortcoming related to weight measures is that most studies solely rely on BMI to evaluate excess weight. A key weakness with BMI is that the measure does not distinguish between different types of body mass such as fat, muscle and skeletal tissue. In addition, BMI does not account for the distribution of the body fat. This is a relevant weakness also for studying the labour market penalty related to obesity, because an abdominal fat distribution has been linked to increased risk of cardiovascular diseases and type 2 diabetes (Snijder et al., 2005), which are among the leading causes of mortality in the advanced countries.

There are numerous ways to measure the distribution of body fat, but usually, abdominal obesity is assessed by the waist-to-hip ratio (WHR). Only a few studies in our selective survey used measures other than BMI to evaluate excess weight (Bozoyan & Wolbring, 2011; Böckerman et al., 2019; Johansson et al., 2009; Kinge, 2017; Mosca, 2013). Based on these studies, it seems that the link between obesity and labour market outcomes does not depend remarkably on the measure of fat mass. Thus, although BMI has its shortages, it seems to be a sufficient measure to assess obesity in relatively large samples. Also, according to Snijder et al. (2005), in large epidemiological studies BMI captures the most of relevant variation in body mass but other measures, such as WHR, can provide additional insights. In medical literature, BMI alone is considered neither a valid measure of obesity nor an adequate predictor of obesity-related illnesses.

Novel Outcomes and the Role of Moderators and Mediators

There are important economic and policy outcomes that have not been considered much in the existing empirical literature. An examination of social income transfers as a potential compensation mechanism for the lost earnings due to obesity is particularly relevant in Europe. Danish (Kjellberg et al., 2017) and Finnish (Böckerman et al., 2019) evidences according to which high BMI increases the probability of receiving social income transfers, supports the conclusion that excess weight has an adverse effect on labour market outcomes and that social income transfers are necessary to compensate these losses. Social income transfers can be considered as forms of negative externalities of obesity and these costs are also borne by non-obese individuals.

Future studies could also pay more attention to policy-relevant mediators and moderators. As stated previously, both health and discrimination may mediate the link between excess weight and labour market outcomes. However, the relative importance of these potential mediators is largely unknown, and their mechanisms should be explored in greater depth.

Future research could also further consider the role of policy-relevant moderators in the relationship between weight and labour market outcome. Most studies focus on the gender differences, but there may be other relevant aspects, such as differences in family background or labour market institutions, which may substantially moderate the link between obesity and labour market outcomes. The explorative findings of Garcia and Quintana-Domeque (2006) suggest that examining the moderating role of labour market institutions and culture increase our understanding of the heterogeneous links between obesity and labour market outcomes in various European countries. Investigating the role of culture is challenging but, for example, the World Values Survey that contains rich information about attitudes could be used to provide novel insights on this topic.

Conclusions

Empirical research has established three stylised facts regarding the labour market penalty of obesity in Europe. The first stylised fact is that there is a negative link between excess weight and labour market outcomes. Obesity is linked to significantly lower earnings, lower levels of employment and higher probability of entering sick leave or exiting from paid employment through disability pension.

The second stylised fact is that the negative link between excess weight and labour market outcomes is surprisingly robust across European countries, given that there are substantial country differences in labour market institutions, culture and the prevalence of obesity (see Marques et al., 2017). However, although the negative links between excess weight, earnings and employment have been documented across Europe, there are also notable cross-country differences in these relationships. For example, the obesity-related wage penalty seems to be stronger in southern Europe compared to northern European countries (Atella et al., 2008; Brunello & D'Hombres, 2007), and while many studies have shown that women suffer from a larger obesity-related wage penalty than men, there also seem to be countries where the opposite applies (e.g. Atella et al., 2008; Dackehag et al., 2015). Future empirical studies should therefore examine the drivers of these differences more closely.

The third stylised fact is that women in Europe seem to suffer less from obesity in terms of lower earnings compared to American women. Thus, the difference in the wage penalty of obesity among women vs. men seems to be smaller in Europe than in the U.S. Again, there is also significant heterogeneity in gender-segregated results by country in Europe. This contradicts, to some extent, the findings from the U.S., wherein white women in particular suffer from a substantial wage penalty (Cawley, 2007).

In this literature review, we focused on the indirect costs of obesity that stem from weaker labour market attachment and lower earnings associated with obesity. Based on empirical findings, these costs constitute a significant burden to the society which may even exceed the direct costs resulting from excess weight. The direct and indirect costs of obesity combined with the increasing prevalence of obesity in most European countries highlight the need for policies and practices that prevent obesity.

References

Amin, V., Böckerman, P., Viinikainen, J., Smart, M. C., Bao, Y., Kumari, M., et al. (2017). Gene-environment interactions between education and body mass: Evidence from the UK and Finland. *Social Science and Medicine, 195*, 12–16.

Amiri, S., & Behnezhad, S. (2019). Body mass index and risk of sick leave: A systematic review and meta-analysis. *Clinical Obesity, 9*(6), e12334.

Andersen, J. R., Hernæs, U. J., Hufthammer, K. O., & Våge, V. (2015). Employment status and sick-leave following obesity surgery: A five-year prospective cohort study. *PeerJ, 3*, e1285.

Asgeirsdottir, T. L. (2011). Do body weight and gender shape the work force? The case of Iceland. *Economics and Human Biology, 9*(2), 148–156.

Atella, V., Pace, N., & Vuri, D. (2008). Are employers discriminating with respect to weight?: European evidence using quantile regression. *Economics and Human Biology, 6*(3), 305–329.

Böckerman, P., & Vainiomäki, J. (2013). Stature and life-time labor market outcomes: Accounting for unobserved differences. *Labour Economics, 24*, 86–96.

Böckerman, P., Cawley, J., Viinikainen, J., Lehtimäki, T., Rovio, S., Seppälä, I., et al. (2019). The effect of weight on labor market outcomes: An application of genetic instrumental variables. *Health Economics, 28*(1), 65–77.

Bozoyan, C., & Wolbring, T. (2011). Fat, muscles, and wages. *Economics and Human Biology, 9*(4), 356–363.

Bramming, M., Jørgensen, M. B., Christensen, A. I., Lau, C. J., Egan, K. K., & Tolstrup, J. S. (2019). BMI and labor market participation: A cohort study of transitions between work, unemployment, and sickness absence. *Obesity, 27*(10), 1703–1710.

Brunello, G., & d'Hombres, B. (2007). Does body weight affect wages? Evidence from Europe. *Economics and Human Biology, 5*, 1–19.

Burgess, S., Daniel, R. M., Butterworth, A. S., Thompson, S. G., & EPIC-InterAct Consortium. (2015). Network Mendelian randomization: Using genetic variants as instrumental variables to investigate mediation in causal pathways. *International Journal of Epidemiology, 44*(2), 484–495.

Caliendo, M., & Gehrsitz, M. (2016). Obesity and the labor market: A fresh look at the weight penalty. *Economics and Human Biology, 23*, 209–225.

Caliendo, M., & Lee, W. S. (2013). Fat chance! Obesity and the transition from unemployment to employment. *Economics and Human Biology, 11*(2), 121–133.

Cawley, J. (2004). The impact of obesity on wages. *Journal of Human Resources, 39*, 451–474.

Cawley, J. (2007). The labor market impact of obesity. In Z. J. Acs & A. Lyes (Eds.), *Obesity, business and public policy* (pp. 76–86). Edward Elgar Publishing.

Cawley, J. (2015). An economy of scales: A selective review of obesity's economic causes, consequences, and solutions. *Journal of Health Economics, 43*, 244–268.

Courtney, M. J., Mahawar, K., Burnell, P., Jennings, N., Balupuri, S., Schroeder, N., et al. (2018). Occupational outcomes of obesity surgery – Do the employed return to work, and do the unemployed find work? *Obesity Surgery, 28*(4), 963–969.

Dackehag, M., Gerdtham, U. G., & Nordin, M. (2015). Productivity or discrimination? An economic analysis of excess-weight penalty in the Swedish labor market. *The European Journal of Health Economics, 16*(6), 589–601.

Dee, A., Callinan, A., Doherty, E., O'Neill, C., McVeigh, T., Sweeney, M. R., et al. (2015). Overweight and obesity on the island of Ireland: An estimation of costs. *BMJ Open, 5*(3), e006189.

Dixon, J. B. (2010). The effect of obesity on health outcomes. *Molecular and Cellular Endocrinology, 316*(2), 104–108.

Durand-Moreau, Q., Gautier, A., Becouarn, G., Topart, P., Rodien, P., & Sallé, A. (2015). Employment and professional outcomes in 803 patients undergoing bariatric surgery in a French reference center for obesity. *The International Journal of Occupational and Environmental Medicine, 6*(2), 502–595.

Feigl, A. B., Goryakin, Y., Devaux, M., Lerouge, A., Vuik, S., & Cecchini, M. (2019). The short-term effect of BMI, alcohol use, and related chronic conditions on labour market outcomes: A time-lag panel analysis utilizing European SHARE dataset. *PLoS One, 14*(3), e0211940.

Garcia, J., & Quintana-Domeque, C. (2006). Obesity, employment and wages in Europe. In K. Bolin & J. Cawley (Eds.), *Advances in health and health services research* (Vol. 17: The economics of obesity) (pp. 187–217). Elsevier.

Goettler, A., Grosse, A., & Sonntag, D. (2017). Productivity loss due to overweight and obesity: A systematic review of indirect costs. *BMJ Open, 7*(10), e014632.

Greve, J. (2008). Obesity and labor market outcomes in Denmark. *Economics and Human Biology, 6*(3), 350–362.

Hawkins, S. C., Osborne, A., Finlay, I. G., Alagaratnam, S., Edmond, J. R., & Welbourn, R. (2007). Paid work increases and state benefit claims decrease after bariatric surgery. *Obesity Surgery, 17*(4), 434–437.

Hu, F. (2008). *Obesity epidemiology*. Oxford University Press.

Jans, M. P., van den Heuvel, S. G., Hildebrandt, V. H., & Bongers, P. M. (2007). Overweight and obesity as predictors of absenteeism in the working population of the Netherlands. *Journal of Occupational and Environmental Medicine, 49*(9), 975–980.

Johansson, E., Böckerman, P., Kiiskinen, U., & Heliövaara, M. (2009). Obesity and labour market success in Finland: The difference between having a high BMI and being fat. *Economics and Human Biology, 7*(1), 36–45.

Kinge, J. M. (2016). Body mass index and employment status: A new look. *Economics and Human Biology, 22*, 117–125.

Kinge, J. M. (2017). Waist circumference, body mass index, and employment outcomes. *The European Journal of Health Economics, 18*(6), 787–799.

Kjellberg, J., Larsen, A. T., Ibsen, R., & Højgaard, B. (2017). The socioeconomic burden of obesity. *Obesity Facts, 10*(5), 493–502.

Kline, B., & Tobias, J. L. (2008). The wages of BMI: Bayesian analysis of a skewed treatment–response model with nonparametric endogeneity. *Journal of Applied Econometrics, 23*, 767–793.

Lehnert, T., Stuhldreher, N., Streltchenia, P., Riedel-Heller, S. G., & König, H. H. (2014). Sick leave days and costs associated with overweight and obesity in Germany. *Journal of Occupational and Environmental Medicine, 56*(1), 20–27.

Lindeboom, M., Lundborg, P., & van der Klaauw, B. (2010). Assessing the impact of obesity on labor market outcomes. *Economics and Human Biology, 8*(3), 309–319.

Locke, A. E., Kahali, B., Berndt, S. I., Justice, A. E., Pers, T. H., Day, F. R., et al. (2015). Genetic studies of body mass index yield new insights for obesity biology. *Nature, 518*(7538), 197–206.

Lundborg, P., Bolin, K., Höjgård, S., & Lindgren, B. (2007). Obesity and occupational attainment among the 50+ of Europe. In K. Bolin & J. Cawley (Eds.), *Advances in health and health services research* (Vol. 17: The economics of obesity) (pp. 219–251). Elsevier.

Lundborg, P., Nystedt, P., & Rooth, D. O. (2014). Body size, skills, and income: evidence from 150,000 teenage siblings. *Demography, 51*(5), 1573–1596.

Marques, A., Peralta, M., Naia, A., Loureiro, N., & de Matos, M. G. (2017). Prevalence of adult overweight and obesity in 20 European countries, 2014. *The European Journal of Public Health, 28*(2), 295–300.

Morris, S. (2007). The impact of obesity on employment. *Labour Economics, 14*(3), 413–433.

Mosca, I. (2013). Body mass index, waist circumference and employment: Evidence from older Irish adults. *Economics and Human Biology, 11*(4), 522–533.

Neovious, K., Johansson, K., Kark, M., & Neovius, M. (2009). Obesity status and sick leave: A systematic review. *Obesity Reviews, 10*(1), 17–27.

Neovious, K., Rehnberg, C., Rasmussen, F., & Neovius, M. (2012). Lifetime productivity losses associated with obesity status in early adulthood. *Applied Health Economics and Health Policy, 10*(5), 309–317.

OECD. (2019a). *The heavy burden of obesity: The economics of prevention*. OECD Publishing. https://doi.org/10.1787/67450d67-en

OECD. (2019b). *Health for everyone? Social inequalities in health and health systems*. OECD Publishing. https://doi.org/10.1787/3c8385d0-en

Pampel, F. C., Denney, J. T., & Krueger, P. M. (2012). Obesity, SES, and economic development: A test of the reversal hypothesis. *Social Science and Medicine, 74*(7), 1073–1081.

Paraponaris, A., Saliba, B., & Ventelou, B. (2005). Obesity, weight status and employability: Empirical evidence from a French national survey. *Economics and Human Biology, 3*(2), 241–258.

Pehkonen, J., Viinikainen, J., Böckerman, P., Lehtimäki, T., Pitkänen, N., & Raitakari, O. (2017). Genetic endowments, parental resources and adult health: Evidence form the Young Finns Study. *Social Science and Medicine, 188*, 191–200.

Pineda, E., Sanchez-Romero, L. M., Brown, M., Jaccard, A., Jewell, J., Galea, G., et al. (2018). Forecasting future trends in obesity across Europe: The value of improving surveillance. *Obesity Facts, 11*(5), 360–371.

Radice, R., Zanin, L., & Marra, G. (2013). On the effect of obesity on employment in the presence of observed and unobserved confounding. *Statistica Neerlandica, 67*(4), 436–455.

Reichert, A. R. (2015). Obesity, weight loss, and employment prospects: Evidence from a randomized trial. *Journal of Human Resources, 50*(3), 759–810.

Robroek, S. J., Reeuwijk, K. G., Hillier, F. C., Bambra, C. L., van Rijn, R. M., & Burdorf, A. (2013). The contribution of overweight, obesity, and lack of physical activity to exit from paid employment: A meta-analysis. *Scandinavian Journal of Work, Environment & Health, 39*(3), 233–240.

Roehling, M. V. (1999). Weight-based discrimination in employment: Psychological and legal aspects. *Personnel Psychology, 52*(4), 969–1016.

Roehling, M. V., Pichler, S., & Bruce, T. A. (2013). Moderators of the effect of weight on job-related outcomes: A meta-analysis of experimental studies. *Journal of Applied Social Psychology, 43*(2), 237–252.

Rooth, D. O. (2009). Obesity, attractiveness, and differential treatment in hiring a field experiment. *Journal of Human Resources, 44*(3), 710–735.

Sanz-de-Galdeano, A. (2007). An economic analysis of obesity in Europe: Health, medical care and absenteeism costs. *Documento de Trabajo, 38*.

Sargent, J. D., & Blanchflower, D. G. (1994). Obesity and stature in adolescence and earnings in young adulthood: Analysis of a British birth cohort. *Archives of Pediatrics & Adolescent Medicine, 148*(7), 681–687.

Snijder, M. B., Van Dam, R. M., Visser, M., & Seidell, J. C. (2005). What aspects of body fat are particularly hazardous and how do we measure them? *International Journal of Epidemiology, 35*(1), 83–92.

Stommel, M., & Schoenborn, C. A. (2009). Accuracy and usefulness of BMI measures based on self-reported weight and height: Findings from the NHANES & NHIS 2001-2006. *BMC Public Health, 9*(1), 421.

Swanson, S. A., & Hernán, M. A. (2013). Commentary: How to report instrumental variable analyses (suggestions welcome). *Epidemiology, 24*(3), 370–374.

Tyrrell, J., Jones, S. E., Beaumont, R., Astley, C. M., Lovell, R., Yaghootkar, H., et al. (2016). Height, body mass index, and socioeconomic status: Mendelian randomisation study in UK Biobank. *BMJ, 352*, i582.

van Duijvenbode, D. C., Hoozemans, M. J. M., Van Poppel, M. N. M., & Proper, K. I. (2009). The relationship between overweight and obesity, and sick leave: A systematic review. *International Journal of Obesity, 33*(8), 807–816.

von Hinke, S., Smith, G. D., Lawlor, D. A., Propper, C., & Windmeijer, F. (2016). Genetic markers as instrumental variables. *Journal of Health Economics, 45*, 131–148.

WHO. (2020a). *Global Health Observatory data repository. Prevalence of obesity among adults, BMI ≥ 30, age-standardized, estimates by WHO region*. http://apps.who.int/gho/data/view.main.REGION2480A?lang=en. Accessed 20 Jan 2020.

WHO. (2020b). *Global Health Observatory data repository. Prevalence of overweight among adults, BMI ≥ 25, age-standardized, estimates by WHO region*. http://apps.who.int/gho/data/node.main.A896?lang=en. Accessed 20 Jan 2020.

WHO. (2020c). *Global Health Observatory data repository. Prevalence of obesity among adults, BMI ≥ 30, age-standardized estimates by country*. http://apps.who.int/gho/data/view.main.CTRY2450A?lang=en. Accessed 20 Jan 2020.

Yates, N., Teuner, C. M., Hunger, M., Holle, R., Stark, R., Laxy, M., et al. (2016). The economic burden of obesity in Germany: Results from the population-based KORA studies. *Obesity Facts, 9*(6), 397–409.

Zheng, J., Baird, D., Borges, M. C., Bowden, J., Hemani, G., Haycock, P., et al. (2017). Recent developments in Mendelian randomization studies. *Current Epidemiology Reports, 4*(4), 330–345.

4 Impact of Obesity on Life Expectancy Among Different European Countries, 1975–2012

Nikoletta Vidra, Sergi Trias-Llimós, and Fanny Janssen

Introduction

Obesity is a global epidemic (Finucane et al., 2011), posing a serious health burden at the individual and population levels because it is associated with an increased risk of morbidity (Field et al., 2001), and mortality (Global BMI Mortality Collaboration et al., 2016). Europe currently ranks second worldwide after the USA (Eurostat, 2017). Specifically, since the 1980s obesity prevalence has increased threefold in many European countries (WHO, 2018), reaching an average of 16% in 2014 across the EU member states (Eurostat, 2016).

There are, however, important variations in obesity prevalence levels and trends between men and women and between European countries. Estimates for 2014 indicate that obesity levels varied almost threefold across European countries, ranging from around 10% in Romania and Italy to over 20% in the United Kingdom, Estonia, Hungary, Latvia, and Malta (even 26%) (Eurostat, 2016). Country differences in obesity prevalence levels are related to, among others, differences in the determinants of obesity, such as food intake, physical activity, and socio-economic status (Berghofer et al., 2008). Furthermore, the observed obesity prevalence differences likely also represent differences in the evolution of the obesity epidemic in European countries.

Figures 4.1 and 4.2 illustrate differences in obesity prevalence trends over time, using data from the NCD Risk Factor Collaboration Study (2016) (NCD Risk Factor Collaboration, 2016). For European men obesity prevalence has increased, on average, threefold from 1975 onwards, in line with the threefold increase for American men (Fig. 4.1). Although the increase was slightly lower among men in Eastern Europe, obesity prevalence levels in 2012 are approximately equal for Eastern and Western European

The Chapter is an adaptation of the journal article: Vidra, N., Trias-Llimós, S. and Janssen, F. (2019). Impact of obesity on life expectancy among different European countries: secondary analysis of population-level data over the 1975–2012 period. BMJ Open 9(7): e028086. In addition, input has been used from the popular version of the article: Janssen, F., Vidra, N. and S. Trias-Llimós (2020) Impact of obesity on life expectancy levels and trends in Europe. N-IUSSP: IUSSP's online news magazine. January 13, 2020. See: https://www.niussp.org/article/impact-of-obesity-on-life-expectancy-levels-and-trends-in-europe/#more-4192

The summary above uses sentences from the original abstract of the article in BMJ Open.

N. Vidra
Department for Health Evidence, Radboud University Medical Center, Nijmegen, The Netherlands

S. Trias-Llimós
Center for Demographic Studies (CED-CERCA), Autonomous University of Barcelona, Barcelona, Spain

F. Janssen (✉)
Population Research Centre, Faculty of Spatial Sciences, University of Groningen, Groningen, The Netherlands

Netherlands Interdisciplinary Demographic Institute – KNAW/University of Groningen, The Hague, The Netherlands
e-mail: f.janssen@rug.nl

G. Garcia-Alexander, D. L. Poston, Jr. (eds.), *International Handbook of the Demography of Obesity*, International Handbooks of Population 12, https://doi.org/10.1007/978-3-031-10936-2_4

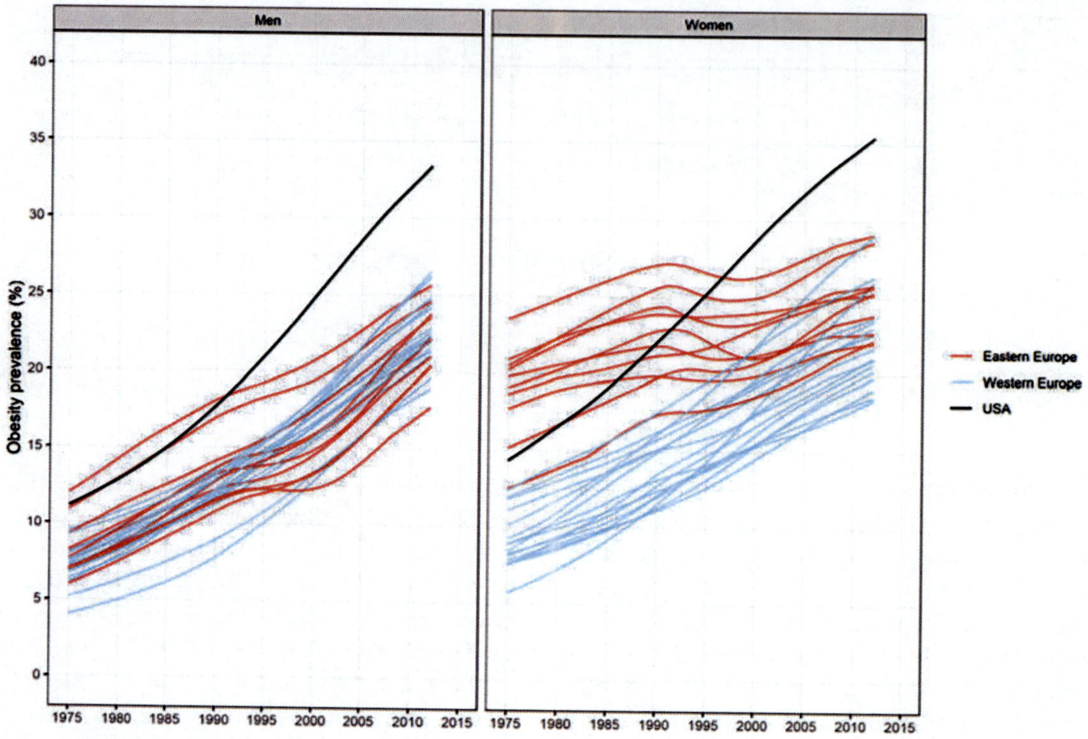

Fig. 4.1 Age-standardized obesity prevalence by sex, by region, 1975–2012, 18–100 years
Eastern Europe: Belarus, Czech Republic, Estonia, Hungary, Latvia, Lithuania, Poland, Russia, Slovakia, Ukraine
Western Europe: Austria, Belgium, Denmark, Finland, France, Iceland, Ireland, Italy, Luxembourg, the Netherlands, Norway, Portugal, Spain, Sweden, Switzerland, UK

men, because of higher obesity prevalence levels in 1975 for Eastern European men. For European women the increase in obesity prevalence between 1975 and 2012 is, on average, twofold. This is less than the increase among European men, and American women (Fig. 4.1). This sex difference in the increase arises predominantly because for women in many Eastern European countries – for which obesity levels were already very high around 1975 – the increase has stalled. For Western European women obesity levels in 2012 were on average 2.5 times higher than in 1975, but still lower than the obesity levels among Eastern European women in 2012.

Examining more closely the trends for individual European countries (Fig. 4.2), additional differences can be observed. For example, increases in obesity prevalence were particularly large among Portuguese, Norwegian and Italian men, and among Irish, Finnish, UK and Norwegian women. Particularly among Estonian, Czechian and Russian women, obesity levels in 2012 were only marginally higher (close to 1.2 times) compared to their already high obesity levels in 1975. Within Western Europe, the smallest increases were observed among Belgian and Italian women, although this still represented an almost twofold increase. Among both men and women, Belarus was the Eastern European country with the highest increase in obesity. For Belarusian men, the increase was even higher than the average in Europe. Please see our discussion for the explanations behind the important differences in the progression of the obesity epidemic for the different European regions.

In light of the worrisome and varying increase in obesity prevalence in Europe, it is essential to obtain a better understanding of how obesity is affecting life expectancy levels and life expectancy trends in Europe as a whole, and in the different European countries. Particularly, the potential impact of the increase in obesity on life

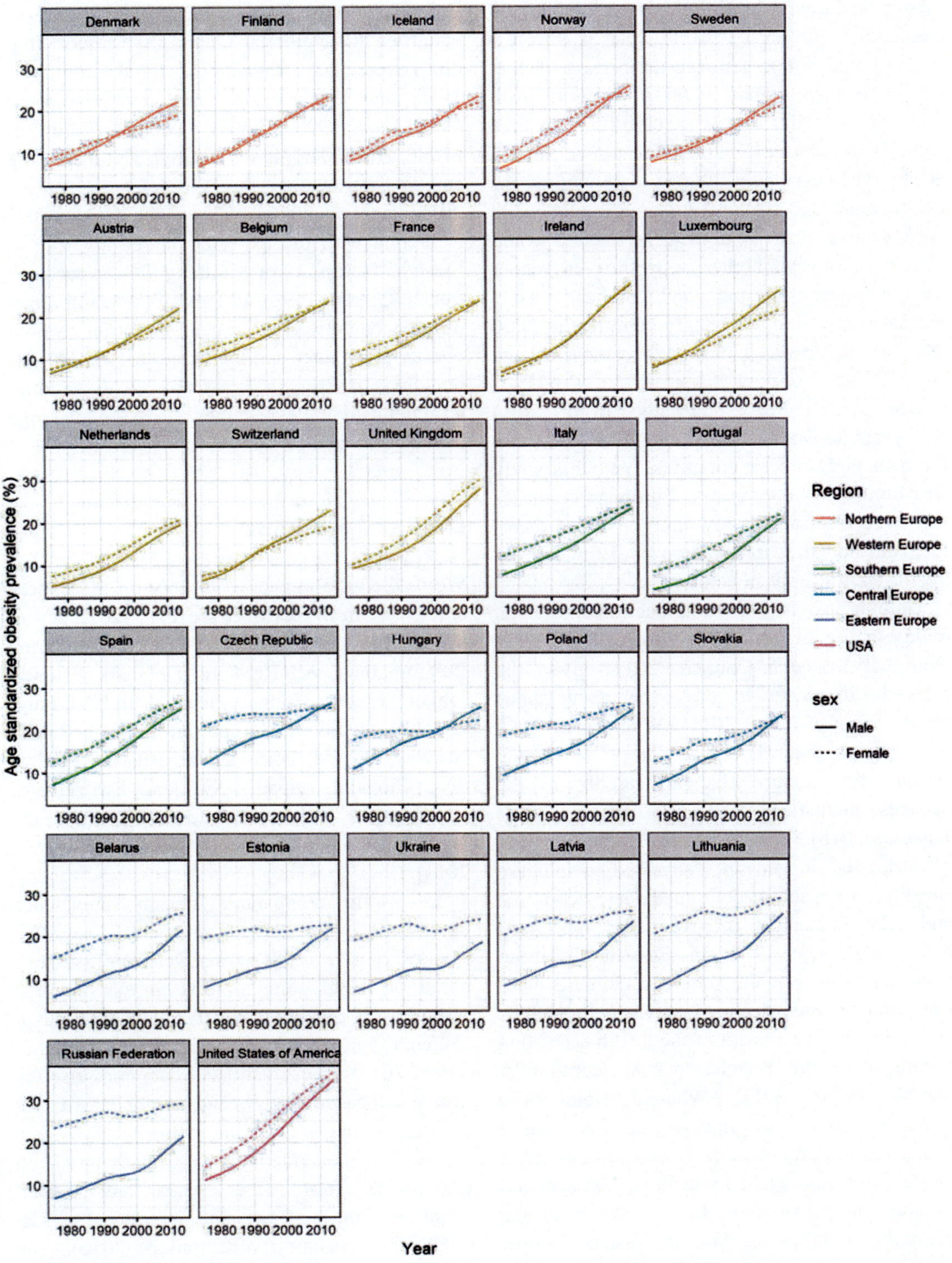

Fig. 4.2 Age-standardised obesity prevalence in 26 European countries*, grouped by 5 regions and USA, 1975–2012, 18–100 years

*Countries within the same region are presented with the same colour

expectancy trends in Europe is as yet largely unknown (Alley et al., 2011). That is, the few existing studies that assessed the impact of obesity on life expectancy at the population level, provided estimates at one specific point in time only (Olshansky et al., 2005; Preston & Stokes, 2011). Olshansky et al. (2005), who studied the USA, found that if obesity was eliminated, life expectancy at birth (e_0) in the USA in 2000 would be 0.21–1.08 years higher, depending on gender and ethnicity. Preston and Stokes (2011) estimated for 16 low-mortality countries in 2006 that the reduction in life expectancy at age 50 (e_{50}) due to obesity was greatest in the USA, at more than 1.5 years; and ranged from 0.50 to 1.19 years for women and from 0.72 to 1.37 years for men in European countries. Yet, this study was limited to 2006, and to European countries that were identified as low-mortality; and therefore, did not offer information over time across the different European contexts.

Gaining insight into the impact of obesity on trends in life expectancy is especially relevant (National Research Council, 2011) given the marked differences in life expectancy trends across Europe (Leon, 2011). Whereas in 1960 life expectancy levels across Europe were quite similar, this picture changed rapidly in the decades thereafter (Vallin & Meslé, 2004; Janssen, 2018). That is, in Western European countries, e_0, in general, continued to increase steadily, as a result of continued socio-economic and related medical progress, and has risen 6–8 years since 1970. In Eastern European countries, however, the previous increase in e_0 stagnated or even declined between the 1970s and the 1980s, as a result of the health crisis that accompanied the policies of the communist regimes (Leon, 2011). Whereas from 1990 onwards e_0 started to improve again for Central Eastern European countries, it was not until 2005 that e_0 increased again for Russia, Ukraine and Belarus, after extremely low e_0 levels at the beginning of the 1990s. Also, in Western Europe, important differences in e_0 trends between individual European countries exist. That is, particularly in Southern European countries increases in e_0 were strong. Whereas the North-Western European countries (especially the Nordic countries, the Netherlands, and the United Kingdom) experienced stagnating e_0 trends around the 1950s and 1960s among men, and around the 1980s and 1990s among women (Vallin & Meslé, 2004), largely due to high and increasing smoking-attributable mortality (Janssen et al., 2015; Janssen, 2020a). This latter development is in line with the expected increasing role of lifestyle factors in determining life expectancy trends (Omran, 1998). In light of these important differences between European countries in both obesity prevalence and life expectancy over time, our aim is to assess the impact of obesity on long-term trends in life expectancy across a wide range of European countries.

Data and Methods

We studied the impact of obesity on life expectancy at birth by sex over the 1975–2012 period in 26 European countries: Austria, Belarus, Belgium, the Czech Republic, Denmark, Estonia, Finland, France, Hungary, Iceland, Ireland, Italy, Latvia, Lithuania, Luxembourg, the Netherlands, Norway, Poland, Portugal, the Russian Federation, Slovakia, Spain, Sweden, Switzerland, Ukraine, the United Kingdom (UK); and the USA as a comparison country (Preston & Stokes, 2011).

Long-term comparable obesity prevalence data (BMI $\geq$ 30 kg/m^2) by country, sex, age (18–19, 20–24, . . ., 85+), and year (1975–2012), based on 1698 population-based measurement studies, were obtained from the NCD Risk Factor Collaboration study (NCD Risk Factor Collaboration, 2016). These validated data comprise the available measured height and weight data of 19.2 million participants from representative data sources, supplemented with estimates based on information from other years and related countries from a Bayesian hierarchical model (NCD Risk Factor Collaboration, 2016). The same model was applied to all countries and it used as input not only the available measured weight and height data, but also covariates that help predict BMI (NCD Risk Factor Collaboration, 2016).

The age- (<50, 50–59, 60–69 and ≥ 70 years) and sex-specific relative risks (RRs) of dying from obesity (see Table 4.1) came from a review of studies mainly conducted in Western Europe and the USA, with the normal-weight category used as the reference group (18.5 ≥ BMI ≤ 25 kg/m^2) (Lobstein & Leach, 2010). These age- and sex-specific RRs were largely in line with the overall European RR of 1.64 recently estimated by the Global BMI Mortality Collaboration (Global BMI Mortality Collaboration et al., 2016). The differences across age groups found in that study, were similar with those reported in our findings (i.e., higher RRs at younger than at older ages), though they were less distinct (Global BMI Mortality Collaboration et al., 2016).

All-cause mortality numbers and exposure population data by single year of age, sex, year, and country were obtained from the Human Mortality Database (Human Mortality Database, 2018). These data are of high quality and are widely used within the demographic community and beyond (Barbieri et al., 2015).

We performed our analyses separately by country and sex, based on data by single year of age (18–100). The obesity prevalence data were turned into single-age prevalence (18–100) by applying Loess smoothing (Cleveland & Loader, 1995). The RRs were turned into single-year RRs (18–100) using linear regression.

To estimate the obesity-attributable mortality fraction (OAMF) – i.e., the share of all-cause mortality due to obesity – we used the Rockhill formula to estimate OAMFs by age (a) and sex (s) (Rockhill et al., 1998).

$$OAMF_{a,s} = \frac{P_{a,s} \cdot (RR_{a,s} - 1)}{1 + (P_{a,s} \cdot (RR_{a,s} - 1))} \qquad (4.1)$$

where P is the obesity prevalence. We then weighted the $OAMF_{a,s}$ with the corresponding number of deaths.

For the estimation of the impact of obesity on life expectancy we needed age-and sex-specific (non-) obesity-attributable mortality rates. These were obtained by multiplying $OAMF_{a,s}$ and $[1-OAMF_{a,s}]$, respectively, with age- and sex-specific all-cause mortality rates.

To ensure comparability across countries, over time, and between men and women, we applied direct age- and sex-standardisation (Preston et al., 2001) to obesity prevalence, obesity-attributable mortality fractions, and obesity-attributable mortality rates, using the European population of 2011 (Eurostat, 2011) as the standard.

To assess the impact of adult obesity on e_0, we calculated for each country the potential gain in life expectancy (PGLE) if obesity-attributable mortality were eliminated, by calendar year and sex, in line with the approach by Preston and Stokes (2011). First, we calculated e_0 by applying standard life table techniques to age-specific all-cause mortality rates (0–100). Second, we applied associated single-decrement life tables (ASDLT) (Preston et al., 2001) to age- and sex-specific non-obesity-attributable mortality rates (0–100) to obtain e_0 if obesity-attributable mortality were eliminated. The PGLE represents the difference between the e_0 based on the ASDLT and the original e_0.

To summarise the changes in PGLE across countries, we estimated the average annual changes in PGLE (in %):

Table 4.1 Age-and sex-specific RRs of dying from obesity from the meta-review from Lobstein and Leach (2010)

	Relative Risk (RR)[a]	
Age	Men	Women
<50	1.55	1.5
50–59	1.539	1.49
60–69	1.5225	1.475
70+	1.495	1.45

[a]Reference group for the RRs: normal weight (18.5 ≥ BMI ≤ 24.9 kg/m^2)

$$\textit{Average annual changes in PGLE}\ (\%) = \frac{\sum_{t=1976}^{2012} \frac{(PGLE_t - PGLE_{t-1})}{PGLE_{t-1}}}{2012 - 1975} 100 \tag{4.2}$$

To assess the impact of obesity on time trends in e_0 between 1975 and 2012, we subtracted the observed change in e_0 from the change in e_0 without obesity. The change in e_0 without obesity was obtained by using the e_0 values from the associated single-decrement life tables applied to non-obesity-attributable mortality for 1975 and 2012.

Results

In presenting the results of our study we will first focus on obesity-attributable mortality levels and PGLE levels in Europe and the USA in 2012, and subsequently discuss the trends over time.

Obesity-Attributable Mortality in Europe and the USA

For the 26 European countries, the age-standardised obesity-attributable mortality fraction (OAMF) was, on average, 11% among men and 10% among women in 2012 (see Table 4.2). For the USA, these estimates were substantially higher; i.e., 15% for both men and women, which is in line with the higher obesity prevalence levels in the USA compared to Europe (see Fig. 4.1). Also, in line with the observed obesity prevalence levels in 2012, the average OAMF levels were about similar between Northern, Western, and Southern Europe combined (Western Europe) and Central and Eastern Europe (Eastern Europe) among men, while among women, the OAMF levels were slightly higher in Eastern Europe compared to Western Europe. Furthermore, the remaining differences between countries in the share of all-cause mortality (OAMF) that is due to obesity in 2012 reflect the observed differences in obesity prevalence between the countries in 2012 (see Fig. 4.2). That is, among men, Ukraine and the Netherlands exhibit the lowest levels of both obesity prevalence and obesity-attributable mortality, whereas UK, Ireland and the Czech Republic exhibit the highest levels. Among women, Denmark, Switzerland and Austria exhibit the lowest levels, whereas Russia, Lithuania and UK exhibit the highest levels.

Impact of Obesity on Life Expectancy Levels in Europe and the USA

The impact of obesity on life expectancy levels in Europe is certainly not negligible. In the 26 European countries in 2012, the potential gain in life expectancy at birth (PGLE) if obesity was eliminated ranged from 0.86 (the Netherlands) to 1.67 years (Lithuania) among men and from 0.66 (Switzerland) to 1.54 years (Russia) among women (see Fig. 4.3 and Table 4.3). Among men in the USA, the PGLE estimate was, at 1.73 years, slightly higher than the highest estimate in Europe. Among women in the USA, the PGLE estimate was, at 1.44 years, the second-highest after the estimate for Russia.

The average PGLE estimate across the 26 European countries was 1.22 years among men and 0.98 years among women. Broken down by region the respective values were 1.08 among men and 0.86 among women in Western European countries, and 1.44 among men and 1.16 among women in Eastern European countries.

Within Western Europe, the impact of obesity was largest in the UK (1.3 years among men; 1.1 years among women) and smallest in Switzerland (0.8 years). Within Eastern Europe, the impact was largest in Russia (1.5 years for both men and women) and smallest in Slovakia (1.3 among men and 1.0 among women).

The abovementioned differences between sexes and regions reflect to a large extent the observed differences in age-standardised obesity prevalence and obesity-attributable mortality (see previous paragraph of the results section). In addition, differences in the age distribution of both obesity and all-cause mortality can have an impact. For example, we observed higher PGLE values among men compared to women in Eastern Europe, despite slightly lower age-standardised obesity prevalence and OAMF

Table 4.2 Age-standardized obesity-attributable mortality fractions (%) in 26 European countries (differentiating Western and Eastern Europe) and the USA 2012, by sex

	Age-standardised obesity-attributable mortality fractions (%) 2012	
Country	Men	Women
Western Europe	10.7	9.6
Austria	10.1	8.4
Belgium	10.8	9.8
Denmark	10.2	8.1
Finland	10.6	9.4
France	10.7	10.0
Iceland	10.6	9.1
Ireland	12.2	11.1
Italy	10.5	10.1
Luxembourg	11.6	9.0
Netherlands	9.1	8.8
Norway	11.5	10.2
Portugal	9.4	9.2
Spain	11.4	11.1
Sweden	10.3	8.7
Switzerland	10.5	8.2
United Kingdom	12.3	12.3
Eastern Europe	10.5	10.7
Belarus	9.8	10.8
Czech Republic	12.0	10.8
Estonia	10.0	9.8
Hungary	11.5	9.6
Latvia	10.5	11.0
Lithuania	11.2	12.1
Poland	11.1	10.9
Russian Federation	9.7	12.1
Slovakia	10.5	9.6
Ukraine	8.6	10.3
Europe	10.6	10.0
United States of America	15.1	14.6
All	10.8	10.2

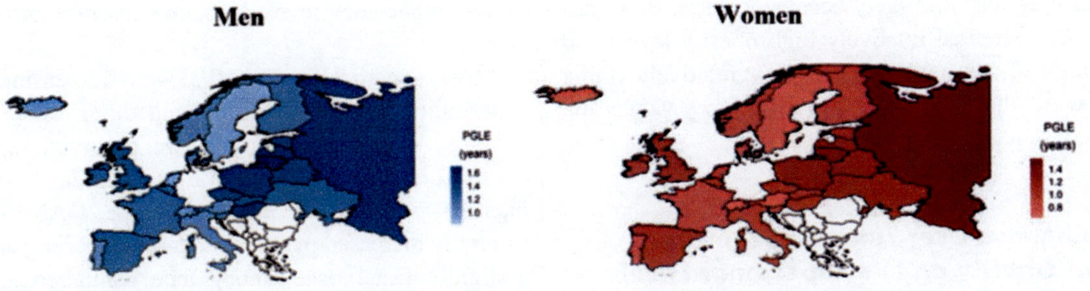

Fig. 4.3 Potential gains in life expectancy at birth (PGLE) if obesity-attributable mortality was eliminated, 26 European countries*, 2012
*Germany, Greece and the Balkan countries were excluded because all-cause mortality data were not available for all studied years from the Human Mortality Database

Table 4.3 Potential gains in life expectancy at birth (PGLE) if obesity-attributable mortality was eliminated, in 26 European countries (differentiating Western and Eastern Europe) and the USA, 1975 and 2012, by sex, 18–100 years

	PGLE 1975		PGLE 2012	
Country	Men	Women	Men	Women
Western Europe	0.42	0.46	1.08	0.87
Austria	0.40	0.39	1.03	0.73
Belgium	0.55	0.61	1.17	0.97
Denmark	0.42	0.46	1.04	0.79
Finland	0.45	0.40	1.19	0.90
France	0.49	0.53	1.18	0.84
Iceland	0.49	0.48	0.97	0.80
Ireland	0.38	0.31	1.21	1.01
Italy	0.44	0.60	1.06	0.93
Luxembourg	0.47	0.42	1.19	0.79
Netherlands	0.29	0.39	0.86	0.88
Norway	0.34	0.39	1.07	0.91
Portugal	0.24	0.41	1.01	0.81
Spain	0.42	0.66	1.22	1.05
Sweden	0.42	0.43	0.91	0.76
Switzerland	0.35	0.35	0.93	0.66
United Kingdom	0.53	0.50	1.27	1.09
Eastern Europe	0.54	0.94	1.44	1.16
Belarus	0.41	0.79	1.41	1.19
Czech Republic	0.70	0.98	1.39	1.03
Estonia	0.55	1.00	1.37	1.04
Hungary	0.64	0.86	1.52	1.04
Latvia	0.58	1.00	1.48	1.18
Lithuania	0.54	1.05	1.67	1.31
Poland	0.57	0.93	1.48	1.19
Russian Federation	0.51	1.26	1.53	1.54
Slovakia	0.43	0.62	1.31	0.96
Ukraine	0.47	0.95	1.25	1.16
Europe	0.47	0.65	1.22	0.98
United States of America	0.69	0.72	1.73	1.44
All	0.47	0.65	1.24	1.00

levels among men. The higher PGLE levels among men are likely because Eastern European men exhibited relatively high obesity levels and high all-cause mortality levels at relatively young ages, whose impact on life expectancy values and consequently PGLE is large.

Changes Over Time in the Impact of Obesity on Life Expectancy Levels in Europe and the USA

In all 26 European countries, the obesity prevalence as well as the share of all-cause mortality due to obesity (obesity-attributable mortality) have increased over time. The impact of obesity on life expectancy levels has, consequently, also grown.

More specifically, OAMFs were increasing over time for all countries and both sexes, although – in line with what we observed for obesity prevalence – not to the same extent (see Figs. 4.4 and 4.5). In Western Europe, OAMFs generally increased over the 1975–2012 period, at a slightly faster pace among men compared to women. In Eastern Europe, by contrast, OAMFs clearly stagnated, and even declined between 1990 and 2000, particularly among women. The overall absolute increase in OAMFs was greatest in the USA, Ireland, and the UK, and smallest in

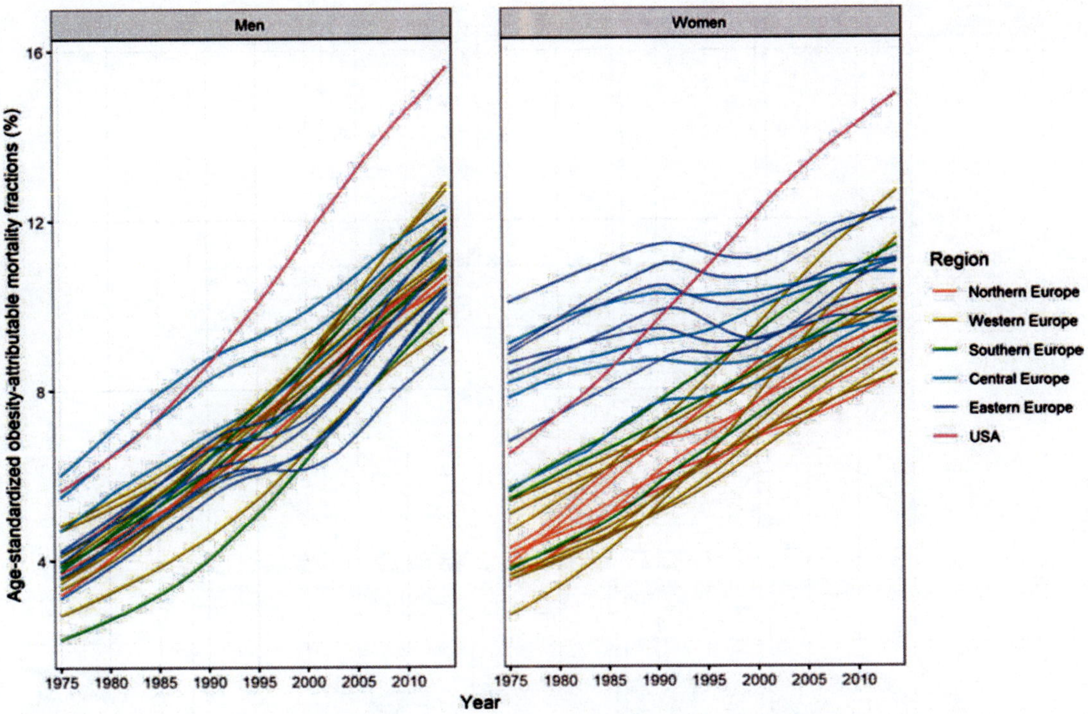

Fig. 4.4 Age-standardised obesity-attributable mortality fractions in 26 European countries* (by 5 regions) and USA, 1975–2014, 18–100 years
*Countries within the same region are presented with the same colour
Central Europe: Czech Republic, Hungary, Poland, Slovakia
Eastern Europe: Belarus, Estonia, Ukraine, Latvia, Lithuania, Russian Federation
Northern Europe: Denmark, Finland, Iceland, Norway, Sweden
Southern Europe: Italy, Portugal, Spain
Western Europe: Austria, Belgium, France, Ireland, Luxembourg, Netherlands, Switzerland, United Kingdom
USA: United States of America

Ukraine and Estonia (women). In Eastern Europe, the increase was highest in Belarus and Slovakia. In Western Europe, the increase was lowest in Belgium and Denmark.

Also, the PGLE due to obesity increased in all of the countries from 1975 to 2012 (see Fig. 4.6). The increase was greater among men (average annual increase of 2.68%) than among women (average annual increase of 1.33%), was largest among men in Portugal and Belarus and among women in Portugal, and was substantial among men and women in Norway. While there was a general increase in PGLE due to obesity, this trend stagnated among women in Eastern Europe from around 1990 onwards, and levelled off after 1995 among women in Denmark and Switzerland (see Fig. 4.7).

Because of the increase in the impact of obesity on life expectancy levels in Europe, obesity has negatively affected life expectancy trends in Europe over time.

Impact of Obesity on Trends in Life Expectancy in Europe and the USA

Table 4.4 and Fig. 4.8 illustrate the effect of obesity on life expectancy trends in the 26 European countries and the USA over the 1975–2012 period.

With the exception of men in Belarus who experienced a decline in life expectancy at birth (e_0), all countries experienced an increase in e_0 over the study period (Table 4.4). On average, e_0

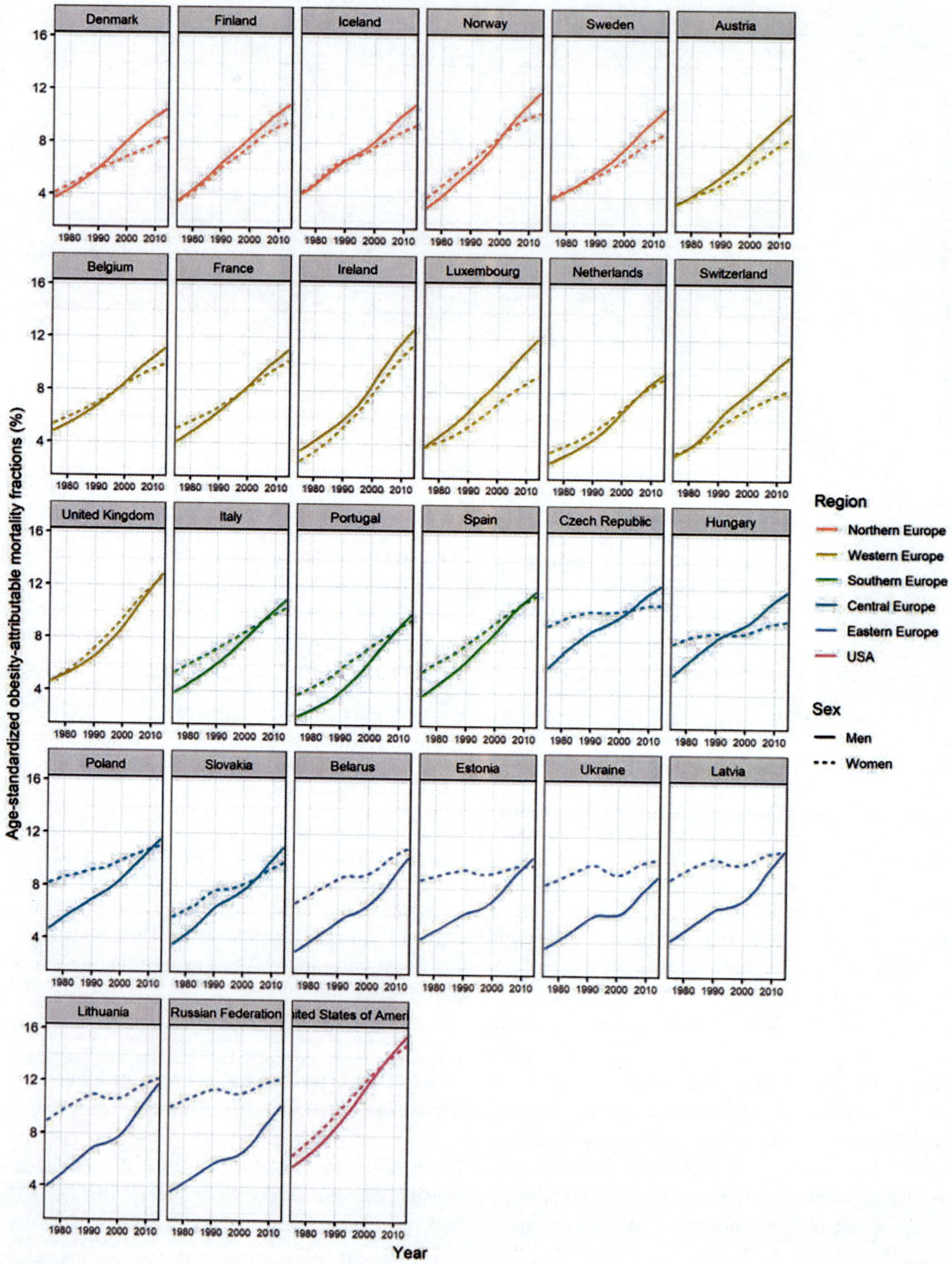

Fig. 4.5 Age-standardised obesity-attributable mortality fractions in 26 European countries*, grouped by 5 regions and USA, 1975–2014, 18–100 years

*Countries within the same region are presented with the same colour

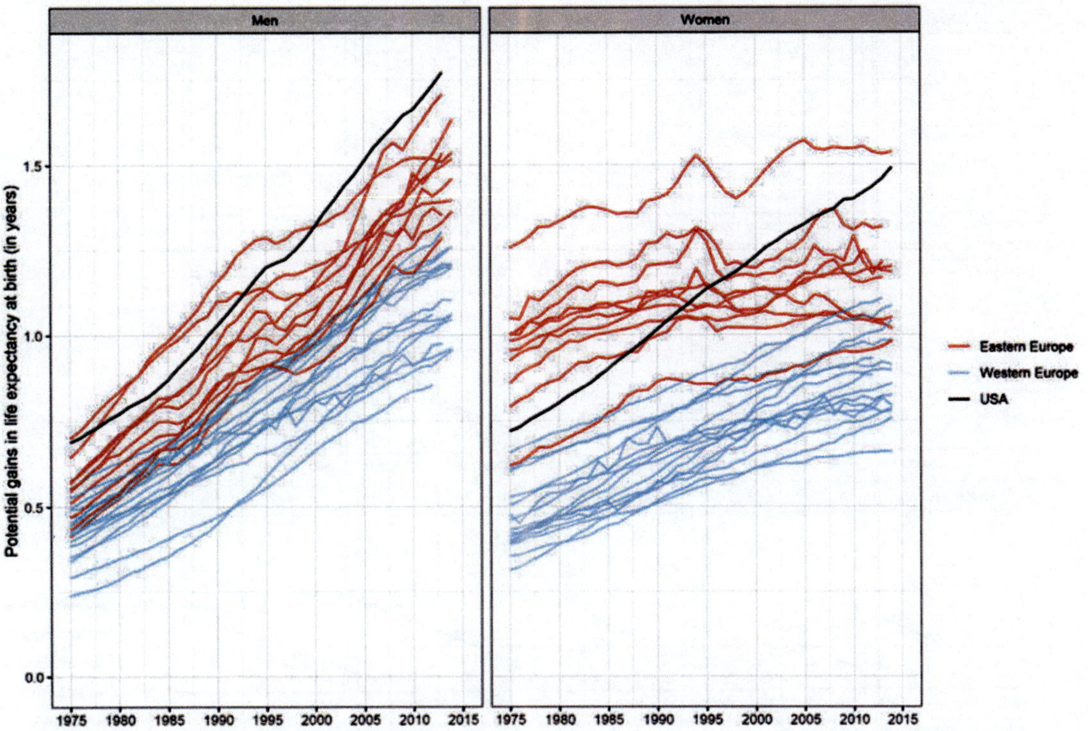

Fig. 4.6 Potential gains in life expectancy at birth (PGLE) if obesity-attributable mortality was eliminated, in 26 European countries* (differentiating Western and Eastern Europe) and the USA, 1975–2012
*Countries within the same region are presented with the same colour
Eastern Europe: Belarus, Czech Republic, Estonia, Hungary, Latvia, Lithuania, Poland, Russian Federation, Slovakia, Ukraine
Western Europe: Austria, Belgium, Denmark, Finland, France, Iceland, Ireland, Italy, Luxembourg, Netherlands, Norway, Portugal, Spain, Sweden, Switzerland, United Kingdom
USA: United States of America

increased between 1975 and 2012 by 7.3 years for men and 6.3 years for women across the 26 European countries. For the USA the increase was slightly higher among men (7.9) but substantially lower among women (4.9). Marked variations across countries were observed, though, with the largest gains accruing to countries in Western Europe (10.0 among men and 7.7 among women). Comparatively, men in Eastern Europe gained 4.0 years and Eastern European women gained 4.6 years, on average.

Yet, all of the countries included in the analysis exhibited reduced increases in life expectancy as a result of the increase in obesity prevalence and obesity-attributable mortality. Without obesity, the average increase in e_0 would have been 8.0 years for men and 6.6 years for women. In other words, without obesity, the average increase in e_0 would have been 0.8 years higher for men and 0.3 years higher for women.

Among men, obesity had the greatest impact on e_0 trends in Lithuania where without obesity the increase in e_0 would have been 1.1 years higher, which is even larger than in the USA where this difference is 1.0 years. Obesity had the smallest impact among men in Iceland and Sweden, where without obesity the increase in e_0 would have been 0.5 years higher. Among women, obesity had the greatest impact on e_0 trends in USA and Ireland (difference of 0.7 years) and the smallest impact in Estonia and the Czech Republic (difference of less than 0.1 year).

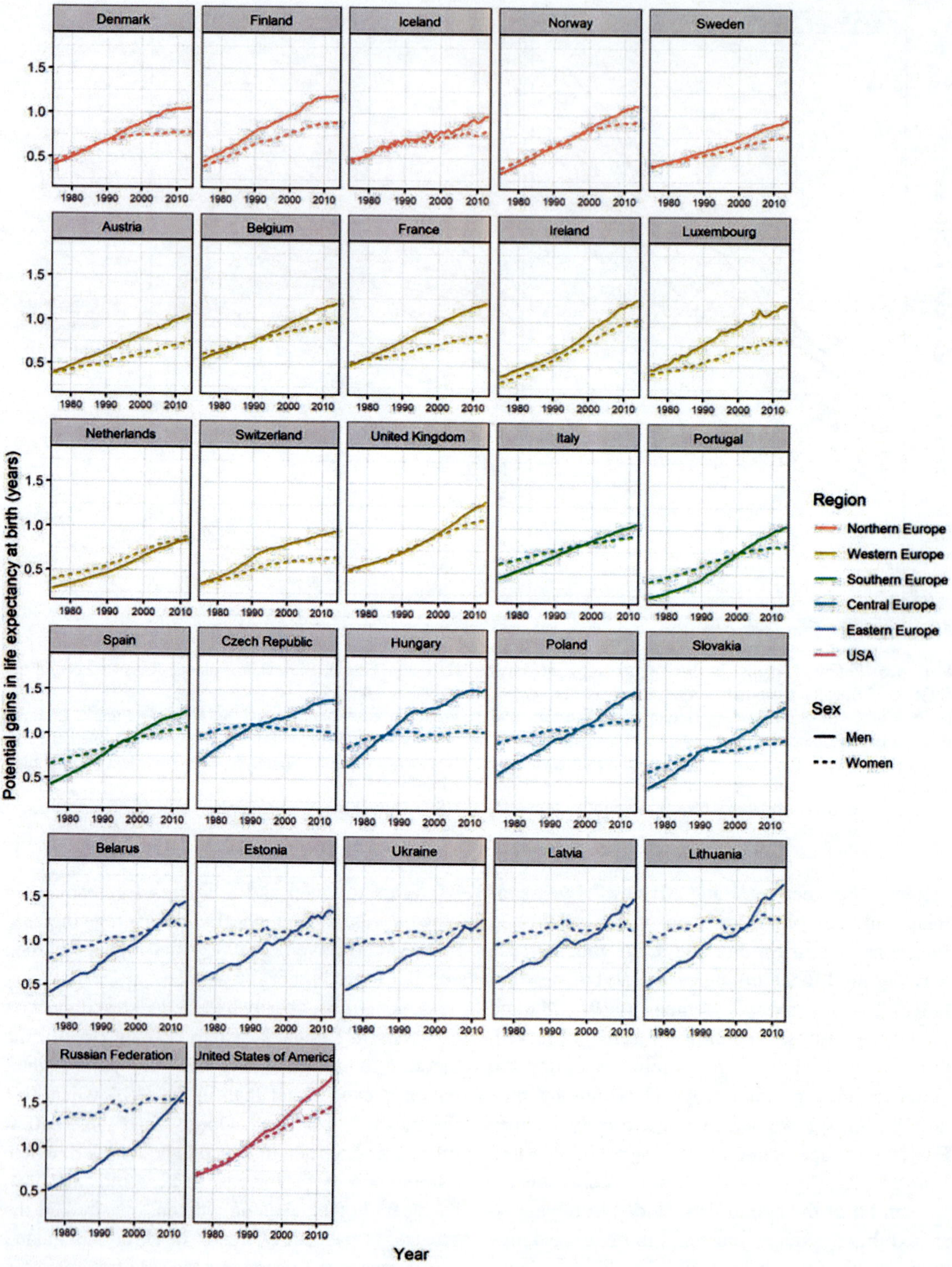

Fig. 4.7 Potential gains in life expectancy at birth (PGLE) if obesity-attributable mortality was eliminated, in 26 European countries*, grouped by 5 regions and USA, 1975–2012, 18–100 years
*Countries within the same region are presented with the same colour

Table 4.4 Impact of obesity on trends in life expectancy at birth (e_0) in 26 European countries and USA 1975–2012, by sex

	Change in e_0 with obesity 2012–1975		Change in e_0 without obesity 2012–1975		Effect of obesity on e_0 change 2012–1975	
Country	Men	Women	Men	Women	Men	Women
Western Europe	9.29	7.32	9.96	7.74	0.66	0.41
Austria	10.62	8.61	11.25	8.95	0.63	0.34
Belgium	8.85	7.63	9.46	7.99	0.61	0.36
Denmark	6.78	5.03	7.40	5.36	0.63	0.33
Finland	10.07	7.26	10.82	7.75	0.74	0.50
France	9.49	7.99	10.17	8.30	0.68	0.31
Iceland	9.02	5.19	9.51	5.51	0.48	0.32
Ireland	9.40	8.40	10.22	9.10	0.83	0.69
Italy	10.19	8.56	10.81	8.89	0.62	0.33
Luxembourg	11.78	9.27	12.50	9.65	0.72	0.37
Netherlands	7.68	5.10	8.26	5.60	0.56	0.49
Norway	7.70	5.33	8.42	5.86	0.74	0.51
Portugal	12.14	10.87	12.91	11.26	0.77	0.40
Spain	8.82	8.75	9.62	9.14	0.79	0.39
Sweden	7.69	5.59	8.18	5.93	0.49	0.33
Switzerland	8.98	6.63	9.55	6.93	0.58	0.30
United Kingdom	9.46	6.96	10.20	7.55	0.74	0.59
Eastern Europe	4.01	4.63	4.92	4.84	0.90	0.22
Belarus	−0.55	1.43	0.46	1.83	1.00	0.40
Czech Republic	7.97	6.98	8.66	7.03	0.69	0.05
Estonia	6.43	6.42	7.26	6.46	0.82	0.04
Hungary	5.29	6.18	6.17	6.36	0.87	0.18
Latvia	4.91	4.53	5.82	4.70	0.90	0.18
Lithuania	2.01	3.80	3.14	4.06	1.13	0.26
Poland	5.90	6.74	6.81	7.00	0.91	0.27
Russian Federation	2.05	2.62	3.06	2.89	1.02	0.28
Slovakia	5.65	5.82	6.52	6.16	0.88	0.34
Ukraine	0.48	1.73	1.26	1.94	0.78	0.21
Europe	7.26	6.29	8.02	6.62	0.75	0.34
United States of America	7.86	4.89	8.90	5.61	1.04	0.71
All	7.28	6.23	8.05	6.59	0.76	0.35

Discussion

Summary of Results

In the 26 European countries studied, the share of mortality due to obesity in 2012 was, on average, 11% among men and 10% among women. PGLE due to obesity in 2012 ranged from 0.86 to 1.73 years among men, and from 0.66 to 1.54 years among women. Overall, PGLE increased between 1975 and 2012, albeit more quickly among men (average annual increase: 2.68%) than among women (1.33%). Among women in Denmark, Switzerland, and Eastern Europe the increase in PGLE levelled off after 1995. Without obesity, the average increase in e_0 between 1975 and 2012 would have been 0.78 years higher among men and 0.30 years higher among women.

Explanation of Results

In 2012, the PGLE due to obesity were, on average, 1.22 years for men and 0.98 years for women

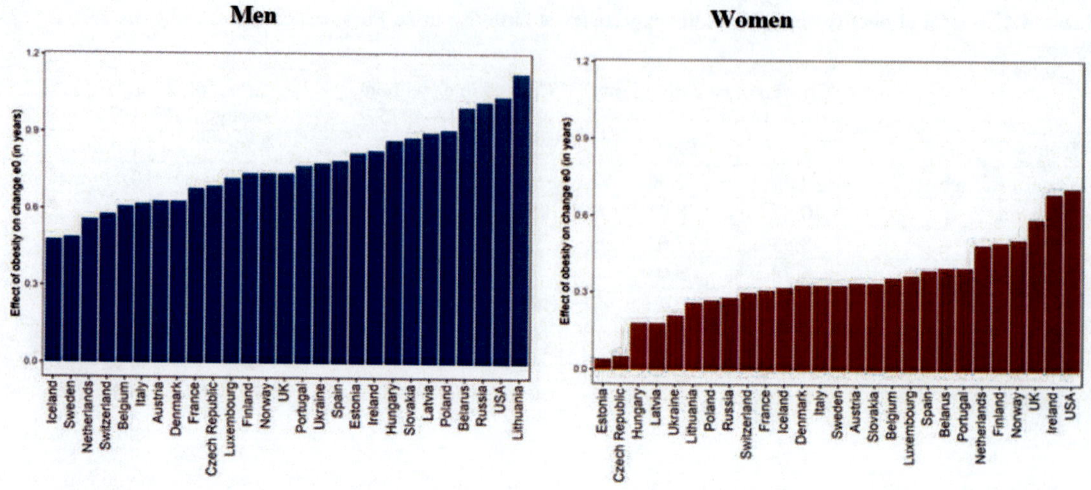

Fig. 4.8 Effect of obesity on change in life expectancy at birth (e0). The additional increase in e0 over the period 1975–2012 had obesity not occurred

Table 4.5 Potential gains in life expectancy at age 50 (PGLE) if obesity-attributable mortality was eliminated, own estimates and those by Preston & Stokes, 2011, in the same countries studied, in 2006

	PGLE e50 2006		
Country	Own estimates	Preston's estimates	Difference
Men			
Austria	0.81	1.00	−0.19
Belgium	0.95	0.98	−0.03
Czech Republic	1.14	1.34	−0.20
Denmark	0.88	0.82	0.06
France	0.94	0.99	−0.05
Italy	0.88	0.90	−0.02
Netherlands	0.69	0.73	−0.04
Poland	1.14	1.37	−0.23
Spain	1.02	1.15	−0.13
Sweden	0.75	0.72	0.03
Switzerland	0.77	0.79	−0.02
United Kingdom	0.99	1.34	−0.35
USA	1.29	1.85	−0.56
Women			
Austria	0.62	0.71	−0.09
Belgium	0.86	0.73	0.13
Czech Republic	0.87	1.01	−0.14
Denmark	0.71	0.62	0.09
France	0.72	0.52	0.2
Italy	0.84	0.57	0.27
Netherlands	0.76	0.69	0.07
Poland	1.08	1.19	−0.11
Spain	0.95	0.87	0.08
Sweden	0.67	0.63	0.04
Switzerland	0.59	0.50	0.09
United Kingdom	0.94	1.23	−0.29
USA	1.18	1.28	−0.10

in the 26 European countries, and 1.73 years for men and 1.43 years for women in the USA. A comparison of our 2006 e_{50} estimates with those of Preston and Stokes (2011) for the same countries uncovered only small differences, except among men in the USA (our estimate was 0.56 years lower) and women in the UK (our estimate was 0.29 years lower) (see Table 4.5). Given that approximately the same methodology was used to estimate the OAMFs, the observed differences are most likely due to the use of different obesity prevalence and risk ratios (RRs) data. Preston & Stokes used prevalence data based on self-reports from the Survey of Health, Ageing and Retirement in Europe for the European countries (except England) and prevalence data based on measured height and weight from nationally representative surveys for England and the USA for years close to 2016, and, in addition, RRs by age, sex and BMI category from the Prospective Studies Collaboration in 2009 (Preston & Stokes, 2011). We, however, used yearly prevalence data from the NCD Risk Factor Collaboration study (2016) based on the available height and weight data from nationally representative surveys and selected BMI predictors, and, in addition, RRs by age and sex based on the review by Lobstein and Leach (2010). Given that the observed differences do not have the same direction for the different countries, we believe that these differences are mainly attributable to the prevalence data used.

To further evaluate our observed PGLE levels, we compared them with our own PGLE estimates for smoking and alcohol (Janssen, 2020b; Trias-Llimós et al., 2018). Our PGLE estimates for smoking were 2.8 for men and 1.0 for women on average in 30 European countries in 2014 (Janssen, 2020a, b), while our average PGLE for obesity was 1.2 for men and 1.0 for women for 26 European countries in 2012. Our PGLE estimates for alcohol were 0.90 years for men and 0.44 years for women in Western Europe, and 2.15 years for men and 1.00 year for women in Eastern Europe (Trias-Llimós et al., 2018); while our average PGLE for obesity was 1.08 among men and 0.86 among women in Western Europe, and 1.44 among men and 1.16 among women in Eastern Europe. Thus, obesity's impact on life expectancy lies between that of smoking and alcohol and can be considered significant.

In our study, we found that PGLE due to obesity was increasing, but that this trend differed across countries and between the sexes. This overall trend can be explained by the general increase in obesity prevalence in European countries (see Figs. 4.1 and 4.2) (NCD Risk Factor Collaboration, 2016) and the resulting growth in the burden of obesity (WHO, 2007), which is also reflected in the OAMFs (Figs. 4.4 and 4.5) in these countries.

At the same time, parts of the observed variation in the increase in PGLE estimates across the USA, Western Europe, and Eastern Europe and between the sexes reflect differences in the onset, the development, and the impact of the obesity epidemic in these countries and in men and women.

Firstly, across the countries studied, the absolute increase in PGLE was largest among women in the USA and second-largest among men in the USA. These observations are in line with evidence showing that between 1980 and 2008, obesity increased much more in the USA than in Europe (Doak et al., 2012; Finucane et al., 2011). This rapid progression of the obesity epidemic in the USA and its large impact on life expectancy has been attributed to an increasingly obesogenic environment caused by factors such as changes in food preparation and processes that promote the consumption of calorically dense foods, and a pronounced decrease in physical activity levels (Cutler et al., 2003).

Secondly, the obesity epidemic has progressed more slowly in Western Europe than in the USA (Finucane et al., 2011; NCD Risk Factor Collaboration, 2016). However, obesity levels in countries like the UK and Ireland are rapidly approaching those in the USA (OECD, 2012), as our PGLE estimates also show. These countries share cultural characteristics related to dietary and physical activity patterns, such as widespread fast food consumption, an increasing prevalence of sedentary lifestyle, and extensive stigmatization of obese people (Donahue, 2018) which aggravates the health effects of obesity and hampers behavioural change.

Thirdly, in the Eastern European countries, the PGLE trends track the evolution of the obesity epidemic in that region. Obesity prevalence levels have been higher in Eastern Europe than in Western Europe in the 1970s and early 1980s (see Fig. 4.1), which suggests that the epidemic started earlier in Eastern Europe. As a result of this earlier onset, the impact of obesity (as expressed in terms of OAMF and PGLE) in the 1970s and 1980s was at times even greater in Eastern Europe than in the USA, especially among women. While there are many potential explanations for this early onset of the obesity epidemic in Eastern Europe, the available data indicate that the main factors were the relatively high total energy supply and intake in Eastern Europe in those years (Zatonski & Bhala, 2012). The overall progress of the obesity epidemic was, however, lower in Eastern Europe than in Western Europe, and the increase was not constant (Finucane et al., 2011). Indeed, in Eastern Europe, increases in obesity prevalence (Bray & Bouchard, 2003; Finucane et al., 2011), OAMFs, and PGLE stagnated in the 1980–2008 period, especially in the 1990s (Bray & Bouchard, 2003; Finucane et al., 2011). However, as these countries started the study period with higher obesity prevalence levels, Eastern Europe still has higher recent average PGLE levels than Western Europe. The pattern of stagnation observed in Eastern Europe could be explained by the decrease in energy supplies at the beginning of the 1990s in Eastern Europe (Silventoinen et al., 2004) resulting from the dramatic economic and political changes that these countries were undergoing in this period (Bray & Bouchard, 2003; Malik et al., 2013; WHO, 2007). The finding that obesity prevalence stagnated among women in these countries in particular, might be related to the fact that women with low socio-economic status (SES) are more prone to food scarcity because of higher energy expenditure (Monteiro et al., 2004).

Fourthly, in Western Europe, a stagnation in PGLE levels was observed among women in Denmark and Switzerland after 1995. This finding seems to be in line with studies reporting a levelling-off of mean BMI since the 1990s (Wilkins et al., 2017); and in specific sub-populations, such as adults with high SES in regions within Switzerland, Italy, France, and Finland (Silventoinen et al., 2004). Although dietary and physical activity information is spreading equally across socioeconomic groups, those with higher SES have a greater ability and capacity to adopt a healthier dietary and physical activity pattern (Robertson et al., 2007). In addition, it appears that higher SES women in particular are more health-conscious, have healthier food habits, and are more prone to follow nutritional recommendations (Fagerli & Wandel, 1999) as they are under greater social pressure to be thin (Psaltopoulou et al., 2017). Similarly, countries with higher income levels and lower levels of inequality (WHO, 2014), like Switzerland and Denmark, tend to have lower obesity levels, especially among women.

When we considered the impact of obesity on life expectancy in the 26 European countries, we found that without obesity, the increase in e_0 between 1975 and 2012 would have been, on average, 0.78 years higher among men and 0.30 years higher among women. These figures account for approximately 10% of the average change in e_0 between 1975 and 2012 among men, and 5% among women. It is therefore clear that the impact of obesity on changes in e_0 should not be ignored. Moreover, the impact of obesity on life expectancy levels and on life expectancy trends is likely to further increase, as previous studies have also suggested (Alley et al., 2011). There are several indicators pointing in that direction, including evidence that obesity's impact is already substantially greater in the USA (13% among men and 15% among women) than in Europe; obesity prevalence is increasing in most European countries (see Figs. 4.1 and 4.2); obesity is increasing in severity; and the duration of obesity is rising in younger generations (Alley et al., 2011).

Evaluation of Data and Methods

Using the recent advances in obesity data, it is now possible to study the impact of obesity on life expectancy for a large number of countries and a long period of time. Two methodological issues warrant our attention, however.

First, in calculating the share of mortality due to obesity (OAMF), which also forms the basis for our PGLE calculations, we were hindered by limitations in the available prevalence and RRs data, which also affected the method used. As has previously been documented, OAMF estimates are sensitive to the data and the methods used (Flegal et al., 2015).

In selecting obesity prevalence data, we used the longest validated time series based on population-based measurement studies that are suitable for studying the impact of obesity on long-term life expectancy trends across Europe (NCD Risk Factor Collaboration, 2016). For those countries with less available obesity data – especially Eastern European countries, a portion of the data we used were merely the result of modelling. Thus, the resulting estimates should be treated with some caution. By contrast, for Western European countries, most of the data we used pertain to measured data (NCD Risk Factor Collaboration, 2016). Table 4.6 gives the confidence intervals around the age-standardised prevalence estimates for each country by sex in order, as to provide more information on the relative reliability of the data for the different countries in our analysis.

Table 4.6 Age-standardised obesity prevalence and 95% confidence intervals, in 26 European countries (differentiating Western and Central Eastern Europe) and USA, 18–100 years in 2012

	Age-standardised obesity prevalence (%) and 95% confidence intervals			
Country	Men		Women	
Western Europe				
Austria	21.1	(14.7; 28.2)	19.1	(13.4; 25.5)
Belgium	22.9	(17.3; 29.1)	22.7	(17.1; 28.9)
Denmark	21.3	(15.5; 27.9)	18.4	(13.1; 24.5)
Finland	22.3	(17.1; 28.2)	21.7	(16.7; 27.3)
France	22.6	(16.3; 29.6)	23.1	(16.9; 29.9)
Iceland	22.3	(15.6; 29.8)	21.0	(14.7; 28.3)
Ireland	26.2	(19.4; 33.8)	26.0	(19.5; 33.2)
Italy	22.3	(17.0; 28.1)	23.5	(18.1; 29.6)
Luxembourg	24.9	(17.6; 32.9)	20.7	(14.3; 28.0)
Netherlands	18.9	(13.8; 24.5)	20.3	(15.3; 25.8)
Norway	24.5	(18.5; 31.2)	23.7	(18.0; 30.2)
Portugal	19.6	(13.8; 26.4)	21.1	(15.0; 28.1)
Spain	24.2	(18.5; 30.5)	26.4	(20.3; 32.8)
Sweden	21.6	(16.3; 27.4)	19.8	(14.7; 25.6)
Switzerland	22.0	(16.3; 28.3)	18.6	(13.1; 24.8)
United Kingdom	26.5	(22.3; 31.2)	29.1	(24.8; 33.6)
Eastern Europe				
Belarus	20.4	(13.6; 28.5)	25.4	(17.7; 34.1)
Czech Republic	25.6	(18.9; 33.4)	25.2	(18.3; 33.0)
Estonia	21.0	(16.0; 26.8)	22.7	(17.4; 28.8)
Hungary	24.6	(17.9; 32.0)	22.1	(15.4; 29.8)
Latvia	22.2	(15.2; 30.2)	25.8	(18.4; 34.5)
Lithuania	23.8	(16.9; 31.8)	28.7	(21.2; 37.1)
Poland	23.6	(18.0; 29.7)	25.7	(19.5; 32.5)
Russian Federation	20.4	(14.8; 26.8)	29.1	(22.6; 36.2)
Slovakia	22.2	(15.7; 29.6)	22.2	(15.8; 29.6)
Ukraine	17.7	(11.2; 25.7)	23.9	(16.3; 32.5)
USA	33.4	(27.5; 39.5)	35.5	(29.7; 41.5)

Because age- and sex-specific RRs of mortality associated with obesity are not readily available by country and year, we have decided to apply to all of the countries studied age- and sex-specific RRs from Western European and US populations that are largely suitable for our setting, as has previously been done (Preston & Stokes 2011). Although RRs could differ slightly across contexts, studies that compared RRs across continents found only small differences in RRs between Europe and North America (Global BMI Mortality Collaboration et al., 2016). Consequently, we do not expect to observe large differences between individual countries. In addition, as time-variant European RRs were not available, we had to apply time-constant RRs even though it is possible that changes in the association of obesity with mortality (which could, for example, occur because of improvements in the treatment of chronic diseases) could have affected the impact of obesity on life expectancy. Previous studies that assessed changes over time in the association of obesity with mortality did so only for the US, and, unfortunately, provided mixed evidence, with some of these studies reporting a decline (Flegal et al., 2005; Mehta & Chang, 2011; Yu, 2012), and others finding an increase (Yu, 2016). Therefore, before implementing time-variant European RRs, more information on their direction is required. Similarly, comparable country-specific RRs are urgently needed. In addition, the choice of these RRs along with their reference group might exert an effect in our estimates. Based on the available data, only a fairly simple – albeit common applied –methodology, i.e. the weighted sum method could be applied (Flegal et al., 2015) to estimate the OAMFs. The application of a more advanced methodology (Flegal et al., 2015) could have affected the OAMFs and thus the PGLE levels, but less the trends (Vidra et al., 2018). The lack of information on the uncertainty of the RRs we used limited us in estimating confidence intervals for the OAMFs and PGLEs.

Second, besides being the result of the OAMFs, the PGLE estimates can also be affected by all-cause mortality levels and trends as age- and sex-specific all-cause mortality rates are used to estimate PGLE. Since all-cause mortality fluctuated greatly in Eastern Europe in the analysed period (Leon, 2011), short-term variations in PGLE in Eastern European countries should be treated with more caution.

Conclusion and Implications

Obesity clearly has a negative impact on both life expectancy levels and trends in Europe. The differences we observed in the impact of obesity across countries and between the sexes can be linked to contextual factors (economic conditions, obesogenic environment, energy supplies), as well as to differences in people's ability and capacity to adopt healthier lifestyles.

It is likely that in the future obesity will have a larger impact on mortality and life expectancy in Europe, as obesity prevalence and obesity-attributable mortality continue to increase in the majority of countries. These trends will have important health, economic, and social implications. Specifically, the increasing prevalence of obesity among European populations, and especially at younger ages, will lead to an increased prevalence of obesity-related disorders, as well as to increases in the mortality burden associated with obesity and in obesity's effects on life expectancy and quality of life.

It is, therefore, crucial that effective health interventions are designed to tackle the obesity epidemic and its increasing effects on public health. Based on the results of our study, we recommend the development of country-specific, multi-sectoral interventions aimed at both individual behaviour and contextual factors. For instance, the combination of individual context-specific nutritional interventions regarding health and lifestyle with addressing the negative effects of the obesogenic environment in which people live (e.g. planning for healthier surroundings, promoting the industry to develop healthier products) and with tackling socio-economic inequalities, could constitute an intervention that addresses obesity at multiple levels and could thus be more effective.

Future Research Directions

Given the large impact of the obesity epidemic, continuous and effective monitoring of its progress is essential. This requires addressing the limitations of the current estimates of obesity-attributable mortality. In our view, three main research directions could address this issue. Firstly, the collection of obesity prevalence data that cover a long period of time and are comparable across context. For this purpose, longitudinal studies that provide obesity data based on measured height and weight are needed, particularly for those countries where existing obesity data are very scarce (e.g. Eastern European countries). Secondly, the collection of comparable country-specific RR data by age and sex, and the examination of their changes over time would, in our view, have important added value for the accurate estimation of obesity-attributable mortality for the different European countries and its trends over time. Thirdly, it would be good to explore indexes other than BMI to capture obesity and, subsequently, estimate obesity-attributable mortality. That is, although a Body Mass Index of ≥ 30 kg/m^2 is the most widely used measure of obesity, it also has several limitations (National Research Council, 2011). For example, the measure does not give any information on body fat and muscle composition, does not distinguish between central and peripheral obesity, and it is a static measure, which – for example – does not accurately deal with ageing-related changes in the body composition. Therefore, it might be worthwhile to examine for European countries whether the use of other indexes, including BMI trajectories, maximum weight in the lifespan, waist circumstance, and waist-to-hip-ratio could better capture obesity, and to explore the potential role of the duration of obesity on mortality risk.

With more comparable, detailed, and accurate data, the estimation of the mortality burden of obesity can be further improved and, in addition, its future course and future impact on society can be better predicted.

Acknowledgements The authors are grateful to Professor Majid Ezatti and Dr. James Bentham (Faculty of Medicine, School of Public Health at Imperial College London); Dr. Gretchen A. Stevens (World Health Organization); and the NCD Risk Factor Collaboration (NCD-RisC) (www.ncdrisc.org) for sharing the obesity data.

This work is financed by the Netherlands Organisation for Scientific Research (NWO) as part of the research programme "Smoking, alcohol, and obesity, ingredients for improved and robust mortality projections, grant no. 452-13-001". See www.futuremortality.com.

References

Alley, D. E., Lloyd, J., & Shardell, M. (2011). Can obesity account for cross-national differences in life expectancy trends? In E. M. Crimmins, S. H. Preston, & B. Cohen (Eds.), *International differences in mortality at older ages: Dimensions and sources, panel on understanding divergent trends in longevity in high-income countries* (pp. 164–192). National Academies Press.

Barbieri, M., Wilmoth, J. R., Shkolnikov, V. M., Glei, D., Jasilionis, D., Jdanov, D., et al. (2015). Data resource profile: The human mortality database (HMD). *International Journal of Epidemiology, 44*(5), 1549–1556. https://doi.org/10.1093/ije/dyv105

Berghofer, A., Pischon, T., Reinhold, T., Apovian, C. M., Sharma, A. M., & Willich, S. N. (2008). Obesity prevalence from a European perspective: A systematic review. *BMC Public Health, 8*(1), 200–210.

Bray, G. A., & Bouchard, C. (2003). *Handbook of obesity: Etiology and pathophysiology* (2nd ed.). CRC Press Taylor & Francis Group.

Cleveland, W. S., & Loader, C. (1995). *Smoothing by local regression: Principles and methods*. AT & T Bell Laboratories.

Cutler, D. M., Glaeser, E. L., & Shapiro, J. M. (2003). Why have Americans become more obese? *The Journal of Economic Perspectives, 17*(1), 93–118.

Doak, C. M., Wijnhoven, T. M., Schokker, D. F., Visscher, T. L., & Seidell, J. C. (2012). Age standardization in mapping adult overweight and obesity trends in the WHO European region. *Obesity Reviews: An Official Journal of the International Association for the Study of Obesity, 13*(2), 174–191.

Donahue, J. (2018). Obesity in the US and UK. *Journal of Nutrition & Food Sciences, 8*(4), 1–5.

Eurostat. (2011). *Census data*. Retrieved from https://ec.europa.eu/CensusHub2/query.do?step=selectHyperCube&qhc=false

Eurostat. (2016). European health interview survey – Almost 1 adult in 6 in the EU is considered obese –

Share of obesity increases with age and decreases with education level. *Eurostat News Release*. Retrieved from http://ec.europa.eu/eurostat/documents/2995521/7700898/3-20102016-BP-EN.pdf/c26b037b-d5f3-4c05-89c1-00bf0b98d646

Eurostat. (2017). *Overweight and obesity – BMI statistics*. Retrieved from http://ec.europa.eu/eurostat/statistics-explained/index.php/Overweight_and_obesity_-_BMI_statistics

Fagerli, R. A., & Wandel, M. (1999). Gender differences in opinions and practices with regard to a "healthy diet". *Appetite, 32*(2), 171–190. S0195-6663(98)90188-X.

Field, A. E., Coakley, E. H., Must, A., Spadano, J. L., Laird, N., Dietz, W. H., et al. (2001). Impact of overweight on the risk of developing common chronic diseases during a 10-year period. *Archives of Internal Medicine, 161*(13), 1581–1586. ioi00652.

Finucane, M. M., Stevens, G. A., Cowan, M. J., Danaei, G., Lin, J. K., Paciorek, C. J., et al, Global Burden of Metabolic Risk Factors of Chronic Diseases Collaborating Group (Body Mass Index). (2011). National, regional, and global trends in body-mass index since 1980: Systematic analysis of health examination surveys and epidemiological studies with 960 country-years and 9.1 million participants. *Lancet, 377*(9765), 557–567.

Flegal, K. M., Graubard, B. I., Williamson, D. F., & Gail, M. H. (2005). Excess deaths associated with underweight, overweight, and obesity. *JAMA, 293*(15), 1861–1867. 293/15/1861.

Flegal, K. M., Panagiotou, O. A., & Graubard, B. I. (2015). Estimating population attributable fractions to quantify the health burden of obesity. *Annals of Epidemiology, 25*(3), 201–207. https://doi.org/10.1016/j.annepidem.2014.11.010

Global BMI Mortality Collaboration, Di Angelantonio, E., Bhupathiraju, S., Wormser, D., Gao, P., Kaptoge, S., et al. (2016). Body-mass index and all-cause mortality: Individual-participant-data meta-analysis of 239 prospective studies in four continents. *Lancet (London, England), 388*(10046), 776–786. https://doi.org/10.1016/S0140-6736(16)30175-1

Human Mortality Database. (2018). *University of California, Berkeley (USA), and Max Planck Institute for Demographic Research (Germany)*. Retrieved from http://www.mortality.org

Janssen, F. (2018). Differences in longevity in Europe. *The European Actuary, 8*(3), 30–33.

Janssen, F. (2020a). Similarities and differences between sexes and countries in the mortality imprint of the smoking epidemic in 34 low-mortality countries, 1950-2014. *Nicotine & Tobacco Research, 22*(7), 1210–1220.

Janssen, F. (2020b). The role of smoking in country differences in life expectancy across Europe, 1985-2014. *Nicotine & Tobacco Research*. https://doi.org/10.1093/ntr/ntaa011

Janssen, F., Rousson, V., & Paccaud, F. (2015). The role of smoking in changes in the survival curve: An empirical study in 10 European countries. *Annals of Epidemiology, 25*(4), 243–249.

Leon, D. A. (2011). Trends in European life expectancy: A salutary view. *International Journal of Epidemiology, 40*(2), 271–277. https://doi.org/10.1093/ije/dyr061

Lobstein, T., & Leach, R. J. (2010). *Workpackage 7: Overweight and obesity report on data collection for overweight and obesity prevalence and related relative risks*. Retrieved from http://www.dynamo-hia.eu/dsresource?type=pdf&disposition=inline&objectid=rivmp:232795&versionid=&subobjectname=

Malik, V. S., Willett, W. C., & Hu, F. B. (2013). Global obesity: Trends, risk factors and policy implications. *Nature Reviews. Endocrinology, 9*(1), 13–27. https://doi.org/10.1038/nrendo.2012.199

Mehta, N. K., & Chang, V. W. (2011). Secular declines in the association between obesity and mortality in the United States. *Population and Development Review, 37*(3), 435–451.

Monteiro, C. A., Conde, W. L., Lu, B., & Popkin, B. M. (2004). Obesity and inequities in health in the developing world. *International Journal of Obesity and Related Metabolic Disorders, 28*(9), 1181–1186. https://doi.org/10.1038/sj.ijo.0802716

National Research Council. (2011). The role of obesity. In E. M. Crimmins, S. H. Preston, & B. Cohen (Eds.), *Explaining divergent levels of longevity in high-income countries* (pp. 43–55). National Academies Press.

NCD Risk Factor Collaboration. (2016). Trends in adult body-mass index in 200 countries from 1975 to 2014: A pooled analysis of 1698 population-based measurement studies with 19.2 million participants. *Lancet (London, England), 387*(10026), 1377–1396. S0140-6736(16)30054-X.

OECD. (2012). *Obesity update 2012*. Retrieved from http://www.oecd.org/els/health-systems/49716427.pdf

Olshansky, S. J., Passaro, D. J., Hershow, R. C., Layden, J., Carnes, B. A., Brody, J., et al. (2005). A potential decline in life expectancy in the United States in the 21st century. *The New England Journal of Medicine, 352*(11), 1138–1145. 352/11/1138.

Omran, A. R. (1998). The epidemiologic transition theory revisited thirty years later. *World Health Statistics Quarterly, 52*, 99–119.

Preston, S. H., & Stokes, A. (2011). Contribution of obesity to international differences in life expectancy. *American Journal of Public Health, 101*(11), 2137–2143. https://doi.org/10.2105/AJPH.2011.300219

Preston, S. H., Heuveline, P., & Guillot, M. (2001). *Demography*. Blackwell.

Psaltopoulou, T., Hatzis, G., Papageorgiou, N., Androulakis, E., Briasoulis, A., & Tousoulis, D. (2017). Socioeconomic status and risk factors for cardiovascular disease: Impact of dietary mediators. *Hellenic Journal of Cardiology: HJC = Hellenike*

Kardiologike Epitheorese, 58(1), 32–42. S1109-9666 (17)30040-4.

Robertson, A., Lobstein, T., & Knai, C. (2007). *Obesity and socio-economic groups in Europe: Evidence review and implications for action*. European Commission.

Rockhill, B., Newman, B., & Weinberg, C. (1998). Use and misuse of population attributable fractions. *American Journal of Public Health, 88*(1), 15–19.

Silventoinen, K., Sans, S., Tolonen, H., Monterde, D., Kuulasmaa, K., Kesteloot, H., et al. (2004). Trends in obesity and energy supply in the WHO MONICA project. *International Journal of Obesity and Related Metabolic Disorders: Journal of the International Association for the Study of Obesity, 28*(5), 710–718. https://doi.org/10.1038/sj.ijo.0802614

Trias-Llimós, S., Kunst, A. E., Jasilionis, D., & Janssen, F. (2018). The contribution of alcohol to the east-west life expectancy gap in Europe from 1990 onward. *European Journal of Epidemiology, 47*(3), 731–739.

Vallin, J., & Meslé, F. (2004). Convergences and divergences in mortality: A new approach of health transition. *Demographic Research, 2*(2), 11–44.

Vidra, N., Bijlsma, M. J., & Janssen, F. (2018). Impact of different estimation methods on obesity-attributable mortality levels and trends: The case of The Netherlands. *International Journal of Environmental Research and Public Health, 15*(10), 2146. https://doi.org/10.3390/ijerph15102146

WHO. (2007). *The challenge of obesity in the WHO european region and the strategies for response: Summary*. World Health Organization, Regional Office for Europe.

WHO. (2014). *Obesity and inequities. Guidance for addressing inequities in overweight and obesity*. World Health Organization, Regional Office for Europe.

WHO. (2018). *Obesity*. Retrieved from http://www.euro.who.int/en/health-topics/noncommunicable-diseases/obesity/obesity

Wilkins, E., Wilson, L., Wickramasinghe, K., Bhatnagar, P., Leal, J., Luengo-Fernandez, R., et al. (2017). *European cardiovascular disease statistics 2017*. European Heart Network.

Yu, Y. (2012). Reexamining the declining effect of age on mortality differentials associated with excess body mass: Evidence of cohort distortions in the United States. *American Journal of Public Health, 102*(5), 915–922. https://doi.org/10.2105/AJPH.2011.300237

Yu, Y. (2016). The changing body mass-mortality association in the United States: Evidence of sex-specific cohort trends from three national health and nutrition examination surveys. *Biodemography and Social Biology, 62*(2), 143–163.

Zatonski, W. A., & Bhala, N. (2012). Changing trends of diseases in Eastern Europe: Closing the gap. *Public Health, 126*(3), 248–252. https://doi.org/10.1016/j.puhe.2011.11.017

5 Obesity with Chinese Characteristics? Prevalence and Determinants of Overweight and Obesity in China

Jiaxin Gu, Yue Yuan, Kenneth C. Land, and Qiang Fu

Introduction

The prevalence rates of overweight and obesity have greatly increased in recent decades with the worldwide trends of industrialization, urbanization, and globalization. In many Western countries, the rapidly increasing obesity epidemic has already become an alarming public health issue (Popkin & Doak, 1998; Wang et al., 2002, 2007a, b). However, only recently have scholars begun to pay serious attention to the prevalence and determinants of overweight and obesity in the most populated country in the world, the People's Republic of China.

Although the obesity epidemic in China is still at an early stage as compared to Western countries, this emerging issue, if left unabated, has the potential to become a substantial public health burden in China and worldwide (Gu et al., 2005; Wang et al., 2007a, b). Further studies investigating the temporal patterns, trends, determinants, and implications of China's growing burden of overweight and obesity are thus clearly warranted. Importantly, the potential obesity epidemic in China, like in any other country, is not merely an anthropometric question but deeply rooted in its socio-cultural context. We need to recognize that the social, cultural, and institutional contexts in contemporary China can differ in striking ways from well-studied Euro-American contexts. In this regard, scholars cannot fully understand the pathogenesis of obesity in China unless the Chinese characteristics of obesity, if they exist, have been seriously considered.

To assess how the obesity epidemic is unfolding in China, as well as to inform policies and intervention programs for effectively combatting the country's obesity epidemic, this chapter reviews studies that address the following topics regarding overweight and obesity in China: age trajectories, sex disparities, socioeconomic and behavioral disparities, and temporal or long-term trajectories. A summary table of all the articles we reviewed on obesity and overweight in China is in the Appendix. We were particularly interested in identifying and articulating any characteristics of obesity that are unique to the Chinese context. Accordingly, we provide some discussion of the socio-cultural characteristics of the obesity epidemic in China so that readers can better assess whether the epidemic is rooted in the country's society, culture, and institutional changes in the last few decades. We begin our chapter with a brief description of the significance of studying overweight and obesity in China, and proceed

J. Gu · Q. Fu (✉)
Department of Sociology, University of British Columbia, Vancouver, BC, Canada
e-mail: qiang.fu@ubc.ca

Y. Yuan
School of Public Policy and Administration, Xi'an Jiaotong University, Xi'an, Shaanxi, China

K. C. Land
Social Science Research Institute, Duke University, Durham, NC, USA

G. Garcia-Alexander, D. L. Poston, Jr. (eds.), *International Handbook of the Demography of Obesity*, International Handbooks of Population 12, https://doi.org/10.1007/978-3-031-10936-2_5

with some definitional and measurement issues in this field.

The Significance of Studying Overweight and Obesity in China

The World Health Organization (WHO) defines obesity as a condition in which excess body fat negatively impacts health, and it has recognized obesity as a disease since 1997 (World Health Organization, 2000). Obesity may pose a serious public health problem, significantly reduce life expectancy, generate substantial financial burdens for central/federal and local governments, and impede social and economic development (Field et al., 2001; Wang et al., 2007a, b; Wolf & Colditz, 1998; Zhao et al., 2008).

A large body of literature has suggested that the economic cost attributable to overweight and obesity accounts for 2–7% of a nation's total healthcare expenditures in Western countries (Katzmarzyk & Janssen, 2004; Segal et al., 1994; Wolf & Colditz, 1998). A study based on the 2003 National Nutrition and Health Survey in China found that costs associated with overweight and obesity, which was estimated to be 21.11 billion Yuan in 2003, had become a major component of the total medical costs for chronic diseases (Zhao et al., 2008). The study further suggested that the percentage of medical costs attributable to obesity in China's total healthcare expenditure was already comparable to or even higher than that in Australia and Canada, and a substantial increase in China's medical costs related to obesity is expected for more recent years.

China's market transformation began in 1978 and has since led to the country's rapid economic growth, accelerated urbanization, and massive rural-to-urban migration. For example, the annual growth rate of urbanization was over 9% from 1978 to 2007, and the corresponding proportion of China's urban population increased from 17.0% in 1978 to 43.5% in 2018 (Cao et al., 2012). Economic growth and urbanization throughout China have brought about major transitions in diets, lifestyles, and physical activity, together with a changing image of body weight. In particular, people who resided in economically developed cities in China were more likely to shift towards Western lifestyles (Wang et al., 2007a, b). With urbanization and economic development, more individuals in China will be exposed to high-fat diets, sedentary behaviors, and other risk factors for obesity, which may lead to a potential loss in (active) life expectancy (Calle et al., 1999; Field et al., 2001; Zhao et al., 2008). When coupled with China's huge population size (approximately 1.4 billion), the country's continuing obesity epidemic will exacerbate the global burden of chronic diseases.

Surveys and Measures

The availability of reliable data has been a critical issue for scholars studying the obesity epidemic in China for two reasons. First, anthropometric data collected by domestic scholars or agencies are largely unavailable for public use. Second, international collaboration in (anthropometric) data collection is often subject to the approval, sanction, or support from local authorities, and its political sensitivity may vary over time. The China Health and Nutrition Survey (CHNS) has thus become a common data source used by scholars in this field. As an open cohort survey that tracks the health status and nutritional conditions of Chinese over time, the CHNS is implemented using a random multi-stage cluster sampling method to collect information from multiple provinces in China (Popkin et al., 1995a, b). Since its first wave in 1989, this household-based survey has provided valuable information including demographic, economic, social, and behavioral questions related to overweight and obesity in China (Wang et al., 2007a, b). Numerous studies based on the CHNS generally suggest that over time more Chinese people have become overweight or obese (Du et al., 2002; Fu & George, 2015a, b; Gu et al., 2005).

One obvious reason behind the CHNS's popularity in the field is that it is arguably the only long-term, nationally representative survey of its kind that is readily available for scholarly use. However, other nationally representative surveys conducted by state or academic institutions to examine the health status of Chinese people do exist. For example, results based on the Chinese National Survey on Students' Constitution and Health (CNSSCH) were used to establish measures for screening overweight and obesity among school-aged children (Ji, 2005). Yet, the CNSSCH, together with other similar survey datasets collected by Chinese agencies, are often, if not always, unavailable for (international) scholars without certain connections.

A consensus on the best measure of overweight and obesity has not been reached, but some measures are used more often than others in empirical studies. Simple measures/thresholds for adulthood overweight and obesity categories from the WHO are based on a body mass index, or BMI (calculated by the weight in kilograms divided by the square of the height in meters) of ≥ 25 and BMI $\geq$ 30, respectively. For children and adolescents below the age of 18, their BMI cutoff points for overweight and obesity are age-specific and the growth curves of BMI cutoff points pass to the adulthood cutoff points at age 18 (Cole et al., 2000; Ji, 2005). The WHO also proposed more detailed BMI cutoff points for screening different levels of overweight status: the normal weight category (between 18.5 and 24.99), Grade 1 overweight (between 25.0 and 29.99), Grade 2 overweight (between 30.0 and 39.99), and Grade 3 overweight (40.0 or higher) (World Health Organization, 1995). BMI is used most often by scholars across the globe for consistency. Yet, research on self-reporting of height and weight suggest that people tend to over-report their height and under-report their weight when a tall and thin body image is desirable (Calle et al., 1999).

Several studies have suggested that the measures of overweight and obesity recommended by the WHO may not be applicable to Asian populations for two reasons: (1) these measures were primarily derived from evidence collected in Western societies; (2) different racial/ethnic groups have different body fat content (Wang et al., 1994; WHO Expert Consultation, 2004; Zhou, 2002). For example, Asians generally show more upper-body subcutaneous fat than whites do (Wang et al., 1994). In other words, Asians have a higher percent of body fat than whites with the same level of BMI (WHO Expert Consultation, 2004; Zhou, 2002). Consequently, it is argued that the BMI cutoff points for overweight and obesity should be lower for Asian populations, including Chinese (WHO Expert Consultation, 2004).

Other, probably more reliable, indicators for overweight and obesity also exist. For example, central obesity, often measured by waist circumference, is considered a better indicator than BMI in some circumstances (Yusuf et al., 2005). According to the guidelines of the International Diabetes Federation for Chinese populations, a waist circumference of between $\geq$90 cm and $\geq$80 cm could be employed to define central obesity for men and women, respectively (Alberti et al., 2006). Although it is preferred for researchers and health professionals to measure both BMI and waist circumference in overweight and obesity, certain measurement instruments may be difficult to deploy in remote areas, rural villages, and poor communities, or in populations with lower cognitive capacity (e.g., children and the most elderly).

Childhood and Elderly Obesity

The Childhood Obesity Epidemic in China

Epidemiological studies have long found that childhood obesity leads to negative health outcomes. Obese children tend to experience higher risks of hypertension, blood clotting, cardiovascular diseases, cerebrovascular diseases, diabetes, and many other chronic diseases (Balcer et al., 1999; Ebbeling et al., 2002; Strauss, 2000). They are also more likely to develop adulthood obesity and experience physical and/or mental issues (e.g., lower self-esteem) in later stages of life, which contributes to higher levels of morbidity and mortality (Freedman et al., 2005; Must & Strauss, 1999; Wang & Veugelers, 2008).

Since the 1990s, the world has witnessed an unprecedented growth in overweight and obese children. Approximately 4.2% of children worldwide were overweight or obese in 1990, and the prevalence rate increased to 6.7% in 2010 (Wang & Lim, 2012). One meta-analysis conducted by Wang and Lobstein (2006) examined the temporal patterns of childhood obesity in more than 60 countries and found an increase in the combined prevalence rate of childhood overweight and obesity in all countries except for Russia and Poland during the 1990s. A study published in *The Lancet* in 2002 recognized the childhood obesity epidemic as an ongoing global public-health crisis (Ebbeling et al., 2002). With rapid economic growth and social transformation, consumption-based and sedentary lifestyles have been quickly adopted by many Chinese families, especially those living in urban areas, hence contributing to China's obesity epidemic (Popkin, 1998).

Though China was once heavily hit by the Great Famine and lost millions of lives from 1958 to 1961, nowadays the country is keeping pace with the global trend of childhood obesity. In 2000, the prevalence rates of obesity among school-aged children and adolescents in urban China were comparable to those in developed countries (Ji & Cheng, 2008). Using the Chinese National Survey on Students' Constitution and Health (CNSSCH), Song et al. (2019) investigated obesity trends among those aged 7–18 based on the WHO's BMI reference criteria and found that the overweight prevalence rates increased from 1.1% to 20.4% between 1985 and 2014. Fu and Land (2015a, b) investigated the temporal pattern of childhood overweight and obesity using the China Health and Nutrition Survey from 1989 to 2009 and found an upward trend during this period across sociodemographic groups. They further identified an upward trend for those born before 2000 and showed that the obesity prevalence rate among school-aged children rose from 3.2% for those born before 1965 to 12.4% for those born between 1995 and 2000. To understand the causes behind the unprecedented rise of childhood obesity and overweight in China, we further explore social determinants of obesity in the Chinese context.

Birth Weight, Dietary Patterns, and Lifestyle

Birth weight is often viewed as a precursor of the later growth of one's body weight. David Barker (2012) proposed the developmental origins of health and disease (DOHaD) hypothesis, stating that prenatal features such as fetal and maternal nutrition may affect the risks of chronic diseases in later stages of life. The hypothesis suggested that those with low birth weight tend to remain small during infancy, and experience rapid growth in weight and BMI afterwards (Barker, 2012). Similarly, macrosomia, whereby one's birth weight is equal to or larger than 4 kg, may also be a predictor of high body weight during infancy, childhood, and even adolescence (Pan et al., 2019; Wang et al., 2009; Yu et al., 2008). Evidence from recent studies recognized birth weight as a risk factor for obesity during infancy and early childhood; yet, the findings remain inconsistent (Monasta et al., 2010; Yu et al., 2011). Some reported a U-shape correlation between birth weight and obesity among pre-school children, suggesting that individuals in higher or lower than normal birth weight groups tend to be obese or overweight (Hua et al., 2007). Others have proposed that there is a linear association between birth weight and childhood obesity: heavier newborns are at a higher risk of being obese compared to those with lighter birth weight (Zhang et al., 2009, 2017). Moreover, a J-shape relationship between birth weight and childhood BMI suggests that individuals born with very low birth weight (lower than 1.5 kg) have the highest risk of being obese during childhood (Yuan et al., 2015).

Shifting dietary patterns associated with rapid development have led to increased consumption of sugar-sweetened beverages. The consumption of regular sugar-sweetened beverages (SSBs) is known to be related to childhood obesity. Shang et al. (2012) found that, compared to regular milk drinkers, children who regularly consumed SSBs had a higher prevalence rate of normal and abdominal obesity. For children and adolescents, both eating habits and dietary patterns affect their likelihood of being obese. Based on a survey of individuals aged 7–17 from seven provinces in China, Zeng et al. (2018) identified eating at a rapid speed as an important predictor of general and abdominal obesity. Zhang et al. (2015) identified three major dietary patterns among Chinese families: modern or Western (featuring a high intake of milk and eggs, along with fast food and snacking), traditional northern (featuring regular consumption of cereals such as wheat and tubers), and traditional southern (characterized by the consumption of a combination of vegetables, rice, and meat), and further examined their relationship with obesity. Their findings suggested that children with modern or traditional northern diets, which contain high-fat and high-carbohydrate foods, showed higher levels of obesity, even after adjusting for total energy intake. Similar studies have largely lent support to this conclusion, though the categorization of dietary patterns may vary (Liu et al., 2019a, b; Shang et al., 2012). However, some studies have reported a non-significant association between dietary patterns and childhood obesity in China (Rutayisire et al., 2018).

Social Disparities in Childhood Obesity

Social disparities in childhood obesity have been widely documented. Studies based on the Western context often report a negative association between socioeconomic status (SES) and childhood obesity, whereby children from a disadvantaged group (e.g., racial or ethnic minorities, those living in a disadvantaged neighborhood or low-income family) are more likely to be obese (Ebbeling et al., 2002; Singh et al., 2010). Yet, a different pattern was observed in China: the prevalence rates of childhood obesity tend to be higher among those from advantaged groups (He et al., 2014), which might be attributable to prolonged sedentary behaviors and the consumption of energy-dense food among children from urban or rich families.

Regional income inequality plays a prominent role in shaping the country's childhood obesity. Chen et al. (2011) found that those living in urban areas tend to have a higher BMI as well as a higher prevalence of obesity and overweight than their counterparts in rural areas. In their study, Zhang et al. (2020a, b) analyzed individuals younger than 18 years old from the China Hypertension Survey (CHS) and showed that the highest prevalence rate of overweight (40.9%) was among individuals in Beijing, while the lowest was among residents in Guangxi (14.6%); the highest prevalence of obesity was observed among residents in Tianjin (12.2%) and lowest in Hainan (1.3%). As Popkin and Du (2003) argued, such regional disparities in overweight among Chinese children may also be attributable to differences in dietary patterns (a detailed discussion of how dietary patterns and the ongoing nutrition transition in China lead to various obesity and overweight risks among different populations can be found in the subsequent sections). In 2004, about one fifth of individuals in Beijing aged 18 and younger were overweight or obese (Shan et al., 2010). In 2014, the prevalence rates of childhood overweight and obesity in Shanghai reached 36% and 21%, respectively, exceeding the corresponding prevalence rates in the United States (Martinson et al., 2015).

Some studies also suggest that the increase in overweight and obesity is more salient among rural children and adolescents than among their urban peers. Cui et al. (2010) observed that, from 1991 to 2006, the overweight prevalence rates among urban children and adolescents increased from 6.9% to 16.6%, and the corresponding increase was from 4.5% to 12.0% in rural areas. Dong et al. (2018) found that the rural-urban disparities in overweight and obesity decreased from 2010 to 2014. Fu and George (2015a, b) applied growth-curve models on a longitudinal dataset from the China Health and Nutrition Survey (CHNS) and suggested that, though urban children reported a higher prevalence rate of overweight than their rural peers, this rural-urban disparity started to diminish after age 13 and a crossover was observed.

Children born and raised in high-income families generally had higher prevalence rates of obesity and overweight than their peers in low- and medium-income families (Cui et al., 2010; He et al., 2014). Parental education is another important predictor of childhood obesity and overweight in China (He et al., 2014), although some argued that it only affects boys (Martinson et al., 2015). Interestingly, the impacts of certain social characteristics on childhood obesity do not stay the same over time. Fu and George (2015a, b) assessed socioeconomic gradients in China's reform era and found that parental state-sector employment, once a risk factor in 1997, had become a protective factor for childhood obesity by 2007. The crossover is possibly associated with a shifting perception of obesity. Prevalence rates of overweight and obesity tend to rise faster among boys than girls (Cui et al., 2010; Yu et al., 2011). The sex disparity among school-aged children is more salient in China's urban areas. In 2005, the prevalence rates of obesity and overweight had reached 32.5% for boys and 17.6% for girls in major coastal cities located in northern China (Ji & Cheng, 2008).

Policy changes have also influenced childhood obesity in China. With the implementation of China's family-planning policy since the early 1980s, many Chinese families living in urban areas were restricted to having only one child (Gu et al., 2007). Children who were born as the only child in their family often face high expectations from their parents, and sometimes grandparents. It has been argued that these children experience the so-called "six-pocket syndrome," whereby their parents and grandparents concentrate their resources and attention on the only child in the family (French & Crabbe, 2010). Scholars found that these children in one-child families exhibited higher levels of obesity as a result of overfeeding (Wang & Zhai, 2013; Zhang et al., 2020a, b). With China's recent move to a universal two-child policy in 2015, followed by a three-child policy in 2021 (Zeng & Hesketh, 2016), the impact of these evolving family-planning policies on childhood obesity deserves further attention.

Obesity and Overweight Among Elderly Adults

When it comes to the ideal body image for the elderly in China, an old saying goes, "a wealthy elderly cannot trade money for a lean body" (*you qian nan mai lao lai shou*). This traditional Chinese view is in line with modern scientific findings, which suggest that the onset of many chronic diseases including hypertension, cardiovascular diseases, and diabetes are positively linked with body weight (Fan et al., 2016; Salihu et al., 2009; Waaler, 1987).

In recent decades, studies often have reported rising prevalence rates of overweight and obesity among the middle-aged and elderly population in China. Based on the China Health and Retirement Longitudinal Study (CHARLS), Song et al. (2018) concluded that the prevalence rates of overweight, obesity, and central obesity among middle-aged and elderly adults rose by 4%, from 1.5% in 2011 to 5.6% in 2015. Zhi et al. (2004) conducted a cross-sectional study on individuals aged 65 and older in Hong Kong and showed that the prevalence rates of overweight were 42.1% for females and 36.6% for males. Elderly women in China are more likely than elderly men to be obese (Zhi et al., 2004).

Different from the research focus on socioeconomic gradients in childhood obesity, research on the elderly population in China tends to focus on the association between overweight/obesity and other diseases or physical conditions. Sarcopenic obesity refers to the scenario in which an individual experiences age-related loss of muscle mass and strength along with an increase in fat mass (Zamboni et al., 2008). Du et al. (2019) analyzed individuals 65 and older from a community-based sample in Shanghai and found that 7% of males and 2.4% of females had sarcopenic obesity. A more recent study by Chen et al. (2021) found that 3% of the Chinese elderly had sarcopenic obesity, and a balanced dietary pattern such as a lacto-ovo vegetarian diet effectively prevented the elderly from getting sarcopenic obesity. Meng et al. (2014) compared the prevalence rates of sarcopenic obesity among those aged 80 years and older in China. They concluded that the prevalence rates would be lowered by 6.6% if the relative appendicular skeletal muscle index (RASM) instead of the weight-adjusted skeletal muscle index definition (SMI) was used. For the elderly population in China, proper measures addressing both the building of body fat and the loss of muscle are warranted.

Sex Disparities and Related Causes of Obesity/Overweight

While studies have suggested that the prevalence of adulthood overweight/obesity has dramatically increased in nearly all age groups and regions in the past few decades (Popkin et al., 1995a, b; Wang et al., 2007a, b; Wildman et al., 2008; Xi et al., 2012), sex disparities in obesity have been well documented. However, little is known about the recent trends and related determinants of sex differences in the Chinese context. The purpose of this section is to provide an overview of the sex patterns of overweight/obesity, which may vary with factors including the area of residence, income, and educational attainment. First and foremost, China's rural-urban divide (Fu & Ren, 2010) is a major driver of the sex disparity in obesity, and its impact on urban males is particularly salient. From 1989 to 1991, there was an increase in the proportion of overweight and obese males in both rural and urban areas, with a larger increase observed for males residing in urban areas; for their female counterparts, the increase in the overweight prevalence within the same period was only observed among women living in rural areas (Popkin et al., 1995a, b). Another study analyzing survey data collected from 1993 to 2009 suggested similar trends: a rapid increase in obesity was observed among men residing in urban areas; by contrast, women living in less urbanized regions had an increasing prevalence of obesity (Xi et al., 2012). Using the Health Service Household Interview Surveys of Hunan Province in 2013 and 2018, Hua et al. (2020) found that compared with rural residents and females, urban residents and males show higher prevalence rates of overweight and obesity. Gao et al. (2016) studied the rural-urban disparities in obesity and overweight among Chinese women and found that those living in rural areas showed higher rates of obesity and overweight than their urban peers.

It has been suggested that sex disparities in obesity might be attributable to differences in dietary patterns and physical activity between urban and rural areas. For example, high-fat diets and large portion sizes appear to be more prevalent in urban areas (Li et al., 2018; Wildman et al., 2008). A sharp decrease in physical activity and a more sedentary lifestyle such as watching TV, playing video games, and surfing the internet is also more visible in urban areas (Gu et al., 2005; Xi et al., 2012). In particular, due to China's rapid urbanization process, a large number of rural residents, especially male migrant workers, moved to cities and engaged in non-agricultural activities that require less energy consumption (Pei et al., 2015).

Second, past studies have not reached a consensus on the relationship between income level and the prevalence rates of overweight/obesity among sex-specific groups. Popkin et al. (1995a, b) used longitudinal data from the 1989 to 1991 China Health and Nutrition Survey (CHNS) to study sociodemographic disparities in obesity. By classifying income level as low, middle, and high (Popkin et al., 1995a, b), their overall results indicated that there was an increasing prevalence of overweight and obesity across all male groups, with the largest increase in the high-income group and the smallest increase in the low-income group. For women, the high- and middle-income categories showed an increase in the overweight prevalence, whereas there was a decline in the low-income category. In contrast, Zhang et al. (2017) analyzed the results from a regional survey conducted in 2005 and demonstrated that higher monthly income significantly decreased the odds of being obese among women, but such a relationship was absent among men (Zhang et al., 2017).

Although there appeared to be an inverse linear relationship between increased income level and healthier lifestyles (Kim et al., 2004), men tend to have less healthy lifestyles as their income levels increase. Meanwhile, two studies indicated that, as compared to women, men had an increased likelihood of exposure to drinking and/or smoking (Hou et al., 2013; Pei et al.,

2015), which is considered to be a risk factor of being overweight. Likewise, it was noted that males, especially those living in urban areas and with a high level of income, are more likely to consume high-calorie foods and have a less healthy lifestyle.

Furthermore, it is well-known that an educational gradient exists in health behaviors, whereby educational attainment influences access to information and knowledge, which in turn leads to different lifestyles and overweight status (Cutlera & Lleras-Muney, 2010). However, the relationship between the educational gradient and overweight seems to be moderated by sex. Overall, the prevalence rates of overweight by levels of educational attainment doubled for women and tripled for men over the period of study (Jones-Smith et al., 2012). In particular, there was a significant association between low (<primary school) educational attainment and the odds of being overweight among Chinese women, while an opposite relationship was observed among men: better educated men in China (>secondary school) are more likely to be overweight (Jones-Smith et al., 2012).

In this regard, one possible explanation is that better educated women are more likely to take advantage of health-related knowledge, maintain healthy dietary habits, and engage in physical exercise (Cutlera & Lleras-Muney, 2010). It may also relate to a preference for a thinner body image among women (especially among those who are better educated) in recent years (Wang et al., 2007a, b). Therefore, better educated women achieved the lowest level of overweight as compared with other socio-demographic groups.

Besides these more common risk factors accounting for sex disparities in obesity/overweight, several studies have investigated the long-term impacts of undernutrition during early life on obesity in later adulthood (Liu et al., 2019a, b; Song 2012; Wang et al., 2010). Their evidence showed that females who experienced early nutritional deprivation exhibited more adverse impacts on being overweight than did males. Consistent with these findings, Liu et al. (2019a, b) further found that an early-life exposure to the Great Chinese Famine resulted in a higher prevalence of abdominal obesity among females later in life (Liu et al., 2019a, b).

Finally, Pei et al. (2015) investigated the age-specific effects on obesity for both sexes. Even though the prevalence rates of obesity rose with age (Pei et al., 2015; Tian et al., 2016), salient sex disparities in adolescents and adults made it difficult to draw a definite conclusion. Among adolescents, urban girls living in high-income households showed higher odds of being overweight (Zhai et al., 2013), while rural boys are more likely to be overweight (Guo et al., 2013). Among adults, men have a higher prevalence rate of overweight than women from age 18 to 54 (Tian et al., 2016; Wang et al., 2016), and both men and women reached the peak of overweight prevalence around the age of 45–54, followed by a slight decrease in older age groups (Gu et al., 2005).

Socioeconomic and Behavioral Disparities

Since the early 1980s, Chinese people have substantially benefited from improved health care, technological advances, and economic growth. Yet, the beneficial social changes in the era of China's market transformation, which include, but are not limited to, urbanization, globalization, and modernization, have also led to progression of the obesity epidemic (Fu & Land, 2015a, b). Specifically, a major shift in the lifestyles, physical activity, and dietary patterns of Chinese people may contribute to the country's imbalance in energy intake and expenditure. Socioeconomic status (SES) and behavioral disparities in obesity have attracted wide scholarly attention. Next, we review a series of socioeconomic and behavioral determinants of obesity in reform-era China.

Rapid economic growth in China over the last few decades has led to socioeconomic inequalities, which have profound implications for the country's rising obesity epidemic. As posited by theorists of China's market transformation (Bian & Logan, 1996; Fu & Lin, 2013; Oi, 1997; Zhou, 2000), broader socioeconomic status, especially connections with political power, largely shapes one's access to various social resources and benefits. For those who are in an advantageous position to benefit from institutional changes, their higher socioeconomic status serves as a protective factor against overweight and obesity because they have better nutritional knowledge, healthier lifestyles, and easier access to medical care (Link, 2008). In contrast, individuals with lower socioeconomic status tend to be less knowledgeable about the causes and consequences of obesity, face more constraints on their dietary choices, and find it more challenging to adjust their lifestyles (Link & Phelan, 1995; Phelan & Link, 2005).

Extant studies of socioeconomic gradients in obesity have focused on three main socioeconomic indicators in China: income, education, and occupation. For empirical studies based on different time periods and surveys, mixed findings have been reported on the relationship between income and obesity. Popkin et al. (1995a, b) used two waves of the China Health and Nutrition Survey in 1989 and 1991 and found that BMI was positively associated with household income. In comparison with those who are lower-income, individuals with higher income tended to have more fat intake and a lower level of physical activity, yet less energy intake. Using data gathered from Tianjin in 2005, Zhang et al. (2017) found that higher monthly income was associated with lower odds of being overweight/obese among women, but not among men.

Higher educational attainment is often viewed as an effective protector against obesity (Monteiro et al., 2007). However, there were also mixed findings pertaining to educational differences in obesity in the Chinese context. Some studies reported that the odds of being obese or overweight vary with different levels of educational attainment over time (Jones-Smith et al., 2012; Zhang et al., 2017). During the 1990s, they found that there was no significant educational difference in obesity. But, in more recent years, educational disparities in obesity became more salient – better educated women have lower odds of being overweight, whereas better educated men tend to be overweight, as compared to their less educated counterparts. Yet, among children, there was not a significant association between education and overweight in China from 1997 to 2016, after controlling for other socio-demographic and temporal factors (Fu & Land, 2015a, b).

The effect of occupation on obesity/overweight in China remains mixed. Shimokawa et al. (2009) categorized occupations into heavy, medium, and sedentary sectors and suggested that the likelihood of being obese was higher among workers in medium and sedentary sectors. By investigating the prevalence rates of obesity and overweight among urban adults in Northeast China, Wang et al. (2012) found that men with white-collar jobs had a high risk of being obese or overweight, but women with white-collar jobs were at a lower risk. For women, another study revealed that working in non-manual sectors and retirement were risk factors for overweight/obesity (Zhang et al., 2017).

These mixed findings provide a compelling opportunity to understand how the obesity epidemic in China is manifested differently than that in other societies. The changing socioeconomic gradients in obesity appear to highlight one intriguing question whose answer has eluded scholars of China's massive social and economic transformation: what is the most meaningful way of measuring social stratification in reform-era China? If power is viewed by theorists as the primary basis of stratification, indicators of socioeconomic status established in Western contexts may not provide an adequate proxy for power, class, or status in the Chinese context (Fu & George, 2015a, b). In this regard, employment in the state sector (governments, institutes, and state-owned enterprises) is shown to be a protective factor against overweight and obesity in urban China (Fu & George, 2015a, b; Li & Zimmer,

2013). However, the protective effect of state-sector employment is not consistent over time. Using the China Health and Nutrition Survey, Shi et al. (2020) examined temporal patterns of overweight prevalence rates among individuals working in state versus non-state sectors, and observed an interesting occupational crossover. The prevalence rates of overweight remained low for individuals with non-state sector employment in earlier years; yet, they surpassed the prevalence rates of overweight for their state-sector counterparts after 2006 and kept growing. This finding is consistent with the reversal hypothesis on the association between SES and obesity/overweight – the association between obesity/overweight and high SES shifts from positive to negative during rapid social and economic development (Pampel et al., 2012). As clearly documented in the market-transformation literature (Bian & Logan, 1996; Zhou, 2000), state-sector employees in China are often entitled to a wide range of work and family benefits which do not exist for individuals outside state sectors. With the development of agricultural production and the growing popularity of sedentary lifestyles along with China's economic reforms, individuals working in state sectors may be at a higher risk of being obese in the early years of economic transformation because they had easier access to high-energy and high-fat diets and could afford sedentary lifestyles compared to their non-state-sector counterparts (Fu & George, 2015a, b). Furthermore, such occupational difference in obesity gradually diminished if not reversed alongside China's economic growth and industrial upgrading. On the one hand, economic growth has shifted the dietary structure of more of the Chinese population towards higher-fat and high-protein diets, which was once considered to be a privilege for high SES individuals (Fu & George, 2015a, b; Zhai et al., 2009). Sedentary lifestyles also became more prevalent with the rise of service sectors in China. On the other hand, as posited by Phelan and Link (2005), high-SES individuals (e.g., state-sector employees) have earlier and better access to health knowledge and technology, which may have prevented them from becoming obese in recent years.

Dietary Behaviors, Living Environment, and Overweight/Obesity

Unhealthy dietary patterns associated with a lack of nutritional knowledge, disordered eating behaviors, and poor dietary habits have been recognized as risk factors for obesity and overweight (Hurby et al., 2016). The increasing prevalence rates of obesity/overweight in China have been found to be affected by the country's ongoing nutritional transition (Drewnowski & Popkin, 1997; Zhai et al., 2009). While traditional dietary habits in China prefer rice, cereal, and a high content of vegetables, contemporary diets tend to include more processed foods that are higher-calorie and high-fat. This transition possibly led to an increase in people's energy intake in recent years (Zhai et al., 2013).

Certain seasonings/additives that are prevalent in China may play a role in the obesity epidemic. Chili is one of the most commonly used seasonings among Chinese. In fact, people from several provinces in China prefer spicy food. As the Chinese saying goes, "Sichuan people do not fear their food being spicy; Being spicy is not a fearful matter to Hubei people; Hunan people fear that their food is not spicy"(Jiang, 2009, p. 4). According to the China Kadoorie Biobank study, a project designed to assess the burden of chronic diseases in China, adults who frequently consumed spicy food were at a higher risk of being obese in China (Sun et al., 2014). Nonetheless, Shi et al. found that chili intake was negatively associated with the risk of overweight/obesity (Shi et al., 2017). In addition to chili, He et al. found that Chinese adults who consumed more monosodium glutamate (MSG) were more likely to be overweight (He et al., 2011).

China's nutritional transition is a product of the country's economic growth, urban transformation, and agricultural development. People now have access to more meat, vegetables, and fruit, and their spending at grocery stores and dining has grown annually, which inevitably leads to more energy intake (Shi et al., 2005). Shi et al. showed that children from high SES families are more likely to consume soft drinks and fast food on a daily basis, as compared with children from low SES families (Shi et al., 2017). Due to China's rapid pace of urbanization and massive rural-urban migration, more individuals from rural or low SES families have shifted their dietary habits from more traditional diets to processed foods (Lu et al., 2016). A more salient increase in obesity has also been observed among rural residents in more recent years (Tian et al., 2016).

The physical environment also matters. Living in places with higher temperatures in the summer has been recognized as an obesogenic factor that increases the likelihood of obesity (Zhang et al., 2020a, b). Air pollution, normally measured at a concentration of PM 2.5, is another risk factor that possibly leads to higher prevalence of obesity and overweight (Cawley, 2015). Air pollution may influence body weight through either biophysical channels such as metabolic dysfunction or chronic diseases (An et al., 2018) or behavioral mechanisms: people may reduce the frequency of their outdoor activity and increase the duration of sedentary behaviors (Li et al., 2015; McConnell et al., 2015). Such a behavioral effect of air pollution is more salient among women and the elderly in China (Li et al., 2015). Individuals living in areas with a higher average PM 2.5 concentration show significantly higher risks of obesity and overweight, regardless of sex (Deschenes et al., 2020; Zhang et al., 2020a, b). The link between air pollution and the obesity epidemic in the Chinese context warrants further research attention.

Physical Activity and Sedentary Lifestyle and Overweight/Obesity

Reduced physical activity and sedentary lifestyles are viewed as important risk factors for overweight/obesity (Lu et al., 2016; Mushtag et al., 2011). In general, lower levels of physical activity are associated with a higher risk of obesity (Popkin et al., 1995a, b). Studies on the association between physical activity and overweight/obesity mainly investigated the effects of work-related activities, household activity, and leisure-time activities (Owen et al., 2000).

Work-related activities including commuting are significantly associated with the risk of obesity (Monda et al., 2008; Xu et al., 2017; Yuan et al., 2021). China's urban planning, which followed the self-contained Soviet model of "microdistrict" (Lu, 2006), once emphasized the link between work and residence, but this link has been severed with the shift towards commodified gated communities and the separation between work and residence (Fu & Land, 2015a, b). Due to the growing separation between work and residence, urban residents nowadays rely more on automobiles (Fu & Land, 2015a, b).

Meanwhile, more intensified land use in urban China has decreased the public or communal spaces, including parks and playgrounds. These changes in urban planning have been shown to reduce opportunities for physical activity such as walking and cycling, and discourage neighborly interactions (e.g., outdoor play) within a neighborhood (Fu & Land, 2015a, b; Lu, 2006). One study showed that physically active forms of transportation, such as walking and cycling, reduced the likelihood of being obese among adult males (Yuan et al., 2021). Likewise, owning a vehicle significantly increased one's odds of being obese (Bell et al., 2012).

Interestingly, the sex disparity in overweight/obesity might be linked to work-related activities: the association between the levels of work-related activity and obesity/overweight in China was significant among male employees but non-significant among females (Xu et al., 2017; Yuan et al., 2021). As expected, the use of labor-saving devices is associated with lower energy expenditure at home (Lanningham-Foster et al., 2012). Meanwhile, the growing popularity of entertainment and electronic devices such as smartphones, computers, and televisions in our daily lives often leads to reduced physical activity and prolonged sedentary time. Greater access to these devices among high SES children in China possibly explains the socioeconomic gradient in childhood obesity (Shi et al., 2005; Zhai et al., 2013).

The Global Context of China's Obesity Epidemic

Our understanding of China's obesity epidemic should be situated within the global context of obesity. The last few decades witnessed drastic and worldwide increases in overweight and obesity (Popkin & Doak, 1998; Seidell & Halberstadt, 2015; Wang et al., 2002). From 1980 to 2008, the worldwide prevalence rate of obesity nearly doubled; the population of overweight adults (BMI $\geq$ 25) is estimated to be 1.5 billion, one third of which were obese in 2008 (Finucane et al., 2011). A more recent study suggested that the combined prevalence rate of overweight and obesity rose by 27.5% among adults from 1980 to 2013, while the total number of overweight children and adults was estimated to be 2.1 billion as of 2013 (Ng et al., 2014).

While obesity is already perceived as a major public-health concern in industrialized countries and economically advanced regions (Caballero, 2007; Seidell & Halberstadt, 2015), it is relatively uncommon in middle-to-low income countries and its presence, if it exists at all, is possibly confined to high SES individuals in these countries (Monteiro et al., 2004). However, the obesity epidemic may unfold differently across nations, regions, and time periods (Heitmann et al., 2004; World Health Organization, 2000). Studies based on developed countries such as Australia, England, and the United States show that the obesity epidemic develops in a non-linear way (Keith et al., 2006; Olds & Harten, 2001; Prentice & Jebb, 1995). Over the past four decades, the prevalence rates of obesity in the United States remained high but tended to stabilize in recent years (Zhao et al., 2018). Data from the United Kingdom suggested that the overall trend of overweight and obesity among school children leveled off around the 2000s (Mitchell et al., 2007; Stamatakis et al., 2010); yet, the socioeconomic disparities have widened, with English children from low socioeconomic groups being more likely to be overweight (Stamatakis et al., 2010). In general, more recent data suggest that the prevalence rates of overweight and obesity appeared to level off in developed countries (Flegal et al., 2010; Rokholm et al., 2010; Stamatakis et al., 2010), whereas the corresponding rates began to take off in less developed countries (Popkin & Gordon-Larsen, 2004). These findings highlight an urgent need for understanding the trends of obesity in China, a developing country with the largest population in the world.

As the world's most populous country, China has witnessed a sustained increase in the size of its overweight and obese population in different sex groups and nearly all age groups since the 1990s (Wang et al., 2007a, b; Xi et al., 2012). Evidence shows that the overall rates of overweight and obesity rose from about 9% to 42% between 1988 and 2012 (Zhao et al., 2018). The proportion of overweight or obese individuals increased 13.7% among men and 7.9% among women over the 11-year period from 1989 to 2000 (Wang et al., 2007a, b). Moreover, significant increases have been observed in urban areas, especially large cities (Wang et al., 2007a, b). For example, the annual increase of the overweight/obesity prevalence in Beijing was faster than the national average (Wang et al., 2007a, b). Striking increases were also identified among children and adolescents (Rokholm et al., 2010): the prevalence rate of overweight and obesity among school-aged children increased from 14% in 1995 to 34.2% in 2005 (Ji & Cheng, 2009).

Understanding the forces behind the obesity epidemic in China is worthwhile and important. The obesity epidemic in the Western context might be attributable to more sedentary lifestyles and a nutritional transition towards processed foods and high-fat, high-calorie diets (Popkin & Doak, 1998). Many developing countries including China are no exceptions to this nutrition transition, which is accompanied by the growing popularity of fast food and physical inactivity at home or work (Popkin, 1994). But beyond these dietary and behavioral changes (Wang et al., 2002), the obesity epidemic in China is also deeply rooted in the country's profound social, economic, and cultural changes since the socialist era. For example, it has been found that birth cohorts who were born during the Great Chinese Famine were more likely to be overweight in adulthood (Fu & Land, 2015a, b; Wang et al., 2010). In the reform era (after the late 1970s), urbanization and marketization are possibly two major driving forces shaping the obesity epidemic in China.

Chinese cities in the socialist era possessed important design features (e.g., the link between work and residence) which discouraged the use of vehicles, created walkable neighborhoods, and once protected urban residents against obesity (Fu & Lin, 2013; Lu, 2006). China's rapid urbanization since the 1980s essentially has meant a massive shift towards an obesogenic environment, mega cities built for cars, and the rise of gated communities (Caballero, 2007; Fu & Land, 2015a, b; Gu et al., 2005; Reynolds et al., 2012), which account for a strong, if not perfect, correlation between China's urbanization index and the time trajectory of overweight prevalence rates (Fu & Land, 2015a, b).

The rural-urban difference in overweight prevalence rates increased from 4.5% in 1989 to 8.3% in 2000 (Wang et al., 2007a, b). In particular, urban men showed the largest increase, from 5.4% in 1989 to 16.5% in 2000 (Wang et al., 2007a, b). Hou (2008) analyzed the China Health and Nutrition Survey and found that urban adults were more likely to be overweight than rural residents; however, the rural-urban difference disappears after controlling for individual lifestyles. Living in more urbanized areas with more restaurants and grocery stores increases the likelihood of being obese (Zhang et al., 2020a, b). Using a nationally representative sample of Chinese adults from 31 provinces, Zhang et al. (2019) revealed that the prevalence of abdominal obesity tends to be higher in the northern and western areas but lower in the southern and eastern areas in China, which is possibly attributable to different weather conditions and dietary patterns.

China has already moved towards a market-oriented economy, which substantially improved the living conditions of its people (Wang et al., 2007a, b; Zhao et al., 2018). For the Chinese population that previously experienced a scarcity economy in the pre-reform era and one of the greatest famines in human history, China's rapid economic growth since the 1980s has unleashed a soaring demand for high-fat and high-protein diets. Accordingly, Chinese people have consumed less cereals but more animal-source foods since the early 1980s (Wang et al., 2007a, b). Instead of solely centering on the individual-level risk factors and the patterns of obesity and overweight, scholars should focus on the synergy between individual characteristics and the obesogenic environment (including but not limited to the built environment, natural environment, regional disparities, and macro-level social changes) to obtain a comprehensive understanding of the ongoing obesity epidemic in China, along with its adverse consequences for the population.

Although the prevalence rates of obesity in some developed countries have tended to be stable in recent years, it should be noted that the obesity epidemic in China shows no signs of leveling off. It is well documented that obesity is an important risk factor for cardiovascular disease, Type 2 diabetes mellitus, cancer, osteoarthritis, and other diseases (Seidell & Halberstadt, 2015). In particular, similar to what is observed in developed countries, cardiovascular disease is already one of the leading causes of death in China (Reynolds et al., 2012; Zalesin et al., 2008). If the rising obesity epidemic is left unabated, China may face much more pronounced health, fiscal, and social burdens (Gu et al., 2005).

Appendix: Summary of Articles Reviewed on Obesity and/or Overweight in China

Article	Survey/data	Measurement		Sample size	Study population
		Obesity	Overweight		
Bell et al. (2012)	China Health and Nutrition Survey 1997	BMI ≥ 25	*N/A*	4741	20–55 years
Zhi et al. (2004)	Data collected from clients of the Elderly Health Centers (EHCs) governed by the Department of Health of the Government of the Hong Kong Special Administrative Region	BMI ≥ 25	*N/A*	56,167	≥65 years
Chen et al. (2011)	Chinese National Survey on Students' Constitution and Health 2005	BMI ≥ 28	BMI 24–27.9	231,326	7–18 years
Chen et al. (2021)	People aged >= 60 years	Waist circumference ≥85 cm in males and ≥80 cm in females	*N/A*	3795	≥60 years
Cui et al. (2010)	China Health and Nutrition Survey (CHNS) 1991, 1993, 1997, 2000, 2004, and 2006	International Obesity Task Force BMI cutoffs (BMI ≥ 30) & BMI cutoffs by the Working Group on Obesity in China (BMI ≥ 28)	International Obesity Task Force cutoff BMI ≥ 25 & Working Group of Obesity in China cutoff BMI ≥ 24	13,442	7–17 years
Deschenes et al. (2020)	China Health and Nutrition Survey 1989–2015	BMI ≥ 30	BMI ≥ 25	13,741	≥18 years
Dong et al. (2018)	Chinese National Survey on Students' Constitution and Health 1995–2014	International Obesity Task Force BMI reference	*N/A*	943,128	7–17 years
Du et al. (2019)	Data collected from community-dwelling older residents from the Zhoujiaqiao community, Shanghai	Body fat above the 60th percentile of the present study sample of the same sex	*N/A*	631	65–89 years
Fan et al. (2016)	The Shanghai Elderly Cardiovascular Health Study (SHECHS)	BMI ≥ 28	24 ≤ BMI < 28	3950	≥65 years

(continued)

Article	Survey/data	Measurement		Sample size	Study population
		Obesity	Overweight		
Fu and George (2015a)	China Health and Nutrition Survey (CHNS) 1993, 1997, 2000, 2004, and 2006	*N/A*	International Obesity Task Force BMI reference	1694	2–11 years
Fu and George (2015b)	China Health and Nutrition Survey (CHNS) 1997, 2000, 2004, and 2006	*N/A*	International Obesity Task Force BMI reference	7292	1–18 years
Fu and Land (2015a)	China Health and Nutrition Survey (CHNS) 1989, 1991, 1993, 1997, 2000, 2004, 2006, and 2009	*N/A*	International Obesity Task Force BMI reference	54,370	18–64 years
Fu and Land (2015b)	China Health and Nutrition Survey (CHNS) 1989–2009	*N/A*	For 2–18 years: International Obesity Task Force BMI cut-points; For aged above 18: BMI $\geq$ 25	25,152	2–25 years
Gao et al. (2016)	Chinese National Breast Cancer Screening Program	BMI $\geq$ 28	BMI 24–27.9	1,210,762	35–59 years
Gu et al. (2005)	International Collaborative Study of Cardiovascular Disease in ASIA (InterASIA) 2000–2001	*N/A*	BMI $\geq$ 25	15,540	35–74 years
Guo et al. (2013)	Data collected from students in Liaoning Province July 2010 to January 2011	Weight class based on the International Obesity Task Force	*N/A*	4094	5–18 years
He et al. (2011)	China Health and Nutrition Survey (CHNS) 1991–2006	*N/A*	BMI $\geq$ 25 and WHO reference for Asians BMI $\geq$ 23	10,095	18–65 years
He et al. (2014)	China Health and Nutrition Survey 1991–2006	Aged 7–18 years: BMI cutoffs according to the Working Group of Obesity in China reference	Age 2–6 years: international BMI cutoffs	10,186	2–18 years
Hou (2008)	China Health and Nutrition Survey 2000	BMI $\geq$ 30	BMI $\geq$ 25	7684	25–65 years
Hou et al. (2013)	Shanghai Diabetes Study (SHDS) 1998–2001	BMI $\geq$ 30	BMI $\geq$ 25	9289	20–74 years
	Shanghai Diabetes Study II (SHDS II) 2007–2008	BMI $\geq$ 28	*N/A*		

(continued)

Article	Survey/data	Measurement		Sample size	Study population
		Obesity	Overweight		
Hua et al. (2007)	A cohort study generated from school-aged children (7–11 years in round 1, and 16–20 years in the follow-up round) in elementary schools in Beijing	BMI ≥ 28	24 ≤ BMI < 28	672	7–11 years
Hua et al. (2020)	Health Service household interview surveys of Hunan Province 2013 and 2018	BMI ≥ 28	BMI 24–27.9	24,282	≥18 years
Ji (2005)	Chinese National Survey on Students' Constitution and Health 2000	BMI ≥ 28	BMI ≥ 24	216,620	School students aged 7–18 years old
Ji and Cheng (2008)	Chinese National Survey on Students' Constitution and Health 2005	BMI ≥ 28	BMI ≥ 24	226,602	7–18 years
Ji and Cheng (2009)	Chinese National Survey on Students' Constitution and Health 1985, 1991, 1995, 2000, and 2005	BMI ≥ 28	*N/A*	226,602	7–18 years
Jones-Smith et al. (2012)	China Health and Nutrition Survey (CHNS) 1989–2006	*N/A*	BMI ≥ 25	13,806	18–50 years
Li et al. (2015)	33 Communities Chinese Health Study (33CHS)	BMI ≥ 30	BMI ≥ 25	24,845	18–74 years
Li and Zimmer (2013)	China Health and Nutrition Survey (CHNS) 1989, 1991, 1993, 1997, 2000, 2004, and 2006	BMI ≥ 95th percentile	*N/A*	Over 1700	2–18 years
Liu et al. (2019a)	China Nutrition and Health Survey 2010–2012	BMI and Chinese standards age- and gender-specific BMI z-scores	BMI and Chinese standards age- and gender-specific BMI z-scores	7988	6–17 years
Liu et al. (2019b)	China Nutrition and Health Survey 2002 and 2010–2012	BMI ≥ 28	24 ≤ BMI < 28	35,578	Adults

(continued)

Article	Survey/data	Measurement		Sample size	Study population
		Obesity	Overweight		
Martinson et al. (2015)	Child Well-Being Study of Shanghai in 2014	Cutoff points of the US Centers for Disease Control and Prevention	*N/A*	2000	Aged 7 years
Meng et al. (2014)	Data collected from the elderly in Beijing with a comparison of 75 healthy volunteers (men) aged 20–40 years	BMI ≥ 27.5	BMI 23.0–27.4	176	Aged 80 and above
Monda et al. (2008)	China Health and Nutrition Survey 1991, 1993, 1997, and 2000	BMI ≥ 30	BMI ≥ 25	9405	18–55 years
Pan et al. (2019)	Chengdu Maternal and Child Health Management System (CMCHMS)	WHO Growth reference weight-for-length/height z score ≥1.645	*N/A*	1767	Infants ≤3 years old
Pei et al. (2015)	Data collected from adults living in rural areas of Hanzhong, Shaanxi Province	BMI ≥ 28	BMI 24–27.9	3030	18–80 years
Popkin et al. (1995a)	China Health and Nutrition Survey 1989 and 1991	BMI ≥ 27 (severely overweight)	BMI ≥ 25	3981	20–45 years
Popkin et al. (1995b)	China Health and Nutrition Survey 1989 and 1991	BMI as the outcome	*N/A*	3901	20–45 years
Reynolds et al. (2012)	The International Collaborative Study of Cardiovascular Disease in Asia (InterASIA) 2000–2001	BMI ≥ 30	BMI 25.0–29.9	15,540	35–74 years
		BMI ≥ 28	BMI ≥ 24		
Rutayisire et al. (2018)	Data collected from children in kindergartens in Anhui and Jiangsu	BMI cutoff: 85th percentile	*N/A*	8900	3–6 years
Shan et al. (2010)	Data collected from resident communities for children living in Beijing for at least 6 months	International Obesity Task Force sex- and age-specific BMI cutoffs and other measures	BMI ≥ 25	21,198	2–18 years
Shang et al. (2012)	Data collected from children living in 6 provincial capital cities (Harbin, Beijing, Jinan, Shanghai, Chongqing, and Guangzhou)	BMI ≥ 95th percentile using age- and sex-specific BMI cutoff points	*N/A*	6974	6–13 years

(continued)

Article	Survey/data	Measurement		Sample size	Study population
		Obesity	Overweight		
Shi et al. (2017)	China Health and Nutrition Survey 1991, 1993, 1997, 2000, 2004, 2006, 2009, and 2011	*N/A*	BMI ≥ 25	126,884	20–75 years
Shi et al. (2020)	China Health and Nutrition Survey (CHNS) 1989–2011	*N/A*	BMI ≥ 24	39,106	18–60 years
Song et al. (2018)	China Health and Retirement Longitudinal Study (CHARLS) 2011	BMI ≥ 27.5	BMI 23.0–27.4	9557	≥45 years
Song et al. (2019)	Chinese National Survey on Students' Constitution and Health 1985, 1995, 2000, 2005, 2010, and 2014	*N/A*	WHO 2007 reference: BMI > one standard deviation	1,489,953	7–18 years
Sun et al. (2014)	China Kadoorie Biobank (CKB) study	BMI, percentage body fat (BF%), waist circumference (WC), and waist-to-height ratio (WHtR)	*N/A*	434,556	30–79 years
Tian et al. (2016)	A cross-sectional nationwide survey conducted by the China Physical Fitness Surveillance Center to monitor physical health in the Chinese population (2000, 2005, 2010, and 2014)	BMI ≥ 27.5	BMI 23.0–27.5	616,676	20–59 years
Wang et al. (2002)	China Health and Nutrition Surveys 1991 and 1997	BMI ≥ 30	BMI ≥ 25	5702	6–18 years
Wang et al. (2007a, b)	China National Nutrition Survey 1992 (CNNS92)	BMI ≥ 28	BMI 24–27.9	78,704	≥18 years
	China National Nutrition and Health Survey (CNNHS02)			209,849	
Wang et al. (2007a, b)	China Health and Nutrition Survey 1989–2000	BMI ≥ 30	BMI ≥ 25	13,080	20–45 years

(continued)

Article	Survey/data	Measurement		Sample size	Study population
		Obesity	Overweight		
Wang et al. (2009)	Data collected from live-born individuals who participated in the US-China collaborative study of periconceptional folic acid supplementation and neural tube defects in the 1990s	The Working Group on Obesity in China BMI reference	*N/A*	2870	Cohorts born in 1993 to 1995
Wang et al. (2010)	Annual physical evaluations from 2006 to 2008 in the Public Health Center of the First Affiliated Hospital of Chongqing Medical University in Chongqing	BMI $\geq$ 28	BMI 24–27.9	17,023	Cohort born in 1956–1964
Wang et al. (2012)	Control Hypertension and Other Risk Factors to Prevent Stroke with Nutrition Education in Urban Area of Northeast China (CHPSNE study) 2009	BMI $\geq$ 27.5	BMI 25–27.5	25,196	18–74 years
Wang et al. (2016)	Jilin Provincial Chronic Disease Survey 2012	BMI $\geq$ 28	BMI 24–28	20,839	18–79 years
Wildman et al. (2008)	China National Hypertension Survey 1991 and the follow-up study 1999–2000	Primary analysis: BMI $\geq$ 30; Secondary analysis: BMI $\geq$ 28	Primary analysis: BMI $\geq$ 25 Secondary analysis: BMI $\geq$ 24	15,716	45–79 years
Xu et al. (2017)	Zhejiang Metabolic Syndrome Prevalence Survey	BMI $\geq$ 28	BMI 24–28.0	6739	18–69 years
Xi et al. (2012)	China Health and Nutrition Survey 1993–2009	BMI $\geq$ 27.5	BMI 25–27.49	52,621	Aged 18 and above
Yuan et al. (2015)	A survey of metabolic syndrome conducted among children and adolescents in 6 geographically representative areas in 2010	BMI $\geq$ 95th percentile	85th percentile $\leq$ BMI < 95th percentile	16,580	7–17 years

(continued)

Article	Survey/data	Measurement		Sample size	Study population
		Obesity	Overweight		
Yuan et al. (2021)	China National Nutrition and Health Survey (CNNHS) 2010–2012	*N/A*	BMI $\geq$ 25	23,112	$\geq$18 years
Yu et al. (2008)	Data collected from singleton children born between 1998 and 31 May 2001, living in Huangpu District, Shanghai and receiving care at local health centers	High Weight-for-Length/Height: z-score $\geq$ 1.68 (WHO reference)	*N/A*	918	1–3 years
Zeng et al. (2018)	A national survey of school-aged children and adolescents in China (the baseline survey of a school-based obesity prevention and intervention program)	BMI $\geq$ 95th percentile	*N/A*	50,037	7–17 years
Zhang et al. (2009)	Data collected from children in selected kindergartens in Tianjin	Obesity I: age- and gender-specific BMI between the 95th and 97.6th percentiles	BMI between the 85th and 95th percentiles	15,852	3–6 years
		Obesity II: age- and gender-specific BMI more than the 97.7th percentiles	*N/A*		
Zhang et al. (2015)	China Health and Nutrition Survey (CHNS) 2011	BMI > 95th percentile	85th percentile < BMI $\leq$ 95th percentile	1282	7–17 years
Zhang et al. (2017)	Diabetes Mellitus in Tianjin (DM-TJ) 2005	BMI $\geq$ 28	BMI 24–27.9	7351	20–79 years
Zhang et al. (2019)	China Hypertension Survey	Abdominal Obesity: Waist Circumference $\geq$ 90 cm for men, and Waist Circumference $\geq$ 85 cm for women	*N/A*	441,306	$\geq$15 years
Zhang et al. (2020a, b)	China Chronic Disease and Risk Factors Surveillance (CCDRFS) 2013–2014	BMI $\geq$ 28	*N/A*	179,347	$\geq$18 years

(continued)

Article	Survey/data	Measurement		Sample size	Study population
		Obesity	Overweight		
Zhao et al. (2008)	National Nutrition and Health Survey 2002	BMI ≥ 28	BMI 24–27.9	39,834	Adults
	A cohort study on cardiovascular disease and its risk factors in Chinese adults			143,521	
	Third National Health Service Survey 2003			24,900	
Zhai et al. (2013)	A population-based survey conducted among school-aged children in Chengdu, China (2013)	Working Group on Obesity in China (WGOC) BMI cutoff	Working Group on Obesity in China (WGOC) BMI cutoff	853	7–12 years

References

Alberti, G., Zimmet, P., Shaw, J., & Grundy, S. M. (2006). The IDF consensus worldwide definition of the metabolic syndrome. *The Lancet, 366*, 1059–1062. www.idf.org/webdata/docs/Metac_syndrome_def.pdf

An, R., Ji, M., Yan, H., & Guan, C. (2018). Impact of ambient air pollution on obesity: A systematic review. *International Journal of Obesity, 42*(6), 1112–1126.

Balcer, L. J., Liu, G., Forman, S., Pun, K., Volpe, N., Galetta, S., & Maguire, M. (1999). Idiopathic intracranial hypertension: Relation of age and obesity in children. *Neurology, 52*(4), 870–870.

Barker, D. J. (2012). Developmental origins of chronic disease. *Public Health, 126*(3), 185–189.

Bell, A. C., Ge, K., & Popkin, B. M. (2012). The road to obesity or the path to prevention: Motorized transportation and obesity in China. *Obesity, 10*(4), 277–283.

Bian, Y., & Logan, J. R. (1996). Market transition and the persistence of power: The changing stratifiation system in urban China. *American Sociological Review, 61*(5), 739–758.

Caballero, B. (2007). The global epidemic of obesity: An overview. *Epidemiology Review, 29*(1), 1–5.

Calle, E. E., Thun, M. J., Petrelli, J. M., Rodriguez, C., & Heath, C. W. (1999). Body-mass index and mortality in a prospective cohort of U.S. adults. *New England Journal of Medicine, 341*(15), 1097–1105.

Cao, G. Y., Chen, G., Pang, L. H., Zheng, X. Y., & Nilsson, S. (2012). Urban growth in China: Past, prospect, and its impacts. *Population and Environment, 33*(2–3), 137–160.

Cawley, J. (2015). An economy of scales: A selective review of obesity's economic causes, consequences, and solutions. *Journal of Health Economics, 43*, 244–268.

Chen, T. J., Modin, B., Ji, C. Y., & Hjern, A. (2011). Regional, socioeconomic and urban-rural disparities in child and adolescent obesity in China: A multilevel analysis. *Acta Paediatrica, 100*(12), 1583–1589.

Chen, F., Xu, S., Cao, L., Wang, Y., Tian, H., Hu, J., et al. (2021). Lacto-ovo vegetarian dietary pattern is protective against sarcopenic obesity: A cross-sectional study of elderly Chinese. *Nutrition, 91–92*, 111386.

Cole, T. J., Bellizzi, M. C., Flegal, K. M., & Dietz, W. H. (2000). Establishing a standard definition for child overweight and obesity worldwide: International survey. *Bmj Clinical Research, 320*(7244), 1240–1243.

Cui, Z., Huxley, R., Wu, Y., & Dibley, M. J. (2010). Temporal trends in overweight and obesity of children and adolescents from nine Provinces in China from 1991–2006. *International Journal of Pediatric Obesity, 5*(5), 365–374.

Cutlera, D. M., & Lleras-Muney, A. (2010). Understanding differences in health behaviors by education. *Journal of Health Economics, 29*, 1–28.

Deschenes, O., Wang, H., Wang, S., & Zhang, P. (2020). The effect of air pollution on body weight and obesity: Evidence from China. *Journal of Development Economics, 145*, 102461.

Dong, Y., Ma, J., Song, Y., Ma, Y., Dong, B., Zou, Z., & Prochaska, J. J. (2018). Secular trends in blood pressure and overweight and obesity in Chinese boys and girls aged 7 to 17 years from 1995 to 2014. *Hypertension, 72*(2), 298–305.

Drewnowski, A., & Popkin, B. M. (1997). The nutrition transition: New trends in the global diet. *Nutrition Reviews, 55*(2), 31–43.

Du, S., Lu, B., Zhai, F., & Popkin, B. M. (2002). A new stage of the nutrition transition in China. *Public Health Nutrition, 5*(1A), 169–174.

Du, Y., Wang, X., Xie, H., Zheng, S., Wu, X., Zhu, X., et al. (2019). Sex differences in the prevalence and adverse outcomes of sarcopenia and sarcopenic obesity in community dwelling elderly in East China using the AWGS criteria. *BMC Endocrine Disorders, 19*(1), 1–11.

Ebbeling, C. B., Pawlak, D. B., & Ludwig, D. S. (2002). Childhood obesity: Public-health crisis, common sense cure. *The Lancet, 360*(9331), 473–482.

Fan, H., Li, X., Zheng, L., Chen, X., Wu, H., Ding, X., et al. (2016). Abdominal obesity is strongly associated with cardiovascular disease and its risk factors in elderly and very elderly community-dwelling Chinese. *Scientific Reports, 6*(1), 1–9.

Field, A. E., Coakley, E. H., Must, A., Spadano, J. L., Laird, N., Dietz, W. H., et al. (2001). Impact of overweight on the risk of developing common chronic diseases during a 10-year period. *Archives of Internal Medicine, 161*(13), 1581–1586.

Finucane, M. M., Stevens, G. A., Cowan, M. J., Danaei, G., Lin, J. K., Paciorek, C. J., et al. (2011). National, regional, and global trends in body-mass index since 1980: Systematic analysis of health examination surveys and epidemiological studies with 960 country-years and 9· 1 million participants. *The Lancet, 377*(9765), 557–567.

Flegal, K. M., Carroll, M. D., Ogden, C. L., & Curtin, L. R. (2010). Prevalence and trends in obesity among US adults, 1999-2008. *JAMA, 303*(3), 235–241.

Freedman, D. S., Khan, L. K., Serdula, M. K., Dietz, W. H., Srinivasan, S. R., & Berenson, G. S. (2005). The relation of childhood BMI to adult adiposity: The Bogalusa Heart Study. *Pediatrics, 115*(1), 22–27.

French, P., & Crabbe, M. (2010). *Fat China: How expanding waistlines are changing a nation*. Anthem Press.

Fu, Q., & George, L. K. (2015a). Sex, socioeconomic and regional disparities in age trajectories of childhood BMI, underweight and overweight in China. *Asian Population Studies, 11*(2), 134–148.

Fu, Q., & George, L. K. (2015b). Socioeconomic determinants of childhood overweight and obesity in China: The long arm of institutional power. *Sociology of Health & Illness, 37*(6), 805–822.

Fu, Q., & Land, K. C. (2015a). Does urbanisation matter? A temporal analysis of the socio-demographic gradient in the rising adulthood overweight epidemic in China, 1989–2009. *Population, Space and Place, 23*(1). https://doi.org/10.1002/psp.1970

Fu, Q., & Land, K. C. (2015b). The increasing prevalence of overweight and obesity of children and youth in China, 1989–2009: An age–period–cohort analysis. *Population Research and Policy Review, 34*(6), 901–921.

Fu, Q., & Lin, N. (2013). Local state marketism: An institutional analysis of China's urban housing and land market. *Chinese Sociological Review, 46*(1), 3–24.

Fu, Q., & Ren, Q. (2010). Educational inequality under China's rural–urban divide: The Hukou system and returns to education. *Environment and Planning A, 42*(3), 592–610.

Gao, Y., Huang, Y., Song, F., Dai, H., Wang, P., Li, H., et al. (2016). Urban-rural disparity of overweight/obesity distribution and its potential trend with breast cancer among Chinese women. *Oncotarget, 7*(35), 56608.

Gu, D., Reynolds, K., Wu, X., Jing, C., & Jiang, H. (2005). Prevalence of the metabolic syndrome and overweight among adults in China. *The Lancet, 365*(9468), 1398–1405.

Gu, B., Wang, F., Guo, Z., & Zhang, E. (2007). China's local and national fertility policies at the end of the twentieth century. *Population and Development Review, 33*, 129–147.

Guo, X., Zheng, L., Li, Y., Zhang, X., Yu, S., Yang, H., et al. (2013). Prevalence and risk factors of being overweight or obese among children and adolescents in Northeast China. *Pediatric Research, 74*(4), 443–449.

He, K., Du, S., Xun, P., Sangita, S., Wang, H., Zhai, F., & Barry, P. (2011). Consumption of monosodium glutamate in relation to incidence of overweight in Chinese adults: China Health and Nutrition Survey (CHNS). *American Journal of Clinical Nutrition, 6*, 1328–1336.

He, W., James, S. A., Merli, M. G., & Zheng, H. (2014). An increasing socioeconomic gap in childhood overweight and obesity in China. *American Journal of Public Health, 104*(1), e14–e22.

Heitmann, B. L., Stroger, U., Mikkelsen, K. L., Holst, C., & Sorensen, T. I. (2004). Large heterogeneity of the obesity epidemic in Danish adults. *Public Health Nutrition, 7*(3), 453–460.

Hou, X. (2008). Urban – Rural disparity of overweight, hypertension, undiagnosed hypertension, and untreated hypertension in China. *Asia-Pacific Journal of Public Health, 20*(2), 159–169.

Hou, X., Liu, Y., Lu, H., Ma, X., Hu, C., Bao, Y., & Jia, W. (2013). Ten-year changes in the prevalence of overweight, obesity and central obesity among the Chinese adults in urban Shanghai, 1998–2007 – Comparison of two cross-sectional surveys. *BMC Public Health, 13*, 1064.

Hruby, A., Manson, J. E., Qi, L., Malik, V. S., Rimm, E. B., Sun, Q., et al. (2016). Determinants and consequences of obesity. *American Journal of Public Health, 106*(9), 1656–1662.

Hua, Q., Tan, J., Liu, Z., Liu, R., & Yang, Z. (2007). A cohort study on the correlation between birth weight, simple obesity, blood lipids, blood glucose and blood pressure from childhood to adolescence. *Zhonghua Nei Ke Za Zhi, 46*(11), 923–925.

Hua, J., Zhang, L., Gao, D., Huang, Y., Ning, P., Cheng, P., et al. (2020). Prevalence of overweight and obesity among people aged 18 years and over between 2013 and 2018 in Hunan, China. *International Journal of Environmental Research and Public Health, 17*(11), 4048.

Ji, C.-Y. (2005). Report on childhood obesity in China (1) body mass index reference for screening overweight and obesity in Chinese school-age children. *Biomedical and Environmental Sciences, 18*(6), 390–400.

Ji, C. Y., & Cheng, T. O. (2008). *Prevalence and geographic distribution of childhood obesity in China in 2005*. Elsevier.

Ji, C. Y., & Cheng, T. O. (2009). Epidemic increase in overweight and obesity in Chinese children from 1985 to 2005. *International Journal of Cardiology, 132*(1), 1–10. https://doi.org/10.1016/j.ijcard.2008.07.003

Jiang, W. (2009). Chapter one: Introduction. In *Acquisition of word order in Chinese as a foreign language* (pp. 1–22). De Gruyter Mouton.

Jones-Smith, J. C., Gordon-Larsen, P., Siddiqi, A., & Popkin, B. M. (2012). Emerging disparities in overweight by educational attainment in Chinese adults (1989–2006). *International Journal of Obesity, 36*(6), 866–875.

Katzmarzyk, P. T., & Janssen, I. (2004). The economic costs associated with physical inactivity and obesity in Canada: An update. *Canadian Journal of Applied Physiology, 29*(1), 90–115.

Keith, S. W., Redden, D. T., Katzmarzyk, P. T., Boggiano, M. M., Hanlon, E. C., Ben Ca, R. M., et al. (2006). Putative contributors to the secular increase in obesity: Exploring the roads less traveled. *International Journal of Obesity, 30*(11), 1585–1594.

Kim, S., Symons, M., & Barry, M. P. (2004). Contrasting socioeconomic profiles related to healthier lifestyles in China and the United States. *American Journal of Epidemiology, 159*(2), 184–191.

Lanningham-Foster, L., Nysse, L. J., & Levine, J. A. (2012). Labor saved, calories lost: The energetic impact of domestic labor-saving devices. *Obesity, 11*(10), 1178–1181.

Li, Y., & Zimmer, Z. (2013). Child and adolescent obesity and employment sector in urban China. *Asian Population Studies, 9*(3), 264–279.

Li, M., Qian, Z., Vaughn, M., Boutwell, B., Ward, P., Lu, T., et al. (2015). Sex-specific difference of the association between ambient air pollution and the prevalence of obesity in Chinese adults from a high pollution range area: 33 communities Chinese health study. *Atmospheric Environment, 117*, 227–233.

Li, Y. Z., Liu, D., Dong, M. Y., Zhang, J., Jing, Z. W., & Wen, H. Z. (2018). Challenges brought about by rapid changes in Chinese diets: Comparison with developed countries and implications for further improvement. *Biomedical and Environmental Sciences: BES, 31*(10), 781–786.

Link, B. G. (2008). Epidemiological sociology and the social shaping of population health. *Journal of Health and Social Behavior, 49*(4), 367–384.

Link, B. G., & Phelan, J. C. (1995). Social conditions as fundamental causes of disease. *Journal of Health and Social Behavior, 1995*, 80–94.

Liu, D., Yu, D.-M., Zhao, L.-Y., Fang, H.-Y., Zhang, J., Wang, J.-Z., et al. (2019a). Exposure to famine during early life and abdominal obesity in adulthood: Findings from the Great Chinese Famine during 1959–1961. *Nutrients, 11*, 903.

Liu, D., Zhao, L.-Y., Yu, D.-M., Ju, L.-H., Zhang, J., Wang, J.-Z., & Zhao, W.-H. (2019b). Dietary patterns and association with obesity of children aged 6–17 years in medium and small cities in China: Findings from the CNHS 2010–2012. *Nutrients, 11*(1), 3.

Lu, D. (2006). *Remaking Chinese urban form: Modernity, scarcity and space, 1949–2005*. Routledge.

Lu, J., Bi, Y., & Ning, G. (2016). Curbing the obesity epidemic in China. *The Lancet Diabetes and Endocrinology, 4*(6), 470–471.

Martinson, M. L., Chang, Y.-L., Han, W.-J., & Wen, J. (2015). Social determinants of childhood obesity in Shanghai, China: A cross-sectional child cohort survey. *The Lancet, 386*, S50.

McConnell, R., Shen, E., Gilliland, F. D., Jerrett, M., Wolch, J., Chang, C.-C., et al. (2015). A longitudinal cohort study of body mass index and childhood exposure to secondhand tobacco smoke and air pollution: The Southern California Children's Health Study. *Environmental Health Perspectives, 123*(4), 360–366.

Meng, P., Hu, Y. X., Fan, L., Zhang, Y., Zhang, M. X., Sun, J., et al. (2014). Sarcopenia and sarcopenic obesity among men aged 80 years and older in B eijing: Prevalence and its association with functional performance. *Geriatrics & Gerontology International, 14*, 29–35.

Mitchell, R. T., Mcdougall, C. M., & Crum, J. E. (2007). Decreasing prevalence of obesity in primary schoolchildren. *Archives of Disease in Childhood, 92*(2), 153–154.

Monasta, L., Batty, G., Cattaneo, A., Lutje, V., Ronfani, L., Van Lenthe, F., & Brug, J. (2010). Early-life determinants of overweight and obesity: A review of systematic reviews. *Obesity Reviews, 11*(10), 695–708.

Monda, K. L., Adair, L. S., Zhai, F., & Popkin, B. M. (2008). Longitudinal relationships between occupational and domestic physical activity patterns and body weight in China. *European Journal of Clinical Nutrition, 62*(11), 1318–1325.

Monteiro, C. A., Moura, E. C., Conde, W. L., & Popkin, B. M. (2004). Socioeconomic status and obesity in adult populations of developing countries: A review. *Bulletin of the World Health Organization, 82*(12), 940–946.

Monteiro, C. A., Conde, W. L., & Popkin, B. M. (2007). Income-specific trends in obesity in Brazil:

1975–2003. *American Journal of Public Health, 97*(10), 1808–1812.

Mushtaq, M. U., Gull, S., Mushtaq, K., Shahid, U., Shad, M. A., & Akram, J. (2011). Dietary behaviors, physical activity and sedentary lifestyle associated with overweight and obesity, and their socio-demographic correlates, among Pakistani primary school children. *International Journal of Behavioral Nutrition and Physical Activity, 8*(1), 130.

Must, A., & Strauss, R. S. (1999). Risks and consequences of childhood and adolescent obesity. *International Journal of Obesity, 23*(2), S2–S11.

Ng, M., Fleming, T., Robinson, M., Thomson, B., & Graetz, N. E. A. (2014). Global, regional, and national prevalence of overweight and obesity in children and adults during 1980–2013: A systematic analysis for the Global Burden of Disease Study 2013. *The Lancet, 384*(9945), 776–781.

Oi, J. C. (1997). *The evolution of local state corporatism.* Harvard University Press.

Olds, T. S., & Harten, N. R. (2001). One hundred years of growth: The evolution of height, mass, and body composition in Australian. *Human Biology, 73*(5), 727–727.

Owen, N., Leslie, E., Salmon, J., & Fotheringham, M. J. (2000). Environmental determinants of physical activity and sedentary behavior. *Exercise and Sport Sciences Reviews, 28*(4), 153–158.

Pampel, F. C., Denney, J. T., & Krueger, P. M. (2012). Obesity, SES, and economic development: A test of the reversal hypothesis. *Social Science & Medicine, 74*(7), 1073–1081.

Pan, X.-F., Tang, L., Lee, A. H., Binns, C., Yang, C.-X., Xu, Z.-P., et al. (2019). Association between fetal macrosomia and risk of obesity in children under 3 years in Western China: A cohort study. *World Journal of Pediatrics, 15*(2), 153–160.

Pei, L., Cheng, Y., Kang, Y., Yuan, S., & Yan, H. (2015). Association of obesity with socioeconomic status among adults of ages 18 to 80 years in rural Northwest China. *BMC Public Health, 15*, 160.

Phelan, J. C., & Link, B. G. (2005). Controlling disease and creating disparities: A fundamental cause perspective. *Journal of Gerontology, 60*(Special Issue 2), S27–S33.

Popkin, B. M. (1994). The nutrition transition in low-income countries: An emerging crisis. *Nutrition Reviews, 52*(9), 285–298.

Popkin, B. M. (1998). The nutrition transition and its health implications in lower-income countries. *Public Health Nutrition, 1*(1), 5–21.

Popkin, B. M., & Doak, C. M. (1998). The obesity epidemic is a worldwide phenomenon. *Nutrition Reviews, 56*(4), 106–114.

Popkin, B. M., & Du, S. (2003). Dynamics of the nutrition transition toward the animal foods sector in China and its implications: A worried perspective. *The Journal of Nutrition, 133*(11), 3898S–3906S.

Popkin, B. M., & Gordon-Larsen, P. (2004). The nutrition transition: Worldwide obesity dynamics and their determinants. *International Journal of Obesity, 28*, S2–S9.

Popkin, B. M., Paeratakul, S., Ge, K., & Zhai, F. (1995a). Body weight patterns among the Chinese: Results from the 1989 and 1991 China Health and Nutrition Surveys. *American Journal of Public Health, 85*(5), 690–694. https://doi.org/10.2105/AJPH.85.5.690

Popkin, B. M., Paeratakul, S., Zhai, F., & Ge, K. (1995b). Dietary and environmental correlates of obesity in a population study in China. *Obesity Research, 3*(S2), 135s–143s.

Prentice, A. M., & Jebb, S. A. (1995). Obesity in Britain: Gluttony or sloth? *BMJ, 311*(7002), 437–439.

Reynolds, K., Gu, D., Whelton, P. K., Wu, X., Duan, X., Mo, J., et al. (2012). Prevalence and risk factors of overweight and obesity in China*. *Obesity, 15*(1), 10–18.

Rokholm, B., Baker, J. L., & Sorensen, T. I. A. (2010). The levelling off of the obesity epidemic since the year 1999 – A review of evidence and perspectives. *Obesity Reviews, 11*(12), 835–846.

Rutayisire, E., Wu, X., Huang, K., Tao, S., Chen, Y., Wang, S., & Tao, F. (2018). Dietary patterns are not associated with overweight and obesity in a sample of 8900 Chinese preschool children from four cities. *Journal of Nutritional Science, 7*, e24.

Salihu, H. M., Bonnema, S. M., & Alio, A. P. (2009). Obesity: What is an elderly population growing into? *Maturitas, 63*(1), 7–12.

Segal, L., Carter, R., & Zimmet, P. (1994). The cost of obesity: The Australian perspective. *PharmacoEconomics, 5*(Suppl 1), 45–52.

Seidell, J. C., & Halberstadt, J. (2015). The global burden of obesity and the challenges of prevention. *Annals of Nutrition & Metabolism, 66*(2), 7–12.

Shan, X. Y., Xi, B., Cheng, H., Hou, D. Q., Wang, Y., & Mi, J. (2010). Prevalence and behavioral risk factors of overweight and obesity among children aged 2–18 in Beijing, China. *International Journal of Pediatric Obesity, 5*(5), 383–389.

Shang, X. W., Liu, A. L., Zhang, Q., Hu, X. Q., Du, S. M., Jun, M., et al. (2012). Report on childhood obesity in China (9): Sugar-sweetened beverages consumption and obesity. *Biomedical and Environmental Sciences, 25*(2), 125–132.

Shi, Z., Lien, N., Kumar, B. N., & Holmboe-Ottesen, G. (2005). Socio-demographic differences in food habits and preferences of school adolescents in Jiangsu Province, China. *European Journal of Clinical Nutrition, 59*, 1439–1448.

Shi, Z., Riley, M., Taylor, A. W., & Page, A. (2017). Chilli consumption and the incidence of overweight and obesity in a Chinese adult population. *International Journal of Obesity, 41*(7), 1074–1079.

Shi, Z., Gu, J., & Fu, Q. (2020). Social change and health inequalities – Evidence from the fifth phase of the epidemiologic transition in urban China. *Sociological Studies, 2020*(6), 160–185.

Shimokawa, S., Chang, H. H., & Pinstrup-Andersen, P. (2009). Understanding the differences in obesity among working adults between Taiwan and China. *Asia Pacific Journal of Clinical Nutrition, 18*(1), 88–95.

Singh, G. K., Siahpush, M., & Kogan, M. D. (2010). Rising social inequalities in US childhood obesity, 2003–2007. *Annals of Epidemiology, 20*(1), 40–52.

Song, S. (2012). Does famine influence sex ratio at birth? Evidence from the 1959–1961 Great Leap Forward Famine in China. *Proceedings of the Royal Society B: Biological Sciences, 279*(1739), 2883–2890. https://doi.org/10.1098/rspb.2012.0320

Song, P., Wang, H., Xia, W., Chang, X., Wang, M., & An, L. (2018). Prevalence and correlates of hyperuricemia in the middle-aged and older adults in China. *Scientific Reports, 8*(1), 1–9.

Song, Y., Agardh, A., Ma, J., Li, L., Lei, Y., Stafford, R. S., & Prochaska, J. J. (2019). National trends in stunting, thinness and overweight among Chinese school-aged children, 1985–2014. *International Journal of Obesity, 43*(2), 402–411.

Stamatakis, E., Wardle, J., & Cole, T. J. (2010). Childhood obesity and overweight prevalence trends in England: Evidence for growing socioeconomic disparities. *International Journal of Obesity, 34*(1), 41–47.

Strauss, R. S. (2000). Childhood obesity and self-esteem. *Pediatrics, 105*(1), e15–e15.

Sun, D., Lv, J., Chen, W., Li, S., & Guo, Y. (2014). Spicy food consumption is associated with adiposity measures among half a million Chinese people: The China Kadoorie Biobank study. *BMC Public Health, 14*(1), 982–1001.

Tian, Y., Jiang, C., Wang, M., Cai, R., Zhang, Y., He, Z., et al. (2016). BMI, leisure-time physical activity, and physical fitness in adults in China: Results from a series of national surveys, 2000–14. *The Lancet Diabetes and Endocrinology, 4*(6), 487–497.

Waaler, H. T. (1987). Hazard of obesity-the Norwegian experience. *Acta Medica Scandinavica, 222*(S723), 17–21.

Wang, Y., & Lim, H. (2012). The global childhood obesity epidemic and the association between socio-economic status and childhood obesity. *International Review of Psychiatry, 24*(3), 176–188.

Wang, Y., & Lobstein, T. (2006). Worldwide trends in childhood overweight and obesity. *International Journal of Pediatric Obesity, 1*(1), 11–25.

Wang, F., & Veugelers, P. (2008). Self-esteem and cognitive development in the era of the childhood obesity epidemic. *Obesity Reviews, 9*(6), 615–623.

Wang, H., & Zhai, F. (2013). Programme and policy options for preventing obesity in China. *Obesity Reviews, 14*, 134–140.

Wang, J., Thornton, J. C., Russell, M., Burastero, S., Heymsfield, S., & Pierson, R. N. (1994). Asians have lower body mass index (BMI) but higher percent body fat than do whites: Comparisons of anthropometric measurements. *American Journal of Clinical Nutrition, 60*(1), 23–28.

Wang, Y., Monteiro, C., & Popkin, B. M. (2002). Trends of obesity and underweight in older children and adolescents in the United States, Brazil, China, and Russia. *American Journal of Clinical Nutrition, 75*(6), 971–977.

Wang, H., Du, S., Zhai, F., & Popkin, B. M. (2007a). Trends in the distribution of body mass index among Chinese adults, aged 20–45 years (1989–2000). *International Journal of Obesity, 31*, 272–278.

Wang, Y., Mi, J., Shan, X. Y., Wang, Q. J., & Ge, K. Y. (2007b). Is China facing an obesity epidemic and the consequences? The trends in obesity and chronic disease in China. *International Journal of Obesity, 31*(1), 177–188.

Wang, Y., Gao, E., Wu, J., Zhou, J., Yang, Q., Walker, M., et al. (2009). Fetal macrosomia and adolescence obesity: Results from a longitudinal cohort study. *International Journal of Obesity, 33*(8), 923–928.

Wang, Y., Wang, X., Kong, Y., Zhang, H. J., & Zeng, Q. (2010). The Great Chinese Famine leads to shorter and overweight females in Chongqing Chinese population after 50 years. *Obesity, 18*(3), 588–592.

Wang, H., Wang, J., Liu, M.-M., Wang, D., Liu, Y.-Q., Zhao, Y., et al. (2012). Epidemiology of general obesity, abdominal obesity and related risk factors in urban adults from 33 communities of Northeast China: The CHPSNE study. *BMC Public Health, 12*(1), 1–10.

Wang, R., Zhang, P., Gao, C., Li, Z., Xin, L., Song, Y., et al. (2016). Prevalence of overweight and obesity and some associated factors among adult residents of Northeast China: A cross-sectional study. *BMJ Open, 6*(7), e010828.

WHO Expert Consultataion. (2004). Appropriate body-mass index for Asian populations and its implications for policy and intervention strategies. *Lancet, 363*(9403), 157–163.

Wildman, R. P., Gu, D., Muntner, P., Wu, X., Reynolds, K., Duan, X., et al. (2008). Trends in overweight and obesity in Chinese adults: Between 1991 and 1999–2000. *Obesity, 16*(6), 1448–1453.

Wolf, A. M., & Colditz, G. A. (1998). Current estimates of the economic cost of obesity in the United States. *Obesity Research, 6*(2), 97–106.

World Health Organization. (1995). Physical status: The use and interpretation of anthropometry. Report of a WHO Expert Committee. *Geneva, Switzerland, WHO, 1995, 854*(6), 1–452.

World Health Organization. (2000). *Report of a WHO Consultation. Obesity: Preventing and managing the global epidemic* (WHO technical report series 894). World Health Organiztion.

Xi, B., Liang, Y., He, T., Reilly, K. H., Hu, Y., Wang, Q., et al. (2012). Secular trends in the prevalence of general and abdominal obesity among Chinese adults, 1993-2009. *Obesity Reviews, 13*(3), 287–296.

Xu, C. X., Zhu, H. H., Fang, L., Hu, R. Y., Wang, H., Liang, M. B., et al. (2017). Gender disparity in the associations of overweight/obesity with occupational activity, transport to/from work, leisure-time physical activity, and leisure-time spent sitting in working adults: A cross-sectional study. *Journal of Epidemiology, 27*, 401–407.

Yu, Z., Sun, J., Haas, J., Gu, Y., Li, Z., & Lin, X. (2008). Macrosomia is associated with high weight-for-height in children aged 1–3 years in Shanghai, China. *International Journal of Obesity, 32*(1), 55–60.

Yu, Z., Han, S., Zhu, G., Zhu, C., Wang, X., Cao, X., & Guo, X. (2011). Birth weight and subsequent risk of obesity: A systematic review and meta-analysis. *Obesity Reviews, 12*(7), 525–542.

Yuan, Z.-P., Yang, M., Liang, L., Fu, J.-F., Xiong, F., Liu, G.-L., et al. (2015). Possible role of birth weight on general and central obesity in Chinese children and adolescents: A cross-sectional study. *Annals of Epidemiology, 25*(10), 748–752.

Yuan, F., Gong, W., Ding, C., Li, H., Feng, G., Ma, Y., et al. (2021). Association of physical activity and sitting time with overweight/obesity in Chinese occupational populations. *Obesity Facts, 14*, 1–7.

Yusuf, S., Hawken, S., Ounpuu, S., Bautista, L., Maria, G. F., Patrick, C., et al. (2005). Obesity and the risk of myocardial infarction in 27,000 participants from 52 countries: A case-control study. *Lancet, 366*(9497), 1640–1649.

Zalesin, K. C., Franklin, B. A., Miller, W. M., Peterson, E. D., & McCullough, P. A. (2008). Impact of obesity on cardiovascular disease. *Endocrinology and Metabolism Clinics of North America, 37*(3), 663–684.

Zamboni, M., Mazzali, G., Fantin, F., Rossi, A., & Di Francesco, V. (2008). Sarcopenic obesity: A new category of obesity in the elderly. *Nutrition, Metabolism, and Cardiovascular Diseases, 18*(5), 388–395.

Zeng, Y., & Hesketh, T. (2016). The effects of China's universal two-child policy. *The Lancet, 388*(10054), 1930–1938.

Zeng, X., Cai, L., Ma, J., Ma, Y., Jing, J., & Chen, Y. (2018). Eating fast is positively associated with general and abdominal obesity among Chinese children: A national survey. *Scientific Reports, 8*(1), 1–8.

Zhai, F., Wang, H., Du, S., He, Y., Wang, Z., Ge, K., & Popkin, B. M. (2009). Prospective study on nutrition transition in China. *Nutrition Reviews, 67*(suppl_1), S56–S61.

Zhai, J., Xue, H., Luo, J., Zhang, L., & Cheng, G. (2013). Associations between socioeconomic status and overweight among urban children aged 7-12 years in Chengdu, Southwest China. *Asia Pacific Journal of Clinical Nutrition, 27*(3), 617–623.

Zhang, X., Liu, E., Tian, Z., Wang, W., Ye, T., Liu, G., et al. (2009). High birth weight and overweight or obesity among Chinese children 3–6 years old. *Preventive Medicine, 49*(2–3), 172–178.

Zhang, J., Wang, H., Wang, Y., Xue, H., Wang, Z., Du, W., et al. (2015). Dietary patterns and their associations with childhood obesity in China. *British Journal of Nutrition, 113*(12), 1978–1984.

Zhang, H., Hu, H., Song, F., Xu, W., Pallard-Borg, S., & Qi, X. (2017). Relation of socioeconomic status to overweight and obesity: A large population-based study of Chinese adults. *Annals of Human Biology, 44*(6), 495–501.

Zhang, L., Wang, Z., Wang, X., Chen, Z., Shao, L., Tian, Y., et al. (2019). Prevalence of abdominal obesity in China: Results from a cross-sectional study of nearly half a million participants. *Obesity, 27*(11), 1898–1905.

Zhang, J., Xu, P., & Liu, F. (2020a). One-child policy and childhood obesity. *China Economic Review, 59*, 100938.

Zhang, X., Zhang, M., Zhao, Z., Huang, Z., Deng, Q., Li, Y., et al. (2020b). Obesogenic environmental factors of adult obesity in China: A nationally representative cross-sectional study. *Environmental Research Letters, 15*(4), 044009.

Zhao, W., Zhai, Y., Hu, J., Wang, J., Yang, Z., Kong, L., & Chen, C. (2008). Economic burden of obesity-related chronic diseases in Mainland China. *Obesity Reviews, 9*(Suppl. 1), 62–67.

Zhao, L. Y., Liu, D., Mei, Y. D., Zhang, J., Wang, J. Z., & Zhao, W. H. (2018). Challenges brought about by rapid changes in Chinese diets: Comparison with developed countries and implications for further improvement. *Biomedical and Environmental Sciences, 31*(10), 73–78.

Zhi, B. L., Sai, Y. H., Wai, M. C., Kin, S. H., Mun, P. L., Leung, G. M., & Tai, H. L. (2004). Obesity and depressive symptoms in Chinese elderly. *International Journal of Geriatric Psychiatry, 19*(1), 68–74.

Zhou, X. (2000). Economic transformation and income inequality in urban China: Evidence from panel data. *American Journal of Sociology, 105*(4), 1135–1174.

Zhou, B. F. (2002). Effect of body mass index on all-cause mortality and incidence of cardiovascular diseases – Report for meta-analysis of prospective studies on optimal cut-off points of body mass index in Chinese adults. *Biomedical and Environmental Sciences, 15*(3), 245.

Part II

Obesity and Demographic Processes, Structures, and Characteristics

The chapters in Part II focus on demographic processes, structures, and characteristics. Neil K. Mehta offers an in-depth discussion of the mortality risks associated with obesity and offers compelling evidence in support of its continued impacts in Chap. 6. In fact, his chapter provides a review of the methodological challenges that have likely led to an underestimation of its effects on mortality. He further offers a review of the aggregate level evidence of obesity's effects in high-income countries.

In Chap. 7, Garcia-Alexander and Marroquin describe the research on obesity in immigrant groups. They review patterns of obesity among migrants to the United States and discuss the theories that have been applied in an effort to understand why immigrants appear to arrive at healthier weights and gain weight with additional time spent in the U.S. For instance, scholars have examined how acculturation may promote obesity via changing dietary patterns. These authors also describe the structural forces (social, political, environmental, and economic conditions) that may limit access to healthy foods and opportunities for physical activity and increase risk of exposure to unhealthy environments.

Frisco and her colleagues (Chap. 8) review the literature developed by population health researchers to understand persistent racial and ethnic disparities in rates of overweight and obesity. Their thorough discussion offers a framework for researchers in this area as it emphasizes the importance of contributions made by demographers. For instance, they delineate how the default American lifestyle, characterized by overconsumption and sedentary activity patterns, may be avoided with higher levels of education. They further emphasize the macroenvironment and how structural disadvantage leads to greater risk of obesity in racial and ethnic minorities. Finally, their discussion of needed research points to several key areas that are underdeveloped and could contribute significantly to our understanding of the factors that promote disparate outcomes.

In Chap. 9, Krueger and his colleagues describe patterns of socioeconomic and racial and ethnic disparities in overweight and obesity. They highlight the tools demographers might use to more effectively identify the factors that drive disparities and to examine differences in cumulative exposure experienced by different racial/ethnic and SES groups. In addition, they review the literature on the mechanisms that lead to disparities with a focus on those with plausible population impacts and offer suggestions for future research.

Falbo and Lin close out this section with a review of the literature on sibling effects on the development of overweight and obesity in Chap. 10. They consider these effects across multiple countries and observe that sibling absence is associated with greater BMI. They describe the theories that help to explain this association and suggest that sibling effects on diet and activity patterns appear to drive these effects on obesity.

6 Obesity and Mortality

Neil K. Mehta

Introduction

A key topic in the demography of obesity is the effect obesity has on mortality among individuals and in populations. While the topic of obesity and mortality has elicited several well-publicized controversies on just how damaging it is (Flegal et al., 2005; Mokdad et al., 2004; Couzin, 2005), there is a growing consensus that obesity substantially shortens lifespan and, at the aggregate level, is a major threat to national mortality improvements. Estimating the magnitude of obesity's effect on mortality, nonetheless, remains an area of lively scientific inquiry, and key methodological challenges and knowledge gaps remain.

More than 40 years have past since obesity levels began rising rapidly, initially in the United States and then followed in other high- and middle-income countries. Many of these countries continue to experience rising levels and since 2000 nearly every country globally is experiencing appreciable increases in obesity levels (NCD Risk Factor Collaboration, 2016). The persistence of the growth as well as its spread suggests that obesity will have far-reaching and long-lasting consequences for aggregate mortality patterns. Researchers are just beginning to uncover these consequences.

In this Chapter, I will provide an overview of some key methodological issues related to estimating the magnitude of the obesity-mortality association, differentiating issues pertinent to the individual and population levels. As this Chapter appears in a volume on demography, I will preference obesity's impact on aggregate mortality patterns—usually at the national level. The estimation of aggregate impacts, however, often relies on estimates of the individual-level death risks associated with obesity. It is therefore prudent to start at the individual level. Much of the earlier controversies have in fact been focused on how best to identify these individual-level risks. I will review the salient issues pertinent to the individual level including a discussion on causal inference. I will go on to review the current evidence on obesity's effect on aggregate mortality patterns. Given that much of the evidence on obesity's aggregate effects come from high-income countries, I will focus my discussion on these countries. I will briefly discuss issues pertinent to low- and middle-income countries.

Most studies rely on the body mass index (BMI) as an indicator of weight status with a BMI ≥ 30.0 kg/m^2 defining obesity. I will adhere to this convention. Waist circumference, the waist-to-hip ratio and body fat percentage are alternative indicators of adiposity that may have distinct advantages in clinical settings. At a population level, however, BMI correlates well with

N. K. Mehta (✉)
School of Public and Population Health, The University of Texas Medical Branch, Galveston, TX, USA
e-mail: nemehta@utmb.edu

G. Garcia-Alexander, D. L. Poston, Jr. (eds.), *International Handbook of the Demography of Obesity*, International Handbooks of Population 12, https://doi.org/10.1007/978-3-031-10936-2_6

these alternative indicators (Flegal et al., 2009; Vazquez et al., 2007) and BMI should be a sufficient metric to evaluate the aggregate mortality consequences of high BMI.

Obesity's effect on mortality is determined by its multi-faceted and deleterious effects on organ function, the immune system and metabolism. There is a rich literature on obesity's far-reaching consequences to normal physiological processes (e.g., Redinger, 2007; Hu, 2008). These mechanisms will not be covered here but two are worth mentioning.

The first is obesity's relation to insulin resistance and pancreatic β-cell dysfunction which combine to form the development of type 2 diabetes mellitus (Galicia-Garcia et al., 2020). Concomitant to the rise of obesity has been the alarming increase in diabetes levels globally (Lin et al., 2020). Estimates of the population attributable risk fractions of diabetes associated with obesity are high (Flegal et al., 2015; Dai et al., 2020), although epidemiological evidence linking obesity to diabetes trends and levels within and across countries still needs to be conducted. The role that adiposity plays on altering healthy pancreatic cellular function is central to the relationship between obesity and diabetes (Klein et al., 2022; Galicia-Garcia et al., 2020). Physical inactivity appears to be a common cause of both obesity and diabetes.

The second mechanism became prominent during the COVID-19 pandemic whereby obesity emerged as a main risk factor for dying after a COVID-19 infection (Popkin et al., 2020; Hendren et al., 2021). This risk is thought to be a function of impaired immunity, chronic inflammation, and a high liability to blood clots (Demeulemeester et al., 2021). These findings may have implications for obesity-related death risks associated with other infectious diseases. Obesity's effect on mortality may be enhanced in contexts where infectious disease levels are high and endemic—a situation that exists in many low-income countries, many of whom are experiencing rising obesity levels (Templin et al., 2019).

Estimating the Relative Risks of Death Associated with Obesity for Purposes of Measuring Obesity's Aggregate Mortality Effect

Measuring the aggregate mortality consequences of obesity will often rely on estimates of the relative risks of dying from obesity for individuals. Identifying the appropriate relative risks to use is challenging because of the dynamic nature of human body weight: individuals can enter and exit an obese state at any time during life. In an ideal scenario we would have information on obesity prevalence for a birth cohort at each age throughout life. We would also have information on the mortality differential between obese and non-obese individuals at each age.

Figure 6.1 depicts this ideal scenario for hypothetical birth cohorts. It shows obesity prevalence (P) and the relative risk of death (RR, which is the mortality ratio) associated with being obese relative to non-obese at 10-year age groups for cohorts born 10-years apart. The main question of interest is what the mortality experience of the cohort would have been if none of its members were ever obese. With the requisite information in Fig. 6.1, we would answer the question by calculating the number and fraction of deaths attributable to obesity at each age and for the life of the cohort. An assumption is that the observed mortality ratios reflect a causal effect of obesity (issues of causality are discussed below). Attributable deaths can then be converted to effects on life expectancy and life-years lost for the cohorts using standard demographic tools. If we are interested in the cumulative effect of obesity for all cohorts alive in a given year, then we can sum the cohort-specific attributable deaths in a given period.

Such an ideal approach is rarely, if ever, used to identify the aggregate effect of obesity on mortality because the requisite cohort history data is usually unavailable. The usual approach is to estimate the relative risk of death associated with obesity in a period using observational health survey data that are linked to prospective

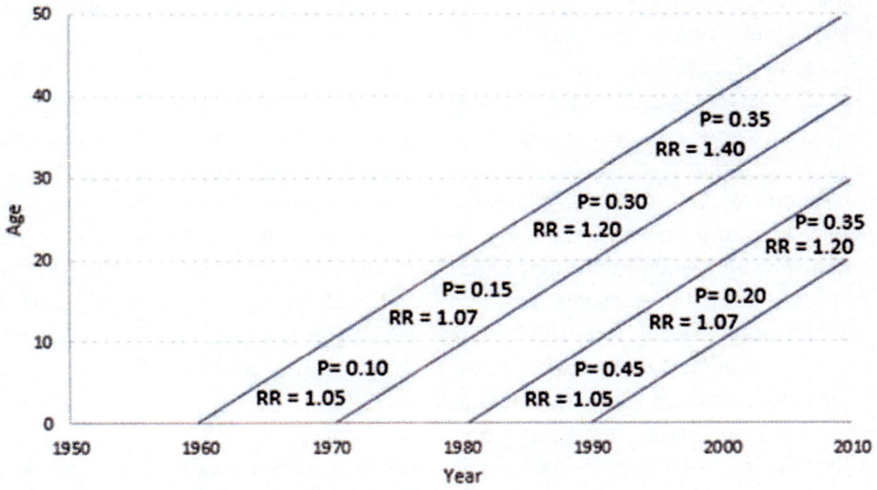

Fig. 6.1 Lexis diagram with obesity prevalence and mortality ratios associated with obesity for hypothetical birth cohorts

data on deaths. Obesity data is normally available at a single-point-in-time for a respondent. Multivariate models adjusting for age, cigarette smoking, socioeconomic status, and other key confounders are implemented to identify the independent relative risks of death associated with obesity. These relative risks are then used as an input to calculate attributable risk fractions to answer the question of how many deaths would be averted in a given year if obesity were eliminated from the population. This approach, utilized by a large number of studies, is the primary way we have assessed obesity's aggregate impact on mortality.

At least for the United States, estimates of the attributable fraction of deaths from obesity using this approach have varied substantially ranging from about 5% to 15% of adult deaths in the United States in the early 2000s (Flegal et al., 2005; Mokdad et al., 2004; Mehta & Chang, 2009). Sources of the discrepant findings have been discussed previously (Mehta & Chang, 2009, 2011; Mehta, 2015) and include the studies' treatment of age as an effect modifier and the representativeness of the population samples used.

This oft-used approach to calculate attributable fractions of death associated with obesity has important nuances. It is a period measure and only under specific conditions will it reflect the experience of a birth cohort. One such condition is that the age-specific prevalence of obesity has remained constant, which of course it has not. In current contexts, more recent cohorts have experienced a higher prevalence of obesity than earlier cohorts at similar ages.

Even if one is interested in the period effect, that is the number of deaths attributable to obesity in a given year or period, the oft-calculated attributable risk has important theoretical underpinnings that are generally not discussed in the epidemiological literature. The underlying counterfactual question is: what would mortality be if obesity were hypothetically eliminated from the population? The common attributable risk estimate is based on eliminating obesity at a single point in time, namely at the time of the survey when obesity is measured or reported. The estimate does not explicitly account for deaths that occurred in the period due to earlier-in-life obesity unless strong assumptions are made (e.g., that the mortality risks associated with obesity observed in the period fully encapsulates its cumulative historical impact).

An important reason that obesity at the time of survey will not reflect the full historical impact of obesity is that of disease-induced weight loss (which is often termed "reverse causation" in the literature). Obesity increases the risk of a wide array of diseases many of which in turn lead to weight loss. These diseases include many common cancers, heart failure, renal failure, and respiratory conditions (Hu, 2008). Disease-induced weight loss appears to arise early in the course of a disease and individuals may experience weight loss or low body weight for years prior to dying indicating sizeable exposure to this process at the population level. Alley et al. (2010), for example, using the longitudinal Baltimore Longitudinal Study of Aging, find that weight loss begins 5–10 years before a cardiovascular death. The result is that some deaths occurring to nonobese individuals in the period may be partly attributable to historical obesity but are missed entirely in the attributable risk calculation. Moreover, the presence of high disease levels among those with low body weight could bias downward the estimates of the relative risks of death associated with obesity in regression models as these disease states often go unobserved in the survey (controlling for disease states in the regression model also raises issues of causal ordering in that diseases are postulated to be on the causal pathway between obesity and death). A sizeable body of evidence indicates that disease-induced weight loss is a key source of bias for the estimation of relative risks (for example, see Stokes & Preston, 2016a, c; Lawlor et al., 2006).

Also of note is that the attributable risk estimate is highly sensitive to the magnitude of the underlying relative risks used in its calculation. Small differences in the relative risks used can result in rather large and meaningful changes in attributable risk estimates as an earlier study has demonstrated (Flegal et al., 2004). The model specification that is used to estimate the relative risk, including the covariates in the model and any relevant interactions, can have important bearings on the magnitude of the relative risk estimates and in turn on estimates of the fraction of deaths attributable to obesity.

Despite these limitations, the common period-based attributable risk calculations have an important place in the valuation of obesity's aggregate impact on mortality in part because obesity's role can be compared to other major risk factors for mortality such as cigarette smoking. In a comprehensive analysis by the Global Burden of Disease 2019 Risk Factor Collaborators, which produced estimates of attributable deaths for 87 risk factors across 204 countries/territories, high BMI placed fifth and sixth in women and men, respectively, in a ranking of risk factors by their attributable mortality (Murray et al., 2020).

Causal Identification of the Mortality Risks Associated with Obesity

As noted, attributable risk estimates imply a causal interpretation. A key concern is whether the individual-level relative risks of death associated with obesity, which the attributable risk relies on, are causal in nature. These relative risks are almost always generated from observational data and unobserved selection into body weight categories poses a threat to identification. I highlight three key threats to identification.

The first threat, which was discussed above, pertains to disease-induced weight loss. The bidirectional relationships between health and weight status cannot always be handled with traditional regression techniques. Disease-induced confounding can be reduced by limiting the sample to healthy respondents (with a loss in generalizability) or by increasing the time lag between the timing of the measurement of obesity and the beginning of the exposure period. For example, with cross-sectional survey data linked to prospective death data one can eliminate the first few years of prospective follow-up and model exposure only after this exclusion, or alternatively include an interaction of weight status with follow-up time. The rationale is that some deaths occurring in the early part of the follow-up occur in individuals who had experienced disease-induced weight loss prior to the time of survey. Evidence, nonetheless, suggests that excluding the first 3–5 years of follow-up has only modest effects on the estimated magnitude of the relative risks (Mehta & Chang, 2009; Flegal et al., 2007; Allison et al., 1999). This finding may be because disease-induced weight loss is a longer-term process and elimination of early part of the follow-up is not an effective strategy to account for disease-induced weight loss.

Confounding by physical activity is a related concern. Activity level is a key input of weight status and has independent effects on mortality (Rockhill et al., 2001). Activity levels, nonetheless, are closely tied to underlying health status and if one includes it as a covariate in a model it may act to "control" for processes on the causal pathway between obesity and death (e.g., high body weight → poor health → low activity → death), thus reducing the estimated relative risks associated with obesity. There is no clear solution to this issue in cross-sectional survey settings. Leveraging long-run longitudinal datasets with information on physical activity and body weight at earlier times in the life-course appear beneficial (Nordstoga et al., 2019).

Second, the treatment of cigarette smoking as either a confounder or effect modifier requires careful consideration and has been a central issue in earlier controversies over the estimation of obesity attributable deaths. Cigarette smoking and body weight are usually negatively correlated in contemporary populations (Chiolero et al., 2008). This relation is partly attributable to nicotine being an appetite suppressor (Audrain-McGovern & Benowitz, 2011). Cigarette smoking is also associated with a high disease burden and average low weight among smokers is likely attributable to their disease burden. It is also one of the strongest risk factors for mortality. Exclusion of cigarette smoking in statistical models would therefore lead to estimates of relative risks associated with obesity that are biased downward. While most studies do control for cigarette smoking based on self-reports of the behavior (e.g., current, former, never), residual confounding will likely remain as the requisite data capturing smoking intensity, duration, and cigarette type are often unavailable. Moreover, the correlation between cotinine, a bio-indicator of nicotine presence, and self-reports of smoking are moderate at best (Stram et al., 2002).

Studies report that the relative risks associated with obesity are higher among never smokers compared to current smokers indicating an effect modification (Stokes & Preston, 2016b, c). The reasons for this effect modification are not fully understood and may be partly a function of higher baseline mortality among current smokers and a higher role for disease-induced confounding in this population, which would lead to downwardly biased estimates for obesity's effect.

Third, obesity is correlated with social and economic factors that are themselves strongly linked to mortality. Failure to control for these factors may lead to overestimated risks. Evidence suggests that controls for key socioeconomic characteristics such as educational attainment and race/ethnicity do reduce the magnitude of relative risks of death associated with obesity (Preston et al., 2018). While most studies do control for select socioeconomic factors, confounding may remain. For example, controls for early life conditions such as childhood socioeconomic status and adverse childhood events that may strongly influence life-course body weight trajectories are rarely included in statistical models. So too are psychosocial factors related to discrimination and other stresses that have been shown to affect dietary and activity patterns and are also more broadly associated with health.-Further work identifying the confounding role of social experiences—particularly earlier in life ones—would be valuable.

Despite the challenges of using observational data, there are reasons to believe that relative risks derived from observational settings can provide useful estimates of the causal effect of obesity on mortality. One approach is to compare the effects of obesity in settings where selection into obesity may differ such as differences across countries. Few of these international comparisons have been conducted. Mehta et al. (2017) compared the obesity-mortality association in the United States and Finland using nationally representative surveys from each country. The authors found no significant difference in risks. The Prospective Studies Collaboration (2009) examined data from 57 datasets across Western Europe and the United States and reported to significant heterogeneity in the relative risks of an ischemic heart disease death associated with high BMI. I am not aware of studies that have examined heterogeneity in risks across low- and middle-income countries, which would be useful.

Studies using traditional instrumental variable approaches have also demonstrated the deleterious effects of a high BMI supporting findings reported from observational studies. One approach has been to use Mendelian randomization (Emdin et al., 2017), which uses sets of genes associated with body weight as a source of random variation. This approach has been made possible by the availability of large population-level repositories, which collect genetic information and follow individuals over time, such as the UK Biobank (Collins, 2012). For studies of BMI and mortality, a genetic risk score is assigned to each individual from sets of genetic variants associated with BMI. The risk score is treated as an instrumental variable in that it is assumed to exert an influence on BMI but is unconfounded with other risk factors and has no effect on mortality other than that through BMI. These studies generally conclude that BMI is positively and causally related to heart disease risks and mortality (Jenkins et al., 2021; Richmond et al., 2014; Nordestgaard et al., 2012; Wade et al., 2018). For example, Wade et al. (2018) use this approach on the UK Biobank and find that the dose-response effect of BMI on CVD mortality is stronger using the instrumental, compared with observational, approach. Smith et al. (2009) use offspring BMI as an instrument for own BMI in a sample of Swedish parent-son pairs. They also conclude that the magnitude of the obesity-mortality association has been underestimated in studies using conventional regression techniques.

Evidence supporting the causal effect of obesity on mortality can also be surmised from experimental data. Studies of bariatric surgery that contain a "control" group indicate that those who received the surgery experienced lower mortality compared to those who did not (Carlsson et al., 2020; Adams et al., 2007; Sjöström et al., 2007). These studies, however, were not experiments in the true sense because they did not randomize participants into control and treatment groups. Experimental studies on non-human mammals find that caloric restriction and weight loss is associated with sizeable reductions in mortality (Colman et al., 2009; Weindruch & Sohal, 1997; Weindruch & Walford, 1982; Vasselli et al., 2005).

Incorporating Obesity Histories to Obtain More Accurate Estimates of the Death Risks Associated with Obesity

As noted, much of the evidence base for obesity's effect on mortality has been from studies using data on obesity at a single point in time. There, however, has always been interest in incorporating information on an individual's obesity history.

There are varied reasons for this interest. First, the incorporation of weight history data can lend itself well to understanding cohort-patterned effects of obesity on mortality. Second, researchers are inherently interested in understanding the links between body weight dynamics over the life course and health. For example, whether obesity exhibits duration effects, that is whether the time one spends obese is positively associated with mortality or health, can provide valuable information on an individual's health risk from obesity-related conditions. Researchers are also interested in the effects of weight change and weight cycling at different stages of the life course to guide clinical and public health practice (Wannamethee et al., 2002; Kritchevsky et al., 2015). Third, the use of obesity history data can be an effective tool to reduce biases caused by disease-induced weight loss, which we return to below.

The number of papers that incorporate information obesity at multiple time points during the life course has grown rapidly over the last decade. Earlier studies, for example, have used the longitudinal U.S. Framingham Heart Study to identify the effect of obesity duration on mortality in individuals (Abdullah et al., 2011b) (and also on diabetes, see Abdullah et al., 2011a).

The obesity history of an individual goes well beyond a simple count of the number of years one has been obese. Preston et al. (2013) have provided a detailed typology of the elements of obesity histories that have been modelled in studies of obesity and mortality. They identified four primary types: (1) additive, (2) duration, (3) weight change, and (4) interactive. Additive models treat each BMI observation for an individual as additive effects in a regression model. So, for example, BMI at the time of survey is entered additively with BMI at an earlier time in the life-course. Duration of obesity models count the number of years an individual has been obese. Weight change specifications model the effects of weight change explicitly. Interactive models allow for the effects of BMI at a particular stage in the life course to be dependent on the level of BMI at another stage in the life course. An important contribution of Preston et al. (2013) is that the authors evaluated the specifications based on ease of interpretability and variance of mortality explained. They showed that basic versions of these specifications often form a nested structure and can be tested using likelihood-ratio tests. Using the two criteria assessed, the authors concluded that duration of obesity models performed the best.

Preston et al. (2013) leveraged data on respondent-reported weight histories available in the cross-sectional National Health and Nutrition Examination Survey (NHANES). Various NHANES have asked respondents to report body weight at different ages (e.g., weight at age 25) or time points (e.g., weight 10 years ago). While these measures may be imperfect, they have in some instances been shown to be strongly correlated with previously measured weight even among older adults (Perry et al., 1995; Stevens et al., 1990). Thus, if longitudinal data is not available researchers should consider the use of retrospectively reported body weight that may be available in cross-sectional data.

One characteristic of an individual's weight history that was not assessed by Preston et al. (2013) was an individual's lifetime peak or maximum lifetime body weight. Maximum BMI has since been increasingly used and evaluated. Maximum BMI is often ascertained from a survey question asking respondents about highest lifetime body weight. It can also be inferred more directly in long-running panels (e.g., by taking the highest BMI observed across waves).

Mehta et al. (2014) used longitudinal data on adults from the Health 2000 survey of Finland and found that an individual's peak BMI (since age 20 years) was more strongly related to mortality compared to BMI taken at the time of survey. Table 6.1, taken from Mehta et al. (2014), shows that the excess hazards associated with peak obesity (BMI >= 30) were nearly twice as strong as the hazards associated with obesity (BMI >= 30) at the time of survey: 42% vs. 21% (with reference to a BMI < 25; Table 6.1). Stokes (2014) reported a similar pattern in a sample of never smoking adults ages 50–84 years in the cross-sectional NHANES, which asks about lifetime maximum body weight. The author found that the hazard ratio (HR) of death associated with obese class I (BMI,

Table 6.1 Hazard ratios of death comparing peak BMI and BMI at Time of Survey in the Health 2000 Survey of Finland (ages 50–74 years at time of survey)

BMI categories	Overall peak BMI	Survey BMI
BMI < 25.0	Ref.	Ref.
Overweight (25.0–29.9)	1.08 (0.79, 1.48)	1.08 (0.82, 1.43)
Obese (≥30.0)	1.42 (1.04, 1.95)	1.22 (0.91, 1.65)

Source: Mehta et al. (2014, Table 3, p. 709) (Reproduced with permission)
Note: Each measure is entered into a separate model. Baseline BMI is BMI at time of survey in 2000–2001. Overall peak BMI is the peak BMI from the retrospective reports of weight at earlier ages (ages 20, 30, 40, and 50 years) and survey BMI. Cox proportional hazard models adjusted for attained age, sex, educational attainment, and cigarette smoking. Deaths were followed through December 31, 2011 (deaths = 335). Estimates reflect sample weighting

30.0–34.9) at maximum was 1.67 (relative to a BMI of 18.5–24.9). The corresponding HR for BMI at time of survey was 1.31-thus, the excess hazard associated with the maximum variable was approximately twice that of the time at survey variable (67% vs. 31%) in line with the finding by Mehta et al. (2014).

Stokes and Preston (2016a) provide a rigorous evaluation of the performance of maximum body weight in statistical models of mortality. They find that models using the maximum specification performed better—according to parsimony and goodness of fit—to models relying on BMI at the time of survey. The authors also show that the "normal" BMI category (BMI, 25.0–29.9) at the time of survey, often used as the reference category, contains a large percentage of respondents who were heavier in early life, lost weight, and carry high mortality. The authors conclude that disease-induced weight loss is a major source of bias when estimating risks based on BMI at time of survey. With respect to the validity of the measure and potential reporting biases, Stokes and Preston (2016a) state that compared to retrospective reports of body weight at specific ages: "[s]elf-reported maximum weight may be subject to less error because the question does not require remembering to a specific age or period in time but simply one feature of a weight trajectory." (Stokes & Preston, 2016a, 576)

Evidence of Obesity's Role on Aggregate Mortality Levels and Trends

Scientists have been increasingly concerned with how rising obesity levels globally are affecting national mortality levels and trends. However, there have been few studies that have addressed this issue, and most have been focused on the United States and Europe. In an early paper, Olshansky et al. (2005) postulated that rising obesity in the United States would lead to a leveling off and potentially a decline in life expectancy at birth and at older ages by 2050. The paper did not provide a formal projection, but rather contextualized an analysis of obesity's effect on life expectancy in 2000 within existing official mortality projections.

Nevertheless, since 2010 U.S. life expectancy growth has been flat, which is a sharp deviation in trend from previous decades. Between 2014 and 2017 U.S. life expectancy experienced three year-over-year declines, which is an almost unprecedented phenomena in recent mortality history. Much of the focus on stalling U.S. life expectancy has focused on the roles of the opioid epidemic and adverse trends in mortality among the working aged (Woolf & Schoomaker, 2019; The National Academies of Science, Engineering, and Medicine, n.d.).

However, work by Mehta et al. (2020) show that the stall in U.S. life expectancy growth since 2010 is almost exclusively a function of stalling declines in mortality from cardiovascular disease. CVD mortality declines have the main driver in life expectancy improvements in most high-income countries since at least the 1950s. However, since 2010, CVD mortality declines have stalled in the United States, and to a lesser extent in other high-income countries (Lopez & Adair, 2019). Figure 6.2, taken from Mehta et al. (2020), show results from a counterfactual exercise designed to compare the effects of trends in CVD mortality with that of drug-overdose mortality on trends in U.S. life expectancy at age 25 years. The figure shows that between 2010 and 2017, actual U.S. life expectancy at age 25 years increased by 0.07 years in women and declined by 0.04 years in men. If drug-overdose deaths did not rise over this period life expectancy at age 25 years in 2017 would have been higher by 0.14 years in women and by 0.36 years in men. In contrast, if CVD mortality declines had not stalled after 2010, life expectancy at age 25 years in 2017 would have been 1.14 years higher in women and men. The authors show that stalls in CVD mortality declines are prominent at both younger and older ages.

Whether rising obesity has been the prime factor responsible for the post-2010 stall in U.S. CVD mortality and overall life expectancy remains to be seen. Preston et al. (2018) showed that rising obesity between 1988 and 2011, as measured using maximum BMI, reduced

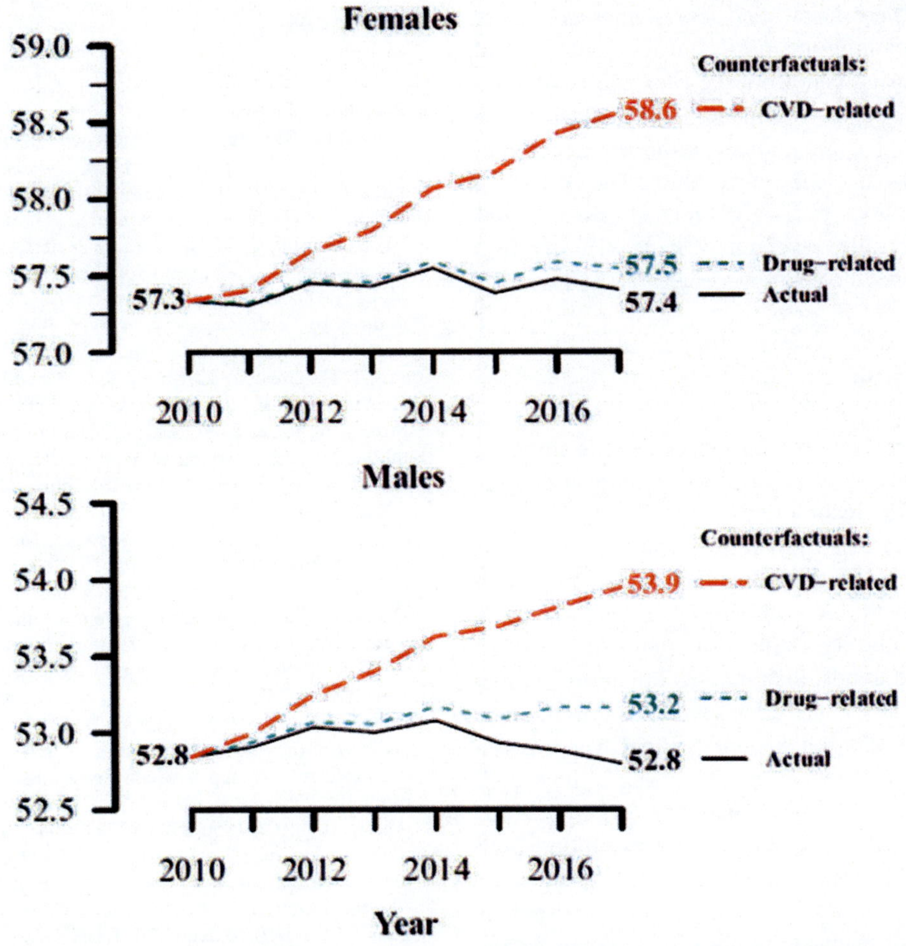

Fig. 6.2 A comparison of the contribution of stalling declines in CVD mortality and rising drug overdose deaths to U.S. life expectancy at age 25 trends. (*Source:* Fig. 6.2 in Mehta et al., 2020, 6999) (Reproduced under Creative Commons License CC BY-NC-ND 4.0, https://creativecommons.org/licenses/by-nc-nd/4.0/legalcode)

U.S. life expectancy at age 40 in 2011 by 0.9 years and was a main contributor to a widening gap in mortality between the United States and peer countries (in that the U.S. disadvantage in mortality grew over this period). A few studies have attempted to project the effects of rising obesity on future U.S. mortality patterns (Stewart et al., 2009; Preston et al., 2014; Soneji & King, 2011). These studies conclude that obesity will be a main factor in stymieing continued U.S. life expectancy improvements gained from reductions in cigarette smoking, medical care and other factors. Of course, the lingering effects of the COVID-19 pandemic now need to be taken into account.

Evidence on the aggregate effect of obesity on national mortality patterns outside the United States is still building. Preston and Stokes (2011) found that obesity reduced 2006 life expectancy at age 50 years by an average of 0.73 years and 0.98 years in women and men, respectively, in 13 high income countries not including the United States (for the United States the estimated effects were 1.54 years (women) and 1.85 years (men)). Similar effects were reported by Vidra et al. (2019) who provided an analysis over the 1975–2012 period for several European countries. Janssen et al. (2021) project that life expectancy will continue to rise in Europe through 2065 despite rising obesity levels. There have been less studies conducted outside of high-income countries. Palloni et al. (2015), using data from the Mexican Health and Aging Survey, estimate that obesity has contributed to a 2–3 year loss in life expectancy at age 50 years in the early 2000s. The OECD has projected that overweight-related diseases will hold back life expectancy in Mexico by over 4 years over the next few decades (OECD, 2019).

Conclusion

I argue here that there have been notable advances in the study of obesity and mortality over the past decade. The incorporation of weight history data and the careful evaluation of statistical models that incorporate these data has been an important advancement. So too has been the increasing focus on obesity's effect on aggregate mortality levels and trends, including its effect on national life expectancy. There are several contributions to be made that would benefit the field. The first is a more comprehensive understanding of how obesity has shaped the mortality experience of cohorts, particularly for cohorts exhibiting high levels of obesity in early life. Part of this project involves reconstructing and documenting cohort histories of exposure to obesity including details on the age-specific incidence of obesity (e.g., Rafei et al., 2022) and age-specific estimates of cumulative exposure. Second, more surveys internationally could collect retrospective information on weight histories. Efforts would be needed to validate these data, but the costs associated with collection may be relatively low. Third, science and policy would benefit from continued efforts at identifying the role of obesity in stalling U.S. life expectancy and slowing improvements in other high-income countries. And fourth, there is a need to reduce the disparity in the number of obesity-mortality studies between higher and lower income countries. This reduction can be achieved by promoting data collection efforts internationally and increasing funding to researchers in middle- and lower-income countries.

References

Abdullah, A., Stoelwinder, J., Shortreed, S., Wolfe, R., Stevenson, C., Walls, H., de Courten, M., & Peeters, A. (2011a). The duration of obesity and the risk of type 2 diabetes. *Public Health Nutrition, 14*(01), 119–126. https://doi.org/10.1017/S1368980010001813

Abdullah, A., Wolfe, R., Stoelwinder, J. U., de Courten, M., Stevenson, C., Walls, H. L., & Peeters, A. (2011b). The number of years lived with obesity and the risk of all-cause and cause-specific mortality. *International Journal of Epidemiology, 40*(4), 985–996. https://doi.org/10.1093/ije/dyr018

Adams, T. D., Gress, R. E., Smith, S. C., Chad Halverson, R., Simper, S. C., Rosamond, W. D., LaMonte, M. J., Stroup, A. M., & Hunt, S. C. (2007). Long-term mortality after gastric bypass surgery. *New England Journal of Medicine, 357*(8), 753–761. https://doi.org/10.1056/NEJMoa066603

Alley, D. E., Jeffrey Metter, E., Griswold, M. E., Harris, T. B., Simonsick, E. M., Longo, D. L., & Ferrucci, L. (2010). Changes in weight at the end of life: Characterizing weight loss by time to death in a cohort study of older men. *American Journal of Epidemiology, 172*(5), 558–565. https://doi.org/10.1093/aje/kwq168

Allison, D. B., Faith, M. S., Heo, M., Townsend-Butterworth, D., & Williamson, D. F. (1999). Meta-analysis of the effect of excluding early deaths on the estimated relationship between body mass index and mortality. *Obesity Research, 7*(4), 342–354. https://doi.org/10.1002/j.1550-8528.1999.tb00417.x

Audrain-McGovern, J., & Benowitz, N. L. (2011). Cigarette smoking, nicotine, and body weight. *Clinical Pharmacology and Therapeutics, 90*(1), 164–168. https://doi.org/10.1038/clpt.2011.105

Carlsson, L. M. S., Sjöholm, K., Jacobson, P., Andersson-Assarsson, J. C., Svensson, P.-A., Taube, M., Carlsson, B., & Peltonen, M. (2020). Life expectancy after bariatric surgery in the Swedish obese subjects study. *New England Journal of Medicine, 383*(16), 1535–1543. https://doi.org/10.1056/NEJMoa2002449

Chiolero, A., Faeh, D., Paccaud, F., & Cornuz, J. (2008). Consequences of smoking for body weight, body fat distribution, and insulin resistance. *The American Journal of Clinical Nutrition, 87*(4), 801–809.

Collins, R. (2012). What makes UK biobank special? *Lancet (London, England), 379*(9822), 1173–1174. https://doi.org/10.1016/S0140-6736(12)60404-8

Colman, R. J., Anderson, R. M., Johnson, S. C., Kastman, E. K., Kosmatka, K. J., Mark Beasley, T., Allison, D. B., et al. (2009). Caloric restriction delays disease onset and mortality in rhesus monkeys. *Science (New York, N.Y.), 325*(5937), 201–204. https://doi.org/10.1126/science.1173635

Couzin, J. (2005). Public health. A heavyweight battle over CDC's obesity forecasts. *Science (New York, N. Y.), 308*(5723), 770–771. https://doi.org/10.1126/science.308.5723.770

Dai, H., Alsalhe, T. A., Chalghaf, N., Riccò, M., Bragazzi, N. L., & Jianhong, W. (2020). The global burden of disease attributable to high body mass index in 195 countries and territories, 1990–2017: An analysis of the global burden of disease study. *PLoS Medicine, 17*(7), e1003198. https://doi.org/10.1371/journal.pmed.1003198

Demeulemeester, F., de Punder, K., van Heijningen, M., & van Doesburg, F. (2021). Obesity as a risk factor for severe COVID-19 and complications: A review. *Cell, 10*(4), 933. https://doi.org/10.3390/cells10040933

Emdin, C. A., Khera, A. V., & Kathiresan, S. (2017). Mendelian randomization. *JAMA, 318*(19), 1925–1926. https://doi.org/10.1001/jama.2017.17219

Flegal, K. M., Graubard, B. I., & Williamson, D. F. (2004). Methods of calculating deaths attributable to obesity. *American Journal of Epidemiology, 160*(4), 331–338. https://doi.org/10.1093/aje/kwh222

Flegal, K. M., Graubard, B. I., Williamson, D. F., & Gail, M. H. (2005). Excess deaths associated with underweight, overweight, and obesity. *JAMA, 293*(15), 1861–1867. https://doi.org/10.1001/jama.293.15.1861

Flegal, K. M., Graubard, B. I., Williamson, D. F., & Gail, M. H. (2007). Impact of smoking and preexisting illness on estimates of the fractions of deaths associated with underweight, overweight, and obesity in the US population. *American Journal of Epidemiology, 166*(8), 975–982. https://doi.org/10.1093/aje/kwm152

Flegal, K. M., Shepherd, J. A., Looker, A. C., Graubard, B. I., Borrud, L. G., Ogden, C. L., Harris, T. B., Everhart, J. E., & Schenker, N. (2009). Comparisons of percentage body fat, body mass index, waist circumference, and waist-stature ratio in adults. *The American Journal of Clinical Nutrition, 89*(2), 500–508. https://doi.org/10.3945/ajcn.2008.26847

Flegal, K. M., Panagiotou, O. A., & Graubard, B. I. (2015). Estimating population attributable fractions to quantify the health burden of obesity. *Annals of Epidemiology, 25*(3), 201–207. https://doi.org/10.1016/j.annepidem.2014.11.010

Galicia-Garcia, U., Benito-Vicente, A., Jebari, S., Larrea-Sebal, A., Siddiqi, H., Uribe, K. B., Ostolaza, H., & Martín, C. (2020). Pathophysiology of type 2 diabetes mellitus. *International Journal of Molecular Sciences, 21*(17), E6275. https://doi.org/10.3390/ijms21176275

Hendren, N. S., de Lemos, J. A., Ayers, C., Das, S. R., Rao, A., Carter, S., Rosenblatt, A., et al. (2021). Association of body mass index and age with morbidity and mortality in patients hospitalized with COVID-19. *Circulation, 143*(2), 135–144. https://doi.org/10.1161/CIRCULATIONAHA.120.051936

Hu, F. (2008). Obesity and mortality. In H. Frank (Ed.), *Obesity epidemiology*. Oxford University Press.

Janssen, F., Bardoutsos, A., El Gewily, S., & De Beer, J. (2021). Future life expectancy in Europe taking into account the impact of smoking, obesity, and alcohol. Edited by Belinda Nicolau, Eduardo Franco, Ugofilippo Basellini, and Collin Payne. *eLife, 10*(July), e66590. https://doi.org/10.7554/eLife.66590

Jenkins, D. A., Wade, K. H., Carslake, D., Bowden, J., Sattar, N., Loos, R. J. F., Timpson, N. J., Sperrin, M., & Rutter, M. K. (2021). Estimating the causal effect of BMI on mortality risk in people with heart disease, diabetes and cancer using Mendelian randomization. *International Journal of Cardiology, 330*(May), 214–220. https://doi.org/10.1016/j.ijcard.2021.02.027

Klein, S., Gastaldelli, A., Yki-Järvinen, H., & Scherer, P. E. (2022). Why does obesity cause diabetes? *Cell Metabolism, 34*(1), 11–20. https://doi.org/10.1016/j.cmet.2021.12.012

Kritchevsky, S. B., Beavers, K. M., Miller, M. E., Kyla Shea, M., Houston, D. K., Kitzman, D. W., & Nicklas, B. J. (2015). Intentional weight loss and all-cause mortality: A meta-analysis of randomized clinical trials. *PLoS One, 10*(3), e0121993. https://doi.org/10.1371/journal.pone.0121993

Lawlor, D. A., Hart, C. L., Hole, D. J., & Smith, G. D. (2006). Reverse causality and confounding and the associations of overweight and obesity with mortality. *Obesity (Silver Spring, Md.), 14*(12), 2294–2304. https://doi.org/10.1038/oby.2006.269

Lin, X., Yufeng, X., Pan, X., Jingya, X., Ding, Y., Sun, X., Song, X., Ren, Y., & Shan, P.-F. (2020). Global, regional, and national burden and trend of diabetes in 195 countries and territories: An analysis from 1990 to 2025. *Scientific Reports, 10*(1), 14790. https://doi.org/10.1038/s41598-020-71908-9

Lopez, A. D., & Adair, T. (2019). Is the long-term decline in cardiovascular-disease mortality in high-income countries over? Evidence from National Vital Statistics. *International Journal of Epidemiology*. https://doi.org/10.1093/ije/dyz143

Mehta, N. K. (2015). Obesity and mortality. In J. D. Wright (Editor-in-Chief), *International encyclopedia of the social & behavioral sciences* (2nd ed., Vol. 17, pp. 75–81). Elsevier.

Mehta, N. K., & Chang, V. W. (2009). Mortality attributable to obesity among middle-aged adults in the United States. *Demography, 46*(4), 851.

Mehta, N. K., & Chang, V. W. (2011). Obesity and mortality. In J. Cawley (Ed.), *Handbook of the social science of obesity*. Oxford University Press.

Mehta, N. K., Stenholm, S., Elo, I. T., Aromaa, A., Heliövaara, M., & Koskinen, S. (2014). Weight histories and mortality among Finnish adults: The role of duration and peak body mass index. *Epidemiology, 25*(5), 707–710. https://doi.org/10.1097/EDE.0000000000000147

Mehta, N., Elo, I., Stenholm, S., Aromaa, A., Heliövaara, M., & Koskinen, S. (2017). International differences in the risk of death from smoking and obesity: The case of the United States and Finland. *SSM—Population Health, 3*(December), 141–152. https://doi.org/10.1016/j.ssmph.2016.12.001

Mehta, N. K., Abrams, L. R., & Myrskylä, M. (2020). US life expectancy stalls due to cardiovascular disease, not drug deaths. *Proceedings of the National Academy of*

Sciences, 117(13), 6998–7000. https://doi.org/10.1073/pnas.1920391117

Mokdad, A. H., Marks, J. S., Stroup, D. F., & Gerberding, J. L. (2004). Actual causes of death in the United States, 2000. *JAMA, 291*(10), 1238–1245. https://doi.org/10.1001/jama.291.10.1238

Murray, C. J. L., Aravkin, A. Y., Zheng, P., Abbafati, C., Abbas, K. M., Abbasi-Kangevari, M., Abd-Allah, F., et al. (2020). Global burden of 87 risk factors in 204 countries and territories, 1990–2019: A systematic analysis for the global burden of disease study 2019. *The Lancet, 396*(10258), 1223–1249. https://doi.org/10.1016/S0140-6736(20)30752-2

NCD Risk Factor Collaboration. (2016). Trends in adult body-mass index in 200 countries from 1975 to 2014: A pooled analysis of 1698 population-based measurement studies with 19·2 million participants. *Lancet (London, England), 387*(10026), 1377–1396. https://doi.org/10.1016/S0140-6736(16)30054-X

Nordestgaard, B. G., Palmer, T. M., Benn, M., Zacho, J., Tybjærg-Hansen, A., Smith, G. D., & Timpson, N. J. (2012). The effect of elevated body mass index on ischemic heart disease risk: Causal estimates from a Mendelian randomisation approach. *PLoS Medicine, 9*(5), e1001212. https://doi.org/10.1371/journal.pmed.1001212

Nordstoga, A. L., Zotcheva, E., Svedahl, E. R., Nilsen, T. I. L., & Skarpsno, E. S. (2019). Long-term changes in body weight and physical activity in relation to all-cause and cardiovascular mortality: The HUNT study. *International Journal of Behavioral Nutrition and Physical Activity, 16*(1), 45. https://doi.org/10.1186/s12966-019-0809-2

OECD. (2019). *The heavy burden of obesity: The economics of prevention* (OECD health policy studies). OECD Publishing. https://doi.org/10.1787/67450d67-en

Olshansky, S. J., Passaro, D. J., Hershow, R. C., Layden, J., Carnes, B. A., Brody, J., Hayflick, L., Butler, R. N., Allison, D. B., & Ludwig, D. S. (2005). A potential decline in life expectancy in the United States in the 21st century. *The New England Journal of Medicine, 352*(11), 1138–1145. https://doi.org/10.1056/NEJMsr043743

Palloni, A., Beltrán-Sánchez, H., Novak, B., Pinto, G., & Wong, R. (2015). Adult obesity, disease and longevity in Mexico. *Salud Pública de México, 57*(0 1), S22–S30.

Perry, G. S., Byers, T. E., Mokdad, A. H., Serdula, M. K., & Williamson, D. F. (1995). The validity of self-reports of past body weights by U.S. adults. *Epidemiology (Cambridge, Mass.), 6*(1), 61–66.

Popkin, B. M., Shufa, D., Green, W. D., Beck, M. A., Algaith, T., Herbst, C. H., Alsukait, R. F., Alluhidan, M., Alazemi, N., & Shekar, M. (2020). Individuals with obesity and COVID-19: A global perspective on the epidemiology and biological relationships. *Obesity Reviews, 21*(11), e13128. https://doi.org/10.1111/obr.13128

Preston, S. H., & Stokes, A. (2011). Contribution of obesity to international differences in life expectancy. *American Journal of Public Health*, AJPH.2011.300219. https://doi.org/10.2105/ajph.2011.300219

Preston, S. H., Mehta, N. K., & Stokes, A. (2013). Modeling obesity histories in cohort analyses of health and mortality. *Epidemiology, 24*(1), 158–166. https://doi.org/10.1097/EDE.0b013e3182770217

Preston, S. H., Stokes, A., Mehta, N. K., & Cao, B. (2014). Projecting the effect of changes in smoking and obesity on future life expectancy in the United States. *Demography, 51*(1), 27–49. https://doi.org/10.1007/s13524-013-0246-9

Preston, S. H., Vierboom, Y. C., & Stokes, A. (2018). The role of obesity in exceptionally slow US mortality improvement. *Proceedings of the National Academy of Sciences, 115*(5), 957–961. https://doi.org/10.1073/pnas.1716802115

Prospective Studies Collaboration. (2009). Body-mass index and cause-specific mortality in 900 000 adults: Collaborative analyses of 57 prospective studies. *The Lancet, 373*(9669), 1083–1096. https://doi.org/10.1016/S0140-6736(09)60318-4

Rafei, A., Elliott, M. R., Jones, R. E., Riosmena, F., Cunningham, S. A., & Mehta, N. K. (2022). Obesity incidence in U.S children and young adults: A pooled analysis. *American Journal of Preventive Medicine, S0749-3797*(22), 00066–00066. https://doi.org/10.1016/j.amepre.2021.12.021

Redinger, R. N. (2007). The pathophysiology of obesity and its clinical manifestations. *Gastroenterology & Hepatology, 3*(11), 856–863.

Richmond, R. C., Smith, G. D., Ness, A. R., den Hoed, M., McMahon, G., & Timpson, N. J. (2014). Assessing causality in the association between child adiposity and physical activity levels: A Mendelian randomization analysis. *PLoS Medicine, 11*(3), e1001618. https://doi.org/10.1371/journal.pmed.1001618

Rockhill, B., Willett, W. C., Manson, J. E., Leitzmann, M. F., Stampfer, M. J., Hunter, D. J., & Colditz, G. A. (2001). Physical activity and mortality: A prospective study among women. *American Journal of Public Health, 91*(4), 578–583.

Sjöström, L., Kristina Narbro, C., Sjöström, D., Karason, K., Larsson, B., Wedel, H., Lystig, T., et al. (2007). Effects of bariatric surgery on mortality in Swedish obese subjects. *New England Journal of Medicine, 357*(8), 741–752. https://doi.org/10.1056/NEJMoa066254

Smith, G. D., Sterne, J. A. C., Fraser, A., Tynelius, P., Lawlor, D. A., & Rasmussen, F. (2009). The association between BMI and mortality using offspring BMI as an indicator of own BMI: Large intergenerational mortality study. *BMJ, 339*(December), b5043. https://doi.org/10.1136/bmj.b5043

Soneji, S., & King, G. (2011). The future of death in America. *Demographic Research, 25*(1), 1–38. https://doi.org/10.4054/DemRes.2011.25.1

Stevens, J., Keil, J. E., Waid, L. R., & Gazes, P. C. (1990). Accuracy of current, 4-year, and 28-year self-reported body weight in an elderly population. *American Journal of Epidemiology, 132*(6), 1156–1163. https://doi.org/10.1093/oxfordjournals.aje.a115758

Stewart, S. T., Cutler, D. M., & Rosen, A. B. (2009). Forecasting the effects of obesity and smoking on U.S. life expectancy. *New England Journal of Medicine, 361*(23), 2252–2260. https://doi.org/10.1056/NEJMsa0900459

Stokes, A. (2014). Using maximum weight to redefine body mass index categories in studies of the mortality risks of obesity. *Population Health Metrics, 12*(1), 6. https://doi.org/10.1186/1478-7954-12-6

Stokes, A., & Preston, S. H. (2016a). Revealing the burden of obesity using weight histories. *Proceedings of the National Academy of Sciences, 113*(3), 572–577. https://doi.org/10.1073/pnas.1515472113

Stokes, A., & Preston, S. H. (2016b). How smoking affects the proportion of deaths attributable to obesity: Assessing the role of relative risks and weight distributions. *BMJ Open, 6*(2), e009232. https://doi.org/10.1136/bmjopen-2015-009232

Stokes, A., & Preston, S. H. (2016c). How dangerous is obesity? Issues in measurement and interpretation. *Population and Development Review, 42*(4), 595–614. https://doi.org/10.1111/padr.12015

Stram, D. O., Huberman, M., & Anna, H. W. (2002). Is residual confounding a reasonable explanation for the apparent protective effects of beta-carotene found in epidemiologic studies of lung cancer in smokers? *American Journal of Epidemiology, 155*(7), 622–628. https://doi.org/10.1093/aje/155.7.622

Templin, T., Hashiguchi, T. C. O., Thomson, B., Dieleman, J., & Bendavid, E. (2019). The overweight and obesity transition from the wealthy to the poor in low- and middle-income countries: A survey of household data from 103 countries. *PLoS Medicine, 16*(11), e1002968. https://doi.org/10.1371/journal.pmed.1002968

The National Academies of Science, Engineering, and Medicine. (n.d.). *High and rising mortality rates among working-age adults* (Consensus study reports). The National Academies Press.

Vasselli, J. R., Weindruch, R., Heymsfield, S. B., Xavier Pi-Sunyer, F., Boozer, C. N., Yi, N., Wang, C., Pietrobelli, A., & Allison, D. B. (2005). Intentional weight loss reduces mortality rate in a rodent model of dietary obesity. *Obesity Research, 13*(4), 693–702. https://doi.org/10.1038/oby.2005.78

Vazquez, G., Duval, S., Jacobs, D. R., & Silventoinen, K. (2007). Comparison of body mass index, waist circumference, and waist/hip ratio in predicting incident diabetes: A meta-analysis. *Epidemiologic Reviews, 29*, 115–128. https://doi.org/10.1093/epirev/mxm008

Vidra, N., Trias-Llimós, S., & Janssen, F. (2019). Impact of obesity on life expectancy among different European countries: Secondary analysis of population-level data over the 1975–2012 period. *BMJ Open, 9*(7). https://doi.org/10.1136/bmjopen-2018-028086

Wade, K. H., Carslake, D., Sattar, N., Smith, G. D., & Timpson, N. J. (2018). BMI and mortality in UK biobank: Revised estimates using Mendelian randomization. *Obesity (Silver Spring, Md.), 26*(11), 1796–1806. https://doi.org/10.1002/oby.22313

Wannamethee, S. G., Shaper, A. G., & Walker, M. (2002). Weight change, weight fluctuation, and mortality. *Archives of Internal Medicine, 162*(22), 2575–2580. https://doi.org/10.1001/archinte.162.22.2575

Weindruch, R., & Sohal, R. S. (1997). Caloric intake and aging. *The New England Journal of Medicine, 337*(14), 986–994.

Weindruch, R., & Walford, R. L. (1982). Dietary restriction in mice beginning at 1 year of age: Effect on lifespan and spontaneous cancer incidence. *Science, 215*(4538), 1415–1418. https://doi.org/10.1126/science.7063854

Woolf, S. H., & Schoomaker, H. (2019). Life expectancy and mortality rates in the United States, 1959-2017. *JAMA, 322*(20), 1996. https://doi.org/10.1001/jama.2019.16932

7 Obesity and Immigration

Ginny Garcia-Alexander and Amethyst Morgan Marroquin

Introduction

International migration refers to the movement of individuals across national borders, and the individuals who move across these borders are referred to as immigrants. Though mobility slowed considerably during the COVID-19 pandemic, international migration grew substantially between 2000 and 2020, with the majority of moves attributed to labor or family migration (UN, 2020). As has traditionally been the case, the United States remains the top receiver of immigrants from a variety of countries.

Given the growth and diversity of international migrants to the U.S., a large body of research has concentrated on the health of these individuals. This area of investigation offers fruitful avenues for understanding the social causes of health as researchers are able to examine the influence of changing social environments on wellbeing (Bakhtiari, 2021). However, as with migration studies more generally, migrant health outcomes are shaped by a complex array of factors. Those who migrate do so for different reasons, some are voluntary while others are involuntary, which has implications for their current and future health status. Similarly, their personal characteristics may encourage healthy behaviors or make them more or less healthy upon arrival. The destinations in which they settle also influence health outcomes based on existing infrastructure and policies that may hinder or support their access to care, or promote unsafe working conditions, among other things.

With respect to how overweight and obesity may be linked to immigration, population research has offered examinations of the prevalence of overweight and obesity and/or related comorbidities based on national origin, with evidence suggesting that immigrants tend to have lower rates of obesity than native-born individuals. These findings have led to a focus on the role of acculturation since overall patterns suggest that increased duration of time in the United States increases the likelihood of weight gain. This chapter reviews patterns of obesity among migrants to the United States, including its prevalence among new arrivals and among those who have been in the United States for longer periods of time. It also covers the relevant theories that have been applied to this area of study along with the methodological approaches employed by demographers who study obesity. The final portion of the chapter describes some of the directions for future research in this area.

G. Garcia-Alexander (✉) · A. M. Marroquin
Department of Sociology, University of Texas at San Antonio, San Antonio, TX, USA
e-mail: ginny.garcia@utsa.edu

G. Garcia-Alexander, D. L. Poston, Jr. (eds.), *International Handbook of the Demography of Obesity*, International Handbooks of Population 12, https://doi.org/10.1007/978-3-031-10936-2_7

Literature Review

The United States Context

The United States is known as an immigration country, in the sense that its policies allow for migrants to enter legally, and it has long been a destination for international migrants. In fact, the U.S. hosts the largest number of migrants worldwide; approximately 51 million people, or about one-sixth of the U.S. population, are foreign-born (UN, 2020). Migration flows to the United States have shifted over time, with post-1965 waves primarily composed of immigrants from Latin America and Asia. Though, it should be noted that the diversity of immigrants has been increasing over time. As of 2019, Latin American countries represented approximately 50% of the total immigrant population (a large but decreasing proportion immigrated from Mexico); Asian countries accounted for approximately 31% of the total; the remaining share was from a diverse mix of countries (MPI, 2021) (Fig. 7.1). Given the increasing share and diversity of immigrants to the U.S., it is important to understand how different groups fare with respect to the burden of overweight and obesity as well as the forces that shape these outcomes.

Because the U.S. hosts more immigrants than any other country, it is useful to understand this context as the United States has been contending with rising rates of overweight and obesity for a number of decades. Among the adult population, rates of overweight and obesity were 73.6% and 42.5% in 2018, respectively (Fryar et al., 2020). Many have argued that such high rates of obesity are attributable to obesity-promoting, or toxic food environments, that encourage energy-dense diets and sedentary lifestyles (Geier & Brownell, 2006; Swinburn et al., 1999). A related concept is the Global Nutrition Transition, which describes the shift in dietary patterns that have been observed across the globe (Popkin, 2006). This concept offers useful insights into global nutritional shifts that have brought health consequences including rapidly rising rates of obesity.

Popkin (2006) outlines five nutritional patterns to describe populations with later patterns, or stages, resulting from urbanization, economic development, and globalization processes. These include: (1) Hunter Gatherer societies; (2) Early Agriculture (characterized by famine); (3) Receding famine and rising incomes (characterized by improved nutrition); (4) Overeating and Obesity-Related Diseases (increased fat, sugar, and processed food consumption and less active lifestyles); and (5) Behavioral Change (improved diet quality). It is important to note the shift from pattern 3 to pattern 4 is representative of the shift from traditional to Western diets. In this stage, technological changes brought by economic

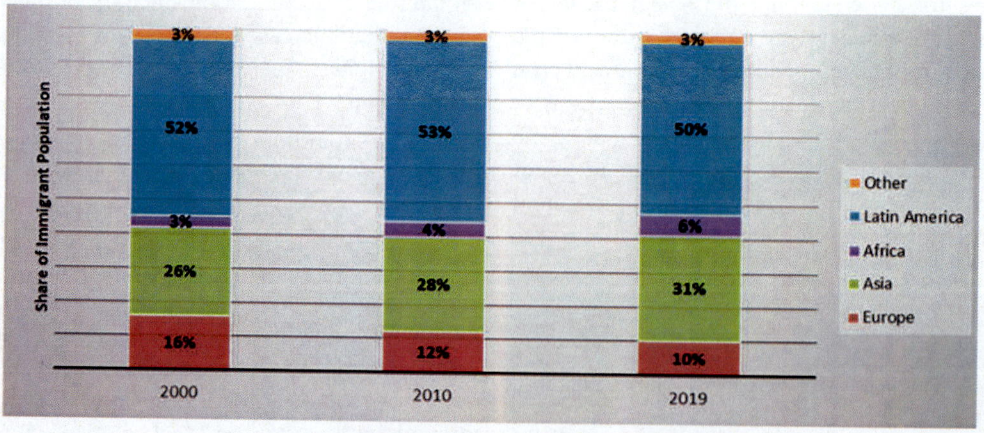

Fig. 7.1 US immigrant population by region of birth, 2000–2019. (Source: Migration Policy Institute Data Hub (tabulation of data from the US Census Bureau 2000 Decennial Census and 2010 to 2019 ACS))

growth lead to increased levels of sedentary behavior, increased consumption of energy dense processed foods, and escalating levels of obesity (Popkin, 2006). The United States is largely characterized by pattern 4. Indeed, the U.S. has long been well ahead of other countries with respect to poor diet quality, lack of physical activity, and levels of overweight and obesity (Popkin, 2017). Pattern 5 reflects a stage in which individuals adopt behavioral changes that improve diet quality and increase levels of physical activity in order to improve health. This appears to have emerged to some extent in the U.S., but is largely limited to well-educated native-born individuals (Hao & Kim, 2009; Rivera et al., 2004).

Beyond the United States, changes in food consumption and obesity prevalence are occurring across the globe. Many immigrant sending countries are thought to be rapidly transitioning toward pattern 4 (Popkin et al., 2012). For example, Mexico, which remains the single largest contributor to the immigrant population in the U.S. (approximately 24% in 2019), saw dramatic increases of 47% and 160% in overweight and obesity prevalence, respectively between 1988 and 1999 (Rivera et al., 2004). Other Latin American countries such as Chile and Brazil also saw an increased prevalence of overweight/obesity in this timeframe (Rivera et al., 2004). Asian countries that are contributing an increased share of immigrants to the U.S. have recently seen similar changes (Abarca-Gomez et al., 2017). These and many other countries are experiencing what is referred to as a dual, or double burden of malnutrition and overweight/obesity (Prentice, 2006; WHO, 2022). Recent findings indicate that individuals in poorer and rural populations suffer from hunger and dietary deficiencies, while simultaneously individuals in higher SES and urban populations have lower levels of physical activity and exhibits excess consumption of sugar and fat (Joy et al., 2017). Some researchers have even pointed to a triple burden which refers to, "the coexistence of food insecurity, undernutrition, and overweight and obesity" (Alaimo et al., 2020: 316).

In a number of middle and low-income countries, recent patterns suggest a trend toward poorer diet quality and increasing mean body mass index (BMI) (Kang et al., 2021). These changes signal important oncoming changes in the health of migrants to the U.S. in the coming decades. Yet, rates of overweight and obesity remain comparatively lower in these countries, and recent arrivals to the United States continue to have somewhat of an advantage in body composition in comparison to native-born individuals.

Patterns and Prevalence of Obesity Among Immigrants to the United States

Among immigrants, studies reflect obesity prevalence rates ranging from 12.5% to 16% across all countries of origin (Choi, 2011; Goel et al., 2004). As mentioned previously, immigrants appear to arrive with healthier body compositions. Indeed, a number of studies have confirmed that immigrants have lower average BMIs than natives (Antecol & Bedard, 2006; Cunningham et al., 2008). However, investigations of subgroup variations indicate a high degree of heterogeneity across groups. One study observed a higher prevalence of overweight or obesity in migrants from Mexico, Central America, and the Caribbean and a lower prevalence among Asians (Oza-Frank & Narayan, 2010). Another observed higher prevalence of overweight and obesity in the same three regions as well as the Indian subcontinent (Commodore-Mensah et al., 2018). These findings are consistent with those proposed by the Global Nutrition Transition in the sense that countries that are further along in development have higher rates of overweight and obesity, which is reflected in higher average BMIs on arrival.

Yet, despite the fact that overweight and obesity are on the rise in sending countries, the existing body of evidence indicates that immigrant arrivals tend to gain weight rapidly upon arrival rather than arrive at an unhealthy weight (Cunningham et al., 2008; Van Hook et al., 2012). Accordingly, the tendency to gain weight with additional time spent in the U.S. has been the focus of much investigation. The following section explores the proccsses involved with these changes.

The Hispanic Paradox

A perspective that has received a great deal of attention in studies of immigrant health is the Hispanic Paradox. This refers to the commonly observed phenomenon of morbidity and mortality advantages among Hispanic immigrants, despite their lower socioeconomic status (Markides & Coreil, 1986; Markides & Eschbach, 2005). A number of studies have successfully illustrated its applicability to health and mortality outcomes (Franzini et al., 2001; Hummer et al., 2007; Ruiz et al., 2013). These paradoxical findings have been attributed to several possibilities. Selective migration refers to the idea that immigrants are selected on the basis of health. It encompasses the healthy migrant effect, which suggests that those who are in good health are more likely to immigrate given the physical and economic demands of the migration process. This argument has received strong support and has been replicated in several settings (Kennedy et al., 2015; Riosmena et al., 2017). Selective migration further encompasses "salmon bias," which posits that those who are in poor health are more likely to return to their countries of origin in late-life thereby producing an undercount of migrant mortality. This argument has received less support, though several have found evidence of limited contributions to the Hispanic mortality advantage (Palloni & Arias, 2004; Turra & Elo, 2008). Finally, selection processes may be bolstered by cultural supports, e.g., traditional diets and health behaviors, that contribute to health advantages in immigrants (Abraido-Lanza et al., 2005; Bostean, 2013).

The argument that immigrants are healthier on arrival is well-established in the literature (Antecol & Bedard, 2006; Markides & Eschbach, 2011). With respect to overweight and obesity prevalence, studies have repeatedly confirmed lower average BMI scores among new immigrants compared to the general population and their native-born counterparts (Popkin & Udry, 1998; Gordon-Larsen et al., 2003). In addition, longer duration in the U.S. has generally been associated with worsening outcomes in body composition. Studies attempting to quantify when the shift toward unhealthy body composition in migrants occurs suggest it happens relatively quickly. For example, Antecol and Bedard (2006) found that immigrant BMIs converged with American BMIs in 10 or 15 years for females and males, respectively. Goel et al. (2004) similarly observed that years of residence is significantly associated with obesity for different immigrant groups after 10 years. Kaplan et al. (2004) observed an increasing prevalence of obesity with each increase in the number of years spent in the U.S. among Hispanic immigrants, with the highest prevalence among those here 15 or more years.

A study combining 15 years of cross-sectional data to create synthetic cohorts of immigrants extended this work to suggest that there are important variations across and within immigrant groups. Specifically, Hispanic immigrants (but not Asian or white immigrants), those with less education, and those who arrived at a younger age had increased obesity with increased duration of time in the US (Kaushal, 2009). Bates et al. (2008) also observed a positive association between duration in US and BMI, but demonstrated differences on the basis of country of origin and generational status. A review of the literature similarly observed that those who migrate at younger ages are more likely to have overweight/obesity than those who migrate at older ages (Oza-Frank & Cunningham, 2010). Overall, the existing body of evidence suggests a positive association between duration of time in the US and overweight/obesity prevalence, but variations on the basis of a number of factors warrant ongoing investigation. In addition, the mechanisms that lead to increasing levels of overweight and obesity among immigrants remain unclear and are the subject of ongoing study.

Acculturation and Overweight/Obesity

A significant portion of the literature linking health and migration focuses on the subsequent deterioration of health, placing attention on how and why health advantages enjoyed by immigrants decline with greater time spent in the U.S. (Abraido-Lanza et al., 2005; Acevedo-

Garcia et al., 2010). The acculturation hypothesis suggests that as migrants spend more time in the US, their health behaviors converge with those of native-born individuals. This argument stems from assimilation theory, which describes the process of incorporation into the host society, and the related concept of acculturation, broadly referring to the process by which immigrants adopt the patterns, norms, and practices of the host society (Gordon, 1964). An extension of this theory is segmented assimilation (Portes & Zhou, 1993; Portes & Rumbaut, 2006), which describes several possibilities for the incorporation of migrants including: traditional, straight-line assimilation and upward mobility; maintenance of cultural identity, i.e., selective acculturation; and downward assimilation with blocked access to opportunities. These varying trajectories have different implications for health outcomes, thus the body of work (largely focused on Latinos) suggests a complex relationship between acculturation and health (Lara et al., 2005). In broad strokes, studies suggest positive impacts on self-reported health and use of preventive services, and negative impacts on substance use and dietary practices (Lara et al., 2005). Accordingly, an area that has been the focus of many scholars of obesity is how exposure to American lifestyles worsens diet and weight-related outcomes.

Acculturation has been posited to produce deleterious outcomes in overweight and obesity via changing dietary patterns. The term dietary acculturation refers to the shift from healthier, traditional diets toward those of the host country (Akresh, 2007; Satia-Abouta et al., 2002). Several studies suggest declining diet quality in those who are higher on various measures of acculturation (e.g. Aldrich & Variyam, 2000; Batis et al., 2011; Van Hook et al., 2014). For example, Van Hook et al. (2016) confirm the importance of acculturation in predicting unhealthy eating. They observed that multiple indicators of acculturation including language spoken at interview, exposure to US eating behaviors, and media exposure, were strongly associated with less healthy diets among Mexican-origin children. Similarly, Soto et al. (2017) found that in families with more acculturated children, diet quality was poorer in mothers. Another study observed an association between greater linguistic acculturation and lower consumption of fruits and vegetables (Creighton et al., 2012). However, the authors were careful to point out that while acculturation is associated with diet quality, it does not appear to account for generational differences in obesity.

Though numerous studies have observed worsening diet quality among those who are higher on acculturation, it is important to note that some studies have produced inconsistent patterns. One study observed that diet quality appears to be improved in children whose parents are more acculturated (Chaparro et al., 2014). Another observed that acculturation was not associated with diet quality in Chinese immigrants, though these authors did observe an association between acculturation and dietary moderation (Liu et al., 2010). With respect to the related concept of physical activity, studies have found higher levels of physical activity among those with a higher degree of acculturation, but a lack of association with obesity (Barcenas et al., 2007). Singh et al. (2011) observed that adjustments for physical activity had little effect on obesity outcomes. Thus, it is worth noting that health behaviors such as diet quality and physical activity are associated with overweight/obesity, but they do not appear to fully account for weight gain among migrants.

A review of studies focused on research using standardized measures of acculturation observed a generally positive association between acculturation and BMI, but suggested a more complex pattern that varied by gender, socioeconomic status, and country of origin (Delavari et al., 2013); with the authors pointing to several explanatory mechanisms including SES and the role of the nutrition transition in promoting weight gain. Another review of studies among Latino youth emphasized the mixed results and pointed to the need for ongoing studies that examine mediating and moderating influences on this association (McLeod et al., 2016). In a study attempting to highlight the role of migration decisions and ties to home and US cultures, it was observed that these factors did relate to weight status in Latino immigrants, but they did not influence BMI among Asian groups (Gorman et al., 2016). In addition, these authors observed that SES underlies the association between BMI and acculturation. Finally, a study attempting to establish the role of acculturation by including well-developed measures of acculturation in addition to duration and generation revealed a lack of association between these measures and obesity (Creighton et al., 2012).

In sum, the literature linking acculturation and weight gain has not yielded definitive conclusions or clear explanatory mechanisms. Inconsistencies in findings may be attributable to poor conceptualization and measurement of acculturation. In fact, the review conducted by McLeod et al. (2016) indicated that in more than half of the studies identified, a definition of acculturation was not provided by the study authors. This was also observed in Broesch and Hadley's (2012) review of the literature. Additionally, critics have called attention to problems with the use of proxy measures of acculturation (e.g. time spent in the U.S., age at immigration) as they do not adequately reflect the extent or complexity of the acculturation process (Lara et al., 2005). This has led to calls for more robust and consistently applied measures of the acculturation process, and more recent work has attempted to incorporate fuller measures of the acculturation process (e.g. Creighton et al., 2012; Gorman et al., 2016; Van Hook et al., 2016).

Other criticisms have centered on inadequate use of existing theoretical models, minimal attention to the heterogeneity of immigrant groups, and a lack of emphasis on differences in socioeconomic status that are known to affect health status (Creighton et al., 2012; Hunt et al., 2004; Lara et al., 2005; Zambrana & Carter-Pokras, 2010). In addition, the lack of attention to immigration and settlement context have prompted concerns from immigration scholars (Cabassa, 2003; Lara et al., 2005). Contextual factors including the political, economic, and social context of the host and new society likely mediate the association between acculturation and various health outcomes; while individual factors, such as reason for migration or stress, are likely to moderate this association (Lara et al., 2005). Ongoing work is needed to identify the mechanisms that explain the shift toward unhealthy body composition in migrants.

Finally, some scholars have argued for a broader shift in the way that acculturation is treated in health research (Hunt et al., 2004). Their arguments are rooted in the desire to avoid explanations that attribute health inequalities to individual behavior patterns that are culturally rooted, rather than to structural causes. Widespread acceptance of acculturation as the primary driver of health outcomes has led to overemphasis on personal health behaviors and a potential lack of focus on upstream factors. These scholars have called for increased interdisciplinarity and greater awareness of the contexts that shape immigrant experiences in order to better capture and describe impacts on health. All in all, the literature on the association between acculturation and overweight and obesity suggests a mixed set of outcomes. Importantly, heavy focus on acculturation as the primary mechanism for worsening outcomes in migrants directs attention away from the role of structural mechanisms that contribute to the prevalence of overweight and obesity. These factors are considered in the following section.

Structural Causes of Obesity

Though lifestyle differences likely play some role in weight gain, scholars have increasingly called attention to the structural forces that shape these patterns. These include the social, political, environmental, and economic conditions and opportunities that promote energy-dense diets and sedentary lifestyles and lead to increased obesity prevalence (Sturm & An, 2014). Examples of the physical environment include urban design, presence of food outlets, and modes of transportation; the social environment encompasses social norms, exposure to marketing, family, and community; and the political and economic environment refers to such things as taxes, subsidies, and labeling, among others. Accordingly, the immigration process may lead to weight gain as immigrants encounter a lack of access to healthy foods, economic constraints that limit food options, blocked access to opportunities for physical activity and/or changing working conditions, exposure to worsening social conditions, and greater exposure to highly processed or fast food.

Studies have increasingly connected neighborhood contexts with health and obesity outcomes (see also Chap. 13). For example, neighborhoods with limited opportunities for physical activity have been consistently associated with increased BMI (Black & Macinko, 2008) as have those with high concentrations of poverty (Boardman et al., 2005). With respect to the role of the neighborhood context for immigrants, prior work has documented mixed associations. Some suggest that immigrant concentration is positively correlated with obesity. Accordingly, Grafova et al. (2008) found in a study of older adults that men living in highly concentrated immigration areas had higher odds of obesity. A study of Latinos in Utah observed that Latino residential isolation was significantly linked to obesity risk (Wen & Maloney, 2011). Isasi et al.' (2015) investigation of four urban areas revealed that exposure to obesogenic, i.e. obesity-promoting, environments was an important risk factor for obesity. A more recent study observed that high co-ethnic concentration was associated with increased waist circumference in Chinese and Latino immigrants (Lê-Scherban et al., 2019). Several potential mechanisms for these patterns have been proposed including the possibility that high immigrant concentrations may promote weight gain via increased opportunities for social gatherings (and increased food consumption) or because these areas are characterized by limited access to opportunities for physical activity and/or limited access to healthy foods. It has also been posited that worsening outcomes in body composition may be attributable to neighborhood disadvantage, which is a common feature of areas with high immigrant concentrations.

On the other hand, a study of the role of residential segregation found lower obesity prevalence among Mexican-American women in highly segregated contexts, pointing to some potential protection offered by enclaves (Kershaw et al., 2013). This is generally consistent with prior findings indicating that a greater concentration of immigrants has beneficial health effects (Eschbach et al., 2004); a finding that has been attributed to the presence of social supports and resources that are health promoting. For example, Hispanic residential concentration may lead to greater demand for and availability of healthier options. Indeed, studies have shown improved diet quality (Dubowitz et al., 2008) and access to healthy foods (Osypuk et al., 2009) in areas with more immigrants. Others have suggested that greater access to social networks and support confers protection against chronic stress and overeating (Nobari et al., 2013). However, areas with higher concentrations of immigrants have also been shown to exhibit poorer neighborhood quality (less safety, social cohesion, opportunities for recreation) (Osypuk et al., 2009). Thus, immigrant communities may have characteristics that simultaneously promote and inhibit weight gain. Additional research is needed to better understand how these mechanisms operate, and the extent to which overweight and obesity are buffered or exacerbated in ethnic enclaves.

The social environment has increasingly gained attention as scholars have shown that discrimination and racism are consistently linked with poorer physical and mental health outcomes (Williams & Mohammed, 2013). These concepts have also been linked to obesity-related outcomes (see Chap. 12 for a review of this research). The heightened sense of fear and stress related to immigration status has been shown to have measurable impacts on a number of health outcomes including food insecurity and poorer general health (Perreira & Pedroza, 2019). Similarly, acculturation stress may increase obesity risk via increased allostatic load (D'Alonzo et al., 2012). Studies that account for the reason(s) prompting individuals to migrate may provide some insight into this process. For example, a recent study found that immigrants who migrated for economic or family reasons have better health outcomes than those who migrate to seek asylum (Giuntella ct al., 2018). However, more work is needed to determine how experiences with discrimination translate into poorer health, both across diverse immigrant groups and in comparison, to native-born counterparts. Beyond the individual-level, the mechanisms that promote differential exposure to discrimination among immigrants with differential risk for poorer health outcomes are increasingly important to understand. However, this has received comparatively less attention in the literature.

The political context of a host country shapes immigration experiences, and immigration policies that are designed to be exclusionary can shape health in several ways. Despite the fact that public sentiment has largely shifted in favor of greater openness and acceptance of immigrants over time, political rhetoric has grown increasingly divisive (Hout & Maggio, 2021) and immigration policies have become increasingly restrictive. Massey (2021) argues that policies designed to criminalize migration will translate into barriers to integration. This may result in a host of negative outcomes that indirectly and directly impact health outcomes. Directly, the political context may shape immigrant health outcomes by hindering access to care or creating unsafe conditions for immigrants. For example, one study illustrated how counties that hosted Trump rallies saw an incredible increase in Latino hate crimes in 2018 (Canizales & Vallejo, 2021). Examinations of historical episodes have shown how negative sentiment can translate into racialized health policies and subsequent poorer health outcomes in groups that have been targeted (Molina, 2011). At present, the Affordable Care Act (ACA) does not cover undocumented migrants. In addition, those who are legally authorized but who have been in the country less than 5 years do not qualify for Medicaid (Ortega et al., 2015). These gaps in care may lead to a lack of information about the health-related impacts of weight gain and/or delayed care for obesity-related outcomes such as diabetes. Studies have also shown a chilling effect on immigrant participation in policies such as the Supplemental Nutritional Assistance Program (SNAP) (Perreira & Pedroza, 2019), which could promote weight gain as food insecurity has been found to predict overweight/obesity in female immigrants (Ryan-Ibarra et al., 2017). Indirectly, a negative political context may further promote conditions that worsen obesity-related outcomes. For example, increasingly restrictive policies driven by nativist sentiment may lead to greater segregation of immigrant communities and fewer community investments in these areas, thereby leading to worsening physical conditions, reduced opportunities for upward mobility, decreased social cohesion, and/or decreased political organization – all of which may have important implications for weight-related outcomes and necessitate further investigation.

Changing immigrant settlement patterns pose additional health challenges as immigrants settle in areas that have previously not had large immigrant populations. Some studies have observed a mortality advantage in migrants who settle in new and minor destinations compared to those in traditional destinations (Fenelon, 2017). This is potentially attributable to selection effects, with those who migrate to new destinations representing those who are least likely to have to rely on contacts and the most upwardly mobile. Medical screening practices, potentially accelerated in the context of COVID-19, may further advantage immigrants, as efforts to restrict entry of immigrants may bias entry toward the youngest and healthiest (Bakhtiari, 2021). These individuals may experience improved health outcomes throughout the life course. However, an increasingly restrictive environment may encourage downward trajectories for those who utilize unofficial channels for entry into the US as well as legal immigrants who are perceived as non-white. As suggested by segmented assimilation theory (Portes & Zhou, 1993), these individuals will likely encounter a host of obstacles resulting in worsening health. Additionally, others have expressed concerns over the lack of infrastructure in communities experiencing an influx of immigrants (Ortega et al., 2015; Viruell-Fuentes et al., 2012). It is of further concern that much of the growth in Latino populations has occurred in states that have not expanded insurance coverage, which restricts access to- and use of health care and may lead to worsening disparities.

Much of the prior work on obesity has focused on the characteristics of immigrants and how their habits change with additional time spent in the US. Proposed hypotheses for improved health in recent immigrants include health selection and acculturation. Health selection suggests that healthier and/or more advantaged individuals migrate (Akresh & Frank, 2008). Acculturation-related arguments suggest individuals who migrate adopt the norms and practices of the host culture, which are comparatively unhealthy, and this leads to a worsening of health over time. Neither of these explanations have led to consistent findings and both necessitate further investigation into pre-immigration experiences and contexts into which immigrants settle. Furthermore, a majority of past research has emphasized individual behaviors and focused on attempts to preserve traditional cultural characteristics that might offer protection from weight gain. This approach misses the importance of the forces that shape individual behaviors. However, growing awareness of the importance of the social and physical environment has led to increased efforts to identify and understand the structural forces that shape poorer health outcomes. Strategies should continue to focus on quantifying the effects of structural forces, e.g., food policy and immigration policies, that underlie changes in body composition. In addition, focusing on the characteristics of the setting into which migrants settle and how this increased exposure leads to deterioration of initial health advantages will broaden our understanding of the mechanisms involved. Importantly, this approach redirects efforts at obesity prevention toward the structural causes of poor health.

Methodological Approaches and Challenges

Data availability has limited investigation into the study of obesity among immigrants. For example, the ability to accurately track changing patterns of overweight and obesity prevalence globally is hampered by the fact that longitudinal trends related to obesity prevalence are available for only a handful of countries (Popkin et al., 2012). In the US, several sources of data are available that provide access to numerous measures of health at the individual-level, however these often include limited measures of migration status or history. Conversely, data sources that provide a rich history with respect to the migration process may be limited in their health measures. However, sources of data (e.g. Mexican Family Life Survey) that provide access to migration histories, health outcomes over time, as well as biomarkers are becoming more readily available, and should be increasingly utilized in this type of research.

The vast majority of research on overweight and obesity in immigrants utilizes cross-sectional data, which only provides the ability to examine associations at a single point in time. This type of data is not a reliable means through which to assess the immigration process and its variations over the life course. Cohort analysis is preferred over cross-sectional analyses given that it is better able to investigate risks in one cohort relative to another. Accordingly, some have pointed to the importance of examining cohorts as compositional differences in groups may explain differential outcomes observed on the basis of years spent in the US (e.g. Ro et al., 2015). Longitudinal studies also offer opportunities to better understand how time spent in the US translates into worsening outcomes and how this may vary for different groups. While several studies have examined mortality risk using longitudinal designs, comparatively fewer have used this approach to examine the factors that are associated with weight gain among immigrants. One exception is the work conducted by Albrecht et al. (2015) which combines longitudinal individual-level data with neighborhood characteristics. Their work indicates that new arrivals experienced faster declines and highlighted the importance of the neighborhood context in reducing these effects. Yet, there is an ongoing need to pinpoint the explanatory mechanisms behind this process and to utilize longitudinal data sources that are generalizable. In addition, multilevel studies that can account for the complexity of the processes that contribute to obesity prevalence are also needed. These models can also be useful for modeling longitudinal data. A variety of factors at the individual and contextual level shape obesity-related outcomes, and designs that can account for these varying inputs will be needed, both to determine the relative contributions and to inform meaningful recommendations for improvement.

Another problem that has plagued research in this area relates to a lack of focus on pre- and post-immigration contexts. Accordingly, scholars should increasingly utilize bi- and multinational data to compare the experiences and environment prior to immigration as a way to better understand the importance and relative contribution of changes in these contexts. One noteworthy study used a novel approach to examine the social environment by comparing individuals who were likely to migrate versus those who were not likely to migrate in the pre-immigration environment. These authors illustrated that body composition was not measurably different in future Mexico-US migrants compared to non-migrants and argued that poorer health outcomes in migrants are more likely the product of exposures to social and environmental stressors (Martinez-Cardoso & Geronimus, 2021). Studies such as this contribute to gaps in knowledge surrounding the influence of host country impacts and pre-migration characteristics and additional work of this kind is needed.

Many scholars have called attention to issues with the measurement and conceptualization of acculturation in prior studies (Abraido-Lanza et al., 2016; McLeod et al., 2016), and many of the studies that observe associations with obesity do so on the basis of simplistic measures such as time spent in the U.S. or generational status. This has led to recommendations that surveys and public health practitioners collect more information on acculturation measures (Lara et al., 2005). Several have called for the use of scales and multidimensional measures to provide a clearer understanding of how acculturation may relate to body composition. Increased use of comprehensive measures is needed to continue to disentangle the role of acculturation on health. However, the lack of consistency in findings linking acculturation and weight gain may suggest an overemphasis on this concept. In addition, it has been argued that acculturation may be acting as a proxy for some other concept, such as exposure to discrimination (Abraido-Lanza et al., 2016). Scholars should increasingly attempt to identify underlying factors that may account for this association via mediation analyses. In addition, the use of qualitative data and interdisciplinary approaches may further broaden our understanding of the web of factors that explain this complex association.

Future Research

An understudied area in research on overweight/obesity in immigrants is the examination of mechanisms leading to these outcomes in diverse migrant groups. Most of the studies in migration have concentrated on Latinos. However, an increasingly large proportion of migrants to the United States comes from a diverse mix of countries. One study examined the prevalence of overweight and obesity in immigrants from an array of countries with results suggesting considerable heterogeneity across groups (Commodore-Mensah et al., 2018). However, little is known about initial risk factors, or how social, political, and physical contexts might explain these outcomes. Inconsistent findings across immigrant subgroups suggest the need for continued investigation of the trajectories of various groups as well as their experiences pre-arrival. It is also necessary to differentiate between immigrants who migrate for different reasons. Future studies should consider how reason for migration as well as reception on arrival translates into worsening obesity-related outcomes. More broadly, as the diversity of immigrants continues to expand, it is necessary to conduct ongoing studies of their health profiles that account for the role of both lifestyle and structural factors.

Many have underscored the role of economic factors as a more plausible explanation for rising obesity than cultural explanations. Future work should adequately account for the potentially confounding role of SES in studies that utilize measures of acculturation. Immigrant groups have differential experiences with respect to their success post-immigration. The extent to which some encounter blocked opportunities for advancement should continue to be explored. Studies also need to account for the role of discrimination among immigrants and should increasingly look for ways to adequately capture its effects at the individual and community-level. For example, some studies have utilized socially assigned race as means through which to examine this possibility. Though limited, the work in this area suggests that individuals who are perceived as white have better health status than those who are perceived as minorities (Jones et al., 2008). Ongoing work is needed to determine how experiences of discrimination contribute to worsening health outcomes.

Findings of rapidly deteriorating health among immigrants to the United States underscore the need for ongoing studies of the social environment. The social environment has increasingly become more hostile to immigrants (Viruell-Fuentes et al., 2012), which has the potential to result in an array of negative health outcomes for immigrants. Structural racism manifests in institutions and policies that may worsen exposure to discrimination and other conditions that promote poorer health outcomes. Furthermore, broad policy support for the exclusion of immigrants from social programs and health benefits may exacerbate obesity-related comorbidities as these individuals may delay care and present with more advanced illness. Future work should investigate the extent to which a lack of willingness to extend social safety net access to immigrants will translate into excess costs and higher burdens of morbidity and mortality.

Recently, scholars have called attention to a global syndemic, which refers to the interaction between obesity, climate change, and undernutrition (Swinburn et al., 2019). These authors outline the urgent need for global action on obesity, which has been effectively prevented by powerful commercial interests. They further describe the need for greater recognition of the systemic nature of obesity as it is the outcome of policies and a global food system that lead to malnutrition and climate change. For example, the food system relies on large-scale, agricultural production of commodities, which is designed to maximize the financial benefits of transnational corporations rather than promote the health of societies. This type of intensive agricultural system, in addition to the energy necessary for the transportation and processing of these products, leads to reliance on nutrient-poor, energy-dense foods that simultaneously raise the risk of obesity and malnutrition as well as generate a significant amount of total greenhouse gas emissions (Swinburn et al., 2019). Future work should concentrate on capturing the effects of food policies and linking them with poorer outcomes in order to encourage structural changes.

Recent evidence suggests that nearly all countries are experiencing dramatic shifts in consumption and activity patterns with subsequent increases in obesity (Popkin, 2017; Swinburn et al., 2019). As conditions continue to deteriorate in sending countries, the initial advantage in body composition that has been observed among new immigrants may lessen. On the other hand, increasingly restrictive screening practices tied to COVID-19 and nativist sentiments may enhance selection effects and lead to healthier immigrants. Additional work is needed to investigate these possibilities. In addition, work that emphasizes an ecological approach is necessary to both establish the importance of structural factors and to parse out the competing effects of these two opposing sets of factors.

Conclusion

Demographers have made significant and noteworthy contributions to the study of obesity and immigration. Our understanding of the prevalence, rates of increase, and factors contributing to overweight and obesity in immigrant populations have advanced rapidly in the past few decades. However, there has been a lack of attention to the heterogeneity of immigrant groups. In addition, important questions remain about the mechanisms that lead to worsening body composition with additional time spent in the US, and how this is a product of social, political, and environmental contexts. Population health researchers should increasingly focus their efforts on identifying and understanding the root, or structural, causes of overweight and obesity via the use of multinational data sources and modeling strategies that appropriately account for the longitudinal and multi-level nature of the immigration and weight gain process. Importantly, population researchers are uniquely positioned to leverage perspectives from multiple disciplines to conduct these studies and provide nuanced interpretations of the complex web of factors that surround immigration processes as well as obesity prevalence.

References

Abarca-Gómez, L., Abdeen, Z. A., Hamid, Z. A., Abu-Rmeileh, N. M., Acosta-Cazares, B., Acuin, C., et al. (2017). Worldwide trends in body-mass index, underweight, overweight, and obesity from 1975 to 2016: A pooled analysis of 2416 population-based measurement studies in 128·9 million children, adolescents, and adults. *The Lancet, 390*(10113), 2627–2642. https://doi.org/10.1016/S0140-6736(17)32129-3

Abraído-Lanza, A. F., Chao, M. T., & Flórez, K. R. (2005). Do healthy behaviors decline with greater acculturation?: Implications for the Latino mortality paradox. *Social Science & Medicine, 61*(6), 1243–1255. https://doi.org/10.1016/j.socscimed.2005.01.016

Abraído-Lanza, A. F., Echeverría, S. E., & Flórez, K. R. (2016). Latino immigrants, acculturation, and health: Promising new directions in research. *Annual Review of Public Health, 37*(1), 219–236. https://doi.org/10.1146/annurev-publhealth-032315-021545

Acevedo-Garcia, D., Bates, L. M., Osypuk, T. L., & McArdle, N. (2010). The effect of immigrant generation and duration on self-rated health among US adults 2003–2007. *Social Science & Medicine, 71*(6), 1161–1172. https://doi.org/10.1016/j.socscimed.2010.05.034

Akresh, I. R. (2007). Dietary assimilation and health among Hispanic immigrants to the United States. *Journal of Health and Social Behavior, 48*(4), 404–417. https://doi.org/10.1177/002214650704800405

Akresh, I. R., & Frank, R. (2008). Health selection among new immigrants. *American Journal of Public Health, 98*(11), 2058–2064. https://doi.org/10.2105/ajph.2006.100974

Alaimo, K., Chilton, M., & Jones, S. J. (2020). Chapter 17 – Food insecurity, hunger, and malnutrition. In B. P. Marriott, D. F. Birt, V. A. Stallings, & A. A. Yates (Eds.), *Present knowledge in nutrition* (11th ed., pp. 311–326). Academic.

Albrecht, S. S., Osypuk, T. L., Kandula, N. R., Gallo, L. C., Lê-Scherban, F., Shrager, S., & Diez Roux, A. V. (2015). Change in waist circumference with longer time in the United States among Hispanic and Chinese immigrants: The modifying role of the neighborhood built environment. *Annals of Epidemiology, 25*(10), 767–772.e762. https://doi.org/10.1016/j.annepidem.2015.07.003

Aldrich, L., & Variyam, J. N. (2000). Acculturation erodes the diet quality of U.S. Hispanics. *Food Review (Washington, DC), 23*(1), 51–55.

Antecol, H., & Bedard, K. (2006). Unhealthy assimilation: Why do immigrants converge to American health status levels? *Demography, 43*(2), 337–360.

Bakhtiari, E. (2021). Migration and health. In W. C. Cockerham (Ed.), *The Wiley Blackwell companion to medical sociology*. Wiley.

Barcenas, C. H., Wilkinson, A. V., Strom, S. S., Cao, Y., Saunders, K. C., Mahabir, S., et al. (2007). Birthplace, years of residence in the United States, and obesity among Mexican-American adults. *Obesity, 15*(4), 1043–1052. https://doi.org/10.1038/oby.2007.537

Bates, L. M. S. D. S. M., Acevedo-Garcia, D. P. M. P. A. U. R. P., Alegría, M. P., & Krieger, N. P. (2008). Immigration and generational trends in body mass index and obesity in the United States: Results of the National Latino and Asian American Survey, 2002-2003. *American Journal of Public Health, 98*(1), 70–77.

Batis, C., Hernandez-Barrera, L., Barquera, S., Rivera, J. A., & Popkin, B. M. (2011). Food acculturation drives dietary differences among Mexicans, Mexican Americans, and Non-Hispanic Whites. *The Journal of Nutrition, 141*(10), 1898–1906. https://doi.org/10.3945/jn.111.141473

Black, J. L., & Macinko, J. (2008). Neighborhoods and obesity. *Nutrition Reviews, 66*(1), 2–20. https://doi.org/10.1111/j.1753-4887.2007.00001.x

Boardman, J. D., Onge, J. M. S., Rogers, R. G., & Denney, J. T. (2005). Race differentials in obesity: The impact of place. *Journal of Health and Social Behavior, 46*(3), 229–243. https://doi.org/10.1177/002214650504600302

Bostean, G. (2013). Does selective migration explain the Hispanic paradox? A comparative analysis of Mexicans in the U.S. and Mexico. *Journal of Immigrant and Minority Health, 15*(3), 624–635. https://doi.org/10.1007/s10903-012-9646-y

Broesch, J., & Hadley, C. (2012). Putting culture back into acculturation: Identifying and overcoming gaps in the definition and measurement of acculturation. *The Social Science Journal, 49*(3), 375–385. https://doi.org/10.1016/j.soscij.2012.02.004

Cabassa, L. J. (2003). Measuring acculturation: Where we are and where we need to go. *Hispanic Journal of*

Behavioral Sciences, 25(2), 127–146. https://doi.org/10.1177/0739986303025002001

Canizales, S. L., & Vallejo, J. A. (2021). Latinos & racism in the Trump era. *Daedalus, 150*(2), 150–164. https://doi.org/10.1162/daed_a_01852

Chaparro, M. P., Langellier, B. A., Wang, M. C., Koleilat, M., & Whaley, S. E. (2014). Effects of parental nativity and length of stay in the US on fruit and vegetable intake among WIC-enrolled preschool-aged children. *Journal of Immigrant and Minority Health, 17*(2), 333–338. https://doi.org/10.1007/s10903-014-0097-5

Choi, J. Y. (2011). Prevalence of overweight and obesity among US immigrants: Results of the 2003 New Immigrant Survey. *Journal of Immigrant and Minority Health, 14*(6), 1112–1118. https://doi.org/10.1007/s10903-011-9560-8

Commodore-Mensah, Y., Selvin, E., Aboagye, J., Turkson-Ocran, R.-A., Li, X., Himmelfarb, C. D., et al. (2018). Hypertension, overweight/obesity, and diabetes among immigrants in the United States: An analysis of the 2010-2016 National Health Interview Survey. *BMC Public Health, 18*(1), 773–773. https://doi.org/10.1186/s12889-018-5683-3

Creighton, M. J., Goldman, N., Pebley, A. R., & Chung, C. Y. (2012). Durational and generational differences in Mexican immigrant obesity: Is acculturation the explanation? *Social Science & Medicine, 75*(2), 300–310. https://doi.org/10.1016/j.socscimed.2012.03.013

Cunningham, S. A., Ruben, J. D., & Venkat Narayan, K. M. (2008). Health of foreign-born people in the United States: A review. *Health & Place, 14*(4), 623–635. https://doi.org/10.1016/j.healthplace.2007.12.002

D'Alonzo, K. T., Johnson, S., & Fanfan, D. (2012). A biobehavioral approach to understanding obesity and the development of obesogenic illnesses among Latino immigrants in the United States. *Biological Research for Nursing, 14*(4), 364–374. https://doi.org/10.1177/1099800412457017

Delavari, M., Sønderlund, A. L., Swinburn, B., Mellor, D., & Renzaho, A. (2013). Acculturation and obesity among migrant populations in high income countries – A systematic review. *BMC Public Health, 13*(1), 458. https://doi.org/10.1186/1471-2458-13-458

Dubowitz, T., Subramanian, S. V., Acevedo-Garcia, D., Osypuk, T. L., & Peterson, K. E. (2008). Individual and neighborhood differences in diet among low-income foreign and U.S.-born women. *Women's Health Issues, 18*(3), 181–190. https://doi.org/10.1016/j.whi.2007.11.001

Eschbach, K., Ostir, G. V., Patel, K. V., Markides, K. S., & Goodwin, J. S. (2004). Neighborhood context and mortality among older Mexican Americans: Is there a barrio advantage? *American Journal of Public Health, 94*(10), 1807–1812.

Fenelon, A. (2017). Rethinking the Hispanic paradox: The mortality experience of Mexican immigrants in traditional gateways and new destinations. *International Migration Review, 51*(3), 567–599. https://doi.org/10.1111/imre.12263

Franzini, L., Ribble, J. C., & Keddie, A. M. (2001). Understanding the Hispanic paradox. *Ethnicity & Disease, 11*(3), 496–518.

Fryar, C. D., Carroll, M. D., & Afful, J. (2020). Prevalence of overweight, obesity, and severe obesity among adults aged 20 and over: United States, 1960–1962 through 2017–2018. *NCHS Health E-Stats*. Retrieved from https://www.cdc.gov/nchs/data/hestat/obesity-adult-17-18/obesity-adult.htm

Geier, A. B., & Brownell, K. D. (2006). Acknowledging and reversing the toxic environment. In M. K. Robinson & A. Thomas (Eds.), *Obesity and cardiovascular disease* (pp. 449–466). CRC Press.

Giuntella, O., Kone, Z. L., Ruiz, I., & Vargas-Silva, C. (2018). Reason for immigration and immigrants' health. *Public Health, 158*, 102–109. https://doi.org/10.1016/j.puhe.2018.01.037

Goel, M., McCarthy, E., Phillips, R., & Wee, C. (2004). Obesity among US immigrant subgroups by duration of residence. *JAMA, 292*(23), 2860–2867. https://doi.org/10.1001/jama.292.23.2860

Gordon, M. M. (1964). *Assimilation in American life: The role of race, religion, and national origins*. Oxford University Press on Demand.

Gordon-Larsen, P., Harris, K. M., Ward, D. S., & Popkin, B. M. (2003). Acculturation and overweight-related behaviors among Hispanic immigrants to the US: The National Longitudinal Study of Adolescent Health. *Social Science & Medicine, 57*(11), 2023–2034.

Gorman, B. K., Novoa, C., & Kimbro, R. T. (2016). Migration decisions, acculturation, and overweight among Asian and Latino immigrant adults in the United States. *International Migration Review, 50*(3), 728–757. https://doi.org/10.1111/imre.12168

Grafova, I. B. P., Freedman, V. A. P., Kumar, R. M. A., & Rogowski, J. P. (2008). Neighborhoods and obesity in later life. *American Journal of Public Health, 98*(11), 2065–2071.

Hao, L., & Kim, J. J. H. (2009). Immigration and the American obesity epidemic. *International Migration Review, 43*(2), 237–262. https://doi.org/10.1111/j.1747-7379.2009.00764.x

Hout, M., & Maggio, C. (2021). Immigration, race & political polarization. *Daedalus, 150*(2), 40–55. https://doi.org/10.1162/daed_a_01845

Hummer, R. A., Powers, D. A., Pullum, S. G., Gossman, G. L., & Frisbie, W. P. (2007). Paradox found (again): Infant mortality among the Mexican-origin population in the United States. *Demography, 44*(3), 441–457. https://doi.org/10.1353/dem.2007.0028

Hunt, L. M., Schneider, S., & Comer, B. (2004). Should "acculturation" be a variable in health research? A critical review of research on US Hispanics. *Social Science & Medicine, 59*(5), 973–986. https://doi.org/10.1016/j.socscimed.2003.12.009

Isasi, C. R., Ayala, G. X., Sotres-Alvarez, D., Madanat, H., Penedo, F., Loria, C. M., et al. (2015). Is acculturation related to obesity in Hispanic/Latino adults? Results from the Hispanic Community Health Study/Study of Latinos. *Journal of Obesity, 2015*, 186276. https://doi.org/10.1155/2015/186276

Jones, C. P., Truman, B. I., Elam-Evans, L. D., Jones, C. A., Jones, C. Y., Jiles, R., et al. (2008). Using "socially assigned race" to probe white advantages in health status. *Ethnicity & Disease, 18*(4), 496–504.

Joy, E. J. M., Green, R., Agrawal, S., Aleksandrowicz, L., Bowen, L., Kinra, S., et al. (2017). Dietary patterns and non-communicable disease risk in Indian adults: Secondary analysis of Indian Migration Study data. *Public Health Nutrition, 20*(11), 1963–1972. https://doi.org/10.1017/S1368980017000416

Kang, S., Kang, M., & Lim, H. (2021). Global and regional patterns in noncommunicable diseases and dietary factors across national income levels. *Nutrients, 13*(10), 3595. https://doi.org/10.3390/nu13103595

Kaplan, M. S., Huguet, N., Newsom, J. T., & McFarland, B. H. (2004). The association between length of residence and obesity among Hispanic immigrants. *American Journal of Preventive Medicine, 27*(4), 323–326. https://doi.org/10.1016/j.amepre.2004.07.005

Kaushal, N. (2009). Adversities of acculturation? Prevalence of obesity among immigrants. *Health Economics, 18*(3), 291–303. https://doi.org/10.1002/hec.1368

Kennedy, S., Kidd, M. P., McDonald, J. T., & Biddle, N. (2015). The healthy immigrant effect: Patterns and evidence from four countries. *Journal of International Migration and Integration, 16*(2), 317–332. https://doi.org/10.1007/s12134-014-0340-x

Kershaw, K. N., Albrecht, S. S., & Carnethon, M. R. (2013). Racial and ethnic residential segregation, the neighborhood socioeconomic environment, and obesity among blacks and Mexican Americans. *American Journal of Epidemiology, 177*(4), 299–309. https://doi.org/10.1093/aje/kws372

Lara, M., Gamboa, C., Kahramanian, M. I., Morales, L. S., & Bautista, D. E. H. (2005). Acculturation and Latino health in the United States: A review of the literature and its sociopolitical context. *Annual Review of Public Health, 26*(1), 367–397. https://doi.org/10.1146/annurev.publhealth.26.021304.144615

Lê-Scherban, F., Albrecht, S. S., Osypuk, T. L., Sánchez, B. N., & Diez Roux, A. V. (2019). Long-term neighborhood ethnic composition and weight-related outcomes among immigrants: The Multi-Ethnic Study of Atherosclerosis. *Health & Place, 58*, 102147. https://doi.org/10.1016/j.healthplace.2019.102147

Liu, A., Berhane, Z., & Tseng, M. (2010). Improved dietary variety and adequacy but lower dietary moderation with acculturation in Chinese women in the United States. *Journal of the American Dietetic Association, 110*(3), 457–462. https://doi.org/10.1016/j.jada.2009.11.016

Markides, K. S., & Coreil, J. (1986). The health of Hispanics in the southwestern United States: An epidemiologic paradox. *Public Health Reports (1974), 101*(3), 253–265.

Markides, K. S., & Eschbach, K. (2005). Aging, migration, and mortality: Current status of research on the Hispanic paradox. *The Journals of Gerontology: Series B, 60*(Special_Issue_2), S68–S75. https://doi.org/10.1093/geronb/60.Special_Issue_2.S68

Markides, K. S., & Eschbach, K. (2011). Hispanic paradox in adult mortality in the United States. In *International handbook of adult mortality* (pp. 227–240). Springer Netherlands.

Martinez-Cardoso, A. M., & Geronimus, A. T. (2021). The weight of migration: Reconsidering health selection and return migration among Mexicans. *International Journal of Environmental Research and Public Health, 18*(22), 12136. https://doi.org/10.3390/ijerph182212136

Massey, D. S. (2021). The bipartisan origins of white nationalism. *Daedalus, 150*(2), 5–22. https://doi.org/10.1162/daed_a_01843

McLeod, D. L., Buscemi, J., & Bohnert, A. M. (2016). Becoming American, becoming obese? A systematic review of acculturation and weight among Latino youth. *Obesity Reviews, 17*(11), 1040–1049. https://doi.org/10.1111/obr.12447

Migration Policy Institute (MPI). (2021). *U.S. immigration trends*. Retrieved from https://www.migrationpolicy.org/programs/data-hub/us-immigration-trends#source

Molina, N. (2011). Borders, laborers, and racialized medicalization Mexican immigration and US public health practices in the 20th century. *American Journal of Public Health (1971), 101*(6), 1024–1031. https://doi.org/10.2105/AJPH.2010.300056

Nobari, T. Z., Wang, M.-C., Chaparro, M. P., Crespi, C. M., Koleilat, M., & Whaley, S. E. (2013). Immigrant enclaves and obesity in preschool-aged children in Los Angeles County. *Social Science & Medicine, 1982*(92), 1–8. https://doi.org/10.1016/j.socscimed.2013.05.019

Ortega, A. N., Rodriguez, H. P., & Bustamante, A. V. (2015). Policy dilemmas in Latino health care and implementation of the affordable care act. *Annual Review of Public Health, 36*(1), 525–544. https://doi.org/10.1146/annurev-publhealth-031914-122421

Osypuk, T. L., Diez Roux, A. V., Hadley, C., & Kandula, N. R. (2009). Are immigrant enclaves healthy places to live? The Multi-ethnic Study of Atherosclerosis. *Social Science & Medicine (1982), 69*(1), 110–120. https://doi.org/10.1016/j.socscimed.2009.04.010

Oza-Frank, R., & Cunningham, S. A. (2010). The weight of US residence among immigrants: A systematic review. *Obesity Reviews, 11*(4), 271–280. https://doi.org/10.1111/j.1467-789X.2009.00610.x

Oza-Frank, R., & Narayan, K. M. V. (2010). Overweight and diabetes prevalence among US immigrants. *American Journal of Public Health, 100*(4), 661–668. https://doi.org/10.2105/AJPH.2008.149492

Palloni, A., & Arias, E. (2004). Paradox lost: Explaining the Hispanic adult mortality advantage. *Demography, 41*(3), 385–415. https://doi.org/10.1353/dem.2004.0024

Perreira, K. M., & Pedroza, J. M. (2019). Policies of exclusion: Implications for the health of immigrants and their children. *Annual Review of Public Health, 40*(1), 147–166. https://doi.org/10.1146/annurev-publhealth-040218-044115

Popkin, B. M. (2006). Global nutrition dynamics: The world is shifting rapidly toward a diet linked with noncommunicable diseases. *The American Journal of Clinical Nutrition, 84*(2), 289–298. https://doi.org/10.1093/ajcn/84.2.289

Popkin, B. M. (2017). Relationship between shifts in food system dynamics and acceleration of the global nutrition transition. *Nutrition Reviews, 75*(2), 73–82. https://doi.org/10.1093/nutrit/nuw064

Popkin, B. M., & Udry, J. R. (1998). Adolescent obesity increases significantly in second and third generation U.S. immigrants: The National Longitudinal Study of Adolescent Health. *The Journal of Nutrition, 128*(4), 701–706. https://doi.org/10.1093/jn/128.4.701

Popkin, B. M., Adair, L. S., & Ng, S. W. (2012). Global nutrition transition and the pandemic of obesity in developing countries. *Nutrition Reviews, 70*(1), 3–21. https://doi.org/10.1111/j.1753-4887.2011.00456.x

Portes, A., & Rumbaut, R. G. (2006). *Immigrant America: A portrait*. University of California Press.

Portes, A., & Zhou, M. (1993). The new second generation: Segmented assimilation and its variants. *The Annals of the American Academy of Political and Social Science, 530*(1), 74–96. https://doi.org/10.1177/0002716293530001006

Prentice, A. M. (2006). The emerging epidemic of obesity in developing countries. *International Journal of Epidemiology, 35*(1), 93–99.

Riosmena, F., Kuhn, R., & Jochem, W. C. (2017). Explaining the immigrant health advantage: Self-selection and protection in health-related factors among five major national-origin immigrant groups in the United States. *Demography, 54*(1), 175–200. https://doi.org/10.1007/s13524-016-0542-2

Rivera, J. A., Barquera, S., González-Cossío, T., Olaiz, G., & Sepúlveda, J. (2004). Nutrition transition in Mexico and in other Latin American countries. *Nutrition Reviews, 62*(suppl_2), S149–S157. https://doi.org/10.1111/j.1753-4887.2004.tb00086.x

Ro, A., Geronimus, A., Bound, J., Griffith, D., & Gee, G. (2015). Cohort and duration patterns among Asian immigrants: Comparing trends in obesity and self-rated health. *Biodemography and Social Biology, 61*(1), 65–80. https://doi.org/10.1080/19485565.2014.950721

Ruiz, J. M. P., Steffen, P. P., & Smith, T. B. P. (2013). Hispanic mortality paradox: A systematic review and meta-analysis of the longitudinal literature. *American Journal of Public Health, 103*(3), E52–E60.

Ryan-Ibarra, S., Sanchez-Vaznaugh, E. V., Leung, C., & Induni, M. (2017). The relationship between food insecurity and overweight/obesity differs by birthplace and length of US residence. *Public Health Nutrition, 20*(4), 671–677. https://doi.org/10.1017/S1368980016002858

Satia-Abouta, J., Patterson, R. E., Neuhouser, M. L., & Elder, J. (2002). Dietary acculturation: Applications to nutrition research and dietetics. *Journal of the American Dietetic Association, 102*(8), 1105–1118. https://doi.org/10.1016/S0002-8223(02)90247-6

Singh, G. K., Siahpush, M., Hiatt, R. A., & Timsina, L. R. (2011). Dramatic increases in obesity and overweight prevalence and body mass index among ethnic-immigrant and social class groups in the United States, 1976–2008. *Journal of Community Health, 36*(1), 94–110. https://doi.org/10.1007/s10900-010-9287-9

Soto, S. H., Arredondo, E. M., Marcus, B., Shakya, H. B., Roesch, S., & Ayala, G. X. (2017). Effects of Latino children on their mothers' dietary intake and dietary behaviors: The role of children's acculturation and the mother-child acculturation gap. *Social Science & Medicine, 1982*(191), 125–133. https://doi.org/10.1016/j.socscimed.2017.09.004

Sturm, R., & An, R. (2014). Obesity and economic environments. *CA: A Cancer Journal for Clinicians, 64*(5), 337–350. https://doi.org/10.3322/caac.21237

Swinburn, B., Egger, G., & Raza, F. (1999). Dissecting obesogenic environments: The development and application of a framework for identifying and prioritizing environmental interventions for obesity. *Preventive Medicine, 29*(6), 563–570. https://doi.org/10.1006/pmed.1999.0585

Swinburn, B. A., Kraak, V. I., Allender, S., Atkins, V. J., Baker, P. I., Bogard, J. R., et al. (2019). The global syndemic of obesity, undernutrition, and climate change: The Lancet Commission report. *The Lancet, 393*(10173), 791–846. https://doi.org/10.1016/S0140-6736(18)32822-8

Turra, C. M., & Elo, I. T. (2008). The impact of salmon bias on the Hispanic mortality advantage: New evidence from social security data. *Population Research and Policy Review, 27*(5), 515–530. https://doi.org/10.1007/s11113-008-9087-4

United Nations (UN) Department of Economic and Social Affairs, Population Division. (2020). *International migration 2020 highlights* (ST/ESA/SER.A/452).

Van Hook, J., Baker, E., Altman, C. E., & Frisco, M. L. (2012). Canaries in a coalmine: Immigration and overweight among Mexican-origin children in the US and Mexico. *Social Science & Medicine (1982), 74*(2), 125–134. https://doi.org/10.1016/j.socscimed.2011.10.007

Van Hook, J., Quiros, S., & Frisco, M. L. (2014). The food similarity index: A new measure of dietary acculturation based on dietary recall data. *Journal of Immigrant and Minority Health, 17*(2), 441–449. https://doi.org/10.1007/s10903-014-0107-7

Van Hook, J., Quiros, S., Frisco, M. L., & Fikru, E. (2016). It is hard to swim upstream: Dietary acculturation among Mexican-origin children. *Population Research and Policy Review, 35*(2), 177–196. https://doi.org/10.1007/s11113-015-9381-x

Viruell-Fuentes, E. A., Miranda, P. Y., & Abdulrahim, S. (2012). More than culture: Structural racism, intersectionality theory, and immigrant health. *Social Science & Medicine, 75*(12), 2099–2106. https://doi.org/10.1016/j.socscimed.2011.12.037

Wen, M., & Maloney, T. N. (2011). Latino residential isolation and the risk of obesity in Utah: The role of neighborhood socioeconomic, built-environmental, and subcultural context. *Journal of Immigrant and Minority Health, 13*(6), 1134–1141. https://doi.org/10.1007/s10903-011-9439-8

Williams, D. R., & Mohammed, S. A. (2013). Racism and health I: Pathways and scientific evidence. *The American Behavioral Scientist (Beverly Hills), 57*(8), 1152–1173. https://doi.org/10.1177/0002764213487340

World Health Organization (WHO). (2022). *Double burden of malnutrition.* Retrieved from https://apps.who.int/nutrition/double-burden-malnutrition/en/#:~:text=The%20double%20burden%20of%20malnutrition,populations%2C%20and%20across%20the%20lifecourse

Zambrana, R. E., & Carter-Pokras, O. (2010). Role of acculturation research in advancing science and practice in reducing health care disparities among Latinos. *American Journal of Public Health, 100*(1), 18–23. https://doi.org/10.2105/ajph.2008.138826

8 Racial and Ethnic Disparities in U.S. Obesity Prevalence: What Have We Learned from Demographic and Population Health Science?

Michelle L. Frisco, Kelsey Shaulis, Jennifer Van Hook, and Robert A. Hummer

Introduction

United States (U.S.) adults are the heaviest in comparison with adults in all other Organization for Economic Co-operation and Development (OECD) countries (Organization for Economic Co-operation and Development, 2017). The most recent estimates based on measured assessments of height and weight, which are used to compute weight categories based on body mass index (BMI), indicate that 42.4% of all U.S. adults have BMIs of 30 or above and are therefore considered obese (Hales et al., 2020). Nineteen percent of all U.S. children are also classified as obese based on their BMI percentile (Fryar et al., 2020). These estimates pre-date the Covid-19 pandemic, which early evidence suggests further increased weight for many Americans and might exacerbate the U.S. obesity prevalence (Bhutani et al., 2021; Zachary et al., 2020).

These obesity estimates are higher than ever before recorded and have increased fourfold or even more over the past half-century (Parikh et al., 2007; Sabin et al., 2015). This trend is concerning because obesity is one of the leading causes of premature mortality and disability in the U.S. (Al Snih et al., 2007, Censin et al., 2019; National Academies of Sciences and Medicine, 2021). Moreover, obesity is not equally distributed across U.S. subpopulations. There are wide racial and ethnic disparities in the obesity risk of U.S. women, men and children.

According to the most recent estimates based on data from the 2017–2018 National Health and Nutrition Examination Survey (NHANES), racial/ethnic differences in obesity are especially large among women. The age-adjusted obesity prevalence among non-Hispanic white women is 39.8%, while the age-adjusted obesity prevalence among Black and Hispanic women is significantly higher. More than half (56.9%) of Black women and 43.7% of Hispanic women in the U.S. are obese (Hales et al., 2020). Asian American women have the lowest obesity prevalence, with 17.2% estimated to be obese.

The most recent NHANES estimates for men find that disparities in the age-adjusted obesity prevalence are especially wide when white men (44.7%) and Asian American men (17.5%) are compared, but much narrower when white men are compared to Hispanic (45.7%) and Black (41.1%) men (Hales et al., 2020). Moreover, differences between Black and white men are not statistically significant.

NHANES estimates of racial/ethnic differences in childhood obesity follow similar

M. L. Frisco (✉) · K. Shaulis · J. Van Hook
Department of Sociology & Criminology, The Pennsylvania State University, University Park, PA, USA
e-mail: mlf112@psu.edu

R. A. Hummer
Department of Sociology, University of North Carolina at Chapel Hill, Chapel Hill, NC, USA

G. Garcia-Alexander, D. L. Poston, Jr. (eds.), *International Handbook of the Demography of Obesity*, International Handbooks of Population 12, https://doi.org/10.1007/978-3-031-10936-2_8

patterns, with the prevalence of obesity lowest among Asian American children ages 2–19 and highest among Hispanics in this age range. While 8.7% of Asian American children are considered obese, the percentages for white children (16.2%), Black children (24.2%), and Hispanic children (25.6%) are much higher (Fryar et al., 2020). This study also finds that there is very little difference in the prevalence of obesity between white boys and girls and between Hispanic boys and girls, but there is a relatively large gap in the percentage of obese Black boys (19.4%) versus girls (29.1%).

The increase in the obesity prevalence over the last five decades and the substantial racial/ethnic inequities in obesity prevalence have led to a wide body of research aimed at better understanding both phenomena. This research has been conducted by scholars across many disciplinary fields. In this review, we focus attention on some of the most important contributions that demographers and population health researchers have made to knowledge about racial/ethnic disparities in obesity during the last two decades.

These contributions include the advancement of conceptual models that help to explain why racial and ethnic disparities in obesity have arisen (e.g., Glass & McAtee, 2006; Mirowsky & Ross, 2015; Phelan & Link, 2015) and a substantial body of research on the risk of obesity among Hispanics in the U.S., including the important roles that nativity, acculturation, and low socioeconomic status have in shaping Hispanics' obesity risk. Further, we spend considerable time reviewing research aimed at understanding Black women's high obesity risk and we review research that indicates that not all Asian American groups exhibit similar levels of obesity. We also address a new and bourgeoning body of research on how obesity shapes racial and ethnic disparities in longevity. We conclude by discussing ongoing issues and challenges for demographers and population health researchers who want to further advance scholarship on racial/ethnic disparities in obesity and propose areas for future research direction.

The Obesogenic Nature of the U.S. Society and Its Implications for Racial/Ethnic Disparities in Obesity

Demographers and population health scientists largely view population-level trends in obesity risk as driven by macrolevel changes in human environments. For example, the expansion of highly efficient food production and distribution systems since World War II have enabled food producers to inundate the U.S. with large quantities of inexpensive calorie-dense food (Popkin, 2008). The result is that the U.S. food environment is characterized by an overabundance of foods of minimal nutritional value (Nestle, 2002). These changes constrain and shape people's eating behavior and have led to dramatic shifts in diet and the prevalence of obesity and obesity-related morbidity. Also contributing to the obesogenic nature of the U.S. are large declines in physical activity that are a function of the changing nature of work, suburbanization, and leisure activities (Brownson et al., 2005).

Mirowsky and Ross (2015) argue that these changes in diet and physical activity have resulted in a "default American lifestyle" and that recognizing its risks is important for health. They argue that education is critical for avoiding the default American lifestyle and the health risks that come with it. Other scholars apply similar ideas to disparities in obesity that fall along the lines of race, ethnicity and nativity (e.g., Frisco et al., 2016).

Glass and McAtee (2006) also address uneven risks of the macroenvironment for health with their conception of "risk regulators" that constrain and alter the costs and benefits of health behaviors related to diet, physical activity, stress, and sleep, ultimately making it more difficult for some people to maintain health than others. In the case of U.S. racial/ethnic inequities in obesity, demographers and population health scientists implicate structural disadvantages that arise due to factors such as racism, social isolation and low socioeconomic status as important risk regulators. Even for health behaviors that seem to involve personal choice, such as food preferences, structural factors loom large, as we discuss in more detail below.

Demographers and population health researchers are also quick to point out that racial/ethnic disparities in obesity can only be fully understood with explicit acknowledgement that race and ethnicity are not biological constructs. Instead, they are social constructs with shared meaning that reflect differences in power and relations that change across time (Waters, 2002). As such, the disparate obesity risks faced by men, women, and children in different racial/ethnic groups largely reflect patterns of inequality in the U.S. that arise because of the U.S. social structure and the way that racial/ethnic groups are situated within it.

Obesity Among U.S. Hispanics

Disparities in obesity between U.S. Hispanics and whites have been studied extensively by demographers and population health researchers for two primary reasons. Hispanics are at higher risk of obesity than white peers and this disparity runs counter to typical patterns of the epidemiological paradox, which is also known as the Hispanic health paradox. Generally, Hispanics live longer and have many health outcomes that are better than U.S.-born whites and Blacks despite their lower socioeconomic status (Hamilton, 2015; Markides & Coreil, 1986).

The Hispanic health paradox recognizes that foreign-born and U.S.-born Hispanics both have longer life expectancies than U.S.-born whites, but immigrants are especially advantaged. Thus, an early line of investigation on Hispanic-white obesity disparities focused on immigrants. Following one of the first nationally representative studies to show that in general, immigrants had a lower obesity risk than U.S.-born adults (Goel et al., 2004), several studies corroborated this finding among Hispanic adults across multiple surveys including the National Health Interview Survey (NHIS) (Antecol & Bedard, 2006), comparisons of respondents in the New Immigrant Survey and NHANES (Akresh, 2008), and the 2002–2003 National Latino and Asian American Survey (NLAAS) (Bates et al., 2008).

Riosmena et al. (2013) went on to show that among Mexican-origin adults, U.S.-born Mexicans were significantly more likely to be obese than U.S.-born whites, but Mexican immigrants were not. In fact, when return migrants were accounted for, Mexican immigrants had a *lower* obesity prevalence than U.S.-born whites. This fits with other research that finds that despite increasing obesity prevalence in Mexico, obesity has not increased among U.S. Mexican immigrants (Ro & Fleischer, 2014). Rather, Mexican immigrants are significantly less likely to be obese than Mexican nationals who remain in Mexico. This finding is consistent with the "healthy migrant effect" whereby healthier people with lower obesity prevalence are more likely to be selected into migration streams.

Research also suggests that disparities in the obesity prevalence between Hispanic immigrants and U.S.-born Hispanics have widened over time (Krueger et al., 2014; Park et al., 2009), a trend evident in subgroups of Mexican-origin, Cuban-origin and Puerto-Rican[1] origin adults (Krueger et al., 2014). This is at least in part due to birth cohort changes in the risk of obesity. Across 10-year birth cohorts born between 1920 and 1990, the prevalence of obesity among Hispanic immigrants and U.S.-born whites are quite similar, but the obesity prevalence of U.S.-born Hispanics becomes significantly higher than both previously mentioned groups among cohorts born after 1950 (Van Hook et al., 2020).

Weight *gain* is also higher for U.S.-born Hispanic adults than foreign-born Hispanics. Analysis of the Los Angeles Family and Neighborhood Survey (L.A. FANS) found that U.S.-born Hispanic women gain more weight between survey waves (a 6–8 year period) than their foreign-born female peers and U.S.-born white women (Ullmann et al., 2013). A similar pattern is

[1] We recognize that Puerto Ricans born in Puerto Rico are U.S. nationals and U.S. citizens but use the term "immigrant" to distinguish those born in the mainland U.S. and the commonwealth of Puerto Rico.

observed for men, but differences between U.S.-born and foreign-born Hispanic men are not statistically significant.

In analyses of nationally representative data where generational status and ethnicity are evaluated separately, weight gain during the transition from adolescence to adulthood is slower for immigrants, net of race/ethnicity, and Hispanics tend to gain weight faster than whites (Harris et al., 2009). Thus, it is unsurprising that analyses of the same data source found that foreign-born Hispanics tend to gain weight more slowly than U.S.-born Hispanics, but the foreign-born advantage is not as large for Hispanics relative to other ethnic subgroups (Jackson, 2011).

In summary, studies on ethnicity, nativity, generational status and body weight among adults suggest that the prevalence and trends in obesity among Hispanics are not entirely inconsistent with the Hispanic health paradox. On average, Hispanic immigrants continue to have a health advantage. It is U.S.-born Hispanics who are particularly vulnerable to obesity.

Among Hispanic children, research has also investigated differences in the obesity risk of children by generational status and parental nativity. Some studies find that first-generation Hispanic adolescents are as lean as whites and leaner than second- and third-generation co-ethnic peers (Popkin & Udry, 1998) because of differences in acculturation, diet and physical (in)activity (Gordon-Larsen et al., 2003). Other studies of younger children with at least one immigrant parent (not exclusively Hispanic) find them to be more vulnerable to obesity than children of U.S.-born parents (Baker et al., 2015, Balistreri & Van Hook, 2011; Van Hook & Baker, 2010). Yet other studies find no generational differences in obesity among children and adolescents (Buttenheim et al., 2013, Hamilton et al., 2011, Li et al., 2011; Liu et al., 2009).

One reason for this mixed evidence is the different data sources analyzed across studies. Another reason is that sex, generational status, and age intersect in ways that shape Hispanic children's obesity risk. Evidence from studies using multiple data sources indicate that boys in immigrant households are particularly vulnerable to obesity (Balistreri & Van Hook, 2011, Frisco et al., 2016; Van Hook & Baker, 2010).

Moreover, among Mexican-origin youth, first- and second-generation girls have a much lower obesity risk than first- and second-generation boys and Mexican-origin girls in immigrant households face no greater risk of obesity than U.S.-born white girls; only third-plus generation Mexican-origin girls have a higher obesity risk than their white U.S.-born peers (Frisco et al., 2016). This sharply contrasts with the risk of obesity observed for *all* Mexican-origin boys regardless of generational status. They are more likely to be obese than other groups, with gaps between whites and both first- and second-generation boys that widen substantially between the ages of 3 and 12 (Frisco et al., 2016).

A prevailing explanation for the heightened obesity risk of U.S.-born Hispanic adults and male children of immigrants is acculturation. It is generally associated with the adoption of an American-style diet (Van Hook et al., 2015). Hispanic immigrants tend to bring customs and traditions of their country of origin to the U.S.—including those around food—and this lack of acculturation helps to protect Hispanic immigrants from obesity (Abraído-Lanza et al., 2006) whereas the adoption of an Americanized diet typical of the "default American lifestyle" is associated with weight gain and obesity among Hispanics (Frisco et al., 2019b).

The importance of acculturation is supported by studies finding that BMI and the risk of obesity increases as duration of U.S. residence increases (Akresh, 2008; Antecol & Bedard, 2006; Kaplan et al., 2004; Sanchez-Vaznaugh et al., 2008). Additionally, lower levels of acculturation among girls may underlie the low obesity prevalence observed among Mexican-origin girls (Frisco et al., 2016). Girls in Mexican-origin immigrant families grow up in more protected environments than boys (Bean et al., 2015), and girls in immigrant households have more limited personal freedom and more familial responsibilities than boys (Bean et al., 2015; Valenzuela, 1999). Conversely, boys in immigrant households more freely interact with peers and nonfamilial social institutions (Martinez, 1999).

Nevertheless, the idea that acculturation alone leads to unhealthy eating has been criticized for underemphasizing the stress and hazards associated with many immigrants' low socioeconomic status, discrimination, and work (Viruell-Fuentes et al., 2012). Indeed, acculturation for Hispanics often occurs in the context of socioeconomic disadvantage. One study of adults showed that even though weight disparities between Mexican Americans and Mexican immigrants are due almost entirely to Mexican American's greater acculturation, Mexican Americans' low socioeconomic status drives disparities in weight between them and whites by increasing stress and unhealthy eating (Frisco et al., 2019b). In addition, among Mexican-origin children, those with U.S.-born parents had less healthy diets than those in immigrant households, but only among children in families with lower socioeconomic status (Martin et al., 2015).

Further muddying the water on whether and how acculturation shapes obesity risk is research showing that children of immigrants who had less exposure to the U.S. are *more* likely to experience early and sustained overweight throughout elementary and middle school, particularly among boys (Balistreri & Van Hook, 2011) and that boys with parents raised outside of the U.S. are particularly heavy and prone to weight gain (Van Hook & Baker, 2010). The authors of these studies speculate that this is because less acculturated parents are less familiar with the obesogenic nature of U.S. society.

Note also that some studies suggest that migration during sensitive periods of childhood like school entry may be more important for immigrants' obesity risk than acculturation. In a study that disentangled how age at arrival and duration of U.S. residence were related to unhealthy eating, only age at arrival mattered. Immigrants who came to the U.S. as school-aged children had less healthy diets than those arriving at younger or older ages, a finding that was attributed to the stress and social exclusion children of Hispanic immigrants face at school (Van Hook et al., 2018). This finding and explanation is concordant with evidence of increased obesity risk for children of immigrants when they first start school. Weight gain during kindergarten, first and second grade drove disparities in weight between U.S.-born whites and Hispanic children of immigrants but not U.S.-born white and U.S-born Hispanic children (Frisco et al., 2019a).

Before turning away from research on U.S. Hispanics' obesity risk, we want to point readers to the broader body of research on dietary acculturation and unhealthy eating among Hispanics. For brevity, we only bring a few of these studies into this paper, but there are several other excellent studies that interested readers can review for more information (e.g., Akresh, 2008, Batis et al., 2011, Dondero et al., 2018, Pérez-Escamilla & Putnik, 2007).

Obesity Among Black Women

As noted previously, Black women exhibit a higher obesity prevalence than any other group defined by the intersection of sex and race/ethnicity. Black women's health risks due to weight become even more apparent when estimates of overweight and obesity are considered together—80.6% of Black women are obese or overweight (The Office of Minority Health, 2020). The disproportionate obesity burden faced by Black women is associated with their higher risk of hypertension, cardiovascular disease (Go et al., 2013), diabetes (Krishnan et al., 2007), and all-cause mortality (Boggs et al., 2011) relative to white women.

Cross-sectional data suggests that Black women's disproportionate obesity risk relative to other groups first emerges among 12–19 year-olds, although the percentage of Black girls that is obese among 6–11 year-olds is also higher than all other groups except for Hispanic young women (Ogden et al., 2018). Analysis of data from the National Longitudinal Survey of Youth 1997 cohort also reveals that Black young women have the highest adolescent BMI among sex-specific racial groups and the greatest increase in BMI over time (Hargrove, 2018).

Analyses of NHIS data collected from 1976–2002 further show how patterns of obesity are distinctive for Black women across birth cohorts and age (Reither et al., 2009). Black women are heavier, on average, than Black men and non-Black men and women across all birth cohorts, but obesity rose very sharply for black women among cohorts born after 1955. Indeed, their probability of being obese has risen more precipitously than other groups from age 18 through midlife.

Demographers and population health researchers have conducted research aimed at understanding why Black women in the U.S. exhibit such a high obesity risk relative to other groups. Many of these studies discuss determinants of obesity such as diet, stress, and discrimination. Yet, it is important to note that structural racism is an upstream macro-level phenomenon that contributes to these determinants of obesity and that racism is now acknowledged as a fundamental cause of health inequalities (Phelan & Link, 2015) such as Black women's high obesity risk relative to other women.

Analysis of the NHANES using decomposition techniques investigated how the two proximate determinants of obesity—caloric intake and energy expenditures—contributed to black-white obesity disparities. Only one of these downstream determinants--caloric input--significantly contributed to black-white obesity disparities (Johnston & Lee, 2011). This finding is in line with what is generally known about weight and weight change. Diet and caloric intake are more important predictors than physical activity because of the flexibility of the human body to adjust to energy expenditures (Dugas et al., 2011; Pontzer et al., 2012).

Caloric intake likely contributes to black-white disparities in obesity among U.S. women because Black women face very high levels of chronic stress. On average, black women in the U.S. face so much more exposure to stressors than white women that it contributes to disparities in biological aging (Geronimus et al., 2010). Chronic stress is associated with the consumption of more energy-dense foods that are high in sugar and fat (O'Connor & Conner, 2011; Torres & Nowson, 2007).

Evidence suggests that stress is a contributing factor to overall Black-white disparities in obesity (which are driven by women given the very similar obesity prevalence of white and black men) (Cuevas et al., 2020). See Chap. 12 in this *Handbook* for additional discussion of these findings. There is also evidence that a significant stressor in the lives of Black adults contributes to disparities in the waist circumference of black and white women—perceptions of unfair police treatment towards relatives and close friends (McFarland et al., 2018).

Recent research has also explicitly shown the role that racism plays in black women's high obesity risk. Among participants in the Black Women's Health Study, measures of everyday racism and lifetime racism were positively associated with an increased incidence of obesity (Cozier et al., 2014). Indicators of structural racism, such as racial segregation, have also been linked to black women's high obesity risk. In racially integrated census tracts in Baltimore, black-white disparities in obesity among women are not evident (Bleich et al., 2010). Yet in California, an analysis of the relationship between low food access and obesity found that black women's risk for obesity was greater in high-poverty, high-black neighborhoods than in similar low-black neighborhoods (Gailey & Bruckner, 2019).

Nonetheless, studies have shown that neighborhood-level racial isolation, social disorder and community disadvantage are related to women's obesity risk, but cannot fully explain significant differences between black and white women (Chang et al., 2009; Robert & Reither, 2004). This is likely because of the many other ways that structural racism influences black women's lives.

For example, studies have investigated the importance of discrimination. Its salience for obesity is not exclusive to black women. Perceptions of discrimination are a risk factor for many sex and racial/ethnic minority groups (Hunte, 2011; Hunte & Williams, 2009). Yet there are some ways in which discrimination is especially salient for black women's weight. For example, experiencing racial discrimination has been linked to excessive weight gain during pregnancy, which is an important determinant of later life obesity (Reid et al., 2016). Hicken et al. (2018) also recently disentangled how experiences of discrimination shaped the weight of black and white women. They found that perceptions of everyday discrimination were not related to Black women's waist circumference. Instead, it was the stress that Black women live with on an everyday basis as a result of the necessary vigilance to avoid and prepare for discrimination that was associated with waist circumference.

Obesity Among Asians

Although this chapter's introduction notes that on average Asian American adults and children generally have a lower obesity prevalence than all other racial/ethnic groups, this does not mean that Asian Americans do not experience health risks associated with weight. For example, Asian American adults are leaner than U.S.-born whites, but across the BMI distribution, Asian Americans are at a significantly higher risk of metabolic syndrome, or the cluster of conditions like abdominal adiposity, high blood pressure, and abnormal cholesterol/triglyceride levels that increase the risk of heart disease, stroke and type 2 diabetes (Palaniappan et al., 2011).

Moreover, patterns of weight, weight gain and obesity are not uniform across Asian American subgroups. As is the case among Hispanics, U.S.-born Asian Americans have a higher obesity prevalence than immigrants (Lauderdale & Rathouz, 2000) and generational status is associated with BMI and obesity risk (Bates et al., 2008). In fact, the study just cited indicates that while 6.9% of first-generation Asian adult participants in the 2002–2003 NLAAS were obese, the percentage of obese nearly doubled (13.5%) and quadrupled (24.2%), respectively, among second- and third-plus generation Asian Americans.

Also consistent with most research on Hispanics, BMI and obesity prevalence vary with duration of U.S. residence among the foreign-born (Gee et al., 2008; Lauderdale & Rathouz, 2000; Ro et al., 2015). This association is especially evident for women (Ro & Bostean, 2015).

Obesity prevalence also varies by country of origin. In the 2002–2003 NLAAS, only 2.5% of Vietnamese in the U.S. and 4.3% of Chinese adults were obese, but 11.3% of other Asian American adults and 17.3% of Filipino adults were obese, with the prevalence of obesity being especially high for third-plus generation Filipinos (33.3%). This estimate is comparable to estimates of obesity among the U.S. population as a whole at the time when the NLAAS was conducted (Ogden et al., 2006). Estimates from the 1992–1995 NHIS largely confirm this finding. Among women and men in the U.S., those of Vietnamese descent were leanest and those of Filipino descent were heaviest, but Japanese men and Asian Indian women also had a higher obesity risk than other Asian Americans (Lauderdale & Rathouz, 2000).

Although the obesity prevalence varies among Asian American subgroups, Chinese, Filipino, and other Asian American adolescents all gain weight at a similar rate as non-Hispanic whites, and Filipinos remain heavier than their other Asian American peers across time (Albrecht & Gordon-Larsen, 2013). The overweight and obesity prevalence has also been growing among Asian American subgroups over time. From 1992 to 2011, the obesity prevalence doubled for Chinese, Asian Indian, Japanese, and Hawaiian/Pacific Islanders and tripled among Filipinos (Singh & Lin, 2013). Yet the obesity prevalence does not appear to change across adult birth cohorts of Asian Americans, possibly due to healthy migrant selection into U.S. immigration streams (Ro et al., 2015).

Studies have identified factors that place Asian American adults at greater and lesser risk of obesity besides generational status and duration of U.S. residence. As is the case among Black women, racial discrimination is one factor that is associated with an increased BMI and obesity risk and these associations become stronger with longer duration of U.S. residence (Gee et al., 2008). Economic hardship is also associated with an increased obesity risk among Asian American young women (but not men) during the transition to adulthood (Scharoun-Lee et al., 2009). Conversely, an indicator of biculturalism as measured using dual-language use is protective against obesity (Wang et al., 2011). Discrimination and language use also help explain why duration of U.S. residence is related to Asian American women's obesity risk (Ro & Bostean, 2015).

As is observed for adults, the prevalence of obesity is not the same for all Asian American children in the U.S. Among four-year-old children in the 2001 Early Childhood Longitudinal Study Birth Cohort (ECLS-B), 26% of Asian American youth are overweight and 13% are obese, but these prevalence estimates vary by mother's country of origin. Relative to whites, of whom 36% were overweight or obese, Chinese-American children (23.5%) and Asian-Indian children (15.6%) had a lower risk of overweight or obesity, while Vietnamese-American children had a higher risk of overweight or obesity (34.7%) (Jain et al., 2012) despite the evidence that Vietnamese women in the U.S. were actually quite lean relative to other groups in the late 1990s (Lauderdale & Rathouz, 2000). While there are differences in the sample of Vietnamese mothers in the ECLS-B study and the total sample of Vietnamese women who participated in the NHIS, the contrast in results for Vietnamese children versus adult women is suggestive of a disadvantage for second- and third-plus generation Vietnamese youth in the U.S.

Chinese adolescents are also leaner than non-Hispanic whites along with their Filipino peers among a national school-based cohort of 1994–1995 7th–12th graders, but as is the case among adults, Asian Americans born in the United States are more than twice as likely to be obese as first-generation peers (Popkin & Udry 1998). California data collected more than a decade later in 2007–2012 for a sample of Asian American adolescents suggests that the prevalence of overweight and obesity is lowest among Japanese adolescents and *highest* among Filipino adolescents (Cook et al., 2017), which contradicts the study just cited.

In California, Asian American adolescents in high- or middle-level SES groups are less likely to be overweight or obese than their ethnic counterparts in low-SES groups (Cook et al., 2017). This finding is concordant with qualitative research on Chinese and Korean immigrant parents' body size evaluations and feeding practices. Parents who were food insecure during childhood perceived that their children should weigh more than they do, allowed their children to consume more soda and sweets, did less monitoring, and had lower concerns about children's weight and diet (Cheah & Van Hook, 2012). In general, these findings regarding family socioeconomic status and parents' deprivation during childhood reflect evidence that immigrant parents who were socialized in contexts where food insecurity and material deprivation was common but obesity was rare may be less attuned to obesity risks in obesogenic cultures (Van Hook & Balistreri, 2007). This again points to the ways that social structure and social position in it, contributes to racial/ethnic variability in obesity prevalence.

Racial/Ethnic Disparities in Obesity and Longevity

Olshansky et al. (2005) first hypothesized that increased obesity prevalence could potentially reduce life expectancy in the U.S. Since then, demographers have played a major role in showing how obesity contributes to life expectancy, racial/ethnic disparities in life expectancy, and to life expectancy projections. Mehta and Chang (2009) analyzed data from the 1992 Health and Retirement Study (HRS) and found that class II/III obesity (a BMI of 35.0 kg/m^2 or higher) was associated with 40% and 62% increases in the mortality of women and men, respectively. Other research suggests that the increase in BMI over the decades spanning 1998–2011 reduced life expectancy at age 40 by .9 years and accounted for 186,000 excess deaths (Preston et al., 2018) and that the impact that obesity has on mortality grows stronger as people age (Masters et al., 2013a).

Given the racial/ethnic disparities in obesity previously discussed, it is unsurprising that obesity contributes to racial/ethnic disparities in mortality. For example, analysis of NHIS data finds that over 20 years spanning 1986–2006, the estimated percentage of adult deaths associated with overweight and obesity among Black and white women was 26.8% and 21.7%, respectively, whereas the opposite pattern is observed among men. Overweight and obesity were associated with only 5% of deaths among Black men and 15.6% of deaths among white men (Masters et al., 2013a, b). Thus, it is unsurprising that other research has found that among women (but not men) ages 40–79, differences in body weight account for nearly 30% of black-white disparities in mortality (Elo et al., 2017).

Frisco et al. (2019c) also investigated how obesity shaped racial/ethnic disparities in life expectancy and healthy life expectancy by conducting simulations under hypothetical conditions that obesity (and smoking) were eliminated from society. With the elimination of obesity alone, they found that Black women would gain 1.7 years of total life expectancy and 3.7 years of healthy life expectancy, gains that are large enough to reduce black-white disparities in total life expectancy among women to statistical non-significance (Frisco et al., 2019c). The elimination of obesity would also lead to gains for Black men but not to the degree necessary to eliminate black-white disparities in total and healthy life expectancy (Frisco et al., 2019c).

With respect to Hispanics, Frisco et al. (2019c) found that the elimination of obesity would actually allow foreign-born Hispanic women to make small gains in total and healthy life expectancy over white women and that disparities between U.S.-born Hispanic and white women would largely be unchanged. Results were similar among men, although foreign-born Hispanic men's advantage in healthy life expectancy would be reduced to statistical non-significance.

More recent research examines the role that obesity has in the epidemiological paradox. This work estimates cohort changes in life expectancy among Hispanics and non-Hispanic whites that are attributable to cohort changes in obesity (and smoking) (Van Hook et al., 2020). The study finds that foreign-born Hispanic adults' life expectancy advantage is likely to persist but U.S.-born Hispanics' life expectancy advantage over whites is likely to wane and possibly disappear entirely among men due to increases in the prevalence of obesity among U.S.-born Hispanics and their high mortality risk due to obesity.

To date, research has not explored how obesity contributes to disparities in mortality between white and Asian American adults. Yet, a high BMI is associated with increased mortality risk among Asian Americans as is the case among adults more generally (Park et al., 2014).

Limitations of Research to Date and Future Research Directions

While demographers and population health researchers have made many contributions to our understanding of U.S. racial/ethnic disparities in obesity, there are limitations to the contributions made, many of which stem from data availability at the national level and the trade-offs of using different data sources. For example, the NHANES and NHIS, two longstanding U.S. health surveillance studies with information on weight and height, are cross-sectional. This limits research on changes in weight and obesity over time among individuals.

Yet, the NHANES study has many strengths. It includes *measured* height and weight and other adiposity indicators including waist circumference and body composition as determined from dual energy x-ray absorptiometry, which uses x-ray beams to differentiate soft tissue from bone. The NHANES also includes limited data on weight histories, information about the proximate determinants of weight—including physical activity and detailed food diaries— and biomarker data that help to capture stress and nutrition. The trade-off of this data's richness, though, is a relatively small sample size and less detail about race and ethnicity. Black, white and Hispanic adults and children can be differentiated, but only one sub-group of Hispanics is identified (those of Mexican-origin) and other racial/ethnic subgroups are classified as 'other.' Until recently, it was impossible to identify Asian Americans and it is still impossible to identify Asian subgroups. Sample size issues can also arise when researchers aim to investigate more fine-grained categories of generational status.

Conversely, the large number of cases in the NHIS and detail on ethnicity and national origin allow researchers to study more fine-grained detail about the importance of race, national origin and ethnicity for obesity, but the NHIS includes only a self-reported measure of height and weight to calculate BMI and obesity. Demographers and population health researchers have developed innovative ways to correct these self-reports (Baker et al., 2015; Van Hook et al., 2020), but there are still likely biases that arise in estimates of self-reports because of racial/ethnic differences in weight over- and under-estimation (Wen & Kowaleski-Jones, 2012) and gender and racial/ethnic differences in how well BMI more generally taps body fatness (Burkhauser & Cawley, 2008). Another NHIS limitation is its utility for studying racial/ethnic disparities in childhood obesity. Information on height and weight is unavailable for children younger than 12.

Finally, the public use versions of both NHANES and NHIS are individual-level data sets that lack contextual information. Neither data source provides detailed geographic identifiers or information about neighborhood, community, or state environments. Also, the NHANES contains limited information about respondents' immediate families and households. Researchers may access community and household contextual data in a Federal Statistical Research Data Center (RDC), but the process for obtaining access is time consuming and expensive. As such, the NHANES and NHIS are very useful for patterns and trends, but more limited with regard to understanding how the social environment shapes racial/ethnic disparities in obesity.

Longitudinal studies commonly analyzed by demographers to study obesity include tremendous strengths in following individuals across time and often contain very rich predictors of obesity at multiple levels of influence, but also have limitations. For example, the NLSY79 and NLSY97 include only self-reported data on height and weight and more limited detail on race and ethnicity than the NHIS. Add Health and the newly-released High School and Beyond (HS&B): Midlife Follow-up have school-based sampling frames, which poses limitations for studying Hispanic immigrants such as Mexicans because of the share of Mexican-born adolescents who migrate to the U.S. and never enroll in U.S. schools (Oropesa & Landale, 2009). Given the propensity of leaner immigrant children and adults to be selected into U.S. immigration streams (Ro & Fleischer, 2014; Van Hook et al., 2012), this suggests school-based studies of obesity among immigrants and the U.S.-born may underestimate the advantage of immigrants.

That said, one important advantage of these longitudinal studies is their ability to estimate change in weight over time from adolescence through midlife, the time in the life course where obesity and body weight tends to peak (Hales et al., 2020). In addition, Add Health and the HS&B: Midlife Follow-up both have limited adiposity measures earlier in the life course, but both studies have expanded the range of measures available later in the life course (these data are currently available in Add Health and are being collected in the latest HS&B: Midlife Follow-up wave currently being fielded). Add Health and HS&B also have data on multi-level predictors of body weight, ranging from thousands of contextual measures at multiple levels to important biomarkers within individuals (Add Health currently contains these data and the HS&B is currently collecting biomarker data).

Nationally representative longitudinal data on young children include the 2000 ECLS-B study, the ECLS-K:1998–1999 and the ECLS-K:2011, which all include measured indicators of children's height and weight. A limitation of each study is by design. They are studies of specific developmental and educational windows, and therefore follow children only to age 5 in the case of ECLS-B or fifth or eighth grade in the case of the ECLS-K studies. To our knowledge, there have been no new longitudinal, nationally representative studies of children from birth to age 5 in over twenty-years. A new ECLS-K study is currently being fielded. Assuming that the study continues to assess height and weight, this will allow for longitudinal comparisons of racial/ethnic disparities in obesity across three cohorts of elementary school-aged children from three decades.

We do not highlight the limitations of the data sources just discussed as criticisms. Instead, our goal is to point out reasons why findings about disparities in obesity by race, ethnicity, nativity, and generational status may be inconsistent and the importance of triangulating across different data sources to fully understand disparities. We also note limits so that future data collection efforts can be enhanced. Moreover, we urge demographers and population health researchers to continue to use methodological innovations to overcome limitations of existing data sources.

There are other blind spots about racial/ethnic disparities in obesity caused by limitations of national data sources and limited research attention. For example, Native Americans and Alaska Natives are more likely to be obese than whites (Office of Minority Health, 2020), yet they have received little research attention from demographers due to their small numbers in national studies.

Moreover, although demographers have made great strides in pushing forward research on immigration, nativity and obesity, there is still room for advances in knowledge. For example, the salience of being undocumented and having undocumented parents despite the stressful nature of these statuses is largely unexplored. This is largely due to the difficulty in collecting reliable data on legal status and on obtaining clearance to analyze federal data sources that allow for inferences about it. One recent study using data from Los Angeles does point to a high obesity risk among undocumented immigrants (Altman & Bachmeier, 2021) yet future research on this topic and how it influences women, men and children is warranted.

More research is also needed on how different waves of immigration from disparate Asian countries shapes the risk of obesity among adults and children, and to flesh out the small body of research on obesity among U.S.-born blacks and Black immigrants from different regions. Prior research suggests that Black immigrants have a lower obesity risk than their U.S.-born peers (Mehta et al., 2015) but greater odds of diabetes (Horlyck-Romanovsky et al., 2019). This contradiction along with the contradiction in Asian Americans' low overall obesity risk but higher risk of metabolic syndrome along the BMI continuum (Palaniappan et al., 2011) suggests the need for more demographic research aimed at understanding how disparities in weight translate into different disparities in morbidity.

We also must note that the attention given to Black women's obesity vulnerability by demographers is not nearly as extensive as the attention given to other groups despite the fact that Black women are heavier than all other groups defined by sex and race/ethnicity. We find this to be a serious limitation to demographic contributions about racial/ethnic disparities in obesity. More research must be done that produces a greater understanding of structural factors that place Black women at such a high obesity risk, where risks are especially concentrated, and how to reduce obesity among black women.

Finally, we should note that all estimates described above about how obesity shapes mortality, life expectancy, and racial/ethnic disparities in both outcomes come from studies conducted prior to the Covid-19 pandemic that began in Spring 2020 and is ongoing at the time that this review was written. Obesity and obesity-related comorbidities including diabetes and hypertension all place Covid-19 patients at increased risk of death, hospitalization, and long-term disease (Kalligeros et al., 2020; Klang et al., 2020; Popkin et al., 2020).

In addition, provisional estimates of reductions in life expectancy in 2020 indicate sharp racial/ethnic disparities, and Covid-19 deaths are the largest driver of these reductions (Arias et al., 2021). White women's and men's life expectancy declines are estimated to be 1.1 year and 1.3 year, respectively. Estimates are much larger among racial and ethnic minorities. Hispanic and black women are estimated to lose 2.0 and 2.4 years of life, respectively, and Hispanic and black men are estimated to lose 3.7 and 3.3 years of life, respectively. These staggering declines suggest that the ways that obesity is shaping racial/ethnic disparities in total and healthy life expectancy in a pandemic and post-pandemic world are still far from understood. This unfortunately offers another ripe area of future research.

References

Abraído-Lanza, A. F., Armbrister, A. N., Flórez, K. R., & Aguirre, A. N. (2006). Toward a theory-driven model of acculturation in public health research. *American Journal of Public Health, 96*(8), 1342–1346.

Akresh, I. R. (2008). Overweight and obesity among foreign-born and U.S.-born Hispanics. *Biodemography and Social Biology, 54*(2), 183–199.

Al Snih, S., Ottenbacher, K. J., Markides, K. S., Kuo, Y.-F., Eschbach, K., & Goodwin, J. S. (2007). The effect of obesity on disability vs mortality in older Americans. *Archives of Internal Medicine, 167*(8), 774–780.

Albrecht, S. S., & Gordon-Larsen, P. (2013). Ethnic differences in body mass index trajectories from adolescence to adulthood: A focus on Hispanic and Asian subgroups in the United States. *PLoS One, 8*(9), e72983.

Altman, C. E., & Bachmeier, J. D. (2021). The weight of being unauthorized? Legal status variation in the association between us exposure and obesity among Hispanic immigrants in Los Angeles. *Journal of Immigrant and Minority Health.*

Antecol, H., & Bedard, K. (2006). Unhealthy assimilation: Why do immigrants converge to American health status levels?*. *Demography, 43*(2), 337–360.

Arias, E., Betzaida, T.-V., Ahmad, F., & Kochanek, K. (2021). *Provisional life expectancy estimates for 2020.* National Center for Health Statistics.

Baker, E. H., Rendall, M. S., & Weden, M. M. (2015). Epidemiological paradox or immigrant vulnerability? Obesity among young children of immigrants. *Demography, 52*(4), 1295–1320.

Balistreri, K. S., & Van Hook, J. (2011). Trajectories of overweight among U.S school children: A focus on social and economic characteristics. *Maternal and Child Health Journal, 15*(5), 610–619.

Bates, L. M., Acevedo-Garcia, D., Alegría, M., & Krieger, N. (2008). Immigration and generational trends in body mass index and obesity in the United States: Results of the National Latino and Asian American survey, 2002–2003. *American Journal of Public Health, 98*(1), 70–77.

Batis, C., Hernandez-Barrera, L., Barquera, S., Rivera, J. A., & Popkin, B. M. (2011). Food acculturation drives dietary differences among Mexicans, Mexican Americans, and non-hispanic whites123. *The Journal of Nutrition, 141*(10), 1898–1906.

Bean, F. D., Brown, S. K., Bachmeier, J. D., Brown, S., & Bachmeier, J. (2015). *Parents without papers: The progress and pitfalls of Mexican American integration.* Russell Sage Foundation.

Bhutani, S., vanDellen, M. R., & Cooper, J. A. (2021). Longitudinal weight gain and related risk behaviors during the covid-19 pandemic in adults in the us. *Nutrients, 13*(2), 671.

Bleich, S. N., Thorpe, R. J., Sharif-Harris, H., Fesahazion, R., & LaVeist, T. A. (2010). Social context explains race disparities in obesity among women. *Journal of Epidemiology & Community Health, 64*(5), 465–469.

Boggs, D. A., Rosenberg, L., Cozier, Y. C., Wise, L. A., Coogan, P. F., Ruiz-Narvaez, E. A., & Palmer, J. R. (2011). General and abdominal obesity and risk of death among black women. *The New England Journal of Medicine, 365*(10), 901–908.

Brownson, R. C., Boehmer, T. K., & Luke, D. A. (2005). Declining rates of physical activity in the United States: What are the contributors? *Annual Review of Public Health, 26*(1), 421–443.

Burkhauser, R. V., & Cawley, J. (2008). Beyond BMI: The value of more accurate measures of fatness and obesity in social science research. *Journal of Health Economics, 27*(2), 519–529.

Buttenheim, A. M., Pebley, A. R., Hsih, K., Chung, C. Y., & Goldman, N. (2013). The shape of things to come? Obesity prevalence among foreign-born vs. us-born Mexican youth in California. *Social Science & Medicine, 78*, 1–8.

Censin, J. C., Peters, S. A. E., Bovijn, J., Ferreira, T., Pulit, S. L., Mägi, R., Mahajan, A., Holmes, M. V., & Lindgren, C. M. (2019). Causal relationships between obesity and the leading causes of death in women and men. *PLoS Genetics, 15*(10), e1008405.

Chang, V. W., Hillier, A. E., & Mehta, N. K. (2009). Neighborhood racial isolation, disorder and obesity. *Social Forces, 87*(4), 2063–2092.

Cheah, C. S. L., & Van Hook, J. (2012). Chinese and Korean immigrants' early life deprivation: An important factor for child feeding practices and Children's body weight in the United States. *Social Science & Medicine, 74*(5), 744–752.

Cook, W. K., Tseng, W., Tam, C., John, I., & Lui, C. (2017). Ethnic-group socioeconomic status as an indicator of community-level disadvantage: A study of overweight/obesity in Asian American adolescents. *Social Science & Medicine, 184*, 15–22.

Cozier, Y. C., Jeffrey, Y., Coogan, P. F., Bethea, T. N., Rosenberg, L., & Palmer, J. R. (2014). Racism, segregation, and risk of obesity in the black Women's health study. *American Journal of Epidemiology, 179*(7), 875–883.

Cuevas, A. G., Chen, R., Slopen, N., Thurber, K. A., Wilson, N., Economos, C., & Williams, D. R. (2020). Assessing the role of health Behaviors, socioeconomic status, and cumulative stress for racial/ethnic disparities in obesity. *Obesity, 28*(1), 161–170.

Dondero, M., Van Hook, J., Frisco, M. L., & Martin, M. A. (2018). Dietary assimilation among Mexican children in immigrant households: Code-switching and healthy eating across social institutions. *Journal of Health and Social Behavior, 59*(4), 601–624.

Dugas, L. R., Harders, R., Merrill, S., Ebersole, K., Shoham, D. A., Rush, E. C., Assah, F. K., Forrester, T., Durazo-Arvizu, R. A., & Luke, A. (2011). Energy expenditure in adults living in developing compared with industrialized countries: A meta-analysis of doubly Labeled water studies. *The American Journal of Clinical Nutrition, 93*(2), 427–441.

Elo, I. T., Mehta, N., & Preston, S. (2017). The contribution of weight status to black-White differences in mortality. *Biodemography and Social Biology, 63*(3), 206–220.

Frisco, M. L., Quiros, S., & Van Hook, J. (2016). One size may not fit all: How obesity among Mexican-origin youth varies by generation, gender, and age. *Demography, 53*(6), 2031–2043.

Frisco, M., Baumgartner, E., & Van Hook, J. (2019a). The weight of school entry: Weight gain among Hispanic children of immigrants during the elementary school years. *Demographic Research, 40*(5), 95–120.

Frisco, M. L., Martin, M. A., & Van Hook, J. (2019b). Socioeconomic status and acculturation: Why Mexican Americans are heavier than Mexican immigrants and whites. In R. Frank (Ed.), *Advances in medical sociology* (Vol. 19, pp. 71–96). Bingley.

Frisco, M. L., Van Hook, J., & Hummer, R. A. (2019c). Would the elimination of obesity and smoking reduce U.S. racial/ethnic/nativity disparities in Total and healthy life expectancy? *SSM – Population Health, 7*, 100374.

Fryar, C. D., Carroll, M. D., & Afful, J. (2020). *Prevalence of overweight, obesity, and severe obesity among children and adolescents aged 2–19 years: United States, 1963–1965 through 2017–2018* (Vol. NCHS Health E-Stats). National Center for Health Statistics.

Gailey, S., & Bruckner, T. A. (2019). Obesity among black women in food deserts: An "omnibus" test of differential risk. *SSM – Population Health, 7*, 100363.

Gee, G. C., Ro, A., Gavin, A., & Takeuchi, D. T. (2008). Disentangling the effects of racial and weight discrimination on body mass index and obesity among Asian Americans. *American Journal of Public Health, 98*(3), 493–500.

Geronimus, A. T., Hicken, M. T., Pearson, J. A., Seashols, S. J., Brown, K. L., & Cruz, T. D. (2010). Do us black women experience stress-related accelerated biological aging? *Nature, 21*(1), 19–38.

Glass, T. A., & McAtee, M. J. (2006). Behavioral science at the crossroads in public health: Extending horizons, envisioning the future. *Social Science & Medicine, 62*(7), 1650–1671.

Go, A. S., Mozaffarian, D., Roger, V. L., Benjamin, E. J., Berry, J. D., Borden, W. B., Bravata, D. M., Dai, S., Ford, E. S., Fox, C. S., Franco, S., Fullerton, H. J., Gillespie, C., Hailpern, S. M., Heit, J. A., Howard, V. J., Huffman, M. D., Kissela, B. M., Kittner, S. J., et al. (2013). Heart disease and stroke statistics—2013 update: A report from the American Heart Association. *Circulation, 127*(1), e6–e245.

Goel, M. S., McCarthy, E. P., Phillips, R. S., & Wee, C. C. (2004). Obesity among U.S immigrant subgroups by duration of residence. *JAMA, 292*(23), 2860–2867.

Gordon-Larsen, P., Harris, K. M., Ward, D. S., & Popkin, B. M. (2003). Acculturation and overweight-related Behaviors among Hispanic immigrants to the us: The National Longitudinal Study of adolescent health. *Social Science & Medicine, 57*(11), 2023–2034.

Hales, C. M., Carroll, M. D., Fryar, C. D., & Ogden, C. L. (2020). *Prevalence of obesity and severe obesity among adults: United States, 2017–2018*. National Center for Health Statistics.

Hamilton, E. R. (2015). Epidemiological paradox. In S. Loue & M. Sajatovic (Eds.), *Encyclopedia of immigrant health* (pp. 630–631). Springer.

Hamilton, E. R., Cardoso, J. B., Hummer, R. A., & Padilla, Y. C. (2011). Assimilation and emerging health disparities among new generations of U.S. children. *Demographic Research, 25*, 783–818.

Hargrove, T. W. (2018). Intersecting social inequalities and body mass index trajectories from adolescence to early adulthood. *Journal of Health and Social Behavior, 59*(1), 56–73.

Harris, K. M., Perreira, K. M., & Lee, D. (2009). Obesity in the transition to adulthood: Predictions across race/ethnicity, immigrant generation, and sex. *Archives of Pediatrics & Adolescent Medicine, 163*(11), 1022–1028.

Hicken, M. T., Lee, H., & Hing, A. K. (2018). The weight of racism: Vigilance and racial inequalities in weight-related measures. *Social Science & Medicine, 199*, 157–166.

Horlyck-Romanovsky, M. F., Wyka, K., Echeverria, S. E., Leung, M. M., Fuster, M., & Huang, T. T.-K. (2019). Foreign-born blacks experience lower odds of obesity but higher odds of diabetes than us-born blacks in new York City. *Journal of Immigrant and Minority Health, 21*(1):47–55.

Hunte, H. E. R. (2011). Association between perceived interpersonal everyday discrimination and waist circumference over a 9-year period in the midlife development in the United States cohort study. *American Journal of Epidemiology, 173*(11), 1232–1239.

Hunte, H. E. R., & Williams, D. R. (2009). The association between perceived discrimination and obesity in a population-based multiracial and multiethnic adult sample. *American Journal of Public Health, 99*(7), 1285–1292.

Jackson, M. I. (2011). Foreign-born health integration during the transition to adulthood: The case of weight. *Social Science Research, 40*(5), 1419–1433.

Jain, A., Mitchell, S., Chirumamilla, R., Zhang, J., Horn, I. B., Lewin, A., & Jennifer Huang, Z. (2012). Prevalence of obesity among young Asian-American children. *Childhood Obesity, 8*(6), 518–525.

Johnston, D. W., & Lee, W.-S. (2011). Explaining the female black-White obesity gap: A decomposition analysis of proximal causes. *Demography, 48*(4), 1429–1450.

Kalligeros, M., Shehadeh, F., Mylona, E. K., Benitez, G., Beckwith, C. G., Chan, P. A., & Mylonakis, E. (2020). Association of Obesity with disease severity among patients with coronavirus disease 2019. *Obesity, 28*(7), 1200–1204.

Kaplan, M. S., Huguet, N., Newsom, J. T., & McFarland, B. H. (2004). The association between length of residence and obesity among Hispanic immigrants. *American Journal of Preventive Medicine, 27*(4), 323–326.

Klang, E., Kassim, G., Soffer, S., Freeman, R., Levin, M. A., & Reich, D. L. (2020). Severe obesity as an independent risk factor for Covid-19 mortality in hospitalized patients younger than 50. *Obesity, 28*(9), 1595–1599.

Krishnan, S., Rosenberg, L., Luc Djoussé, L., Cupples, A., & Palmer, J. R. (2007). Overall and central obesity and risk of type 2 diabetes in U.S. black women. *Obesity, 15*(7), 1860–1866.

Krueger, P. M., Coleman-Minahan, K., & Rooks, R. N. (2014). Race/ethnicity, nativity and trends in BMI among U.S. adults. *Obesity, 22*(7), 1739–1746.

Lauderdale, D. S., & Rathouz, P. J. (2000). Body mass index in a us National Sample of Asian Americans: Effects of nativity, years since immigration and socioeconomic status. *International Journal of Obesity, 24*(9), 1188–1194.

Li, N., Strobino, D., Ahmed, S., & Minkovitz, C. S. (2011). Is there a healthy foreign born effect for childhood obesity in the United States? *Maternal and Child Health Journal, 15*(3), 310–323.

Liu, J., Probst, J. C., Harun, N., Bennett, K. J., & Torres, M. E. (2009). Acculturation, physical activity, and obesity among Hispanic adolescents. *Ethnicity & Health, 14*(5), 509–525.

Markides, K. S., & Coreil, J. (1986). The health of Hispanics in the Southwestern United States: An epidemiologic paradox. *Public Health Reports, 101*(3), 253–265.

Martin, M. A., Van Hook, J. L., & Quiros, S. (2015). Is socioeconomic incorporation associated with a healthier diet? Dietary patterns among Mexican-origin children in the United States. *Social Science & Medicine, 147*, 20–29.

Martinez, E. (1999). Mexican American/Chicano families. In H. McAdoo (Ed.), *Family ethnicity: Strength in diversity* (pp. 121–134). Sage.

Masters, R. K., Powers, D. A., & Link, B. G. (2013a). Obesity and us mortality risk over the adult life course. *American Journal of Epidemiology, 177*(5), 431–442.

Masters, R. K., Reither, E. N., Powers, D. A., Claire Yang, Y., Burger, A. E., & Link, B. G. (2013b). The impact of obesity on us mortality levels: The importance of age and cohort factors in population estimates. *American Journal of Public Health, 103*(10), 1895–1901.

McFarland, M. J., Taylor, J., & McFarland, C. A. S. (2018). Weighed down by discriminatory policing: Perceived unfair treatment and black-White disparities in waist circumference. *SSM – Population Health, 5*, 210–217.

Mehta, N. K., & Chang, V. W. (2009). Mortality attributable to obesity among middle-aged adults in the United States. *Demography, 46*(4), 851–872.

Mehta, N. K., Elo, I. T., Ford, N. D., & Siegel, K. R. (2015). Obesity among U.S.- and foreign-born blacks by region of birth. *American Journal of Preventive Medicine, 49*(2), 269–273.

Mirowsky, J., & Ross, C. E. (2015). Education, health, and the default American lifestyle. *Journal of Health and Social Behavior, 56*(3), 297–306.

National Academies of Sciences, Engineering and Medicine. (2021). High and rising mortality rates among working-age adults. In K. M. Harris, M. K. Majmundar, & T. Becker (Eds.), *Washington*. The National Academies Press.

Nestle, M. (2002). *Food politics: How the food industry influences nutrition and health*. University of California Press.

O'Connor, D. B., & Conner, M. (2011). Effects of stress on eating behavior. In R. J. Contrada & A. Baum (Eds.), *The handbook of stress science: Biology, psychology, and Health* (pp. 275–286). Springer.

Office of Minority Health. (2020). *Obesity and American Indians/Alaska Natives*. The Office of Minority Health.

Ogden, C. L., Carroll, M. D., Curtin, L. R., McDowell, M. A., Tabak, C. J., & Flegal, K. M. (2006). Prevalence of overweight and obesity in the United States, 1999-2004. *JAMA, 295*(13), 1549–1555.

Ogden, C. L., Fryar, C. D., Hales, C. M., Carroll, M. D., Aoki, Y., & Freedman, D. S. (2018). Differences in obesity prevalence by demographics and urbanization in us children and adolescents, 2013–2016. *JAMA, 319*(23), 2410–2418.

Olshansky, S. J., Passaro, D. J., Hershow, R. C., Layden, J., Carnes, B. A., Brody, J., Hayflick, L., Butler, R. N., Allison, D. B., & Ludwig, D. S. (2005). A potential decline in life expectancy in the United States in the 21st century. *New England Journal of Medicine, 352*(11), 1138–1145.

Organization for Economic Co-operation and Development. (2017). *Obesity update*. Organisation for Economic Co-operation and Development.

Oropesa, R. S., & Landale, N. S. (2009). Why do immigrant youths who never Enroll in U.S. schools matter? School enrollment among Mexicans and non-Hispanic whites. *Sociology of Education, 82*(3), 240–266.

Palaniappan, L. P., Wong, E. C., Shin, J. J., Fortmann, S. P., & Lauderdale, D. S. (2011). Asian Americans have greater prevalence of metabolic syndrome despite lower body mass index. *International Journal of Obesity, 35*(3), 393–400.

Parikh, N. I., Pencina, M. J., Wang, T. J., Lanier, K. J., Fox, C. S., D'Agostino, R. B., & Vasan, R. S. (2007). Increasing trends in incidence of overweight and obesity over 5 decades. *The American Journal of Medicine, 120*(3), 242–50.e2.

Park, J., Myers, D., Kao, D., & Min, S. H. (2009). Immigrant obesity and unhealthy assimilation: Alternative estimates of convergence or divergence, 1995–2005. *Social Science & Medicine, 69*(11), 1625–1633.

Park, Y., Wang, S., Kitahara, C. M., Moore, S. C., Berrington, A., de Gonzalez, L., Bernstein, E. T., Chang, A. J., Flint, D. M., Freedman, J. M., Gaziano, R. N., Hoover, M. S., Linet, M. P., Robien, K., Schairer, C., Sesso, H. D., White, E., Willcox, B. J., Thun, M. J., et al. (2014). Body mass index and risk of death in Asian Americans. *American Journal of Public Health, 104*(3), 520–525.

Pérez-Escamilla, R., & Putnik, P. (2007). The role of acculturation in nutrition, lifestyle, and incidence of type 2 diabetes among Latinos. *The Journal of Nutrition, 137*(4), 860–870.

Phelan, J. C., & Link, B. G. (2015). Is racism a fundamental cause of inequalities in health? *Annual Review of Sociology, 41*(1), 311–330.

Pontzer, H., Raichlen, D. A., Wood, B. M., Mabulla, A. Z. P., Racette, S. B., & Marlowe, F. W. (2012). Hunter-gatherer energetics and human obesity. *PLoS One, 7*(7), e40503.

Popkin, B. M. (2008). *The world is fat: The fads, trends, policies, and products that are fattening the human race*. Avery-Penguin Press.

Popkin, B. M., & Richard Udry, J. (1998). Adolescent obesity increases significantly in second and third generation U.S. immigrants: The National Longitudinal Study of adolescent health. *The Journal of Nutrition, 128*(4), 701–706.

Popkin, B. M., Shufa, D., Green, W. D., Beck, M. A., Algaith, T., Herbst, C. H., Alsukait, R. F., Alluhidan, M., Alazemi, N., & Shekar, M. (2020). Individuals with obesity and Covid-19: A global perspective on the epidemiology and biological relationships. *Obesity Reviews, 21*(11), e13128.

Preston, S. H., Vierboom, Y. C., & Stokes, A. (2018). The role of obesity in exceptionally slow us mortality improvement. *Proceedings of the National Academy of Sciences, 115*(5), 957–961.

Reid, A. E., Rosenthal, L., Earnshaw, V. A., Lewis, T. T., Lewis, J. B., Stasko, E. C., Tobin, J. N., & Ickovics, J. R. (2016). Discrimination and excessive weight gain during pregnancy among black and Latina young women. *Social Science & Medicine, 156*, 134–141.

Reither, E. N., Hauser, R. M., & Yang, Y. (2009). Do birth cohorts matter? Age-period-cohort analyses of the obesity epidemic in the United States. *Social Science & Medicine, 69*(10), 1439–1448.

Riosmena, F., Wong, R., & Palloni, A. (2013). Migration selection, protection, and acculturation in health: A binational perspective on older adults. *Demography, 50*(3), 1039–1064.

Ro, A., & Bostean, G. (2015). Duration of U.S. stay and body mass index among Latino and Asian immigrants: A test of theoretical pathways. *Social Science & Medicine, 144*, 39–47.

Ro, A., & Fleischer, N. (2014). Changes in health selection of obesity among Mexican immigrants: A binational examination. *Social Science & Medicine, 123*, 114–124.

Ro, A., Geronimus, A., Bound, J., Griffith, D., & Gee, G. (2015). Cohort and duration patterns among Asian immigrants: Comparing trends in obesity and self-rated health. *Biodemography and Social Biology, 61*(1), 65–80.

Robert, S. A., & Reither, E. N. (2004). A multilevel analysis of race, community disadvantage, and body mass index among adults in the us. *Social Science & Medicine, 59*(12), 2421–2434.

Sabin, M. A., Kao, K.-T., Juonala, M., Baur, L. A., & Wake, M. (2015). Viewpoint article: Childhood obesity – Looking back over 50 years to begin to look forward. *Journal of Paediatrics and Child Health, 51*(1), 82–86.

Sanchez-Vaznaugh, E. V., Ichiro Kawachi, S. V., & Subramanian, Brisa N. Sánchez and Dolores Acevedo-Garcia. (2008). Differential effect of birthplace and length of residence on body mass index (Bmi) by education, gender and race/ethnicity. *Social Science & Medicine, 67*(8), 1300–1310.

Scharoun-Lee, M., Adair, L. S., Kaufman, J. S., & Gordon-Larsen, P. (2009). Obesity, race/ethnicity and the multiple dimensions of socioeconomic status during the transition to adulthood: A factor analysis approach. *Social Science & Medicine, 68*(4), 708–716.

Singh, G. K., & Lin, S. C. (2013). Dramatic increases in obesity and overweight prevalence among Asian subgroups in the United States, 1992–2011. *ISRN Preventive Medicine, 2013*, e898691.

The Office of Minority Health. (2020). *Obesity and African Americans*. Office of Minority Health.

Torres, S. J., & Nowson, C. A. (2007). Relationship between stress, eating behavior, and obesity. *Nutrition, 23*(11), 887–894.

Ullmann, S. H., Goldman, N., & Pebley, A. R. (2013). Contextual factors and weight change over time: A comparison between U.S. Hispanics and other population sub-groups. *Social Science & Medicine, 90*, 40–48.

Valenzuela, A. (1999). Gender roles and settlement activities among children and their immigrant families. *American Behavioral Scientist, 42*(4), 720–742.

Van Hook, J., & Balistreri, K. S. (2007). Immigrant generation, socioeconomic status, and economic development of countries of origin: A longitudinal study of body mass index among children. *Social Science & Medicine, 65*(5), 976–989.

Van Hook, J., & Baker, E. (2010). Big boys and little girls: Gender, acculturation, and weight among young

children of immigrants. *Journal of Health and Social Behavior, 51*(2), 200–214.
Van Hook, J., Baker, E., Altman, C. E., & Frisco, M. L. (2012). Canaries in a coalmine: Immigration and overweight among Mexican-origin children in the US and Mexico. *Social Science & Medicine (1982), 74*(2), 125–134.
Van Hook, J., Quiros, S., & Frisco, M. L. (2015). The food similarity index: A new measure of dietary acculturation based on dietary recall data. *The Journal of Immigrant and Minority Health, 17*(2), 441–449.
Van Hook, J., Quirós, S., Dondero, M., & Altman, C. E. (2018). Healthy eating among Mexican immigrants: Migration in childhood and time in the United States. *Journal of Health and Social Behavior, 59*(3), 391–410.
Van Hook, J., Frisco, M. L., & Graham, C. E. (2020). Signs of the end of the paradox? Cohort shifts in smoking and obesity and the Hispanic life expectancy advantage. *Sociological Science, 7*, 391–414.
Viruell-Fuentes, E., Miranda, P. Y., & Abdulrahimc, S. (2012). More than culture: Structural racism, intersectionality theory, and immigrant health. *Social Science & Medicine, 75*(12), 2099–2106.
Wang, S., Quan, J., Kanaya, A. M., & Fernandez, A. (2011). Asian Americans and obesity in California: A protective effect of biculturalism. *Journal of Immigrant and Minority Health, 13*(2), 276–283.
Waters, M. C. (2002). The social construction of race and ethnicity: Some examples from demography. In N. Denton & S. Tolnay (Eds.), *American diversity*. SUNY Press.
Wen, M., & Kowaleski-Jones, L. (2012). Sex and ethnic differences in validity of self-reported adult height, weight and body mass index. *Ethnicity & Disease, 22*(1), 72–78.
Zachary, Z., Brianna, F., Brianna, L., Garrett, P., Jade, W., Alyssa, D., & Mikayla, K. (2020). Self-quarantine and weight gain related risk factors during the covid-19 pandemic. *Obesity Research & Clinical Practice, 14*(3), 210–216.

9 Race/Ethnic and Socioeconomic Disparities in Obesity

Patrick M. Krueger, Shawna F. Bayerman, and Eric N. Reither

Introduction

Race/ethnic and socioeconomic status (SES) disparities in obesity have important implications for the health and wellbeing of the U.S. population. Obesity is associated with adverse outcomes including discrimination in the workplace and health care settings, elevated levels of disability and morbidity, reduced earnings, increased risks of death, and limited access to health care. Thus, efforts to close race/ethnic and SES disparities in obesity may reduce disparities in other important outcomes. Our chapter describes current disparities in obesity, reviews evidence about the mechanisms that likely give rise to disparities in obesity, and considers the major policy and intervention frameworks that may support efforts to shift disparities in obesity in the U.S. population.

P. M. Krueger (✉)
Department of Health & Behavioral Sciences, University of Colorado Denver, Denver, CO, USA

University of Colorado Population Center, Boulder, CO, USA
e-mail: Patrick.krueger@ucdenver.edu

S. F. Bayerman · E. N. Reither
University of Colorado Denver, Denver, CO, USA

Surveillance and Measurement

Disparities

Race/ethnic and SES disparities in obesity are substantial. Among adults in 2017–2018, 42% of non-Hispanic whites were obese (BMI $\geq$ 30.0), compared to 50% of non-Hispanic blacks, 45% of Hispanics, and just 17% of non-Hispanic Asians (Hales et al., 2020). Although the prevalence of obesity is lower among Asians than among other race/ethnic groups, evidence suggests that Asian subpopulations may experience health risks at a lower BMI than other race/ethnic groups (Jih et al., 2014). Among children in 2017–2018, 16% of non-Hispanic whites were obese (BMI $\geq$ 95th percentile on growth charts), compared to 24% of non-Hispanic blacks, 26% of Hispanics, and 9% of Asians (Fryar et al., 2020). Important disparities by SES are also present. The prevalence of obesity is 12 percentage points lower among those who have a college degree than among those who have a high school degree or less education, and is 8 percentage points lower among those who are >350% of the federal poverty line than among those who are $\leq$130% of the federal poverty line (Ogden et al., 2018).

Notably, growth in the burden of obesity is not shared equally by all. Demographic and epidemiologic research finds increasing obesity across most groups in the U.S. in recent decades, with the fastest increases among blacks and Mexican

G. Garcia-Alexander, D. L. Poston, Jr. (eds.), *International Handbook of the Demography of Obesity*, International Handbooks of Population 12, https://doi.org/10.1007/978-3-031-10936-2_9

Americans, and slower increases among Asians of Indian descent, immigrants, and those with higher income or education (Ford et al., 2011; Krueger et al., 2014; Ogden et al., 2018). Drawing on age-period-cohort models, demographers find that birth cohorts play a central role in driving the increases in obesity over time (Masters et al., 2013; Reither et al., 2009; Yang et al., 2021). Within cohorts, blacks tend to have higher body masses than whites, in addition to persistent disadvantages across age groups. Body mass also increases across birth cohorts for all education groups. These findings emphasize that cohorts may be more important than period effects for driving disparities in our population, suggesting the need to identify the early life factors that drive obesity.

Self-Reports Versus Objective Measures

Demographers rely on population samples to study obesity, and some of those samples rely on self-reported heights and weights (the measures used to calculate body mass and obesity). However, self-reported heights and weights may be biased due to social desirability, lack of knowledge, or rounding errors. Individuals tend to report taller heights and lower weights than observed with objective measures, leading to under-estimates of obesity (Gorber et al., 2007). One study finds that only 57% of adults who are underweight (i.e., BMI < 18.5), based on objectively measured heights and weights, are classified as underweight when using self-reported heights and weights. Similarly, only 72% of those who are extremely obese (i.e., BMI > 40), based on objective measures, fall into that same group when relying on self-reported heights and weights (Stommel & Schoenborn, 2009).

The accuracy of self-reported heights and weights varies across race/ethnic groups and by SES, potentially confounding efforts to understand the magnitude, determinants, or consequences of disparities in body mass that are measured from self-reports. Among adults, blacks and some Hispanic groups tend to overestimate their self-reported heights relative to whites, and those with college degrees tend to underestimate their weight relative to those with less than a high school education (Stommel & Schoenborn, 2009). These differences do not always translate into significant differences in average body masses from objectively measured and self-reported measures, although college-educated individuals do have significantly lower body masses when using self-reported heights and weights rather than objective measures (Stommel & Schoenborn, 2009). Among adolescents, correlations between observed and self-reported heights, weights, and body masses range from 0.79 to 0.95, and the correlation between self-reported and observed body masses is significantly smaller for blacks than for whites (Strauss, 1999). Notably, errors in self-reported measures and observed measures appear constant across time for all race/ethnic groups (Hattori & Sturm, 2013).

Although understanding the impact of misreported heights and weights on mean levels of body mass is important, errors in self-reports may have a larger impact on understanding disparities at either end of the body mass distribution. This is especially problematic given that race/ethnic differences in average body mass understate the vast over-representation of blacks and Native Americans among the most obese, and Asian Americans among the underweight (Denney et al., 2004). To our knowledge, no comparable work has examined whether the shape of the body mass distribution differs across levels of SES, suggesting a direction for future research. For example, lower SES individuals may have divergent experiences and be concentrated at the tails of the body mass distribution (e.g., very obese and underweight), whereas lower SES individuals may be more likely to gravitate to the normal weight or overweight points in body mass distribution.

Population surveys increasingly include objective measures of height and weight (e.g., National Health and Nutrition Examination Survey, National Longitudinal Study of Adolescent Health, Health, and Retirement Study). Measured heights and weights may be especially important during adolescence and at older ages, when body mass can change rapidly, with important implications for race/ethnic and SES disparities.

Incidence and Prevalence

Most research on obesity focuses on prevalence—the obesity status of individuals at the time of measurement. Prevalence measures are useful for describing race/ethnic or socioeconomic disparities in body mass at a given moment in time, or for tracking disparities over time. Fewer studies examine rates of new cases of obesity, or rates of recovery from obesity. Demographers, however, have methodological tools for examining rates of incidence and recovery (e.g., survival models) and the time spent in specific states (e.g., life tables). These tools are useful for identifying factors that are associated with transitions to higher or lower body masses in the population, and to understand which groups are likely to spend more or less time at specific body masses.

A handful of studies show that the incidence of obesity is higher among black and Hispanic children than among whites, and is higher among children in lower income families than in higher-income families (Cunningham et al., 2014; Gordon-Larsen et al., 2004; Strauss & Knight, 1999; Tran et al., 2016). Further, among children, transitions from obese or overweight statuses to normal weight are relatively common (Gordon-Larsen et al., 2004; Tran et al., 2016). Multistate life tables show that children who are obese at age 3 can expect to live 3.1 of the next 13 years in the normal weight status if they are white, 1.9 years in the normal weight status if they are Asian, 1.4 years in the normal weight status if they are black, and just 0.9 years in the normal weight status if they are Hispanic (Tran et al., 2016). Blacks and Hispanics are especially unlikely, relative to whites or Asians, to transition to lower body masses throughout childhood.

Studies of incidence and recovery require longitudinal data with repeated measures of height and weight ideally focused at stages of the life course (e.g., childhood, old age) where body masses may change frequently. Studies like these could allow us to advance research on body mass disparities in several ways. First, researchers could examine how often individuals in the population lose weight, in the absence of major interventions, and how that weight loss varies across race/ethnic and SES groups. Second, researchers could examine whether the factors that drive disparities in new cases of obesity differ from the factors that drive disparities in recovery to lower body masses. Third, researchers could examine the duration of time spent in normal weight, overweight, or obese statuses over some span of time, allowing them to consider the impact of cumulative exposures to a given body mass status to health outcomes among race/ethnic and SES groups.

Mechanisms

Numerous studies have examined the mechanisms that drive race/ethnic and SES disparities in obesity. We review studies that consider the behavioral, biological, neighborhood, and social mechanisms that could plausibly have population-level impacts. The diversity of mechanisms considered reflects the failure of simple behavioral interventions to reverse the tide of the obesity pandemic, and the breadth of factors that give rise to disparities in obesity. Throughout, we note areas where additional research might advance the literature.

Behaviors

Diet and Physical Activity Diet (caloric intake) and physical activity (energy output) together create energy balance—when caloric intake exceeds energy output, then individuals gain weight. Current trends in caloric intake and physical activity suggest that the prevalence of obesity will increase in the future, and racial and SES disparities will continue to widen (Basu et al., 2014). Modest changes in caloric intake and physical activity could reduce the prevalence of obesity in the coming decades, but those changes would have to be larger among non-whites and low-SES groups to close those disparities. For example, even if blacks reduced their caloric intake by over 500-kilocalories per day, black-white disparities in obesity would persist into the future, due to metabolic constraints in how fast individuals can lose weight. Further, individuals with lower SES would need to reduce caloric intake by 72 kilocalories per day, or increase physical activity by 14 minutes per day, to achieve the same prevalence of obesity as the middle-income population (Basu et al., 2014).

The consumption of calorically dense foods varies across race/ethnic and SES groups, and may partially explain disparities in obesity. For example, the frequency of eating fast food is higher among blacks than among whites, and among those with 12 years of schooling than among those with college degrees (Kant et al., 2015). Similarly, the consumption of sugar-sweetened beverages is higher among black, Mexican American, and non-Mexican Hispanic populations than among whites, and higher among those with less education or income than among those with higher SES (Bleich et al., 2018; Han & Powell, 2013). Low water consumption is associated with higher consumption of sugar-sweetened beverages (Rosinger et al., 2019). Remarkably, one-fifth of the U.S. population reports no water consumption on a given day. Tap water consumption is lower among blacks and Hispanics relative to whites, and among those with less education than among those with more education (Rosinger et al., 2018).

Overall diet quality also varies across race/ethnic and SES groups. Compared to white children, Hispanic children are more likely to eat greens, beans, seafood, and plant proteins, whereas black children are less likely to eat whole fruits or dairy (Thomson et al., 2018). Among adults, poor quality diets (based on standards from the American Heart Association) are more common among blacks and Hispanics, relative to whites, and among less educated adults compared to those with more education (Rehm et al., 2016).

Research on Mexican immigrants to the U.S. shows that diet quality decreases with each successive generation in the U.S. Notably, a decline in diet quality is greatest among migrants from low-SES backgrounds, which is consistent with segmented assimilation theory (Martin et al., 2015). Further, higher levels of linguistic acculturation (e.g., being more fluent in English and speaking English in more contexts) among migrants are associated with lower consumption of fruits and vegetables (Creighton et al., 2012). Although concepts including acculturation and assimilation have been criticized due to poor conceptualization and measurement, more rigorous approaches drawn from anthropology might more directly measure how norms, values, and beliefs change in diverse ways as immigrants spend time in the U.S. (Broesch & Hadley, 2012).

Food insecurity—wherein households have limited or uncertain access to healthy foods—may also partially account for disparities in obesity. Households that are food insecure may look for foods that are affordable, calorically dense, and comforting; unfortunately, that results in poorer quality diets. Some research finds that lower income food insecure adults consumed lower quality diets compared with their lower income food secure counterparts (Leung et al., 2014), suggesting that food insecurity is associated with poorer diets independent of poverty. However, other research finds that food insecurity is not associated with poorer diets or overweight among children, after adjusting for poverty (Bhattacharya et al., 2004). When focusing on race/ethnic disparities, research shows that food insecurity is associated with poorer quality diets among non-Hispanic whites and Asians, but not among blacks or Hispanics (Leung & Tester, 2019). Looking across studies, food insecurity is important in its own right, but its role in driving disparities in obesity is unclear.

Physical activity has declined over time in the U.S., and those declines are associated with increasing obesity (Church et al., 2011). Disparities in leisure-time, work-related, and active transportation-related physical activity may help to explain race/ethnic and SES disparities in obesity. Education is positively associated with leisure-time physical activity and negatively associated with work-related physical activity (Scholes & Bann, 2018). Adults with less than a high school degree are most likely to engage in active transportation-related physical activity. Further, whites have higher levels of both leisure-time and work-related physical activity compared to blacks and Hispanics, but blacks and Hispanics have higher levels of active transportation-related physical activity (Scholes & Bann, 2018). Adolescents show similar patterns; non-Hispanic whites are most likely to meet recommendations for physical activity, followed by Hispanics, non-Hispanic blacks, and Asians (Katzmarzyk et al., 2017).

Disparities in types of sports pursued may also help to explain race/ethnic and SES disparities in physical activity. More educated adults are more likely to undertake all types of leisure-time physical activity, including team sports (e.g., basketball, soccer), fitness activities (e.g., running, weight lifting), and activities that typically require specialized facilities (e.g., swimming, golf) (Saint Onge & Krueger, 2011). Compared to whites, blacks and Mexican Americans are more likely to engage in team and fitness sports, and those disparities widen with education. Disparities in types of physical activity may matter for obesity across the life course because participation in team-based sports and some fitness activities may be more difficult to maintain at the older ages when injuries and declines in cardiovascular function may be more common (Saint Onge & Krueger, 2011). Physical activity in childhood and adolescence, including participation in sports, is predictive of physical activity in early adulthood. This is vexing given that children from lower SES backgrounds are less likely to engage in sports after school than children from wealthier backgrounds, presaging future disparities in obesity (Turner et al., 2015).

Sleep Duration Short sleep duration may be linked to obesity through several pathways. First, experimental studies find that short sleep duration is associated with hormonal dysregulation, including decreases in leptin (a hormone that reduces appetite) and increases in ghrelin (a hormone that stimulates appetite) (Omisade et al., 2010; Spiegel et al., 2004). Second and relatedly, short sleep is associated with snacking more frequently and preferences for foods with more saturated fats and sugar, and less protein (Al Khatib et al., 2017). Finally, short sleep may leave individuals too fatigued to engage in physical activity, although evidence for this mechanism remains mixed (Al Khatib et al., 2017).

Short sleep and sleep disturbances vary across race/ethnicity and SES. Among adults, sleep durations of less than 6 h per night are more common among blacks, Mexican Americans, other Hispanics, and Chinese Americans than among whites (Chen et al., 2015; Krueger & Friedman, 2009). Among adolescents, more black and Asian girls sleep less than 7 h per night (compared to white girls), and more black, Hispanic, and Asian boys sleep less than 7 h (compared to white boys) (Reither et al., 2014). Evidence also shows that exposure to discrimination is associated with sleep disturbances, sleepiness, and difficulty falling asleep (Yip et al., 2020). Higher levels of education and income are associated with higher odds of sleeping 7–8 h per night, whereas lower education and income are associated with higher odds of sleeping 6 or fewer hours or 9 or more hours per night (Basner & Dinges, 2018; Krueger & Friedman, 2009). Long work hours are also associated with shorter sleep durations (Krueger & Friedman, 2009).

Evidence that sleep duration mediates race/ethnic disparities in obesity and related outcomes is uneven. Narcisse et al. (2018) demonstrate that trouble falling asleep, trouble staying asleep, and short sleep duration each explained between 1% and 16% of the association between food insecurity and obesity among whites, Hispanics, Asians, and Native Hawaiian-Pacific Islanders. Other studies, however, have found no evidence that sleep duration mediates race/ethnic disparities in obesity (Piccolo et al., 2013; Reither et al., 2014). Although theory suggests that sleep should mediate the association between SES and obesity (Van Cauter et al., 1999), empirical tests are lacking. Using longitudinal data to test whether sleep duration or sleep quality explains SES disparities in obesity could advance our understanding of the origins of disparate obesity outcomes.

Some evidence shows that the association between sleep duration and BMI varies by race/ethnicity. Data from adolescents and adults show that the association between short sleep and weight gain (Spaeth et al., 2013) or obesity (Jean-Louis et al., 2015; Reither et al., 2014) is stronger among blacks than among whites. When focusing on Hispanic subgroups, some research finds that sleep is inversely associated with body mass among Mexican Americans, but not among Cuban Americans or Puerto Ricans (Knutson, 2011). In conclusion, improved sleep quality and quantity may help to reduce obesity, but the benefits vary across groups.

Screen Time and Sedentary Behaviors - Sedentary behavior—including sitting, watching television or other electronic devices, and driving—is associated with obesity independently of the frequency of physical activity (Kim et al., 2016). Even individuals who are very active spend substantial time in sedentary activities throughout the day. Three mechanisms might link sedentary activity to obesity. First, sedentary behavior leads to metabolic dysfunction, resulting in increased total cholesterol, triglycerides, and insulin resistance (Hamburg et al., 2007). Second, sedentary behavior and screen time allows individuals an opportunity to snack and diminishes recognition of satiety. Specifically, both adults and children tend to eat fewer fruits and vegetables, and consume more calorically dense snacks, beverages, and fast foods, when engaging in screen time (Pearson & Biddle, 2011). Third, screen time can displace time spent on sleep and physical activity (Chahal et al., 2013), behaviors that can protect against obesity. As a result, evidence demonstrates that more frequent sedentary activity is associated with increased body mass and prospective weight gain (Mun et al., 2018).

Notable disparities in screen time or other sedentary activities have been observed. Children who are non-white and from lower income families tend to have more screen time than children who are white or from wealthier families, based on parent reports (Haughton et al., 2016; Tandon et al., 2012). However, those disparities disappear when using accelerometer-derived time in sedentary activities (Carson & Kuzik, 2017). Among adults, accelerometer data shows that income is associated with higher levels of moderate and vigorous activity, but also more time spent in sedentary activities (Shuval et al., 2017). These patterns suggest that sedentary behaviors may help to explain disparities in body mass, although drawing on objective measures of activity, and adjusting for time spent in moderate or vigorous activity, may be essential for future research.

Smoking Cigarette smoking is associated with obesity, and may play a role in shaping disparities in obesity. Smoking can reduce appetite, and smokers often note concerns about weight gain as a barrier to quitting smoking. Smoking is associated with obesity for several reasons (Audrain-McGovern & Benowitz, 2011). First, smoking activates neurological pathways that reduce appetite (Mineur et al., 2011). Second, smoking can increase the activity of enzymes in adipose tissue which can lead to reduced body weight (Carney & Goldberg, 1984). Third, smoking cessation can lead to an increase in snacking as a means of coping with withdrawal (Audrain-McGovern & Benowitz, 2011). Finally, smoking is associated with insulin resistance and central fat accumulation (Houston et al., 2006; Shimokata et al., 1989). As a result, current smokers are often less likely to be obese than never smokers and former smokers are more likely to be obese than never smokers (Audrain-McGovern & Benowitz, 2011). Over time, however, the lifetime consumption of cigarettes is positively associated with body mass among both current and former smokers (Dare et al., 2015).

Substantial racial/ethnic and socioeconomic disparities are present in smoking behavior. Those who have less education and lower incomes have higher rates of smoking in the U.S. (Pampel et al., 2010). Youth smoking is highest among American Indians, followed by whites, while Hispanics, blacks, and Asians have the lowest rates of current smoking. Among adults, a striking 42% of American Indians are current smokers, followed by whites and blacks at 37%, Hispanics at 23%, and Asians at 15% (Garrett et al., 2011). Some research, however, shows that smoking and obesity are especially likely to co-occur among blacks relative to whites, as well as among the less educated and those with lower family incomes (Healton et al., 2006), suggesting that smoking and obesity may be elements of a shared lifestyle. We are not aware of longitudinal studies that specifically examine whether smoking mediates race/ethnic or SES disparities in obesity. Efforts to understand the role of smoking for disparities in obesity are especially pressing, given the joint contributions of obesity and smoking to survival and other health outcomes.

Maternal smoking may also shape disparities in obesity. Maternal smoking is associated with the development of pediatric obesity. Although maternal smoking is associated with low birthweight, those low birthweight infants tend to experience faster gains in weight than normal weight infants and are more likely to become obese in childhood (Ino, 2010). Hispanic and black children are more often exposed to maternal smoking than are whites, although those differences are reduced after adjusting for SES (Taveras et al., 2010). As such, maternal smoking may play a larger role in explaining SES disparities in child obesity than in accounting for race/ethnic disparities.

Breastfeeding Breastfeeding may be an important factor in obesity prevention for both the mother and baby. Breastfeeding may help infants to regulate caloric intake and provide infants with nutrients and bioactive factors that affect their growth (Bartok & Ventura, 2009). Less than half of infants are breastfed for the first 6 months of life, and Healthy People 2020 set goals to increase the share of infants that are breastfed at 6 months and 1 year of age (U.S. Department of Health and Human Services, 2013). Indeed, the percentage of infants who are breastfed for at least 6 months is lower among blacks and Hispanics than among whites, and is lower among those with a high school degree or less than among those with some college or a college degree (Xiang et al., 2019), suggesting that encouraging breastfeeding and reducing barriers to breastfeeding may help to reduce disparities in obesity (Thompson & Bentley, 2013).

Breastfeeding is also associated with maternal obesity. Some studies suggest that exclusive breastfeeding, especially for longer durations, may be associated with weight loss among postpartum women (Neville et al., 2014). Breastfeeding, however, varies across SES and race/ethnicity. Higher levels of maternal and paternal education are associated with higher odds of mothers ever breastfeeding. Further, mothers who are white or foreign-born Latinas have among the highest odds of ever breastfeeding, whereas blacks, Asians, and U.S.-born Latinas have among the lowest odds of ever breastfeeding (Heck et al., 2006; Louis-Jacques et al., 2017). Interventions aimed at increasing breastfeeding in an effort to increase postpartum weight loss show mixed results. One study in Belarus was able to increase exclusive breastfeeding via hospital-based behavior interventions, but found no effect on postpartum weight loss (Kramer et al., 2009). A second study used a cell phone app to encourage breastfeeding among low income women in the U.S., but the app did not successfully increase breastfeeding (Lewkowitz et al., 2020). Efforts to design interventions that promote breastfeeding in diverse U.S. populations are crucial for testing the effect of breastfeeding on postpartum weight loss.

Biological Factors

Developmental Origins of Health and Disease The developmental origins of health and disease perspective emphasizes that prenatal and postnatal environments can impact birth characteristics and subsequent disease risk throughout the life course. Both observational studies of humans and experimental studies of animal models find that prenatal and perinatal exposures to poor nutrition or inadequate calories can result in physiologic changes that are adaptive to low-nutrition environments, but that may lead to subsequent increased likelihood of diabetes, hypertension, and obesity (Gluckman & Hanson, 2004). Among humans, maternal obesity, gestational weight gain, poor nutrition, and excessive nutrition are associated with subsequent child obesity via the intrauterine environment (Dabelea & Crume, 2011; Perng et al., 2019), by altering fetal metabolism, hormone production, or sensitivity to those hormones. In turn, those changes shape fetal organ development and subsequent metabolic set points (Gluckman et al., 2008).

We are aware of only one study that examines whether maternal obesity explains race/ethnic disparities in children's obesity. The researchers found that parental body mass explains almost 40% of the black/white gap in children's body mass, and almost 20% of the Hispanic/white gap in children's body mass (Taveras et al., 2013). We are not aware of any studies that examine whether maternal body mass explains SES disparities in child obesity, suggesting a useful direction for future research.

The developmental origins of health and disease perspective also suggest that prenatal environments can drive epigenetic changes that shape race/ethnic and SES disparities in obesity. Epigenetic changes can change gene activity, and can sometimes be passed from one generation to the next, but do not change the structure of DNA itself. For example, paternal obesity has been associated with hypo-methylation of the insulin-like growth factor gene (IGF2) among newborns (Soubry et al., 2013), which has been associated with obesity in children (Ács et al., 2017).

Race/ethnicity and SES may be linked to sets of exposures during developmental stages when epigenetic changes are most likely to occur. Race/ethnic minorities experience historical processes, prejudice, and discrimination that may result in epigenetic changes (Osborne-Majnik et al., 2013). Further, SES might directly impact access to resources like food. Some research shows that having a black father or a less educated mother is associated with epigenetic changes (as observed in umbilical cord blood) that are associated with low birth weight, which is linked to subsequent cardiovascular disease, diabetes, and obesity (King et al., 2015).

Genetics A large body of literature suggests that individuals are genetically predisposed to obesity. Heritability estimates show that genetic factors account for 72% of the variability in obesity among twins and 46% of the variability in obesity among families (Stryjecki et al., 2018). This provides support for the heritable nature of obesity. However, genetic factors may do little to explain race/ethnic differences in obesity. Heritability estimates do not vary across families from different ethnic backgrounds (Stryjecki et al., 2018). Further, most published twin studies have been conducted in predominantly white populations, and provide little insight into understanding the contribution of genetics to race/ethnic disparities in obesity (Harden & Koellinger, 2020).

Genome-wide association studies (GWAS) have demonstrated that obesity is heritable in more diverse populations (Domingue et al., 2014). However, genetic factors are weakly associated with observed race/ethnicity or education, suggesting that they may be poorly poised to explain disparities across groups (Harden & Koellinger, 2020). As a result, genetic factors likely have little power to explain race/ethnic or educational disparities in obesity (Boardman et al., 2010; Boardman et al., 2015).

The thrifty gene hypothesis suggests that genetic differences may predispose some race/ethnic groups differentially to obesity, given ancestral environments that are selected for those genes (Locke et al., 2015). For example, one GWAS in an isolated population of 3072 Samoans found a genetic variant that is unique to this population, predisposing them to obesity (Minster et al., 2016). When expressed, this gene plays a role in decreasing energy use and increasing fat storage. When looking across race/ethnic groups, however, the thrifty-gene hypothesis receives little support. One large study finds little support for the positive selection of single-nucleotide polymorphisms (SNPs) that are associated with obesity, and of the few that were found, five favored leanness rather than obesity (Wang & Speakman, 2016). Further, most of these mutations had occurred prior to the last 30,000 years, suggesting that they did not take place in the context of more recent shifts in agriculture or food systems. Genetic variation may contribute to obesity risk, but in diverse populations, it may do little to account for disparities in obesity.

Neighborhood Context

Neighborhoods are often the places where individuals eat at restaurants, go grocery shopping, exercise, sleep, and experience pollution—all of which may shape obesity risk (also see Chap. 13). Neighborhoods are also segregated by race/ethnicity and SES, suggesting that they may impact disparities in obesity.

Neighborhoods and Food A food desert refers to a low-income neighborhood where a large number of residents have poor access to healthy foods, based on distance from supermarkets, supercenters, or large grocery stores. The food desert literature assumes that people will purchase and consume healthy foods (e.g., fruits, vegetables, and whole grains) if they are available. However, the literature on food deserts and obesity is mixed.

In a nationally representative survey of adults in the U.S., living in a food desert was positively associated with obesity (Testa & Jackson, 2019). Other studies find a null relationship between obesity and food deserts (Cummins et al., 2014). A recent quasi-experimental study shows that opening a grocery store in a food desert leads to few dietary changes and may, in fact, increase the consumption of less healthy foods (Campbell et al., 2020). When stratified by race and ethnicity, one study finds that whites living in food deserts are more likely to be obese than blacks, even though African Americans are more likely to reside in food deserts (Walker et al., 2010). In contrast, a study on African American women with low food access shows that those living in high-poverty neighborhoods are more likely to be obese compared to their counterparts in low-poverty neighborhoods (Gailey & Bruckner, 2019).

Food swamps are neighborhoods with substantial access to unhealthy food options (Fleischhacker et al., 2011). Some research suggests that a lack of access to healthy food may have less impact on obesity than an abundance of unhealthy options (Cooksey-Stowers et al., 2017). For example, minorities and low-income communities are disproportionately targeted by advertising for fast food, snack foods, and sugary beverages (Cassady et al., 2015; Nguyen et al., 2020). Further, communities where the gap between black and white earnings is greatest have relatively more fast food access than grocery store access (Bell et al., 2019). Future research that draws on a more complete inventory of food environments—including food swamps, food deserts, access to food from personal gardens or hunting, or food sold in retail outlets that primarily sell non-food items (e.g., pharmacies)—could clarify the diverse food resources available to broad segments of the population. That research could, in turn, clarify the role of community food access and disparities in obesity.

Neighborhoods and Physical Activity Neighborhoods also offer residents different opportunities to engage in physical activity. Neighborhoods that have access to parks, green spaces, trails, or that are more walkable, are associated with greater physical activity among residents (Smith et al., 2017), and lower levels of obesity (Lee et al., 2019a). But those benefits are not shared equally. Some evidence shows that parks in high-poverty areas are utilized less than parks in more affluent areas (Park et al., 2018). Other research shows that Latinos are more likely to use neighborhood trails for walking or jogging than whites, and those with less education use fewer areas of the trail than do those who are more educated (Kraft et al., 2018). A full test of whether the physical amenities can explain disparities is limited. One example finds that amenities do little to explain race/ethnic or SES disparities. The association between amenities and obesity is stronger among low income than among high income children, but only in rural areas, and the association between amenities and obesity is weaker among Hispanic children than among whites in both urban and rural areas (Uzochukwu, 2017).

Access to outdoor amenities may have little impact on obesity if they appear unsafe or if perceptions of crime are common (Fish et al., 2010). Public spaces like parks and trails that have poor lighting, high levels of crime (or perceptions of crime), and graffiti or other vandalism, may be used less often by individuals in the area (Kraft et al., 2018). For example, parks in high-poverty or minority neighborhoods are often underutilized, due to physical disorder (e.g., graffiti, broken glass) as well as social disorder (e.g., public drinking) (Douglas et al., 2018; Park et al., 2018). Indeed, one study finds that access to safe parks is associated with lower odds of physical inactivity among adolescents who are Asian, white, or from low income families (Babey et al., 2008).

Neighborhoods and Sleep Neighborhoods may impact sleep through diverse mechanisms including concerns about safety, excess light, and noise (Hale et al., 2019). Non-whites and low income populations are more likely to live in neighborhoods with greater exposure to noise pollution due to nearby airports or highways (Muzet, 2007). Further, the housing stock in neighborhoods can affect sleep disparities. Mobile homes are common in lower income communities but are often more poorly constructed than houses or apartments, making it harder for residents to limit noise exposure and control temperature. As a result, those who live in mobile homes are more likely to experience short sleep durations, although blacks are more likely to report short sleep duration than whites even in houses or apartments (Johnson et al., 2018). Noisy neighborhoods are more strongly associated with disrupted sleep among Hispanics than among whites, and are more strongly associated with short sleep durations among both Hispanics and blacks than among whites (Koinis-Mitchell et al., 2019). Ultimately, community barriers to sleep may drive disparities in obesity.

Neighborhoods and Environmental Pollution A recent body of literature suggests that environmental pollution may contribute to obesity through mechanisms including metabolic dysregulation, elevating the risks of other chronic diseases that are associated with obesity, or by preventing individuals from being physically active (An et al., 2018). Indeed, one study shows that exposure to air pollution from automobile traffic is associated with a nearly 14% increase in body mass (Jerrett et al., 2014). Another study suggests that long-term exposure to nitrogen dioxide (a common pollutant) is associated with higher fasting blood-lipid levels, especially among those who are already obese (Kim et al., 2019). These findings are especially concerning, given that air pollution—from sources including automobile traffic, industrial pollution, landfills, or hazardous waste sites—is generally higher among low income or nonwhite populations, than among whites or those with higher household incomes (Clark et al., 2014; Gray et al., 2013). Although this research suggests that air pollution may explain disparities in obesity, empirical tests are lacking. Demographers may be well poised to do this research with access to administrative, geo-spatial, and surveillance data.

Social Connectedness

Social Networks Social networks may influence obesity if one's family, friends, or classmates support lifestyles that drive weight gain or weight loss, or support norms about body image that encourage weight gain or weight loss (Christakis & Fowler, 2007). For example, peers can support obesogenic behaviors such as fast food consumption (Fortin & Yazbeck, 2015). However, the association between social network characteristics and obesity may be spurious if individuals are more likely to befriend individuals who have a similar body mass (i.e. homophily) or if unobserved factors (e.g., school, work, or family characteristics) drive both network connections and obesity (Cohen-Cole & Fletcher, Cohen-Cole & Fletcher, 2008a, b; Zhang et al., 2018). A recent review of longitudinal studies suggests that network characteristics may drive obesity in a reciprocal manner. Individuals form connections with people who have similar risks of obesity, who then go on to share similarly obesogenic environments, and then go on to influence each other's weight related behaviors (Zhang et al., 2018).

Social network characteristics are associated with disparities in obesity. A cross-sectional study suggests that white females are more likely to be overweight if their friends are also overweight, but that association does not emerge among blacks and Hispanics (Bruening et al., 2015). That study, however, does not clarify whether peer influences determine white females' body masses, or whether white females simply choose friends who have similar levels of obesity. A longitudinal study that adjusted for school-level variables and attempted to account for reverse-causality, found that being obese is associated with having fewer friends and lower levels of social integration among white females, but not among blacks or Hispanics (Ali et al., 2012). Aside from the structure of social networks (e.g., number of friends, degree of integration), the characteristics of the people in those networks may also influence obesity. Among black and Hispanic adults, having more friends or family members who are obese is associated with viewing heavier weights as normal (Winston et al., 2015). Network size and SES are also associated with obesity. Higher SES adolescents generally have wider social networks and lower levels of obesity, but social network structure did not vary across the obesity status of adolescents (Arias et al., 2018). Thus, SES may do little to explain any associations between network characteristics and obesity. Taken together, future research could continue to examine whether social networks play a causal role in shaping disparities in obesity, and, if so, untangling the mechanisms at play.

Social Support Social support—including encouragement, accountability, and modeling of healthy behaviors from family, friends, or coworkers—can support obesity prevention and weight loss efforts (Lemstra et al., 2016; Umberson, 1992). Social support from diverse sources may inform race/ethnic and SES disparities in obesity. For example, children in low-income income families have higher body masses, but that association is weaker for children who have greater social support from grandparents (Lindberg et al., 2016). Other research shows that social support within school settings is associated with higher levels of physical activity for children across income groups, and for Hispanics and blacks, but not for whites or Asians (Babey et al., 2015). Social support from parents also matters. Compared to children of white parents, children of English-speaking Hispanic parents have 7.7 times the odds of being overweight or obese in the absence of social support, but that association is reduced by almost 80% if children of English-speaking Hispanic parents have access to social support (Watt et al., 2012). And finally, social support from family and friends is associated with increased physical activity among both white and Hispanic children (Vazquez & Schuler, 2020).

Policy and Population-Level Interventions

Efforts to reduce disparities in obesity depend, in part, on policy and intervention efforts that have population-level impacts.

Randomized Clinical Trials for Obesity Interventions

Some interventions have successfully reduced obesity and its sequelae. A recent meta-analysis of randomized controlled trials (RCTs) finds strong evidence that nutritional intervention programs conducted in obese adult populations significantly reduce the future risk of cardiovascular events and all-cause mortality (Ma et al., 2017). This same study shows that dietary interventions also reduce the subsequent risk of death from cardiovascular disease. In addition, surgical options may reduce disease incidence and extend longevity in overweight adults. A systematic review and meta-analysis of bariatric surgery found that it reduces the risk of stroke, myocardial infarction, and premature mortality by 50%, relative to overweight subjects treated with non-surgical options (Kwok et al., 2014). Recent meta-analyses also show that obesity intervention programs are effective in slowing weight gain among children (Liu et al., 2019; Scott-Sheldon et al., 2020), which could promote the primary prevention of obesity if implemented early in the life course.

This evidence is encouraging and runs counter to the narrative among some clinicians and scholars that obesity intervention programs are "futile" (Havrankova, 2012). However, existing research seldom includes disadvantaged populations. Only one of the RCTs considered by Ma et al. (2017) was conducted in a non-Hispanic Black sample of U.S. adults. Moreover, financial, cultural, and other barriers (e.g., health insurance coverage) can prohibit the widespread adoption of effective interventions, particularly in disadvantaged communities. Indeed, members of disadvantaged communities may lack the resources, knowledge, or power to benefit from any given intervention (Masters et al., 2015; Pampel et al., 2012). For example, food deserts in some areas present structural challenges to the widespread adoption of programs and policies designed to alter dietary behaviors among residents of these communities. Efforts to overcome these barriers might require broader structural shifts such as housing vouchers to move to better resourced neighborhoods (Ludwig et al., 2011).

Social Policies and Large-Scale Interventions

In addition to tailoring small-scale intervention programs to disadvantaged groups, it is important to understand how findings from relatively small intervention programs could scale into social policies that maximize population health returns on public investments (Roundtable on Population Health Improvement, 2015). Although not obesity interventions per se, nutritional assistance programs in the U.S. are currently the most influential social policies with respect to dietary options, behaviors, and related changes in body habitus. To date, evidence on these programs is mixed.

The Supplemental Nutrition Assistance Program (SNAP) is one such program. With a typical annual budget in excess of 60 billion dollars that reaches approximately 40 million households each month, SNAP—formerly known as the food stamp program—is by far the largest nutritional intervention program in the U.S. (Tiehen, 2020). SNAP targets lower income families, and eligibility depends on both income and asset criteria. Unfortunately, a considerable body of evidence suggests that, as historically configured, SNAP benefits create incentives that encourage poor diet, weight gain, and obesity. For instance, children, adolescents, and adults who receive SNAP-subsidized groceries are more likely to drink sugar-sweetened beverages than SNAP-eligible persons who do not receive benefits (Twarog et al., 2020). Perhaps in part due to sugary beverage consumption, adolescent and adult SNAP recipients are more likely to be obese and exhibit poor cardiometabolic health, relative to low income persons who do not use SNAP (Leung et al., 2017; Leung & Rimm, 2015). Moreover, the county-level prevalence of obesity is positively associated with SNAP-authorized convenience stores, suggesting that SNAP benefits are sometimes used to purchase high-calorie items of low nutritional value (Houghtaling et al., 2021).

However, it is important to acknowledge that some research indicates that SNAP benefits can support a healthy diet and body mass. For instance, analyses of data from the Panel Study of Income Dynamics found that low-income children with access to SNAP benefits have lower long-term risks of developing obesity and related conditions (e.g., diabetes) than other disadvantaged children (Hoynes et al., 2012). Similarly, a study of the National Longitudinal Survey of Youth-1979 data finds that, among SNAP recipients, access to higher levels of SNAP benefits reduced average weight and the probability of obesity (Almada & Tchernis, 2018).

Evidence suggests that health outcomes related to nutritional-support programs are malleable and dependent on specific policy provisions. To illustrate, in 2009 the Special Supplemental Nutrition Program for Women, Infants, and Children (WIC) improved recipients' food packages (e.g., by including more fruits and vegetables), which encouraged healthier overall food purchasing behaviors (e.g., buying items with less sodium and sugar) among WIC-eligible households (Ng et al., 2018). In addition, improved nutritional standards for school-lunch programs implemented in 2010 by the U.S. Department of Agriculture have resulted in healthier diets and lower odds of overweight and obesity among children and adolescents (Welker et al., 2016). Recent evidence suggests that these improved nutritional standards are associated with reduced obesity risk, especially among children in poverty (Kenney et al., 2020).

In addition to SNAP and other federally-supported nutrition programs, scholars and policymakers have begun to explore interventions that are specifically designed to limit weight gain and reduce obesity prevalence. Perhaps the clearest illustration of such policies is the implementation of soda taxes in some U.S. cities, which are levied to reduce consumption of sugar sweetened beverages (SSBs) by increasing financial costs to consumers. In 2014, Berkeley, California levied a one cent per-ounce excise tax on SSBs; after 3 years, consumption of SSBs declined significantly among Berkeley residents but remained constant in comparison cities of Oakland and San Francisco, which did not tax SSBs until 2017 and 2018, respectively (Lee et al., 2019b). A similar policy in Philadelphia, Pennsylvania, had modest effects on reducing SSB consumption, overall, but significantly reduced the intake of SSBs among African-American children and adults (Cawley et al., 2019). Although this policy had limited benefits for overall population health, it benefited a sub-population with higher obesity risk, potentially preventing further widening of obesity disparities in the future.

Finally, it is imperative to recognize that human behavior occurs within institutional and environmental contexts that constrain the choices available to individuals. One way to shift environmental contexts is to move from one neighborhood to another, leading to improvement (or deterioration) in access to well-stocked supermarkets, walkable sidewalks and/or trails, and healthcare facilities. Extant research strongly suggests but has not yet definitively shown that moving from disadvantaged neighborhoods to wealthier ones reduces obesity risks through these and other mechanisms (Drewnowski et al., 2019). Another, more subtle way to alter choice sets is to "nudge" people toward healthier options. For instance, workplaces can increase access to and improve the visibility of healthy snack options, nudging employees toward lower-calorie diets. A meta-analysis of dietary interventions designed to test behavioral nudges concluded that altering "choice architecture" is likely an effective public health strategy to reduce obesity prevalence (Arno & Thomas, 2016). An implication of these studies is that reducing obesity disparities in the U.S. will require new policies that support access to healthy choices, especially for its most disadvantaged citizens.

Conclusion

Race/ethnic and SES disparities in obesity are persistent, and may continue to widen in the future. A complex set of behavioral, biological, neighborhood, and social mechanisms contribute to these disparities, although existing research does little to systematically compare each of these sets of mechanisms. The literature also describes some policy levers or interventions that may be useful for closing disparities or reducing overall disparities, if configured appropriately. Urgent efforts to improve our understanding of disparities and to design policies and interventions to close those disparities are warranted, given the long-term consequences of obesity disparities for population health.

References

Ács, O., Péterfia, B., Hollósi, P., Luczay, A., Török, D., & Szabó, A. (2017). Methylation status of CYP27B1 and IGF2 correlate to BMI SDS in children with obesity. *Obesity Facts, 10*, 353–362.

Al Khatib, H. K., Harding, S. V., Darzi, J., & Pot, G. K. (2017). The effects of partial sleep deprivation on energy balance: A systematic review and meta-analysis. *European Journal of Clinical Nutrition, 71*, 614–624.

Ali, M. M., Amialchuk, A., & Rizzo, J. A. (2012). The influence of body weight on social network ties among adolescents. *Economics & Human Biology, 10*, 20–34.

Almada, L. N., & Tchernis, R. (2018). Measuring effects of SNAP on obesity at the intensive margin. *Economics and Human Biology, 31*, 150–163.

An, R., Ji, M., Yan, H., & Guan, C. (2018). Impact of ambient air pollution on obesity: A systematic review. *International Journal of Obesity, 42*, 1112–1126.

Arias, N., Calvo, M. D., Benítez-Andrades, J. A., Álvarez, M. J., Alonso-Cortés, B., & Benavides, C. (2018). Socioeconomic status in adolescents: A study of its relationship with overweight and obesity and influence on social network configuration. *International Journal of Environmental Research and Public Health, 15*, 2014.

Arno, A., & Thomas, S. (2016). The efficacy of nudge theory strategies in influencing adult dietary behaviour: A systematic review and meta-analysis. *BMC Public Health, 16*, 676.

Audrain-McGovern, J., & Benowitz, N. L. (2011). Cigarette smoking, nicotine, and body weight. *Clinical Pharmacology and Therapeutics, 90*, 164–168.

Babey, S. H., Hastert, T. A., Hongjian, Y., & Richard Brown, E. (2008). Physical activity among adolescents: When do parks matter? *American Journal of Preventive Medicine, 34*, 345–348.

Babey, S. H., Wolstein, J., & Diamant, A. L. (2015). Adolescent physical activity: Role of school support, role models, and social participation in racial and income disparities. *Environment and Behavior, 48*, 172–191.

Bartok, C. J., & Ventura, A. K. (2009). Mechanisms underlying the association between breastfeeding and obesity. *International Journal of Pediatric Obesity, 4*, 196–204.

Basner, M., & Dinges, D. F. (2018). Sleep duration in the United States 2003–2016: First signs of success in the fight against sleep deficiency? *Sleep*, 41.

Basu, S., Seligman, H., & Winkleby, M. A. (2014). A metabolic-epidemiological microsimulation model to estimate the changes in energy intake and physical activity necessary to meet the Healthy People 2020 obesity objective. *American Journal of Public Health, 104*, 1209–1216.

Bell, C. N., Kerr, J., & Young, J. L. (2019). Associations between obesity, obesogenic environments, and structural racism vary by county-level racial composition. *International Journal of Environmental Research and Public Health, 16*.

Bhattacharya, J., Currie, J., & Haider, S. (2004). Poverty, food insecurity, and nutritional outcomes in children and adults. *Journal of Health Economics, 23*, 839–862.

Bleich, S. N., Vercammen, K. A., Koma, J. W., & Li, Z. (2018). Trends in beverage consumption among children and adults, 2003-2014. *Obesity, 26*, 432–441.

Boardman, J. D., Blalock, C. L., Corley, R. P., Stallings, M. C., Domingue, B. W., McQueen, M. B., Crowley, T. J., Hewitt, J. K., Ying, L., & Field, S. H. (2010). Ethnicity, body mass, and genome-wide data. *Biodemography and Social Biology, 56*, 123–136.

Boardman, J. D., Domingue, B. W., & Daw, J. (2015). What can genes tell us about the relationship between education and health? *Social Science & Medicine, 1982*(127), 171–180.

Broesch, J., & Hadley, C. (2012). Putting culture back into acculturation: Identifying and overcoming gaps in the definition and measurement of acculturation. *The Social Science Journal, 49*, 375–385.

Bruening, M., MacLehose, R., Eisenberg, M. E., Kim, S., Story, M., & Neumark-Sztainer, D. (2015). Friends like me: Associations in overweight/obese status among adolescent friends by race/ethnicity, sex, and friendship type. *Childhood Obesity, 11*, 722–730.

Campbell, C., Pinedo, M. M. C., Midgette, W., & Vieira, J. (2020). The consequences of living in a small-town food desert: Mixed methods evidence from a quasi-experiment. *Social Currents, 7*, 563–581.

Carney, R. M., & Goldberg, A. P. (1984). Weight gain after cessation of cigarette smoking. *New England Journal of Medicine, 310*, 614–616.

Carson, V., & Kuzik, N. (2017). Demographic correlates of screen time and objectively measured sedentary time and physical activity among toddlers: A cross-sectional study. *BMC Public Health, 17*, 187.

Cassady, D. L., Liaw, K., Soederberg, L. M., & Miller. (2015). Disparities in obesity-related outdoor advertising by neighborhood income and race. *Journal of Urban Health, 92*, 835–842.

Cawley, J., Frisvold, D., Hill, A., & Jones, D. (2019). The impact of the Philadelphia beverage tax on purchases and consumption by adults and children. *Journal of Health Economics, 67*, 102225.

Chahal, H., Fung, C., Kuhle, S., & Veugelers, P. J. (2013). Availability and night-time use of electronic entertainment and communication devices are associated with short sleep duration and obesity among Canadian children. *Pediatric Obesity, 8*, 42–51.

Chen, X., Wang, R., Zee, P., Lutsey, P. L., Javaheri, S., Alcántara, C., Jackson, C. L., Williams, M. A., & Redline, S. (2015). Racial/ethnic differences in sleep disturbances: The multi-ethnic study of atherosclerosis (MESA). *Sleep, 38*, 877–888.

Christakis, N. A., & Fowler, J. H. (2007). The spread of obesity in a large social network over 32 years. *New England Journal of Medicine, 357*, 370–379.

Church, T. S., Thomas, D. M., Tudor-Locke, C., Katzmarzyk, P. T., Earnest, C. P., Rodarte, R. Q., Martin, C. K., Blair, S. N., & Bouchard, C. (2011). Trends over 5 decades in US occupation-related physical activity and their associations with obesity. *PLoS One, 6*, e19657.

Clark, L. P., Millet, D. B., & Marshall, J. D. (2014). National patterns in environmental injustice and inequality: Outdoor NO 2 air pollution in the United States. *PLoS One, 9*, e94431.

Cohen-Cole, E., & Fletcher, J. M. (2008a). Detecting implausible social network effects in acne, height, and headaches: Longitudinal analysis. *BMJ, 337*, a2533.

Cohen-Cole, E., & Fletcher, J. M. (2008b). Is obesity contagious? Social networks vs. environmental factors in the obesity epidemic. *Journal of Health Economics, 27*, 1382–1387.

Cooksey-Stowers, K., Schwartz, M. B., & Brownell, K. D. (2017). Food swamps predict obesity rates better than food deserts in the United States. *International Journal of Environmental Research and Public Health, 14*.

Creighton, M. J., Goldman, N., Pebley, A. R., & Chung, C. Y. (2012). Durational and generational differences in Mexican immigrant obesity: Is acculturation the explanation? *Social Science & Medicine, 75*, 300–310.

Cummins, S., Flint, E., & Matthews, S. A. (2014). New neighborhood grocery store increased awareness of food access but did not alter dietary habits or obesity. *Health Affairs, 33*, 283–291.

Cunningham, S. A., Kramer, M. R., & Narayan, K. M. (2014). Incidence of childhood obesity in the United States. *The New England Journal of Medicine, 370*, 403–411.

Dabelea, D., & Crume, T. (2011). Maternal environment and the transgenerational cycle of obesity and diabetes. *Diabetes, 60*, 1849.

Dare, S., Mackay, D. F., & Pell, J. P. (2015). Relationship between smoking and obesity: A cross-sectional study of 499,504 middle-aged adults in the UK general population. *PLoS One, 10*, e0123579–e0123579.

Denney, J. T., Krueger, P. M., Rogers, R. G., & Boardman, J. D. (2004). Race/ethnic and sex differentials in body mass among US adults. *Ethnicity & Disease, 14*, 389–398.

Domingue, B. W., Belsky, D. W., Harris, K. M., Smolen, A., McQueen, M. B., & Boardman, J. D. (2014). Polygenic risk predicts obesity in both white and black young adults. *PLoS One, 9*, e101596.

Douglas, J. A., Briones, M. D., Bauer, E. Z., Trujillo, M., Lopez, M., & Subica, A. M. (2018). Social and environmental determinants of physical activity in urban parks: Testing a neighborhood disorder model. *Preventive Medicine, 109*, 119–124.

Drewnowski, A., Arterburn, D., Zane, J., Aggarwal, A., Gupta, S., Hurvitz, P. M., Moudon, A. V., Bobb, J., Cook, A., Lozano, P., & Rosenberg, D. (2019). The moving to health (M2H) approach to natural experiment research: A paradigm shift for studies on built environment and health. *SSM Popul Health, 7*, 100345.

Fish, J. S., Ettner, S., Ang, A., & Brown, A. F. (2010). Association of perceived neighborhood safety on body mass index. *American Journal of Public Health, 100*, 2296–2303.

Fleischhacker, S. E., Evenson, K. R., Rodriguez, D. A., & Ammerman, A. S. (2011). A systematic review of fast food access studies. *Obesity Reviews, 12*, e460–e471.

Ford, E. S., Li, C., Zhao, G., & Tsai, J. (2011). Trends in obesity and abdominal obesity among adults in the United States from 1999–2008. *International Journal of Obesity, 35*, 736–743.

Fortin, B., & Yazbeck, M. (2015). Peer effects, fast food consumption and adolescent weight gain. *Journal of Health Economics, 42*, 125–138.

Fryar, C. D., Carroll, M. D., & Afful, J. (2020). *Prevalence of overweight, obesity, and severe obesity among children and adolescents aged 2–19 years: United States, 1963–1965 through 2017–2018*. E-Stats.

Gailey, S., & Bruckner, T. A. (2019). Obesity among black women in food deserts: An "omnibus" test of differential risk. *SSM-population health, 7*, 100363.

Garrett, B. E., Dube, S. R., Trosclair, A., Caraballo, R. S., & Pechacek, T. F. (2011). Cigarette smoking – United States, 1965–2008. *Morbidity and Mortality Weekly Report, 60*, 109–113.

Gluckman, P. D., & Hanson, M. A. (2004). Living with the past: Evolution, development, and patterns of disease. *Science, 305*, 1733.

Gluckman, P. D., Hanson, M. A., Cooper, C., & Thornburg, K. L. (2008). Effect of in utero and early-life conditions on adult health and disease. *The New England Journal of Medicine, 359*, 61–73.

Gorber, S., Connor, M., Tremblay, D. M., & Gorber, B. (2007). A comparison of direct vs. self-report measures for assessing height, weight and body mass index: A systematic review. *Obesity Reviews, 8*, 307–326.

Gordon-Larsen, P., Adair, L. S., Nelson, M. C., & Popkin, B. M. (2004). Five-year obesity incidence in the transition period between adolescence and adulthood: The National Longitudinal Study of adolescent health. *The American Journal of Clinical Nutrition, 80*, 569–575.

Gray, S. C., Edwards, S. E., & Miranda, M. L. (2013). Race, socioeconomic status, and air pollution exposure in North Carolina. *Environmental Research, 126*, 152–158.

Hale, L., James, S., Xiao, Q., Billings, M. E., & Johnson, D. A. (2019). Chapter 7 – Neighborhood factors associated with sleep health. In M. A. Grandner (Ed.), *Sleep and health* (pp. 77–84). Academic.

Hales, C. M., Carroll, M. D., Fryar, C. D., & Ogden, C. L. (2020). Prevalence of obesity and severe obesity among adults: United States, 2017-2018. In *NCHS data brief, no 360*. National Center for Health Statistics.

Hamburg, N. M., McMackin, C. J., Huang, A. L., Shenouda, S. M., Widlansky, M. E., Schulz, E., Gokce, N., Ruderman, N. B., Keaney Jr, J. F., & Vita, J. A. (2007). Physical inactivity rapidly induces insulin resistance and microvascular dysfunction in healthy volunteers. *Arteriosclerosis, Thrombosis, and Vascular Biology, 27*, 2650–2656.

Han, E., & Powell, L. M. (2013). Consumption patterns of sugar-sweetened beverages in the United States. *Journal of the Academy of Nutrition and Dietetics, 113*, 43–53.

Harden, K. P., & Koellinger, P. D. (2020). Using genetics for social science. *Nature Human Behaviour, 4*, 567–576.

Hattori, A., & Sturm, R. (2013). The obesity epidemic and changes in self-report biases in BMI. *Obesity, 21*, 856–860.

Haughton, C. F., Wang, M. L., & Lemon, S. C. (2016). Racial/ethnic disparities in meeting 5-2-1-0 recommendations among children and adolescents in the United States. *The Journal of Pediatrics, 175*(188–194), e1.

Havrankova, J. (2012). Is the treatment of obesity futile? YES. *Canadian Family Physician, 58*, 508–510.

Healton, C. G., Vallone, D., McCausland, K. L., Xiao, H., & Green, M. P. (2006). Smoking, obesity, and their co-occurrence in the United States: Cross sectional analysis. *BMJ, 333*, 25–26.

Heck, K. E., Braveman, P., Cubbin, C., Chávez, G. F., & Kiely, J. L. (2006). Socioeconomic status and breastfeeding initiation among California mothers. *Public Health Reports, 121*, 51–59.

Houghtaling, B., Kniola, D., & Misyak, S. (2021). Supplemental nutrition assistance program (SNAP)-authorized grocery, convenience, dollar, and restaurant or delivery service settings are associated with increased obesity prevalence in Virginia. *American Journal of Health Promotion, 35*, 127–130.

Houston, T. K., Person, S. D., Pletcher, M. J., Liu, K., Iribarren, C., & Kiefe, C. I. (2006). Active and passive smoking and development of glucose intolerance among young adults in a prospective cohort: CARDIA study. *BMJ, 332*, 1064–1069.

Hoynes, H. W., Schanzenbach, D., Almond, D., & National Bureau of Economic Research. (2012). *Long run impacts of childhood access to the safety net* (NBER working paper series no 18535, (Pp. 1 online resource (47 pages))). National Bureau of Economic Research.

Ino, T. (2010). Maternal smoking during pregnancy and offspring obesity: Meta-analysis. *Pediatrics International, 52*, 94–99.

Jean-Louis, G., Youngstedt, S., Grandner, M., Williams, N. J., Sarpong, D., Zizi, F., & Ogedegbe, G. (2015). Unequal burden of sleep-related obesity among black and white Americans. *Sleep Health, 1*, 169–176.

Jerrett, M., McConnell, R., Wolch, J., Chang, R., Lam, C., Dunton, G., Gilliland, F., Lurmann, F., Islam, T., & Berhane, K. (2014). Traffic-related air pollution and obesity formation in children: A longitudinal, multilevel analysis. *Environmental Health, 13*, 1–9.

Jih, J., Mukherjea, A., Vittinghoff, E., Nguyen, T. T., Tsoh, J. Y., Fukuoka, Y., Bender, M. S., Tseng, W., & Kanaya, A. M. (2014). Using appropriate body mass index cut points for overweight and obesity among Asian Americans. *Preventive Medicine, 65*, 1–6.

Johnson, D. A., Thorpe, R. J., McGrath, J. A., Jackson, W. B., & Jackson, C. L. (2018). Black–white differences in housing type and sleep duration as well as sleep difficulties in the United States. *International Journal of Environmental Research and Public Health, 15*.

Kant, A. K., Whitley, M. I., & Graubard, B. I. (2015). Away from home meals: Associations with biomarkers of chronic disease and dietary intake in American adults, NHANES 2005–2010. *International Journal of Obesity, 39*, 820–827.

Katzmarzyk, P. T., & I-Min Lee, Corby K Martin, and Steven N Blair. (2017). Epidemiology of physical activity and exercise training in the United States. *Progress in Cardiovascular Diseases, 60*, 3–10.

Kenney, E. L., Barrett, J. L., Bleich, S. N., Ward, Z. J., Cradock, A. L., & Gortmaker, S. L. (2020). Impact of the healthy, hunger-free kids act on obesity trends. *Health Affairs, 39*, 1122–1129.

Kim, Y., Barreira, T. V., & Kang, M. (2016). Concurrent associations of physical activity and screen-based sedentary behavior on obesity among US adolescents: A latent class analysis. *Journal of Epidemiology, 26*, 137–144.

Kim, J. S., Chen, Z., Alderete, T. L., Toledo-Corral, C., Lurmann, F., Berhane, K., & Gilliland, F. D. (2019). Associations of air pollution, obesity and cardiometabolic health in young adults: The Meta-AIR study. *Environment International, 133*, 105180.

King, K., Murphy, S., & Hoyo, C. (2015). Epigenetic regulation of Newborns' imprinted genes related to gestational growth: Patterning by parental race/ethnicity and maternal socioeconomic status. *Journal of Epidemiology and Community Health, 69*, 639–647.

Knutson, K. L. (2011). Association between sleep duration and body size differs among three Hispanic groups. *American Journal of Human Biology, 23*, 138–141.

Koinis-Mitchell, D., Boergers, J., Kopel, S. J., McQuaid, E. L., Farrow, M. L., & LeBourgeois, M. (2019). Racial and ethnic disparities in sleep outcomes among urban children with and without asthma. *Sleep Health, 5*, 532–538.

Kraft, A. N., Nunez, J., Tarlov, E., Slater, S., & Zenk, S. N. (2018). Racial/ethnic and educational differences in perceptions and use of a new urban trail. *Ethnicity & Health*, 1–16.

Kramer, M. S., Matush, L., Vanilovich, I., Platt, R. W., Bogdanovich, N., Sevkovskaya, Z., Dzikovich, I., Shishko, G., Collet, J.-P., Martin, R. M., Smith, G. D., Gillman, M. W., Chalmers, B., Hodnett, E., & Shapiro, S. (2009). A randomized breast-feeding promotion intervention did not reduce child obesity in Belarus. *The Journal of Nutrition, 139*, 417S–421S.

Krueger, P. M., & Friedman, E. M. (2009). Sleep duration in the United States: A cross-sectional population-based study. *American Journal of Epidemiology, 169*, 1052–1063.

Krueger, P. M., Coleman-Minahan, K., & Rooks, R. N. (2014). Race/ethnicity, nativity, and trends in BMI among U.S. adults. *Obesity, 22*, 1739–1746.

Kwok, C. S., Pradhan, A., Khan, M. A., Anderson, S. G., Keavney, B. D., Myint, P. K., Mamas, M. A., & Loke, Y. K. (2014). Bariatric surgery and its impact on cardiovascular disease and mortality: A systematic review and meta-analysis. *International Journal of Cardiology, 173*, 20–28.

Lee, K. H., Heo, J., Jayaraman, R., & Dawson, S. (2019a). Proximity to parks and natural areas as an environmental determinant to spatial disparities in obesity prevalence. *Applied Geography, 112*, 102074.

Lee, M. M., Falbe, J., Schillinger, D., Basu, S., McCulloch, C. E., & Madsen, K. A. (2019b). Sugar-sweetened beverage consumption 3 years after the Berkeley, California, sugar-sweetened beverage tax. *American Journal of Public Health, 109*, 637–639.

Lemstra, M., Bird, Y., Nwankwo, C., Rogers, M., & Moraros, J. (2016). Weight loss intervention adherence and factors promoting adherence: A meta-analysis. *Patient Preference and Adherence, 10*, 1547.

Leung, C. W., & Rimm, E. B. (2015). Misinterpretation of SNAP participation, diet, and weight in low-income adults. *American Journal of Public Health, 105*, e1.

Leung, C. W., & Tester, J. M. (2019). The association between food insecurity and diet quality varies by race/ethnicity: An analysis of National Health and nutrition examination survey 2011-2014 results. *Journal of the Academy of Nutrition and Dietetics, 119*, 1676–1686.

Leung, C. W., Epel, E. S., Ritchie, L. D., Crawford, P. B., & Laraia, B. A. (2014). Food insecurity is inversely associated with diet quality of lower-income adults. *Journal of the Academy of Nutrition and Dietetics, 114*(1943–1953), e2.

Leung, C. W., Tester, J. M., Rimm, E. B., & Willett, W. C. (2017). SNAP participation and diet-sensitive Cardiometabolic risk factors in adolescents. *American Journal of Preventive Medicine, 52*, S127–S137.

Lewkowitz, A. K., López, J. D., Carter, E. B., Duckham, H., Strickland, T., Macones, G. A., & Cahill, A. G. (2020). Impact of a novel smartphone application on low-income, first-time mothers' breastfeeding rates: A randomized controlled trial. *American Journal of Obstetrics & Gynecology MFM, 2*, 100143.

Lindberg, L., Ek, A., Nyman, J., Marcus, C., Ulijaszek, S., & Nowicka, P. (2016). Low grandparental social support combined with low parental socioeconomic status is closely associated with obesity in preschool-aged children: A pilot study. *Pediatric Obesity, 11*, 313–316.

Liu, Z., Xu, H. M., Wen, L. M., Peng, Y. Z., Lin, L. Z., Zhou, S., Li, W. H., & Wang, H. J. (2019). A systematic review and meta-analysis of the overall effects of school-based obesity prevention interventions and effect differences by intervention components. *International Journal of Behavioral Nutrition and Physical Activity, 16*, 95.

Locke, A. E., Kahali, B., Berndt, S. I., Justice, A. E., Pers, T. H., Day, F. R., Powell, C., Vedantam, S., Buchkovich, M. L., & Yang, J. (2015). Genetic studies of body mass index yield new insights for obesity biology. *Nature, 518*, 197–206.

Louis-Jacques, A., Deubel, T. F., Taylor, M., & Stuebe, A. M. (2017). Racial and ethnic disparities in U.-S. breastfeeding and implications for maternal and child health outcomes. *Seminars in Perinatology, 41*, 299–307.

Ludwig, J., Sanbonmatsu, L., Gennetian, L., Adam, E., Duncan, G. J., Katz, L. F., Kessler, R. C., Kling, J. R., Lindau, S. T., Whitaker, R. C., & McDade, T. W. (2011). Neighborhoods, obesity, and diabetes — A randomized social experiment. *New England Journal of Medicine, 365*, 1509–1519.

Ma, C., Avenell, A., Bolland, M., Hudson, J., Stewart, F., Robertson, C., Sharma, P., Fraser, C., & MacLennan, G. (2017). Effects of weight loss interventions for adults who are obese on mortality, cardiovascular disease, and cancer: Systematic review and meta-analysis. *BMJ, 359*, j4849.

Martin, M. A., Van Hook, J. L., & Quiros, S. (2015). Is socioeconomic incorporation associated with a healthier diet? Dietary patterns among Mexican-origin children in the United States. *Social Science & Medicine, 147*, 20–29.

Masters, R. K., Reither, E. N., Powers, D. A., Claire Yang, Y., Burger, A. E., & Link, B. G. (2013). The impact of obesity on US mortality levels: The importance of age and cohort factors in population estimates. *American Journal of Public Health, 103*, 1895–1901.

Masters, R. K., Link, B. G., & Phelan, J. C. (2015). Trends in education gradients of 'preventable' mortality: A test of fundamental cause theory. *Social Science & Medicine, 127*, 19–28.

Mineur, Y. S., Abizaid, A., Rao, Y., Salas, R., DiLeone, R. J., Gündisch, D., Diano, S., De Biasi, M., Horvath, T. L., Gao, X.-B., & Picciotto, M. R. (2011). Nicotine decreases food intake through activation of POMC neurons. *Science, 332*, 1330.

Minster, R. L., Hawley, N. L., Chi-Ting, S., Sun, G., Kershaw, E. E., Cheng, H., Buhule, O. D., Lin, J., Tuitele, J., & Naseri, T. (2016). A thrifty variant in CREBRF strongly influences body mass index in Samoans. *Nature Genetics, 48*, 1049–1054.

Mun, J., Kim, Y., Farnsworth, J. L., Suh, S., & Kang, M. (2018). Association between objectively measured sedentary behavior and a criterion measure of obesity among adults. *American Journal of Human Biology, 30*, e23080.

Muzet, A. (2007). Environmental noise, sleep and health. *Sleep Medicine Reviews, 11*, 135–142.

Narcisse, M.-R., Long, C. R., Felix, H., Rowland, B., Bursac, Z., & McElfish, P. A. (2018). The mediating role of sleep quality and quantity in the link between food insecurity and obesity across race and ethnicity. *Obesity, 26*, 1509–1518.

Neville, C. E., McKinley, M. C., Holmes, V. A., Spence, D., & Woodside, J. V. (2014). The relationship between breastfeeding and postpartum weight change—A systematic review and critical evaluation. *International Journal of Obesity, 38*, 577–590.

Ng, S. W., Hollingsworth, B. A., Busey, E. A., Wandell, J. L., Miles, D. R., & Poti, J. M. (2018). Federal nutrition program revisions impact low-income households' food purchases. *American Journal of Preventive Medicine, 54*, 403–412.

Nguyen, K. H., Glantz, S. A., Palmer, C. N., & Schmidt, L. A. (2020). Transferring racial/ethnic marketing strategies from tobacco to food corporations: Philip Morris and Kraft General Foods. *American Journal of Public Health, 110*, 329–336.

Ogden, C. L., Carroll, M. D., Fakhouri, T. H., Hales, C. M., Fryar, C. D., Li, X., & Freedman, D. S. (2018). Prevalence of obesity among youths by household income and education level of head of household – United States 2011–2014. *MMWR. Morbidity and Mortality Weekly Report, 67*, 186–189.

Omisade, A., Buxton, O. M., & Rusak, B. (2010). Impact of acute sleep restriction on cortisol and leptin levels in young women. *Physiology & Behavior, 99*, 651–656.

Osborne-Majnik, A., Qi, F., & Lane, R. H. (2013). Epigenetic mechanisms in fetal origins of health and disease. *Clinical Obstetrics and Gynecology, 56*, 622.

Pampel, F. C., Krueger, P. M., & Denney, J. T. (2010). Socioeconomic disparities in health behaviors. *Annual Review of Sociology, 36*, 349–370.

Pampel, F. C., Denney, J. T., & Krueger, P. M. (2012). Obesity, SES, and economic development: A test of the reversal hypothesis. *Social Science & Medicine, 74*, 1073–1081.

Park, S., Han, B., Cohen, D. A., & Derose, K. P. (2018). Contributions of neighborhood parks to physical activity in high-poverty urban Neighborhoods. *Journal of Urban Health, 95*, 881–887.

Pearson, N., & Biddle, S. J. H. (2011). Sedentary behavior and dietary intake in children, adolescents, and adults: A systematic review. *American Journal of Preventive Medicine, 41*, 178–188.

Perng, W., Oken, E., & Dabelea, D. (2019). Developmental overnutrition and obesity and type 2 diabetes in offspring. *Diabetologia, 62*, 1779–1788.

Piccolo, R. S., Yang, M., Bliwise, D. L., Klar Yaggi, H., & Araujo, A. B. (2013). Racial and socioeconomic disparities in sleep and chronic disease: Results of a longitudinal investigation. *Ethnicity & Disease, 23*, 499.

Rehm, C. D., Peñalvo, J. L., Afshin, A., & Mozaffarian, D. (2016). Dietary intake among US adults, 1999-2012. *JAMA, 315*, 2542–2553.

Reither, E. N., Hauser, R. M., & Yang, Y. (2009). Do birth cohorts matter? Age-period-cohort analyses of the obesity epidemic in the United States. *Social Science & Medicine, 69*, 1439–1448.

Reither, E. N., Krueger, P. M., Lauren Hale, E., Reiter, M., & Peppard, P. E. (2014). Ethnic variation in the association between sleep and body mass among US adolescents. *International Journal of Obesity, 38*, 944–949.

Rosinger, A. Y., Herrick, K. A., Wutich, A. Y., Yoder, J. S., & Ogden, C. L. (2018). Disparities in plain, tap and bottled water consumption among US adults: National Health and Nutrition Examination Survey (NHANES) 2007–2014. *Public Health Nutrition, 21*, 1455–1464.

Rosinger, A. Y., Bethancourt, H., & Francis, L. A. (2019). Association of Caloric Intake from sugar-sweetened beverages with water intake among US children and young adults in the 2011–2016 national health and nutrition examination survey. *JAMA Pediatrics, 173*, 602–604.

Roundtable on Population Health Improvement. (2015). Paying for population health improvement: An overview. In *Financing population health improvement: Workshop summary: Institute of medicine*. National Academies Press.

Saint Onge, J. M., & Krueger, P. M. (2011). Education and racial-ethnic differences in types of exercise in the United States. *Journal of Health and Social Behavior, 52*, 197–211.

Scholes, S., & Bann, D. (2018). Education-related disparities in reported physical activity during leisure-time, active transportation, and work among US adults: Repeated cross-sectional analysis from the National Health and Nutrition Examination Surveys, 2007 to 2016. *BMC Public Health, 18*, 926.

Scott-Sheldon, L. A. J., Hedges, L. V., Cyr, C., Young-Hyman, D., Khan, L. K., Magnus, M., King, H., Arteaga, S., Cawley, J., Economos, C. D., Haire-Joshu, D., Hunter, C. M., Lee, B. Y., Kumanyika, S. K., Ritchie, L. D., Robinson, T. N., & Schwartz, M. B. (2020). Childhood obesity evidence base project: A systematic review and meta-analysis of a new taxonomy of intervention components to improve weight status in children 2-5 years of age, 2005-2019. *Childhood Obesity, 16*, S221–S248.

Shimokata, H., Muller, D. C., & Andres, R. (1989). Studies in the distribution of body fat: III. Effects of cigarette smoking. *JAMA, 261*, 1169–1173.

Shuval, K., Li, Q., Gabriel, K. P., & Tchernis, R. (2017). Income, physical activity, sedentary behavior, and the 'weekend warrior' among U.S. adults. *Preventive Medicine, 103*, 91–97.

Smith, M., Hosking, J., Woodward, A., Witten, K., MacMillan, A., Field, A., Baas, P., & Mackie, H. (2017). Systematic literature review of built environment effects on physical activity and active transport – An update and new findings on health equity. *International Journal of Behavioral Nutrition and Physical Activity, 14*, 158.

Soubry, A., Schildkraut, J. M., Murtha, A., Wang, F., Huang, Z., Bernal, A., Kurtzberg, J., Jirtle, R. L., Murphy, S. K., & Hoyo, C. (2013). Paternal obesity is associated with IGF2 hypomethylation in newborns: Results from a Newborn epigenetics study (NEST) cohort. *BMC Medicine, 11*, 1–10.

Spaeth, A. M., Dinges, D. F., & Goel, N. (2013). Effects of experimental sleep restriction on weight gain, caloric intake, and meal timing in healthy adults. *Sleep, 36*, 981–990.

Spiegel, K., Tasali, E., Penev, P., & Van Cauter, E. (2004). Brief communication: Sleep curtailment in healthy young men is associated with decreased leptin levels, elevated ghrelin levels, and increased hunger and appetite. *Annals of Internal Medicine, 141*, 846–850.

Stommel, M., & Schoenborn, C. A. (2009). Accuracy and usefulness of BMI measures based on self-reported weight and height: Findings from the NHANES & NHIS 2001-2006. *BMC Public Health, 9*, 1–10.

Strauss, R. S. (1999). Comparison of measured and self-reported weight and height in a cross-sectional sample of young adolescents. *International Journal of Obesity, 23*, 904–908.

Strauss, R. S., & Knight, J. (1999). Influence of the home environment on the development of obesity in children. *Pediatrics, 103*, e85–e85.

Stryjecki, C., Alyass, A., & Meyre, D. (2018). Ethnic and population differences in the genetic predisposition to human obesity. *Obesity Reviews, 19*, 62–80.

Tandon, P. S., Zhou, C., Sallis, J. F., Cain, K. L., Frank, L. D., & Saelens, B. E. (2012). Home environment relationships with children's physical activity, sedentary time, and screen time by socioeconomic status. *International Journal of Behavioral Nutrition and Physical Activity, 9*, 1–9.

Taveras, E. M., Gillman, M. W., Kleinman, K., Rich-Edwards, J. W., & Rifas-Shiman, S. L. (2010). Racial/ethnic differences in early-life risk factors for childhood obesity. *Pediatrics, 125*, 686–695.

Taveras, E. M., Gillman, M. W., Kleinman, K. P., Rich-Edwards, J. W., & Rifas-Shiman, S. L. (2013). Reducing racial/ethnic disparities in childhood obesity: The role of early life risk factors. *JAMA Pediatrics, 167*, 731–738.

Testa, A., & Jackson, D. B. (2019). Food insecurity, food deserts, and waist-to-height ratio: Variation by sex and race/ethnicity. *Journal of Community Health, 44*, 444–450.

Thompson, A. L., & Bentley, M. E. (2013). The critical period of infant feeding for the development of early disparities in obesity. *Social Science & Medicine, 97*, 288–296.

Thomson, J. L., Tussing-Humphreys, L. M., Goodman, M. H., & Landry, A. S. (2018). Diet quality in a nationally representative sample of American children by sociodemographic characteristics. *The American Journal of Clinical Nutrition, 109*, 127–138.

Tiehen, Laura. 2020. "The food assistance landscape: Fiscal year 2019 annual report.".

Tran, M. K., Krueger, P. M., McCormick, E., Davidson, A., & Main, D. S. (2016). Body mass transitions through childhood and early adolescence: A multistate life table approach. *American Journal of Epidemiology, 183*, 643–649.

Turner, R. W., Perrin, E. M., Coyne-Beasley, T., Peterson, C. J., & Skinner, A. C. (2015). Reported sports participation, race, sex, ethnicity, and obesity in US adolescents from NHANES physical activity (PAQ_D). *Global Pediatric Health, 2*, 2333794X15577944.

Twarog, J. P., Peraj, E., Vaknin, O. S., Russo, A. T., Woo Baidal, J. A., & Sonneville, K. R. (2020). Consumption of sugar-sweetened beverages and obesity in SNAP-eligible children and adolescents. *Primary Care Diabetes, 14*, 181–185.

U.S. Department of Health and Human Services. (2013). *Office of disease prevention and health promotion. Healthy people 2020*. http://www.healthypeople.gov/2020/

Umberson, D. (1992). Gender, marital status, and the social control of health behavior. *Social Science and Medicine, 34*, 907–917.

Uzochukwu, K. (2017). The associations between neighborhood constructs, physical activity, and childhood obesity: Understanding race and income disparities. *Journal of Urban Affairs, 39*, 421–435.

Van Cauter, E., & Spiegel, K. (1999). Sleep as a mediator of the relationship between socioeconomic status and health: A hypothesis. *Annals of the New York Academy of Sciences, 896*, 254–261.

Vazquez, C., & Schuler, B. (2020). Adolescent physical activity disparities by parent nativity status: The role of social support, family structure, and economic hardship. *Journal of Racial and Ethnic Health Disparities, 7*, 1079–1089.

Walker, R. E., Keane, C. R., & Burke, J. G. (2010). Disparities and access to healthy food in the United States: A review of food deserts literature. *Health & Place, 16*, 876–884.

Wang, G., & Speakman, J. R. (2016). Analysis of positive selection at single nucleotide polymorphisms associated with body mass index does not support the "thrifty gene" hypothesis. *Cell Metabolism, 24*, 531–541.

Watt, T. T., Martinez-Ramos, G., & Majumdar, D. (2012). Race/ethnicity, acculturation, and sex differences in the relationship between parental social support and children's overweight and obesity. *Journal of Health Care for the Poor and Underserved, 23*, 1793–1805.

Welker, E., Lott, M., & Story, M. (2016). The school food environment and obesity prevention: Progress over the last decade. *Current Obesity Reports, 5*, 145–155.

Winston, G., Phillips, E., Wethington, E., Wells, M., Devine, C. M., Peterson, J., Wansink, B., Ramos, R., & Charlson, M. (2015). The relationship between social network body size and the body size norms of black and Hispanic adults. *Preventive Medicine Reports, 2*, 941–945.

Xiang, A. H., Chow, T., Mora-Marquez, J., Martinez, M. P., Wang, X., Wei, Y., Panganiban, M. B., Richter, P. M., & Schneider, D. I. (2019). Breastfeeding persistence at 6 months: Trends and disparities from 2008 to 2015. *The Journal of Pediatrics, 208*, 169–175.e2.

Yang, Y. C., Walsh, C. E., Johnson, M. P., Belsky, D. W., Reason, M., Curran, P., Aiello, A. E., Chanti-Ketterl, M., & Harris, K. M. (2021). Life-course trajectories of body mass index from adolescence to old age: Racial and educational disparities. *Proceedings of the National Academy of Sciences, 118*, e2020167118.

Yip, T., Cheon, Y. M., Wang, Y., Cham, H., Tryon, W., & El-Sheikh, M. (2020). Racial disparities in sleep: Associations with discrimination among ethnic/racial minority adolescents. *Child Development, 91*, 914–931.

Zhang, S., de la Haye, K., Ji, M., & An, R. (2018). Applications of social network analysis to obesity: A systematic review. *Obesity Reviews, 19*, 976–988.

Sibling Effects on the Development of Obesity

10

Toni Falbo and Shengjie Lin

The goal of this chapter is to investigate what is known about sibling effects on the development of body mass, overweight, and obesity and to identify the underlying causes of these sibling effects. This chapter will apply theories typically associated with sibling effects on intelligence and achievement to understanding sibling effects on physical growth, particularly the development of excess body mass. Finally, the chapter will make recommendations for reducing or eliminating the sibling effects currently found on the development of obesity.

Sibling Theory

Traditionally, resource dilution theories (Blake, 1981, 1989; Downey, 2001) have argued that families containing larger numbers of children will have fewer resources available to invest in each child, compared to families containing smaller numbers of children. Consequently, children with more siblings will attain diminished outcomes because their parents invested less in their development (Becker & Tomes, 1976).

Within the field of psychology, parental resources are viewed as taking many forms and include *material resources*, such as money for college, *cognitive resources*, such as time spent reading to the child, and *interpersonal resources*, such as attention and affection (Hertwig et al., 2002). Parental investments of these resources have been shown to promote their children's development in terms of such outcomes as educational attainment, vocabulary, and emotional well-being (Blake, 1981; Downey, 2001; Lin et al., 2021). However, the field of psychology has not examined potential sibling effects on the development of obesity or overweight in children. This is changing (Lin & Falbo, 2022; Ruggiero et al., 2021).

The present chapter will review the research literature about sibling effects on the development of obesity. To foreshadow the contents of this chapter, a large and growing body of research points to the conclusion that children with fewer siblings, most notably those without siblings, develop higher BMIs and are more likely to reach thresholds indicating overweight or obese status than children growing up with more siblings. Thus, in the case of the development of body mass, children with few or no siblings attain the worst outcomes, despite the greater quantities of resources available to them.

The research literature about sibling effects includes correlational studies between the number of siblings or birth order and BMI, as well as, the likelihood of overweight and obesity. Sibship size reflects the total number of children within a family and is directly linked to resource dilution.

T. Falbo (✉)
Department of Educational Psychology, University of Texas at Austin, Austin, TX, USA
e-mail: toni@prc.utexas.edu

S. Lin
Yale Center for Emotional Intelligence, Yale University, New Haven, CT, USA

G. Garcia-Alexander, D. L. Poston, Jr. (eds.), *International Handbook of the Demography of Obesity*, International Handbooks of Population 12, https://doi.org/10.1007/978-3-031-10936-2_10

Birth order and sibship size are thought to interact in determining the resources available to each child. Families are dynamic and most do not achieve their ultimate sibship size all at once; instead, children accumulate in families gradually over time, and depart as they mature into adulthood.

Hertwig et al. (2002) created a model of parental investment that takes into account this gradual addition and eventual subtraction of each child in a family. The Hertwig et al. model argues that the first child born in a family receives all available parental investments until their first sibling is born. As each new child enters the family, parents divide their total resources among the children, resulting in a gradual reduction in the investments available for each child. However, as children leave the family as adults, the total amount of parental investment available for the remaining children rebounds, gradually allowing more parental investment in the remaining children. Eventually, all but the last child leaves the family, and this last child receives all available parental investment, achieving a situation similar to that experienced by only children.

Overall, the Hertwig et al. model predicts that children who never had a sibling receive the greatest investments from their parents, with firstborns and last borns receiving somewhat less parental investment over the course of their childhoods, while middle borns receive the least amount of parental investment, because they are unlikely to spend time within the family as only children. Hertwig et al. reported that the evidence from studies of birth order and sibship size was consistent with expectations from their model. However, their review of the relevant literature focused on such outcomes as vaccinations and educational aspirations and did not include the development of body mass, overweight, or obesity.

Sibling Absence and Obesity: The Evidence

Evidence has been accumulating that the absence of siblings during childhood is associated with greater likelihood of obesity or overweight. Table 10.1 presents a summary of some of the studies that have examined sibling effects on BMI and the likelihood of overweight or obesity.

One early study (Patterson et al., 1997) of U.S. girls (ages 9 and 10 years old) reported that the odds for obesity was 60% higher for girls without siblings than for girls with three or more siblings. Another study of low-income U.S. children yielded results indicating similar sibling effects. Specifically, Mosli et al. (2015) examined a sample of children, ranging in age from 4 to 8 years, and found that only children and last-born children were more likely to be overweight or obese than children who had younger siblings.

Furthermore, this enhanced likelihood of developing overweight or obesity among only or last borns is not limited to low-income children. Mosli et al. (2016a, b) conducted a longitudinal analysis of data from a sample of firstborn babies, recruited from 10 sites across the U.S. Their heights and weights were measured during home visits, at 15, 24, 36, 54 months of age and at their entry into first grade. The results indicated that children who arrived at first grade without a sibling had significantly higher BMI z scores than those who acquired a sibling during their first 6 years. Mosli calculated that those children who arrived at first grade without a sibling had 2.94 greater odds of obesity compared to children who obtained a sibling when they were between 36 and 54 months old.

Analyses of other U.S. data extended this finding to fifth graders. Using data from Early Childhood Longitudinal Studies-K (ECLS-K), Datar (2017) examined the relationship between sibship size and the likelihood of childhood obesity and found a significant and negative relationship between number of siblings and the likelihood of obesity. The most striking results, however, indicated that those without siblings had higher BMI percentile scores and were more likely to reach the obesity threshold than those with one, two, or three or more siblings, regardless of birth order.

Two articles published in 2018 reviewed collections of studies examining the relationship

Table 10.1 Summary of studies

References	Study		Sample		Independent and dependent variables in analysis		Major relevant findings
	Design	Setting	Sample size	Age group	Sibling measures	Obesity measures	
Chen et al. (2012)	Cross-sectional	Taiwan	9 to 14-year-old participants (n = 7930)	Children and adolescents	Single children vs. Children with siblings Sibship size (number of older/younger siblings)	Overweight and obesity	Children who had more siblings had less likelihood of obesity and overweight
Chen and Escarce (2010)	Longitudinal	USA	Kindergarten (n = 14,493); Third grade (n = 11,855); Fifth grade (n = 10,036)	Children and adolescents	Single children vs. Children with siblings	BMI and obesity	Single children had higher BMI and greater likelihood of obesity than children with sibling
Chen and Escarce (2014)	Longitudinal	USA	Kindergarten to eighth grade (n = 6551);	Children and adolescents	Sibship size (single children/1 sibling/2 or more siblings)	BMI and obesity	Single children had higher BMI and greater likelihood of obesity than children with 2 or more siblings Single children had a larger increase in BMI from kindergarten through eighth grade than children with 2 or more siblings
Datar (2017)	Cross-sectional	USA	Fifth grade (n = 10,080)	Children	Sibship size (single children/1 sibling/ 2 siblings/3 or more siblings)	BMI and obesity	Larger sibship size were associated with lower BMI and lower likelihood of obesity
Formisano et al. (2014)	Cross-sectional and longitudinal	8 European countries (Belgium, Cyprus, Estonia, Germany, Hungary, Italy, Spain, and Sweden)	Cross-sectional analysis: 2 to 9-year-old children (n = 12,350); Longitudinal analysis: 5 to 9-year-old children (n = 5236)	Children	Sibship size (single children/1 sibling/2 or more siblings)	BMI and overweight/ obesity	Cross-sectional analysis: the higher the sibship size, the lower the BMI; Longitudinal analysis: the more siblings living in the household, the lower likelihood of overweight/obesity

(continued)

Table 10.1 (continued)

References	Study		Sample		Independent and dependent variables in analysis		Major relevant findings
	Design	Setting	Sample size	Age group	Sibling measures	Obesity measures	
Ghosh and Bandyopadhyay (2006)	Cross-sectional	India	Adult female (n = 171)	Young adults	Birth order (first tertile, second tertile) Sibship size (first tertile, second tertile)	BMI	Larger sibship size were associated with lower BMI
Haugaard et al. (2013)	Cohort sampling	Denmark	13-year-old children (n = 2,9327); obese young man (n = 323) and controls of young men (n = 575)	Children and young adults	Birth order (1/2/3/4/5 or more) Sibship size (single child/2 siblings/3 siblings/4 siblings/5 or more siblings)	Obesity	Single children had higher likelihood of obesity among both children and young adult samples
Hu et al. (2017)	Cross-sectional	China (rural)	Children less than 5 years old (n = 1686)	Children	Birth order (single/1/2/3 or more)	BMI	Single children had *lower* likelihood of overweight and obesity than the second and third-born or younger children
Lin and Falbo (2022)	Longitudinal	USA	7 to 12-grade adolescents to adult (n = 3563)	Adolescents to middle-age adults	Birth order (single/first/middle/last) Sibship size (single/1/2/3 or more)	BMI	Single children had higher BMI than those with siblings from adolescence to middle adulthood Single children had higher BMI than middle-born, but not last-born participants
Mosli et al. (2015)	Cross-sectional	USA	4 to 8 year-old low-income children (n = 274)	Children	Birth order (single/oldest/middle/youngest)	Overweight and obesity	Single children and last-born children were more likely to be overweight or obese than children who had young siblings

Mosli et al. (2016a, b)	Longitudinal	USA	15-moth to first grade (n = 697)	Children	Children with no siblings born by first grade vs. Children with a sibling born by first grade	BMI	Children who did not have a sibling in first grade had higher BMI than those who acquired a sibling during their first six years
Patterson et al. (1997)	Cross-sectional	USA	9- and 10-year-old low-income female (n = 2379)	Children	Sibship size (single/1/2/3 or more)	Obesity	Girls without siblings had higher likelihood of obesity than girls with three or more siblings
Rodrigues et al. (2020)	Cross-sectional	Portugal	7 to 15-year-old participants (n = 542)	Children and adolescents	Single children vs. Children with siblings	BMI	Single children were taller and heavier than children with siblings, although no BMI differences were found
Santiago et al. (2012)	Cross-sectional	Spain	6 to 12-year-old (n = 3101)	Children	Single children vs. Children with siblings	Overweight	Boys without siblings had higher likelihood of overweight than boys who had siblings
Tian and von Cramon-Taubadel (2020)	Longitudinal	China	17-year-old and younger (n = 4414)	Children and adolescents	Single children vs. Children with siblings	BMI, overweight, and obesity	Single children had higher BMI and greater likelihood of overweight and obesity
Ochiai et al. (2012)	Cross-sectional	Japan	Fourth grade (n = 4026)	Children	Birth order (single/oldest/middle/youngest); Sibship size (single/1/2 or more)	Overweight	Single and youngest children had greater likelihood of overweight than children with younger siblings

between sibling variables and BMI, overweight, and obesity. The Meller et al. (2018) review involved a quantitative synthesis of 14 studies examining sibling effects, and included studies of children, adolescents, and adults. The Park and Cormier (2018) review consisted of a qualitative synthesis of 22 studies and focused on children and adolescents. Both reviews included data from the U.S. as well as other nations, and came to the same conclusion, even though the collection of studies reviewed by each were largely non-overlapping. The chief conclusion of both reviews was that the children who grow up without siblings have significantly higher BMI than others; therefore, children without siblings were more likely to reach the threshold indicating overweight or obesity status than were those growing up with siblings.

Persistence of Sibling Effects These findings about the effects of growing up without siblings on the development of body mass raise concern because childhood obesity is a strong predictor of adult obesity (Simmonds et al., 2016). Unfortunately, there is evidence that these sibling effects found in childhood and adolescence persist well into adulthood.

Specifically, Lin and Falbo (2022) used data from the National Longitudinal Study of Adolescent to Adult Health (Add Health) and followed a cohort who were initially in grades 7–12 in 1994–1995, through five waves, spanning adolescence to middle adulthood. The results illuminated many aspects of sibling effects by considering birth order effects as well as sibship size effects. The study found that those who had grown up without siblings had significantly higher BMIs than those who grew up with siblings, and this difference persisted throughout the duration of the longitudinal study. That is, the sibling effects on BMI, first observed in adolescence, did not disappear after people left their families of origin, but persisted into their middle age. Furthermore, the Lin and Falbo findings provide evidence about the dynamics of sibling absence within families and consequently, the dynamics of sibling effects on BMI.

In creating sibling categories for use in their analyses, Lin and Falbo used items from the first and fifth waves of Add Health to identify sample members without siblings, as well as their respective comparison groups. The sibling item for the first wave of Add Health reflected the desire of the originators of Add Health to identify full biological siblings. This led to identifying single children in terms of being the only child of their biological parents, regardless of whether they had adopted, half, or step siblings. In the Lin and Falbo study, the BMIs of these single children were compared to the BMIs of other birth orders: firstborns, middle borns, and last borns.

In contrast, the sibling item from the fifth wave of Add Health reflected the desire to identify those participants who never had any sort of sibling, and the BMIs of these single children were compared to the BMIs of other sibship sizes, notably, one, two, and three or more siblings. As one might expect, the first-wave indicator of single-child status found more of them (17.6%) than did the fifth-wave indicator (4.3%) in the Add Health sample.

Thus, the Lin and Falbo study examined separately two types of sibling effects on body mass. In terms of sibship size, the findings were consistent with the findings of other studies, with higher BMIs for those who reported never having a sibling, compared to those with one, two, or three or more siblings, and this difference was significant at each wave. These results suggest that receiving undivided investments from parents may lead to undesirable outcomes, notably the development of too much body mass, and this greater body mass was found to stay with single children as they had matured into middle age.

The Lin and Falbo findings about birth order provide nuance to the sibship size findings. When single children were identified in terms of being the only biological child of their parents, they had higher BMIs than middle borns and this was true for each wave. As children grow up, middle borns are typically surrounded by siblings within their households, compared to the other birth order categories. This finding of a lower body mass among people who were middle children in their families suggests that more continuous sibling presence during childhood may be protective against excessive body mass. In contrast, the Lin and Falbo findings indicate that the BMIs of single children were never significantly different from the BMIs of last borns, across all the waves. Last borns have no younger siblings and they may reside in the household for extended periods as the sole child after their older siblings leave home.

International Similarities and Differences Sibling effects on the likelihood of children developing overweight or obesity have been reported by several international studies, including those based on data from Taiwan (Chen et al., 2012), Japan (Ochiai et al., 2012), Denmark (Haugaard et al., 2013), and India (Ghosh & Bandyopadhyay, 2006). In terms of Taiwan, Chen et al. selected a sample of children (9–14 years) from 14 Taiwanese communities and found that the likelihood of obesity and overweight was significantly less for children who had more siblings, although other factors, such as parental smoking and birth weight, were also found to be important predictors. Ochiai et al. conducted a study of the physical development of a sample of fourth grade children (9 and 10 years) in one Japanese town and reported that only and last-born children were more likely to be overweight than children with younger siblings. A study of samples of Danish adolescents and young adults (Haugaard et al., 2013) found that being a single or last-born child was associated with obesity. Finally, a study of young college women in Bengal, India (Ghosh & Bandyopadhyay, 2006) found that sibship size was negatively associated with body mass.

Studies in China have arrived at similar conclusions about sibling effects, at least for children growing up in urban environments. Tian and von Cramon-Taubadel (2020) used data from child participants (17 years or younger), using four waves (2004, 2006, 2009, and 2011) of the China Health and Nutrition Survey. The findings indicated that single children had higher BMIs and were more likely to be overweight and obese than children growing up with siblings. However, this sibling effect was not present among rural children without siblings and generally less likely in girls. The reduced likelihood of becoming overweight or obese among Chinese only children in rural areas was also reported by Hu et al. (2017), based on data from the China Family Panel Studies, consisting of a nationally representative sample.

Mechanisms of Sibling Effects

Findings of sibling effects on BMI and obesity are correlational and do not demonstrate direct, causal connections between siblings and the development of body mass. Instead, there is evidence that these observed sibling effects reflect dietary and activity patterns associated with various birth orders and sibship sizes.

The Ecology of the Single-Child Family in the U.S The single-child family was disparaged early within the history of psychology, as evidenced by the statements of one of the founders of American psychology, G. Stanley Hall. He portrayed single-child families as fundamentally pathogenic, with mothers overprotecting and overindulging their single children, thereby thwarting their normal development (Brill, 1922; Fenton, 1928). This view was so persuasive that little research about these families was conducted until much later in the twentieth century when Feiring and Lewis (1987) videotaped the interactions between family members during dinner time, comparing the qualities of single-child mealtimes to those of mealtimes with multiple children. Although the Feiring and Lewis sample consisted of only 47 families, all of whom contained one three-year-old child and were White and middle-class, the differences they observed provide insights into the mealtime differences between the families of single versus multiple children.

Specifically, Feiring and Lewis found that mealtimes for multiple-child families were child-centered, noisy, and chaotic, with children likely to arrive at the table and leave it at will. In contrast, they noted that single-child families had quieter, more adult-oriented mealtimes, with the meal starting when all family members arrived at the dinner table and only ended later when the parents perceived that the child had finished their meal. Taken together, these findings suggest that children without siblings have more opportunity to consume calories at mealtime.

More recently, two other studies about time use and companionship patterns provide a deeper description of the ecology of the single-child family. Both studies were based on large, representative samples of U.S. children or adolescents. The first study (Dunifon et al., 2017) used diary data from children ranging in age from 6 and 12 years, based on the Child Development Supplement of the Panel Study of Income Dynamics. The authors found that children without siblings spent more time with their parents than did children with siblings. In contrast, children with siblings spent half of their discretionary time engaged with their siblings, including more time in unstructured play. The second study (Wikle et al., 2019) used data from the nationally representative American Time Use Survey to compare the patterns of adolescents (15–18 years) who were living with and without siblings. They found that adolescents without siblings spent more time alone than did adolescents with siblings, although the amount of time spent with peers was equivalent for those with and without siblings. Together, these findings suggest that the ecology of the one-child family can be described as more adult-centric, with more time spent alone or with a parent, while the ecology of the multiple-child family is more child-centric, with substantial time for interactions between siblings.

Diet There is some evidence that children growing up without siblings have more obesogenic diets than children growing up with siblings. For example, based on ECLS-K data, Datar (2017) found that fifth grade children growing up without siblings reported drinking more sugary soda, eating more fast food, and buying more junk food in school than children with three or more siblings. Similarly, for adolescents, Lin and Falbo (2022) found more frequent fast-food consumption among those who never had a sibling, compared to those with one, two, or three or more siblings.

Similarly, Tian and von Cramon-Taubadel (2020) found that urban Chinese only children had more obesogenic diets than did children growing up with siblings. These single children were found to be more likely to eat meals prepared outside the home and to eat more Western fast food and drink more soft drinks than children with siblings. The results also indicated that while these single children ate more meat, fish, milk products and eggs than those with siblings, they also ate less plant-based foods, such as cereals and vegetables.

Physical Activity Various studies have suggested that children growing up without siblings engage in more sedentary activities, such as reading and television watching, than children with siblings. According to Blake (1981), who combined data from the Health Examination Survey, with the Youth in Transition survey, and the High School and Beyond survey, children and adolescents with no siblings spent more time playing alone than did their peers with siblings. Another early study (Claudy, 1984) of the preferred activities of single children was based on analyses of data from Project TALENT, a U.-S. national sample of adolescents conducted in 1960. Claudy reported that only children were more likely to engage in activities that were *solitary*, such as collecting stamps, *intellectual*, such as reading, and *artistic*, such as music, while adolescents who had siblings were more likely to report engaging in activities that were *group-oriented*, such as team sports, or *practical*, such as cooking.

Studies of more recent cohorts of U.S. children and adolescents have reported that children without siblings may spend more time in sedentary activities than children with siblings. Datar (2017) reported that the fifth graders growing up without siblings watched more television than those with siblings. Likewise, Lin and Falbo (2022) found that single and last-born adolescents reported spending more time viewing screens, including watching television and videos and playing electronic games, than did first or middle borns.

One consequence of a more sedentary lifestyle for children growing up without siblings is that they develop less physical fitness than their peers. Rodrigues et al. (2020) conducted a study of Portuguese children, ranging in age from 7–15 years, and found that those who grew up without siblings scored substantially less in fitness, based on several indices, including hand grip and standing long jump, than those who grew up with siblings.

Sibling Absence as the Cause of Obesity Epidemics

Increases in the proportion of families with just one child have been blamed for the obesity epidemic in the U.S. and China. Notably, Datar (2017) argued that the higher prevalence of children growing up without siblings in the U.S. accounted for up to 13% of the increase in childhood obesity between the late 1960s and 2008. Similarly, Tian and von Cramon-Taubadel (2020) argued that China's One-Child Policy[1] contributed to the current prevalence of obesity and overweight in China, because this policy resulted in more single-child families and single children are more likely to be obese/overweight (see Chap. 5 in this *Handbook* for additional discussion). Tian and von Cramon-Taubadel went further when they suggested that the problem of obesity in China will be greatly reduced by the new Chinese family planning policy that promotes the two or three-child family.

Given the evidence reviewed in this chapter, are single-child families the cause of obesity epidemics? Will eliminating single-child families solve the problem of widespread obesity? There are two lines of evidence that suggest the elimination of single-child families will not solve the public health problem of obesity.

The first line of evidence comes from two studies suggesting that rural Chinese children growing up without siblings do not have excessive body mass. These two studies of Chinese children and adolescents (Hu et al., 2017; Tian & von Cramon-Taubadel, 2020) found that single children growing up in rural China had less access to Western style fast food and more opportunities for physical activity.

The second line of evidence comes from the Lin and Falbo findings about the gradual increase in body mass across all waves of the longitudinal Add Health data. They found that every sibling group crossed the threshold of obesity by the time they attained middle age, with the exception of middle borns, who scored just under the obesity threshold at the last wave. Note also that Lin and Falbo found that the BMIs of last borns were never significantly different from the BMIs of single children, indicating that simply having siblings does not eliminate the potential for the development of excessive body mass.

The accumulated evidence described in this chapter suggests that sibling effects on diet and physical activity are the primary cause of sibling effects on obesity. The solution to the problem of sibling absence and excessive body mass can best be addressed by focusing on the diets and physical activities of children who experience all or much of their childhoods without siblings. Eating less junk food and less fast food, while engaging in more active lifestyles, will benefit the physical development of everyone, but especially children experiencing sibling absence. Parents with just one child at home, even if this child eventually becomes a firstborn, or parents with just one child left at home, should be alerted to their elevated risk of creating an obesogenic environment within their family.

Implications for Theories

Traditional theories addressing sibling effects on children's outcomes are based on the assumption that more parental investment in children leads to better outcomes. Indeed, the research evidence generally supports the expectation that more

[1] China's one-child policy was launched in 1980 and was in effect until 2016. It has resulted in as many as 100 million one-child families (Feng et al., 2016).

parental resources, in the form of money for college and time for conversation and expressions of care, leads to better outcomes for children. There are no thresholds for too much vocabulary, too much education, or too much well-being. But for body mass, there are thresholds defining too much, too little, and ideal levels. Children and adolescents can develop too much body mass, which can lead to persistent and negative psychological, social, and medical consequences. For example, too much body mass can lead to social isolation (Hajek et al., 2021) as well the development of such diseases as diabetes (Felber & Golay, 2002). Thus, dilution theories may need to add an asterisk about the limitations of these notions about parental investment when considering the development of body mass.

Conclusion

This chapter has presented the evidence regarding sibling effects on the development of body mass in children, adolescents, and young adults. The general finding is that children growing up with more siblings develop smaller body masses than those growing up without siblings. Indeed, multiple studies have found that the absence of siblings during childhood is associated with greater likelihood of obesity or overweight.

Given what is known now about the dangers of sibling absence for children's development of obesity, these findings suggest that parents with just one child at home should invest more in healthy diets and physical activities for this child. Avoiding frequent fast-food consumption and sedentary activities, including screen time, will require parents to make more strategic investments in their children.

References

Becker, G. S., & Tomes, N. (1976). Child endowments and the quantity and quality of children. *Journal of Political Economy, 84*(4), S143–S162.

Blake, J. (1981). Family size and the quality of children. *Demography, 18*(4), 421–442.

Blake, J. (1989). *Family size and achievement*. University of California Press.

Brill, A. A. (1922). *Psychoanalysis—Its theories and practical applications*. Saunders.

Chen, A. Y., & Escarce, J. J. (2010). Peer reviewed: Family structure and childhood obesity, early childhood longitudinal study—kindergarten cohort. *Preventing Chronic Disease*, 7, A50.

Chen, A. Y., & Escarce, J. J. (2014). Family structure and childhood obesity: An analysis through 8th grade. *Maternal and Child Health Journal, 18*(7), 1772–1777.

Chen, Y. C., Chen, P. C., Hsieh, W. S., Portnov, B. A., Chen, Y. A., & Lee, Y. L. (2012). Environmental factors associated with overweight and obesity in Taiwanese children. *Pediatric and Perinatal Epidemiology, 26*(6), 561–571.

Claudy, J. G. (1984). The only child as a young adult: Results from project talent. In T. Falbo (Ed.), *The single child family* (pp. 211–252). Guilford Press.

Datar, A. (2017). The more the heavier? Family size and childhood obesity in the US. *Social Science & Medicine, 180*, 143–151.

Downey, D. B. (2001). Number of siblings and intellectual development: The resource dilution explanation. *American Psychologist, 56*(6–7), 497–504.

Dunifon, R., Fomby, P., & Musick, K. (2017). Siblings and children's time use in the United States. *Demographic Research, 37*, 1611–1624.

Feiring, C., & Lewis, M. (1987). The ecology of some middle class families at dinner. *International Journal of Behavioral Development, 10*(3), 377–390.

Felber, J. P., & Golay, A. (2002). Pathways from obesity to diabetes. *International Journal of Obesity, 26. Suppl, 2*, 39–45.

Feng, W., Gu, B., & Cai, Y. (2016). The End of China's One-Child Policy. *Studies in Family Planning, 47*(1), 83–86. https://doi.org/10.1111/j.1728-4465.2016.00052.x

Fenton, N. (1928). The only child. *Journal of Genetic Psychology, 35*, 546–556.

Formisano, A., Hunsberger, M., Bammann, K., Vanaelst, B., Molnar, D., Moreno, L. A., & Siani, A. (2014). Family structure and childhood obesity: Results of the IDEFICS Project. *Public Health Nutrition, 17*(10), 2307–2315.

Ghosh, J. R., & Bandyopadhyay, A. R. (2006). Income, birth order, siblings, and anthropometry. *Human Biology*, 733–741.

Hajek, A., Kretzler, B., & Konig, H. H. (2021). The association between obesity and social isolation as well as loneliness in the adult population: A systematic review. *Diabetes, Metabolic Syndrome and Obesity: Target and Therapy, 14*, 2765–2773.

Haugaard, L. K., Ajslev, T. A., Zimmermann, E., Ängquist, L., & Sørensen, T. I. (2013). Being an only or last-born child increases later risk of obesity. *PLoS One, 8*(2), e56357.

Hertwig, R., Davis, J. N., & Sulloway, F. J. (2002). Parental investment: how an equity motive can produce inequality. *Psychological Bulletin, 128*(5), 728–745.

Hu, J., Ding, N., Zhen, S., Liu, Y., & Wen, D. (2017). Who is more likely to be obese or overweight among siblings? A nationally representative study in rural China. *PLoS One, 12*(11), e0187693.

Lin, S., Falbo, T., Qu, W., Wang, Y., & Feng, X. (2021). Chinese only children and loneliness: Stereotypes and realities. *American Journal of Orthopsychiatry, 91*(4), 531–544.

Lin, S., & Falbo, T. (2022). Sibling absence and body mass index: From adolescence to adulthood. *Pediatric. Obesity*, e12899.

Meller, F. O., Loret de Mola, C., Assunção, M. C. F., Schäfer, A. A., Dahly, D. L., & Barros, F. C. (2018). Birth order and number of siblings and their association with overweight and obesity: a systematic review and meta-analysis. *Nutrition Reviews, 76*(2), 117–124.

Mosli, R. H., Lumeng, J. C., Kaciroti, N., Peterson, K. E., Rosenblum, K., Baylin, A., & Miller, A. L. (2015). Higher weight status of only and last-born children. Maternal feeding and child eating behaviors as underlying processes among 4–8 year olds. *Appetite, 92*, 167–172.

Mosli, R. H., Kaciroti, N., Corwyn, R. F., Bradley, R. H., & Lumeng, J. C. (2016a). Effect of sibling birth on BMI trajectory in the first 6 years of life. *Pediatrics, 137*(4), e20152456.

Mosli, R. H., Miller, A. L., Peterson, K. E., Kaciroti, N., Rosenblum, K., Baylin, A., & Lumeng, J. C. (2016b). Birth order and sibship composition as predictors of overweight or obesity among low-income 4-to 8-year-old children. *Pediatric Obesity, 11*(1), 40–46.

Ochiai, H., Shirasawa, T., Ohtsu, T., Nishimura, R., Morimoto, A., Obuchi, R., et al. (2012). Number of siblings, birth order, and childhood overweight: a population-based cross-sectional study in Japan. *BMC Public Health, 12*(1), 1–7.

Park, S. H., & Cormier, E. (2018). Influence of siblings on child health behaviors and obesity: A systematic review. *Journal of Child and Family Studies, 27*(7), 2069–2081.

Patterson, M. L., Stern, S., Crawford, P. B., McMahon, R. P., Similo, S. L., Schreiber, G. B., et al. (1997). Sociodemographic factors and obesity in preadolescent black and white girls: NHLBI's Growth and Health Study. *Journal of the National Medical Association, 89*(9), 594–600.

Rodrigues, L. P., Lima, R. F., Silva, A. F., Clemente, F. M., Camões, M., Nikolaidis, P. T., et al. (2020). Physical fitness and somatic characteristics of the only child. *Frontiers in Pediatrics, 8*, 324.

Ruggiero, C. F., McHale, S. M., Paul, I. M., & Savage, J. S. (2021). Learned Experience and Resource Dilution: Conceptualizing Sibling Influences on Parents' Feeding Practices. *International Journal of Environmental Research and Public Health, 18*(11), 5739.

Santiago, S., Zazpe, I., Cuervo, M., & Martínez, J. A. (2012). Perinatal and parental determinants of childhood overweight in 6–12 years old children. *Nutrición Hospitalaria, 27*(2), 599–605.

Simmonds, M., Llewellyn, A., Owen, C. G., & Woolacott, N. (2016). Predicting adult obesity from childhood obesity: a systematic review and meta-analysis. *Obesity Reviews, 17*(2), 95–107.

Tian, X., & von Cramon-Taubadel, S. (2020). Are only children in China more likely to be obese/overweight than their counterparts with siblings? *Economics & Human Biology, 37*, 100847.

Wikle, J. S., Ackert, E., & Jensen, A. C. (2019). Companionship patterns and emotional states during social interactions for adolescents with and without siblings. *Journal of Youth and Adolescence, 48*, 2190–2206.

Part III

Emerging Areas of Study

Population researchers have increasingly contributed to our understanding of the causes and consequences of obesity. This section offers a sampling of emerging areas of investigation that offer promising opportunities for future research efforts. For example, the social environment has increasingly been recognized as a contributor to overweight and obesity. One important aspect of this is religion. In Chap. 11, Hill and his colleagues provide an extensive review of the findings linking religion and body mass in national and international context. Further, they discuss how this area of study has evolved. Overall, they observe mixed evidence with some findings indicating a lack of association and others indicating that religion is associated with greater body mass. They suggest a number of ways to advance our understanding of this understudied association, both theoretically and methodologically.

Another important area of study relates to the role of stress and discrimination. Cuevas and his colleagues (Chap. 12) describe how stress is conceptualized, outline the biobehavioral pathways that link stress and obesity, and describe psychosocial risk factors for obesity. They review the literature in this area and close with a discussion of needed research. Lopez and Anderson (Chap. 13) thoroughly review the literature on the role of the neighborhood environment as it relates to obesity. They describe the importance of an ecological approach to the study of obesity as it shifts the focus away from individuals and toward the opportunity structures that influence individual decisions and behaviors. Finally, Kennel and his colleagues (Chap. 14) use patient records from emergency medical services to document pain related outcomes in patients with obesity. They describe the literature on weight bias and undertake an analysis to determine the extent to which patients with obesity may have poorer outcomes in an EMS setting. Interestingly, they observe that patients with obesity may have a treatment advantage – though these outcomes vary by gender.

11 Fit for Christ or Gluttons for God? An Overview of Research on Religion and Body Mass

Terrence D. Hill, Samantha M. Galindo, and Amy M. Burdette

Introduction

Over the past three decades, numerous studies have shown that religious involvement – indicated by observable identities, feelings, beliefs, activities, and experiences in relation to a spiritual, divine, or supernatural entity – is associated with *better* health across the life course. This general pattern has been remarkably consistent across indicators of health behavior (e.g., drinking and smoking), mental health (e.g., depression and anxiety), physical health (e.g., disability and allostatic load), and all-cause and cause-specific mortality risk (Burdette et al., 2018; Ellison & Levin, 1998; George et al., 2002; Hill et al., 2011, 2016; Idler, 2004, 2011; Koenig et al., 2012; Krause & Hayward, 2016). In contrast to these more established literatures, surprisingly little attention has been devoted to body mass and related outcomes (e.g., body image and eating disorders). As obesity rates continue to rise in various subpopulations of the United States (Hales et al., 2020; Ogden et al., 2020; Zhang et al., 2020), the health sciences should prioritize research on understudied social determinants. Religion is clearly understudied and, more importantly, often associated with *greater* body mass across a range of populations (Koenig et al., 2012; Yeary et al., 2017). Understanding this unique risk profile is one way to advance the social epidemiology of body mass *and* religion and health research, which tends to overemphasize the ways in which religion might promote population health.

In this chapter, we provide an overview of the religion and body mass literature. Along the way, we consider (1) the nature and extent of the association between religion and body mass in population-based studies of adults conducted in the United States and other countries, (2) explanations for why religion might be associated with body mass, (3) subgroup variations in the association between religion and body mass, and (4) several important avenues for future research. Although we intend for this collection of studies to be representative of the field, we do not consider it to be exhaustive. The general aim of this review is to update and extend previous reviews (Koenig et al., 2012; Yeary et al., 2017) and to spark greater attention to this important area of body mass research.

T. D. Hill (✉) · S. M. Galindo
Department of Sociology, The University of Texas at San Antonio, San Antonio, TX, USA
e-mail: terrence.hill@utsa.edu

A. M. Burdette
Professor of Sociology and an Associate of the Pepper Institute on Aging and Public Policy, Florida State University, Tallahassee, FL, USA

G. Garcia-Alexander, D. L. Poston, Jr. (eds.), *International Handbook of the Demography of Obesity*, International Handbooks of Population 12, https://doi.org/10.1007/978-3-031-10936-2_11

Studies of Religion and Body Mass

The United States Context

The study of religion and body mass began over half a century ago. Goldblatt et al.' (1965) study of "social factors in obesity" highlighted the roles of socioeconomic status, gender, and immigration in midtown Manhattan. Although the abstract revealed "suggestive relationships between ethnic and religious factors and obesity. . .for both sexes" (Goldblatt et al., 1965:97), these associations were only briefly mentioned in the discussion section. The authors explained that they had "found differences among respondents of different religions" and noted that "Lutherans, for example, were more often obese (24%) than Episcopalians (3%), but any statement made about the Lutherans and Episcopalians reflects also the difference between respondents of German and of British extraction" (Goldblatt et al., 1965:101). The authors went on to qualify that they "did not have enough cases to sift out the effects of religion per se" (Goldblatt et al., 1965:101).

Nearly two decades later, Gottlieb and Green (1984) used data from the *National Survey of Personal Health Practices and Consequences* to explore the health effects of "life events, social network, and life-style." Church participation was conceptualized as "social network involvement." The authors used life insurance tables to estimate the "ideal weight for height" for women and men. The study showed that church participation was associated with "unfavorable weight" in women. For women, this meant being outside of the "favorable weight" interval between 10% below and 9.9% above ideal weight for height. Interestingly, church participation was *unrelated* to ideal weight for height in men.

After another 13 years had passed, we started to see a consistent stream of research on religion and body mass. Lapane et al.' (1997) study of the *Pawtucket Heart Health Program* was among the first to focus on "religion and cardiovascular disease risk." In this instance, religion was operationalized as membership in a "religiously-affiliated social organization." Body mass was indicated by the traditional body mass index (BMI). Consistent with Gottlieb and Green (1984), Lapane et al. (1997:160) showed that "church members were *more* likely to be greater than 20% overweight." Although the authors failed to offer any substantive theoretical explanations for the observed differences between church members and non-church members, they concluded that "religious organizations" should be used for "cardiovascular disease prevention efforts."

Idler and Kasl's (1997) analysis of data from the New Haven site of the *Established Populations for the Epidemiologic Study of the Elderly* also focused on religion. Drawing on the research of Emile Durkheim, Idler and Kasl (1997:S294) theorized that "religions tend to promote healthy life styles as part of their overall regulative function." In fact, these authors were among the first to hypothesize that "religious involvement" would be associated with a *healthier* weight. The authors employed three measures of religious involvement, including religious affiliation, church attendance, and subjective religiousness (an index of two items tapping religious feelings and religious coping). Body mass was operationalized as the BMI. The analyses compared white Protestants, black Protestants, Jews, and respondents of other faiths or no religious leanings to Roman Catholics. Only one difference was observed among these comparisons: Jewish respondents tended to weigh *less* than Roman Catholics. While religious attendance was *unrelated* to body mass, subjective religiousness was *positively* associated with body mass. Although the finding for subjective religiousness is generally consistent with previous studies linking religion with greater body mass, the authors failed to reconcile with their expectation that religious involvement would be associated with a healthier weight. The reported difference between Jews and Roman Catholics was also never discussed.

The following year, Ferraro (1998) used state ecological data and national survey data from the first wave of the *Americans' Changing Lives* study to examine various associations between religion and body mass at different levels of analysis. The ecological data showed that while the state percentage of Baptists was associated with *higher* rates of obesity, the percentage of non-affiliates (no religious affiliation) was associated with *lower* rates of obesity. Interestingly, the percentage of church members and the percentage of Catholics were both *unrelated* to state obesity rates. Although the national survey data indicated no religious affiliation differences in BMI scores, regression analyses revealed that religious practice (an index of attendance, reading religious books, and consuming religious television or radio) was associated with *higher* BMI scores, *higher* rates of obesity (being greater than one standard deviation above sex-specific BMI means), and *lower* rates of thinness (being less than one standard deviation below sex-specific BMI means). In contrast to the effects of religious practice, religious salience (the importance of religious or spiritual beliefs in daily life) and religious comfort (seeking spiritual comfort and support to cope with life stress) were both *unrelated* to all three BMI outcomes.

In addition to providing the first multilevel analysis, the author offered the most thorough theoretical treatment of the association between religion and body mass. Ferraro (1998:225–226) referred to doctrines and beliefs concerning the "sinfulness" of gluttony, the sanctification of the body as the "temple of the Holy Spirit," and "moderation in all things" to explain how religion could be "oriented to maintaining a reasonable body weight." To explain why "many 'firm believers' do not have 'firm bodies,'" Ferraro (1998:238) speculated about how heavier religious people might seek "consolation and comfort from religion and from eating" to cope with the social structural disadvantages of being a racial and ethnic minority and of low socioeconomic status. To our knowledge, this was the first ever theory to explain why religion might be associated with a heavier weight.

The next study of "religion and body weight" appeared five years later. Kim et al.' (2003) analysis of data from the *National Survey of Midlife Development in the United States* examined a range of religion measures, including religious affiliation, religious practice (attendance), religious application (application of religious and spiritual beliefs), religious social support (seeking religious comfort), religious identity (belief in the importance of marrying someone of their same faith), and religious commitment (importance of religion and spirituality). Among men, conservative Protestants (e.g., Southern Baptists and Pentecostals) and mainline Protestants (e.g., Methodists and Lutherans) exhibited higher BMI scores than those with no religious preference, and religious practices, religious social support, religious commitment, and religious identity were all *positively* associated with BMI scores. Among women, *none* of the religion measures were associated with BMI. Along with providing such a detailed empirical analysis, Kim et al. (2003) were the first to review the cumulative literature by referencing previous studies of religion and body mass. Following previous work, Kim et al. (2003:469) expected that religion would "contribute to decreased body weight in several ways." Their discussion referenced religious beliefs that linked fasting with purity and the sanctification of the body with healthier diets and more active lifestyles. They also extended prior theoretical work by identifying a range of new potential mechanisms to explain why religion might be associated with body mass. They proposed that religion could decrease body weight through religious coping with stress and social support in weight loss. Grappling with the glaring disconnect between their theory (suggesting that religion should be associated with a lower BMI) and their data (showing that religion is associated with a higher BMI in men), Kim et al. (2003:475) concluded with the first defining statement of religion and body mass research: "Given the abundance of literature showing religion's positive effect on health status, religion correlating with better physical health and greater body weight appears to be inconsistent, since being overweight is associated with poorer health."

Approximately three years later, researchers began to theorize about how religion might be associated with a greater BMI. Departing significantly from previous research, Cline and Ferraro (2006:270) started by noting the "consistency across" studies showing "that religion is related to higher body weight." They then described a range of potential explanations. They noted that religious doctrine often discourages smoking (nicotine is an appetite suppressant) and encourages eating through religious social gatherings, including "Sunday School donuts," "church pot-luck dinners," and other "high-fat foods" (Cline & Ferraro, 2006, p. 271). The authors suggested that religious organizations may be "a consoling and welcoming setting for people who are obese and seeking protection from social stigma" and speculated that religious media practice in one's home (e.g., viewing religious television programs) may be a sedentary behavior that is easily combined with "food and beverages." (Cline & Ferraro, 2006, p. 271). In addition to these important theoretical advances, the study leveraged three waves of data from the *Americans' Changing Lives* survey to provide the first longitudinal examination of the association between religion and body mass. Cline and Ferraro (2006:271) noted the methodological importance of establishing causal order in this case: "Religion may have an effect on body weight, but body weight may also influence religion." The authors explored several dimensions of religion, including religious affiliation, religious attendance, religious salience (importance of religious and spiritual beliefs in daily life), religious media practice (reading religious books and watching or listening to religious programs), and consolation (seeking spiritual or religious support). Among women, the longitudinal analyses indicated that while religious attendance was associated with *lower* rates of obesity, Baptist affiliation and religious media practice were associated with *higher* rates of obesity. Religion was mostly *unrelated* to obesity among men. The only exception was consolation, which was associated with *lower* rates of obesity.

In one of the largest national studies, Gillum (2006) used data from the *Third National Health and Nutrition Examination Survey* to examine the association between religious attendance and direct measurements of body mass. In contrast with previous research, Gillum (2006:655) began with the null hypothesis that "frequent attendance at religious services is not associated with prevalence of overweight or obesity in adults of all ages independent of sociodemographic variables, cigarette smoking, and health status." In the full sample, with basic control variables, frequent attendance at religious services was associated with *higher* rates of overweight/obesity (combined). Interestingly, this association was fully mediated by smoking status. In other words, greater religious participation increased the likelihood of overweight/obesity by lowering the likelihood of smoking. The authors also reported that religious attendance was *unrelated* to body mass in obesity-specific models. Although the study claimed to focus on women and men, the only gender-specific analyses focused on women. In these models, religious attendance was *unrelated* to body mass. The authors failed to present or describe any gender-specific analyses for men. Based on these results, Gillum (2006:658) concluded that because the association between religious attendance and body mass was mediated by smoking, "religiousness" "likely is not etiologically important, contrary to what some prior reports claimed."

Merrill and Hillam (2006) used data from the *Utah Health Status Survey* to explore religious affiliation differences in body mass. Their results showed that "Latter-day Saints (LDS or Mormons)" tended to exhibit *greater* BMI scores and *higher* rates of obesity than Protestants, Catholics, people of other religious faiths, and people with no religious affiliation. Moreover, the LDS were the only religious group to differ from people with no religious affiliation. Merrill and Hillam (2006:43) explained that "despite doctrine in the LDS church that strongly discourages use of tobacco, alcohol, coffee or tea, and sexual promiscuity, and encourages moderation in all things, overeating is not emphasized as a sin." The authors noted that "acceptance of overweight people is common in the church and religion in general" (p. 43). They also identified several potential mechanisms related to health lifestyles, including lower rates of smoking, caffeine use (caffeine increases metabolism), and physical activity.

In 2009, Yeary and colleagues used data from the *Foods of our Delta Study*, a sample of adults living in the rural Mississippi Delta region, to test several potential mediators of the association between religion and body mass. Religion measures included religious affiliation, religious attendance, religious importance, religious media use (radio and television), and frequency of prayer. Body mass was assessed with the BMI. Potential mediators included smoking, nutrition (calories and total fat from foods), and exercise. Among blacks, religion was *unrelated* to body mass. Among whites, only religious media use was associated with *greater* BMI scores. *None* of the other religion measures were associated with body mass. Among whites, the association between religious media use was only partially mediated by smoking, but not nutrition or exercise. The authors failed to offer any substantive explanations for their mediators (e.g., how smoking mediates the effects of religious media use), for why religion was mostly unrelated to body mass in blacks and whites, or for why religious media use was only associated with body mass among whites.

The following year, Ayers et al.' (2010) examined the impact of religious socialization on women of Korean descent living in California. In this case, socialization was indicated by receiving messages "discouraging excessive eating" and "encouraging exercise" from religious leadership and congregants. Personal religious involvement was measured by religious attendance. The BMI was used as the outcome of interest. Although religious attendance increased the probability of being overweight or obese, receiving messages about excessive eating and exercise from religious leaders and congregants lowered the probability of being overweight or obese. Ayers et al. (2010:545) concluded that, in accordance with the behavioral ecological model, the "communication content within religious institutions may reduce the probability of Korean women being overweight or obese."

Adding to the body of work confirming the link between religion and overweight/obesity, Feinstein et al. (2010, 2012) published two studies of religious involvement and obesity. Using data from the *National Heart, Lung, and Blood Institute's Multi-Ethnic Study of Atherosclerosis*, Feinstein et al. (2010) showed that frequency of religious participation, frequency of prayer or meditation, and feelings of spirituality (e.g., feeling God's presence) tended to *increase* the probability of obesity (BMI). Their longitudinal follow-up using data from the *Coronary Artery Risk Development in Young Adults* study indicated that "frequent religious participants are more likely to become obese between young adulthood and middle age" (Feinstein et al., 2012, p. 117). The authors concluded that "the presence of a significant longitudinal association between religiosity and obesity even after adjustment for demographics highlights a need for anti-obesity interventions targeted specifically at religious groups" (Feinstein et al., 2012, p. 120).

In the same year, Reeves et al.' (2012) analysis of data from the *Jackson Heart Study*, a sample of black Americans living in the southeastern United States, indicated that organized religious activity (religious attendance and religious activities), frequency of private prayer or meditation, and daily spiritual experiences (e.g., feeling God's love) were all unrelated to body mass. According to Reeves et al. (2012:44), "the positive relationships between religion and body weight found in large multiethnic samples do not apply to African Americans." However, this conclusion was directly contradicted by Dodor's (2012) examination of data from the *National Longitudinal Study of Adolescent Health* (African Americans ages 28–34). In this study, religious attendance and frequency of prayer *increased* the probability of obesity, while religious importance and religious coping were unrelated to body mass. Dodor (2012:461) concluded that "highly religious African Americans are at high risk for obesity" and that "African American denominations need to advocate much more effectively than before for faith-based practices that espouse lifestyles beneficial to health and protection against obesity."

In 2013, Bharmal and colleagues' analysis of data from the *California Asian Indian Tobacco Use Survey* found that religiosity (an index of religious identity, salience of spiritual beliefs, and observance of religious holidays) was associated with *higher* average BMI scores and *greater* odds of being overweight or obese among Asian Indian immigrants. Interestingly, these associations were observed for Hindus and Sikhs, but not for Muslims. Bharmal et al. (2013:319) explained that, compared with Muslims, Hindus and Sikhs may engage in fewer ritualized physical activities, drink more alcohol, consume more foods that are "high in saturated fat and refined sugar," and fast less often each year.

Hill et al.' (2014) examination of data from the *National Social Life, Health, and Aging Project* showed that religious attendance was associated with *lower* BMI scores based on direct measurements and a lower probability of being underweight. Hill et al. (2014:778–779) concluded that, among older adults, "the mechanisms through which religious attendance might be associated with lower body mass (e.g., congregational support for healthy lifestyles, sanctification of the body, self-control, lower stress, better mental health, lower consumption of alcohol, and greater physical activity) would seem to exceed the mechanisms in favor of greater body mass (e.g., poor eating habits, lower rates of smoking, and religious media consumption)."

Two years later, Krause and Hayward (2016) used data from the *Landmark Spirituality and Health Survey* to examine the effects of anxious attachment to God (e.g., "I often worry about whether God is pleased with me."), spiritual support (e.g., "How often does someone in your congregation help you to know God better?"), religious affiliation, church attendance, and frequency of prayer on obesity (BMI). Their results showed that having an anxious attachment to God *increased* the probability of being obese, especially among respondents with lower levels of spiritual support. The data also indicated that the combined groups of black Protestants and evangelicals were *more* likely to be obese than other respondents. Church attendance and prayer were both *unrelated* to body mass. The authors concluded that spiritual support may effectively help people to cope with the stress of having an anxious attachment to God.

In 2018, Godbolt and colleagues used data from the *Health and Retirement Study* to examine race and gender variations in the association between religious attendance and direct measurements of BMI scores, waist circumference (waist measurements at the navel), and waist-to-height ratio (waist circumference divided by height). This study was the first to examine the effects of religion on more precise measures of body mass like waist circumference and waist-to-height ratio. The authors argued that this was important because BMI scores are primarily measured through imprecise self-reports of height and weight. BMI scores also fail to account for the difference between fat and nonfat mass from bone and muscle. Measures like waist circumference, waist-to-hip ratio, and waist-to-height ratio are more precise and more sensitive to the physiological stress response (i.e., allostatic load) than more general BMI scores.

In the full sample of older adults, church attendance was *unrelated* to BMI scores and *inversely* associated with waist circumference and waist-to-height ratio. Although not the focus of the study, the data also showed that mainline Protestants, evangelical protestants, and Catholics tended to exhibit *greater* body mass (BMI, waist circumference, and waist-to-height ratio) than non-affiliates. The BMI scores were *comparable* among black Protestants, respondents of other faiths, and non-affiliates. There was some evidence that black Protestants exhibited *greater* waist circumference and waist-to-height ratio than non-affiliates. Among older women, church attendance was *unrelated* to BMI scores and *inversely* associated with waist circumference and waist-to-height ratio. Among older white women, attendance was either *protective* or *unrelated* to body mass. Among older black women, attendance was consistently associated with *increased* body mass. Religious attendance was *unrelated* to body mass among men, regardless of race. The authors concluded that, among older adults, the effects of church attendance on body mass may be protective among white women and deleterious among black women.

In a follow-up study of longitudinal data from the *Health and Retirement Study*, Suh et al.' (2019) showed that, among older adults, religious attendance was *unrelated* to four-year changes in BMI scores and waist circumference. These results are important because they seem to suggest some degree of health selection into religious attendance. When prior body mass was controlled, church attendance was *unrelated* to subsequent changes in body mass. These findings further complicate the conclusions of Godbolt et al. (2018) because their analyses failed to control for prior body mass.

In the following year, Bentley-Edwards et al.' (2020) analysis of data from the *National Survey of American Life* examined the effects of religious affiliation and religious attendance on obesity in black women and men. Their analyses failed to observe any differences in rates of obesity by religious affiliation. Although religious attendance *increased* the probability of being obese among black men, attendance was *unrelated* to body mass among black women. Bentley-Edwards et al. (2020:3065) suggested that gendered roles within the church may help to explain their findings, noting that black men "may embody a 'superman role,' experiencing overwhelm from church and other social contexts that undermine self-care, promote obesity and other adverse health outcomes."

We end our review of U.S. studies of religion and body mass with Nie's (2021) recent multilevel examination of the effects of county-level religious contexts (percentage Catholic and percentage conservative Protestant) and individual-level religious affiliation and general religiosity (an index of attendance, religious importance, scripture reading, and frequency of prayer) on BMI scores. While individuals in counties with larger percentages of Catholics tended to report *lower* BMI scores, individuals in counties with larger percentages of conservative Protestants tended to report *higher* BMI scores. At the same time, personal religiosity was *inversely* associated with BMI scores. Religious affiliation was also *unrelated* to body mass. Nie (2021) concluded that research on religion and body mass should move beyond "simply studying the implications of individual religiosity."

The International Context

As far as we can tell, the international study of religion and body mass began four decades ago in The Netherlands. Baecke et al.' (1983) study of "socio-demographic variables and body mass" in Dutch adults explored the roles of religious affiliation and church attendance. Their analyses revealed that Lutheran women and men tended to exhibit *higher* BMI scores than non-Lutherans. Interestingly, these findings supported the very first comparison of Lutherans and Episcopalians (Goldblatt et al., 1965). While religious attendance was associated with *lower* BMI scores among men, attendance was *unrelated* to body mass among women.

Nearly two decades later, van Lenthe et al. (2000) used data from the Dutch longitudinal *GLOBE* study to examine the association between religious affiliation and body mass over six years. In contrast to Baecke et al. (1983), van Lenthe et al. (2000) compared Roman Catholics and respondents of other religious faiths to non-affiliates. In this study, religious affiliation was *unrelated* to body mass at baseline and six-year changes in body mass.

In 2014, Kortt and Dollery examined the effects of religious affiliation, religious importance, and religious attendance on BMI scores in Australia. Among men, Catholics and Baptists tended to exhibit *higher* BMI scores than non-affiliates, while other Protestants, non-Christians, Jews, and other Christians were *comparable* to non-affiliates. Religious importance and religious attendance were also *unrelated* to BMI scores among men. Among women, non-Christians tended to exhibit *lower* BMI scores than non-affiliates, and other Christians tended to exhibit *higher* BMI scores. Catholics, other Protestants, Baptists, and Jews were also *comparable* to non-affiliates. Although religious importance was associated with *lower* BMI scores among women, religious attendance was *unrelated* to body mass.

The following year, Lycett (2015) used data from the *Health Survey for England* to explore the effects of religious affiliation on multiple indicators of body mass (BMI and waist-to-hip ratio). Although having any religious affiliation was associated with *higher* BMI scores, these patterns were largely driven by Catholics and other Christians. Buddhists exhibited *lower* BMI scores. Having any religious affiliation was also associated with *higher* waist-to-hip ratios, but these disparities were largely accounted for by men who identify as Catholic, other Christian, or Sikh. Interestingly, these associations persisted with adjustments for smoking, alcohol consumption, and physical activity.

In 2017, Hill and colleagues employed longitudinal data from the *Mexican Health and Aging Study* to examine the effects of religious participation (frequency of participation in events organized by churches) on direct measurements of BMI scores and waist-to-hip ratio over the nine-year study period. Their results showed that while baseline religious participation was associated with *lower* waist-to-hip ratios among older Mexicans, religious participation was *unrelated* to BMI scores. Changes in religious participation were also *unrelated* to BMI scores and waist-to-hip ratios.

Most recently, Svensson et al.' (2020) analysis of data collected through the Danish *Early Detection and Prevention* project examined the effects of religious attendance and prayer/mediation on the probability of being overweight (BMI). This study failed to observe any multivariate associations between religion and body mass in the full sample or gender-stratified models.

Summary

Over the past five decades, studies of religion and body mass have employed a range data sources, several indicators of body mass based on self-reports and direct measurements (i.e., ideal weight for height, BMI, waist circumference, waist-to-height ratio, and waist-to hip-ratio), and numerous dimensions of religion (i.e., religious affiliation, religious attendance, religiosity, subjective religiousness, religious salience, frequency of prayer, religious socialization, frequency of meditation, God attachments, spiritual beliefs, spiritual support, religious coping, religious media use, religious social distancing, and observance of religious holidays). The studies in our review reported approximately 563 unique statistical tests, including some measure of religion and some measure of body mass. In nearly 69% of tests, religion was unrelated to body mass. In roughly 27% of tests, religion was associated with greater body mass. In nearly 4% of tests, religion was associated with leaner body mass. Our review is generally consistent with the findings of previous reviews. For example, Koenig et al. (2012) found that the plurality of studies (not tests) reported no association. Their second most common finding was a positive association between religion and body mass. Again, studies showing an inverse association between religion and body mass were least common. The most recent review by Yeary et al. (2017) also tends to support these general conclusions. Although null associations are most common in the literature overall, the most common pattern of statistical significance indicates that religion is associated with greater body mass. In terms of religious identification, conservative Protestant populations consistently exhibited greater body mass.

Mediators of Religion and Body Mass

Obesogenic Mechanisms

There are several potential explanations for why religion might be associated with greater body mass. To begin with, gluttony is not a sin that churches tend to focus on, and many religious organizations use food as a means for socializing (Cline & Ferraro, 2006; Hill et al., 2014; Kortt & Dollery, 2014; Merrill & Hillam, 2006; Yeary et al., 2017). Both of these tendencies would make excessive eating or other poor eating habits an "acceptable vice" or "acceptable substitute" for behaviors defined as deviant among churchgoers. Religious media practice (e.g., through religious television and radio shows) is also common in some religious groups (Cline & Ferraro, 2006; Hill et al., 2014; Kortt & Dollery,

2014; Yeary et al., 2009). These sedentary practices could be easily ritualized and combined with poor dietary practices (e.g., snacking).

Other health-related behaviors could also play a role (Ayers et al., 2010; Bharmal et al., 2013; Cline & Ferraro, 2006; Gillum, 2006; Hill et al., 2014; Kim et al., 2003; Merrill & Hillam, 2006; Yeary et al., 2009, 2017). When religious groups discourage behaviors like smoking and caffeine consumption, they essentially deter behavior that would otherwise suppress one's appetite or increase one's metabolism. Religious adults could also be less motivated to manage their weight because they are more likely to engage in long-term monogamous relationships and less likely enter dating and marriage markets. The idea is that actively pursuing new partners could conceivably reduce the pressure to diet and exercise to seem more attractive.

When religious populations exhibit larger body masses, processes related to reference groups and social control could be at play (Bharmal et al., 2013; Cline & Ferraro, 2006; Kim et al., 2003; Kortt & Dollery, 2014; Nie, 2021; Ruiz & Acevedo, 2015). If your reference groups tend to have larger body masses, your personal weight standards could be stretched because a few extra pounds may go unnoticed. In contrast, if your social comparisons tend to have smaller body masses, your personal standards could be more restricted to conform to the group. If your reference groups and social comparisons tend to be larger, it is plausible that the stigma associated with being larger could be lower (e.g., the probability of accusations about the sinfulness of gluttony).

Leptogenic Mechanisms

There are also several potential explanations for why religion might be associated with slimmer body mass. Although there is widespread speculation in the literature about overeating at church gatherings and snacking through hours of televangelism, numerous studies show that religious involvement tends to favor healthier diets, greater physical activity, lower rates of alcohol consumption, and better sleep quality (Dodor, 2012; Ellison et al., 2009; Garcia et al., 2013; Hill et al., 2006, 2007, 2016, 2018; Idler & Kasl, 1997; Koenig et al., 2012; Mahoney et al., 2005; Reeves et al., 2012; Strawbridge et al., 2001; Svensson et al., 2020; Wallace & Forman, 1998). These lifestyle patterns are crucial considerations because they represent some of the most consistent predictors of healthy body mass (Asghari et al., 2017; Beccuti & Pannain, 2011; Bouchard et al., 1993; Traversy & Chaput, 2015).

There are several theories for these healthy lifestyle patterns. Religious groups regularly adhere to general religious principles like "moderation in all things" and the sanctity of the physical body as the "temple of the Holy Spirit" (Ayers et al., 2010; Boyatzis et al., 2007; Ferraro, 1998; Hill et al., 2011; Horton, 2015; Kent et al., 2016; Mahoney et al., 2005; Merrill & Hillam, 2006; Ruiz & Acevedo, 2015; Yeary et al., 2020). Religious involvement also contributes to greater self-control by conditioning "moral muscles" through years of ritual adherence (e.g., regular religious attendance), moral socialization (e.g., ideas about the sinfulness of gluttony and sloth), self-examination (e.g., through confession and prayer), and social control (e.g., social sanctions within the religious community) (DeWall et al., 2014; Geyer & Baumeister, 2005; McCullough & Willoughby, 2009; Pascoe et al., 2016; Welch et al., 2006). Religious involvement may also reduce motivations for risky behavior (e.g., heavy drinking and over-eating) by promoting supportive social ties, feelings of hope and optimism, a sense of meaning and purpose, and better mental health (Ellison & Levin, 1998; George et al., 2002; Hill et al., 2011; Idler, 2004; Koenig et al., 2012; Krause & Hayward, 2016).

Chronic stress is another potential mechanism linking religion and leaner body mass. Recent studies consistently show that religious involvement is associated with lower levels of allostatic load or the chronic activation of the physiological stress response (Hill et al., 2014, 2016, 2017; Maselko et al., 2007; Suh et al., 2019). In the first major stage of the stress response (the sympathetic response), the hypothalamus (in the brain) signals the adrenal glands to release a stress hormone called adrenaline (or epinephrine) to ready the body for fight-or-flight. In the second major stage (the parasympathetic response), the hypothalamus signals the adrenal glands to release another stress hormone called cortisol to switch off and compensate for the sympathetic response. In an effort to replenish energy reserves depleted during the initial fight-or-flight response, cortisol converts food into stored fats and acts on the brain to induce hunger and food-seeking behavior. When cortisol levels are chronically high, energy is stored as fat around the abdomen, which increases the risk of central obesity (McEwen, 2002). Religious involvement could conceivably protect against greater body mass by buffering physiological processes related to allostatic load. It is interesting that religion can be simultaneously (in the same study) unrelated to BMI scores and inversely associated with waist circumference, waist-to-height ratio, and waist-to-hip ratio (Godbolt et al., 2018; Hill et al., 2017).

Summary

Although these mechanisms are at least theoretically viable, there is little empirical evidence for any of them (Yeary et al., 2017). Smoking has received the most research support to explain why religion might be associated with greater body mass (Gillum, 2006; Kim et al., 2003; Yeary et al., 2009), but this pathway is far from conclusive (Feinstein et al., 2010; Lycett, 2015). Other obesogenic mechanisms like unhealthy eating habits and sedentary lifestyles also lack corroboration (Dodor, 2012; Lycett, 2015; Yeary et al., 2009). To our knowledge, none of the likely explanations for why religion might be associated with leaner body mass have been formally tested. Because studies rarely find any inverse associations between religion and body mass, the literature has mostly abandoned this theoretical possibility. This is unfortunate because the protective effects of religion are consistently observed in certain segments of the population (e.g., older adults and women). In our view, the theories for why religion might be associated with slimmer body mass are more plausible than the theories for why religion might be associated with greater body mass.

Moderators of Religion and Body Mass

Gender and Race

The literature often assumes that the association between religion and body mass is inconsistent across subgroups. For example, studies regularly stratify their analyses by gender and race to show different associations for women and men (Ayers et al., 2010; Baecke et al., 1983; Bentley-Edwards et al., 2020; Cline & Ferraro, 2006; Gillum, 2006; Godbolt et al., 2018; Gottlieb & Green, 1984; Kim et al., 2003; Kortt & Dollery, 2014; Lycett, 2015; Merrill & Hillam, 2006; Svensson et al., 2020; van Lenthe et al., 2000), and blacks and whites (Bentley-Edwards et al., 2020; Dodor, 2012; Godbolt et al., 2018; Reeves et al., 2012; Yeary et al., 2009).

The studies in our review reported approximately 388 null statistical tests, which indicate no association between some measure of religion and some measure of body mass. Roughly 20% of these null tests applied to populations of women, and 21% applied to populations of men. Our review revealed 152 positive associations between religion and body mass. Almost 13% of these tests applied to populations of women, and another 13% applied to populations of men. We could find only 23 inverse associations. About 43% of these tests applied to populations of women, while only 13% applied to populations of men. For the most part, across statistical tests, the association between religion and body does not appear to vary much by gender. Contingent on a larger sample of inverse associations, religion may be more protective for women than men.

When we compare the frequency of null associations by race, we see that approximately 13% of these tests applied to black populations, and only 4% applied to white populations. There are too few race-specific positive or negative tests to produce any meaningful percentages. The probability of observing no association between religion and body mass seems to be higher in black populations than white populations.

Age

Although no studies stratified their analyses by age, we compared the results of studies based on samples of older adults (50 and older) with studies of other samples of adults (18 and older). Studies of older adults accounted for 3% of null tests, 5% of positive tests, and 35% of negative tests. This suggests that the probability of observing a protective effect of religion on body mass may be higher in older populations.

Summary

To our knowledge, there are no established theories for any of these variations. This raises several important questions: Why might religion be more protective among women and older adults? Why might religion have a weaker impact (positive or negative) on body mass in black populations? Understanding how the association between religion and body mass may differ across demographic subgroups is important because religious institutions are not independent of broader systems of social stratification (Godbolt et al., 2018).

Directions for Future Research

Although body mass is an important indicator of population health, this outcome has been surprisingly understudied in the religion and health literature. In an effort to advance the social epidemiology of body mass, we provided an overview of the religion and body mass literature. We considered the nature and extent of the association between religion and body mass in population-based studies of adults conducted in the United States and other countries. We outlined several theoretical and empirical explanations for why religion might be associated with body mass. We also summarized studies of subgroup variations in the association between religion and body mass. Where should the literature go from here?

Theoretical Issues

Our review of the literature raised several fundamental theoretical questions. Why are some measures of religion associated with body mass when others are not? How can some religion measures be associated with greater body mass while others are associated with lesser body mass? How can the same measure of religion (e.g., religious attendance) be associated with greater body mass in one population and lesser body mass in another? Why are so many associations between religion and body mass null? The religion and body mass literature is woefully under-theorized. In the future, researchers will need to move beyond generic conceptualizations of their religion measures. When studies measure religious attendance, they should theorize about the role of religious attendance, not general religiousness. When studies propose mediators or moderators, they should formulate precise hypotheses and thorough explanations for any proposed mechanisms or subgroups variations. Theorizing in these ways and about a broader range of mediators and moderators would help researchers to address these fundamental questions.

Although studies of religion and body mass have employed a range of religion measures, the "dark side" of religion has been understudied in the literature. Over the last decade, the broader study of religion and health has increasingly focused on the ways in which religious struggles may undermine population health. Stauner and colleagues (Stauner et al., 2016:1) define religious struggles as "tension and conflict about sacred matters within oneself, with others, and with the supernatural." There are three general dimensions of religious struggles: interpersonal, intrapersonal, and divine/demonic (Exline et al., 2014). Interpersonal struggles refer to religious-based conflicts with family, friends, or less intimate relations within one's religious group or broader community. Intrapersonal struggles refer to intrapsychic battles with one's own religious beliefs and behavior, including struggles with internalized morality standards, religious doubts, and the search for meaning in life. While divine struggles refer to negative beliefs about or strained relationships with God or another higher power, demonic struggles refer to ominous beliefs about the devil or other evil spirits. The only study in our review to engage with the concept of religious struggles indicated that having an anxious attachment to God could *increase* the probability of being obese (Krause & Hayward, 2016). In the same study, church attendance and prayer were both *unrelated* to body mass. As more studies of religion and body mass incorporate measures of religious struggles, it will be necessary to document the new net effects of standard measures of religious involvement. If religious involvement is associated with religious struggles, the dark side of religion could, depending on the nature of the associations, confound or suppress associations between religion and body mass. For example, it will be interesting to see the degree to which the obesogenic effects of conservative Protestant faith and religious attendance are actually attributable to indicators of religious struggles.

We also observed that the literature is generally limited in terms of theoretical models. Most studies in the literature focus on the direct effects of religion. To a lesser extent, studies have also explored simple mediation and moderation models. One way to advance the complexity of future research is to employ more complex theoretical models like suppression, moderated mediation, and mediated moderation. Suppression occurs when one observes little or no association between two variables until a third (suppressor) variable is controlled (Wheaton, 1985). For example, the positive association between religious attendance and body mass could be, at least theoretically, suppressed by stress. The idea is that religious attendance would be even more obesogenic if it were not inversely associated with stress, which increases body mass. Moderated mediation occurs when a mediation process varies across subgroups (Hayes, 2013). For example, does smoking mediate the association between religion and body mass in women and men (not just the full sample)? Mediated moderation occurs when a subgroup variation is mediated or explained. For example, if the effects of religion on body mass are stronger for whites, what factors might underlie these subgroup variations? Finally, more multilevel models are needed in the literature. For example, Nie (2021) recently used multilevel models to distinguish between the effects of contextual-level religion (county percent Catholic) and individual-level religion (personal Catholic identification) on individual-level body mass. These models can also assess cross-level interactions to formally test whether the effects are contingent on each other. In this case, Nie (2021) showed that the association between percentage Catholic and body mass was not limited to Catholic respondents. This suggest that Catholic context can matter for individuals of different religious faiths. Models along these lines would really add to the theoretical complexity of the literature.

The significance of the literature could also be amplified through the extension of basic theoretical models. Could what we know about the association between religion and body mass help to explain the effects of religion on physical health and mortality risk? Nam (2013) showed that obesity could suppress the positive association between religious attendance and better self-rated health. The general interpretation is that religious attendance would promote even better self-rated health if it were not associated with a greater risk of obesity. In this study, once obesity was controlled, the association between religious attendance and self-rated health became more pronounced. Body mass could also serve as a mediator of religion and health in certain populations. For example, in older adults, religious attendance can lower the probability of being underweight (Hill et al., 2014). Could this pattern help to explain why religious attendance is often associated with longer life expectancies among older adults? Future research could conceivably test these theoretical models (suppression and mediation) using a range of health and mortality outcomes. Religion could also function to buffer the effects of other risk factors for obesity and other health outcomes. In this case, the direct and indirect effects of religion are unimportant because religion is framed as a moderator of other risk factors. For example, Pirutinsky and colleagues (2012) tested whether religious coping could buffer the effects of poor emotional functioning on obesity. Ferraro (1998) also tested whether various religion measures could buffer the effects of body mass on symptoms of happiness and depression. Connecting with other models of obesity and natural outcomes of body mass (e.g., indicators of mental health, physical health, and mortality) would easily enhance the significance of the literature. Why is studying religion and body mass important? Because this research base helps us to understand the social patterning of body mass and a range of other important health outcomes.

Another way to extend previous theoretical models is to incorporate outcomes that are conceptually related to body mass, including, for example, birthweight, biomarkers linked to cardiovascular and metabolic functioning (e.g., blood pressure and cholesterol levels), weight perceptions, body beliefs (e.g., body image, body esteem, and body satisfaction), and eating disorders. Previous research has shown that maternal religious attendance can be protective against low birth weight (Burdette et al., 2012). This is association is important because low birth weight is associated with greater body mass throughout the life course (Hirschler et al., 2008; Ribeiro et al., 2015). Ribeiro et al. (2015:340) explain "that both cardiometabolic events and obesity originate from intrauterine nutritional deficiency" and "a food supply that is excessive to the metabolic needs of the organism in early life stages." When a baby experiences low birth weight and "nutritional deficiency" or starvation, the baby's metabolism slows down to compensate for the lack of nutrition. Slower metabolisms then burn fewer calories, which means more energy is stored as fat in the body. Although some research suggests that religious involvement is associated with lower levels of blood pressure, total cholesterol, and non-high-density lipoprotein cholesterol, religious involvement is typically unrelated to glycosylated hemoglobin or glucose levels (Das & Nairn, 2016; Hill et al., 2014, 2017; Koenig et al., 1998; Suh et al., 2019). It should be noted that these biomarker studies are generally inconsistent with the obesogenic effects of religious involvement. If religious involvement is associated with greater body mass, body mass could be suppressing these associations. The idea is that religious adults would have even lower blood pressures and cholesterol levels if they were not more likely to be obese. In older populations, religious attendance is associated with lower BMI scores and better biological functioning, which is, of course, entirely consistent.

Other related literatures center on body beliefs, weight perceptions, dieting, eating disorders, and severe weight loss. Studies show that several dimensions of religious involvement are consistently associated with healthier body images and greater body esteem and body satisfaction (Boyatzis et al., 2006, 2007; Boyatzis & Quinlan, 2008; Forthun et al., 2003; Goulet et al., 2017; Holman, 2012; Homan, 2012; Homan & Boyatzis, 2009, 2010; Inman, 2014; Kim, 2006; Mahoney et al., 2005; Smith et al., 2004; Tiggemann & Hage, 2019). Researchers have also linked religious beliefs and behaviors with lower levels of dieting, eating disorders and related emotional distress, and severe weight loss (Boyatzis & Quinlan, 2008; Henderson & Ellison, 2015; Homan & Cavanaugh, 2013; Homan & Lemmon, 2014; Joughin et al., 1992). Some evidence even suggests that religious adults are more likely to underestimate their body weight (Kim, 2007; Ruiz & Acevedo, 2015). Several theories underlie these associations. Some argue that religious institutions provide a "social enclave from societal norms of thinness" (Kim, 2007:122). Others emphasize secure attachments to God and the belief that God will love you "no matter what [you] look like" (Boyatzis & Quinlan, 2008:201). These patterns and theories could conceivably contribute to the continued development of religion and body mass research. The obesogenic effects of religion could be at least partially explained by healthier body images, underestimates of body weight, and lower rates of dieting. All of these patterns suggest that religious people may be less likely to interpret their weight as problematic. Under these conditions, weight management strategies become less salient.

Methodological Issues

We also observed several methodological issues in our review. First and foremost, most studies of religion and body mass are cross-sectional. Although this is typical of many literatures, we are concerned that null findings seem to characterize existing longitudinal studies of religion and body mass. Is this due to body mass selection? In other words, are heavier adults drawn to institutions of religion in the first place? To answer these questions, researchers will need to prioritize longitudinal studies and more advanced longitudinal designs (e.g., fixed-effects models, event history of obesity transitions, and growth curve analyses of body mass trajectories).

It is also necessary to address the high rate of null findings in the religion and body mass literature. Are these patterns true (a theoretical problem), or are they merely methodological artifacts? If religion can be positively and negatively associated with body mass, these opposing processes could counteract each other to produce null associations between religion and body mass. There is also the possibility of undiagnosed suppression patterns. These concerns should also continue to motivate researchers to seriously think about why specific religion measures are uniquely associated with body mass.

Mediators have been discussed, but these analyses are limited. There are two general approaches to testing mediation models. The "coefficient change" approach assesses the change in the coefficient for the focal predictor across nested models (i.e., before and after the mediator variable is added to the regression equation). This is the most common approach in the literature. Researchers essentially "eye-ball" the statistically significant associations between religion and body mass before and after a supposed mediator is controlled (e.g., smoking). If the association between religion and body mass is noticeably reduced or attenuated to insignificance, the authors conclude that mediation has occurred. The problem is that studies rarely test whether the magnitude of the change in the religion coefficient is statistically significant. There are formal tests for this (e.g., Clogg et al., 1995). More fundamentally, the coefficient change approach has become old-fashioned. The preferable "indirect effect" approach assesses the statistical significance of an indirect effect (i.e., the product of two coefficients, the coefficient for the effect of the focal predictor on the mediator and the coefficient for the effect of the mediator on the outcome). This approach is more intuitive than the coefficient change approach because it requires information for each link in the proposed causal process ($X \rightarrow M$ and $M \rightarrow Y$). It is important to note that, unlike the coefficient change approach, the indirect effect approach does not require a statistically significant direct effect of X on Y (i.e., religion → body mass). MacKinnon (2008:68) explains that the direct effect of X on Y "is controversial because it is possible that the relation between the independent variable and the dependent variable may be nonsignificant, yet there can still be substantial mediation." More recently, Hayes (2013:88) has noted that "[m] ediation analysis as practiced in the 21st century no longer imposes evidence of a simple association between X and Y as a precondition." In the future, researchers should begin to incorporate more indirect effect approaches to mediation (Hayes, 2013; MacKinnon, 2008; Sobel, 1982; VanderWeele, 2015).

Moderation analyses also have issues. There are two general ways to assess moderation. The most common method in the religion and body mass literature is to stratify the sample to see the association between religion and body mass in different subgroups (e.g., women and men). While this method is informative in a descriptive sense, it does not offer a formal test of subgroups variations. A formal test would involve an interaction term or an extra test that directly compares the coefficients observed in different subgroups (Aiken & West, 1991; Hayes, 2013; Paternoster et al., 1998). Although these types of tests are rare in the literature, they are needed to support more precise conclusions about subgroup variations.

Conclusion

Our overview of religion and body mass research revealed a literature that is complex and underdeveloped, both theoretically and methodologically. Although a large majority of studies show that religion is unrelated to body mass, a non-trivial percentage of previous work suggests that religion tends to favor greater body mass. The least common finding is that religion is associated with leaner body mass. Additional research is needed to establish: (1) more precise theories of mediation and moderation (e.g., explanations for the obesogenic effects of religion); (2) the role of religious struggles (e.g., religious doubts); (3) more advanced theoretical models (e.g., moderated mediation); (4) broader model extensions (e.g., the stress-buffering effects of religion); (5) theoretical and empirical connections to related literatures (e.g., birth weight and body image); (6) more rigorous longitudinal designs (e.g., growth curve models of body mass trajectories); (7) viable alternative explanations for the high rate of null findings (e.g., undiagnosed suppression patterns); and (8) more advanced tests of mediation and moderation (e.g., indirect effects with bias corrected bootstrap confidence intervals). Studies along these lines will no doubt contribute to a more detailed and systematic understanding of religious variations in body mass and related outcomes.

References

Aiken, L., & West, S. (1991). *Multiple regression: Testing and interpreting interactions*. Sage Publications.

Asghari, G., Mirmiran, P., Yuzbashian, E., & Azizi, F. (2017). A systematic review of diet quality indices in relation to obesity. *British Journal of Nutrition, 117*, 1055–1065.

Ayers, J. W., Hofstetter, C. R., Irvin, V. L., Song, Y., Park, H. R., Paik, H. Y., & Hovell, M. F. (2010). Can religion help prevent obesity? Religious messages and the prevalence of being overweight or obese among Korean women in California. *Journal for the Scientific Study of Religion, 49*, 536–549.

Baecke, J. A. H., Burema, J., Frijters, J., Hautvast, J. G., & van der Wiel-Wetzels, W. A. (1983). Obesity in young Dutch adults: I, socio-demographic variables and body mass index. *International Journal of Obesity and Related Metabolic Disorders, 7*, 1–12.

Beccuti, G., & Pannain, S. (2011). Sleep and obesity. *Current Opinion in Clinical Nutrition and Metabolic Care, 14*, 402–412.

Bentley-Edwards, K. L., Carr, L. T. B., Robbins, P. A., Conde, E., Zaw, K., & Darity, W. A. (2020). Investigating denominational and church attendance differences in obesity and diabetes in Black Christian men and women. *Journal of Religion and Health, 59*, 3055–3070.

Bharmal, N., Kaplan, R. M., Shapiro, M. F., Kagawa-Singer, M., Wong, M. D., Mangione, C. M., et al. (2013). The association of religiosity with overweight/obese body mass index among Asian Indian immigrants in California. *Preventive Medicine, 57*, 315–321.

Bouchard, C., Depres, J. P., & Tremblay, A. (1993). Exercise and obesity. *Obesity Research, 1*, 133–147.

Boyatzis, C. J., & Quinlan, K. B. (2008). Women's body image, disordered eating, and religion: A critical review of the literature. In R. Piedmont (Ed.), *Research in the social scientific study of religion* (pp. 183–208). Brill.

Boyatzis, C. J., Trevino, K. M., Manning, A. E., & Quinlan, K. B. (2006). The role of religion and spirituality in women's body image and eating behavior: Qualitative and quantitative approaches and clinical implications. *Counseling and Spirituality, 25*, 29–51.

Boyatzis, C. J., Kline, S., & Backof, S. (2007). Experimental evidence that theistic-religious body affirmations improve women's body image. *Journal for the Scientific Study of Religion, 46*, 553–564.

Burdette, A. M., Weeks, J., Hill, T. D., & Eberstein, I. W. (2012). Maternal religious attendance and low birth weight. *Social Science & Medicine, 74*, 1961–1967.

Burdette, A. M., Hill, T. D., Webb, N. S., Ford, J. A., & Haynes, S. H. (2018). Religious involvement and substance use among urban mothers. *Journal for the Scientific Study of Religion, 57*, 156–172.

Cline, K. M., & Ferraro, K. F. (2006). Does religion increase the prevalence and incidence of obesity in adulthood? *Journal for the Scientific Study of Religion, 45*, 269–281.

Clogg, C. C., Petkova, E., & Haritou, A. (1995). Statistical methods for comparing regression coefficients between models. *American Journal of Sociology, 100*, 1261–1293.

Das, A., & Nairn, S. (2016). Religious attendance and physiological problems in late life. *The Journals of Gerontology Series B: Psychological Sciences and Social Sciences, 71*, 291–308.

DeWall, C. N., Pond, R. S., Jr., Carter, E. C., McCullough, M. E., Lambert, N. M., Fincham, F. D., & Nezlek, J. B. (2014). Explaining the relationship between religiousness and substance use: Self-control matters. *Journal of Personality and Social Psychology, 107*, 339–351.

Dodor, B. (2012). The impact of religiosity on health behaviors and obesity among African Americans. *Journal of Human Behavior in the Social Environment, 22*, 451–462.

Ellison, C. G., & Levin, J. S. (1998). The religion-health connection: Evidence, theory, and future directions. *Health Education & Behavior, 25*, 700–720.

Ellison, C., Lee, J., Krause, N., Hill, T., & Marcum, J. (2009). Faith and fitness: Religious beliefs, congregational support, and exercise in a nationwide survey of Presbyterians. In A. Ai & M. Ardelt (Eds.), *Faith and well-being in later life: Linking theories with evidence in an interdisciplinary inquiry* (pp. 165–184). Nova Science Publishers.

Exline, J. J., Pargament, K. I., Grubbs, J. B., & Yali, A. M. (2014). The religious and spiritual struggles scale: Development and initial validation. *Psychology of Religion and Spirituality, 6*, 208–222.

Feinstein, M., Liu, K., Ning, H., Fitchett, G., & Lloyd-Jones, D. M. (2010). Burden of cardiovascular risk factors, subclinical atherosclerosis, and incident cardiovascular events across dimensions of religiosity: The multi-ethnic study of atherosclerosis. *Circulation, 121*, 659–666.

Feinstein, M., Liu, K., Ning, H., Fitchett, G., & Lloyd-Jones, D. M. (2012). Incident obesity and cardiovascular risk factors between young adulthood and middle age by religious involvement: The coronary artery risk development in young adults (CARDIA) study. *Preventive Medicine, 54*, 117–121.

Ferraro, K. F. (1998). Firm believers? Religion, body weight, and well-being. *Review of Religious Research, 39*, 224–244.

Forthun, L. F., Pidcock, B. W., & Fischer, J. L. (2003). Religiousness and disordered eating: Does religiousness modify family risk? *Eating Behaviors, 4*, 7–26.

Garcia, G., Ellison, C. G., Sunil, T. S., & Hill, T. D. (2013). Religion and selected health behaviors among Latinos in Texas. *Journal of Religion and Health, 52*, 18–31.

George, L., Ellison, C., & Larson, D. (2002). Explaining the relationships between religious involvement and health. *Psychological Inquiry, 13*, 190–200.

Geyer, A., & Baumeister, R. (2005). Religion, morality, and self-control. In R. F. Paloutzian & C. L. Park (Eds.), *Handbook of the psychology of religion and spirituality* (pp. 412–432). Guilford Press.

Gillum, R. F. (2006). Frequency of attendance at religious services, overweight, and obesity in American women and men: The Third National Health and Nutrition Examination Survey. *Annals of Epidemiology, 16*, 655–660.

Godbolt, D., Vaghela, P., Burdette, A. M., & Hill, T. D. (2018). Religious attendance and body mass: An examination of variations by race and gender. *Journal of Religion and Health, 57*, 2140–2152.

Goldblatt, P. B., Moore, M. E., & Stunkard, A. J. (1965). Social factors in obesity. *Journal of the American Medical Association, 192*, 1039–1044.

Gottlieb, N. H., & Green, L. W. (1984). Life events, social network, life-style, and health: An analysis of the 1979 National Survey of Personal Health Practices and Consequences. *Health Education Quarterly, 11*, 91–105.

Goulet, C., Henrie, J., & Szymanski, L. (2017). An exploration of the associations among multiple aspects of religiousness, body image, eating pathology, and appearance investment. *Journal of Religion and Health, 56*, 493–506.

Hales, C. M., Carroll, M. D., Fryar, C. D., & Ogden, C. L. (2020). Prevalence of obesity and severe obesity among adults: United States, 2017–2018. In *NCHS Data Brief, no 360*. National Center for Health Statistics.

Hayes, A. F. (2013). *Introduction to mediation, moderation, and conditional processes analysis: A regression-based approach*. Guilford Press.

Henderson, A. K., & Ellison, C. G. (2015). My body is a temple: Eating disturbances, religious involvement, and mental health among young adult women. *Journal of Religion and Health, 54*, 954–976.

Hill, T. D., Burdette, A. M., Ellison, C. G., & Musick, M. A. (2006). Religious attendance and the health behaviors of Texas adults. *Preventive Medicine, 42*, 309–312.

Hill, T. D., Ellison, C. G., Burdette, A. M., & Musick, M. A. (2007). Religious involvement and healthy lifestyles: Evidence from the survey of Texas adults. *Annals of Behavioral Medicine, 34*, 217–222.

Hill, T. D., Burdette, A. M., & Idler, E. (2011). Religious involvement, health status, and mortality risk. In R. Settersten & J. Angel (Eds.), *Handbook of sociology of aging* (pp. 533–546). Springer.

Hill, T. D., Rote, S. M., Ellison, C. G., & Burdette, A. M. (2014). Religious attendance and biological functioning: A multiple specification approach. *Journal of Aging and Health, 26*, 766–785.

Hill, T. D., Burdette, A. M., & Bradshaw, M. (2016). Health and biological functioning. In D. Yamane (Ed.), *Handbook on religion and society* (pp. 11–28). Springer.

Hill, T. D., Rote, S. M., & Ellison, C. G. (2017). Religious participation and biological functioning in Mexico. *Journal of Aging and Health, 29*, 951–972.

Hill, T. D., DeAngelis, R., & Ellison, C. G. (2018). Religious involvement as a social determinant of sleep: An initial review and conceptual model. *Sleep Health, 4*, 325–330.

Hirschler, V., Bugna, J., Roque, M., Gilligan, T., & Gonzalez, C. (2008). Does low birth weight predict obesity/overweight and metabolic syndrome in elementary school children? *Archives of Medical Research, 39*, 796–802.

Holman, A. (2012). Religion and the body: An overview of the insertions of religion in the empirical psycho-social research lines on the body. *European Journal of Science and Theology, 8*, 127–134.

Homan, K. J. (2012). Attachment to God mitigates negative effect of media exposure on women's body image. *Psychology of Religion and Spirituality, 4*, 324.

Homan, K. J., & Boyatzis, C. J. (2009). Body image in older adults: Links with religion and gender. *Journal of Adult Development, 16*, 230–238.

Homan, K. J., & Boyatzis, C. J. (2010). The protective role of attachment to God against eating disorder risk factors: Concurrent and prospective evidence. *Eating Disorders, 18*, 239–258.

Homan, K. J., & Cavanaugh, B. N. (2013). Perceived relationship with god fosters positive body image in college women. *Journal of Health Psychology, 18*, 1529–1539.

Homan, K. J., & Lemmon, V. A. (2014). Attachment to God and eating disorder tendencies: The mediating role of social comparison. *Psychology of Religion and Spirituality, 6*, 349–357.

Horton, S. E. (2015). Religion and health-promoting behaviors among emerging adults. *Journal of Religion and Health, 54*, 20–34.

Idler, E. (2004). Religious observance and health: Theory and research. In K. Schaie, N. Krause, & A. Booth (Eds.), *Religious influences on health and well-being in the elderly* (pp. 20–43). Springer.

Idler, E. (2011). Religion and adult mortality. In R. Rogers & E. Crimmins (Eds.), *International handbook of adult mortality* (pp. 345–377). Springer.

Idler, E. L., & Kasl, S. V. (1997). Religion among disabled and nondisabled persons I: Cross-sectional patterns in health practices, social activities, and well-being Ellen. *The Journals of Gerontology Series B: Psychological Sciences and Social Sciences, 52*, S294–S305.

Inman, M. L. (2014). The effects of religious-body affirmations and religious commitment on men's body esteem. *Psychology of Religion and Spirituality, 6*, 330–337.

Joughin, N., Crisp, A. H., Halek, C., & Humphrey, H. (1992). Religious belief and anorexia nervosa. *International Journal of Eating Disorders, 12*, 397–406.

Kent, L. M., Morton, D. P., Ward, E. J., Rankin, P. M., Ferret, R. B., Gobble, J., & Diehl, H. A. (2016). The influence of religious affiliation on participant responsiveness to the complete health improvement program (CHIP) lifestyle intervention. *Journal of Religion and Health, 55*, 1561–1573.

Kim, K. H. C. (2006). Religion, body satisfaction and dieting. *Appetite, 46*, 285–296.

Kim, K. H. C. (2007). Religion, weight perception, and weight control behavior. *Eating Behaviors, 8*, 121–131.

Kim, K. H., Sobal, J., & Wethington, E. (2003). Religion and body weight. *International Journal of Obesity, 27*, 469–477.

Koenig, H., George, L., Hays, J., Larson, D., Cohen, H., & Blazer, D. (1998). The relationship between religious activities and blood pressure in older adults. *International Journal of Psychiatry in Medicine, 28*, 189–213.

Koenig, H. G., King, D., & Carson, V. B. (2012). *Handbook of religion and health*. Oxford University Press.

Kortt, M. A., & Dollery, B. (2014). Religion and BMI in Australia. *Journal of Religion and Health, 53*, 217–228.

Krause, N., & Hayward, R. (2016). Religion, health, and aging. In L. George & K. Ferraro (Eds.), *Handbook of aging and the social sciences* (pp. 251–270). Elsevier.

Lapane, K. L., Lasater, T. M., Allan, C., & Carleton, R. A. (1997). Religion and cardiovascular disease risk. *Journal of Religion and Health, 36*, 155–164.

Lycett, D. (2015). The association of religious affiliation and body mass index (BMI): An analysis from the health survey for England. *Journal of Religion and Health, 54*, 2249–2267.

MacKinnon, D. P. (2008). *Introduction to statistical mediation analysis*. Lawrence Erlbaum.

Mahoney, A., Carels, R. A., Pargament, K. I., Wachholtz, A., Edwards Leeper, L., Kaplar, M., & Frutchey, R. (2005). The sanctification of the body and behavioral health patterns of college students. *The International Journal for the Psychology of Religion, 15*, 221–238.

Maselko, J., Kubzansky, L., Kawachi, I., Seeman, T., & Berkman, L. (2007). Religious service attendance and allostatic load among high-functioning elderly. *Psychosomatic Medicine, 69*, 464–472.

McCullough, M. E., & Willoughby, B. L. (2009). Religion, self-regulation, and self-control: Associations, explanations, and implications. *Psychological Bulletin, 135*, 69–93.

McEwen, B. S. (2002). *The end of stress as we know it.* Joseph Henry Press.

Merrill, R. M., & Hillam, S. (2006). Religion and body weight in Utah. *Utah's Health: An Annual Review, 11*, 40–50.

Nam, S. (2013). The effects of religious attendance and obesity on health by race/ethnicity. *Osong Public Health and Research Perspectives, 4*, 81–88.

Nie, F. (2021). Body mass index in religious contexts: Exploring the multilevel influences of religion. *Journal of Religion and Health, 60*, 1160–1178.

Ogden, C. L., Fryar, C. D., Martin, C. B., Freedman, D. S., Carroll, M. D., Gu, Q., & Hales, C. M. (2020). Trends in obesity prevalence by race and Hispanic origin – 1999–2000 to 2017–2018. *Journal of the American Medical Association, 324*, 1208–1210.

Pascoe, A. E., Hill, T. D., Mossakowski, K. N., & Johnson, R. J. (2016). Religious involvement and perceptions of control: Evidence from the Miami-Dade health survey. *Journal of Religion and Health, 55*, 862–873.

Paternoster, R., Brame, R., Mazerolle, P., & Piquero, A. (1998). Using the correct statistical test for the equality of regression coefficients. *Criminology, 36*, 859–866.

Pirutinsky, S., Rosmarin, D. H., & Holt, C. L. (2012). Religious coping moderates the relationship between emotional functioning and obesity. *Health Psychology, 31*, 394–397.

Reeves, R. R., Adams, C. E., Dubbert, P. M., Hickson, D. A., & Wyatt, S. B. (2012). Are religiosity and spirituality associated with obesity among African Americans in the Southeastern United States (the Jackson Heart Study)? *Journal of Religion and Health, 51*, 32–48.

Ribeiro, A. M., de Carvalho Lima, M., de Lira, P. I. C., & da Silva, G. A. P. (2015). Low birth weight and obesity: Causal or casual casual association? *Revista Paulista de Pediatria, 33*, 340–348.

Ruiz, A. L., & Acevedo, G. A. (2015). True believers? Religion, physiology, and perceived body weight in Texas. *Journal of Religion and Health, 54*, 1221–1237.

Smith, M. H., Richards, P. S., & Maglio, C. J. (2004). Examining the relationship between religious orientation and eating disturbances. *Eating Behaviors, 5*, 171–180.

Sobel, M. (1982). Asymptotic intervals for indirect effects in structural equation models. In S. Leinhart (Ed.), *Sociological methodology* (pp. 290–312). Jossey-Bass.

Stauner, N., Exline, J. J., Grubbs, J. B., Pargament, K. I., Bradley, D. F., & Uzdavines, A. (2016). Bifactor models of religious and spiritual struggles: Distinct from religiousness and distress. *Religions, 7*, 68.

Strawbridge, W. J., Shema, S. J., Cohen, R. D., & Kaplan, G. A. (2001). Religious attendance increases survival by improving and maintaining good health behaviors, mental health, and social relationships. *Annals of Behavioral Medicine, 23*, 68–74.

Suh, H., Hill, T. D., & Koenig, H. G. (2019). Religious attendance and biological risk: A national longitudinal study of older adults. *Journal of Religion and Health, 58*, 1188–1202.

Svensson, N. H., Hvidt, N. C., Nissen, S. P., Storsveen, M. M., Hvidt, E. A., Søndergaard, J., & Thilsing, T. (2020). Religiosity and health-related risk behaviours in a secular culture—Is there a correlation? *Journal of Religion and Health, 59*, 2381–2396.

Tiggemann, M., & Hage, K. (2019). Religion and spirituality: Pathways to positive body image. *Body Image, 28*, 135–141.

Traversy, G., & Chaput, J. P. (2015). Alcohol consumption and obesity: An update. *Current Obesity Reports, 4*, 122–130.

Van Lenthe, F. J., Droomers, M., Schrijvers, C. T. M., & Mackenbach, J. P. (2000). Socio-demographic variables and 6 year change in body mass index: Longitudinal results from the GLOBE study. *International Journal of Obesity, 24*, 1077–1084.

VanderWeele, T. (2015). *Explanation in causal inference: Methods for mediation and interaction*. Oxford University Press.

Wallace, J. M., Jr., & Forman, T. A. (1998). Religion's role in promoting health and reducing risk among American youth. *Health Education & Behavior, 25*, 721–741.

Welch, M. R., Tittle, C. R., & Grasmick, H. G. (2006). Christian religiosity, self-control and social conformity. *Social Forces, 84*, 1605–1623.

Wheaton, B. (1985). Models for the stress-buffering functions of coping resources. *Journal of Health and Social Behavior, 26*, 352–364.

Yeary, K. H. K., Jo, C. H., Simpson, P., Gossett, J. M., Johnson, G. S., McCabe-Sellers, B. J., et al. (2009). Religion and body weight in an underserved population. *Race, Gender & Class, 16*, 82–98.

Yeary, K. H. C. K., Sobal, J., & Wethington, E. (2017). Religion and body weight: A review of quantitative studies. *Obesity Reviews, 18*, 1210–1222.

Yeary, K. H. C. K., Moore, P. C., & Sobal, J. (2020). Religion and body weight among African-American adults attempting to lose weight: An exploratory study. *Journal of Religion and Health, 59*, 758–771.

Zhang, Y., Yang, J., Hou, W., & Arcan, C. (2020). Obesity trends and associations with types of physical activity and sedentary behavior in US adults: National Health and Nutrition Examination Survey, 2007-2016. *Obesity, 29*, 240–250.

12 Psychosocial Stressors and Obesity

Adolfo G. Cuevas, Natalie Eckert, and Keri Carvalho

Obesity has become a perilous public health issue in the United States (US) (Flegal et al., 2016). Approximately 4 out of 10 adults in the US have obesity, more than a three-fold increase over the 12% rate observed in 1991 (Ogden et al., 2020). Projections indicate that by 2030, approximately half of all US adults will have obesity, with disproportionately high prevalence among racial/ethnic minorities and women (Ward et al., 2019). Compared to people with healthy weight, individuals with obesity have an increased risk of morbidity—including diabetes, cardiovascular disease, and colorectal cancer—and early mortality (Arteaga et al., 2014; Calle et al., 2003; Calle & Kaaks, 2004; Renehan et al., 2008; Vucenik & Stains, 2012). As a consequence of continually rising obesity prevalence, it is expected that the excessive burden of obesity-related morbidity and mortality will soar. While the etiology of obesity remains unclear, researchers agree that obesity is a multifactorial, preventable disease that involves a complex interaction between environmental factors, genetic factors, and lifestyle behaviors. Growing bodies of research are beginning to recognize psychological and social (psychosocial) stress as an important environmental risk factor of obesity. This chapter is organized into four sections. First, we introduce the topic of stress and provide a description of how stress is commonly conceptualized in the literature. Second, we draw attention to the biobehavioral pathways that undergird the association between psychosocial stress and obesity risk. Third, we highlight six prominent psychosocial stressors that have been identified as obesogenic risk factors. In the final section, we describe some future research directions that would help advance our understanding of psychosocial stress and obesity.

What Is Stress?

Stress is typically defined as one's environmental demands exceeding their resources for adapting to the situation (Cohen et al., 2007; Schneiderman et al., 2005). The intensity and duration of stressful stimuli are important determinants of health risk and, thus, stressful stimuli are typically categorized as acute or chronic. Acute stressors are forms of stress that come and go quickly and are often physical, e.g., hunger or thirst, rather than psychological, e.g., shooting the winning point free throw in a basketball game. Although they are short-lived events, acute stressors can have harmful effects on one's health, such as increased mortality, pain, anxiety, and depression and decreased self-rated health (Garfin et al., 2018). Conversely, chronic stressors occur over

A. G. Cuevas (✉)
NYU School of Global Public Health, New York, NY, USA
e-mail: Adolfo.cuevas@nyu.edu

N. Eckert · K. Carvalho
Department of Community Health, Tufts University, Medford, MA, USA

G. Garcia-Alexander, D. L. Poston, Jr. (eds.), *International Handbook of the Demography of Obesity*, International Handbooks of Population 12, https://doi.org/10.1007/978-3-031-10936-2_12

long periods of time and cause sustained distress. These stressors are typically psychological (e.g., financial strain or discrimination), rather than physical (e.g., experiencing a drought). Chronic, psychological stress has deleterious effects on a wide range of physical and mental health outcomes with compelling evidence that health compromising behaviors and physiological dysregulation may mediate these relationships (Bosch & Bird, 2018). As such, it has been strongly implicated in the onset of major disease and illnesses, including coronary heart disease, diabetes, depression disorder, and early mortality (Cohen et al., 2007; Schneiderman et al., 2005).

Pathways Linking Psychological Stress to Obesity

How can stress contribute to obesity? Stress can increase risk for obesity through biological and behavioral pathways. In this section, we review the known biological pathways that link stress to weight gain. We also review three prominent obesity-related behaviors that are influenced by stress exposure. Mapping the mechanisms connecting stress to obesity risk would allow us to better understand how psychosocial stressors operate to increase the risk for obesity and help us identify key areas for future research and intervention development.

Psychosocial stress may increase the risk of obesity through biological pathways (see Fig. 12.1). Human and animal studies have eloquently demonstrated that stressful events can activate physiological regulatory systems that can lead to visceral obesity (Hewagalamulage et al., 2016; Rodriguez et al., 2015). In humans, exposure to stressful stimuli can affect the hippocampus and amygdala, two key regions of the brain that process safety and threat as well as regulate emotions (Lockwood et al., 2018; McEwen, 2007). These regions modulate stress output, which is comprised of two arms—the hypothalamus-pituitary adrenal (HPA) axis and the sympathetic nervous system (SNS). The SNS, which includes the sympathoadrenal–medullary (SAM) axis, is the first and fastest acting part of the stress response, influencing cardiovascular function, respiration, endocrine, and other systems (Elenkov et al., 2000; Murison, 2016). The SAM system releases additional catecholamines into the bloodstream, causing subsequent changes in blood pressure (BP), breathing, heartbeat, and dilation of blood vessels, and allowing large amounts of glycogen to be released into the muscles (Elenkov et al., 2000). Intertwined within these systems lies the HPA axis, which also functions to maintain homeostasis during stressful events. The hypothalamus releases hormones (e.g., corticotropin-releasing factor and arginine vasopressin) to activate the pituitary gland. The anterior pituitary gland produces and secretes hormones, particularly adrenocorticotropic hormones, which prompts the adrenal glands to produce glucocorticoids.

Cortisol secretion and inflammation are two biological responses that can lead to an increase in fat storage (see Fig. 12.1). Cortisol, the main glucocorticoid in humans, allows the body to adapt to stress by providing a temporary surge in energy, modulating immune cells, reducing sensitivity to pain, and improving memory function (Schneiderman et al., 2005). Chronic secretion of cortisol, however, can lead to weight gain indirectly through increased consumption of "comfort" foods that are high in fat and sugar and directly through abdominal fat deposition (Abraham et al., 2013; DiNicolantonio et al., 2018; Gyllenhammer et al., 2014; Hewagalamulage et al., 2016). Inflammation is also an important feature of the stress response, as it is a fundamental property of the biological systems to maintain homeostasis. Alterations in HPA axis and SNS induces expression of several pro-inflammatory cytokines and anti-inflammatory cytokines (Liu et al., 2017; Sorrells et al., 2009). Chronic HPA axis and SNS responses to stress can lead to immune dysregulation evidenced by a state of low-grade elevations in circulating inflammatory markers (Ehrlich et al., 2016). Chronic inflammation can alter insulin sensitivity and the release of growth hormone, all of which can lead to accumulation of visceral fat (Deng et al., 2016; Lumeng & Saltiel, 2011; Ramos-Nino, 2013).

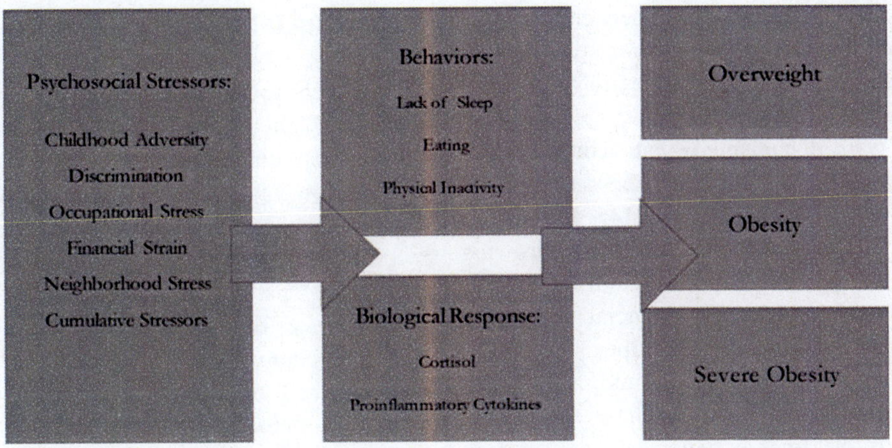

Fig. 12.1 Pathways linking psychosocial stress to obesity

As shown in Fig. 12.1, health compromising behaviors mediate the stress and weight-gain association. People experiencing psychological distress can experience weight gain through increased food consumption (Hruby & Hu, 2015; Scott et al., 2012). Psychosocial stress is generally thought to induce the release of appetite hormones that results in this increase in food consumption (Adam & Epel, 2007; Araiza & Lobel, 2018; Pool et al., 2015; Scott et al., 2012). Individuals with high levels of stress tend to consume foods high in fats and sugar as a way to activate brain reward systems and reduce stress responses (Scott et al., 2012). A seminal study showed that women had a greater preference for foods high in fat or sugar after a stressful episode (Grunberg & Straub, 1992). Since then, several studies have documented the relationship between stress and food intake (Elshurbjy & Ellulu, 2017; Ulrich-Lai et al., 2015; Yau & Potenza, 2013). Adults reporting high levels of stress are almost twice as likely to eat ultra-processed foods (Lopes Cortes et al., 2021). In adolescents, higher self-reported stress levels are associated with increased hunger after stressful events and an increased likelihood of overeating (Debeuf et al., 2018).

Figure 12.1 also indicates that psychosocial stress increases the risk of disease through physical inactivity. The association between stress and physical activity is well-established. In a systematic review of 55 prospective studies, Stults-Kolehmainen and Sinha (2014) found that objective (e.g., reports of major life changes) and subjective forms of stress (e.g., the degree to which situations are appraised as stressful) predicted less physical activity and exercise and more sedentary behavior. For instance, caregivers of spouses with Alzheimer's Disease report higher levels of stress and also report lower exercise 15–18 months later (Vitaliano et al., 1998). In a study of 7066 Danish adults, individuals who appraised current life circumstances as unpredictable or uncontrollable were 90% more likely to become physically inactive 10 years later (Rod et al., 2009). In a study of 2507 community-dwelling older adults, individuals with low stress were more likely to engage in physically active recreations at least three times a week and maintain this level of physical activity over a 4-year period compared to those high in stress (Burton et al., 1999). Much of the literature has corroborated these prospective findings through qualitative, retrospective, and experimental work (Stults-Kolehmainen & Sinha, 2014). For instance, children who were exposed to a stressor—preparing and delivering a videotaped speech—had a 21% reduction in physical activity compared to children who engaged in passive reading (Roemmich et al., 2003). Stults-Kolehmainen and Sinha (2014) point out that few studies employ rigorous experimental designs, which would help solidify our understanding of stress and physical activity. Nevertheless, the prospective studies help establish the temporal sequence between stressors and physical activity, and, therefore, gives us confidence that stress is a risk factor of physical inactivity.

It is well documented that reduced sleep and poor sleep quality predict the development of obesity (Bayon et al., 2014; Beccuti & Pannain, 2011; Zimberg et al., 2012). Growing research indicate that exposure to different psychosocial adversities (e.g., financial stress, job strain) can prevent or disrupt sleep. For instance, in a large population study of African American adults (N = 4683), those exposed to high levels of stress experienced shorter sleep duration and poorer sleep quality (Johnson et al., 2016). Other studies have linked poor sleep quality and poor sleep duration with discrimination exposure, goal-striving stress, financial stress, high job demand (Cain-Shields et al., 2020; Owens et al., 2017; Hall et al., 2008, 2009; Van Laethem et al., 2013). While there is a need for epidemiologic studies to establish sleep as a mediator between different psychosocial stressors and obesity, the existing evidence suggest that stress exposure increase the risk of obesity through poor sleep.

It is important to note that stress does not happen in a vacuum. While stress is a normal part of life that all living humans experience, the type of stress exposure, its duration, and its severity are part of a larger social structure. As such, historically marginalized groups are disproportionately exposed to stressors and experience stress-related diseases. Historical and contemporary policies have downstream effects that significantly expose marginalized groups to poor environmental pollutants and toxins, restricted socioeconomic opportunity, and violence and abuse. Thus, interventions that seek to mitigate the obesogenic effects of stress should attune themselves to policies and laws that influence stressor exposure. While reduction in body mass index at the population-level is the best indicator of a policy's efficacy, it may take years to observe improvements. Therefore, biobehavioral mediators (Fig. 12.1) can serve as early evidence of whether stress-related policies are effective and achieving their targets to reduce obesity.

Psychosocial Stressors and Obesity

Five psychosocial stress domains have been examined in relation to obesity-related phenotypes: childhood adversity, occupational stress (or job strain), financial strain, discrimination, and neighborhood stress. More recently, researchers have examined the multidimensional nature of stress by capturing cooccurrences of multiple psychosocial stressors. The association between each psychosocial stressors and obesity-related phenotypes have been documented. Since the level of evidence varies across the psychosocial stress domains, questions remain about how to best measure stress, the mechanisms involved, and their interaction with genes. We review recent findings in each of these areas, and offer directions for future research.

Childhood Adversity

Childhood adversity can occur when a person experiences single or cumulative stressful events prior to the age of 18. These experiences can include emotional and physical neglect by caregivers; different forms of abuse; exposure to poverty; and parental incarceration, divorce, mental illness, and alcohol or substance misuse, among others (Felitti et al., 1998). The operationalization of adverse childhood experiences (ACEs) has begun to expand to experiences such as moving, discrimination, pregnancy, bullying, and educational disruption (e.g., incompletion, suspension, or dropping out) in childhood (Friedman et al., 2015; Gardner et al., 2019; Heerman et al., 2016; Salmela et al., 2019; Wall et al., 2019).

The prevalence of ACEs is high. Almost two out of every three people in the United States report experiencing at least one ACE (Center for Disease Control and Prevention (CDC), 2019). Substantial literature has documented that people exposed to ACEs are at greater risk of several adverse health outcomes in adulthood, including poor self-rated health, chronic diseases, functional limitations, premature mortality, and poor mental health (Felitti et al., 1998). ACEs may also increase the risk of obesity (Fig. 12.1). Numerous studies have demonstrated a positive relationship between the occurrence of adverse experiences in childhood and adult obesity (Danese & Tan, 2014; Wiss & Brewerton, 2020; Schroeder et al., 2021). Adults are 46% more likely to have obesity if they have experienced adversity in their childhood, and each ACE is associated with a 14% increased likelihood of adulthood obesity (Friedman et al., 2015; Wiss & Brewerton, 2020). In childhood, those with self-reported cumulative ACEs are more likely to be obese than those with one ACE or none (Heerman et al., 2016). Because obesity and ACEs are more prevalent in women in the United States (Liu et al., 2013; Ogden et al., 2020), researchers have explored whether the effects of ACEs are stronger for women. Meta-regression analyses reveal that the association between childhood maltreatment and obesity was stronger for women than men (Danese & Tan, 2014). It remains unclear whether some early life adversities (e.g., physical abuse) have greater effects on obesity than other early life exposures (e.g., household challenges). Also, the biobehavioral pathways that link these individual stressors with obesity is not well-understood. This level of analysis can lead more effectual obesity prevention measures that seek to curb obesity in early life.

Occupational Stress

Occupational stress (job strain) can occur when occupational demands exceed one's ability to influence or control aspects of their job (Overgaard et al., 2006). Although occupational stress varies between individuals, jobs, and industries, occupational demands (i.e., time spent working, pace of work, and occupational pressures) can be a source of incredible stress for many workers. Various surveys of workers have revealed that 26–40% of workers feel that their job is very stressful, and 25% of workers report their job being their primary stressor (CDC, 2014). Occupational stress can lead to a wide range of negative health outcomes, including cardiovascular disease, depression, and anxiety (Burns et al., 2016; Kivimäki et al., 2015; Wieclaw et al., 2008). Bolstered by these findings, researchers investigated its association with overweight/obesity. Meta-analysis and systematic review revealed, however, that the association between occupational stress and obesity are mixed (Bhui et al., 2012; Kivimäki et al., 2015). There are multiple reasons for the mixed findings. Individuals possess different eating patterns when under stress. Thus, occupational stress may increase eating in some individuals while decreasing it in others (Kivimäki et al., 2015). Some stressful occupations are also physically demanding, and these workers accrue substantial amounts of physical activity that reduces their risk of obesity (Gudnadottir et al., 2019). Other measures of occupational stress, such as burnout, working the night shift, working more than 40 hours per week, and being in a hostile environment, may better capture the obesogenic effects of occupational stress. These factors have been associated with greater risk of obesity (Armenta-Hernández et al., 2018; Luckhaupt et al., 2014; Sun et al., 2018). Thus, future research should consider exploring the multidimensionality of occupational stress to better elucidate its effects on obesity.

Financial Strain

Financial strain is a perceived or actual economic stressor that occurs when one's economic needs outweigh their resources. It can encompass acute events, such as not having enough financial resources to pay for an unexpected bill without significant sacrifice or prolonged, chronic events, such as worrying about paying rent each month. There are multiple mechanisms by which financial strain can increase the risk of obesity. Those who are financially strained are less likely to have healthy food options or engage in health promoting behaviors (e.g., physical activity) (Carvalho et al., 2016; Conklin et al., 2014a, b). People experiencing financial strain also report greater depressive and anxiety disorder and, as noted previously, compromised sleep quality (Dijkstra-Kersten et al., 2015; Hall et al., 2008; Hall et al., 2009; Okechukwu et al., 2012). A study investigating the effects of financial strain on obesity in college students found that both men and women who reported financial strain were more likely to be obese; however, after the authors controlled for other stressors, the relationship only held for men, who were 14% more likely to be obese if they reported financial strain (Cheng et al., 2020). Longitudinal studies find that financial strain (e.g., difficulty paying bills) is associated with subsequent weight gain among adults (Siahpush et al., 2014; Conklin et al., 2014a, b; Cuevas, 2020; Averett & Smith 2014). Additionally, financial strain may help to explain some of the racial disparities in obesity. In a study investigating possible factors that could result in obesity differences in Black and White adults, researchers not only found that 3.65% of the disparity could be accounted for with financial strain, but also that it was the only stressor with significant effects on racial obesity differences (Cuevas et al., 2019). Financial strain is a byproduct of systemic social and economic policies that create barriers to quality jobs and higher wages, and, therefore, is a mediator between larger structural barriers and obesity. Future research should investigate how local policies (e.g., state minimum wage laws) contribute to financial strain and, in turn, obesity risk. The need to identify the root causes of financial strain can help inform policy level interventions that seek to reduce obesity and racial/ethnic obesity disparities.

Discrimination

Over the last two decades, research has shown that exposure to unfair treatment, often referred to as perceived discrimination, has deleterious effects on physical health. Exposure to discrimination can activate key regulatory physiological systems and influence individuals to engage in obesity-related behaviors to increase their risk of obesity (Cuevas et al., 2020; Lewis et al., 2015). Recent research has shown that exposure to discrimination is associated with increased risk for obesity. For instance, African American men who experienced any major discrimination, such as being denied a bank loan, had a higher likelihood of obesity compared to those who reported no major discrimination (Thorpe et al., 2017). In a study of 1452 adults, Hunte and Williams (2009) found that participants who reported greater everyday discrimination had increased waist circumference over a 9-year period. Similar results were found in a study that examined the effects of racial discrimination on obesity, wherein everyday discrimination was associated with increased incidence of obesity over a 12-year period (Cozier et al., 2014). Discrimination is not limited to race/ethnicity. Individuals and groups can experience other forms of discrimination, including gender, sexual orientation, weight, immigration status, religion, and age. For instance, lesbian women are 2.49 times more likely to have obesity when they report experiences of heterosexist discrimination (Mereish, 2014).

In particular, the association between exposure to weight discrimination and weight gain is well established (Tomiyama, 2014; Sutin & Terraciano, 2013). For instance, one study documented that individuals reporting discrimination based on their weight had a significant weight gain over a three-year time period (Udo & Grilo, 2016). Likelihood of exposure to weight discrimination is directly associated with BMI, with an overall prevalence of 7.3% (Sikorski et al., 2016). However, approximately one in three individuals with morbid obesity experience weight discrimination, which may further exacerbate weight gain. Exposure to weight discrimination has been shown to be pervasive in children and adults. For example, children may be exposed to weight bullying in school and home settings (Puhl et al., 2013), which may affect academic performance and self-esteem. Adults may experience unfair hiring and promotion practices in workplaces (Grant et al., 2014), which can increase exposure to financial strain. The compounding of psychosocial stressors can ultimately lead to higher cumulative stress, and in turn weight gain.

Neighborhood Stress

Stress from the social environment is associated with a wide range of health outcomes, including depression, anxiety, substance abuse, and psychological distress (LeCounte & Swain, 2017). The neighborhood in which one lives exposes groups and individuals to social and environmental stressors, such as truncated employment opportunities, violence, pollutants, and excessive noise (Kwarteng et al., 2017). Exposure to neighborhood physical and social disorder (e.g., graffiti, abandoned buildings, and crime) can induce physiological stress response, resulting in dysregulation of neuroendocrine and inflammatory processes (Browning et al., 2012; Robinette et al., 2016). Neighborhood disorder can also dissuade individuals from engaging in outdoor physical activity (Gomez et al., 2004; Lenhart et al., 2017; Kärmeniemi et al., 2018). Negative perception of the neighborhood physical environment is associated with increases in adiposity (Kwarteng et al., 2017; Powell-Wiley et al., 2013; Pham et al., 2014; Burdette & Needham, 2012). For instance, in a study of 5907 adults, those who rated their neighborhood as unfavorable—measured by neighborhood violence, physical environment, and social cohesion—had 28% greater odds of obesity than those who viewed their neighborhoods favorably (Powell-Wiley et al., 2013). Another study of 2255 adults found that those who perceived their neighborhoods as unsafe had a BMI that was 2.81 kg/m^2 higher than did those who perceived their neighborhoods as safe (Fish et al., 2010). Going beyond individual-level reports, researchers have examined objective forms of neighborhood disorder. One study found that higher neighborhood physical disorder—as measured by rates of police-recorded crime and 311 calls for service—was associated with higher odds of obesity (Mayne et al., 2018). Another study found that neighborhood disorder—as measured by poor sidewalk conditions and greater presence of garbage are associated with obesity risk (Boehmer et al., 2007). The culmination of these findings reveals that both subjective and objective indicators of neighborhood deprivation are important risk factors to obesity.

Cumulative Stress

Psychosocial stressors often coexist in individuals' lives (Sternthal et al., 2011; Wardle et al., 2011). Thus, researchers are beginning to better estimate and characterize the impact of stress by assessing the co-occurrence of stressors and its health sequelae (Evans et al., 2013; Evans & Kim, 2010; Slavich, 2016; Sternthal et al., 2011). Emerging research suggests that exposure to multiple stressors has greater obesogenic effects than single exposures. One study found that those who reported stress exposure in the highest quintiles across 2, 3, or $\geq$4 types of stressors had significantly higher odds of obesity compared to participants who were not in the top quintile of any domain (Cuevas et al., 2019). Those with four or more stressor exposures were 60% more likely to have obesity compared to those with no stressor exposure (Cuevas et al., 2019). These findings provide insight into the role of stress in existing racial/ethnic obesity disparities. Racial/ethnic minorities report experiencing greater exposure to common stressors and race-related stressors than their White counterparts (see Fig. 12.2). Using data from the Chicago Community Adult Health Study (2001–2003), Cuevas et al. (2020) quantified the extent to which health behaviors (fruit and vegetable consumption and physical activity), socioeconomic position, and cumulative stressors (e.g., perceived discrimination, financial strain) each explained differences in obesity prevalence in Black, US-born Hispanic, and non-US-born Hispanic compared with non-Hispanic White participants. Counter to long-held beliefs in the literature, the authors found that socioeconomic position and health behaviors did not explain obesity differences between racial/ethnic minorities and White individuals. However, having high levels of stress in four or more domains explained 4.46% of the differences between Black and White individuals, whereas having high levels of stress in three domains significantly explained 14.13% of differences between US-born Hispanic and White. Taken together, the emerging research suggests that the cumulative burden of psychosocial stressors play a role in obesity risk and that disproportionate exposure

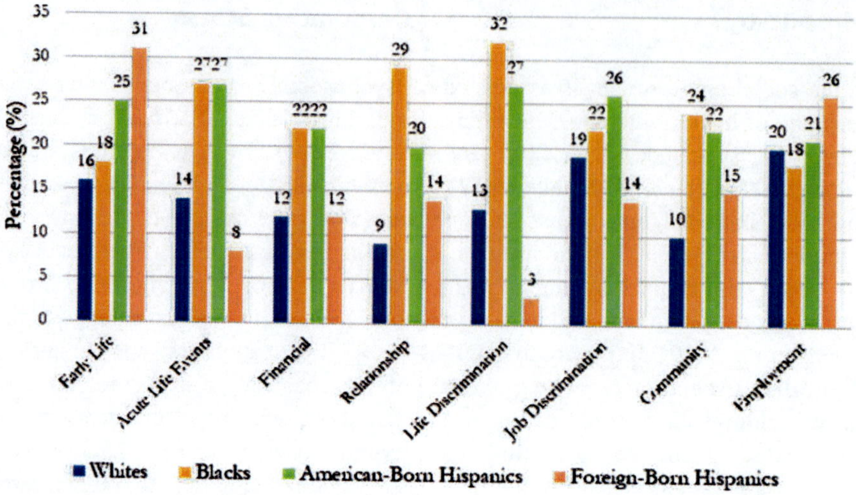

Fig. 12.2 Distribution of psychosocial stressor exposure by race/ethnicity. (Cuevas et al., 2019)

to cumulative stress may contribute to obesity disparities. There is no evidence of variation in the association between cumulative stress and obesity by racial/ethnic groups. Yet, it is unknown whether the pathways between stressors and obesity are similar across groups. Racial/ethnic groups may differ in the ways they cope with certain stressors (e.g., discrimination) and, therefore, future studies should examine the potential differences in stress pathways among racial/ethnic groups. Further, researchers should consider a wider range of stressors that capture the lived experiences of racial/ethnic minorities. For instance, acculturation stress and stress related to documentation status are commonly experienced by immigrants and may influence weight gain. Incorporating other stressors in the operationalizing of cumulative stress would increase statistical power and better represent a source of potential explanatory power of racial/ethnic obesity disparities.

Future Research

Although the literature has established a causal relationship between stress and obesity, there remains a need to identify the psychosocial stressors that increase the risk of obesity. Research has documented the obesogenic effects of childhood adversity, occupational stress, financial strain, neighborhood stress, and the cumulative burden of psychosocial stressors. Still, there are other stressors (e.g., food insecurity, relationship stress, and caregiver stress) that need to be thoroughly examined. As such, research design should be closely considered in the future to help us cross-compare study findings and have a more nuanced understanding of study data.

A Better Understanding of Pathways

Not all stressors are created equal. Individuals cope with each stressor differently, and, thus, the health effects will vary across stressors. Research is still needed to longitudinally assess the association between a wide range of stressors and obesity-related phenotypes. Taking a lifecourse perspective would allow researchers to better pinpoint the temporal order of stress in relation to the onset of obesity. Moreover, to accurately understand the obesogenic effects of psychosocial stressors, their respective measures must capture the level of severity and the duration of the events. For instance, some acute events may be longer in duration and more severe than other events (e.g., experiencing natural disaster). The intensity of the stressor is a major factor in the overall response of the HPA axis (Cohen et al., 2007; Herman et al., 2016; Schneiderman et al., 2005). Including these dimensions to measure would allow us to better understand how psychosocial stressors may physiologically operate.

It would also be helpful to explore how individuals appraise their exposure to stressors and how coping mechanisms increase the onset of obesity. How individuals appraise stressors engender different physiological responses. Potential stressors that individuals can control or manage (challenge appraisal) activates the SNS, whereas potential stressors that exceeds an individual's coping capacity (threat appraisal) provokes the activation of the SNS and HPA axis (Blascovich & Mendes, 2000; Seery, 2011). While it remains unclear whether certain stress appraisal types also lead to different obesity-related behaviors, it is surmisable that different stressors can induce distinct obesity-related behaviors. For instance, experiencing financial stress may not necessarily lead to greater food consumption given that money, or lack thereof, may influence eating practices and behaviors. Likewise, individuals may adopt health promoting behaviors to cope with certain stressors. For instance, African Americans experiencing moderate or high racial discrimination were more physically active than those reporting no discrimination (Borrell et al., 2013).

Gene x Stress Interaction

Genetics play an important role in the determination and risk of obesity. Research suggests that gene-environment (GxE) interaction models enhance the accuracy and precision in the assessment of both genetic and environmental influences on obesity (Burgess et al., 2017; Huang & Hu, 2015; Ottman, 1996; Qi & Cho, 2008; Speakman, 2004). GxE proposes that the genotype of an individual modulates the sensitivity or response to a specific environmental exposure or vice versa (Burgess et al., 2017; Cohen-Woods & Harkess, 2016; Wagner et al., 2013). With innovative methods like the polygenic scores, social scientists can now begin incorporating genetics into stress research. The question remains whether some individuals with genetic risks may be more susceptible to the obesogenic effects of psychosocial stressors (Dalle Molle et al., 2017; Esposito et al., 2018). Determining the interactive effects of psychosocial stressors and genetic risks will be critical to developing personalized intervention strategies and therapeutics. A gene-environment framework can provide insight into identifying individuals who are at high-risk for obesity based on both genetic risks and high exposure to multiple comorbid stressors.

Conclusion

Stress has long been implicated as a risk factor of obesity. Researchers from a variety of disciplines have begun to identify the psychological and social stressors that contribute to obesity risk. There remain critical understudied areas in the literature. There are other stressors that disproportionately affect racial/ethnic minorities (e.g., acculturative stress, food insecurity) that have not been seriously researched within the context of stress and obesity. Moreover, as noted in this chapter, there is an urgent need to better understand the obesogenic effects of well-known psychosocial stressors. As such, there is a need to examine other dimensions of a stressful experience (e.g., severity and duration), short-term and long-term consequences of stressor exposure, and how stressors interact with genetic predisposition. As stakeholders and social scientists continue to combat the rise of obesity, an understanding of the stressors and their root causes can contribute to effectual public health and personalized intervention strategies.

Conflict of Interest No potential conflict of interest was reported by the authors.

References

Abraham, S., Rubino, D., Sinaii, N., Ramsey, S., & Nieman, L. (2013). Cortisol, obesity, and the metabolic syndrome: A cross-sectional study of obese subjects and review of the literature. *Obesity, 21*(1), E105–E117.

Adam, T. C., & Epel, E. S. (2007). Stress, eating and the reward system. *Physiology & Behavior, 91*(4), 449–458. https://doi.org/10.1016/j.physbeh.2007.04.011

Araiza, A. M., & Lobel, M. (2018). Stress and eating: Definitions, findings, explanations, and implications. *Social and Personality Psychology Compass, 12*(4), e12378. https://doi.org/10.1111/spc3.12378

Armenta-Hernández, O. D., Maldonado-Macías, A., García-Alcaraz, J., Avelar-Sosa, L., Realyvasquez-Vargas, A., & Serrano-Rosa, M. A. (2018). Relationship between burnout and body mass index in senior and middle managers from the Mexican manufacturing industry. *International Journal of Environmental Research and Public Health, 15*(3), 541. https://doi.org/10.3390/ijerph15030541

Arteaga, C. L., Adamson, P. C., Engelman, J. A., Foti, M., Gaynor, R. B., Hilsenbeck, S. G., Limburg, P. J., Lowe, S. W., Mardis, E. R., Ramsey, S., Rebbeck, T. R., Richardson, A. L., Rubin, E. H., & Weiner, G. J. (2014). AACR cancer Progress report 2014. *Clinical Cancer Research, 20*(19 Supplement), S1–S112. https://doi.org/10.1158/1078-0432.CCR-14-2123

Averett, S. L., & Smith, J. K. (2014). Financial hardship and obesity. *Economics and Human Biology, 15*, 201–212. https://doi.org/10.1016/j.ehb.2013.12.004

Bayon, V., Leger, D., Gomez-Merino, D., Vecchierini, M.-F., & Chennaoui, M. (2014). Sleep debt and obesity. *Annals of Medicine, 46*(5), 264–272. https://doi.org/10.3109/07853890.2014.931103

Beccuti, G., & Pannain, S. (2011). Sleep and obesity. *Current Opinion in Clinical Nutrition and Metabolic Care, 14*(4), 402–412. https://doi.org/10.1097/MCO.0b013e3283479109

Bhui, K. S., Dinos, S., Stansfeld, S. A., & White, P. D. (2012). A synthesis of the evidence for managing stress at work: A review of the reviews reporting on anxiety, depression, and absenteeism. *Journal of Environmental and Public Health, 2012*, 515874–515821. https://doi.org/10.1155/2012/515874

Blascovich, J., & Mendes, W. B. (2000). *Challenge and threat appraisals: The role of affective cues.*

Boehmer, T. K., Hoehner, C. M., Deshpande, A. D., Ramirez, L. B., & Brownson, R. C. (2007). Perceived and observed neighborhood indicators of obesity among urban adults. *International Journal of Obesity, 31*(6), 968–977.

Borrell, L. N., Kiefe, C. I., Diez-Roux, A. V., Williams, D. R., & Gordon-Larsen, P. (2013). Racial discrimination, racial/ethnic segregation, and health behaviors in the CARDIA study. *Ethnicity & Health, 18*(3), 227–243. https://doi.org/10.1080/13557858.2012.713092

Bosch, M., & Bird, W. (2018). *Oxford textbook of nature and public health: The role of nature in improving the health of a population*. Oxford University Press.

Browning, C. R., Cagney, K. A., & Iveniuk, J. (2012). Neighborhood stressors and cardiovascular health: Crime and C-reactive protein in Dallas, USA. *Social Science & Medicine (1982), 75*(7), 1271–1279. https://doi.org/10.1016/j.socscimed.2012.03.027

Burdette, A. M., & Needham, B. L. (2012). Neighborhood environment and body mass index trajectories from adolescence to adulthood. *Journal of Adolescent Health, 50*(1), 30–37. https://doi.org/10.1016/j.jadohealth.2011.03.009

Burgess, S., Bowden, J., Fall, T., Ingelsson, E., & Thompson, S. G. (2017). Sensitivity analyses for robust causal inference from Mendelian randomization analyses with multiple genetic variants. *Epidemiology, 28*(1), 30–42. https://doi.org/10.1097/EDE.0000000000000559

Burns, R. A., Butterworth, P., & Anstey, K. J. (2016). An examination of the long-term impact of job strain on mental health and wellbeing over a 12-year period. *Social Psychiatry and Psychiatric Epidemiology, 51*(5), 725–733. https://doi.org/10.1007/s00127-016-1192-9

Burton, L. C., Shapiro, S., & German, P. S. (1999). Determinants of physical activity initiation and maintenance among community-dwelling older persons. *Preventive Medicine, 29*(5), 422–430. https://doi.org/10.1006/pmed.1999.0561

Cain-Shields, L. R., Johnson, D. A., Glover, L., & Sims, M. (2020). The association of goal-striving stress with sleep duration and sleep quality among African Americans in the Jackson heart study. *Sleep Health, 6*(1), 117–123.

Calle, E. E., & Kaaks, R. (2004). Overweight, obesity and cancer: Epidemiological evidence and proposed mechanisms. *Nature Reviews Cancer, 4*(8), 579. https://doi.org/10.1038/nrc1408

Calle, E. E., Rodriguez, C., Walker-Thurmond, K., & Thun, M. J. (2003). Overweight, obesity, and mortality from cancer in a prospectively studied cohort of U.-S. adults. *The New England Journal of Medicine, 348*(17), 1625–1638. https://doi.org/10.1056/NEJMoa021423

Carvalho, L. S., Meier, S., & Wang, S. W. (2016). Poverty and economic decision-making: Evidence from changes in financial resources at payday. *American Economic Review, 106*(2), 260–284. https://doi.org/10.1257/aer.20140481

Centers for Disease Control and Prevention. (2019, November 5). *Vital Signs: Adverse childhood experiences*. https://www.cdc.gov/vitalsigns/aces/index.html

Centers for Disease Control and Prevention. (2014, June 6). *STRESS...At Work*. https://www.cdc.gov/niosh/docs/99-101/default.html

Cheng, C. E., Thomas Tobin, C. S., & Weiss, J. W. (2020). Psychological distress, social context, and gender patterns in obesity among a multiethnic sample of U.-S. college students. *Journal of American College*

Health, 1–9. https://doi.org/10.1080/07448481.2020.1817032

Cohen, S., Janicki-Deverts, D., & Miller, G. E. (2007). Psychological stress and disease. *JAMA, 298*(14), 1685–1687. https://doi.org/10.1001/jama.298.14.1685

Cohen-Woods, S., & Harkess, K. (2016). *Gene-environment interactions, stress, and depression*. Springer.

Conklin, A. I., Forouhi, N. G., Brunner, E. J., & Monsivais, P. (2014a). Persistent financial hardship, 11-year weight gain, and health behaviors in the Whitehall II study. *Obesity, 22*(12), 2606–2612. https://doi.org/10.1002/oby.20875

Conklin, A. I., Forouhi, N. G., Suhrcke, M., Surtees, P., Wareham, N. J., & Monsivais, P. (2014b). Variety more than quantity of fruit and vegetable intake varies by socioeconomic status and financial hardship. Findings from older adults in the EPIC cohort. *Appetite, 83*, 248–255. https://doi.org/10.1016/j.appet.2014.08.038

Cozier, Y. C., Yu, J., Coogan, P. F., Bethea, T. N., Rosenberg, L., & Palmer, J. R. (2014). Racism, segregation, and risk of obesity in the black Women's health study. *American Journal of Epidemiology, 179*(7), 875–883. https://doi.org/10.1093/aje/kwu004

Cuevas, A. G., Chen, R., Slopen, N., Thurber, K. A., Wilson, N., Economos, C., & Williams, D. R. (2020). Assessing the role of health Behaviors, socioeconomic status, and cumulative stress for racial/ethnic disparities in obesity. *Obesity, 28*(1), 161–170.

Cuevas, A. G., Chen, R., Thurber, K. A., Slopen, N., & Williams, D. R. (2019). Psychosocial stress and overweight and obesity: Findings from the Chicago community adult health study. *Annals of Behavioral Medicine*. https://doi.org/10.1093/abm/kaz008

Dalle Molle, R., Fatemi, H., Dagher, A., Levitan, R. D., Silveira, P. P., & Dubé, L. (2017). Gene and environment interaction: Is the differential susceptibility hypothesis relevant for obesity? *Neuroscience and Biobehavioral Reviews, 73*, 326–339. https://doi.org/10.1016/j.neubiorev.2016.12.028

Danese, A., & Tan, M. (2014). Childhood maltreatment and obesity: Systematic review and meta-analysis. *Molecular Psychiatry, 19*(5), 544–554. https://doi.org/10.1038/mp.2013.54

Debeuf, T., Verbeken, S., Van Beveren, M., Michels, N., & Braet, C. (2018). Stress and eating behavior: A daily diary study in youngsters. *Frontiers in Psychology, 9*, 2657–2657. https://doi.org/10.3389/fpsyg.2018.02657

Deng, T., Lyon, C. J., Bergin, S., Caligiuri, M. A., & Hsueh, W. A. (2016). Obesity, inflammation, and cancer. *Annual Review of Pathology, 11*, 421–449. https://doi.org/10.1146/annurev-pathol-012615-044359

Dijkstra-Kersten, S. M., Biesheuvel-Leliefeld, K. E., van der Wouden, J. C., Penninx, B. W., & van Marwijk, H. W. (2015). Associations of financial strain and income with depressive and anxiety disorders. *Journal of Epidemiology and Community Health, 69*(7), 660 665.

DiNicolantonio, J. J., Mehta, V., Onkaramurthy, N., & O'Keefe, J. H. (2018). Fructose-induced inflammation and increased cortisol: A new mechanism for how sugar induces visceral adiposity. *Progress in Cardiovascular Diseases, 61*(1), 3–9.

Ehrlich, K. B., Miller, G. E., Rohleder, N., & Adam, E. K. (2016). Trajectories of relationship stress and inflammatory processes in adolescence. *Development and Psychopathology, 28*(1), 127–138.

Elenkov, I. J., Wilder, R. L., Chrousos, G. P., & Vizi, E. S. (2000). The sympathetic nerve—An integrative interface between two supersystems: The brain and the immune system. *Pharmacological Reviews, 52*(4), 595–638.

Elshurbjy, A. J., & Ellulu, M. S. (2017). Association between stress and dietary behaviors among university students: Mini-review. *Med Clin Arch, 1*.

Esposito, G., Azhari, A., & Borelli, J. L. (2018). Gene × environment interaction in developmental disorders: Where do we stand and what's next? *Frontiers in Psychology, 9*. https://doi.org/10.3389/fpsyg.2018.02036

Evans, G. W., & Kim, P. (2010). Multiple risk exposure as a potential explanatory mechanism for the socioeconomic status–health gradient. *Annals of the New York Academy of Sciences, 1186*(1), 174–189. https://doi.org/10.1111/j.1749-6632.2009.05336.x

Evans, G. W., Li, D., & Whipple, S. S. (2013). Cumulative risk and child development. *Psychological Bulletin, 139*(6), 1342.

Felitti, V. J., Anda, R. F., Nordenberg, D., Williamson, D. F., Spitz, A. M., Edwards, V., Koss, M. P., & Marks, J. S. (1998). Relationship of childhood abuse and household dysfunction to many of the leading causes of death in adults: The adverse childhood experiences (ACE) study. *American Journal of Preventive Medicine, 14*(4), 245–258. https://doi.org/10.1016/S0749-3797(98)00017-8

Fish, J. S., Ettner, S., Ang, A., & Brown, A. F. (2010). Association of perceived neighborhood safety with [corrected] body mass index. *American Journal of Public Health, 100*(11), 2296–2303. https://doi.org/10.2105/AJPH.2009.183293

Flegal, K. M., Kruszon-Moran, D., Carroll, M. D., Fryar, C. D., & Ogden, C. L. (2016). Trends in obesity among adults in the United States, 2005 to 2014. *JAMA, 315*(21), 2284–2291. https://doi.org/10.1001/jama.2016.6458

Friedman, E. M., Montez, J. K., Sheehan, C. M., Guenewald, T. L., & Seeman, T. E. (2015). Childhood adversities and adult Cardiometabolic health. *Journal of Aging and Health, 27*(8), 1311–1338. https://doi.org/10.1177/0898264315580122

Gardner, R., Feely, A., Layte, R., Williams, J., & McGavock, J. (2019). Adverse childhood experiences are associated with an increased risk of obesity in early adolescence: A population-based prospective cohort study. *Pediatric Research, 86*(4), 522–528. https://doi.org/10.1038/s41390-019-0414-8

Garfin, D. R., Thompson, R. R., & Holman, E. A. (2018). Acute stress and subsequent health outcomes: A systematic review. *Journal of Psychosomatic Research, 112*, 107–113. https://doi.org/10.1016/j.jpsychores.2018.05.017

Gómez, J. E., Johnson, B. A., Selva, M., & Sallis, J. F. (2004). Violent crime and outdoor physical activity among inner-city youth. *Preventive Medicine, 39*(5), 876–881. https://doi.org/10.1016/j.ypmed.2004.03.019

Grant, S., & Mizzi, T. (2014). Body weight bias in hiring decisions: Identifying explanatory mechanisms. *Social Behavior and Personality, 42*(3), 353–370.

Grunberg, N. E., & Straub, R. O. (1992). The role of gender and taste class in the effects of stress on eating. *Health Psychology: Official Journal of the Division of Health Psychology, American Psychological Association, 11*(2), 97–100. https://doi.org/10.1037//0278-6133.11.2.97

Gudnadottir, U., Cadmus-Bertram, L., Spicer, A., Gorzelitz, J., & Malecki, K. (2019). The relationship between occupational physical activity and self-reported vs measured total physical activity. *Preventive Medicine Reports, 15*, 100908–100908. https://doi.org/10.1016/j.pmedr.2019.100908

Gyllenhammer, L. E., Weigensberg, M. J., Spruijt-Metz, D., Allayee, H., Goran, M. I., & Davis, J. N. (2014). Modifying influence of dietary sugar in the relationship between cortisol and visceral adipose tissue in minority youth. *Obesity, 22*(2), 474–481.

Hall, M., Buysse, D. J., Nofzinger, E. A., Reynolds, C. F., Thompson, W., Mazumdar, S., & Monk, T. H. (2008). Financial strain is a significant correlate of sleep continuity disturbances in late-life. *Biological Psychology, 77*(2), 217–222. https://doi.org/10.1016/j.biopsycho.2007.10.012

Hall, M. H., Matthews, K. A., Kravitz, H. M., Gold, E. B., Buysse, D. J., Bromberger, J. T., Owens, J. F., & Sowers, M. (2009). Race and financial strain are independent correlates of sleep in midlife women: The SWAN sleep study. *Sleep, 32*(1), 73–82.

Heerman, W. J., Krishnaswami, S., Barkin, S. L., & McPheeters, M. (2016). Adverse family experiences during childhood and adolescent obesity. *Obesity (Silver Spring, Md.), 24*(3), 696–702. https://doi.org/10.1002/oby.21413

Herman, J. P., McKlveen, J. M., Ghosal, S., Kopp, B., Wulsin, A., Makinson, R., Scheimann, J., & Myers, B. (2016). Regulation of the hypothalamic-pituitary-adrenocortical stress response. *Comprehensive Physiology, 6*(2), 603–621. https://doi.org/10.1002/cphy.c150015

Hewagalamulage, S. D., Lee, T. K., Clarke, I. J., & Henry, B. A. (2016). Stress, cortisol, and obesity: A role for cortisol responsiveness in identifying individuals prone to obesity. *Domestic Animal Endocrinology, 56*, S112–S120. https://doi.org/10.1016/j.domaniend.2016.03.004

Hruby, A., & Hu, F. B. (2015). The epidemiology of obesity: A big picture. *PharmacoEconomics, 33*(7), 673–689. https://doi.org/10.1007/s40273-014-0243-x

Huang, T., & Hu, F. B. (2015). Gene-environment interactions and obesity: Recent developments and future directions. *BMC Medical Genomics, 8*(Suppl 1), S2. https://doi.org/10.1186/1755-8794-8-S1-S2

Hunte, H. E. R., & Williams, D. R. (2009). The association between perceived discrimination and obesity in a population-based multiracial and multiethnic adult sample. *American Journal of Public Health (1971), 99*(7), 1285–1292. https://doi.org/10.2105/AJPH.2007.128090

Johnson, D. A., Lisabeth, L., Lewis, T. T., Sims, M., Hickson, D. A., Samdarshi, T., et al. (2016). The contribution of psychosocial stressors to sleep among African Americans in the Jackson heart study. *Sleep, 39*(7), 1411–1419.

Kärmeniemi, M., Lankila, T., Ikäheimo, T., Koivumaa-Honkanen, H., & Korpelainen, R. (2018). The built environment as a determinant of physical activity: A systematic review of longitudinal studies and natural experiments. *Annals of Behavioral Medicine, 52*(3), 239–251. https://doi.org/10.1093/abm/kax043

Kivimäki, M., Singh-Manoux, A., Nyberg, S., Jokela, M., & Virtanen, M. (2015). Job strain and risk of obesity: Systematic review and meta-analysis of cohort studies. *International Journal of Obesity, 39*(11), 1597–1600. https://doi.org/10.1038/ijo.2015.103

Kwarteng, J. L., Schulz, A. J., Mentz, G. B., Israel, B. A., & Perkins, D. W. (2017). Independent effects of Neighborhood poverty and psychosocial stress on obesity over time. *Journal of Urban Health, 94*(6), 791–802. https://doi.org/10.1007/s11524-017-0193-7

LeCounte, E. S., & Swain, G. R. (2017). Life expectancy at birth in Milwaukee County: A zip code-level analysis. *Journal of Patient-Centered Research and Reviews, 4*(4), 213–220. https://doi.org/10.17294/2330-0698.1576

Lenhart, C. M., Wiemken, A., Hanlon, A., Perkett, M., & Patterson, F. (2017). Perceived neighborhood safety related to physical activity but not recreational screen-based sedentary behavior in adolescents. *BMC Public Health, 17*(1), 722–722. https://doi.org/10.1186/s12889-017-4756-z

Lewis, T. T., Cogburn, C. D., & Williams, D. R. (2015). Self-reported experiences of discrimination and health: Scientific advances, ongoing controversies, and emerging issues. *Annual Review of Clinical Psychology, 11*(1), 407–440. https://doi.org/10.1146/annurev-clinpsy-032814-112728

Liu, Y., Croft, J. B., Chapman, D. P., Perry, G. S., Greenlund, K. J., Zhao, G., & Edwards, V. J. (2013). Relationship between adverse childhood experiences and unemployment among adults from five US states. *Social Psychiatry and Psychiatric Epidemiology, 48*(3), 357–369. https://doi.org/10.1007/s00127-012-0554-1

Liu, Y.-Z., Wang, Y.-X., & Jiang, C.-L. (2017). Inflammation: The common pathway of stress-related diseases. *Frontiers in Human Neuroscience*, 11. https://doi.org/10.3389/fnhum.2017.00316

Lockwood, K. G., Marsland, A. L., Matthews, K. A., & Gianaros, P. J. (2018). Perceived discrimination and cardiovascular health disparities: A multisystem review and health neuroscience perspective. *Annals of the New York Academy of Sciences, 1428*(1), 170–207. https://doi.org/10.1111/nyas.13939

Lopes Cortes, M., Andrade Louzado, J., Galvão Oliveira, M., Moraes Bezerra, V., Mistro, S., Souto Medeiros, D., Arruda Soares, D., Oliveira Silva, K., Nicolaevna Kochergin, C., Honorato Dos Santos de Carvalho, V. C., Wildes Amorim, W., & Serrate Mengue, S. (2021). Unhealthy food and psychological stress: The association between ultra-processed food consumption and perceived stress in working-class young adults. *International Journal of Environmental Research and Public Health, 18*(8), 3863. https://doi.org/10.3390/ijerph18083863

Luckhaupt, S. E., Cohen, M. A., Li, J., & Calvert, G. M. (2014). Prevalence of obesity among U.S. workers and associations with occupational factors. *American Journal of Preventive Medicine, 46*(3), 237–248. https://doi.org/10.1016/j.amepre.2013.11.002

Lumeng, C. N., & Saltiel, A. R. (2011). Inflammatory links between obesity and metabolic disease. *The Journal of Clinical Investigation, 121*(6), 2111–2117. https://doi.org/10.1172/JCI57132

Mayne, S. L., Jose, A., Mo, A., Vo, L., Rachapalli, S., Ali, H., Davis, J., & Kershaw, K. N. (2018). Neighborhood disorder and obesity-related outcomes among women in Chicago. *International Journal of Environmental Research and Public Health, 15*(7), 1395. https://doi.org/10.3390/ijerph15071395

McEwen, B. S. (2007). Physiology and neurobiology of stress and adaptation: Central role of the brain. *Physiological Reviews, 87*(3), 873–904. https://doi.org/10.1152/physrev.00041.2006

Mereish, E. H. (2014). The weight of discrimination: The relationship between heterosexist discrimination and obesity among lesbian women. *Psychology of Sexual Orientation and Gender Diversity, 1*(4), 356–360. https://doi.org/10.1037/sgd0000056

Murison, R. (2016). The neurobiology of stress. In *Neuroscience of pain, stress, and emotion* (pp. 29–49). Elsevier.

Ogden, C. L., Fryar, C. D., Martin, C. B., Freedman, D. S., Carroll, M. D., Gu, Q., & Hales, C. M. (2020). Trends in obesity prevalence by race and Hispanic origin—1999-2000 to 2017-2018. *JAMA: The Journal of the American Medical Association, 324*(12), 1208–1210. https://doi.org/10.1001/jama.2020.14590

Okechukwu, C. A., El Ayadi, A. M., Tamers, S. L., Sabbath, E. L., & Berkman, L. (2012). Household food insufficiency, financial strain, work–family spillover, and depressive symptoms in the working class: The work, family, and health network study. *American Journal of Public Health, 102*(1), 126–133.

Ottman, R. (1996). Gene–environment interaction: Definitions and study designs. *Preventive Medicine, 25*(6), 764–770.

Overgaard, D., Gamborg, M., Gyntelberg, F., & Heitmann, B. L. (2006). Psychological workload and weight gain among women with and without familial obesity. *Obesity (Silver Spring, Md.), 14*(3), 458–463. https://doi.org/10.1038/oby.2006.60

Owens, S., Hunte, H., Sterkel, A., Johnson, D. A., & Johnson-Lawrence, V. (2017). Association between discrimination and objective and subjective sleep measures in the MIDUS adult sample. *Psychosomatic Medicine, 79*(4), 469.

Pham, D., Ommerborn, M. J., Hickson, D. A., Taylor, H. A., & Clark, C. R. (2014). Neighborhood safety and adipose tissue distribution in African Americans: The Jackson heart study. *PLoS One, 9*(8), e105251. https://doi.org/10.1371/journal.pone.0105251

Pool, E., Delplanque, S., Coppin, G., & Sander, D. (2015). Is comfort food really comforting? Mechanisms underlying stress-induced eating. *Food Research International, 76*, 207–215. https://doi.org/10.1016/j.foodres.2014.12.034

Powell-Wiley, T. M., Ayers, C. R., de Lemos, J. A., Lakoski, S. G., Vega, G. L., Grundy, S., Das, S. R., Banks-Richard, K., & Albert, M. A. (2013). Relationship between perceptions about neighborhood environment and prevalent obesity: Data from the Dallas heart study. *Obesity (Silver Spring, Md.), 21*(1), E14–E21. https://doi.org/10.1002/oby.20012

Puhl, R. M., & King, K. M. (2013). Weight discrimination and bullying. *Best Practice & Research Clinical Endocrinology & Metabolism, 27*(2), 117–127.

Qi, L., & Cho, Y. A. (2008). Gene-environment interaction and obesity. *Nutrition Reviews, 66*(12), 684–694. https://doi.org/10.1111/j.1753-4887.2008.00128.x

Ramos-Nino, M. E. (2013). The role of chronic inflammation in obesity-associated cancers. *ISRN Oncology*, 2013. https://doi.org/10.1155/2013/697521

Renehan, D. A. G., Roberts, D. L., & Dive, C. (2008). Obesity and cancer: Pathophysiological and biological mechanisms. *Archives of Physiology and Biochemistry, 114*(1), 71–83. https://doi.org/10.1080/13813450801954303

Robinette, J. W., Charles, S. T., Almeida, D. M., & Gruenewald, T. L. (2016). Neighborhood features and physiological risk: An examination of allostatic load. *Health & Place, 41*, 110–118. https://doi.org/10.1016/j.healthplace.2016.08.003

Rod, N. H., Grønbæk, M., Schnohr, P., Prescott, E., & Kristensen, T. S. (2009). Perceived stress as a risk factor for changes in health behaviour and cardiac risk profile: A longitudinal study. *Journal of Internal Medicine, 266*(5), 467–475. https://doi.org/10.1111/j.1365-2796.2009.02124.x

Rodriguez, A. C. I., Epel, E. S., White, M. L., Standen, E. C., Seckl, J. R., & Tomiyama, A. J. (2015). Hypothalamic-pituitary-adrenal axis dysregulation and cortisol activity in obesity: A systematic review. *Psychoneuroendocrinology, 62*, 301–318.

Roemmich, J. N., Gurgol, C. M., & Epstein, L. H. (2003). Influence of an interpersonal laboratory stressor on youths' choice to be physically active. *Obesity Research, 11*(9), 1080–1087.

Salmela, J., Mauramo, E., Lallukka, T., Rahkonen, O., & Kanerva, N. (2019). Associations between childhood disadvantage and adult body mass index trajectories: A follow-up study among midlife Finnish municipal employees. *Obesity Facts, 12*(5), 564–574. https://doi.org/10.1159/000502237

Schneiderman, N., Ironson, G., & Siegel, S. D. (2005). STRESS AND HEALTH: Psychological, Behavioral, and biological determinants. *Annual Review of Clinical Psychology, 1*, 607–628. https://doi.org/10.1146/annurev.clinpsy.1.102803.144141

Schroeder, K., Schuler, B. R., Kobulsky, J. M., & Sarwer, D. B. (2021). The association between adverse childhood experiences and childhood obesity: A systematic review. *Obesity Reviews*. https://doi.org/10.1111/obr.13204

Scott, K. A., Melhorn, S. J., & Sakai, R. R. (2012). Effects of chronic social stress on obesity. *Current Obesity Reports, 1*(1), 16–25. https://doi.org/10.1007/s13679-011-0006-3

Seery, M. D. (2011). Challenge or threat? Cardiovascular indexes of resilience and vulnerability to potential stress in humans. *Neuroscience & Biobehavioral Reviews, 35*(7), 1603–1610.

Siahpush, M., Huang, T. T.-K., Sikora, A., Tibbits, M., Shaikh, R. A., & Singh, G. K. (2014). Prolonged financial stress predicts subsequent obesity: Results from a prospective study of an Australian national sample. *Obesity (Silver Spring, Md.), 22*(2), 616–621. https://doi.org/10.1002/oby.20572

Sikorski, C., Spahlholz, J., Hartlev, M., & Riedel-Heller, S. G. (2016). Weight-based discrimination: An ubiquitary phenomenon? *International Journal of Obesity, 40*(2), 333–337.

Slavich, G. M. (2016). Life stress and health: A review of conceptual issues and recent findings. *Teaching of Psychology (Columbia, Mo.), 43*(4), 346–355. https://doi.org/10.1177/0098628316662768

Sorrells, S. F., Caso, J. R., Munhoz, C. D., & Sapolsky, R. M. (2009). The stressed CNS: When glucocorticoids aggravate inflammation. *Neuron, 64*(1), 33–39. https://doi.org/10.1016/j.neuron.2009.09.032

Speakman, J. R. (2004). Obesity: The integrated roles of environment and genetics. *The Journal of Nutrition, 134*(8), 2090S–2105S. https://doi.org/10.1093/jn/134.8.2090S

Sternthal, M. J., Slopen, N., & Williams, D. R. (2011). Racial disparities in health: How much does stress really matter? *Du Bois Review: Social Science Research on Race, 8*(01), 95–113. https://doi.org/10.1017/S1742058X11000087

Stults-Kolehmainen, M. A., & Sinha, R. (2014). The effects of stress on physical activity and exercise. *Sports Medicine (Auckland, N.Z.), 44*(1), 81–121. https://doi.org/10.1007/s40279-013-0090-5

Sun, X. M., Feng, W., Wang, F., Li, P., Li, Z., Li, M., Tse, G., Vlaanderen, J., Vermeulen, R., & Tse, L. A. (2018). Meta-analysis on shift work and risks of specific obesity types. *Obesity Reviews, 19*(1), 28–40. https://doi.org/10.1111/obr.12621

Sutin, A. R., & Terracciano, A. (2013). Perceived weight discrimination and obesity. *PloS One, 8*(7), e70048.

Thorpe, R. J., Parker, L. J., Cobb, R. J., Dillard, F., & Bowie, J. (2017). Association between discrimination and obesity in African-American men. *Biodemography and Social Biology, 63*(3), 253–261. https://doi.org/10.1080/19485565.2017.1353406

Tomiyama, A. J. (2014). Weight stigma is stressful. A review of evidence for the Cyclic Obesity/Weight-Based Stigma model. *Appetite, 82*, 8–15.

Udo, T., & Grilo, C. M. (2016). Perceived weight discrimination, childhood maltreatment, and weight gain in U.S. adults with overweight/obesity. *Obesity (Silver Spring, Md.), 24*(6), 1366–1372. https://doi.org/10.1002/oby.21474

Ulrich-Lai, Y. M., Fulton, S., Wilson, M., Petrovich, G., & Rinaman, L. (2015). Stress exposure, food intake, and emotional state. *Stress (Amsterdam, Netherlands), 18*(4), 381–399. https://doi.org/10.3109/10253890.2015.1062981

Van Laethem, M., Beckers, D. G., Kompier, M. A., Dijksterhuis, A., & Geurts, S. A. (2013). Psychosocial work characteristics and sleep quality: A systematic review of longitudinal and intervention research. *Scandinavian Journal of Work, Environment & Health*, 535–549.

Vitaliano, P. P., Scanlan, J. M., Ochs, H. D., Syrjala, K., Siegler, I. C., & Snyder, E. A. (1998). Psychosocial stress moderates the relationship of cancer history with natural killer cell activity 1,2. *Annals of Behavioral Medicine, 20*(3), 199–208. https://doi.org/10.1007/BF02884961

Vucenik, I., & Stains, J. P. (2012). Obesity and cancer risk: Evidence, mechanisms, and recommendations. *Annals of the New York Academy of Sciences, 1271*(1), 37–43. https://doi.org/10.1111/j.1749-6632.2012.06750.x

Wagner, B., Li, J., Liu, H., & Guo, G. (2013). Gene–environment correlation: Difficulties and a natural experiment–based strategy. *American Journal of Public Health, 103*(Suppl 1), S167–S173. https://doi.org/10.2105/AJPH.2013.301415

Wall, M. M., Mason, S. M., Liu, J., Olfson, M., Neumark-Sztainer, D., & Blanco, C. (2019). Childhood psychosocial challenges and risk for obesity in U.S. men and women. *Translational Psychiatry, 9*(1), 16–16. https://doi.org/10.1038/s41398-018-0341-1

Ward, Z. J., Bleich, S. N., Cradock, A. L., Barrett, J. L., Giles, C. M., Flax, C., Long, M. W., & Gortmaker, S. L. (2019). Projected U.S. state-level prevalence of adult obesity and severe obesity. *New England Journal of Medicine, 381*(25), 2440–2450. https://doi.org/10.1056/NEJMsa1909301

Wardle, J., Chida, Y., Gibson, E. L., Whitaker, K. L., & Steptoe, A. (2011). Stress and adiposity: A meta-analysis of longitudinal studies. *Obesity (Silver Spring,*

Md.), 19(4), 771–778. https://doi.org/10.1038/oby.2010.241

Wieclaw, J., Agerbo, E., Mortensen, P. B., Burr, H., Tuchsen, F., & Bonde, J. P. (2008). Psychosocial working conditions and the risk of depression and anxiety disorders in the Danish workforce. *BMC Public Health, 8*(1), 280–280. https://doi.org/10.1186/1471-2458-8-280

Wiss, D. A., & Brewerton, T. D. (2020). Adverse childhood experiences and adult obesity: A systematic review of plausible mechanisms and meta-analysis of cross-sectional studies. *Physiology & Behavior, 223*, 112964. https://doi.org/10.1016/j.physbeh.2020.112964

Yau, Y. H. C., & Potenza, M. N. (2013). Stress and eating Behaviors. *Minerva Endocrinologica, 38*(3), 255–267.

Zimberg, I. Z., Dâmaso, A., Del Re, M., Carneiro, A. M., de Sá Souza, H., de Lira, F. S., Tufik, S., & de Mello, M. T. (2012). Short sleep duration and obesity: Mechanisms and future perspectives. *Cell Biochemistry and Function, 30*(6), 524–529. https://doi.org/10.1002/cbf.2832

13 The Neighborhood Environment and Overweight/Obesity

Angelica Lopez and Kathryn Freeman Anderson

Introduction

Understanding the various social factors that relate to the prevalence of obesity has become one of the main public health projects over the past several decades as rates of obesity rise. Much of this extant work is predominantly focused on individual-level risk factors, particularly those related to diet and exercise. As such, many of the proposed interventions within medicine and public health alike have focused on altering individual behaviors. However, from an ecological perspective, a long tradition in demography, there may be ways that the environment in which an individual is situated may influence their behaviors and choices. That is, individuals often make choices and behave in a manner that is constrained by their context. Here, we examine how that environment may also influence their health-related behaviors and ultimately weight status. One's local neighborhood creates an opportunity structure that may be obesogenic, or promote obesity, depending on how that environment is organized. In this chapter, we examine the literature on how neighborhood environments relate to the weight status of individuals living in these environments. Understanding the ecological contribution to obesity can also lead us to different policy solutions, from solutions that focus on altering individual-level behavior to solutions that focus on creating environments that promote and encourage healthy behaviors and discourage obesity.

We tackle this topic by addressing two broad kinds of literature and how they relate to overweight/obesity: organizational resources and environmental quality. In the first, organizational resources, we discuss the vast literature on the presence/absence of various establishments that may contribute to BMI. This literature is predominantly focused on food availability and resources for fitness/recreation. The assumption is that the availability of certain kinds of establishments can contribute to lower or higher rates of obesity across the population, depending on the resource in question. In the second, environmental quality, we also consider the quality and safety of the neighborhood environment to factor in how the built, natural, and social environment can be obesogenic as well. This literature is less developed than the former, but provides important insights into the nuanced ways in which neighborhoods inform the study of the demography of obesity. We review these two literatures and provide suggestions for future research.

Authors: Angelica Lopez and Kathryn Freeman Anderson have equally contributed to this chapter.

A. Lopez
T. Denny Sanford School of Social and Family Dynamics, Arizona State University, Tempe, AZ, USA

K. F. Anderson (✉)
Department of Sociology, University of Houston, Houston, TX, USA
e-mail: kateanderson@uh.edu

G. Garcia-Alexander, D. L. Poston, Jr. (eds.), *International Handbook of the Demography of Obesity*, International Handbooks of Population 12, https://doi.org/10.1007/978-3-031-10936-2_13

Organizational Resources

One of the main ways the literature on the demography of obesity argues that neighborhoods may relate to obesity is through access to resources (French et al., 2001). Most often, this refers to formal organizations, such as businesses, community organizations, or associations, which have been hypothesized to relate to obesity by shaping accessibility to different kinds of foods and opportunities for physical activity. This association between resources and obesity may be either beneficial or detrimental, depending on the resource in question. For instance, greater accessibility and presence of physical fitness centers may contribute to lower rates of obesity in an area, while a fast-food restaurant may relate to higher rates of community obesity. We review the work on these associations in detail here.

Food Access and Quality

The primary focus of this literature has been on the distribution of food resources across communities. Scholars in this area have characterized certain environments as health-promoting, i.e. resource-rich, which have a high degree of food provision, measured by both quantity and quality. Food environments that are thought to be linked with increased obesity have been termed toxic food environments or obesogenic environments. These are thought to promote obesity via increased exposure to lower-quality foods and limited access to high-quality healthy food options. This is most evident in the so-called "food deserts" literature. Food deserts broadly refer to geographic areas that lack access to healthy food options within a reasonable distance or time frame, though there is no agreement on the formal definition of this concept (Beaulac et al., 2009; Walker et al., 2010). While some studies have used this term to describe a complete absence of food establishments, more recent scholarship has emphasized healthy food options as the primary distinguishing feature, especially in the context of urban locales (Cummins & Macintyre, 2002). Other work emphasizes the affordability of those available food options as well (Macintyre, 2007). An explosion of interest in "food deserts" has resulted in hundreds of published studies on this topic over the last several decades.

This work has generally found that poor and minority communities are less likely to have a wide variety of essential food resources, though a few studies have produced mixed results depending on the measurement and outcome in question (Beaulac et al., 2009; Walker et al., 2010). Generally, these studies can be grouped into two different projects: studies that examine geographic proximity to stores, and "market-basket" approaches that examine the type and price of food offerings (Beaulac et al., 2009). The vast majority of these studies examine access to food through geographic proximity, measured in a variety of different ways. Moreover, across both types of studies, the vast majority of these are cross-sectional in design, examining the food environment in snapshots in time, and comparing those measures to local demographics and outcomes (Lytle & Sokol, 2017).

Work that uses the geographic approach has analyzed geographic proximity to stores using a number of different methods, including the number of available food stores (density), the distance to various food stores, the number of establishments within a certain distance, and more sophisticated approaches that factor in the street grid, transportation systems, and walkability (Walker et al., 2010; Lytle & Sokol, 2017). This work tells a fairly consistent story where socio-economically disadvantaged areas, as well as areas that contain a majority of racial/ethnic minorities, particularly Black segregated areas, are less likely to have food stores and are more likely to have to travel further distances to get to those locations (Algert et al., 2006; Alwitt & Donley, 1997; Chung & Myers, 1999; Moore & Diez Roux, 2006; Morland et al., 2002a, b; Powell et al., 2007; Zenk et al., 2005). As an example, Zenk et al. (2005) found that factoring in both race and class, Black neighborhoods are farther in terms of average miles from the nearest grocery store. This is especially the case for supermarkets, large chain supermarkets in particular, which are more likely to contain a wide variety of fresh fruits and vegetables, typically at lower prices than convenience stores and small grocers (Anderson, 2017; Bower et al., 2014; Moore & Diez Roux, 2006; Powell et al., 2007). Moore and Diez Roux (2006), for instance, found that low-income areas had four times as many small grocers and convenience stores, and half as many chain supermarkets when compared with more affluent areas. They also found that predominantly racial/ethnic minority areas also had half as many chain supermarkets as predominantly White areas. Similarly, Morland et al. (2002a), in a study of four U.S. states, found that this disparity between Black versus White neighborhoods was even greater, with White neighborhoods having four times the number of chain supermarkets.

The results have been similar in the market-basket approach, though these results are somewhat more mixed than the geographically based studies. These studies are aimed at understanding the availability and price of healthy food options in neighborhoods. This work has shown again that poor and minority (in most studies, Black) neighborhoods tend to have fewer healthy food options on the shelves of their stores, and, where available, that the price of those foods tends to be higher when compared to similar stores in more advantaged neighborhoods (Chung & Myers, 1999; Hall, 1983). In particular, Chung and Meyer (1999) found that chain supermarkets have food prices that are on average 10–40% lower than non-chain grocers, and other work has shown that the food stocked on the shelves of these full supermarkets is healthier (Glanz et al., 2007). However, this finding has been somewhat less consistent with several studies finding no difference in price when adjusted for the quality of the items (Crockett et al., 1992; Hayes, 2000). Further, a few studies have found lower prices in disadvantaged neighborhoods and urban areas generally, though again these same studies found differences in the quality of items available (Block & Kouba, 2007; Horowitz et al., 2004). Alternatively, several studies found a curvilinear relationship where prices were lower in middle-income neighborhoods, and higher in both lower-income and higher-income areas (Alcaly & Klevorick, 1971; Captain & McIntire, 1969; Jetter & Cassady, 2006; MacDonald & Nelson, 1991).

These results also appear to differ substantially by nation (Beaulac et al., 2009; Black et al., 2014). In a systematic review of the evidence, Beaulac et al. (2009) found that these results with regard to food deserts are primarily limited to the United States. While they reviewed articles across several countries, including the UK, Canada, Australia, and New Zealand, the results for the U.S. were more consistent, with substantially more mixed findings outside of the U.S. and, to some degree, the UK. Work conducted outside of the U.S. has had more robust evidence of food deserts when measured across urban versus rural locations, rather than across different types of neighborhoods within urban areas. For example, research from Australia and New Zealand, in particular, has largely found little to no differences in service provision within urban areas, but rural residents must travel farther for food resources, and there are fewer supermarkets, even when adjusting for population size (O'Dwyer & Coveney, 2006; Pearce et al., 2006).

Recent work has also suggested that, especially for outcomes like obesity, the absence of certain food resources is not as salient as the presence of certain types of unhealthy food outlets, particularly fast-food, convenience stores, and liquor stores (Block et al., 2004; Cummins et al., 2005). This work conversely argues that the appropriate term is not "food desert," but rather "food swamp," suggesting that while food may still be available, the poor quality of food detracts from the health benefits that access to food may provide (Cooksey-Stowers et al., 2017). Thus, it is not necessarily total food insecurity that matters, but the quality and type of food. This related body of work has also shown important differences in both neighborhood-level socioeconomic status and race in the accessibility of junk food and fast-food (Blair Lewis et al., 2005; Block et al., 2004; Cummins et al., 2005; Kwate, 2008; Lee, 2012; Morland et al., 2002a). For example, one such study found that predominantly Black neighborhoods have six times the number of fast-food outlets as White neighborhoods (Block et al., 2004). In another investigation, James et al. (2014) found that at the block group level, percent Black, but not poverty, was associated with shorter distances to the nearest fast-food chain.

Furthermore, this work has shown that the location of these organizations has direct consequences on weight status. While most of this work assumes that the location of food resources will affect health-related outcomes, such as eating behaviors or obesity, considerably fewer studies have directly tested this contention (Lytle, 2009). Despite the more limited attention paid to obesity or weight, the extant literature suggests that the local food environment maps onto weight outcomes in the population. In particular, studies have shown that food options relate to fruit and vegetable consumption, where having more full-sized chain supermarkets is related to increased consumption, and conversely, not having these options in close proximity is associated with poorer diet quality (Blitstein et al., 2012; Gibson, 2011; Holsten, 2009; Laraia et al., 2004; Michimi & Wimberly, 2010; Morland et al., 2002a). However, this work is mixed. Some work suggests that this effect is moderated by the sociodemographic characteristics of the local community context (Chen et al., 2010). Similarly, the availability of healthy food stores is related to lower rates of obesity, with some studies relating weight status to dietary habits as well (Morland et al., 2006; Stark et al., 2013; Yan et al., 2015). Additionally, as expected, a greater number of fast-food outlets and convenience stores is also associated with poor diet quality and higher rates of being overweight or obese for both adults and children (Gibson, 2011; Inagami et al., 2006; Ohri-Vachaspati et al., 2013; Stark et al., 2013). However, some work has found no association with BMI/weight status (Holsten, 2009; Jack et al., 2013; Lee, 2012), and one study even found a negative association between fast-food density and BMI among an adolescent sample in New York City (Bader et al., 2013).

In summary, the research on food resources suggests that the local food retail environment is related to the extent to which a neighborhood may be considered obesogenic. Further, this appears to be stratified on the basis of race and class, whereby poor and minority neighborhoods are less likely to have a wide variety of healthy food options in close proximity or easily accessible through public transportation. The evidence for whether or not prices are higher in these areas is mixed, largely depending on the quality of the food available. These studies have been methodologically varied as well, through studies on geographic proximity, such as physical distance to stores and travel times, density of outlets, and market basket approaches, that use either surveys or inventories of stock to examine what is on the shelves of stores and how much they cost. Moreover, while the work on how this relates to weight outcomes is limited, there is evidence that the local food retail environment is related to diet quality and, in turn, overweight/obesity. Most of the studies that directly examine BMI/obesity specifically focus on geographic approaches, as opposed to more in-depth studies examining food quality and pricing (Caspi et al., 2012). The work on the distribution of establishments is well-established and has employed various sophisticated statistical and spatial methods. Further work, especially studies using longitudinal methods of both individual-level weight status over time and the neighborhood context over time (Gibson, 2011), as well as more detailed measures of the local food environment (Caspi et al., 2012), would help build the evidence for whether or not food deserts or swamps impact population obesity.

Recreation

Other work has focused on the ways in which the built environment may promote or discourage physical activity. Similar to the large body of work on food environments, literature on neighborhood resources has also noted a disparity in the distribution of recreational establishments, which may relate to obesogenic environments. As with the food environment, this research overall has generally found that lower income, lower education, and racial/ethnic minority communities are less likely to have both green/park spaces as well as physical fitness facilities either within the community or in a short distance from their home (Duncan et al., 2013; Estabrooks et al., 2003; Hughey et al., 2016; Moore et al., 2008; Popkin et al., 2005; Wilson et al., 2004). Some work, though, has not found a significant relationship in certain geographic locations (Abercrombie et al., 2008). Moreover, this work has found that even when these establishments are within a convenient distance, they tend to be of lower quality without proper maintenance and worn or unsafe equipment (Algert et al., 2006; Duncan et al., 2013; Hughey et al., 2016; Powell et al., 2007; Vaughan et al., 2013).

Additionally, much like with the case of food resources, there is complimentary literature, albeit a more limited body of work, that has directly tested how these resources relate to the weight status of individuals in these areas. For instance, studies have demonstrated that the lack of recreational and park facilities in areas is associated with lower rates of physical activity/fitness and higher rates of being overweight/obese (Berry et al., 2010; Black et al., 2010; Feng et al., 2010; Gordon-Larsen et al., 2006; Humpel et al., 2002; Prince et al., 2011; Sawyer et al., 2017; Schüle & Bolte, 2015). Not all studies have found evidence of this, particularly outside of the U.S. context (Maas et al., 2008). For example, in a study of the Netherlands, Maas et al. (2008) found no relationship between the amount of recreational space in the local environment and physical activity, cycling, or sports. Thus, lacking these resources can have consequences for those communities and may be an important factor in trying to understand population-level rates of obesity across neighborhoods.

Despite this attention to recreation in the literature, a number of limitations remain. In particular, much of this work is limited or qualified in some way. For instance, while these studies have demonstrated strong disparities in access to both quality and quantity of recreational facilities, the majority of this literature at present is limited to an understanding of the spatial distribution of these resources, rather than how residents interact with these spaces, and whether or not having or lacking these facilities hinders their ability to stay sufficiently physically active (McNeill et al., 2006; Sawyer et al., 2017). More detailed studies on the frequency and utilization of such resources, as well as behavior within those spaces, such as the amount and type of exercise performed, would be necessary to fill this gap. Similarly, the extant work is often limited or qualified in scope by either population, geographic area, or methods. For example, while Gordon-Larsen et al. (2006) conducted a sophisticated study and found evidence of this pathway using a national sample, their study was limited to adolescent participants. Alternatively, Black et al. (2010) established that neighborhoods featuring greater access to fitness facilities decreased the risk of obesity, but their study area was limited to New York City. To build a causal pathway between the presence/absence of recreational facilities/space and BMI, we need more studies in more locations, particularly studies that test each part of this mechanistic pathway in a causal fashion (Berry et al., 2010).

Environmental Quality

While the research on community organizational resources focuses on the availability of a particular resource that may be obesogenic, the research on environmental quality focuses on how different characteristics of neighborhoods are favorable to weight status or overall health. Beyond the access and availability of resources, this work on the quality of the built environment has focused on several major areas, such as urban design, including the aesthetic qualities of urban spaces, land use and zoning, transportation systems, neighborhood reputation and safety, and the social organization of the community (Black & Macinko, 2008). For instance, as an extension of the literature just reviewed, a neighborhood may have a park location that, in theory, could be used for exercise and outdoor recreation. However, if that location is not well-maintained, safe from crime, or accessible on foot, the potential for that park to encourage exercise is limited. An existing body of literature has examined how the built environment contributes to other measures of health (Diez Roux & Mair,

2010; Evans 2003; Mujahid et al., 2008). For instance, a lack of recreation facilities and low walkability in neighborhoods has been linked to higher rates of hypertension and diabetes, while high levels of neighborhood disorder have been linked to depressive symptoms among residents (Diez Roux & Mair, 2010; Muhahid et al., 2008). In this section, we discuss the myriad of ways that the quality of the neighborhood built, natural, and social environment may contribute to weight outcomes.

Walkability

Neighborhood walkability refers to the availability of walking infrastructure that facilitates walking as a form of transportation and recreational activity (Casagrande et al., 2011; Cutts et al., 2009). This includes sidewalks and their components, such as connections to other sidewalks, obstructions, the number of stop signs, crosswalks, etc. (Boehmer et al., 2007; Casagrande et al., 2011). Researchers may measure neighborhood walkability rates by considering the available walking infrastructure, the number of minutes it takes residents to walk from their home to a recreational facility, and the number of walkable destinations near their vicinity (Booth et al., 2005). Some studies indicate that residents from high walkability neighborhoods have a lower prevalence rate for obesity (Boehmer et al., 2007; Booth et al., 2005; King et al., 2011; Kowaleski-Jones et al., 2018). This may be because higher walkability neighborhoods are conducive to outdoor physical activities, such as walking and running (Booth et al., 2005; King et al., 2011). For instance, Booth et al. (2005) found that residents from a high walkability neighborhood sample performed 63 more minutes of exercise per week than residents from low walkability neighborhoods.

However, a recent epidemiological review of the literature on neighborhood walkability and obesity found the relationship inconclusive (Wei et al., 2020). Other neighborhood factors (i.e., segregation, crime) may reverse, nullify, or moderate the association (Casagrande et al., 2011; Cutts et al., 2009). For instance, a study on neighborhoods in Phoenix, Arizona, found residents from high walkability neighborhoods to be more vulnerable to obesity (Cutts et al., 2009). However, the sampled high walkability neighborhoods also happened to be predominantly Latino or Black and had high crime levels (Cutts et al., 2009). Comparatively, another study, conducted in Baltimore, Maryland, revealed that individuals living in predominantly white neighborhoods with high walkability had lower rates of obesity; however, this was not the case for individuals living in predominantly Black neighborhoods (Casagrande et al., 2011). The researchers theorized that the racial discrepancy may be attributable to higher leisure time among whites in high SES neighborhoods or lower perceived neighborhood safety levels in predominantly black neighborhoods (Casagrande et al., 2011). Lastly, Sandy and colleagues (2000) found the presence and length of trails near children's homes to be associated with a significant decrease in BMI. Specifically, among children 8 years of age or older, the addition of 100 meters of trail near their homes decreases the probability of being obese by 1.6%. However, this was only the case if the crime rate in the neighborhood was low; otherwise, the relationship would reverse, and the trail length near residents' homes would lead to a higher BMI. In neighborhoods with a high rate of violent crime, trails near residents' homes may provide more space for violent criminal activity near residents' homes. The researchers theorize that in neighborhoods with a high rate of violent crime, trails near residents' homes may provide more open space for violent activity to occur and draw criminal activities closer to residents' homes, resulting in decreased feelings of neighborhood safety, and increasing BMI (Sandy et al., 2013).

Neighborhood Land Use

In conjunction with neighborhood walkability, prior research has focused on mixed land use and neighborhood obesity rates. Land use is an aspect of neighborhood design that has been linked to obesity given its influence on the prevalence of residents walking or taking public transportation to a nearby interesting site or recreational area. Land use refers to the type of developments in the area, commercial or residential (Rundle et al., 2007). For example, a neighborhood with low mixed land use would consist of primarily residential developments (houses) with little else in terms of stores, restaurants, and other destinations. Conversely, high mixed land use consists of an equal distribution of the types of developments in the neighborhood.

To assess land use, researchers typically survey neighborhood residents or use data from tax assessors, aerial shots, and global positioning system technology to assess the type and number of non-residential destinations near neighborhoods and the distance it takes residents to reach these destinations (Boehmer et al., 2007; Booth et al., 2005; Rundle et al., 2009). Multiple studies suggest that residents of neighborhoods with high mixed land use have a lower prevalence of obesity, potentially through its relationship to walkability (Booth et al., 2005; Brown et al., 2009; Lopez & Hynes, 2006; Rundle et al., 2007, 2009; Yamada et al., 2012). For instance, Boehmer et al. (2007) found the absence of non-residential destinations and interesting sites to be associated with a higher obesity rate. Moreover, obese residents were twice as likely to report not having an interesting destination within a 10-min walk from their home. This finding supports prior research indicating higher physical activity levels in neighborhoods with high mixed land use (Boehmer et al., 2007).

Notably, high mixed land use is also related to increased public transportation (Lopez & Hynes, 2006; Rundle et al., 2007). This is because an increase in nearby non-residential destinations leads to a higher rate of walking and biking to these locations, and a reduced reliance on personal vehicles (Boehmer et al., 2007; Booth et al., 2005). As a result, mixed land use supports the expansion of public transportation near neighborhoods and further facilitates walking and biking as a form of transportation (Booth et al., 2005; Lopez & Hynes, 2006; Rundle et al., 2007). Similarly, research indicates that a higher density of bus and subway stops is associated with lower obesity rates (Rundle et al., 2007).

Green Space

Green spaces or green belts consist of parks, gardens, adjacent natural land, and vegetation (Astell-Burt et al., 2014). Prior research indicates that green spaces improve the neighborhood's aesthetic, increase the perception of neighborhood safety, improve mental health, and promote outdoor physical activities, all of which may relate to population obesity (Dadvand et al., 2014). As such, some research indicates that neighborhood green spaces also lead to lower obesity rates. Dadvand et al. (2014) found that children residing in neighborhoods near forests have a 25% lower prevalence of obesity and a 39% lower prevalence of excessive screen time. The researchers contend that proximity to forests decreases sedentary activities (electronics usage) and increases health-promoting behavior such as exercising. At the same time, Mylona et al. (2020) found neighborhoods with a high proximity to green space to be 21% less likely to be located in an obesity hotspot. Interestingly, vegetation can also lead to a lower prevalence of obesity. For example, a study on New York City low-income neighborhoods revealed that children ages 3–5 who live in a neighborhood with a higher tree street density (75 vs. 25%) are 12% less likely to be obese (Lovasi et al., 2013).

Prior research on obesity and children also suggests that access to parks and playgrounds may lower BMI and propensity for obesity (Fan & Jin, 2014; Hughey et al., 2016; Hughey et al., 2017). However, the association may be dependent on several sociodemographic factors (Fan & Jin, 2014; Hughey et al., 2017). For instance, in the United States, the association between neighborhood parks and decreased propensity for obesity occurs mainly among girls (Fan & Jin, 2014; Hughey et al., 2017). Furthermore, Fan and Jin (2014) found the association to be stronger among pre-adolescents, non-Hispanic whites, residents of unsafe neighborhoods, and youth from neighborhoods without community centers. Although international research on parks and obesity also finds accessibility to playgrounds to lower the prevalence of obesity among children, no specific sociodemographic factors are significant. For instance, in a Canadian study, Veugelers et al. (2008) found that children with access to playgrounds and parks spend less time using electronics, are more likely to engage in sports, and are less likely to be obese. Notably, there is plenty of literature on childhood obesity and green space. Future research would benefit from examining the impact of green space on middle-aged and older adults.

Neighborhood Social Environment

In addition to research on neighborhood aesthetics within the built environment and obesity, there is growing literature on the effects of the neighborhood social environment on obesity prevalence (Suglia et al., 2016). The "[n]eighborhood social environment refers to relationships, groups, and social processes that exist between individuals and groups who live and work in a neighborhood" (Carroll-Scott et al., 2013, p. 3). This refers to social processes such as collective efficacy, social cohesion, social support, and social networks within a neighborhood. Prior research on the effects of the neighborhood social environment has found low levels of social cohesion, trust, and perceived neighborhood safety to be detrimental to multiple health outcomes, including obesity (Carroll-Scott et al., 2013).

Much of the literature on the neighborhood social environment focuses on collective efficacy. Collective efficacy measures social cohesion and the likelihood that community members will coalesce and work towards the community's wellbeing (Cecil-Karb & Grogan-Kaylor, 2009; Cohen et al., 2006; Franzini et al., 2009; Kimbro et al., 2011). To measure collective efficacy, researchers typically administer surveys that measure social cohesion and informal social control at the neighborhood level. Although studies on collective efficacy and obesity vary, most emphasize the role of social cohesion, or unity among neighborhood residents, in creating a safer environment. Cohen et al. (2006) proposed two ways in which collective efficacy can indirectly contribute to a higher risk of obesity. First, low collective efficacy has been shown to increase stress, commonly captured with allostatic load, which may increase BMI through a surplus in cortisol production. Second, low levels of neighborhood collective efficacy can result in unsafe, disordered neighborhoods, leading to decreased physical exercise opportunities outside of residents' homes. Moreover, the literature indicates that high levels of perceived collective efficacy among neighborhood residents may decrease violent crimes, which has implications for the stress process as it relates to health and obesity (Sampson et al., 1997).

Some limited work suggests a relationship between perceived levels of collective efficacy in neighborhoods and obesity. For instance, Cohen et al. (2006) found that individuals living in low efficacy neighborhoods are 52% more likely to be overweight than individuals living in neighborhoods with average collective efficacy. Moreover, the study also found low collective efficacy to be associated with being at risk of obesity and having a higher BMI (Cohen et al., 2006).

Because of the growing rates of obesity in children, more recent scholarship has studied the effects of similar social processes on children's propensity for obesity and obesity conducive behaviors (Carroll-Scott et al., 2013; Franzini et al., 2009). This literature primarily focuses on collective efficacy (or social cohesion) and the perception of neighborhood safety. Researchers theorize that low levels of trust and cohesion towards their neighbors may lead parents to limit the time their children spend outdoors and, therefore, increase the probability that their children will partake in sedentary activities (e.g., watching television). For example, in a study of fifth-grade students, Franzini et al. (2009) found physical exercise to mediate neighborhood collective efficacy and obesity among children. More specifically, the researchers found low collective efficacy, socialization of children, social exchange, social ties, and perceived neighborhood safety to lead to a lower physical activity score, and lower physical activity was associated with a higher level of obesity. Notably, other research has been unable to establish a direct connection between social cohesion and obesity rates among children; nonetheless, their findings still suggest that social cohesion affects the frequency of exercise (Carroll-Scott et al., 2013).

Additional research focuses on the effects of neighborhood network diversity and social ties on obesity. However, the research findings remain inconclusive. For example, Carroll-Scott et al. (2013) found an increase in the number of neighborhood social ties to be associated with increased consumption of healthy and unhealthy foods and exercise throughout the week among children. Yet, the association between the number of social ties and obesity was not significant. However, in another study, Christakis and Fowler (2007) found the type of social tie, not geographic distance, to be associated with obesity. More specifically, if Individual A and Individual B, who is obese, consider themselves to be friends, the risk of Individual A becoming obese increases by 171%. Notably, this is not the case if they are just neighbors. The researchers theorize individuals are more likely to accept weight gain among close social ties and therefore be more likely to accept weight gain in themselves, in effect, engaging in activities that promote weight gain (Christakis & Fowler, 2007).

Neighborhood SES and Segregation

In the United States, racial/ethnic minorities often live in segregated neighborhoods that are frequently underfunded, have a high level of physical disorder, and a high level of crime, resulting in deleterious health effects (Cuevas et al., 2020; Krivo et al., 2009). For instance, low SES neighborhoods have a higher number of nearby fast-food restaurants, fewer food options at supermarkets, fewer facilities for physical recreation, and more substantial neighborhood physical disorder than high SES neighborhoods (Booth et al., 2005, Greves Grow et al., 2010; Sharifi et al., 2016). Existing literature suggests that these conditions may lead to obesogenic behaviors regardless of individual SES or educational attainment among some minority groups.

A growing body of literature has further examined the effects of various dimensions of segregation on obesity prevalence among Latinos and Blacks. In a study of residential isolation and immigrant concentration among Latinos living in Utah, Wen and Maloney (2011) found residential isolation to be associated with an increased prevalence of obesity among Latinos and Latinas, even after controlling for neighborhood immigrant concentration. The researchers measured residential isolation by calculating the percentage of Latinos per census tract. In this process, they considered immigrant concentration by using the number of new Latino immigrants within the last 5 years and the number of linguistically isolated households. In another study, Kershaw et al. (2013) used the isolation index as a measure of residential segregation for Blacks and Latinos. The researchers found residential segregation to be associated with obesity only among Black women and Latinas. Interestingly, while Black women living in highly segregated neighborhoods have an increased prevalence of obesity, the reverse is true for Latina women for whom living in highly segregated neighborhoods lowers their prevalence of obesity. Kershaw et al. (2013) theorize that the inverse relationship between Black and Latina women could be because of the protective health factors that enclaves offer to recent migrant Latina women. More research is needed to examine the effect of migration on the relationship between neighborhood racial/ethnic segregation and obesity.

Crime and Perceptions of Neighborhood Safety

The literature on the neighborhood social environment also focuses on the effect of violent and residential crime on rates of obesity. Crime and social disorder may contribute to higher rates of obesity through two main pathways. First, crime rates may elevate stress levels that result in higher rates of obesity (Chang, 2006). Second, high crime rates may lead to neighborhood residents feeling too unsafe to perform physical exercise outside of their homes, even if there is space for outdoor activities (Chang et al., 2009; Sandy et al., 2013). This is also applicable to children since parents in high-crime neighborhoods may be more inclined to limit their children's time outside. Lovasi et al. (2013) found that children ages 3–5 living in neighborhoods in the 75th percentile for homicide had a 22% higher propensity for obesity than children living in 25th percentile neighborhoods. But, studies focused on crime have documented inconsistent findings based on the type of crime. For example, Carroll-Scott et al. (2013) could not demonstrate a link between violent crime and obesity among pre-adolescents; however, the results suggest property crime rates are associated with BMI. The researchers theorize that property crimes reflect a lack of social order in the neighborhood and discourage outside activities. Furthermore, another study indicates that although neighborhood violent crime rate is not directly associated with obesity, it helps explain racial discrepancies in obesity rates (Stolzenberg et al., 2019). Blacks and Latinos are more likely to be obese and have a higher BMI than whites in neighborhoods with a high violent crime rate.

As an extension of this work on objective indicators of crime rate, research has also examined subjective perceptions of crime and safety as it relates to obesity. These researchers contend that subjective measures of crime (i.e., perception of neighborhood safety) are more accurate indicators of obesity than objective measures (Fish et al., 2010; Richardson et al., 2017). Multiple studies suggest that an increase in perception of neighborhood safety is associated with lower obesity rates among neighborhood residents (Borrell et al., 2016; Burdette et al., 2006; Fish et al., 2010; Richardson et al., 2017). Perception of neighborhood safety is related to obesity levels through stress hormone production, physical exercise, and food diet (Fish et al., 2010). Even though Datar et al. (2013) were unable to establish a link between parents' perception of neighborhood safety and their child's risk for obesity, their findings suggest that the children of parents who perceive their neighborhood as unsafe watch more hours of television and perform less physical activity.

In summary, the quality of a multitude of neighborhood characteristics (walkability, land use, parks and green spaces, collective efficacy, crime, and perceived neighborhood safety) may result in a higher prevalence of obesity. However, the literature indicates that there is no single pathway through which higher obesity rates may occur (Sandy et al., 2013). For example, the presence of sidewalks may not lead to lower obesity rates if residents find their neighborhood unsafe or have no interesting places to go. Additionally, studies have indicated differences in effect size among different socio-demographics (i.e., low/high income, girls/boys, preadolescent/adolescent) (Fan & Jin, 2014; Hughey et al., 2017). Future research should focus on discerning the mechanisms behind some of these differences. Notably, because of the childhood obesity epidemic, prior literature mainly samples school-aged children. Future research in this area should consider including other age cohorts, such as middle-aged adults and the aging population. On the same note, the literature on environmental quality and racial/ethnic minorities is also limited. Because of the persistent patterns of racial neighborhood segregation in the United States, it is essential to consider the impact of racial segregation on the relationship between environmental quality and obesity prevalence.

Conclusions and Future Directions

Overall, this work demonstrates the various ways that neighborhood environments can relate to population obesity. While some nuance within the literature exists concerning the extent or context in which such environments contribute to obesity, the overarching story is that the built and social environments of neighborhoods relate to what people eat, how and if they recreate, and how safe or comfortable they feel in their neighborhoods. All of these can contribute to obesity rates across neighborhoods. We reviewed two facets of this literature. First, we covered the literature on the organizational environment in terms of the number and types of establishments that may lead to differing rates of obesity. This perspective largely focuses on the opportunity structure, in terms of available neighborhood resources, for diet and exercise. We also reviewed the literature on the quality of the neighborhood environment and how the built and social conditions within neighborhoods relate to rates of obesity. This work goes a step beyond to examine how aspects of neighborhoods, such as walkability, land use, sociability, and crime, can both create opportunities for movement and give a neighborhood a particular feeling that may either reduce or promote stress. Both of these can relate to the demography of obesity.

Despite the rich and growing body of work, we offer several points for improvement. In general, we argue for greater variety in how we think about obesogenic environments, both in terms of what is considered, as well as how that is measured and analyzed. First, we need to expand our thinking of what is considered an obesogenic environment. While recent work, especially in the area of environmental quality has demonstrated the myriad of ways that neighborhoods can affect weight status, the vast majority of this literature is still focused on how these factors influence individual-level diet and physical activity. Research on community organizations more broadly, beyond food and recreation, has also demonstrated that predominantly poor and racial/ethnic minority communities lack a wide variety of establishments, such as retail, health care organizations, social services, and civic society (Allard et al., 2003a; b; Alwitt & Donley, 1997; Anderson, 2017; Galaskiewicz et al., 2013; Schuetz et al., 2012; Small & Stark, 2005; Smiley et al., 2010). Although many of these types of establishments are not often linked to health (with the exception of health care) or even associated with health in our popular understandings of health, including overweight/obesity, future work should consider if and how these types of establishments contribute to the differential obesity rates that we observe across communities.

Previous work has suggested that social services and civic life can contribute to the overall well-being and mental health of residents (Allard, 2009; Hill et al., 2005; House et al., 1988; Small, 2009; Umberson et al., 2010). It would be reasonable to assume that organizations that provide social support and community vitality could also play a role in the individuals' weight status, as social support can reduce stress and lead to positive coping mechanisms. However, the extant literature on the impact of community organizations on health outcomes tends to suffer from an individual-level focus on the potential sources of "calories in" (food) and "calories out" (exercise) (French et al., 2001). Taking a more holistic view of the human body and the various ways that the available organizational resources can impact weight status and gain would make meaningful advances to this literature.

Second, we argue for greater methodological variety. While this area of the literature has seen an explosion of interest over the past several decades, many of the studies cited here use similar methodological and measurement approaches. For example, in a recent review of the work published on food, Lytle and Sokol (2017) found that although there have been hundreds of studies published on the topic in recent years, the vast majority of them (65%) use geographic proximity to measure access, and the overwhelming majority (86.1%) are cross-sectional. Moreover, they note that few of these studies provide any metrics for the reliability and validity of these constructs. While their review only examines the literature on food specifically, that is arguably the most developed body of literature reviewed here. A greater variety of measurements and validation of those measures would improve the development of this literature and provide further evidence of these associations.

Furthermore, to demonstrate in a causal fashion the link between neighborhood environments and obesity, we need more studies that directly test this relationship through longitudinal design and mediation analyses. Many of the studies infer an impact but do not leverage over time data to demonstrate a causal chain. Similarly, many of the mechanisms are inferred, but again not directly measured or tested. For example, in much of this work, especially on neighborhood establishments, it is assumed that the presence/absence of a neighborhood condition will be related to obesity, because that resource is elsewhere associated with weight status (Black & Macinko 2008). Few studies that link together all parts of the causal chain in a mediation analysis could better serve this literature, as well as inform public health interventions. Studies using biomarkers of the stress response, for example, could serve to further this work. This research is also heavily quantitative, with few qualitative studies that might paint a richer picture of the processes by which people experience their neighborhoods and obesogenic environments.

Third, the literature could consider more holistically how neighborhoods relate to obesity. Most of the literature focuses on pinpointing one particular feature of a neighborhood (e.g., crime) or one particular type of establishment (e.g., supermarkets) rather than considering how these pieces fit together to create a total environment and how these various factors may mediate or moderate the observed relationships, with few exceptions (Hughey et al., 2017; Sandy et al., 2013). This work is also primarily focused on objective aspects of the built and natural environment, rather than how residents of their neighborhoods perceive environments with some notable exceptions (Fish et al., 2010; Richardson et al., 2017). The literature could benefit from more work that tackles the perceived and objective facets of the neighborhood environment and how these uniquely contribute to population obesity.

In sum, this work points to a nuanced picture of how neighborhoods can relate to obesity. It is clear that different environments can produce an environmental context that is either obesogenic or salubrious to health. These patterns fall on similar lines to many other features of inequality in our society through socioeconomic status and race. As we remain a highly segmented and stratified society, including residential spaces, we see these patterns bear out in our neighborhoods by patterning weight across the population.

References

Abercrombie, L. C., Sallis, J. F., Conway, T. L., Frank, L. D., Saelens, B. E., & Chapman, J. E. (2008). Income and racial disparities in access to public parks and private recreation facilities. *American Journal of Preventive Medicine, 34*(1), 9–15. https://doi.org/10.1016/j.amepre.2007.09.030

Alcaly, R. E., & Klevorick, A. K. (1971). Food prices in relation to income levels in new York City. *The Journal of Business, 44*(4), 380–397.

Algert, S. J., Agrawal, A., & Lewis, D. S. (2006). Disparities in access to fresh produce in low-income neighborhoods in Los Angeles. *American Journal of Preventive Medicine, 30*(5), 365–370. https://doi.org/10.1016/j.amepre.2006.01.009

Allard, S. W. (2009). *Out of reach: Place, poverty, and the new American welfare state*. Yale University Press.

Allard, S. W., Rosen, D., & Tolman, R. M. (2003a). Access to mental health and substance abuse services among women receiving welfare in Detroit. *Urban Affairs Review, 38*(6), 787–807. https://doi.org/10.1177/1078087403038006002

Allard, S. W., Tolman, R. M., & Rosen, D. (2003b). The geography of need: Spatial distribution of barriers to employment in metropolitan Detroit. *Policy Studies Journal, 31*(3), 293–307. https://doi.org/10.1111/1541-0072.00023

Alwitt, L. F., & Donley, T. D. (1997). Retail stores in poor urban neighborhoods. *Journal of Consumer Affairs, 31*(1), 139–164.

Anderson, K. F. (2017). Racial residential segregation and the distribution of health-related organizations in urban Neighborhoods. *Social Problems, 64*(2), 256–276. https://doi.org/10.1093/socpro/spw058

Astell-Burt, T., Feng, X., & Kolt, G. S. (2014). Greener neighborhoods, slimmer people? Evidence from 246 920 Australians. *International Journal of Obesity, 38*(1), 156–159. https://doi.org/10.1038/ijo.2013.64

Bader, M. D. M., Schwartz-Soicher, O., Jack, D., Weiss, C. C., Richards, C. A., Quinn, J. W., Lovasi, G. S., Neckerman, K. M., & Rundle, A. G. (2013). More neighborhood retail associated with lower obesity among New York City public high school students. *Health & Place, 23*(0), 104–110. https://doi.org/10.1016/j.healthplace.2013.05.005

Beaulac, J., Kristjansson, E., & Cummins, S. (2009). A systematic review of food deserts, 1966–2007. *Preventing Chronic Disease, 6*(3), 10.

Berry, T. R., Spence, J. C., Blanchard, C. M., Cutumisu, N., Edwards, J., & Selfridge, G. (2010). A longitudinal and cross-sectional examination of the relationship between reasons for choosing a neighbourhood, physical activity and body mass index. *International Journal of Behavioral Nutrition and Physical Activity, 7*, 11. https://doi.org/10.1186/1479-5868-7-57

Black, J. L., & Macinko, J. (2008). Neighborhoods and obesity. *Nutrition Reviews, 66*(1), 2–20. https://doi.org/10.1111/j.1753-4887.2007.00001.x

Black, J. L., Macinko, J., Dixon, L. B., & Fryer, G. E., Jr. (2010). Neighborhoods and obesity in New York City. *Health & Place, 16*(3), 489–499. https://doi.org/10.1016/j.healthplace.2009.12.007

Black, C., Moon, G., & Baird, J. (2014). Dietary inequalities: What is the evidence for the effect of the neighbourhood food environment? *Health & Place, 27*(0), 229–242. https://doi.org/10.1016/j.healthplace.2013.09.015

Blair Lewis, L., Sloane, D. C., Nascimento, L. M., Diamant, A. L., Guinyard, J. J., Yancey, A. K., & Flynn, G. (2005). African Americans' access to healthy food options in South Los Angeles restaurants. *American Journal of Public Health, 95*(4), 668–673. https://doi.org/10.2105/AJPH.2004.050260

Blitstein, J. L., Snider, J., & Evans, W. D. (2012). Perceptions of the food shopping environment are associated with greater consumption of fruits and vegetables. *Public Health Nutrition, 15*(06), 1124–1129. https://doi.org/10.1017/S1368980012000523

Block, D., & Kouba, J. (2007). A comparison of the availability and affordability of a market basket in two communities in the Chicago area. *Public Health Nutrition, 9*(7), 837–845. https://doi.org/10.1017/PHN2005924

Block, J. P., Scribner, R. A., & DeSalvo, K. B. (2004). Fast food, race/ethnicity, and income: A geographic analysis. *American Journal of Preventive Medicine, 27*(3), 211–217. https://doi.org/10.1016/j.amepre.2004.06.007

Boehmer, T. K., Hoehner, C. M., Deshpande, A. D., Brennan Ramirez, L. K., & Brownson, R. C. (2007). Perceived and observed neighborhood indicators of obesity among urban adults. *International Journal of Obesity, 31*(6), 968–977. https://doi.org/10.1038/sj.ijo.0803531

Booth, K. M., Pinkston, M. M., & Poston, W. S. C. (2005). Obesity and the built environment. *Journal of the American Dietetic Association, 105*(5), S110–S117. https://doi.org/10.1016/j.jada.2005.02.045

Borrell, L. N., Graham, L., & Joseph, S. P. (2016). Associations of Neighborhood safety and Neighborhood support with overweight and obesity in US children and adolescents. *Ethnicity & Disease, 26*(4), 469–476. https://doi.org/10.18865/ed.26.4.469

Bower, K. M., Thorpe, R. J., Jr., Rohde, C., & Gaskin, D. J. (2014). The intersection of neighborhood racial segregation, poverty, and urbanicity and its impact on food store availability in the United States. *Preventive Medicine, 58*(0), 33–39. https://doi.org/10.1016/j.ypmed.2013.10.010

Brown, B. B., Yamada, I., Smith, K. R., Zick, C. D., Kowaleski-Jones, L., & Fan, J. X. (2009). Mixed land use and walkability: Variations in land use measures and relationships with BMI, overweight, and obesity. *Health & Place, 15*(4), 1130–1141. https://doi.org/10.1016/j.healthplace.2009.06.008

Burdette, H. L., Wadden, T. A., & Whitaker, R. C. (2006). Neighborhood safety, collective efficacy, and obesity in women with young children. *Obesity, 14*(3), 518–525. https://doi.org/10.1038/oby.2006.67

Captain, O. B., & McIntire, M. S. (1969). Cost and quality of food in poverty and non-poverty urban areas. *Journal of the American Dietetic Association, 55*(6), 569–571.

Carroll-Scott, A., Gilstad-Hayden, K., Rosenthal, L., Peters, S. M., McCaslin, C., Joyce, R., & Ickovics, J. R. (2013). Disentangling neighborhood contextual associations with child body mass index, diet, and physical activity: The role of built, socioeconomic, and social environments. *Social Science & Medicine, 95*, 106–114. https://doi.org/10.1016/j.socscimed.2013.04.003

Casagrande, S. S., Gittelsohn, J., Zonderman, A. B., Evans, M. K., & Gary-Webb, T. L. (2011). Association of Walkability with Obesity in Baltimore City, Maryland. *American Journal of Public Health, 101*(S1), S318–S324. https://doi.org/10.2105/AJPH.2009.187492

Caspi, C. E., Sorensen, G., Subramanian, S. V., & Kawachi, I. (2012). The local food environment and diet: A systematic review. *Health & Place, 18*(5), 1172–1187. https://doi.org/10.1016/j.healthplace.2012.05.006

Cecil-Karb, R., & Grogan-Kaylor, A. (2009). Childhood body mass index in community context: Neighborhood safety, television viewing, and growth trajectories of BMI. *Health & Social Work, 34*(3), 169–177. https://doi.org/10.1093/hsw/34.3.169

Chang, V. W. (2006). Racial residential segregation and weight status among US adults. *Social Science & Medicine, 63*(5), 1289–1303. https://doi.org/10.1016/j.socscimed.2006.03.049

Chang, V. W., Hillier, A. E., & Mehta, N. K. (2009). Neighborhood racial isolation, disorder and obesity. *Social Forces, 87*(4), 2063–2092.

Chen, S., Florax, R. J. G. M., Snyder, S., & Miller, C. C. (2010). Obesity and access to chain grocers. *Economic Geography, 86*(4), 431–452. https://doi.org/10.1111/j.1944-8287.2010.01090.x

Christakis, N. A., & Fowler, J. H. (2007). The spread of obesity in a large social network over 32 years. *New England Journal of Medicine, 357*(1), 370–379. https://doi.org/10.1056/NEJMsa066082

Chung, C., & Myers, S. L. (1999). Do the poor pay more for food? An analysis of grocery store availability and food Price disparities. *The Journal of Consumer Affairs, 33*(2), 276.

Cohen, D. A., Finch, B. K., Bower, A., & Sastry, N. (2006). Collective efficacy and obesity: The potential influence of social factors on health. *Social Science & Medicine, 62*(3), 769–778. https://doi.org/10.1016/j.socscimed.2005.06.033

Cooksey-Stowers, K., Schwartz, M., & Brownell, K. D. (2017). *Food swamps predict obesity rates better than food deserts in the United States* (Vol. 14).

Crockett, E. G., Clancy, K. L., & Bowering, J. (1992). Comparing the cost of a thrifty food plan market basket in three areas of New York state. *Journal of Nutrition Education, 24*(1, supplement 1), 71S–78S. https://doi.org/10.1016/S0022-3182(12)80146-4

Cuevas, A. G., Kawachi, I., Ortiz, K., Pena, M., Reitzel, L. R., & McNeill, L. H. (2020). Greater social cohesion is associated with lower body mass index among African American adults. *Preventive Medicine Reports, 18*, 101098. https://doi.org/10.1016/j.pmedr.2020.101098

Cummins, S., & Macintyre, S. (2002). "Food deserts": Evidence and assumption in health policy making. *BMJ [British Medical Journal], 325*(7361), 436–438. https://doi.org/10.2307/25452163

Cummins, S. C. J., McKay, L., & MacIntyre, S. (2005). McDonald's restaurants and neighborhood deprivation in Scotland and England. *American Journal of Preventive Medicine, 29*(4), 308–310. https://doi.org/10.1016/j.amepre.2005.06.011

Cutts, B. B., Darby, K. J., Boone, C. G., & Brewis, A. (2009). City structure, obesity, and environmental justice: An integrated analysis of physical and social barriers to walkable streets and park access. *Social Science & Medicine, 69*(9), 1314–1322. https://doi.org/10.1016/j.socscimed.2009.08.020

Dadvand, P., Villanueva, C. M., Font-Ribera, L., Martinez, D., Basagaña, X., Belmonte, J., Vrijheid, M., Gražulevičienė, R., Kogevinas, M., & Nieuwenhuijsen, M. J. (2014). Risks and benefits of green spaces for children: A cross-sectional study of associations with sedentary behavior, obesity, asthma, and allergy. *Environmental Health Perspectives, 122*(12), 1329–1335. https://doi.org/10.1289/ehp.1308038

Datar, A., Nicosia, N., & Shier, V. (2013). Parent perceptions of Neighborhood safety and Children's physical activity, sedentary behavior, and obesity: Evidence from a national longitudinal study. *American Journal of Epidemiology, 177*(10), 1065–1073. https://doi.org/10.1093/aje/kws353

Diez Roux, A., & V., & Mair, C. (2010). Neighborhoods and health. *Annals of the New York Academy of Sciences, 1186*(1), 125–145. https://doi.org/10.1111/j.1749-6632.2009.05333.x

Duncan, D. T., Kawachi, I., White, K., & Williams, D. R. (2013). The geography of recreational open space: Influence of neighborhood racial composition and neighborhood poverty. *Journal of Urban Health: Bulletin of the New York Academy of Medicine, 90*(4), 618–631. https://doi.org/10.1007/s11524-012-9770-y

Estabrooks, P. A., Lee, R. E., & Gyurcsik, N. C. (2003). Resources for physical activity participation: Does availability and accessibility differ by neighborhood socioeconomic status? *Annals of Behavioral Medicine, 25*(2), 100–104. https://doi.org/10.1207/s15324796abm2502_05

Evans, G. (2003). The built environment and mental health. *Journal of Urban Health, 80*(4), 536–555. https://doi.org/10.1093/jurban/jtg063

Fan, M., & Jin, Y. (2014). Do Neighborhood parks and playgrounds reduce childhood obesity? *American Journal of Agricultural Economics, 96*(1), 26–42. https://doi.org/10.1093/ajae/aat047

Feng, J., Glass, T. A., Curriero, F. C., Stewart, W. F., & Schwartz, B. S. (2010). The built environment and obesity: A systematic review of the epidemiologic evidence. *Health & Place, 16*(2), 175–190. https://doi.org/10.1016/j.healthplace.2009.09.008

Fish, J. S., Ettner, S., Ang, A., & Brown, A. F. (2010). Association of perceived neighborhood safety on body mass index. *American Journal of Public Health, 100*(11), 2296–2303. https://doi.org/10.2105/AJPH.2009.183293

Franzini, L., Elliott, M. N., Cuccaro, P., Schuster, M., Gilliland, M. J., Grunbaum, J. A., Franklin, F., & Tortolero, S. R. (2009). Influences of physical and social Neighborhood environments on children's physical activity and obesity. *American Journal of Public Health, 99*(2), 271–278. https://doi.org/10.2105/ajph.2007.128702

French, S. A., Story, M., & Jeffery, R. W. (2001). Environmental influences on eating and physical activity. *Annual Review of Public Health, 22*(1), 309.

Galaskiewicz, J., Mayorova, O. V., & Duckles, B. M. (2013). Studying the roles of nonprofits, government, and business in providing activities and services to youth in the Phoenix metropolitan area. *The Annals of the American Academy of Political and Social Science, 647*, 50–82. https://doi.org/10.2307/23479095

Gibson, D. M. (2011). The neighborhood food environment and adult weight status: Estimates from longitudinal data. *American Journal of Public Health, 101*(1), 71–78. https://doi.org/10.2105/AJPH.2009.187567

Glanz, K., Sallis, J. F., Saelens, B. E., & Frank, L. D. (2007). Nutrition environment measures survey in stores (NEMS-S): Development and evaluation. *American Journal of Preventive Medicine, 32*(4), 282–289. https://doi.org/10.1016/j.amepre.2006.12.019

Gordon-Larsen, P., Nelson, M. C., Page, P., & Popkin, B. M. (2006). Inequality in the built environment underlies key health disparities in physical activity and obesity. *Pediatrics, 117*(2), 417–424. https://doi.org/10.1542/peds.2005-0058

Greves Grow, H. M., Cook, A. J., Arterburn, D. E., Saelens, B. E., Drewnowski, A., & Lozano, P. (2010). Child obesity associated with social disadvantage of Children's Neighborhoods. *Journal of Social Science and Medicine, 71*(3), 584–591. https://doi.org/10.1016/j.socscimed.2010.04.018

Hall, B. F. (1983). Neighborhood differences in retail food stores: Income versus race and age of population. *Economic Geography, 59*(3), 282–295. https://doi.org/10.2307/143417

Hayes, L. R. (2000). Are prices higher for the poor in new York City? *Journal of Consumer Policy, 23*(2), 127–152. https://doi.org/10.1023/A:1006421500820

Hill, T. D., Ross, C. E., & Angel, R. J. (2005). Neighborhood disorder, psychophysiological distress, and health. *Journal of Health and Social Behavior, 46*(2), 170–186.

Holsten, J. E. (2009). Obesity and the community food environment: A systematic review. *Public Health Nutrition, 12*(3), 397–405. https://doi.org/10.1017/s1368980008002267

Horowitz, C. R., Colson, K. A., Hebert, P. L., & Lancaster, K. (2004). Barriers to buying healthy foods for people with diabetes: Evidence of environmental disparities. *American Journal of Public Health, 94*(9), 1549–1554.

House, J. S., Landis, K. R., & Umberson, D. (1988). Social relationships and health. *Science, 241*(4865), 540–545.

Hughey, S. M., Walsemann, K. M., Child, S., Powers, A., Reed, J. A., & Kaczynski, A. T. (2016). Using an environmental justice approach to examine the relationships between park availability and quality indicators, neighborhood disadvantage, and racial/ethnic composition. *Landscape and Urban Planning, 148*(supplement C), 159–169. https://doi.org/10.1016/j.landurbplan.2015.12.016

Hughey, M. S., Kaczynski, A. T., Child, S., Moore, J. B., Porter, D., & Hibbert, J. (2017). Green and lean: Is neighborhood park and playground availability associated with youth obesity? Variations by gender, socioeconomic status, and race/ethnicity. *Preventive Medicine, 95*, S101–S108. https://doi.org/10.1016/j.ypmed.2016.11.024

Humpel, N., Owen, N., & Leslie, E. (2002). Environmental factors associated with adults' participation in physical activity: A review. *American Journal of Preventive Medicine, 22*(3), 188–199. https://doi.org/10.1016/S0749-3797(01)00426-3

Inagami, S., Cohen, D. A., Finch, B. K., & Asch, S. M. (2006). You are where you shop: Grocery store locations, weight, and neighborhoods. *American Journal of Preventive Medicine, 31*(1), 10–17. https://doi.org/10.1016/j.amepre.2006.03.019

Jack, D., Neckerman, K., Schwartz-Soicher, O., Lovasi, G. S., Quinn, J., Richards, C., Bader, M., Weiss, C., Konty, K., Arno, P., Viola, D., Kerker, B., & Rundle, A. (2013). Socio-economic status, neighbourhood food environments and consumption of fruits and vegetables in New York City. *Public Health Nutrition, 16*(07), 1197–1205.

James, P., Arcaya, M. C., Parker, D. M., Tucker-Seeley, R. D., & Subramanian, S. V. (2014). Do minority and poor neighborhoods have higher access to fast-food restaurants in the United States? *Health & Place, 29*, 10–17.

Jetter, K. M., & Cassady, D. L. (2006). The availability and cost of healthier food alternatives. *American Journal of Preventive Medicine, 30*(1), 38–44. https://doi.org/10.1016/j.amepre.2005.08.039

Kershaw, K. N., Albretch, S. S., & Carnethon, M. R. (2013). Racial and ethnic residential segregation, the Neighborhood socioeconomic environment, and obesity among blacks and Mexican Americans. *American Journal of Epidemiology, 177*(4), 299–309. https://doi.org/10.1093/aje/kws372

Kimbro, R. T., Brooks-Gunn, J., & McLanahan, S. (2011). Young children in urban areas: Links among neighborhood characteristics, weight status, outdoor play, and television watching. *Social Science & Medicine, 72*(5), 668–676. https://doi.org/10.1016/j.socscimed.2010.12.015

King, A. C., Sallis, J. F., Frank, L. D., Saelens, B. E., Cain, K., Conway, T. L., Chapman, J. E., Ahn, D. K., & Kerr, J. (2011). Aging in neighborhoods differing in walkability and income: Associations with physical activity and obesity in older adults. *Social Science & Medicine, 73*(10), 1525–1533. https://doi.org/10.1016/j.socscimed.2011.08.032

Kowaleski-Jones, L., Zick, C., Smith, K. R., Brown, B., Hanson, H., & Fan, J. (2018). Walkable neighborhoods and obesity: Evaluating effects with a propensity score approach. *SSM – Population Health, 6*, 9–15. https://doi.org/10.1016/j.ssmph.2017.11.005

Krivo, L. J., Peterson, R. D., & Kuhl, D. C. (2009). Segregation, racial structure, and Neighborhood violent crime. *American Journal of Sociology, 114*(6), 1765–1802. https://doi.org/10.1086/597285

Kwate, N. O. A. (2008). Fried chicken and fresh apples: Racial segregation as a fundamental cause of fast food density in black neighborhoods. *Health & Place, 14*(1), 32–44. https://doi.org/10.1016/j.healthplace.2007.04.001

Laraia, B. A., Siega-Riz, A. M., Kaufman, J. S., & Jones, S. J. (2004). Proximity of supermarkets is positively associated with diet quality index for pregnancy. *Preventive Medicine, 39*(5), 869–875. https://doi.org/10.1016/j.ypmed.2004.03.018

Lee, H. (2012). The role of local food availability in explaining obesity risk among young school-aged children. *Social Science & Medicine, 74*(8), 1193–1203. https://doi.org/10.1016/j.socscimed.2011.12.036

Lopez, R. P., & Hynes, H. P. (2006). Obesity, physical activity, and the urban environment: Public health research needs. *Environmental Health, 5*(1), 25. https://doi.org/10.1186/1476-069X-5-25

Lovasi, G. S., Schwartz-Soicher, O., Quinn, J. W., Berger, D. K., Neckerman, K. M., Jaslow, R., Lee, K., & Rundle, A. (2013). Neighborhood safety and green space as predictors of obesity among preschool children from low-income families in new York City. *Preventive Medicine, 57*(3), 189–193. https://doi.org/10.1016/j.ypmed.2013.05.012

Lytle, L. A. (2009). Measuring the food environment: State of the science. *American Journal of Preventive Medicine, 36*(4, Suppl), S134–S144. https://doi.org/10.1016/j.amepre.2009.01.018

Lytle, L. A., & Sokol, R. L. (2017). Measures of the food environment: A systematic review of the field, 2007–2015. *Health & Place, 44*, 18–34. https://doi.org/10.1016/j.healthplace.2016.12.007

Maas, J., Verheij, R. A., Spreeuwenberg, P., & Groenewegen, P. P. (2008). Physical activity as a possible mechanism behind the relationship between green space and health: A multilevel analysis. *BMC Public Health, 8*(1), 206–218.

MacDonald, J. M., & Nelson, P. E. (1991). Do the poor still pay more? Food price variations in large metropolitan areas. *Journal of Urban Economics, 30*(3), 344–359. https://doi.org/10.1016/0094-1190(91)90054-B

Macintyre, S. (2007). Deprivation amplification revisited; or, is it always true that poorer places have poorer access to resources for healthy diets and physical activity? *The International Journal of Behavioral Nutrition and Physical Activity, 4*, 32–32. https://doi.org/10.1186/1479-5868-4-32

McNeill, L. H., Kreuter, M. W., & Subramanian, S. V. (2006). Social environment and physical activity: A review of concepts and evidence. *Social Science & Medicine, 63*(4), 1011–1022. https://doi.org/10.1016/j.socscimed.2006.03.012

Michimi, A., & Wimberly, M. C. (2010). Associations of supermarket accessibility with obesity and fruit and vegetable consumption in the conterminous United States. *International Journal of Health Geographics, 9*, 14. https://doi.org/10.1186/1476-072x-9-49

Moore, L. V., & Diez Roux, A. V. (2006). Associations of Neighborhood characteristics with the location and type of food stores. *American Journal of Public Health, 96*(2), 325–331. https://doi.org/10.2105/AJPH.2004.058040

Moore, L. V., Roux, A. V. D., Evenson, K. R., McGinn, A. P., & Brines, S. J. (2008). Availability of recreational resources in minority and low socioeconomic status areas. *American Journal of Preventive Medicine, 34*(1), 16–22. https://doi.org/10.1016/j.amepre.2007.09.021

Morland, K., Wing, S., & Roux, A. D. (2002a). The contextual effect of the local food environment on Residents' diets: The atherosclerosis risk in communities study. *American Journal of Public Health, 92*(11), 1761–1767.

Morland, K., Wing, S., Roux, A. D., & Poole, C. (2002b). Neighborhood characteristics associated with the location of food stores and food service places. *American Journal of Preventive Medicine, 22*(1), 23–29. https://doi.org/10.1016/s0749-3797(01)00403-2

Morland, K., Diez Roux, A. V., & Wing, S. (2006). Supermarkets, other food stores, and obesity: The atherosclerosis risk in communities study. *American Journal of Preventive Medicine, 30*(4), 333–339. https://doi.org/10.1016/j.amepre.2005.11.003

Mujahid, M. S., Diez Roux, A. V., Morenoff, J. D., Raghunathan, T. E., Cooper, R. S., Ni, H., & Shea, S. (2008). Neighborhood characteristics and hypertension. *Journal of Epidemiology, 19*(4), 590–598. https://doi.org/10.1097/EDE.0b013e3181772cb2

Mylona, E. K., Shehadeh, F., Fleury, E., Kalligeros, M., & Mylonakis, E. (2020). Neighborhood-level analysis on the impact of accessibility to fast food and open green spaces on the prevalence of obesity. *The American Journal of Medicine, 133*(3), 340–346.e341. https://doi.org/10.1016/j.amjmed.2019.08.024

O'Dwyer, L. A., & Coveney, J. (2006). Scoping supermarket availability and accessibility by socio-economic status in Adelaide. *Health Promotion Journal of Australia, 17*(3), 240–246. https://doi.org/10.1071/HE06240

Ohri-Vachaspati, P., Lloyd, K., DeLia, D., Tulloch, D., & Yedidia, M. J. (2013). A closer examination of the relationship between children's weight status and the food and physical activity environment. *Preventive Medicine, 57*(3), 162–167. https://doi.org/10.1016/j.ypmed.2013.05.009

Pearce, J., Witten, K., & Bartie, P. (2006). Neighbourhoods and health: A GIS approach to measuring community resource accessibility. *Journal of Epidemiology and Community Health, 60*(5), 389. https://doi.org/10.1136/jech.2005.043281

Popkin, B. M., Duffey, K., & Gordon-Larsen, P. (2005). Environmental influences on food choice, physical activity and energy balance. *Physiology & Behavior, 86*(5), 603–613. https://doi.org/10.1016/j.physbeh.2005.08.051

Powell, L. M., Slater, S., Mirtcheva, D., Bao, Y., & Chaloupka, F. J. (2007). Food store availability and neighborhood characteristics in the United States. *Preventive Medicine, 44*(3), 189–195. https://doi.org/10.1016/j.ypmed.2006.08.008

Prince, S. A., Kristjansson, E. A., Russell, K., Billette, J.-M., Sawada, M., Ali, A., Tremblay, M. S., & Prud'homme, D. (2011). A multilevel analysis of neighbourhood built and social environments and adult self-reported physical activity and body mass index in Ottawa, Canada. *International Journal of Environmental Research and Public Health, 8*(10), 3953–3978. https://doi.org/10.3390/ijerph8103953

Richardson, A. S., Troxel, W. M., Ghosh-Dastidar, M., Hunter, G. P., Beckman, R., Colabianchi, N., Collins, R., & Dubowitz, T. (2017). Pathways through which higher neighborhood crime is longitudinally associated with greater body mass index. *International Journal of Behavioral Nutrition and Physical Activity, 14*(1), 155. https://doi.org/10.1186/s12966-017-0611-y

Rundle, A., Roux, A. V. D., Freeman, L. M., Miller, D., Neckerman, K. M., & Weiss, C. C. (2007). The urban built environment and obesity in new York City: A multilevel analysis. *American Journal of Health Promotion, 21*(4_suppl), 326–334. https://doi.org/10.4278/0890-1171-21.4s.326

Rundle, A., Neckerman, K. M., Freeman, L., Lovasi, G. S., Purciel, M., Quinn, J., Richards, C., Sircar, N., & Weiss, C. (2009). Neighborhood food environment and walkability predict obesity in new York City. *Environmental Health Perspectives, 117*(3), 442–447. https://doi.org/10.1289/ehp.11590

Sampson, R. J., Raudenbush, S. W., & Earls, F. (1997). Neighborhoods and violent crime: A multilevel study of collective efficacy. *Science, 277*(5328), 918–924. https://doi.org/10.1126/science.277.5328.918

Sandy, R., Tchernis, R., Wilson, J., Liu, G., & Zhou, X. (2013). Effects of the built environment on childhood obesity: The case of urban recreational trails and crime. *Economics and Human Biology, 11*(1), 18–29. https://doi.org/10.1016/j.ehb.2012.02.005

Sawyer, A. D. M., Jones, R., Ucci, M., Smith, L., Kearns, A., & Fisher, A. (2017). Cross-sectional interactions between quality of the physical and social environment and self-reported physical activity in adults living in income-deprived communities. *PLoS One, 12*(12), 17. https://doi.org/10.1371/journal.pone.0188962

Schuetz, J., Kolko, J., & Meltzer, R. (2012). Are poor neighborhoods "retail deserts"? *Regional Science and Urban Economics, 42*(1–2), 269–285. https://doi.org/10.1016/j.regsciurbeco.2011.09.005

Schüle, S. A., & Bolte, G. (2015). Interactive and independent associations between the socioeconomic and objective built environment on the neighbourhood level and individual health: A systematic review of multilevel studies. *PLoS One, 10*(4), e0123456. https://doi.org/10.1371/journal.pone.0123456

Sharifi, M., Sequist, T. D., Rifas-Shiman, S. L., Melly, S. J., Duncan, S. T., Horan, C. M., Smith, R. L., Marshall, R., & Taveras, E. M. (2016). The role of Neighborhood characteristics and the built environment in understanding racial/ethnic disparities in childhood obesity. *Preventive Medicine, 91*(1), 102–109. https://doi.org/10.1016/j.ypmed.2016.07.009

Small, M. L. (2009). *Unanticipated gains: Origins of network inequality in everyday life*. Oxford University Press.

Small, M. L., & Stark, L. (2005). Are poor neighborhoods resource deprived? A case study of childcare centers in New York. *Social Science Quarterly, 86*(5), 1013–1036. https://doi.org/10.1111/j.0038-4941.2005.00334.x

Smiley, M. J., Diez Roux, A. V., Brines, S. J., Brown, D. G., Evenson, K. R., & Rodriguez, D. A. (2010). A spatial analysis of health-related resources in three diverse metropolitan areas. *Health & Place, 16*(5), 885–892. https://doi.org/10.1016/j.healthplace.2010.04.014

Stark, J. H., Neckerman, K., Lovasi, G. S., Konty, K., Quinn, J., Arno, P., Viola, D., Harris, T. G., Weiss, C. C., Bader, M. D., & Rundle, A. (2013). Neighbourhood food environments and body mass index among new York City adults. *Journal of Epidemiology and Community Health, 67*(9), 736–742. https://doi.org/10.1136/jech-2013-202354

Stolzenberg, L., D'Alessio, S. J., & Flexon, J. L. (2019). The impact of violent crime on obesity. *Social Sciences, 8*(12), 329.

Suglia, S. F., Shelton, R. C., Hsiao, A., Wang, Y. C., Rundle, A., & Link, B. G. (2016). Why the neighborhood social environment is critical in obesity prevention. *Journal of Urban Health, 93*(1), 206–212. https://doi.org/10.1007/s11524-015-0017-6

Umberson, D., Crosnoe, R., & Reczek, C. (2010). Social relationships and health behavior across life course. *Annual Review of Sociology, 36*.

Vaughan, K., Kaczynski, A., Wilhelm Stanis, S., Besenyi, G., Bergstrom, R., & Heinrich, K. (2013). Exploring the distribution of park availability, features, and quality across Kansas City, Missouri by income and race/ethnicity: An environmental justice investigation. *Annals of Behavioral Medicine, 45*(1), 28–38. https://doi.org/10.1007/s12160-012-9425-y

Veugelers, P., Sithole, F., Zhang, S., & Muhajarine, N. (2008). Neighborhood characteristics in relation to diet, physical activity and overweight of Canadian children. *International Journal of Pediatric Obesity, 3*(1), 152–159. https://doi.org/10.1080/17477160801970278

Walker, R. E., Keane, C. R., & Burke, J. G. (2010). Disparities and access to healthy food in the United States: A review of food deserts literature. *Health & Place, 16*(5), 876–884. https://doi.org/10.1016/j.healthplace.2010.04.013

Wei, J., Wu, Y., Zheng, J., Nie, P., Jia, P., & Wang, Y. (2020). Neighborhood sidewalk access and childhood obesity. *Obesity Reviews*, published online. https://doi.org/10.1111/obr.13057.

Wen, M., & Maloney, T. (2011). Latino residential isolation and the risk of obesity in Utah: The role of neighborhood socioeconomic, built-environmental, and subcultural context. *Journal of Immigrant and Minority Health, 13*(6), 1134–1141. https://doi.org/10.1007/s10903-011-9439-8

Wilson, D. K., Kirtland, K. A., Ainsworth, B. E., & Addy, C. L. (2004). Socioeconomic status and perceptions of access and safety for physical activity. *Annals of Behavioral Medicine, 28*(1), 20–28. https://doi.org/10.1207/s15324796abm2801_4

Yamada, I., Brown, B. B., Smith, K. R., Zick, C. D., Kowaleski-Jones, L., & Fan, J. X. (2012). Mixed land use and obesity: An empirical comparison of alternative land use measures and geographic scales. *The Professional Geographer, 64*(2), 157–177. https://doi.org/10.1080/00330124.2011.583592

Yan, R., Bastian, N. D., & Griffin, P. M. (2015). Association of food environment and food retailers with obesity in US adults. *Health & Place, 33*, 19–24. https://doi.org/10.1016/j.healthplace.2015.02.004

Zenk, S. N., Schulz, A. J., Israel, B. A., James, S. A., Bao, S., & Wilson, M. L. (2005). Neighborhood racial composition, neighborhood poverty, and the spatial accessibility of supermarkets in metropolitan Detroit. *American Journal of Public Health, 95*(4), 660–667. https://doi.org/10.2105/AJPH.2004.042150

14 Treatment and Outcome Disparities for Patients with Obesity in Emergency Medical Services

Jamie Kennel, Hyeyoung Woo, and Ginny Garcia-Alexander

Introduction

Many Americans are categorized as having overweight or obesity, with rates reaching what several scholars consider epidemic levels (e.g., Rubenstein, 2005). In fact, recent body mass index (BMI; kilograms of weight divided by height in meters squared) data from the Center of Disease Control and Prevention indicate that 79% of men and 77% of women over the age of 20 in the U.S. have either overweight (BMI: 25–29), obesity (30–39), or severe obesity (40 and above) with even higher rates among Black and Hispanic individuals (Fryar et al., 2016; Hales et al., 2018).

Much of the prior work on obesity has focused on its links to higher morbidity and mortality. Such studies have revealed that individuals with obesity are more likely to suffer from many chronic health conditions including cardiovascular disease, type 2 diabetes mellitus, respiratory disorders, various cancers, osteoporosis, and gall bladder disease; and emerging evidence indicates they experience more serious COVID-19 symptoms. Moreover, individuals with obesity are more likely to have severe complications and consequences from these conditions leading to increased risks of mortality (Busetto et al., 2020; Manson et al., 1995; Sanchis-Gomer et al., 2020; Visscher & Seidell, 2001). Finally, mounting evidence suggests that obesity is significantly associated with a higher risk for "all-cause" mortality, compared to individuals without obesity (Di Angelantonio et al., 2016; Calle et al., 1999).

In addition to these higher health risks, individuals with obesity also suffer from negative social outcomes. For example, people with obesity often encounter discrimination at school and work, including higher rates of school bullying and school dropout rates, lower rates of employment and income, and slower career progression (Canning & Mayer, 1966; Crandall, 1991; Rubino et al., 2020). In medical settings, individuals with obesity are more likely to experience weight-related bias and receive substandard care when utilizing healthcare services including reduced cancer screening recommendations, fewer diagnostic tests, and reduced time receiving physician-led health education during clinical visits (Lee & Pausé, 2016; Phelan et al., 2014b).

Patients with obesity are also more likely to experience negative interactions with medical providers, characterized by disrespect, condescension, and poorer treatment. This may worsen the morbidity and mortality burden of obese

J. Kennel (✉)
Emergency Medical Services, Oregon Institute of Technology, Wilsonville, OR, USA
e-mail: jamie.kennel@oit.edu

H. Woo
Sociology, Institute for Asian Studies, Portland State University, Portland, OR, USA

G. Garcia-Alexander
Department of Sociology, University of Texas at San Antonio, San Antonio, TX, USA

G. Garcia-Alexander, D. L. Poston, Jr. (eds.), *International Handbook of the Demography of Obesity*, International Handbooks of Population 12, https://doi.org/10.1007/978-3-031-10936-2_14

patients, as such interactions have been shown to increase rates of treatment non-compliance and avoidance of medical care (Amy et al., 2006; Bertakis & Azari, 2005; Budd et al., 2009; Hebl et al., 2003; Lee & Pausé, 2016; Phelan et al., 2014b). Additionally, examples of weight bias in healthcare settings have been associated with substandard treatment (Amy et al., 2006; Bertakis & Azari, 2005; Hebl et al., 2003; Phelan et al., 2015). Despite the evidence that obesity bias can influence the attitudes of healthcare providers as well as their treatment recommendations, the link between obesity and treatment outcomes has only been examined in limited areas of medicine. For example, Emergency Medical Services (EMS) provides medical treatment for an estimated 16 million sick and injured individuals annually, often with acute morbidity and mortality consequences, yet the presence of obesity treatment bias in EMS has not been examined in this context.

In this chapter, we investigate the association between obesity and EMS treatments, using data from patient care records. In the sections below, we first review the theoretical perspectives that shed light on how weight-related bias may operate for individuals with obesity. We also provide a review of research documenting weight-related bias in healthcare settings among those with obesity, including subgroup variations by gender and its manifestations in treatment differences. Then, we offer an analysis of treatment bias in an understudied medical setting (emergency medical services), and discuss implications of these findings and directions for future research.

Background

Obesity is a highly stigmatized condition, and those with obesity face a host of negative consequences including stereotyping, othering, status loss, and discrimination (Link & Phelan, 2001). Public attitudes toward obesity are especially negative and scholars have argued this is due to the attribution of blame or personal responsibility for excess weight. In other words, obesity is presumed to be under a person's control, and they are therefore held personally responsible for their condition (Dejong, 1980). It is for this reason that scholars have suggested that weight bias is so widespread.

Weight bias pervades many aspects of social life and has increased in recent decades (Puhl & Heuer, 2009). In fact, estimates suggest that up to 42% of adults in the United States experience weight-based discrimination (Rubino et al., 2020). As mentioned previously, the presence of weight bias has been well-documented across settings including the workplace and schools. In health settings, weight bias appears to be similarly widespread. One study of women with overweight and obesity observed that 69% experienced weight stigma from a doctor and 52% reported that it occurred repeatedly (Puhl & Brownell, 2006). Yet, it is unclear how common weight bias is in an emergency medicine context and whether this translates into differential practices and outcomes.

Treatment Disparities in Healthcare

In the healthcare system, there is ample empirical evidence of disparities in both the attitudes and treatment recommendations from healthcare providers when people with obesity engage in medical treatment. Many physicians, medical students, and allied health providers stereotype individuals with obesity as "lacking self-discipline", "dishonest", "unintelligent", "noncompliant with treatment", "lazy", and "annoying" (Budd et al., 2009; Phelan et al., 2014b; Teachman & Brownell, 2001). Further, as an indication of the strength of obesity stigma, these negative attitudes toward patients are even found in physicians who specialize in providing treatment to patients with obesity (Schwartz et al., 2003).

Providers have also been shown to be more likely to recommend substandard treatment for people with obesity. For example, while it's understood that people with obesity are more at risk for cervical and ovarian cancer, medical providers are less likely to perform the necessary pelvic exams to screen for these life threatening conditions (Amy et al., 2006). Further, people with obesity report spending less time with medical providers and receive less health education during medical appointments when compared to people without obesity (Bertakis & Azari, 2005; Hebl et al., 2003; Phelan et al., 2015). Some studies have shown that gender moderates the association between weight and bias or discrimination, with women experiencing greater penalties (Schulte et al., 2007). For example, women are more likely to encounter negative attitudes and treatment differences when interacting with medical providers (Anderson et al., 2001; Fikkan & Rothblum, 2012).

On the patient side, negative attitudes and poor treatment across a variety of providers is commonly reported. In fact, one study indicated that patients expect to encounter negative stereotypes and stigma in primary care (Brown et al., 2006); others have documented disrespectful or upsetting comments on the part of providers (Puhl & Brownell, 2006). These negative perceptions and interactions have important implications as they tend to demotivate adherence to obesity interventions. They have also been linked to avoidance of care and delayed use of preventive health screenings for colorectal, breast, cervical cancer, and pelvic exams (Amy et al., 2006; Lee & Pausé, 2016; Puhl & Heuer, 2010).

Emergency Medical Services

Emergency Medical Services (EMS) provides medical treatment for an estimated 16 million sick and injured individuals annually, often with acute morbidity and mortality consequences. It is not known if patients with obesity are more likely to utilize EMS services than patients without obesity. However, there is good reason to believe that patients with obesity may rely on EMS more frequently given their higher health risks along with prior work documenting a higher utilization rate for patients with obesity in healthcare overall (Fuoco, 2010). Further, patients with obesity are more likely to delay medical treatments which may arguably result in increased utilization of EMS services as untreated medical conditions escalate (Rubino et al., 2020).

This study explores evidence of treatment and outcome disparities for obese patients when they interact with EMS medical providers. EMS providers are unlikely to be immune to the negative attitudes towards obese patients found in other areas of medicine as well as in society at large. Thus, it is likely that obesity stigma results in an as yet undocumented negative impact on the quality of EMS treatment and patient outcomes. Further, EMS providers may be even more susceptible to obesity bias for two primary reasons. First, EMS providers are often evaluated on the speed at which various tasks are performed (scene times, transport times, time to perform procedures, etc.) and obese patients often require additional treatment time due to additional scene extrication challenges, the need for additional personnel (e.g., for lifting and moving assistance) or specialized equipment (e.g., a bariatric ambulance). Studies have shown that stereotypes are particularly likely to be used in the presence of time constraints (Burgess, 2010). Thus, EMS providers may be more likely to activate stereotypes, which may lead to treatment disparities. Second, if EMS providers, like other healthcare providers, believe that patients with obesity are more likely to be non-compliant with their treatment recommendations, they may believe that they are being requested to primarily provide transportation to the hospital. This might be perceived as a waste of EMS resources and may further illicit negative attitudes and behaviors from the EMS providers.

This analysis is important for several reasons. First, individuals with obesity are likely to rely more heavily on EMS services as they are both more susceptible to several diseases and often experience more severe consequences from disease. In addition, the role of weight bias impacting treatment and outcomes in EMS is unknown. By addressing the potential reduction in the quality of treatment provided in EMS, this study informs our understanding of how patients with obesity may face bias when using EMS, and our results may lead directly to improvement of treatment and outcomes for these vulnerable patients.

Research Question and Hypothesis

This study investigates the associations between a patient's obesity status and the quality and outcomes of the EMS medical treatment provided for patients who engage with EMS for painful emergencies. We focus on pain-related treatments and outcomes because it is one of the most common reasons that patients request EMS treatment, and pain-related treatment protocols typically allow the provider considerable treatment discretion.[1] To measure these associations, we focus on three distinct, yet sequenced, components of the EMS encounter. The first component is the administration of a pain screening, a process utilized by emergency providers to assess the presence and severity of pain using a 0–10 pain scale. The second component is the receipt of pain medication. Prior studies have documented racial/ethnic disparities in the receipt of pain medication (Hewes et al., 2017; Kennel et al., 2019; Todd et al., 1999), and based on these studies it is expected that having obesity, a stigmatized condition, will reduce the likelihood of receiving pain medication. Third, we examine pain outcomes, based on patient's self-assessment of pain. We look at the difference between a patient's pain level at the beginning and at the conclusion of EMS treatment. It is expected that obesity status will reduce the likelihood of pain screening, pain medication administration, and effective pain reduction during EMS treatment. The specific hypotheses to be tested are:

H-1: When patients receive treatment from EMS providers for traumatic and atraumatic painful emergencies, patients with obesity are less likely to receive a pain screening when compared to patients without obesity, and the association is even more salient for women.

H-2: When patients receive treatment from EMS providers for traumatic and atraumatic painful emergencies, patients with obesity are less likely to receive pain medications when compared to patients without obesity, and the likelihood of receiving pain medications is even lower for women.

H-3: When patients receive treatment from EMS providers for traumatic and atraumatic painful emergencies, obese patients are less likely to have their pain levels reduced when compared to patients without obesity, and the association is stronger for women.

Data, Measures, and Methods

Data

This study utilizes patient care record (PCR) data from 2015 to 2019 for patients who received emergency treatment from EMS services in the City of Vancouver, WA. The City of Vancouver was selected for two primary reasons. First, the City of Vancouver provided access to the complete and private PCR dataset for both the Vancouver Fire Department and American Medical Response (ambulance transport agency), including population-level data access as well as several additional variables not available in public EMS datasets (i.e. NEMSIS: National Emergency Medical Services Information System). Second, the City of Vancouver data structure allows PCR data from multiple EMS agencies that provide concurrent care to a single patient to be consolidated into a single set of treatments. The PCR represents the official EMS medical record, which captures all assessments and treatments provided to the patient during the entire EMS encounter. As is common in many EMS systems, EMS treatment within the City of Vancouver is often, but not always, provided concurrently by paramedics employed by two independent EMS organizations: the contracted ambulance provider, American Medical Response (AMR), and

[1] Prior research has demonstrated that the treatment of pain has been shown to vary on the basis of patient characteristics when clinical uncertainty and or levels of provider treatment discretion is high (Bloche, 2001; Mort et al., 1994; Smedley et al., 2003).

the City of Vancouver Fire Department (VFD). In the current study, PCR data from AMR and VFD were combined to create a new single comprehensive PCR that includes all assessments and treatments provided to the patient from either agency. By selecting data from the years 2015–2019, we capture the most recent years of PCR data available with a single electronic charting environment for each PCR system.

Analytic Sample

All PCRs with a primary impression of either atraumatic pain or a traumatic injury are included. The primary impression value represents the working diagnosis as determined by the EMS team, and from which a treatment plan follows. When two different primary impression values existed for the same patient encounter, we use the value from AMR.[2]

Several exclusion criteria are applied in order to restrict the analysis to patients who were clinically equivalent and eligible for pain treatment. First, patients with a clinical contraindication for receiving pain treatment are excluded, including patients with altered mental status or patients reporting an allergy to pain medications. Patients with an altered mental status (AMS) are identified either through a secondary impression of AMS or as having a charted Glasgow Coma Scale (GCS) of <14. Next, patients with allergies to Ketorolac, Fentanyl, Ketamine, Morphine, or "pain medications" are excluded. Finally, interfacility or scheduled ambulance transports are excluded in order to focus this analysis on patient interactions resulting from 911-initiated calls. The final analytic sample resulted in 18,000 PCRs, of which VFD contributed PCR data in 2513 cases.

[2] AMR provided treatment for the vast majority (98%) of requests for emergency care compared to VFD (14%) in the sample. Additionally, the AMR primary impression value is communicated to the emergency department upon patient drop off at the hospital and is more likely to direct the majority of patient treatment compared to the VFD primary impression.

Outcome Variables

As mentioned above, we measure treatment outcomes at EMS using three variables in this analysis: (1) completion of a pain screening; (2) pain medication administration; and (3) pain reduction. A pain screening procedure, if performed, is captured in the PCR as a value between 0, no pain, to 10, the most severe pain score. For the second variable, we create a dichotomous variable to indicate if any pain medications were administered (yes = 1; no = 0). EMS treatment protocols for the City of Vancouver include the following pain medications: ketorolac, fentanyl, ketamine, and nitrous oxide. While multiple pain medications were available to crews to use, 97% of the time fentanyl was used when a pain medication was administered which limited our ability to analyze differences in the use of different pain medications. For this reason, only fentanyl administration was examined in this analysis. Pain reduction is the final outcome variable of interest. Most patients who received a pain screening received at least two pain scores (98% of patients), allowing for two treatment outcome variables to be created. Based on this information, a variable was created indicating if a patient had a change in their pain score by comparing the beginning pain score to the ending pain score. PCRs with a positive change in pain scores were designated as a pain increase, negative values were designated as a pain decrease, and no change in pain scores were assigned a no change in pain value.

Independent Variable

Our independent variable in this study is obesity status of the patient. Determining obesity status using medical chart data is conventionally calculated using the Body Mass Index (BMI) formula (kg/m^2), incorporating an individual's height and weight data. However, PCR data consistently captures patient weight, but EMS crews do not chart patient height data. To arrive at height data, we use average height data by race and gender using a nationally representative sample from the National Health and Nutrition Examination Surveys (Fryar et al., 2018). Once BMI values were calculated, we categorized cases into not obese (BMI < 30), obese (BMI 30–39), and severely obese (BMI 40 and above) groupings for analysis.

Control Variables

The control variables considered in this analysis include both sociodemographic and clinical variables that may confound the relationship between the primary and outcome variables of interest.

The sociodemographic variables used as controls include patient race, patient gender, patient age, and the patient's insurance status. A single race value was derived for each PCR after evaluating the charted race values from both the AMR and VFD PCRs resulting in the following race categories: White, Black, Asian, Hispanic, Other, Unknown, and "Discordant". The "Other" race category includes "American Indian", "Arab or Middle Eastern", "Native Hawaiian", "Pacific Islander", and "Other Race". The "Discordant" race category included 23 PCRs (0.1% of the total sample) where VFD and AMR charted race values that were in direct and specific conflict (e.g., if, for a single call, one record indicated White and the other record indicated Black). In cases where a specific race value (e.g., Asian or Black) was in conflict with a race value of "other" or "unknown" the more specific race value was maintained.

Patient gender is captured as a binary value (e.g., male, female) in both AMR and VFD datasets. When a null value exists in one dataset and a non-null value in the other, the non-null value was used in the analysis. Where gender values are in direct conflict between datasets, a new "discordant gender" value was created.

Patient age is captured as a continuous variable, expressed in years, in both datasets. When a null value is provided in one dataset and a non-null value in the other, the non-null value was used in the analysis. When both datasets had a patient age value that is not in agreement and is less than 10 years apart, an average of the two values was calculated and used in the analysis. When both datasets have a patient age value that is not in agreement and is greater than 10 years apart, the open text narrative field in each PCR was examined for indications of the correct age. Where the correct age could not be confidently determined, a 'discordant age' value was imputed and treated as missing in the analysis.

Additionally, this analysis uses the patient's health insurance status as a proxy for the patient's socio-economic status (SES). Patient insurance information is captured in an open text field in AMR PCRs that allowed for multiple entries. Each PCR was assigned a single insurance status category based on the patient's 'highest' level of insurance in the following priority order: Private, Medicare, Medicaid, Other Government, No Insurance, and Unknown insurance.

Several clinical variables were used as controls. First, all 30 unique subcategory values within 'traumatic' and 'atraumatic' primary impression values were utilized in the models for each outcome measure analyzed. Primary impressions represent the EMS provider's working diagnosis of the patient's condition. Next, a dichotomous variable was created to document if a pain assessment was performed (1) or not (0) for each case and was used on the models investigating pain medication, and pain reduction outcome variables. Finally, since treatment is expected to vary by the patient's pain level, the patient's first documented pain score (0–10) was incorporated as 11 distinct dichotomous variables, one for each pain score value.

Results

Patient Characteristics

First, we present social/demographic characteristics of patients. As illustrated in Table 14.1, the mean age of EMS patients is 61, and female and white patients with non-private insurance who experienced traumatic

Table 14.1 Demographic characteristics of PCR data by patient weight

	Total		Not Obese (BMI < 30)		Obese (BMI 30–39)		Severely Obese (BMI > 39)		
	n		%	n	%	n	%	n	sig
Total	18,000		67%	11,987	23%	4220	10%	1793	–
Age, y (mean, SD)	61 (22)		62 (24)		58 (20)		56 (17)		0.000
Gender									
Male	43.2%	7769	43.6%	5223	46.6%	1965	32.4%	581	0.000
Female	56.8%	10,231	56.4%	6764	53.4%	2255	67.6%	1212	0.000
Race									
White	81.4%	14,656	83.0%	9944	78.2%	3300	78.8%	1412	0.000
Black	2.9%	519	2.4%	282	3.2%	133	5.8%	104	0.000
Asian	1.3%	226	1.6%	191	0.6%	26	0.5%	9	0.000
Hispanic	3.4%	609	3.0%	358	4.3%	182	3.8%	69	0.000
Other	10.4%	1875	9.5%	1142	13.0%	550	10.2%	183	0.000
Unknown	0.6%	115	0.6%	70	0.7%	29	0.9%	16	0.157
Insurance									
Private	19.3%	3475	18.4%	2206	21.6%	910	20.0%	359	0.000
Medicare	26.1%	4703	27.5%	3292	23.2%	978	24.1%	433	0.000
Medicaid	13.2%	2374	11.9%	1425	14.1%	595	19.7%	354	0.000
Other Gov't	1.8%	330	1.8%	211	2.2%	94	1.4%	25	0.052
No Insurance	20.9%	3753	21.4%	2570	20.5%	867	17.6%	316	0.001
Unknown	18.7%	3365	19.0%	2283	18.4%	776	17.1%	306	0.113
Primary Impressions									
Traumatic Injury	59.3%	10,680	61.7%	7391	56.7%	2392	50.0%	897	0.000
Abdominal Pain	18.4%	3311	17.8%	2132	17.8%	753	23.8%	426	0.000
Back or Body Pain	18.2%	3277	16.5%	1975	21.1%	890	23.0%	412	0.000
Pain Management	4.1%	732	4.1%	489	4.4%	185	3.2%	58	0.118

injury are found to be more common users of EMS, compared to male, non-white patients with private insurance who had acute pain, respectively. Additionally, the characteristics differ by obesity status. For example, compared to patients without obesity, the mean age of patients with severe obesity in this sample was younger (56 vs 62). Also, patients with severe obesity had higher proportions of female patients (68% vs 56%), Black patients (5.8% vs 2.4%), and Hispanic patients (3.8% vs 3.0%), than those without obesity. Patients with severe obesity also had smaller proportions of cases with Medicare or No Insurance, and higher proportions of patients with Private or Medicaid health insurance when compared to patients without obesity.

Next, Table 14.2 shows unadjusted associations between obesity status and treatment outcomes. As shown in Table 14.2, the proportion of patients who received a pain screening is higher among those with obesity or severe obesity, compared to those without obesity (72%, 75%, and 67%, respectively).

Additionally, a larger proportion of patients with obesity or severe obesity reported being in severe pain (pain score of 7–10) when compared to non-obese patients (57%, 63%, and 52%, respectively). Further, both obese and severely obese patients received a higher average total dose of opioid pain medications (115 and 114 mcg compared to 104 mcg). However, it is worth noting that while the average difference of 10–11 mcg represents a statistically significant difference, it has minimal clinical significance. Finally, in looking at changes from initial pain scores to pain scores after EMS treatments, the majority of the sample (66%) reported no change in pain outcomes, 7% reported worsening pain, and 31% reported experiencing a reduction in pain; this self-reported pain change does not

Table 14.2 Clinical characteristics of PCR data by patient weight

	Total		Not Obese (BMI < 30)		Obese (BMI 30–39)		Severely Obese (BMI > 39)		
	n		%	n	%	n	%	n	sig
Total	18,000		67%	11,987	23%	4220	10%	1793	0.000
Patients without Pain Screening	30.7%	5528	32.6%	3910	27.7%	1171	24.9%	447	0.000
Patients with Pain Screening	69.3%	12,472	67.4%	8077	72.3%	3049	75.1%	1346	0.000
No pain (0)	9.0%	1119	10.6%	856	6.7%	203	4.5%	60	0.000
Mild pain (1–3)	13.3%	1655	14.1%	1141	12.8%	389	9.3%	125	0.002
Moderate pain (4–6)	23.4%	2915	23.4%	1892	23.4%	714	23.0%	309	0.103
Severe pain (7–10)	54.4%	6783	51.9%	4188	57.2%	1743	63.3%	852	0.000
Pain Medication Admin Rate Overall (n = 18,000)	19.1%	3434	18.0%	2162	21.3%	900	20.7%	372	0.000
Patients without pain screening (n = 5528)	5.6%	312	5.5%	217	6.1%	72	4.9%	22	0.489
Patients with pain screening (n = 12,472)	25.0%	3122	24.1%	1945	27.2%	828	26.0%	350	0.003
Total Fentanyl Dose Admin, mcg (mean, SD)[a]	107 (54)		104 (53)		113 (54)		115 (57)		0.000
Patients without pain screening	101 (51)		99 (51)		103 (53)		106 (51)		0.784
Patients with pain screening	108 (54)		104 (53)		114 (54)		115 (57)		0.000
Change in Pain Scores (n = 12,472)									
Worsening	6.6%	822	6.5%	526	6.3%	193	7.7%	103	0.237
No change	62.1%	7749	62.8%	5072	61.4%	1873	59.7%	804	0.066
Pain reduction	31.3%	3901	30.7%	2479	32.2%	983	32.6%	439	0.155
Pain reduction 10–19%	5.2%	652	5.1%	409	5.0%	152	6.8%	91	0.028
Pain reduction 20–29%	6.5%	813	6.3%	508	7.1%	215	6.7%	90	0.336
Pain reduction 30–39%	4.0%	495	3.7%	297	4.4%	135	4.7%	63	0.071
Pain reduction 40–49%	2.6%	325	2.7%	215	2.7%	82	2.1%	28	0.438
Pain reduction 50–59%	4.0%	499	3.8%	309	4.4%	134	4.2%	56	0.374
Pain reduction 60–69%	2.7%	340	2.8%	223	2.4%	73	3.3%	44	0.247
Pain reduction 70–79%	1.9%	241	1.9%	153	2.1%	63	1.9%	25	0.823
Pain reduction 80–89%	1.5%	185	1.6%	127	1.3%	41	1.3%	17	0.526
Pain Reduction 90–99%	0.3%	39	0.3%	23	0.4%	12	0.3%	4	0.653
Pain reduction 100%	2.5%	312	2.7%	215	2.5%	76	1.6%	21	0.057

[a]only fentanyl was included as 97% of patients that received pain meds received fentanyl

appear to differ by the patient's obesity status. In the next section, we present results from logistic regression models.

Pain Screening Results

For our first treatment outcome, pain screening, we present results of the association of obesity status with pain screening in Table 14.3.

The results of Model 1, which adjusts for patient race, gender, age, health insurance status, primary impression, and incident year, indicate that compared to patients who are not obese, the odds of receiving a pain screening from EMS is higher for patients with obesity (OR 1.24, $p < .001$), or severe obesity (OR 1.29, $p < .001$). Model 2 includes the interaction term between gender and obesity status using the same adjustments as in Model 1, and the results show that while the odds of receiving a pain screening is higher for patients with obesity compared to patients without obesity, the "obesity advantage" appears attenuated for female patients (OR 0.76,

Table 14.3 Multivariable logistic regression of obesity status on pain screening

	Model 1[a]		Model 2[a]	
Regressor	B	OR	B	OR
Not Obese				
Obese (BMI 30–39)	0.22	1.24***	0.36	1.44***
Severely Obese (BMI > 39)	0.25	1.29***	0.39	1.47***
Female	0.19	1.20***	0.26	1.30***
Female X Obese			−0.27	0.76**
Female X Severely Obese			−0.22	0.81
Constant	0.812		0.812	
Number of Cases	18,000		18,000	
-2 log likelihood	20,411		20,399	
Pseudo R2 (Nagelkerke)	0.135		0.135	

Note: *B* logistic regression coefficient and *OR* odds ratio
$*p < .05$; $**p < .01$; $***p < .001$
[a]Model adjusts for: patient race, patient gender, patient age, patient health insurance, primary impression, and incident year

Table 14.4 Multivariable logistic regression of obesity status on pain medication administration

	Model 1[a]		Model 2[a]	
Regressor	B	OR	B	OR
Not Obese				
Obese (BMI 30–39)	0.11	1.11*	0.23	1.25**
Severely Obese (BMI > 39)	−0.01	0.99	0.26	1.29*
Female	0.05	1.06	0.15	1.16**
Female X Obese			−0.21	0.81*
Female X Severely Obese			−0.41	0.67**
Constant	−1.445		−1.445	
Number of Cases	18,000		18,000	
-2 log likelihood	14,367		14,357	
Pseudo R2 (Nagelkerke)	0.260		0.261	

Note: *B* logistic regression coefficient and *OR* odds ratio
$*p < .05$; $**p < .01$; $***p < .001$
[a]Adjusts for: patient race, patient gender, patient age, patient health insurance, primary impression, pain screening, initial pain score, and incident year

$p < .01$). However, this 'female disadvantage' was not observed among patients with severe obesity.

Pain Medication Results

Next, Table 14.4 shows the results of the logistic regression models examining the relationship between obesity status and pain medication administration.

Similar to the models for the first outcome, Model 1 in Table 14.4 adjusts for patient race, gender, age, health insurance status, primary impression, pain screening, pain scores, and incident year. The results indicate that the odds of receiving pain medication are higher among patients with obesity (OR 11%, $p < .01$).[3] Model 2 presents the results of our interaction analysis between gender and obesity status using the same adjustments as in Model 1. While there is an advantage in receiving pain medications for females (OR 1.16, $p < .01$) this advantage is eliminated for females who have obesity (OR 0.81, $p < .05$) and even more severely

[3] Model estimates were also run on sub-populations with mild (1–3), moderate (4–6), or severe pain (7–10) scores with no significant findings.

Table 14.5 Multivariable multinomial regression of obesity status on pain outcomes

Regressor	Model 1[a] Increased pain B	OR	Decreased Pain B	OR	Model 2[a] Increased pain B	OR	Decreased Pain B	OR
Not Obese								
Obese (BMI 30–39)	0.00	1.01	−0.07	0.94	−0.05	0.96	0.09	1.10
Severely Obese (BMI > 39)	0.32	1.38*	−0.25	0.96	0.55	1.73**	0.15	1.17
Female	0.00	1.00	0.01	1.01	0.02	1.02	0.11	1.12
Female X Obese					0.10	1.10	−0.28	0.75**
Female X Severely Obese					−0.36	0.70	−0.28	0.76
Number of Cases	12,472				12,472			
-2 log likelihood	15,726				15,716			
Pseudo R2 (Nagelkerke)	0.404				0.405			

Note: *B* regression coefficient and *OR* odds ratio
*$p < .05$; **$p < .01$; ***$p < .001$
[a]Adjusts for: patient race, patient gender, patient age, patient health insurance, primary impression, pain screening, initial pain score, pain medication administration, and incident year

reduced for females who have severely obesity (OR 0.67, $p < .01$); while males with obesity or severe obesity receive a benefit, i.e., increased likelihood of receiving pain medications.

Pain Outcome Results

Finally, we present two multinomial logistic regression models (Table 14.5) exploring the relationship obesity status has on the patient's pain outcome (increased pain, no change, or decreased pain). Model 1 results indicates that after adjusting for patient race, gender, age, health insurance status, primary impression, pain screening, pain scores, incident year, and if pain medications were provided, patients with severe obesity are more likely to report an increase in pain levels (OR 1.38, $p < .01$) after EMS treatment. Model 2 presents the interaction results of gender and obesity status using the same adjustments as in model 1, and indicates that while females, overall, did not have evidence of an advantage or disadvantage in this outcome compared to men, women with obesity were more likely to report a reduction in pain (OR 0.75, $p < .01$) after their EMS encounter.

Discussion

Our results indicate several important findings. First, compared to patients without obesity, those with obesity who engage EMS services for painful conditions were more likely to receive a pain screening, report severe pain, and receive pain medications. Second, having obesity or severe obesity negated the advantage that female patients had in all outcome variables studied. We discuss our findings below.

Pain Screening

Counter to our first hypothesis, which predicted reduced likelihood of pain screening for patients with obesity, we observed that patients with obesity or severe obesity were *more* likely to receive a pain screening compared to patients without obesity. This finding was somewhat unexpected as it indicates an area of increased treatment, rather than undertreatment, which has been observed in other medical settings. When a pain screening was performed, patients with obesity and severe obesity were more likely to be in severe pain compared to those without obesity.

Assuming there are not significant differences in how patients with and without obesity experience pain, this is potentially suggestive of delays in health-seeking behavior. Indeed, studies in other areas of healthcare have found that patients with obesity are more likely to defer or skip their healthcare appointments (Amy et al., 2006; Bertakis & Azari, 2005; Lee & Pausé, 2016; Phelan et al., 2014a). Though we are unable to test this directly, it is possible this same utilization pattern, i.e. avoidance or delayed care, is taking place in EMS. Accordingly, patients with obesity may be more likely to engage EMS services for severe or emergent pain; the signs and symptoms of which may be more suggestive of someone in severe pain, encouraging EMS providers to complete a pain screening.

Pain Medications

Patients with obesity were more likely to receive pain medications, however patients with severe obesity were not, when compared to patients without obesity. This finding is also somewhat counter to our second hypothesis that obesity status would have a negative relationship with pain medication administration. These findings may be the result of several influences and interactions. First, given the higher-than-average obesity rate prevalent in the EMS workforce (80%) it is likely that an EMS provider with obesity provided patient treatments. The increased rate of patient and provider obesity concordance may provide a sense of solidarity and increased understanding that serves to influence or overcome the negative effects of obesity bias for obese patients but not for severely obese patients (Brice et al., 2019). While it's been demonstrated that physicians without obesity are more likely than physicians with obesity to more aggressively address obesity related treatments, to our knowledge the association has not been studied in EMS, and it's unclear if the painful conditions and corresponding treatment that instigated EMS service in these cases would be perceived as treatments related to obesity (Wells et al., 1984).

Further, when pain medications were provided, the amount of pain medication administered was clinically equivalent across obesity status. Importantly, the primary pain medication used by EMS providers in this sample of EMS interactions (fentanyl) has a total available dose determination based on the patient's weight (3 mcg/Kg), allowing for a larger dose for patients with obesity or severe obesity (Wittwer et al., 2018). However, the analysis indicates that EMS providers did not take advantage of the larger dosing range available to them. While fentanyl is lipophilic[4] its pharmacokinetic profile is believed to be unaffected by increased adipose tissue, thus current hospital-based recommendations suggest using a patients "ideal" body weight (versus actual body weight or lean body weight) to determine proper dosing (De Baerdemaeker et al., 2004). EMS treatment protocols used by the City of Vancouver do not indicate which patient weight to use, nor provide a recommendation on how best to determine "ideal" body weight when calculating maximum total dosing (Wittwer et al., 2018). Since a commonly understood side effect of administering excessive opioid pain medication is respiratory depression, this result may indicate EMS providers may be unwilling to provide additional opioid pain medications for patients with obesity and severe obesity as management of respiratory difficulties in these patients can be more difficult and have poorer outcomes compared to patients without obesity (Mafort et al., 2016). This represents an area of study that requires further investigation, both from the standpoint of best practices in pain medication administration on the basis of weight and implications for excess dosing in those with obesity.

Our findings further revealed gender discrepancies such that having obesity diminished the likelihood of receipt of pain medication in females. Prior studies have observed that women experience greater penalties related to

[4] Lipophilicity is the affinity of a drug for a lipid environment and has become a critical parameter in understanding how drugs are distributed, metabolized, and cleared once administered.

weight bias in medical settings. It is possible that this this is a manifestation of disparate treatment on the basis of gender. However, additional investigation is needed as it's unclear why this hesitancy may apply to women with obesity but not men with obesity.

Pain Outcomes

We predicted that improvements in pain levels, measured as the change in pain screening scores at the beginning and end of EMS interactions, would be reduced in patients with obesity. In other words, we expected less successful pain management based on prior work suggesting undertreatment in this group. Our hypothesis was not supported in patients with obesity; however, it was supported in patients with severe obesity as they were more likely to report an increase in their pain levels after receiving treatment from EMS crews when compared to patients without obesity. Interestingly, patients with obesity were more likely to receive a pain screening, be in more severe pain, and were more likely to receive pain medications, yet did not show evidence of having their pain reduced any more effectively when compared to patients without obesity. It is possible that the increased dosages were insufficient to address the severe pain found in patients with obesity (as described above). Similarly, patients with severe obesity were also more likely to receive a pain screening and be in severe pain; however, they did not have evidence of an increased likelihood of receiving pain medication, and logically were more likely to report increased pain levels after EMS interaction compared to patients without obesity.

Gender and Obesity in EMS Treatment

For each outcome variable reviewed, women were more disadvantaged by having obesity or severe obesity when compared to men. Regarding pain screening, women without obesity, compared to men without obesity, were more likely to receive a pain screening; however, having obesity eliminates this advantage for women while enhancing it for men. Similarly, women without obesity were more likely to receive pain medication, however having obesity or severe obesity eliminated this advantage for women while, again, enhancing it for men. Finally, regarding pain outcomes, there was no evidence indicating females overall experience different outcomes compared to men; however, obesity once again had a negative impact on women but not men. These findings suggest obesity bias has a gendered relationship which negatively affects women across all three outcomes in our study, consistent with other studies showing an increased penalty for women with obesity compared to men with obesity (Fikkan & Rothblum, 2012).

Limitations

This study has several limitations. First, because we sample PCRs from a single metropolitan area (Vancouver, Washington), our results might not be generalizable to EMS agencies in other locations, especially non-metropolitan areas, and thus applications of our results require cautions. However, these findings represent an important preliminary investigation into this issue and suggest the need for continuing regional and national investigations. Second, despite consolidating PCRs from AMR and VFD into a single event PCR, the unit of analysis in this dataset remains chart-based, rather than patient-based. Thus, we may have inadvertently included over-weight high-utilizer patients at a different rate than normal weight high-utilizer patients. Although frequent utilization of EMS is not common, EMS utilization rates for patients with obesity are unknown in this dataset. Perhaps more importantly, it is not clearly known whether patients with obesity are more likely to use EMS, compared to those without obesity. For these reasons, we are unable to determine whether and how this limitation may impact the results of the study. Third, it is unclear if the average height for patients used to calculate obesity status in our sample matches the national average height estimates. However, given the relatively large dataset used in this study, this limitation is not believed to be substantial. Finally, as has been described elsewhere, BMI is a relatively poor indicator for physical fitness. It is a crude measure simply based on height and weight, not accounting for the amount of body muscle. Thus, men are more likely to be counted as either overweight or obese when they have a more muscular build (Roehling, 2012). However, despite this measurement caveat, a consistent association between BMI and health outcomes has been reported in the literature (Lee & Pausé, 2016). Moreover, given that this potential overcount of muscular men as obese may underestimate the influence of being obese on treatment outcomes, our findings here should be considered as conservative estimates, serving as an important step toward disentangling the complex interactions between health providers and obese patients.

Implications of the Findings and Future Directions

Our findings have several important implications. First, our results offer an important advancement in the study of weight-bias impacts on medical treatment in an understudied context of medicine. Little is known about how weight-related issues manifest in EMS treatment, and our study offers important insights in this area. Importantly, we observed that pain screenings were more likely for patients with obesity. This pattern of treatment suggests a few possibilities worthy of further investigation. Future work should examine the extent to which concordance in patient and provider obesity status improves treatment outcomes. Additionally, avoidance and delayed health-seeking behaviors among those with obesity may lead them to be more likely to utilize EMS for care when symptoms become so severe they cannot be ignored. If this is the case, EMS represents an important source of care for those with obesity and additional investigation is needed to develop best practices in standards of care. This would also seem to represent an ideal site for intervention and educational strategies designed to reduce bias in health settings.

Numerous studies have documented weight bias in medical settings, but few have examined whether this translates into differential practices among providers. Interestingly, we observed that obesity increased the likelihood of both pain screening and receipt of pain medication (though the amount was clinically minor) in the EMS setting. This seems especially noteworthy given that time constraints have been shown to increase stereotyping and worsen care. EMS interactions are arguably time-compressed, yet, our findings suggest that EMS providers may be more sensitive to or aware of the needs of patients with obesity. More work is needed to determine the extent to which this may be the case as well as the mechanisms underlying such an association. Next, these findings also reinforce the importance of an intersectional analysis to improve the understanding of the gendered nature of the effects of obesity stigma. Women were disadvantaged in all outcomes. Though we cannot directly test whether bias is the underlying mechanism, it is a likely contributor given prior studies suggesting greater penalties for women with obesity across various domains. Further investigation is needed to determine why females with obesity are disadvantaged in this context. We hope our results bring awareness to the EMS community regarding the role of obesity bias, especially for women, in influencing EMS treatments. As rates of obesity continue to increase in the general population, particularly in geographic areas with already high rates of obesity, such as the southeastern US, understanding and mitigating EMS obesity treatment disparities is critical for EMS agencies. Additionally, while our study focused on pain management, it is possible that obesity bias may negatively impacts other emergency medical conditions. Finally, our results can be used to inform EMS agencies to create an opportunity to better train and educate health providers in an effort to mitigate treatment disparities.

Going forward, we suggest several areas for future research. First, work is needed to better understand EMS utilization patterns and whether patients with obesity use EMS more often, and if so under what conditions. Second, a more comprehensive understanding of which health conditions, in addition to pain management, are susceptible to substandard care among women with obesity is needed. Without awareness and visibility to the nature of the problem, mitigation of the harmful effects will be less effective. Finally, further exploration of how obesity bias impacts medical treatment disparities for women across sociodemographic subgroups (e.g., race/ethnicity and age) will be important to develop a more fulsome understanding of opportunities to reduce disparities and increase the quality of care for patients.

Conclusion

Obesity status is associated with improvements in some areas of EMS treatment (i.e., pain screening, and pain medication administration). This unexpected finding may suggest that EMS is a unique medical setting in which previously observed patterns of undertreatment for those with obesity are not applicable. It is possible this is attributable to a pattern of delayed care and subsequently emergent/extreme pain among those with obesity, which cannot be ignored. It is also possible that EMS providers are less likely to engage in victim blaming or stereotyping than other medical providers, perhaps due to an increased obesity prevalence in the EMS workforce. These interesting possibilities are worthy of continued investigation, and subsequent work should attempt to confirm similar patterns in other outcomes and directly examine EMS provider attitudes surrounding obesity. If EMS providers are engaging in practices that improve outcomes for those with obesity, it is necessary to determine why and how this occurs. On the other hand, an intersectional analysis shows there is a consistent negative impact on women compared to men across all studied outcomes, and the role of bias may well be impactful in this context. Accordingly, efforts should be made to ensure the highest standard of care for all stigmatized groups.

References

Amy, N. K., Aalborg, A., Lyons, P., & Keranen, L. (2006). Barriers to routine gynecological cancer screening for white and African-American obese women. *International Journal of Obesity, 30*(1), 147–155.

Anderson, C., Peterson, C. B., Fletcher, L., Mitchell, J. E., Thuras, P., & Crow, S. J. (2001). Weight loss and gender: An examination of physician attitudes. *Obesity Research, 9*(4), 257–263.

Baerdemaeker, D., Luc, E. C., Mortier, E. P., & Struys, M. M. R. F. (2004). Pharmacokinetics in obese patients. *Continuing Education in Anesthesia, Critical Care and Pain, 4*(5), 152–155.

Bertakis, K. D., & Azari, R. (2005). The impact of obesity on primary care visits. *Obesity Research, 13*(9), 1615–1623.

Bloche, M. G. (2001). Race and discretion in American medicine. *Yale Journal of Health Policy, Law, and Ethics, 1*, 95–131.

Brice, J. H., Cyr, J. M., Hnat, A. T., Wei, T. L., Principe, S., Thead, S. E., Delbridge, T. R., Winslow, J. E., Studnek, J. R., Fernandez, A. R., & Forrest, E. E. (2019). Assessment of key health and wellness indicators among North Carolina emergency medical service providers. *Prehospital Emergency Care: Official Journal of the National Association of EMS Physicians and the National Association of State EMS Directors, 23*(2), 179–186.

Brown, I., Thompson, J., Tod, A., & Jones, G. (2006). Primary care support for tackling obesity: A qualitative study of the perceptions of obese patients. *British Journal of General Practice, 56*(530), 666–672.

Budd, G. M., Mariotti, M., Graff, D., & Falkenstein, K. (2009). Health care professionals' attitudes about obesity: An integrative review. *Applied Nursing Research, 24*, 127–137.

Burgess, D. J. (2010). Are providers more likely to contribute to healthcare disparities under high levels of cognitive load? How features of the healthcare setting may lead to biases in medical decision making." *Medical Decision Making, 30*(2), 246–57.

Busetto, L., Bettini, S., Fabris, R., Serra, R., Pra, C. D., Maffei, P., Rossato, M., Fioretto, P., & Vettor, R. (2020). Obesity and COVID-19: An Italian snapshot. *Obesity, 28*(9), 1600–1605.

Calle, E. E., Thun, M. J., Petrelli, J. M., Rodriguez, C., & Helath, C. W. (1999). Body-mass index and mortality in a prospective cohort of U.S. adults. *New England Journal Medicine, 341*(15), 1097–1105.

Canning, H., & Mayer, J. (1966). Obesity — Its possible effect on college acceptance. *New England Journal of Medicine, 275*(21), 1172–1174.

Crandall, C. S. (1991). Do heavy-weight students have more difficulty paying for college? *Personality and Social Psychology Bulletin, 17*(6), 606–611.

Dejong, W. (1980). The stigma of obesity : The consequences of naive assumptions concerning the causes of physical deviance. *Journal of Health and Social Behavior, 21*(1), 75–87.

Di Angelantonio, E., Bhupathiraju, S. N., Wormser, D., Gao, P., Kaptoge, S., de Gonzalez, A. B., Cairns, B. J., Huxley, R., Jackson, C. L., Joshy, G., Lewington, S., Manson, J. A. E., Murphy, N., Patel, A. V., Samet, J. M., Woodward, M., Zheng, W., Zhou, M., Bansal, N., et al. (2016). Body-mass index and all-cause mortality: Individual-participant-data meta-analysis of 239 prospective studies in four continents. *The Lancet, 388*(10046), 776–786.

Fikkan, J. L., & Rothblum, E. D. (2012). Is fat a feminist issue? Exploring the gendered nature of weight bias. *Sex Roles, 66*(9–10), 575–592.

Fryar, C. D., Carroll, M. D., & Ogden, C. L. (2016). Prevalence of overweight, obesity, and extreme obesity among adults aged 20 and over: United States, 1960–1962 through 2013–2014. *Health E-Stats*, 1–6.

Fryar, C. D., Kruszon-Moran, D., Qiuping, G., & Ogden, C. L. (2018). Mean body weight, height, waist circumference, and body mass index among adults: United States, 1999–2000 through 2015–2016. *National Health Statistics Reports, 2018*(122), 1999–2000.

Fuoco, M. A. (2010). As obesity increases, so does challenge to EMS. *Pittsburg Post-Gazette*, 2–6.

Hales, C. M., Fryar, C. D., Carroll, M. D., Freedman, D. S., & Ogden, C. L. (2018). Trends in obesity and severe obesity prevalence in US youth and adults by sex and age, 2007–2008 to 2015–2016. *JAMA, 319*(16), 1723–1725.

Hebl, M. R., Xu, J., & Mason, M. F. (2003). Weighing the care: Patients' perceptions of physician care as a function of gender and weight. *International Journal of Obesity, 27*(2), 269–275.

Hewes, H. A., Mengtao, D., Clay Mann, N., Baca, T., & Taillac, P. (2017). Prehospital pain management: Disparity by age and race. *Prehospital Emergency Care, 3127*(October), 1–9.

Kennel, J., Withers, E., Parsons, N., & Woo, H. (2019). Racial/ethnic disparities in pain treatment: Evidence from oregon emergency medical services agencies. *Medical Care* (September):1–6.

Lee, J. A., & Pausé, C. J. (2016). Stigma in practice: barriers to health for fat women. *Frontiers in Psychology, 7*(Dec), 2063.

Link, B. G., & Phelan, J. C. (2001). Conceptualizing stigma. *Annual Review of Sociology, 27*, 363–385.

Mafort, T. T., Rufino, R., Costa, C. H., & Lopes, A. J. (2016). Obesity: Systemic and pulmonary complications, biochemical abnormalities, and impairment of lung function. *Multidisciplinary Respiratory Medicine, 11*(1), 1–11.

Manson, J. E., Willett, W. C., Stampfer, M. J., Colditz, G. A., Hunter, D. J., Hankinson, S. E., Hennekens, C. H., & Speizer, F. E. (1995). Body weight and mortality among women. *The New England Journal of Medicine, 333*(11), 677–685.

Mort, E. A., Weissman, J. S., & Epstein, A. M. (1994). Physician discretion and racial variation in the use of surgical procedures. *Archive of Internal Medicine, 154*, 761–767.

Phelan, J. C., Lucas, J. W., Ridgeway, C. L., & Taylor, C. J. (2014a). Stigma, status, and population health. *Social Science and Medicine, 103*, 15–23.

Phelan, S. M., Clinic, M., Dovidio, J. F., Haven, N., Puhl, R. M., Haven, N., Burgess, D. J., Nelson, D. B., Yeazel, M. W., Hardeman, R., Perry, S., Haven, N., Van Ryn, M., & Clinic, M. (2014b). Implicit and explicit weight bias in a national sample of 4732 medical students: The medical student CHANGES study. *Obesity, 22*(4), 1201–1208.

Phelan, S. M., Burgess, D. J., Yeazel, M. W., Hellerstedt, W. L., Griffin, J. M., & van Ryn, M. (2015). Impact of weight bias and stigma on quality of care and outcomes for patients with obesity. *Obesity Reviews, 16*(4), 319–326.

Puhl, R. M., & Brownell, K. D. (2006). Confronting and coping with weight stigma: An investigation of overweight and obese adults. *Obesity, 14*(10), 1802–1815.

Puhl, R. M., & Heuer, C. A. (2009). The stigma of obesity: A review and update. *Obesity, 17*(5), 941–964.

Puhl, R. M., & Heuer, C. A. (2010). Obesity stigma: Important considerations for public health. *American Journal of Public Health, 100*(6), 1019–1028.

Roehling, P. V. (2012). Fat is a feminist issue, but it is complicated: Commentary on Fikkan and Rothblum. *Sex Roles, 66*(9–10), 593–599.

Rubenstein, A. H. (2005). Obesity: A modern epidemic. *Transactions of the American Clinical and Climatological Association, 116*(1), 103–113.

Rubino, F., Puhl, R. M., Cummings, D. E., Eckel, R. H., Ryan, D. H., Mechanick, J. I., Nadglowski, J., Salas, X. R., Schauer, P. R., Twenefour, D., Apovian, C. M., Aronne, L. J., Batterham, R. L., Berthoud, H. R., Boza, C., Busetto, L., Dicker, D., De Groot, M., Eisenberg, D., et al. (2020). Joint international consensus statement for ending stigma of obesity. *Nature Medicine, 26*(4), 485–497.

Sanchis-Gomer, F., Lavie, C. J., Mehra, M. R., Henry, B. M., & Lippi, G. (2020). Obesity and outcomes in COVID-19: When an epidemic and pandemic collide. *Mayo Clinic Proceedings, 95*(7), 1445–1453.

Schulte, P. A., Wagner, G. R., Ostry, A., Blanciforti, L. A., Cutlip, R. G., Krajnak, K. M., Luster, M., Munson, A. E., O'Callaghan, J. P., Parks, C. G., Simeonova, P. P., & Miller, D. B. (2007). Work, obesity, and occupational safety and health. *American Journal of Public Health, 97*(3), 428–436.

Schwartz, M. B., O'Neal Chambliss, H., Brownell, K. D., Blair, S. N., & Billington, C. (2003). Weight bias among health professionals specializing in obesity. *Obesity Research, 11*(9), 1033–1039.

Smedley, B., Stith, A. Y., & Nelson, A. R. (Eds). (2003). *Unequal treatment: Confronting racial and ethnic disparities in health care*. The National Academies Press.

Teachman, B. A., & Brownell, K. D. (2001). Implicit anti-fat bias among health professionals: Is anyone immune? *International Journal of Obesity, 25*(10), 1525–1531.

Todd, K. H., Deaton, C., D'adamo, A. P., & Goe, L. (1999). Ethnicity and analgesic practice. *Annals of Emergency Medicine, 35*(1), 11–16.

Visscher, T. L. S., & Seidell, J. C. (2001). The public health impact of obesity. *Annual Review of Public Health, 22*, 355–375.

Wells, K. B., Lewis, C. E., Leake, B., & Jr Ware, J. E. (1984). Do physicians preach what they practice? A study of physicians' health habits and counseling practices. *JAMA, 252*(20), 2846–2848.

Wittwer, L. K., Macht, M., Muhr, M., Simukka, E., Ford, S., Jensen, J., Free, C., & Boyce, D.. (2018). SW region patient care protocols – Clark county EMS.

Part IV

Obesity in Sexual Minority Populations

Only recently have demographers begun to examine the connections between sexual orientation and health. Efforts in this area have traditionally been hampered by a lack of high-quality scientific data. However, increased consistency in the measurement of sexual orientation along with greater availability of representative data has allowed for expanded investigation of health-specific outcomes in sexual gender minority (SGM) populations. Accordingly, growing efforts to document and understand sexual minority health are underway. But, notable gaps exist in our understanding of the patterns and mechanisms that explain poorer health outcomes in some of these groups. With respect to overweight and obesity in sexual minorities, the research in this area has been relatively limited and often inconsistent in nature.

To add to what is known about the relationships between overweight and obesity among sexual minorities, the chapters in this section summarize the conceptual issues and concerns surrounding the measurement of sex, gender identity, and sexual orientation. Each offers a review of relevant research on body weight in a specific sexual minority population. In addition, each undertakes analyses using recent data to describe current patterns of overweight and obesity prevalence.

Poston, Engin and Cagatay analyze in Chap. 15 the association between obesity and asexuality. Most human sexuality research has focused on sexuals, with comparatively little attention directed to asexuals. But in recent decades, asexuality is gaining increased attention among social scientists and in the popular media as a separate and distinct sexual orientation. Poston and his colleagues reviewed the research literature and also analyzed U.S. data. They found that the prevalence of obesity is higher for asexual women compared to their sexual and heterosexual counterparts, but the opposite occurs for male asexuals. Their research is an important addition to the body of literature about the relationship between sexual minority status and overweight and obesity.

Baker-Hughes and Poston began Chap. 16 on gay males by asking if gay men are more fit than straight men. Their review of the literature focusing on obesity and overweight among gay and straight males indicated somewhat of a tendency for gay men to be less overweight and less obese than straight men, and thus more fit. The authors then showed that much of the research on male sexuality conceptualizes the phenomenon in terms of three different dimensions, namely, sexual behavior, sexual attraction, and sexual self-identification. Their analyses of U.S. data followed this approach. Using all three dimensions of sexuality one at a time, Baker-Hughes and Poston found that gay males are less likely to be characterized by overweight or obesity than are straight males.

In Chap. 17, Walther and Poston focused on obesity trends and patterns among lesbians and straight women. Some of the research they reviewed found that lesbians appear to have a higher prevalence of obesity than heterosexual women, while other research found little or no relationship. Their empirical analyses of U.S. data also conceptualized sexuality in terms of the three dimensions mentioned above. They found that for the most part lesbians are not significantly different from straight females with respect to obesity and/or overweight. The results of their analyses are not inconsistent with the mixed literature reviewed in their chapter.

In Chap. 18, Davis reviewed the literature on obesity and bisexuality. She first noted that the inclusion of bisexuals in obesity research is relatively new. But she found that for the most part obesity is higher in bisexual females and lesbians compared to heterosexual females, with a slightly elevated risk in lesbians compared to bisexual women. Conversely, the available literature on bisexual males has mixed results. Her empirical analyses of U.S. data are consistent with the research observed in the literature. She found that bisexual women (and lesbians) have a somewhat elevated risk of obesity compared to straight women, and she found the opposite association, and sometimes no association, among bisexual men compared to straight men.

Finally, in Chap. 19, Davis, Compton and Farris investigated trends in obesity among transgendered and cisgendered persons. They reported that the consensus in the literature is that while sexual minorities may have weight-related issues, analyses of the relationships between gender identity and weight are limited. Their examination of the limited literature found that the transgendered are more likely to be food insecure, and this seems to be intensified by the intersectionality of other socioeconomic conditions. Food insecurity, for instance, seems to be more pronounced in transgendered persons of color. Davis and her colleagues than analyzed current U.S. data on obesity and gender identification and found few significant differences in obesity among the three transgendered categories of male to female, female to male, and gender nonbinary, although greater percentages of trans males to females are underweight. They noted that ongoing work is clearly needed to investigate further the extent to which transgender individuals experience weight-related issues.

Obesity Prevalence and Trends in the Asexual and Sexual Populations

15

Dudley L. Poston, Jr., Ceylan Engin, and Yağmur Çağatay

Introduction

This chapter examines the prevalence and distribution of obesity among asexuals and sexuals. Most human sexuality research has focused on sexuals, with comparatively little attention directed to asexuals. Prior work has mainly examined the behavior and characteristics of sexuals, i.e., heterosexuals and homosexuals and bisexuals (Laumann et al., 1994; Black et al., 2003; Baumle et al., 2009; Baumle & Poston, 2011). But the literature reveals that in terms of their sexuality, some individuals do not fall clearly into the heterosexual, homosexual, or bisexual categories. This is a significant oversight as a non-trivial number of persons reports that they are not engaging in sexual activity, and/or that they experience no sexual desire, and/or that they self-identify as asexual (Laumann et al., 1994; Bogaert, 2004, 2012, 2015; Poston & Baumle, 2006, 2010). Moreover, asexuality is gaining increasing attention in the popular media as a separate and distinct sexual orientation (Decker, 2014; Dahl, 2015).

D. L. Poston, Jr. (✉)
Department of Sociology, Texas A & M University, College Station, TX, USA
e-mail: d-poston@tamu.edu

C. Engin
Boğazici University, Istanbul, Turkey

Y. Çağatay
Department of Sociology, Boğazici University, Istanbul, Turkey

Despite the growing attention to the presence of asexuality, we know comparatively little about the prevalence of obesity in the asexual and sexual populations. This chapter addresses this void and endeavors to develop some generalizable information about the prevalence of obesity among asexuals and the extent to which this may be similar to, or different from, its prevalence among sexuals.

We first discuss the conceptualization of sexuality and asexuality because there are several different ways to conceptualize, define and measure the two. We next focus specifically on asexuality, conceptualizing and discussing it according to each of three dimensions of sexual behavior, sexual attraction, and sexual self-identification. We next present a review of the limited literature about obesity in the asexual and sexual populations. Next, to supplement existing work, we offer separate empirical analyses for females and for males of the association between overweight/obesity and asexuality. We conclude with some recommendations for ongoing work in this area.

Throughout the chapter, we use people-first language to describe obesity and its distribution. We mainly use the phrase "people with obesity" instead of the term "obese people"; this indicates the "status (of obesity) as a medical condition and avoids the perpetuation of weight bias" (Garcia-Alexander, 2019: 859; Palad & Stanford, 2018).

G. Garcia-Alexander, D. L. Poston, Jr. (eds.), *International Handbook of the Demography of Obesity*, International Handbooks of Population 12, https://doi.org/10.1007/978-3-031-10936-2_15

Conceptualizing Sexuality and Asexuality

Most of the social science literature conceptualizes sexual orientation with one of two perspectives or approaches, or a combination thereof: essentialism and social constructionism. The essentialist view is one of dimorphism. Founded in biology, it argues that there is an essential biological or psychological characteristic or attribute that is common to all persons and is believed to be a fundamental drive or trait that establishes a person's inclusion into, or not into, one of the sexual categories of heterosexual, homosexual, bisexual or asexual (Laumann et al., 1994: 285; Baumle et al., 2009: 19–20). Heterosexuals are sexually oriented toward persons of the opposite sex, homosexuals toward persons of the same sex, and bisexuals toward persons of both sexes; asexuals are not sexually oriented to any persons. The essentialist view states that a person is designated, or not designated, as homosexual or as heterosexual or as bisexual or as asexual. A binary distinction is made between one who is in that category and one who is not.

The social constructionist view, on the other hand, counters and critiques the essentialist approach. For instance, with regard to heterosexuality and homosexuality, social constructionism argues against the notion of binary categories (Foucault, 1978; Butler, 1990; Seidman, 1996) and suggests that sexual orientation exists along a continuum, with varying degrees of homosexuality/heterosexuality. Social constructionism notes that the concepts, definitions, and practices of sexuality vary across context and cultures (Laumann et al., 1994; Katz, 1995).

The social constructionist arguments, we hold, are just as applicable to asexuality. What is considered to be asexuality for one individual might not be so considered for another. One individual might self-identify as an asexual, but still engage in sexual behavior; another might define their asexuality as the abstention from sexual intercourse (Poston & Baumle, 2010).

Until Alfred Kinsey and his colleagues (1948, 1953) conducted their sexuality research in the 1940s and 1950s, most analyses of sexuality used an essentialist orientation. Kinsey moved sexuality research away from a position of essentialism when he argued that the sexuality of humans is a lot more varied than originally thought. The range of expression he created, known as the "Kinsey scale," is a 7-point index that ranks overall sexuality from completely heterosexual (scored 0) to completely homosexual (scored 6) and everything in-between.

There are several different ways in which sexuality is conceptualized and measured, owing to the different ways sexual orientation has been defined in surveys and conceptualized by researchers. Sexual orientation is usually defined in terms of sexual behavior, sexual attraction, and self-identification (Laumann et al., 1994; Saewyc et al., 2004; Baumle et al., 2009; Poston & Chang, 2015). Regarding the behavior dimension, researchers would ask how does the person behave sexually; do they interact sexually with persons of the same sex, with persons of the opposite sex, or with person of both sexes; or do they not interact sexually? Regarding the dimension of sexual attraction, researchers would ask to whom is the person attracted sexually; are they sexually attracted to persons of the same sex, to persons of the opposite sex, to person of both sexes; or are they not attracted sexually to anyone? Regarding the self-identification dimension, researchers would ask how does the person self-identify, as a homosexual, heterosexual, bisexual, or asexual?

Among social scientists studying sexual orientation, demographers tend to focus more on sexual behavior, psychologists and sexologists tend to focus more on sexual attraction, and sociologists tend to focus more on self-identification. More detailed investigation of these concepts is beyond the scope of this chapter, but the reader is directed to Bogaert (2012) for a detailed discussion of these three dimensions of sexual orientation, as well as several others.

What Is Asexuality?

There is a limited social science literature on asexuality. This is due in part to the presumed low levels of asexuality in human and nonhuman populations. Some researchers hold that levels of asexuality should be low because according to evolutionary models of behavior, "one would expect strong selection pressures against such nonreproductive tendencies" (Bogaert, 2004: 279). But the fact that a behavior has "nonreproductive tendencies" does not necessarily mean that it will have a low prevalence. Indeed Bogaert noted that same-sex sexual attraction "is clearly a nonreproductive orientation; ... [but] its prevalence over time and across societies continues to challenge evolutionary theorists" (Bogaert, 2004: 279).

Like heterosexuality, homosexuality, and bisexuality, asexuality may also be defined in terms of sexual behavior, sexual attraction, and self-identification. We now present a review of the popular and social scientific literature dealing with asexual identity, desire, and behavior.

We first turn first to the common dictionary. *The Oxford English Dictionary* (2000, Volume 1: 682) defines asexuality as "an asexual condition; the absence of sex; without sexuality." The *OED* gives the following three earliest known uses of the term "asexual":

1. "The high estimation of virgin purity ... was advocated by the leaders of thought ...and... the asexual existence...was extolled as virtue in itself" (Eckenstein, 1896: 307).
2. "All doctors will tell you that, athletic or not, women are more asexual than men" (*The Daily Mail*, 1903: 2/7).
3. "I feel I've shot it (i.e., the book) like a bomb against all their false sex and hypocrisy, as my Florentine doctor said, against all their asexual sexuality" (Lawrence, [1928], 1962: 1077).

The *OED* definition of asexuality and the three *OED*-provided earliest uses of the term all represent a behavioral definition. Thus, an asexual is one who does not engage in sexual behavior. This definition is echoed in many studics of asexuality. Asexuals are often viewed as individuals who have "engaged in few or no sexual behaviors" (Rothblum & Brehony, 1993; Brotto et al., 2010: 600). Researchers have quantified the prevalence of asexuality by applying this particular definition of the absence of asexual behavior.

Abbott (2000) has observed in her fascinating account of the history of celibacy over the past 3000 years, from the vestal virgins of Rome, the castrati of Europe, and the eunuchs of China, to the athletes and professional women of the modern day, that more of them were happy and satisfied, than not, with their lack of sexual activity. Also, in a study of clerical celibacy, Cozzens (2006) has noted that Catholic priests who view their celibacy as a charism, a bestowed gift from the Holy Spirit, are more often very happy, than not very happy, with their sexual celibacy.

Another dimension of asexuality asks not about sexual behavior, but about sexual attraction. Is the person sexually attracted to other persons? If they are not, they are designated as asexual. The Asexual Visibility and Education Network (AVEN) (Dore, 2021) defines asexuality as an independence from sexual desire: an asexual is one who is not sexually attracted to other persons. Asexuals defined in terms of sexual attraction might have an emotional closeness to other persons while not being sexually attracted to them (Dore, 2021; Westphal, 2004; Poston & Baumle, 2010). AVEN goes on to note that some asexuals do experience some kind of attraction to particular individuals but prefer to act on the attraction in a non-sexual manner.

Finally, for some persons, asexuality may be determined by one's self-identification rather than by their lack of sexual behavior or sexual attraction. Asexuality may serve as an identity which can be co-opted throughout one's life if the situation warrants. "Asexuality may be an identity, used as a signal to others of a chosen lifestyle. The asexual identification is sometimes used during the 'coming out' process, to inform family and friends of a selected sexual orientation" (Poston & Baumle, 2010: 514; Westphal, 2004). We now discuss the prevalence of asexuality.

Prevalence of Asexuality

Due to limitations tied to the lack of probability samples that measure asexuality, it is difficult to determine the exact number of individuals who are asexual. In fact, the prevalence of asexuality has been shown to differ according to each of the sexuality dimensions of behavior, identification, or attraction (Poston & Baumle, 2010).

Measuring asexuality via the attraction dimension, Bogaert (2004) found that a significant minority (1.05%) of the British population in 1990 claimed to have never felt sexual attraction to anyone. A follow-up study showed the asexual population to be 0.73% in 2000 (Bogaert, 2013). An Australian national survey found 0.4% of the population to never feel sexual attraction, and that women were more likely to report never feeling sexual attraction compared to men (Smith et al., 2003). Poston and Baumle (2010) reported a similar figure using data from the U.S. based 2002 National Survey of Family Growth (NSFG). They found around 0.7% of men and 0.8% of women reporting that they are "unsure" about their sexual attraction. As the authors noted, however, this finding may be an overestimate of asexuality since the "not sure" category can include individuals who are unclear about what attraction means, as well as those who are uncertain about whether they are attracted to men or to women.

Using data from the National Health and Social Life Survey (NHSLS) – one of the leading sex surveys ever conducted in the U.S.- Laumann and his colleagues (1994) found one-third of women and one-seventh of men reported having low sexual desire. Although low or absent desire does not fully capture a lack of sexual attraction (Bogaert, 2012), the absence of desire gives an insight about asexuality.

Nationally representative research that assesses asexuality on the basis of self-identification is even more limited. Using data from the 2014/2015 New Zealand Attitudes and Values Study, Greaves et al. (2017) find that 0.4% of the respondents self-identified themselves as asexuals when answering the question "How would you describe your sexual orientation?" Data from the 2002 NSFG indicate a sizable minority (3.9%) of the respondents selected the category of "something else" as their sexual orientation, selecting it instead of the categories of heterosexual, homosexual, and bisexual. Another 1.8% did not choose any of the categories that were presented to them. We should keep in mind, however, that non-response or "something else" are overinclusive operationalizations of asexuality (Poston & Baumle, 2010).

Regarding the sexual behavior dimension, Poston & Baumle (2010) found 5% of women and 6% of men in the U.S. reporting they have never engaged in sex in their lifetimes. Laumann and his colleagues (1994) found that about 13% of their respondents reporting they had not had sex in the past year, and about 2% indicating that they had never had a sexual experience (Laumann et al., 1994). The research indicates that the dimension of sexual behavior tends to yield the highest prevalence rate for asexuality. However, we should note that sexual behavior is not static across the life course. The fact that people claim to have no sexual activity at one point in time does not necessarily assure future sexual inactivity.

Here it is important to mention that sexual attraction differs from sexual behavior. While asexual individuals generally report lower levels of sexual activity compared to sexual individuals, they may still engage in forms of partnered sexual behavior (Bogaert, 2013; Haydon et al., 2014). Moreover, it is possible that a lack of sexual behavior may be an indication of a lack of opportunity to have sex, or a moral or religious choice not to have sex, rather than an asexual orientation (Bogaert, 2013).

Answering the question about the prevalence of asexuality is not an easy one. The literature indicates that the degree of prevalence depends on which sexuality dimension (attraction, identification, or behavior) is used to conceptualize asexuality. We turn now to a review of the literature on the prevalence of obesity in the asexual and sexual populations.

Asexuals and Sexuals with Obesity: A Review of Literature

While considerable research has examined the relationship between obesity and gender, race, and class (Garawi et al., 2014; Lovejoy et al., 2009; Baskin et al., 2005; Boardman et al., 2005; Puciato & Rozpara, 2020; Rennie & Jebb, 2005; Witkos et al., 2008), we do not know as much about the relationship between sexual orientation and obesity (Newlin Lew et al., 2018; Boehmer et al., 2007; Boehmer & Bowen, 2009; Hsieh & Ruther, 2016; Yean et al., 2013; Azagba et al., 2019; Semlyen et al., 2020; Deputy & Boehmer, 2010). The literature about the association between obesity and asexuality is even more limited. In this section, we discuss the understudied scholarship that examines the prevalence of obesity among asexual and sexual populations, and we introduce some of the mechanisms that might account for linkages between the two.

Body image, eating disorders, and obesity have been shown to have important interconnections (Thompson, 2001), and research suggests that eating disorders and obesity share a set of risk factors (Haines & Neumark-Sztainer, 2006). There also seems to be a close relationship between eating disorders and sexual minority status. Research has shown that compared to their heterosexual counterparts, gay men are more likely to experience eating disorders (Blashill, 2011; Duggan & McCreary, 2004; Yelland & Tiggemann, 2003; Strong et al., 2000), report less satisfaction with their bodies (Yean et al., 2013), and show a greater desire to be thin (Duggan & McCreary, 2004). Relatedly, while the likelihood of being underweight is higher (Semlyen et al., 2020), the risk of obesity is lower for gay and bisexual men compared to heterosexual men (Feldman & Meyer, 2007; Newlin Lew et al., 2018; Azagba et al., 2019; Semlyen et al., 2020; Deputy & Boehmer, 2010).

Evidence concerning the relationship between obesity and sexual minority women is mixed. A few studies (Share & Mintz, 2002; Feldman & Meyer, 2007) find no difference between homosexual and heterosexual women regarding eating disorders. Other research (Bayer et al., 2017; Wichstrøm, 2006; Strong et al., 2000; Schneider et al., 1995) has discovered that lesbians are more prone to eating disorders compared to straight women (Bell et al., 2019). Moreover, lesbians are at a greater risk of obesity than straight women (Newlin Lew et al., 2018; Azagba et al., 2019; Semlyen et al., 2020).

Regarding asexual individuals' perceptions of their bodies, Swami et al. (2019: 3) have reported that asexual people, especially asexual males, hold unfavorable "body images" such as lack of "body appreciation" of themselves and perceived "body acceptance" from others. Asexual women, on the other hand, express that their identity challenges the notion of sexual objectification of women. (Gupta, 2019). Thus, there may be gendered differences in the linkages between asexuality and body image that lead to different overweight and obesity outcomes. To our knowledge, no studies have directly investigated whether body image issues are associated with eating disorders and/or obesity in the asexual population.

It is also unknown whether asexuality may contribute to negative sexual experiences that might worsen weight-related outcomes. This is worth considering given that some asexual people do engage in sexual activities (Brotto et al., 2010; Prause & Graham, 2007; Van Houdenhove et al., 2015), but those who have sexual partners often engage in "unwanted" though "consensual sexual activity" to please their partners. This potentially worsens psychological distress, which may lead to weight gain.

On the other hand, individuals with obesity may be more likely to be desexualized by others. Asexuality has been linked with negative stereotypes including "unattractiveness" (Gerike, 1990); fatness has also been shown to be associated with asexuality (Millman, 1980, Gailey, 2012). Stigma against persons with obesity is in line with these attitudes, as persons with obesity are often viewed as asexual. Thus, obesity may lead to limited opportunities or blocked access to sexual activity (Hayden et al., 2010; Gailey, 2012).

Research has indicated that people with obesity tend to experience a lower quality of sexual life (Sarwer & Steffen, 2015; Taskin Yilmaz et al., 2019; Poggiogalle et al., 2014). Among women with obesity, Cecilio et al. (2014) reported an association between overweight and a lack of sexual desire. Regan's (1996: 1810) research has also revealed that women with obesity are considered to be less "desirable as a sexual partner," "sexually warm," and "sexually responsive," compared to their non-obese counterparts. Exploring the sexual experiences of 34 self-identified fat women, Gailey (2012: 125) reported that these women are "unwilling to engage in sexual relationships" and evidence a lack of appreciation of their bodies.

Concerning men with obesity, they tend to have significantly fewer sexual partners compared to those without obesity (Nagelkerke et al., 2006). Persons with higher BMI classifications tend to have greater disadvantages regarding "sexual enjoyment, desire, and avoidance of sexual encounters" (Kolotkin et al., 2006: 474). Moreover, men with severe obesity (BMI > 40 kg/m^2) tend to experience more problems with sexual functioning, are less satisfied with their body image, and are more reluctant to engage in sexual behavior, compared to those with severe obesity who lost weight by way of bariatric surgery (Sarwer et al., 2012). Accordingly, a lack of sexual behavior or activity seems to be linked with obesity in both men and women.

Yet, research focused on dimensions other than sexual behavior has yielded mixed results. Bogaert (2004, 2013) found no weight differences in asexuals, identified on the basis of sexual attraction, when compared to their sexual counterparts. Using an identification measurement of asexuality, Greaves et al. (2017) also found no statistical association between weight and asexuality. Poston and Baumle's (2010) analysis is consistent with these findings. Using a social constructionist conceptualization of asexuality, they found that neither asexual men nor women were heavier compared to their heterosexual counterparts.

For the most part, however, the empirical research on the relationship between obesity and asexuality is limited and/or inconclusive and needs further investigation. But prior work does indicate an association between obesity and sexual minority status, and that the association may well differ by gender. Gay men seem to have less obesity than heterosexual men. On the other hand, lesbians seem to have more obesity than heterosexual women. It is unclear whether similar associations are present in the asexual population. Given the mixed nature of previous findings and lack of attention to gender-based differences, we will estimate obesity prevalence among asexuals and sexuals by gender using a behavioral measure of asexuality. We hypothesize that female asexuals will have a higher prevalence of overweight or obesity compared to non-asexual females. We further hypothesize that male asexuals will have less overweight and obesity than their non-asexual counterparts. In the next section, we discuss the data used to explore the distribution of obesity among asexuals and sexuals.

Data: 2017–2019 U.S. National Survey of Family Growth

The National Survey of Family Growth (NSFG) is a national multistage probability sample survey of female and male respondents between the ages of 15 and 49 years of age in the non-institutionalized population of the United States. The National Center for Health Statistics has been conducting the NSFG since the 1970s to gather information on fertility and infertility, cohabitation and marriage, contraception use, family life, and general and reproductive health of the U.S. population. The 2017–2019 NSFG contains data for 6141 female respondents and 5206 male respondents, for a total of 11,347 respondents, aged 15–49 (Centers for Disease Control and Prevention, 2021a, b).

We now discuss the NSFG questionnaire items dealing with asexuality and obesity. We first consider the NSFG questions pertaining to the three sexuality dimensions of behavior, attraction, and self-identification. With respect to sexual behavior, the 2017–2019 NSFG includes the following two questions asked of the female respondents, with similar questions asked of the male respondents:

> At any time in your life, have you ever had sexual intercourse with a man, that is, made love, had sex, or gone all the way? Yes or No.
>
> Have you ever had any other sexual experience of any kind with another female? Yes or No.

We have designated females and males who answered "no" to both questions as asexuals on the behavioral dimension of sexuality.

Regarding the sexual attraction dimension of sexuality, the 2017–2019 NSFG asked both female and male respondents the following question:

> People are different in their sexual attraction to other people. Which best describes your feelings? Are you: Only attracted to males, Mostly attracted to males, Equally attracted to males and females, Mostly attracted to females, Only attracted to females, or Not sure?

These response categories do not provide an appropriate classification[1] for asexual individuals. Thus, we did not include the attraction dimension in our quantitative analyses.

We made a similar decision with respect to including asexuals in our analysis who were so designated according to the sexuality dimension of self-identification. The 2017–2019 NSFG asked the female and male respondents the following question pertaining to the self-identification of their sexual orientation:

> Which of the following best represents how you think of yourself? Gay or lesbian, Straight, that is, not gay or lesbian, Bisexual, or Something else?

Observe that in the self-identification question, there is not a specific response of "asexual," which would be the self-identification response[2] of asexuals. Consequently, we decided not to include in our quantitative analysis, asexuals who were so designated according to the dimension of self-identification. Our analysis below of asexuals and sexuals is restricted to respondents based solely on their sexual behavior, or lack thereof.

We turn now to the measurement and conceptualization of obesity. The common standard for categorizing obesity is the body mass index (BMI), a measure for adult men and women of their body fat based on their height and weight according to this formula: one's weight (in kilograms) divided by the square of their height (in meters). The BMI is a "commonly used measure for assessing overweight or underweight men and non-pregnant women" (National Center for Health Statistics, 2020: 7). BMIs less than or equal to 18.5 are categorized as underweight, BMIs between 18.5 and 24.9 are categorized as normal, BMIs of 25.0 to 29.9 are categorized as overweight, and BMIs of 30.0 or higher as obese (CDC, 2021a, b).

The 2017–2019 NSFG includes a variable labeled BMICAT, i.e., BMI category. Following the above BMI formula and its categorical designations, each respondent is assigned one of

[1] There is not a specific response for the NSFG question on sexual attraction for persons who are not sexually attracted to other persons. A response such as "I am not sexually attracted to anyone" would be the likely response for persons who are not sexually attracted to other humans. But such a response was not included on the 2017–2019 NSFG. Some have suggested that a person who does not desire sex with anyone would likely answer the above question as "not sure" (Poston & Baumle, 2010). But, persons who desire sex with, or who are only sexually attracted to, animals, or who only receive sexual gratification from exhibitionism, masochism, fetishism, or other paraphilias would also likely answer the above NSFG question on sexual attraction as "not sure" (Poston & Baumle, 2010: 517–518). So even though the "not sure" response category would include asexuals, it would also include, as well, other persons who may not be asexuals.

[2] Some researchers have suggested that asexuals would most likely answer the self-identification question as "something else" (Poston & Baumle, 2010: 517). But this would also be a likely answer for persons self-identifying as zoosexual, masochist, exhibitionist, or as self-identifying as having a sexual fetish for such items as balloons, breasts, feet, panties, and so forth. Even though the "something else" response would be the most likely response for asexuals, we agree with Mosher and his colleagues that "further study of those who answered, 'something else' ... is needed ... (to be better able) to characterize their sexual and risk behaviors" (Mosher et al., 2005: 14).

the following five categories: 1 = underweight, 2 = normal, 3 = overweight, 4 = obese, and 5 = undefined BMI. Because this information is not collected for pregnant women or for persons in the 15–19 age category, data on the BMICAT variable are only provided in the NSFG for adult males and for adult non-pregnant females. Thus, as we will see below, 1153 of the 6141 female respondents do not receive a score on the BMICAT variable, nor do 1032 the 5206 male respondents.

One final point needs to be mentioned about our analyses of obesity among the asexual and sexual respondents using data from the 2017–2019 NSFG. Because the 2017–2019 NSFG is based on multistage and stratified probability sampling, one cannot make inferences with the data to the larger population of U.S. adults from which the samples were drawn without first considering the complex sampling designs of the NSFG.

Thus, in the empirical analyses reported in the next sections, we use the "svy" suite of statistical sample adjustment methods available in the Stata 17 statistical package (StataCorp, 2021) that introduce survey adjustment estimators. These methods enable us to adjust our analyses according to the various population and strata weights available in the 2017–2019 NSFG.

Results, Female Respondents

In this section we present data on the female respondents, and in the next section on the male respondents. We first determine whether the distribution of BMI categories varies significantly among the asexual and sexual female populations.

The analysis presented in Table 15.1[3] shows that the asexual and sexual groups do not differ significantly with respect to the distribution of the BMI categories; see the F-test value of 1.08, with a P of 0.37. The data in Table 15.1 indicate that 21.5% of female asexuals are in the overweight category, compared to 26.4% of their non-asexual counterparts. Also see that 39.7% of asexuals are designated as obese, compared to 35.6% of sexuals. Thus, women who are asexual on the basis of sexual activity and those who are not asexual have similar percentages in all the BMI categories. They do not differ significantly in their respective distributions of the BMI categories.

We conducted another analysis, similar to that reported in Table 15.1, but did not include respondents with an "Undefined BMI." This analysis compared the distributions of only the four BMI categories of underweight, normal weight, overweight, and obese among the female asexuals and sexuals. We showed, once again, that female asexuals and sexuals do not differ significantly in their distributions of the four basic BMI categories, $F = 1.26$, $P = 0.29$ (table not shown).

We now employ another method to ascertain whether female asexuals differ significantly from female sexuals with respect to obesity. We first estimate a logistic regression equation with the asexual dummy variable (asexual = 1) as the dependent variable, and an obesity dummy variable (obese = 1) as the independent variable. We next estimate four more logistic regression equations, adding additional independent variables to the equations. Though we treat asexuality as the dependent variable in the models, we are not using obesity and the other independent variables in the logistic regression equations to predict the likelihood of a person being asexual versus sexual. Instead, following the approach taken by Bogaert (2004, 2012, 2013) and by Poston and Baumle (2010), we use the results from the logistic regression equations to indicate whether asexuals are significantly different from sexuals with respect to the presence of obesity, after controlling for other independent variables hypothesized to be associated with persons being asexual versus being sexual.

In Table 15.2 we present the results of the five logistic regression equations examining the log

[3] As we noted above, 1153 of the 6141 women in the NSFG did not receive a BMI classification because they were below the age of 20, and/or were pregnant. Our analyses thus are limited to nonpregnant women of ages 20 and older.

Table 15.1 Distributions of BMI categories among the female asexual and female sexual populations, 2017–2019 National Survey of Family Growth: 4988 females, 20–49 years of age (Survey adjusted percentages using NSFG respondent sampling weights)

	Female asexuals		Female sexuals		All females	
	N	%	N	%	N	%
BMI category						
Underweight	10	4.87	116	2.37	126	2.47
Normal weight	63	31.42	1488	33.82	1551	33.72
Overweight	39	21.46	1229	26.36	1268	26.15
Obese	78	39.70	1848	35.55	1926	35.72
Undefined BMI	5	2.55	112	1.91	117	1.93
Total	**195**	**100.00**	**4793**	**100.01**	**4988**	**99.99**

$\chi 2 = 8.83$, $F = 1.08$, $P = 0.3656$

Table 15.2 Logistic regression equation coefficients of female asexuals and sexuals on the independent variable of obesity (yes/no) and other race, Hispanic, and socioeconomic variables: 4871 non-pregnant females, aged 20–49, 2017–2019 National Survey of Family Growth (Survey adjusted coefficients using NSFG respondent sampling weights)

	Model-1		Model-2		Model-3		Model-4		Model-5	
Independent variable	Coef	t	Coef	t	Coef	t	Coef	t	Coef	t
Obese (yes = 1)	0.19	0.82	0.57	2.61	0.67	3.12	0.74	3.40	0.55	2.15
Age (in years)			−0.19	−10.55	−0.19	−10.48	−0.20	−10.06	−0.06	−2.94
Hispanic (yes = 1)			−0.12	−0.47	−0.13	−0.53	−0.25	−1.00	−0.18	−0.57
Black (yes = 1)			−0.77	−2.41	−0.77	−2.42	−0.69	−2.16	−1.03	−3.06
General Health*					−0.15	−1.23	−0.11	−0.85	−0.07	−0.61
Education (years)							0.14	3.13	0.05	0.87
Ever Marry or Cohabit (yes = 1)									−4.80	−4.40
Constant	−3.19	−21.4	2.64	4.03	2.93	4.12	1.28	1.66	−0.03	−0.03

*1 = excellent to 5 = poor

odds relationships between the dummy variable of asexual and several independent variables, including the dummy variable of obesity. Presented for each independent variable is its logit coefficient and its t-test value (t = the logit coefficient divided by its standard error). We use the t-test to evaluate the statistical significance of a logit regression coefficient. T-test values greater than 1.96 indicate that the regression coefficient is statistically significant, with a P-value of 0.05 or lower.

The first column of Table 15.2 presents the logistic regression results with only the one variable of obesity (yes = 1). The logit coefficient of the obesity variable is 0.19, with a t-test value of 0.82. There is no statistically significant relationship between the presence of obesity and asexuality. This is a confirmation of the results discussed earlier, especially those shown in Table 15.1.

But, this is a bivariate relationship, that is, no other independent variables are included in the logit regression equation. We wonder if there might be a relationship between asexuality and obesity if we enter control variables of age and race/ethnicity, as prior research has suggested that asexuals are often younger than sexuals, and that asexuals are less likely than sexuals to be racial and ethnic minorities (Poston & Baumle, 2006). The logit regression equation in Model-2- examines the association between obesity and asexuality, controlling for age (in years) and whether the respondent is Hispanic or Black. The obesity coefficient is 0.57 and is statistically significant, with a t-test value of 2.61.

In Model-3, we add to the equation a general health variable scored from 1 to 5, with 1 representing excellent health and 5 representing poor health. This inclusion is based on evidence that asexuals have poorer health than sexuals

(Bogaert, 2004: 282). The obesity variable retains its significant association with asexuality, indeed there is a small increase in the value of the logit coefficient.

In Model-4 we add to the equation the woman's years of completed education, and in Model-5 we add a variable about whether the respondent has ever-married or cohabited. Prior literature (Bogaert, 2004; Poston & Baumle, 2006) has shown educational attainment to be positively associated with asexuality, and marital or cohabitation status to be negatively associated with asexuality. The obesity coefficient in Model-4 is 0.74, and falls off a bit in Model-5 to 0.55. It is statistically significant in both equations. The obesity coefficient of 0.55 in Model-5 indicates a significant relationship between obesity and whether the person is asexual, controlling for the respondent's age, whether she is Black or Hispanic, her general health, her years of education, and whether she has ever been married or cohabited.

We estimated a second logistic regression equation with the same dependent variable of asexuality and with all the same control variables as shown in Table 15.2. But we expanded the obesity variable to not only include women with obesity but also women who are overweight. We estimated five logit regression equations, just as we did above, but the obesity variable now becomes an overweight/obesity variable. Its logit coefficient in the regression equation with all the independent variables, like the equation in Model-5 in Table 15.2, is 0.57, with a t-test value of 2.10. The overweight/obesity coefficient value of 0.57 indicates that controlling for all the other independent variables shown in Model-5 in Table 15.2, obesity is positively associated with whether the women are asexual (table not shown).

In this section we first showed that the distribution of BMI categories is not statistically different for women according to whether they are asexuals or sexuals. We then estimated logistic regression equations with an asexuality dummy variable as the outcome, and several characteristics variables, including one gauging the presence of obesity, as independent variables. The results of our multivariate analyses indicate that controlling for independent variables based on age, whether the woman is Black or Hispanic, her general health, her years of education, and whether she has ever married or cohabited, women who have obesity, and in a second equation women with obesity or overweight, there are positive relationships between obesity and overweight and whether the woman is asexual. In the next section we repeat the above analyses for male respondents of age 20 and over.

Results, Male Respondents

We now present data on the male respondents, repeating the same analyses we presented above for females. We first examine the distributions of BMI categories among the asexual and sexual male populations to see whether the two distributions are significantly different?

As we noted earlier, BMI data are not included for respondents under age 20. Thus 1032 of the 5206 male respondents do not receive scores on the BMICAT variable. We thus restricted our analysis to those 4174 males who are at least 20 years of age. The results are presented in Table 15.3.

We show in Table 15.3 that the asexual and sexual male populations differ significantly with respect to the distribution of the BMI categories, as indicated by the F-test value of 5.22, with a P of 0.002. The data indicate that 29.2% of the male asexuals are in the overweight category, compared to 39.6% who are not asexual, and that 17.2% of male asexuals are designated as obese, compared to 31.0% of the male sexuals. Male asexuals evidence considerably lower percentages in the overweight and obese categories than do male sexuals. The two groups differ significantly in their distributions of the BMI categories.

We repeated the analysis shown in Table 15.3 but excluded those 63 male respondents with an "Undefined BMI," allowing us to compare the distributions of the four BMI categories of underweight, normal weight, overweight, and obese among the male asexuals and sexuals. The results indicated, again, that male asexuals have lower

Table 15.3 Distributions of BMI categories among the male asexual and male sexual populations, 2017–2019 National Survey of Family Growth: 4174 males, 20–49 years of age (Survey adjusted percentages using NSFG respondent sampling weights)

	Male asexuals		Male sexuals		All males	
	N	%	N		N	%
BMI category						
Underweight	3	2.81	53	1.02	56	1.11
Normal weight	70	48.33	1107	27.17	1177	28.14
Overweight	51	29.15	1502	39.62	1553	39.14
Obese	50	17.17	1275	31.02	1325	30.38
Undefined BMI	7	2.54	56	1.16	63	1.23
Total	**181**	**100.00**	**3993**	**99.99**	**4174**	**100.00**
$\chi 2 = 54.08$, F = 5.22, P = 0.0015						

percentages in the overweight and obese categories than male sexuals. Male asexuals and sexuals differ significantly in their distributions of the four BMI categories, F = 5.94, P = 0.001 (table not shown).

To determine whether male asexuals differ significantly from male sexuals with respect to obesity, we opted next to fit a logistic regression equation with the asexual dummy variable (asexual = 1) as the dependent variable, and an obesity dummy variable (obese = 1) as the independent variable (as we did in Table 15.2 for the female population). Again, our objective is not to employ the obesity variable as a predictor of the likelihood of a male being asexual versus sexual, but rather to determine whether male asexuals are significantly different from male sexuals with respect to the presence of obesity.

Table 15.4 presents the results of four regression equations examining the log odds relationships between the dummy variable of asexual and several independent variables, including the dummy variable of obesity. Presented in the table for each independent variable is its logit coefficient and its t-test value.

The first column of Table 15.4, Model-1, presents the regression results with only the independent variable of obesity (yes = 1). The obesity independent variable has a logit coefficient of −0.76, with a t-test value of −2.62. The association between obesity and being an asexual is negative and statistically significant.

In Models 2 through 4 we have added control variables shown in the literature to be related to whether one is asexual or sexual. The obesity coefficient in Model-2 reports the association between obesity and asexuality, controlling for age and whether the respondent is Hispanic or Black. The obesity coefficient is −0.25 and is not statistically significant. And when we introduce additional independent variables in the equations, as in Model-3 and Model-4, the obesity coefficient continues to be negative, but not statistically significant. We conclude that after controlling for the male respondent's age, whether he is Black or Hispanic, his general health, and his years of education, his being characterized by obesity is not related to whether he is asexual or sexual.

We have estimated a second set of logit regression equations with the same dependent variable of asexuality and with all the same control variables as shown in Table 15.4. But we have expanded the obesity variable to also include the overweight variable. The results of these equations are presented in Table 15.5.

The logit coefficient for the overweight/obesity independent variable in the first logit regression equation, Model-1, is −1.02, with a t-test value of −4.11, indicating a statistically significant negative association between obesity and whether the male is asexual. In Model-2, we add the control variables for age and whether the respondent is Hispanic or Black. The value of the overweight/obese logit coefficient drops to −0.40, with a t of −1.61. Although it is now statistically insignificant, its coefficient value is not far from being significant.

Table 15.4 Logistic regression equation coefficients of male asexuals and sexuals on the independent variable of obesity (yes/no) and other race, Hispanic, and socioeconomic variables: 4111 males, aged 20–49, 2017–2019 National Survey of Family Growth (Survey adjusted coefficients using NSFG respondent sampling weights)

	Model-1		Model-2		Model-3		Model-4	
Independent variable	Coef	t	Coef	t	Coef	t	Coef	t
Obese (yes = 1)	−0.76	−2.62	−0.25	−0.93	−0.26	−1.05	−0.23	−0.96
Age (in years)			−0.21	−6.96	−0.21	−6.93	−0.21	−6.44
Hispanic (yes = 1)			−0.90	−2.28	−0.90	−2.28	−0.80	−2.12
Black (yes = 1)			−1.28	−3.01	−1.27	−3.00	−1.20	−2.93
General Health*					0.03	0.29	0.06	0.54
Education (years)							0.09	1.91
Constant	−2.86	−11.54	3.20	3.88	3.13	3.96	1.97	2.87

*1 = excellent to 5 = poor

Table 15.5 Logistic regression equation coefficients of male asexuals and sexuals on the independent variable of overweight/obese (yes/no) and other race, Hispanic, and socioeconomic variables: 4111 males, aged 20–49, 2017–2019 National Survey of Family Growth (Survey adjusted coefficients using NSFG respondent sampling weights)

	Model-1		Model-2		Model-3		Model-4	
Independent variable	Coef	t	Coef	t	Coef	t	Coef	t
Overweight/Obese (yes = 1)	−1.02	−4.11	−0.40	−1.61	−0.40	−1.72	−0.40	−1.75
Age (in years)			−0.20	−6.65	−0.20	−6.62	−0.21	−6.23
Hispanic (yes = 1)			−0.89	−2.26	−0.89	−2.26	−0.79	−2.09
Black (yes = 1)			−1.27	−2.97	−1.26	−2.95	−1.18	−2.87
General Health*					0.03	0.29	0.07	0.56
Education (years)							0.09	1.97
Constant	−2.43	−8.30	3.22	3.96	3.16	4.03	1.96	2.89

*1 = excellent to 5 = poor

When we add still more control variables in Models 3 and 4, the t-test values and their associated probabilities, reach statistical significance with respect to one-tail tests. One-tail tests may be used when the hypothesis indicates not only the presence of a relationship but also its direction. We are hypothesizing, for males, a negative association between the overweight/obese variable and the asexual variable. The coefficients in both Models 3 and 4 for the overweight/obese variable are negative and statistically significant ($p \leq 0.10$). This supports the hypothesis presented earlier for males about the negative association between being characterized as overweight or obese and being asexual.

In line with prior work on sexual minorities, the results of the univariate and multivariate analyses for females and for males are different. Controlling for several factors shown to be associated with being asexual, we observed a positive association between asexuality and overweight/obesity among females. In contrast, we observed a negative association between asexuality and overweight/obesity among males. Taken together, these findings suggest that some of the mechanisms proposed to account for associations between sexual minority status and overweight/obesity may be similarly relevant for the asexual population and worthy of additional investigation.

Conclusion

In this chapter we have examined the distribution of obesity and overweight among female and male asexuals and sexuals. The demography of obesity literature has tended to focus heavily on sexuals, that is, people who have one or more of the following characteristics: engagement in sexual activity, sexual attraction to other persons, and/or self-identification as homosexual, heterosexual or bisexual. Very little attention has asked about the relationship between obesity and overweight among persons who are asexual.

We first discussed the conceptualization of sexuality and asexuality, considering several different ways to conceptualize, define and measure the two. Importantly, we outlined how asexuality may be conceptualized differently according to sexual behavior, sexual attraction and sexual self-identification. This lack of consistency in conceptualization and measurement has led to inconsistent estimates of the asexual population as it is highly dependent on the sexuality dimension (attraction, identification, or behavior) that is used to conceptualize and measure asexuality (Bogaert, 2004, 2013; Laumann et al., 1994; Smith et al., 2003; Poston & Baumle, 2010). However, the existing research has shown that a significant number of persons report that they are not engaging in sexual activity, and/or not experiencing sexual desire, and/or not self-identifying as sexual.

Our review of the literature revealed limited work examining the relationship between obesity and sexual orientation in general, and asexuality in particular. This literature has demonstrated that gay men have lower odds of obesity compared to heterosexual men, while lesbians have higher odds of obesity compared to heterosexual women. The literature on asexuality and obesity has yielded inconsistent results that appear to vary based on how asexuality is measured. Accordingly, studies that apply attraction or identification-based measures of asexuality have reported a lack of association. Other studies have made linkages between sexual behavior, or lack thereof, and obesity (Sarwer & Steffen, 2015; Poggiogalle et al., 2014). People with obesity are more likely to report asexual behavior (Cecilio et al., 2014; Nagelkerke et al., 2006; Kolotkin et al., 2006), and this association tends to be stronger for women (Gailey 2012). Moreover, people with obesity are often viewed as asexuals, and the negative stereotypes they experience due to obesity often lead to body image issues as well as influence the quality and access to their sexual activity (Millman, 1980, Hayden et al., 2010; Gailey, 2012). The existing body of evidence in this area does not allow us to definitively comment on the directionality of this association. In other words, it is unclear if asexuality leads to weight gain, or, if having obesity leads to a lack of sexual activity. To supplement the existing research, we estimated a series of models, separately for males and females, to determine whether asexual and sexual populations differ in their distributions of overweight and obesity.

Using data from the 2017–2019 National Survey of Family Growth and employing the behavioral dimension of asexuality, we examined the degree of obesity and overweight in asexual females and asexual males, respectively. Our findings are consistent for the most part with those of previous research exploring the prevalence of obesity in lesbian and gay populations. The prevalence of obesity is higher for both asexual and lesbian women compared to their sexual and heterosexual counterparts while it is the opposite for men. We thus add to the body of literature suggesting that sexual minority status is associated with overweight and obesity.

At present, the mechanisms underlying the association between asexuality and overweight or obesity are not known. Given that asexuality reflects sexual minority status, it is possible that this group has differential experiences or characteristics that make them more or less vulnerable to weight gain or eating disturbances. For example, they may have more body image issues or fewer psychosocial resources, which are connected to the risk of overweight or obesity. We noted earlier that prior findings suggest that male homosexuals have more body image issues, eating disorders, and higher risk of underweight. Evidence for homosexual females is more mixed but has revealed higher rates of eating disorders and risk of obesity. Additional work is needed to better understand these associations.

Additionally, we find it important to emphasize the role of gender as it may be considered as a second burden leading to differential risk and gendered asymmetries among sexual minorities. The gender difference in health outcomes comparing asexuals and sexuals needs further investigation.

It is also possible that obesity may lead to greater likelihood of asexuality, at least in behavioral terms, as it may limit sexual opportunities or reduce sexual desire. Because our analysis was cross-sectional, we are unable to address causality. Additional work is needed to determine how obesity may contribute to the presence of behavioral asexuality. Relatedly, data limitations only allowed us to operationalize asexuality via the behavioral dimension. Research needs to be undertaken examining the prevalence of obesity in asexual and sexual populations using identification and attraction dimensions of sexuality to confirm whether these associations exist across all dimensions. These limitations aside, our analysis contributes to the existing body of work documenting differences in obesity and overweight on the basis of sexual minority status. Further, we establish how these patterns differ on the basis of gender and affirm the need for continuing work on the mechanisms underlying these associations.

References

Abbott, E. (2000). *A history of celibacy: From Athena to Elizabeth I, Leonardo da Vinci, Florence nightingale, Ghandi, and Cher*. Scribner.

Azagba, S., Shan, L., & Latham, K. (2019). Overweight and obesity among sexual minority adults in the United States. *International Journal of Environmental Research and Public Health, 16*, 1828.

Baskin, M. L., Ard, J., Franklin, F., & Allison, D. B. (2005). Prevalence of obesity in the United States. *Obesity Reviews: An Official Journal of the International Association for the Study of Obesity, 6*, 5–7.

Baumle, A. K., & Poston, D. L. (2011). The economic cost of homosexuality: Multilevel models. *Social Forces, 89*, 1005–1032.

Baumle, A. K., Compton, D.'. L., & Poston, D. L. (2009). *Same-sex partners: The social demography of sexual orientation*. SUNY Press.

Bayer, V., Robert-McComb, J. J., Clopton, J. R., & Reich, D. A. (2017). Investigating the influence of shame, depression, and distress tolerance on the relationship between internalized homophobia and binge eating in lesbian and bisexual women. *Eating Behaviors, 24*, 39–44.

Bell, K., Rieger, E., & Hirsch, J. K. (2019). Corrigendum: Eating disorder symptoms and proneness in gay men, lesbian women, and transgender and gender non-conforming adults: Comparative levels and a proposed mediational model. *Frontiers in Psychology, 10*, 1540.

Black, D. A., Makar, H. R., Sanders, S. G., & Taylor, L. J. (2003). The earnings effects of sexual orientation. *Industrial and Labor Relation Review, 56*, 449–469.

Blashill, A. J. (2011). Gender roles, eating pathology, and body dissatisfaction in men: A meta-analysis. *Body Image, 8*, 1–11.

Boardman, J. D., Saint Onge, J. M., Rogers, R. G., & Denney, J. T. (2005). Race differentials in obesity: The impact of place. *Journal of Health and Social Behavior, 46*, 229–243.

Boehmer, U., & Bowen, D. J. (2009). Examining factors linked to overweight and obesity in women of different sexual orientations. *Preventive Medicine, 48*, 357–361.

Boehmer, U., Bowen, D. J., & Bauer, G. R. (2007). Overweight and obesity in sexual-minority women: Evidence from population-based data. *American Journal of Public Health, 97*, 1134–1140.

Bogaert, A. F. (2004). Asexuality: Prevalence and associated factors in a national probability sample. *Journal of Sex Research, 41*, 279–287.

Bogaert, A. F. (2012). *Understanding asexuality*. Rowman and Littlefield Publishers.

Bogaert, A. F. (2013). The demography of asexuality. In A. K. Baumle (Ed.), *International handbook on the demography of sexuality* (pp. 275–288). Springer.

Bogaert, A. F. (2015). Asexuality: What it is and why it matters. *The Journal of Sex Research, 52*, 362–379.

Brotto, L. A., Knudson, G., Inskip, J., Rhodes, K., & Erskine, Y. (2010). Asexuality: A mixed-methods approach. *Archives of Sexual Behavior, 39*, 599–618.

Butler, J. (1990). *Gender trouble*. Routledge.

Cecilio, H. P. M., de Cássia Nogueira Sanches, R., Radovanovic, C. A. T., & Marcon, S. S. (2014). Perceptions of obese women on sexuality. *REME, 18*(4).

Centers for Disease Control and Prevention. (2021a). *About the National Survey of family growth*. Centers for Disease Control and Prevention, National Center for Health Statistics, National Survey of Family Growth. https://www.cdc.gov/nchs/nsfg/about_nsfg.htm. Accessed 1 Nov 2021.

Centers for Disease Control and Prevention. (2021b). *Defining adult overweight and obesity*. Retrieved from https://www.cdc.gov/obesity/adult/defining.html

Cozzens, D. (2006). *Freeing celibacy*. Liturgical Press.

Dahl, M. (2015). 5 ways to better understand asexuality. *New York Magazine* (August 10).

Daily Mail. (1903, 10 September). London, England: Associated New Media.

Decker, J. S. (2014). *The invisible orientation: An introduction to asexuality*. Carrel Books.

Deputy, N. P., & Boehmer, U. (2010). Determinants of body weight among men of different sexual orientation. *Preventive Medicine, 51*, 129–131.

Dore, Michael, AVEN Board of Directors and Project Team. (2021). *AVEN: The asexual visibility and education network*. https://www.stonewall.org.uk/about-us/news/aven-%E2%80%93-asexual-visibility-and-education-network. Accessed 3 Nov 2021.

Duggan, S. J., & McCreary, D. R. (2004). Body image, eating disorders, and the drive for muscularity in gay and heterosexual men: The influence of media images: The influence of media images. *Journal of Homosexuality, 47*, 45–58.

Eckenstein, L. (1896). *Women under monasticism*. Cambridge University Press.

Feldman, M. B., & Meyer, I. H. (2007). Eating disorders in diverse lesbian, gay, and bisexual populations. *The International Journal of Eating Disorders, 40*, 218–226.

Foucault, M. (1978). *The history of sexuality: An introduction* (Vol. 1). Vintage Books.

Gailey, J. A. (2012). Fat shame to fat pride: Fat Women's sexual and dating experiences. *Fat Studies, 1*, 114–127.

Garawi, F., Devries, K., Thorogood, N., & Uauy, R. (2014). Global differences between women and men in the prevalence of obesity: Is there an association with gender inequality? *European Journal of Clinical Nutrition, 68*, 1101–1106.

Garcia-Alexander, G. (2019). The demography of obesity (Chapter 33). In D. L. Poston (Ed.), *Handbook of population* (2nd ed., pp. 859–873). Springer.

Gerike, A. E. (1990). On gray hair and oppressed brains. *Journal of Women & Aging, 2*, 35–46.

Greaves, L. M., Barlow, F. K., Huang, Y., Stronge, S., Fraser, G., & Sibley, C. G. (2017). Asexual identity in a New Zealand national sample: Demographics, well-being, and health. *Archives of Sexual Behavior, 46*, 2417–2427.

Gupta, K. (2019). Gendering asexuality and asexualizing gender: A qualitative study exploring the intersections between gender and asexuality. *Sexualities, 22*(7–8), 1197–1216.

Haines, J., & Neumark-Sztainer, D. (2006). Prevention of obesity and eating disorders: A consideration of shared risk factors. *Health Education Research, 21*(6), 770–782. https://doi.org/10.1093/her/cyl094

Hayden, M. J., Dixon, M. E., Dixon, J. B., Playfair, J., & O'Brien, P. E. (2010). Perceived discrimination and stigmatisation against severely obese women: Age and weight loss make a difference. *Obesity Facts, 3*, 7–14.

Haydon, A. A., Cheng, M. M., Herring, A. H., McRee, A.-L., & Halpern, C. T. (2014). Prevalence and predictors of sexual inexperience in adulthood. *Archives of Sexual Behavior, 43*, 221–230.

Houdenhove, V., Ellen, L. G., T'Sjoen, G., & Enzlin, P. (2015). Stories about asexuality: A qualitative study on asexual women. *Journal of Sex & Marital Therapy, 41*, 262–281.

Hsieh, N., & Ruther, M. (2016). Sexual minority health and health risk factors: Intersection effects of gender, race, and sexual identity. *American Journal of Preventive Medicine, 50*, 746–755.

Katz, J. (1995). *The invention of heterosexuality*. Penguin Books.

Kinsey, A. C., Pomeroy, W. B., & Martin, C. E. (1948). *Sexual behavior in the human male*. W.B. Saunders and Company.

Kinsey, A. C., Pomeroy, W. B., Martin, C. E., & Gebhard, P. H. (1953). *Sexual behavior in the human female*. W.B. Saunders and Company.

Kolotkin, R. L., Binks, M., Crosby, R. D., Østbye, T., Gress, R. E., & Adams, T. D. (2006). Obesity and sexual quality of life. *Obesity, 14*, 472–479.

Laumann, E. O., Gagnon, J. H., Michael, R. T., & Michaels, S. (1994). *The social organization of sexuality: Sexual practices in the United States*. The University of Chicago Press.

Lawrence, D. H. ([1928] 1962). *Collected letters* (H. T. Moore, Ed.). Viking Press.

Lovejoy, J. C., A. Sainsbury, and Stock Conference 2008 Working Group. (2009). Sex differences in obesity and the regulation of energy homeostasis. *Obesity Reviews: An Official Journal of the International Association for the Study of Obesity, 10*, 154–167.

Millman, M. (1980). *Such a pretty face: Being fat in America*. WW Norton.

Mosher, W. D., Chandra, A., & Jones, J. (2005). Sexual behavior and selected health measures: Men and women 15–44 years of age, United States, 2002. In *Advance data from vital and health statistics* (Vol. 362). National Center for Health Statistics.

Nagelkerke, N. J. D., Bernsen, R. M. D., Sgaier, S. K., & Jha, P. (2006). Body mass index, sexual behaviour, and sexually transmitted infections: An analysis using the NHANES 1999–2000 data. *BMC Public Health, 6*, 199.

National Center for Health Statistics. (2020). *Public-use data file documentation, 2017–2019 National Survey of family growth, User's guide, appendix 7C*. National Center for Health Statistics. https://www.cdc.gov/nchs/data/nsfg/NSFG-2017-2019-UG-App7c-RestrictedUseRDCvars-508.pdf. Accessed 10 Nov 2021.

Newlin Lew, K., Dorsen, C., & Long, T. (2018). Prevalence of obesity, prediabetes, and diabetes in sexual minority men: Results from the 2014 behavioral risk factor surveillance system. *The Diabetes Educator, 44*, 83–93.

Palad, C. J., & Stanford, F. C. (2018). Use of people-first language with regard to obesity. *The American Journal of Clinical Nutrition, 108*, 201–203.

Poggiogalle, E., Di Lazzaro, L., Pinto, A., Migliaccio, S., Lenzi, A., & Donini, L. M. (2014). Health-related quality of life and quality of sexual life in obese subjects. *International Journal of Endocrinology, 2014*, 847871.

Poston, D. L., & Baumle, A. K. (2006). *A quantitative analysis of asexuality and sexuality in the United States, 2002*. Paper presented at the Annual Meeting of the American Sociological Association, Montreal, Canada, August 14.

Poston, D. L., & Baumle, A. K. (2010). Patterns of asexuality in the United States. *Demographic Research, 23*, 509–530.

Poston, D. L., & Chang, Y.-T. (2015). The conceptualization and measurement of the homosexual, heterosexual and bisexual populations in the United States. In M. N. Hoque & L. B. Potter (Eds.), *Emerging techniques in applied demography* (pp. 359–378). Springer.

Prause, N., & Graham, C. A. (2007). Asexuality: Classification and characterization. *Archives of Sexual Behavior, 36*, 341–356.

Puciato, D., & Rozpara, M. (2020). Demographic and socioeconomic determinants of body mass index in people of working age. *International Journal of Environmental Research and Public Health, 17*, 8168.

Regan, P. C. (1996). Sexual outcasts: The perceived impact of body weight and gender on sexuality1. *Journal of Applied Social Psychology, 26*, 1803–1815.

Rennie, K. L., & Jebb, S. A. (2005). Prevalence of obesity in Great Britain. *Obesity Reviews: An Official Journal of the International Association for the Study of Obesity, 6*, 11–12.

Rothblum, E. D., & Brehony, K. A. (1993). Why focus on romantic but asexual relationships among lesbians? In E. D. Rothblum & K. A. Brehony (Eds.), *Boston marriages: Romantic but asexual relationships among contemporary lesbians* (pp. 3–14). The University of Massachusetts Press.

Saewyc, E. M., Bauer, G. R., Skay, C. L., Resnick, M. D., Reis, E., & Murphy, A. (2004). Measuring sexual orientation in adolescent health surveys: Evaluation of eight school-based surveys. *Journal of Adolescent Health, 35*, 345.

Sarwer, D. B., & Steffen, K. J. (2015). Quality of life, body image and sexual functioning in bariatric surgery patients: Quality of life and sexual functioning. *European Eating Disorders Review: The Journal of the Eating Disorders Association, 23*, 504–508.

Sarwer, D. B., Lavery, M., & Spitzer, J. C. (2012). A review of the relationships between extreme obesity, quality of life, and sexual function. *Obesity Surgery, 22*, 668–676.

Schneider, J. A., O'leary, A., & Jenkins, S. R. (1995). Gender, sexual orientation, and disordered eating. *Psychology & Health, 10*, 113–128.

Seidman, S. (1996). Introduction. In S. Seidman (Ed.), *Queer Theory/Sociology* (pp. 1–29). Wiley-Blackwell Publishers.

Semlyen, J., Curtis, T. J., & Varney, J. (2020). Sexual orientation identity in relation to unhealthy body mass index: Individual participant data meta-analysis of 93 429 individuals from 12 UK health surveys. *Journal of Public Health, 42*, 98–106.

Share, T. L., & Mintz, L. B. (2002). Differences between lesbians and heterosexual women in disordered eating and related attitudes. *Journal of Homosexuality, 42*, 89–106.

Smith, A. M. A., Rissel, C. E., Richters, J., Grulich, A. E., & de Visser, R. O. (2003). Sex in Australia: Sexual identity, sexual attraction and sexual experience among a representative sample of adults. *Australian and New Zealand Journal of Public Health, 27*, 138–145.

StataCorp. (2021). *Stata survey data reference manual, release 17*. StataCorp LLC.

Strong, S. M., Williamson, D. A., Netemeyer, R. G., & Geer, J. H. (2000). Eating disorder symptoms and concerns about body differ as a function of gender and sexual orientation. *Journal of Social and Clinical Psychology, 19*, 240–255.

Swami, V., Laughton, R., Grover, S., & Furnham, A. (2019). Asexuality is inversely associated with positive body image in British adults. *Heliyon, 5*, e02452.

Taskin Yilmaz, F., Kumsar, A. K., & Demirel, G. (2019). The effect of body image on sexual quality of life in obese married women. *Health Care for Women International, 40*, 479–492.

The Oxford English Dictionary. (2000). Second edition. Prepared by J.A. Simpson and E.S.C. Weiner. Clarendon Press.

Thompson, J. K. (2001). *Body image, eating disorders, and obesity: An integrative guide for assessment and treatment*. American Psychological Association.

Westphal, S. P. (2004). Glad to be asexual. *New Scientist, 17*, 7.

Wichstrøm, L. (2006). Sexual orientation as a risk factor for bulimic symptoms. *The International Journal of Eating Disorders, 39*, 448–453.

Witkos, M., Uttaburanont, M., Lang, C. D., & Arora, R. (2008). Costs of and reasons for obesity. *Journal of the Cardiometabolic Syndrome, 3*, 173–176.

Yean, C., Benau, E. M., Dakanalis, A., Hormes, J. M., Perone, J., & Alix Timko, C. (2013). The relationship of sex and sexual orientation to self-esteem, body shape satisfaction, and eating disorder symptomatology. *Frontiers in Psychology, 4*, 887.

Yelland, C., & Tiggemann, M. (2003). Muscularity and the gay ideal: Body dissatisfaction and disordered eating in homosexual men. *Eating Behaviors, 4*, 107–116.

16 Are Gay Men More Fit? Obesity and Overweight Differences Among Gay and Straight Men

Sharon Baker-Hughes and Dudley L. Poston, Jr.

What does it mean to be a gay man in America? Our society has undergone a transition in which the gay man, once vilified, now has a fairly regular representation in the media. This seems to suggest that the public acceptance and understanding of sexuality and sexual orientation may have changed, and that gay men, at least in certain roles, are now more accepted, and perhaps even celebrated. For example, the "gay best friend" has come to be its own genre in mainstream media (Shugart, 2003).

However, increased visibility does not necessarily indicate acceptance, and several have argued that media representations sometimes involve stereotypical portrayals (Raley & Lucas, 2006). Stereotypical gay males may be portrayed as flamboyant, hypersexual, effeminate, fashionable, thin, and preoccupied with body image (Madon, 1997; McLaughlin & Rodriguez, 2017; Rothmann, 2013), These last two stereotypes have potential relevance for several health outcomes, including overweight and obesity.

Like many marginalized identities, sexual orientation and sexuality have been narrowly defined based on certain behaviors, characteristics, and expectations of what it means to be a gay man in America. A hypersexualized view of gay men suggests they are primarily visual creatures, and they desire sexual partners who are well kempt, attractive, and thin. In fact, research suggests that gay men, more so than straight men, place a greater emphasis on physical attractiveness in order to conform to beauty ideals and to be more sexually attractive (Siever, 1996; Wood, 2004). Similarly, the notion that gay men are preoccupied with body issues might suggest a greater tendency to be thin. For the stereotypical gay man, this definition of thin may be somewhat more nuanced based on degree of muscularity. Our collective subconscious may answer the question in the title to our chapter, "Are gay men more fit?" with a resounding "Yes." The evidence, however, may have a more detailed response. In this chapter, we endeavor to answer the question, are gay men less likely to be characterized by obesity or overweight than straight men?

Despite an expansive literature in the last few decades on the qualities and characteristics of gay and straight men, research that explores the prevalence of obesity and overweight in the gay male population is much more limited, especially comparing them to the straight male population. In this chapter, we examine the distribution of weight status (underweight, normal weight, overweight, obese) in gay men. We also examine the likelihood of overweight or obesity in gay males compared to heterosexual males.

S. Baker-Hughes
Blinn College-Bryan Campus, Bryan, TX, USA

D. L. Poston, Jr. (✉)
Department of Sociology, Texas A & M University, College Station, TX, USA
e-mail: d-poston@tamu.edu

G. Garcia-Alexander, D. L. Poston, Jr. (eds.), *International Handbook of the Demography of Obesity*, International Handbooks of Population 12, https://doi.org/10.1007/978-3-031-10936-2_16

We first discuss the main approaches used in the research literature on the conceptualization and measurement of what it means to be a gay or straight man. We next discuss the principal obesity and overweight measure, the Body Mass Index. We examine its utility as the primary indicator of body composition and explore its limitations; this will be especially pertinent to answering our primary question. We next review the rather limited literature about the prevalence of obesity and overweight in the gay male and straight male populations. Our literature review is followed by a discussion of the data we will use in this chapter, namely, the 2017–2019 National Survey of Family Growth. Finally, we present the results of our statistical analyses of the distribution of obesity and overweight among gay and straight males. As was noted in the earlier chapter dealing with asexuals and sexuals, in this *Handbook* we are mainly using people-first language to describe obesity and overweight and their distributions. For example, we will use the phrase "people with obesity" instead of the phrase "obese people"; this indicates the "status (of obesity) as a medical condition and avoids the perpetuation of weight bias" (Kyle & Puhl, 2014; Palad & Stanford, 2018; also see Garcia-Alexander, 2019).

Conceptualizing Sexual Orientation

We noted in an earlier chapter dealing with the asexual and sexual populations that most of the social science literature conceptualizes sexual orientation using one of two perspectives, namely, essentialism or social constructionism. The essentialist point of view argues for an "essential" biological or psychological attribute that establishes a person's sexual orientation (Laumann et al., 1994: 285; Baumle et al., 2009: 19–20; Poston & Chang, 2015). Quantitative measures identify gay males as those who are sexually oriented toward persons of the same sex, straight males as those who are oriented toward persons of the opposite sex, and males who are bisexual as those who are oriented towards persons of both sexes. The social constructionist view, on the other hand, counters and critiques the essentialist approach. It is concerned not only with the conflation of biological sex and gender identity, but also argues against the notion of binary categorizations (Foucault, 1978; Butler, 1990; Seidman, 1996). According to the social constructionist view, sexuality and sexual orientation exist along a continuum, with varying degrees of homosexuality/heterosexuality. The definitions of sexuality thus vary across time, context, and cultures (Laumann et al., 1994; Katz, 1995). See the asexuality chapter by Poston and colleagues in this *Handbook* for more discussion.

Social scientists go about defining and measuring sexual orientation using different approaches. The three most common approaches focus on sexual behavior, sexual attraction, and sexual self-identification (Laumann et al., 1994; Saewyc et al., 2004; Baumle et al., 2009; Poston & Chang, 2015). Researchers using the behavioral dimension ask about one's sexual partners; do they have sex with persons of the same sex or of the opposite sex, or of both sexes? Researchers using the dimension of sexual attraction ask if the respondents are attracted to persons of the same sex, the opposite sex, or both sexes? Finally, researchers using the dimension of sexual self-identification ask how individuals self-identify, as gay, as straight, or as bisexual?

In the earlier chapter in this *Handbook* on asexuality, Poston and his colleagues noted that demographers tend to focus more on sexual behavior, psychologists and sexologists more on sexual attraction, and sociologists more on self-identification. We direct the interested reader to the detailed discussion by Bogaert (2012) of these three dimensions, as well as several other dimensions of sexual orientation. In our empirical analysis, we will examine all three dimensions of sexuality as they relate to weight status.

Conceptualizing Obesity and Overweight

Public health officials and most medical professionals accept the use of the Body Mass

Index (BMI) as the standard for identifying risk factors in adults based on their weight category. The BMI uses a mathematical formula, calculated by dividing a person's weight (in kilograms) by the square of the person's height (in meters). It is a "commonly used measure for assessing overweight or underweight [status] of men and non-pregnant women" (National Center for Health Statistics, 2020: 7). The Centers for Disease Control (CDC) applies the following designations with respect to weight status: BMIs less than 18.5 are categorized as underweight, BMIs between 18.5 and 24.9 are categorized as normal, BMIs of 25.0–29.9 are categorized as overweight, and BMIs of 30.0 or higher as obese (2021, 2022). Public health officials have promoted BMI data tables as a better index for an understanding of weight, and of weight categories, than the historically used MetLife health insurance formula where adult men and women started at a standard height and weight and then added 5 pounds per inch to determine the categories of ideal and overweight (Campos, 2004: 9). The reality is that both height/weight charts, MetLife and BMI, have been built and developed by comparing the same measures and usually provide pretty much the same basic results (Sorkin, 2014).

The primary problem associated with using BMI as the standard for body weight comparisons is that it purports to measure body composition and percentages of body fat based on that composition. This may be problematic. While BMI is calculated using a quantifiable mathematical formula that correlates a person's height and weight, it does not provide an accurate measure of body composition or any measure of body fat (Campos, 2004; Denton & Karpe, 2016; Scerpella et al., 2013). BMI supporters have argued that a pound of fat weighs as much as a pound of muscle. While it is true that one pound equals another, this assertion may illustrate a lack of understanding regarding the role of body composition and its true indication of whether an individual is overweight or obese. Muscle is more dense and compact than is fat. A person who is very athletic and muscular will have a higher BMI using the above mathematical formula but will likely have a lower percentage of fat in their body composition than the categorization would suggest. If the stereotype of gay males as more physically fit and more muscular compared to straight males is accurate, then BMI might be a particularly problematic measure in studying the true risks of obesity as it relates to sexual orientation. Indeed, public health officials often classify athletes as "anyone who is physically active enough to garner the immense health benefits that come from being active" (Campos, 2004: 134).

To further illustrate this point, Campos (2004) has examined these issues in his book *The Obesity Myth: Why America's Obsession with Weight is Hazardous to Your Health*, using BMI data of athletes in the National Football League. Remember that a BMI of 25–29.9 categorizes an individual as overweight and a BMI of 30 or more as obese. According to Campos (2004), BMI data indicate that every single running back in the National Football League is obese. The quarterbacks are all overweight or obese. Also, the running backs, hailed for their quick, fast, and nimble moves are all overweight. The top receivers are likewise overweight. These statistics have not changed significantly in the last 20 years.

The Centers for Disease Control and Prevention (CDC) defines the BMI as a screening tool but highlights on their website that BMI "...does not diagnose body fatness or health..." and urges people to visit their healthcare providers for better measures of body composition and body fat (CDC, 2022). Denton and Karpe (2016) further point out that BMI calculations change as people progress in age, and lose height, a transition which is ignored by simply using BMI. Indeed, they suggest that while BMI tends to overestimate overweight and obesity in athletic populations, it simultaneously underestimates the weight characteristics of thinner people with less lean muscle mass (Denton & Karpe, 2016).

While doctors and public health officials acknowledge that BMI may be less accurate for athletic individuals, they continue to use the measure as their primary screening tool (Denton & Karpe, 2016). The use of BMI as an explanatory factor for health outcomes could be improved by simple steps which could be incorporated by most doctors and medical practices. Scerpella et al. (2013: 40) found that "adding a single skinfold measurement of the biceps and a physical activity score significantly improved the explanatory power of body composition compared to BMI alone." Using these more inclusive elements could better inform people regarding their health risks associated with their weight and body composition.

While the measurement of BMI could certainly be improved, the BMI mathematical formula is the basis for most research. It is fortunate that for most people the mathematical BMI turns out to be moderately related with body composition. Furthermore, BMI is strongly correlated with the negative health outcomes associated with these more direct measures of body fatness (CDC, 2022). The purpose, after all, of measuring, or estimating, the percentage of body weights which consists of fat, muscle, and skeletal frame, is to determine the relative risk to individuals of those physical ailments which are associated with being overweight or obese. According to the CDC (2022), BMI is moderately correlated with both the prevalence of those outcomes and objectively better measures of body composition offered by more direct measures of body fat such as skinfold thickness measurements, bioelectrical impedance, underwater weighing, dual energy x-ray absorptiometry (DXA) and the like (see Denton & Karpe, 2016; Goyanes, 2012; Scerpella et al., 2013 for more detailed discussions of these alternative methods).

Are Gay Males More or Less Likely to Have Overweight and Obesity than Straight Males?

A Review of the Literature

Much of the quantitative research focusing on sexual orientation among U.S. adults links sexuality implicitly or explicitly to health outcomes (Laumann et al., 1994). Indeed, the primary data used by demographers and others to understand and research sexuality, life outcomes, discrimination, and other factors are gathered and sponsored by the Centers for Disease Control and Prevention in their nationally representative studies on health. It is surprising, then, that very little research exists that asks whether having overweight or obesity is related with sexual orientation status in males (Laska et al., 2015; Periera, 2021; Tuthill et al., 2020). Part of this difficulty may lie in the intersection of sexual orientation identities and other minority statuses, such as race, education, and income.

Studies which collect their own data and attempt to answer questions related to health tend to rely on convenience samples (Tuthill et al., 2020) and are often not necessarily representative of the general population. One such study asked men to self-identify their sexual orientation and then compared these with their self-reported responses about their height and weight. The results showed less of a risk of overweight and obesity among males who are gay compared to those who are straight (Tuthill et al., 2020). In a similar study using self-reported data, Periera (2021) found that the stereotypical expectations of gay men as thin and fit were in fact associated with lower risks of being obese and overweight. For example, Carpenter's (2003) research shows that obesity in gay males tends to decrease the likelihood of a partnered relationship compared to the likelihood for straight men, even when controlling for the overall lower percentages of partnerships among gay men. At least one analysis suggests that gay males may actually be at a greater risk of being underweight and malnourished to meet this "body fascist 'no pecs; no sex' world of metropolitan gay masculinity" (Richardson, 2015: 646). Similarly, Laska et al. (2015) found that males who are gay are less likely to engage in strenuous physical activity, perhaps for similar reasons as those for straight women, so as to be more appealing to men.

The results of the limited research are mixed; some find that sexual minority status is associated with healthier weights (Tuthill et al., 2020). Others suggest that in fact, gay men may be at a higher risk for underweight due to perceived pressures to be thin (Periera, 2021; Laska et al., 2015). Still other research has reported no statistically significant difference in the BMI categories of gay males when compared to straight males (Periera, 2021; Richardson, 2015). Researchers have also documented other health related trends with disparities between males who are gay and males who are straight, including a higher incidence of smoking, decreased access to healthcare, and increased mental health issues, which might impact weight and the incidence of obesity (Carpenter, 2003; Laska et al., 2015; Sang et al., 2021; Tuthill et al., 2020).

In this chapter, we attempt to address some of the voids and overcome some of the inconsistencies in the literature just reviewed. While the literature measuring obesity and sexuality is limited, the CDC now offers several nationally representative datasets that include measures of health outcomes, including obesity and overweight, while also including one or more measures of sexual orientation. In an effort to contribute to this limited literature we undertake an empirical analysis that examines the distribution of weight statuses in males on the basis of sexual minority status. We use the most recent cycle of available data from the National Survey of Family Growth (NSFG). We next discuss the data, measures, and findings.

Data: 2017–2019 U.S. National Survey of Family Growth

The National Survey of Family Growth (NSFG) is a multistage probability sample survey of female and male respondents between the ages of 15 and 49 years of age in the United States. Its major purpose is to gather information about the U.S. population on such topics as fertility and infertility, cohabitation and marriage, contraception use, family life, and general and reproductive health. See the more detailed discussion of the NSFG in the earlier chapter on asexuality in this *Handbook*. There are 5206 male respondents in the 2017–2019 NSFG.

Measures

We now discuss the questionnaire items from the NSFG that we will use in our analysis of gay males and straight males pertaining to the three most common dimensions of sexual orientation, namely, sexual behavior, sexual attraction, and sexual self-identification.

Sexual Behavior All of the male respondents in the 2017–2019 NSFG were asked if they have ever had vaginal, oral, or anal sex with a female, and if they have ever had oral or anal sex with a male. Another two questions asked about the same sexual behaviors in the past 12 months. We have categorized gay males as those who report as ever having sex with a male and never having sex with a female. Straight males are designated as those reporting they have ever had sex with a female and have never had sex with a male.

Of the 5206 male respondents, 4207 have valid responses, meaning that they can be categorized as behaving as either straight males or as gay males. According to the behavioral dimension of sexuality, 4126 of these males (98.1%) are categorized as straight, and 81 (1.9%) are categorized as gay.

Sexual Attraction The 2017–2019 NSFG asked male respondents the following question:

> People are different in their sexual attraction to other people. Which best describes your feelings? Are you: Only attracted to males, Mostly attracted to males, Equally attracted to males and females, Mostly attracted to females, Only attracted to females, or Not sure?

We have categorized gay males as those who are only or who are mainly attracted to males, while straight males are those who report they are only or are mainly attracted to females. Of the 5206 male respondents, 5001 of them, are categorized on the attraction dimension as either straight or as gay: 4845 (96.9%) of these males are classified as straight, and 156 (3.1%) are classified as gay.

Self-Identification Finally, with respect to the sexuality dimension of self-identification, the 2017–2019 NSFG asked each male respondent the following question about their identification of their sexual orientation:

> Which of the following best represents how you think of yourself? Gay or lesbian; Straight, that is, not gay; Bisexual; or Something else?

Of the 5206 male respondents in the NSFG, 4921 of them self-identify themselves as either gay (N = 137, 2.8%) or as straight (N = 4784, 97.2%).

Weight Status We noted earlier that the Body Mass Index (BMI) is the standard measure used to classify people as underweight, normal weight, overweight, or obese. BMI is calculated by taking the person's weight (in kilograms) and dividing it by the square of the person's height (in meters). Persons with BMIs less than or equal to 18.5 are categorized as underweight, those with BMIs between 18.5 and 24.9 are categorized as normal, those with BMIs of 25.0–29.9 as overweight, and those of 30.0 or higher as obese. The 2017–2019 NSFG applies these thresholds to assign adults into one of the following five categories: 1 = underweight, 2 = normal, 3 = overweight, 4 = obese, and 5 = undefined BMI. Since BMI is typically restricted to adult men and women, the 2017–2019 NSFG did not develop BMI information for male respondents who are younger than 20 years of age (National Center for Health Statistics, 2020: 7).

Analysis

As mentioned above, 1032 of the 5206 male respondents do not have valid responses on weight status. We further restrict our analyses to those who also have valid responses on the various dimensions of sexuality, thus resulting in analytic samples of 3675 males using the behavior dimension of sexuality, 4028 males using the attraction dimension, and 3960 males using the self-identification dimension.

We mention one last final point about the analyses to be presented below of obesity and overweight among gay male and straight male respondents using data from the 2017–2019 NSFG. The NSFG is a national multistage probability sample survey. Accordingly, the NSFG first sampled large areas in the U.S. consisting of metropolitan areas and counties and cities; and next their neighborhoods; and next their groups of adjacent blocks; and next their housing units; and finally, persons in the sampled households were selected for interview. In addition, minority race and ethnic group members were oversampled. To account for the complex sampling design of the NSFG we will use the "svy" suite of statistical sample adjustment methods available in the Stata 17 statistical package (StataCorp, 2021) that will adjust the analyses according to the various population and strata weights in the NSFG.

Results

We begin our analysis by examining the distribution of the BMI categories among gay males and straight males; we do this three times, categorizing the males as gay or straight each time according to each of the three sexuality dimensions. After undertaking these descriptive analyses, we turn to logistic regression analyses estimating equations with a dependent variable of sexual orientation (gay or straight) and with the independent variables of obese (one set of equations) or obese/overweight (second set of equations); each set contains three equations, one for each of the three sexuality dimensions.

We first present the descriptive analyses. We examine the distribution of all five body mass index (BMI) categories among the gay male and straight male populations to determine whether the distributions differ significantly among the two populations. First, we examine the distribution of BMI categories among males who *behave* sexually as gay or as straight. In the 2017–2019 NSFG, 4207 men were categorized as behaving sexually as either straight or as gay. Of these 4207 respondents, 3675 are at least 20 years of age and thus had valid information on BMI.

Table 16.1 (top panel) presents data on the survey-adjusted distributions of the BMI

Table 16.1 Distributions of BMI categories among gay males and straight males, 20–49 years of age by each of three dimensions of sexuality: 2017–2019 National Survey of Family Growth (Survey adjusted using NSFG respondent sampling weights)

	Behavior dimension of sexuality (N = 3675 males)		
	Gay males	**Straight males**	**All males**
	%	%	%
BMI category			
Underweight	0.43	1.07	1.06
Normal weight	41.85	26.95	27.21
Overweight	32.36	39.94	39.81
Obese	25.36	31.29	31.19
Undefined BMI	0.00	0.74	0.73
TOTAL	**100.00**	**99.99**	**100.00**
χ^2 = 7.41, F = 1.23, P = 0.2998			
	Attraction dimension of sexuality (N = 4028 males)		
	Gay males	**Straight males**	**All males**
	%	%	%
BMI category			
Underweight	0.00	1.10	1.07
Normal weight	46.37	27.58	28.10
Overweight	31.82	39.80	39.58
Obese	21.80	30.65	30.41
Undefined BMI	0.00	0.87	0.84
TOTAL	**99.99**	**99.99**	**100.00**
χ^2 = 20.39, F = 3.11, P = 0.0185			
	Self-identification dimension of sexuality (N = 3960 males)		
	Gay males	**Straight males**	**All males**
	%	%	%
BMI category			
Underweight	0.23	1.13	1.10
Normal weight	41.76	27.49	27.92
Overweight	33.55	39.83	39.64
Obese	24.46	30.68	30.50
Undefined BMI	0.00	0.87	0.84
TOTAL	**100.00**	**99.99**	**100.00**
χ^2 = 12.74, F = 2.17, P = 0.0925			

categories among these 3675 gay males and straight males, according to the behavior dimension of sexuality. The data indicate that a much higher percentage of gay males are in the normal weight category compared to straight males; 41.9% versus 27.0%, respectively. A lower percentage of gay males, 32.4%, are in the overweight category compared to 39.9% of straight males. Similarly, a lower percentage of gay men, 25.4%, compared to straight men, 31.3, falls into the obese category. In sum, compared to straight males, gay males tend to be more characterized by normal weight and less characterized by overweight and obesity.

To determine whether there is a statistically significant difference in the distribution of the five BMI categories among the gay males compared to the distribution among the straight males, we calculated a Pearson χ^2 statistic which was then corrected for the survey design with a "second-order correction" (Rao & Scott, 1984), and converted into an F statistic. The F test of 1.23 indicates that the gay male and straight male groups, categorized by the behavior dimension of sexuality, do not differ significantly with respect to the distribution of the five BMI categories.

We next examine the distributions of the BMI categories among gay and straight males, categorized as being either straight or gay according to the *attraction* dimension of sexuality. Of the male respondents in the NSFG who are between the ages of 20 and 49 (meaning they have valid BMI data), 4028 may be designated as gay or straight according to the sexual attraction dimension. In the second panel of Table 16.1, we present the results of our analyses of the distributions of the BMI categories on the basis of attraction. Nearly twice as many men who report attraction to other men (46%) fall into the normal weight category than men who are attracted to women (28%). A higher percentage of straight males are in both the overweight and obese BMI categories than are gay males. As with the behavioral dimension, those men classified as gay on the basis of sexual attraction have much higher levels of normal weight, and they have less overweight and obesity compared to men who are attracted to women. Moreover, the distribution of the BMI categories is significantly different among the gay males than among the straight males, $F = 3.11$, $P = 0.02$.

Finally, we compare the BMI category distributions among the gay male and straight male populations, distinguishing the groups according to their sexuality *self-identification*. Recall from our earlier discussion that of the male respondents in the 2017–2019 NSFG, more than 95% of them self-identify as either gay or as straight. When we further restrict this group to males between the ages of 20 and 49, we are left with 3960 males.

In the third panel of Table 16.1, we present the distributions of the BMI categories among male groups, categorized by their sexuality self-identification. A larger percentage of men who self-identify as gay are in the normal weight category, 42%, compared to 27.5% of those who identify as straight males. Also, smaller percentages of gay males have overweight or obesity (33.6% and 24.5%) compared to men who self-identify as straight males (39.8% and 30.7%). However, the two distributions are not statistically different from one another, $F = 2.17$, $P = 0.09$.

To summarize the results in Table 16.1, we conducted three analyses comparing the distribution of the five BMI categories among gay males with the distribution among straight males. In all three analyses, we showed higher percentages of gay males compared to straight males in the normal weight category, and lower percentages in the overweight and obese categories. But, only in the analysis classifying the sexual orientation of the respondents according to the sexual attraction dimension did we find the distribution of the BMI categories for gay males to be significantly different from the distribution for straight males.

We now focus on the obesity and overweight variables in our comparisons of gay males with straight males. This will permit a more straightforward test of the hypothesis that gay males are more fit, that is, less characterized by obesity and overweight, than are straight males. First, we have dropped from our analysis those adult males with an "undefined BMI." For males defined as gay or straight according to any of the three sexuality dimensions, males with an "undefined BMI" comprise only between 0.7% and 0.8% of all males. We next created a dummy variable labelled "obesity"; males were assigned a value of 1 if classified with the BMI category of obese, that is, if their BMI was 30.0 or higher, and 0 if they had one of the other three BMI categories of underweight, normal weight, or overweight. We then created a second dummy variable labelled "overweight/obese," scored 1 if the male was classified with either of the two BMI categories of overweight or obese, that is, if their BMI was 25.0 or higher, and 0 if categorized as underweight or normal weight.

But rather than calculating chi-squared statistics based on cross-tabulations of each of the two variables with whether the males are gay or straight, as we reported in Table 16.1, we opted to fit a logistic regression equation with the gay male dummy variable (gay male = 1) as the dependent variable, and the obesity dummy variable (obese = 1) as the independent variable in one equation, and then the overweight/obese dummy variable as the independent variable in a second equation. We are not using the obesity and overweight/obese independent variables in the logistic regression equations to predict the likelihood of a male being gay or straight. We are using the logistic equation results to indicate whether gay males are significantly different from straight males on the overweight/obese variable(s).

In Table 16.2 we present the results of one logistic regression equation examining the log odds relationship between the dummy variable of gay male and the independent variable of obesity, and then the results of a second logistic regression equation but with the independent variable of overweight or obese. We use the t-test to evaluate the statistical significance of a logit regression coefficient; t-test values greater than 1.96 indicate that the regression coefficient is statistically significant, that is, its P-value is 0.05 or lower.

The top third of Table 16.2 presents for gay males and straight males, so designated according to the behavior dimension of sexuality, thc logit equation results of the gay male dummy variable regressed on the obese dummy variable; and next the results of the equation regressing the gay male dummy variable on the overweight or obese dummy variable. The second third of the table presents results for similar equations for gay and straight males classified based on their sexual attraction. And the bottom third of Table 16.2 presents results for gay and straight males designated based on the self-identification of their sexuality.

The results of the first logit regression equation in the top panel of Table 16.2 report the association between obesity (yes/no) and gay male (yes/no). The obesity coefficient is negative as hypothesized, but its value of −0.30 is not statistically significant, with a t-test value of −1.01. Gay males are not significantly different from straight males with respect to obesity. The results of the second logit regression equation in the top panel presents the association between the overweight or obese independent variable (yes/no)

Table 16.2 Logistic regression equation coefficients of gay males versus straight males on the independent variable of obesity (yes/no), and on the independent variable of overweight or obesity (yes/no), by each of three dimensions of sexuality: 2017–2019 National Survey of Family Growth (Survey adjusted using NSFG respondent sampling weights)

	Behavior dimension of sexuality (N = 3646 males)	
Independent variable	**Logit coefficient**	**t statistic**
Obese (yes = 1)	−0.30	−1.01
Constant	−3.94	−17.58
	Behavior dimension of sexuality (N = 3646 males)	
Independent variable	**Logit coefficient**	**t statistic**
Overweight or obese (yes = 1)	−0.62	−1.96
Constant	−3.63	−13.11
	Attraction dimension of sexuality (N = 3990 males)	
Independent variable	**Logit coefficient**	**t statistic**
Overweight (yes = 1)	−0.47	−1.89
Constant	−3.42	−24.32
	Attraction dimension of sexuality (N = 3990 males)	
Independent variable	**Logit coefficient**	**t statistic**
Overweight or obese (yes = 1)	−0.75	−2.95
Constant	−3.08	−16.39
	Self-identification dimension of sexuality (N = 3923 males)	
Independent variable	**Logit coefficient**	**t statistic**
Obese (yes = 1)	−0.33	−1.18
Constant	−3.39	−23.03
	Self-identification dimension of sexuality (N = 3923 males)	
Independent variable	**Logit coefficient**	**t statistic**
Overweight or obese (yes = 1)	−0.58	−2.27
Constant	−3.10	−16.17

and gay male (yes/no). The overweight or obese coefficient is negative as hypothesized and statistically significant; the logit coefficient is −0.62, with a t-test value of 1.96. Gay men are significantly less likely to be obese or overweight compared to straight males.

In the middle panel of Table 16.2 we report the results of two similar logistic regression equations, but here we have designated the males as gay or straight based on the attraction dimension. The results of the first equation in the middle panel show that the obesity coefficient is negative as hypothesized, but its value of −0.47 is not statistically significant. The results from the second equation inform us that the overweight or obese independent variable is significantly related with a male being gay versus being straight; the logit coefficient has a value of −0.75. This indicates that according to the attraction dimension of sexuality, gay males are significantly less likely than straight males to be obese or overweight.

In the bottom panel of Table 16.2, we again fit two logistic regression equations with the dependent variable of the male being gay versus being straight; but the gay/straight classification in these two equations is based on the males' self-identification of their sexuality. In the first logit regression equation we are testing whether there is an association between males with obesity and their sexual orientation of gay versus straight. The logit coefficient is negative as hypothesized but is not statistically significant. In the second equation, we are testing whether the overweight or obese independent variable is significantly associated with males being gay versus straight. This logit coefficient is statistically significant with a value of −0.58, $t = -2.27$. According to the self-identification dimension of sexuality, gay males are significantly less likely than straight males to be obese or overweight.

In this section, we conducted two separate analyses of gay males and straight males, each time designating the males as gay or as straight according to one of three dimensions of sexual orientation. In the first analyses, with the results presented in Table 16.1, we compared the distribution of the five BMI categories among gay males with its distribution among straight males. We first classified the males as gay or straight according to their sexual behavior, we next classified them as gay or straight according to their sexual attraction, and lastly, we classified them according to their sexual self-identification. In all three analyses, we showed higher percentages of gay males compared to straight males in the normal weight category, and lower percentages in the overweight and obese categories. But only in the analysis where we classified the sexual orientation of the males according to the sexual attraction dimension did we find the distribution of the BMI categories for gay males to be significantly different from that for straight males.

In the second set of analyses, we estimated one logistic regression equation with the dependent variable of gay versus straight, and the independent variable of obese (yes = 1); and we estimated a second logistic regression equation but changed the independent variable to overweight/obese (yes = 1). We estimated these equations three different times, each time designating the males as gay or straight based on one of the three dimensions of sexuality; see the results in Table 16.2. In all six equations, the obese independent variable and the overweight or obese independent variable were shown to be negatively related with the gay versus straight dependent variable; but only in the equations with the overweight/obese independent variable were the relationships with the dependent variable statistically significant. We showed that irrespective of how the gay versus straight distinction is conceptualized, gay males are less likely than straight males to be classified as overweight or as obese. These analyses support the commonly held stereotype that gay males are more physically fit than straight males.

Conclusion

We started this chapter with a question asking if gay men are more fit than straight men. We proceeded then to examine the distribution of obesity and overweight among gay and straight men. The literature focusing on obesity and overweight among gay and straight males is limited, with a tendency to argue that gay men tend to be less overweight and less obese than straight men, hence they are more fit. We endeavored in this chapter to test empirically the above relationship.

We first needed to consider the conceptualization of male sexuality. That is, what do we mean when we state that one male is gay and another one is straight? What does it mean to be a gay male, and what does it mean to be a straight male? We showed that research on male sexuality conceptualizes the phenomenon in terms of three different dimensions, namely, sexual behavior, sexual attraction, and sexual self-identification. According to the behavior dimension, men who have sex with men are defined as gay; men who have sex with women are defined as straight. In contrast, the sexual attraction dimension defines gay men as those who are sexually attracted to men, and straight men as those who are sexually attracted to women. Finally, the self-identification dimension defines gay men as those who self-identify as gay, and straight men as those who self-identify as straight.

We then presented our empirical analyses in which we used data from the 2017–2019 National Survey of Family Growth. The 2017–2019 NSFG contains data for 5206 male respondents. We differentiated these men into gay and straight categories depending on how they answered the NSFG questions on sexual behavior, sexual attraction, and sexual self-identification. Based on each of the three dimensions, not all 5206 male respondents ended up being classified as either gay or straight; some ended up being classified as bisexual and some as asexual, and these men were not included in our analyses. Of those male respondents who were gay or straight according to the questions dealing with sexual behavior, 98.1% were classified as straight, and 1.9% as gay. Of those classified according to the sexual attraction question, 96.9% were designated as straight, and 3.1% as gay. And of those males classified according to the sexual self-identification question, 97.3% were defined as straight, and 2.8% as gay. We next examined the degree of obesity and overweight in gay and straight males. Obese and overweight males were less likely to be gay, and more likely to be straight, irrespective of which of the three sexuality dimensions was used to designate whether they were straight or gay.

Using all three dimensions of sexuality one at a time, we found that gay males are less likely to be characterized by overweight or obesity than are straight males. The question asked in the title to our chapter may be answered affirmatively. Yes, gay men do indeed tend to be more fit than straight men. Our empirical findings are consistent with those in the rather limited literature exploring the prevalence of obesity and overweight in the gay and straight male populations.

These results suggest several opportunities for future research. Let us mention one specific future research opportunity, one involving the conceptualization and measurement of sexual orientation in more of a social constructionist manner. That is, rather than defining a gay male in three different ways, as we did in this chapter, namely, as a male who behaves sexually with males, or as a male who is attracted sexually to males, or as a male who self-identifies as gay, in future research we might combine together the three approaches. We would thus define a gay male as a male who behaves sexually with males, and/or who is sexually attracted to males, and/or who self-identifies as gay. This is clearly a much broader conceptualization, and it would also typically result in a larger population of gay males. One analysis, not three analyses, would then be conducted, comparing gay males with straight males.

Alternatively, we could define gay males in not only one way, as just noted, and in not only three ways, as in the analyses in this chapter, but in seven ways, as follows:

- males who behave sexually with males;
- males who are attracted sexually to males;
- males who self-identify as gay;
- males who behave sexually with males and who are attracted sexually to males;
- males who behave sexually with males and who self-identify as gay;
- males who are attracted sexually to males and who self-identify as gay; and

– males who behave sexually with males and who are attracted sexually to males and who self-identify as gay.

Laumann and his colleagues (1994) and Poston and Chang (2015) used the above approach in their analyses of the prevalence of male and female homosexuality and heterosexuality. Both analyses employed Venn diagrams with "overlapping circles to display all the logically possible intersections among different categories" of sexuality (Laumann et al., 1994: 298). Both showed that an essentialist conceptualization of male and female homosexuality, that is one defining a homosexual as one who behaves sexually with same-sex persons, and who is attracted sexually to persons of the same sex, and who self-identifies as homosexual, is much more restrictive than a social constructionist approach. Their research demonstrated the importance of a social constructionist perspective in developing an understanding of sexuality. They noted that "although some individuals provided the same sexual response ... on all three dimensions, most of the respondents gave one sexual response" (Poston & Chang, 2015: 371) to the question on one dimension and another sexual response to the question on another dimension. Using a social constructionist orientation in future research analyses of sexuality will provide us with a much more encompassing understanding of sexuality.

References

Baumle, A. K., Compton, D.'. L., & Poston, D. L., Jr. (2009). *Same-sex partners: The social demography of sexual orientation*. SUNY Press.

Bogaert, A. F. (2012). *Understanding asexuality*. Rowman and Littlefield Publishers.

Butler, J. (1990). *Gender trouble*. Routledge.

Campos, P. F. (2004). *The obesity myth: Why America's obsession with weight is hazardous to your health*. Avery.

Carpenter, C. (2003). Sexual orientation and body weight: Evidence from multiple surveys. *Gender Issues, 21*(3), 60–774.

Centers for Disease Control and Prevention. (2021). *Defining adult overweight and obesity*. Available at: https://www.cdc.gov/obesity/adult/defining.html. Accessed 31 May 2022.

Centers for Disease Control and Prevention. (2022). *All about adult BMI*. Available at: https://www.cdc.gov/healthyweight/assessing/bmi/index.html. Accessed 19 Feb 2022.

Denton, N., & Karpe, F. (2016). Measuring body composition and regional fat mass accurately. *Practical Diabetes, 33*(7), 224–226.

Foucault, M. (1978). *The history of sexuality: An introduction* (Vol. 1). Vintage Books.

Garcia-Alexander, G. (2019). "The demography of obesity." Chapter 33. In D. L. Poston Jr. (Ed.), *Handbook of population* (2nd ed., pp. 859–873). Springer Nature.

Goyanes, C. (2012). The scale lies! *Self, 34*(8), 62.

Katz, J. (1995). *The invention of heterosexuality*. Penguin Books, Inc.

Kyle, T. K., & Puhl, R. M. (2014). Putting people first in obesity. *Obesity, 22*, 1211–1211.

Laska, M. N., VanKim, N. A., Erickson, D. J., Lust, K., Eisenberg, M. E., & Simon Rosser, B. R. (2015). Disparities in weight and weight behaviors by sexual orientation in college students. *American Journal of Public Health, 105*(1), 111–121.

Laumann, E. O., Gagnon, J. H., Michael, R. T., & Michaels, S. (1994). *The social organization of sexuality: Sexual practices in the United States*. The University of Chicago Press.

Madon, S. (1997). What do people believe about gay males? A study of stereotype, content and strength. *Sex Roles, 37*, 663–685.

McLaughlin, B., & Rodriguez, N. S. (2017). Identifying with a stereotype: The divergent effects of exposure to homosexual television characters. *Journal of Homosexuality, 64*, 1196–1213.

National Center for Health Statistics. (2020). *Public-use data file documentation, 2017–2019 National Survey of Family Growth, User's Guide, Appendix 7C*. National Center for Health Statistics. https://www.cdc.gov/nchs/data/nsfg/NSFG-2017-2019-UG-App7c-RestrictedUseRDCvars-508.pdf. Accessed 10 Nov 2021.

Palad, C. J., & Stanford, F. C. (2018). "Use of people-first language with regard to obesity" [Letter to the editor]. *The American Journal of Clinical Nutrition, 108*, 201–203.

Periera, H. (2021). Sexual health determinants of normal weight, overweight, and obese sexual minority men. *Journal of Obesity, 3*, 1–9.

Poston, D. L., & Chang, Y.-T. (2015). The conceptualization and measurement of the homosexual, heterosexual and bisexual populations in the United States. In M. Nazrul Hoque & L. B. Potter (Eds.), *Emerging techniques in applied demography* (pp. 359–378). Springer.

Raley, A. B., & Lucas, J. L. (2006). Stereotype or success? *Journal of Homosexuality, 51*, 19–38.

Rao, J. N. K., & Scott, A. J. (1984). On chi-squared tests for multiway contingency tables with cell proportions estimated from survey data. *Annals of Statistics, 12*, 46–60.

Richardson, N. (2015). Fat gay men: Girth, mirth, and the politics of stigma. *Sociology of Health & Illness, 37*(4), 646–648.

Rothmann, J. (2013). Send in the (gay) clowns: Will & grace and modern family as 'sensibly queer'. *Acta Academica, 45*, 40–83.

Saewyc, E. M., Bauer, G. R., Skay, C. L., Resnick, M. D., Reis, E., & Murphy, A. (2004). Measuring sexual orientation in adolescent health surveys: Evaluation of eight school-based surveys. *Journal of Adolescent Health, 35*, 345e.1–345e.15.

Sang, J. M., Marcus Greatheart, L., Wang, J. B., Lal, A., Card, K. G., Blackwell, E., Lachowsky, N. J., Roth, E. A., Eric, R. S. H., & Moore, D. M. (2021). Assessing bear/cub/otter identity and history of cardiovascular disease among gay, bisexual, and other men who have sex with men in metro Vancouver. *Canadian Journal of Human Sexuality, 30*(1), 78–93.

Scerpella, T. A., Gero, N. M., Ursillo, C. R., Rosenbaum, P. F., & Dowthwaite, J. N. (2013). Improved body composition assessment using biceps skinfold and physical activity score in premenarcheal girls: A DXA-based validation study. *International Journal of Body Composition Research, 11*(2), 35–41.

Seidman, S. (1996). Introduction. In S. Seidman (Ed.), *Queer theory/sociology* (pp. 1–29). Wiley-Blackwell Publishers.

Shugart, H. A. (2003). Reinventing privilege: The new (gay) man in contemporary popular media. *Critical Studies in Media Communication, 20*, 67–91.

Siever, M. D. (1996). The perils of sexual objectification: Sexual orientation, gender, and socioculturally acquired vulnerability to body dissatisfaction and eating disorders. In C. J. Alexander (Ed.), *Gay and lesbian mental health: A sourcebook for practitioners* (pp. 201–226). The Haworth Press, Inc.

Sorkin, J. D. (2014). BMI, age, and mortality: The slaying of a beautiful hypothesis by an ugly fact. *The American Journal of Clinical Nutrition, 99*, 759–760.

StataCorp. (2021). *Stata survey data reference manual, release 17*. StataCorp LLC.

Tuthill, Z., Denney, J. T., & Gorman, B. (2020). Racial disparities in health and health behaviors among gay, lesbian, bisexual, and heterosexual men and women in the BRFSS-SOP. *Ethnicity & Health, 25*(2), 177–188.

Wood, M. J. (2004). The gay male gaze. *Journal of Gay & Lesbian Social Services, 17*, 43–62.

17 Prevalence and Trends in Obesity and Overweight Among U.S. Women: Do Lesbians Differ from Straight Women?

Carol S. Walther and Dudley L. Poston, Jr.

Women in western cultures for centuries have faced enormous pressures to achieve and maintain thinness and various beauty standards (Donaghue & Clemitshaw, 2012). However, some have argued that lesbians, i.e., women with exclusive romantic/sexual attractions to and/or relationships with other women,[1] may be protected from pressures of a body acceptance of thinness (Bowen et al., 2008; Morrison et al., 2004; Yost & Chmielewski, 2011). Eliason and Fogel (2015) have suggested that the status of body acceptance in lesbian communities is a complicated one. Some lesbian communities follow feminist perspectives regarding body acceptance. Indeed, it has been reported that some lesbians specifically rate larger bodies as more attractive than normal weight bodies (Cohen & Tannenbaum, 2001). Some lesbian communities are more accepting of bigger bodies – their own and those of others – than are heterosexual women (Maor, 2012; Morrison et al., 2004; Swami et al., 2010).

Some researchers have found that lesbians are often caught between mainstream heterosexual body norms and their community norms to accept their bodies as they are (Fogel et al. 2009; Kelly, 2007). Others have found that lesbians follow the same norms as heterosexual women when it comes to weight and body acceptance (Huxley et al., 2014; Luis, 2012; Peplau et al., 2009). The limited literature is clearly mixed regarding these issues.

In this chapter, we examine issues of weight and body image among lesbians and heterosexual women. We ask specifically whether the distribution of the basic categories of body mass index (BMI) differs significantly for lesbians compared to the distribution for straight women. We also ask whether lesbians compared to straight women are more or less likely to be characterized by obesity and overweight. Some of the above literature has found that there should be no differences in these outcomes among lesbians and straight women, and some of the literature indicates differences.

This chapter is the third chapter in this *Handbook* dealing with obesity and sexual orientation. Preceding this chapter are chapters focusing on the relationship between obesity and asexuality and the relationship between obesity and gay male sexuality. We invite the reader to refer to these two earlier chapters for detailed discussions of the main approaches used in the research

[1] In this chapter the terms lesbian, sexual minority women, and same-sex females are used interchangeably; the terms gay, gay men, and same-sex males are also used interchangeably.

C. S. Walther (✉)
Department of Sociology, Northern Illinois University, DeKalb, IL, USA
e-mail: cwalther@niu.edu

D. L. Poston, Jr.
Department of Sociology, Texas A & M University, College Station, TX, USA
e-mail: d-poston@tamu.edu

G. Garcia-Alexander, D. L. Poston, Jr. (eds.), *International Handbook of the Demography of Obesity*, International Handbooks of Population 12, https://doi.org/10.1007/978-3-031-10936-2_17

literature on the conceptualization and measurement of human sexuality, as well as issues dealing with the conceptualization and measurement of Body Mass Index (BMI). We will treat these issues below, but in an abbreviated manner.

In the next section we review and summarize some of the literature about the current prevalence and trends of obesity and overweight in the lesbian and heterosexual women populations. Following our review of prevalence and trends, we will discuss the 2017–2019 National Survey of Family Growth, the dataset that we will be using in our analyses. This will be followed by our statistical analyses of obesity and overweight among lesbians and heterosexual women. As noted in other chapters, we will mainly use people-first language to describe obesity and overweight and their distribution among lesbians and heterosexual women (Kyle & Puhl, 2014; Palad & Stanford, 2018; also see Garcia-Alexander, 2019).

Current Prevalence and Trends

Obesity may be defined as "weight that is higher than what is considered healthy for a given height" (Centers for Disease Control and Prevention, 2021b). According to the World Health Organization (2021), the fundamental cause of obesity and overweight is an energy imbalance between calories consumed and calories expended.

The WHO (2021) reports the following two main global trends:

- There has been an increased intake of energy-dense foods that are high in fat and sugars; and an increase in physical inactivity due to the increasingly sedentary nature of many forms of work, changing modes of transportation, and increasing urbanization.
- Changes in dietary and physical activity patterns are often the result of environmental and societal changes associated with development and lack of supportive policies in sectors such as health, agriculture, transport, urban planning, environment, food processing, distribution, marketing, and education.

The WHO (2021) also notes that all the states of the U.S. report obesity rates of at least twenty percent. The highest rates are reported in the Midwestern states (33.9%) and the Southern states (33.3%) states. More specifically, the Centers for Disease Control and Prevention (2022) reports that in 2020, 63% of lesbians were in good health, which is similar to the percentage for heterosexual women. Furthermore, the CDC reports that 19% of lesbians smoked compared to 15% for heterosexual women, and that 37% of lesbians were obese compared to 30% of heterosexual women. Lew et al. (2018) found that White lesbians had a 33% obesity prevalence, African American lesbians a 27.7% obesity prevalence and Hispanic lesbians a 49.1% obesity prevalence, the highest of any of the race-ethnic groups. Another study found that White and African American lesbians had a higher risk of overweight, but among Latinas, sexual minority status was not linked to weight (Deputy & Boehmer, 2014).

Some research has found that lesbians appear to have a higher prevalence of obesity than heterosexual women, no matter the race or ethnicity of the woman (Bowen et al., 2008; Carpenter, 2003; Lew et al., 2018; Semlyen et al., 2019; Simenson et al., 2020; Struble et al., 2010; Tuthill et al., 2020). However, this body of work remains limited as many studies involving sexual minorities may not be generalizable, use small samples, inconsistently apply measures of sexual identity, or may suffer from mismeasurement as sexual minority women may be less likely to disclose (Bowen et al., 2008; Lew et al., 2018).

In consideration of other health outcomes, sexual minority women have higher rates of mental distress, tobacco use, binge drinking, and gastrointestinal conditions than heterosexual women (Caceres et al., 2019; Conron et al., 2010; Dyar et al., 2019; Fredriksen-Goldsen et al., 2012). Co-occurring diseases such as heart attack, stroke, and type 2 diabetes have been reported more often among lesbians. For example, sexual minority women reported higher rates of CVD risk factors. Corliss et al. (2018) reported that lesbians have a much higher incidence of type 2 diabetes than their heterosexual peers. They found that lesbians had higher BMI values which may well have contributed to their type 2 diabetes. In addition to higher odds of multiple co-occurring diseases among lesbians, they also reported lower daily vegetable intake and higher odds of consuming sugar-sweetened beverages. On the other hand, a review of studies revealed higher BMIs in lesbians, but there was no evidence of associated negative health outcomes (Eliason et al., 2015). In summary, several studies have found that lesbians appear to have a higher rate of obesity than heterosexual women, yet this area of research remains limited and more work is needed to investigate this potential association.

In this chapter, we will use current national data for the U.S. to examine some of these issues statistically in an attempt to make some sense of the limited and mixed results in the literature just reviewed. As discussed previously in the asexuality and gay men chapters in this *Handbook*, the U.S. National Survey of Family Growth provides data allowing us to address these issues including measures of health outcomes, such as obesity and overweight and several measures of sexual identity. We next discuss the 2017—2019 U.S. National Survey of Family Growth dataset.

The 2017–2019 U.S. National Survey of Family Growth

The National Survey of Family Growth (NSFG) is a multistage probability sample survey of female and male respondents between the ages of 15 and 49 years of age in the United States. The principal purpose of the NSFG is to gather information about the U.S. population on such topics as fertility and infertility, cohabitation and marriage, contraception use, family life, and general and reproductive health. See the more detailed discussion of the NSFG in the earlier chapter on asexuality and gay men in this *Handbook*. The 2017–2019 NSFG provides data for a nationally representative sample of 6141 female respondents (Centers for Disease Control and Prevention, 2021a).

Measures

We now discuss the questionnaire items from the 2017–2019 NSFG that we will use in addressing and measuring sexuality in our analysis of lesbians and heterosexual women. It has been noted in previous chapters in this *Handbook* that the three most common dimensions of sexuality are sexual behavior, sexual attraction, and sexual self-identification. We first consider the NSFG questions dealing with sexual behavior.

All the female respondents in the 2017–2019 NSFG were asked the following two questions about their sexual behavior:

> At any time in your life, have you ever had sexual intercourse with a man, that is, made love, had sex, or gone all the way? Yes or No. Have you ever had any other sexual experience of any kind with another female? Yes or No.

According to the behavioral dimension of sexuality, we have defined lesbians as those who report as ever having sex with a female and never having sex with a male, and heterosexual females as those reporting they have ever had sex with a male and have never had sex with a female.

Of the 6141 female respondents in the NSFG, 4,275 of them may be categorized according to the behavioral dimension of sexuality as either straight females or as lesbians. Of these females, 4,203 of them, or 98.3%, are categorized as straight females, and 72 of them, or 1.7%, are categorized as lesbians.

We turn next to the sexual attraction dimension of sexuality. In the 2017–2019 NSFG, the following question was asked of the female respondents:

> People are different in their sexual attraction to other people. Which best describes your feelings? Are you: Only attracted to males, Mostly attracted to males, Equally attracted to males and females, Mostly attracted to females, Only attracted to females, or Not sure?

We have categorized lesbians as those who are only, or who are mainly attracted to females, and heterosexual females as those who are only, or who are mainly attracted to males. Of the 6,141 female respondents, 5,518 of them may be categorized on the attraction dimension as either straight or as gay: 5,297 of them, or 96.0%, are classified as straight females, and 221 of them, or 4.0%, are classified as lesbians.

Finally, with respect to the self-identification dimension of sexuality, the 2017–2019 NSFG asked each female respondent the following question about their personal identification of their sexual orientation:

> Which of the following best represents how you think of yourself? Gay or lesbian;
>
> Straight, that is, not gay; Bisexual; or Something else?

Of the 6,141 female respondents in the 2017–2019 NSFG, 5,288 of them self-identify themselves as either lesbian or straight; 159 (3.0%) self-identify as lesbian, and 5,129 (97.0%) self-identify as straight.

The percentages of females classified as lesbian or straight clearly differ according to the dimension of sexuality used for the classification. If we classify the females enumerated in the 2017–2019 NSFG as lesbian or straight according to the behavioral dimension, 98.3% will be designated as straight and 1.7% as lesbian. If we use the question on sexual attraction as the basis for the classification, then 96.0% will be designated as straight and 4.0% as lesbian. If we use the question on self-identification, then 97.0% will be classified as straight and 3.0% as lesbian.

We turn now to the measurement of obesity with data from the NSFG. We noted in earlier chapters that the Body Mass Index (BMI) is the standard measure used to classify people as underweight, normal weight, overweight, or obese. One's BMI is calculated by taking the person's weight (in kilograms) and dividing it by the square of the person's height (in meters). BMIs less than or equal to 18.5 are categorized as underweight, BMIs between 18.5 and 24.9 as normal, BMIs of 25.0–29.9 as overweight, and BMIs of 30.0 or higher as obese.

In the 2017–2019 NSFG, BMIs are calculated only for adult women who are not pregnant. BMI values were not calculated female respondents who were younger than 20 years of age and/or were pregnant at the date of the interview (National Center for Health Statistics, 2020: 7). Consequently, as we will see below, 1153 of the 6141 female respondents in the NSFG were not scored on the BMI variable and thus are not categorized into one of the BMI categories just noted.

We further restrict our analyses of the female respondents to those who also have valid responses on the various dimensions of sexuality. These restrictions result in analytic samples of 4,275 females using the behavior dimension of sexuality, 5,518 females using the attraction dimension, and 5,288 females using the self-identification dimension. Finally, the NSFG is a national multistage probability sample survey and hence has a complex sampling design; everyone in the survey was not sampled randomly. Please see our detailed discussions in earlier chapters of these issues. Therefore, to account for the complex sampling design of the NSFG, we will use in our statistical analyses the "svy" suite of statistical sample adjustment methods available in the Stata 17 statistical package (StataCorp, 2021) that will adjust our analyses according to the various population and strata weights in the NSFG.

Results

Our statistical analyses will be presented in two parts. We will first examine the distribution of the BMI categories among lesbians and straight females. We will undertake these examinations three times, one time for each of the three sexuality dimensions. Following the descriptive analyses, we will then estimate logistic regression equations with a dependent variable of the sexual orientation of the female respondents (lesbian or straight) and independent variables of obese (one equation) or obese/overweight (a second equation). And as was the case above with the descriptive analyses, we will estimate these equation three times, one time for each of the three sexuality dimensions.

In the descriptive analyses, we compare the distribution of all five-body mass index (BMI) categories among the lesbian respondents with its distribution among the straight female respondents to determine whether the BMI distributions differ significantly among the two populations. We first examine the distribution of the categories among females who *behave* sexually as lesbian or as straight. In the 2017–2019 NSFG, 4275 females were categorized as behaving sexually as either straight or as lesbian. Of these respondents, 3726 are at least 20 years of age and are not pregnant, and hence have valid information on BMI.

The top panel of Table 17.1 provides data on the survey-adjusted distributions of the five BMI categories (underweight, normal weight, overweight, obese, and undefined BMI) among these 3,726 lesbians and straight females, according to the behavior dimension of sexuality. The data indicate that a much higher percentage of lesbians, compared to straight females, are in the normal weight category, namely 58.6% versus 34.1%, respectively. A much lower percentage of lesbians (16.7%) is in the overweight category compared straight females (35.4%). Compared to straight females, lesbians appear to be more characterized by normal weight and less characterized by obesity.

However, there is no statistically significant difference in the distributions of the BMI

Table 17.1 Distribution of BMI categories among lesbians and straight females, 20–49 years of age and not pregnant, by each of three dimensions of sexuality: 2017–2019 National Survey of Family Growth (survey adjusted during NSFG respondent sampling weights)

	Behavior dimension of sexuality (N = 3726 females)		
	Lesbians	**Straight females**	**All females**
	%	%	%
BMI category			
Underweight	3.16	2.35	2.36
Normal weight	58.45	34.07	34.28
Overweight	20.28	26.48	26.43
Obese	16.74	35.44	35.28
Undefined BMI	1.37	1.66	1.66
TOTAL	**100.00**	**100.00**	**100.01**
$\chi^2 = 8.95, F = 1.90, P = 0.1386$			
	Attraction dimension of sexuality (N = 4544 females)		
	Lesbians	**Straight females**	**All females**
	%	%	%
BMI category			
Underweight	2.80	2.46	2.47
Normal weight	33.30	34.14	34.12
Overweight	30.78	26.31	26.45
Obese	31.66	35.53	35.40
Undefined BMI	1.46	1.57	1.56
TOTAL	**100.00**	**100.01**	**100.00**
$\chi^2 = 1.82, F = 0.26, P = 0.8236$			
	Self-identification dimension of sexuality (N = 4357 females)		
	Lesbians	**Straight females**	**All females**
	%	%	%
BMI category			
Underweight	3.67	2.57	2.60
Normal weight	36.51	33.81	33.88
Overweight	28.03	26.17	26.22
Obese	31.42	35.97	35.85
Undefined BMI	0.37	1.48	1.45
TOTAL	**100.00**	**100.00**	**100.00**
$\chi^2 = 2.50, F = 0.44, P = 0.7102$			

categories in the two groups of female respondents. We calculated a Pearson $\chi 2$ statistic which was then corrected for the survey design with a "second-order correction" (Rao & Scott, 1984), and converted into an F statistic. The F test of 1.90 indicates that the lesbian and straight female population groups, categorized by the behavior dimension of sexuality, do not differ significantly with respect to the distribution of the five BMI categories.

We next compare the distributions of the BMI categories among lesbians and straight females where we have categorized their sexual orientation according to the *attraction* dimension of sexuality. Of the female respondents in the NSFG who are between the ages of 20 and 49 and who are not pregnant, indicating that they have valid BMI data, 4544 of them may be classified as either lesbian or as straight according to the sexual attraction dimension. In the second panel of Table 17.1, we present the results of our analyses of the distributions of the BMI categories for the two groups of females. The percentages of lesbians in each of the five BMI category groupings are rather similar to the percentages of straight females. The distribution of the BMI categories for the lesbians is not significantly different from the distribution for the straight females, $F = 0.26$, $P = 0.82$.

Lastly, we compare the distributions of the BMI categories among the lesbian and straight female populations, classifying their sexual orientations according to their *self-identification* of their sexual orientation. Of the female respondents in the 2017–2019 NSFG, 5288 of them self-identify as either gay or as straight. When we further restrict this group to females between the ages of 20 and 49 who are not pregnant, we are left with 4,357 respondents for analysis.

In the third panel of Table 17.1, we present the distributions of the BMI categories among the lesbian and straight female groups. As was the case in the previous analysis of women classified according to the attraction dimension of sexuality (panel 2 of Table 17.1), in this analysis of women classified according to their self-identification of their sexuality, there are hardly any differences in their percentages in each of the five BMI category groups. The two distributions of BMI categories are not statistically different from one another, $F = 0.44$, $P = 0.71$.

To summarize the results in Table 17.1, we conducted three analyses comparing the distribution of the five BMI categories for lesbians with the distribution for straight females. In all three analyses, the two distributions of the BMI categories do not differ significantly between the two groups of lesbians and straight females. Lesbians and straight females do not show significantly different distributions of BMI categories, irrespective of how their sexual orientations are conceptualized.

We now turn to the second part of our analysis, the estimation of logistic regression equations involving the independent variables of obesity and overweight and the dependent variable of lesbian/straight. This will permit us to investigate in a more straightforward fashion whether lesbians are more or less characterized than straight females to be obese or to be obese or overweight. Prior to our estimating the logistic regression equations, we dropped from the analyses those adult nonpregnant females with an "undefined BMI." For females defined as lesbian or as straight according to any of the three sexuality dimensions, those with an "undefined BMI" comprise only between 0.4% and 1.5% of all the females in the analysis. We next created a dummy variable labelled "obesity"; females were scored with a value of 1 if they were classified with the BMI category of obese, that is, if their BMI was 30.0 or higher; and they were classified with 0 if they had one of the other three BMI categories of underweight, normal weight, or overweight. We then created a second dummy variable labelled "overweight/obese," scored 1 if the female was classified with either of the two BMI categories of overweight or obese, that is, if their BMI was 25.0 or higher, and 0 if categorized as underweight or normal weight.

For the female respondents, we fitted logistic regression equation with the lesbian dummy variable (lesbian =1) as the dependent variable, and the obesity dummy variable (obese = 1) as the independent variable in one equation, and then the overweight/obese dummy variable as the independent variable in a second equation. We estimated these equations three times, each time classifying females as lesbian or as straight according to one of the three dimensions of sexuality. We want to be clear that we are not using the obesity and overweight/obese independent variables in the logistic regression equations to predict the likelihood of a female being lesbian or straight. Instead, following the approach taken by Bogaert (2004, 2012, 2013) and by Poston and Baumle (2010), we use the results from the logistic regression equations to indicate whether lesbians are significantly different from straight females on the overweight/obese variable(s).

In each panel of Table 17.2 we present the results of one logistic regression equation examining the log odds relationship between the dummy variable of lesbian and the independent variable of obesity, and then the results of a second logistic regression equation but with the independent variable of overweight or obese. We use the t-test to evaluate the statistical significance of each logit regression coefficient; t-test values greater than 1.96 indicate that the regression coefficient is statistically significant, two-tailed, that is, its p-value is 0.05 or lower.

The top third of Table 17.2 presents for lesbians and straight females who are so classified on the basis of the behavior dimension of sexuality, the logit regression equation results of the lesbian dummy variable regressed on the obese dummy variable; and next the results of the equation regressing the lesbian dummy variable on the overweight or obese dummy variable. In the second third of the table, we show results for similar equations for lesbians and straight females who have been classified on the basis of their sexual attraction. And in the bottom panel of Table 17.2 we present the logistic regression equation results for lesbians and straight females who have been so designated on the basis of their self-identification of their sexuality.

Table 17.2 Logistic regression equation coefficient of lesbians versus straight females on the independent variable of obesity (yes/no), and on the independent variable of overweight or obesity (yes/no), by each of three dimensions of sexuality: 2017–2019 National Survey of Family Growth (survey adjusted using NSFG respondent sampling weights)

	Behavior dimension of sexuality (*N*=3653 females)	
Independent variable	**logit coefficient**	***t* statistic**
Obese (yes =1)	−1.01	−1.63
Constant	−4.51	−14.17
	Behavior dimension of sexuality (*N*=3653 females)	
Independent variable	**logit coefficient**	***t* statistic**
Overweight or obese (yes =1)	−1.04	−1.79
Constant	−4.25	−10.07
	Attraction dimension of sexuality (*N*=4459 females)	
Independent variable	**logit coefficient**	***t* statistic**
Overweight (yes =1)	−0.18	−0.71
Constant	−3.32	−23.53
	Attraction dimension of sexuality (*N*=4459 Females)	
Independent variable	**logit coefficient**	***t* statistic**
Overweight or obese (yes =1)	−0.02	−0.08
Constant	−3.39	−13.69
	Self-identification dimension of sexuality (*N*=4281 females)	
Independent variable	**logit coefficient**	***t* statistic**
Obese (yes =1)	−0.22	−0.88
Constant	−3.52	−24.09
	Self-identification dimension of sexuality (N=4281 females)	
Independent variable	**logit coefficient**	***t* statistic**
Overweight or obese (yes =1)	−0.14	−0.51
Constant	−3.51	−17.64

The results of the first logit regression equation in the top panel of Table 17.2 report the association between obesity (yes/no) and lesbian (yes/no). The obesity coefficient is negative, but its value of −1.01 is not statistically significant. Lesbians, identified on the basis of behavior, are not significantly different from straight females with respect to obesity.

The results of the second logit regression equation in the top panel presents the association between the overweight or obese independent variable (yes/no) and the lesbian dependent variable (yes/no). The overweight or obese coefficient is negative and is statistically significant, one tail; the logit coefficient is −1.04, with a t-test value of 1.79; this translates to a one tail probability of 0.039. According to the behavioral dimension of sexuality, lesbians are significantly less likely to be obese or overweight compared to straight females. Looking back at the descriptive results in the top panel of Table 17.1, we found much lower percentages of lesbians in the obese and overweight BMI categories than straight females. The logit results in the top panel of Table 17.2 are consistent with these earlier findings.

In the middle panel of Table 17.2 we report the results of two similar logistic regression equations, with the females classified as lesbian or straight on the basis of the attraction dimension of sexuality. The results of the two logit equations show that both the obesity coefficient (first equation) and the obesity/overweight coefficient (second equation) are not statistically significant. According to the attraction dimension of sexuality, lesbians are not significantly more or less obese, or more or less obese or overweight, compared to straight females.

In the bottom panel of Table 17.2, we again fit two logistic regression equations with the dependent variable of the female being lesbian versus being straight, with the lesbian/straight classification based on their self-identification of their sexuality. The results from the two equations show that the obesity coefficient and the obesity or overweight coefficient are not statistically significant. According to the self-identification dimension of sexuality, lesbians are not significantly more or less likely than straight females to be either obese or obese or overweight.

To summarize our results, we conducted two separate analyses of lesbians and straight females, each time designating the females as lesbian or as straight according to one of the three dimensions of sexual orientation. The results of the first analyses are presented in Table 17.1. We compared the distribution of the five BMI categories among lesbians with its distribution among straight females. We first classified the females as lesbian or straight according to their sexual behavior, and next according to their sexual attraction, and lastly according to their sexual self-identification. In all three analyses, the distributions of the BMI categories in the lesbian populations were not shown to be significantly different from the distributions in the straight female populations. Lesbians and straight females do not differ significantly with regard to their respective percentages in the five BMI categories.

The results of the second set of analyses are presented in Table 17.2. There we estimated one logistic regression equation with the dependent variable of lesbian versus straight, and the independent variable of obese (yes = 1); and we estimated a second logistic regression equation but changed the independent variable to overweight/obese (yes =1). We estimated these equations three different times, each time designating the females as lesbian or straight based on one of the three dimensions of sexuality. In all six equations, the obese independent variable and the overweight or obese independent variable were shown to be negatively related with the lesbian versus straight dependent variable. But for the most part the logit coefficients were not statistically significant. The results in five of the six equations indicated that lesbians are not significantly different from straight females with regard to being obese, or being obese or overweight. Only in the one equation where females were classified as lesbian or straight according to the behavior dimension of sexuality did we find a statistically significant relationship between the obese/overweight independent variable and the lesbian/straight dependent variable. And this coefficient was significant at one tail. We conclude that for the most part lesbians are not significantly different from straight females with respect to obesity or obesity/overweight. The results of these analyses are not inconsistent with the mixed and somewhat inconsistent literature we reviewed earlier about whether lesbians tend to be more or less obese or overweight than straight females. Our results indicate for the most part that lesbians compared to straight women are neither more or less likely to be obese, or obese or overweight. We turn now to a further discussion and conclusion.

Discussion and Conclusion

In this chapter we have reviewed the literature about lesbians, straight females, and obesity. The literature has offered mixed results. Researchers have argued that lesbians may be protected from pressures of a body acceptance of thinness (Bowen et al., 2008; Morrison et al., 2004; Yost & Chmielewski, 2011). Other researchers have found that lesbians are often caught between mainstream heterosexual body norms and their community norms to accept their bodies as they are (Fogel et al., 2009; Kelly, 2007). Others have found that lesbians follow the same norms as heterosexual women when it comes to weight and body acceptance (Huxley et al., 2014; Luis, 2012; Peplau et al., 2009). On the other hand, it has been observed that sexual minority women, in particular, lesbians have higher rates of overweight and obesity. But, this research is relatively underdeveloped and is often based on regional or small samples that may not be reflective of the larger population.

To contribute to the body of work documenting the association between overweight and obesity in lesbians, we undertook an empirical analysis using nationally representative data. As in previous chapters in this *Handbook*, we first defined and considered female sexuality. Using the behavioral dimension of sexuality, 98.3% are classified as straight females while 1.7% are classified as lesbians. Using the attraction dimension, 96.0% are classified as straight females, and 4.0% are classified as lesbians. Based on self-identification, 97% of women are classified as straight, and 3.0% as lesbian. These variations are interesting to note and suggest the need for further investigation, which considers the multi-faceted nature of sexuality.

When we examine our empirical results, we found that there is little statistical difference between lesbians and straight females in bodyweight distribution. Specifically, in Table 17.1 we present three analyses, which reveal that the two distributions of the BMI categories do not differ significantly between the two groups of lesbians and straight females. Interestingly, lesbians have lower percentages in the overweight and obese categories when measured on the basis of attraction. However, lesbians and straight females do not have significantly different distributions of BMI categories, irrespective of how their sexual orientations are conceptualized.

We next turned to six different equations among lesbian and straight females based upon definition of female sexuality. The results in five of the six equations indicated that lesbians are not significantly different from straight females with regard to being obese or overweight. Only in the one equation where females were classified as lesbian or straight according to the behavior dimension of sexuality did we find a statistically significant relationship between the obese/overweight independent variable and the lesbian/straight dependent variable. And this coefficient was significant at one-tail. We conclude that for the most part lesbians are not significantly different from straight females with respect to obesity or obesity/overweight.

The results of these analyses add to the mixed and somewhat inconsistent literature that we reviewed earlier about whether lesbians tend to be more obese or overweight than straight females. As discussed more specifically above, researchers have suggested that lesbians may be: (1) protected from pressures of a body acceptance of thinness (Bowen et al., 2008; Morrison et al., 2004; Yost & Chmielewski, 2011), (2) follow feminist values about body and weight, (3) have more chronic diseases because of being obese or overweight, and/or (4) lesbians and lesbian communities prefer larger body types. For all these debates, in our analyses, lesbians, no matter how female sexuality was defined (attraction, behavior, or self-identification), we find no support for any of these debates. Moreover, all of the obese/overweight coefficients are negative, suggesting that lesbians are less likely to be obese or overweight than straight females. More empirical investigation is clearly needed to determine their risk, as well as the mechanisms that might explain variations in bodyweight.

In conclusion, we have a few limitations and suggestions for future research. First, we did not analyze how age may be a factor in why we see few statistically significant results in our analyses. As people age, their BMI tends to increase. Second, the number of lesbians is small and may have affected our six equations discussed above. Third, we did not analyze lesbian and straight females by race. Some variations by race and ethnicity have been documented previously, and an intersectional approach could provide nuance to findings related to race/ethnicity, female sexuality, and BMI. Fourth, education and social class could also provide valuable information about female sexuality and BMI. Research suggests that the more education and higher socioeconomic status a person has, the more likely they are to have positive health outcomes. Thus, future investigations should consider how these factors relate to bodyweight among lesbians. As the literature in this *Handbook* describes, often sexual and gender minorities are discriminated against in health care and other settings. This too might account for poorer health outcomes and/or variations in BMI.

Future research should continue to examine the inconsistencies present in analyses of overweight and obesity in lesbians in ways that shed light on why this may be the case. For example, we did not analyze all three dimensions of sexuality simultaneously, that is, classify as a lesbian any woman who is attracted sexually to women, behaves sexually with women, and/or self-identifies as a lesbian. This definition is more of a social constructionist approach and may have provided findings that are more robust. Similarly, more robust equations, including variables, such as age, race, ethnicity, education, and social class, could indicate why we found little differences between lesbian and straight females. Nonetheless, our findings utilize a nationally representative, probability sample and therefore add to what is known about the distribution of bodyweight in lesbians compared to straight women. Our lack of findings of significant differences between these two groups suggests the need for additional work in this area.

Acknowledgments We would like to thank Dr. Kari Hickey and Alexandra Lawyer.

References

Bogaert, A. F. (2004). Asexuality: Prevalence and associated factors in a National Probability Sample. *Journal of Sex Research, 41*, 279–287.

Bogaert, A. F. (2012). *Understanding asexuality*. Rowman and Littlefield Publishers.

Bogaert, A. F. (2013). The demography of asexuality. In A. K. Baumle (Ed.), *International Handbook on the Demography of Sexuality* (pp. 275–288). Springer.

Bowen, D. J., Balsam, K. F., & Ender, S. R. (2008). A review of obesity issues in sexual minority women. *Obesity, 16*, 221–228.

Caceres, B. A., Veldhuis, C. B., Hickey, K. T., & Hughes, T. L. (2019). Lifetime trauma and cardiometabolic risk in sexual minority women. *Journal of Women's Health, 38*, 1200–1217.

Carpenter, C. (2003). Sexual orientation and body weight: Evidence from multiple surveys. *Gender Issues, 21*, 60–74.

Centers for Disease Control and Prevention. (2021a). *About the National Survey of family growth*. Centers for Disease Control and Prevention, National Center for Health Statistics, National Survey of Family Growth. Available at: https://www.cdc.gov/nchs/nsfg/about_nsfg.htm. Accessed 1 Nov 2021

Centers for Disease Control and Prevention. (2021b). *Defining adult overweight and obesity*. Centers for Disease Control and Prevention, National Center for Health Statistics, National Survey of Family Growth. Available at: https://www.cdc.gov/obesity/adult/defining.html. Accessed 31 May 2022

Centers for Disease Control and Prevention. (2022). *Adult obesity prevalence maps*. Centers for Disease Control and Prevention, National Center for Health Statistics, National Survey of Family Growth. Available at: https://www.cdc.gov/obesity/data/prevalence-maps.html#states. Accessed 2 June 2022

Cohen, A. B., & Tannenbaum, I. J. (2001). Lesbian and bisexual women's judgments of the attractiveness of different body types. *Journal of Sex Research, 38*, 226–232.

Conron, K. J., Mimiaga, M. J., & Landers, S. J. (2010). A population-based study of sexual orientation identity and gender differences in adult health. *American Journal of Public Health, 100*, 1953–1960.

Corliss, H. L., Van Kim, N. A., Hee-Jin, J., Bryn Austin, S., Hong, B., Wang, M., & Frank, B. H. (2018). Risk of type 2 diabetes among lesbian, bisexual, and heterosexual women: Findings from the nurses' health study II. *Diabetes Care, 41*, 1448–1454.

Deputy, N. P., & Boehmer, U. (2014). Weight status and sexual orientation: Differences by age and within racial and ethnic subgroups. *American Journal of Public Health, 104*(1), 103–109.

Donaghue, N., & Clemitshaw, A. (2012). 'I'm totally smart and a feminist. . .and yet I want to be a waif': Exploring ambivalence towards the thin ideal within the fat acceptance movement. *Women's Studies International Forum, 35*, 415–425.

Dyar, C., Taggart, T. C., Rodriguez-Seijas, C., Thompson, R. G., Elliott, J. C., Hasin, D. S., & Eaton, N. R. (2019). Physical health disparities across dimensions of sexual orientation, race/ethnicity, and sex: Evidence for increased risk among bisexual adults. *Archives of Sexual Behavior, 48*, 225–242.

Eliason, M. J., & Fogel, S. (2015). An ecological framework for sexual minority women's health: Factors associated with greater body mass. *Journal of Homosexuality, 62*, 1–38.

Eliason, M. J., Ingraham, N., Fogel, S. C., Jennifer, L., Richard Mauery, D., Haynes, S., et al. (2015). A systematic review of the literature on weight in sexual minority women. *Women's Health Issues, 25*(2), 162–175.

Fogel, S., Young, L., & Bryan McPherson, J. (2009). The experience of group weight loss efforts among lesbians. *Women & Health, 49*, 540–554.

Fredriksen-Goldsen, K. I., Kim, H.-J., Hoy-Ellis, C. P., Emlet, C. A., Erosheva, E. A., Muraco, A., & Petry, H. (2012). The quality of life of LGBT older adults: Key risk and protective factors. *Gerontologist, 52*, 143–143.

Garcia-Alexander, G. (2019). 'The demography of obesity' Chapter 33. In D. L. Poston Jr. (Ed.), *Handbook of population* (2nd ed., pp. 859–873). Springer Nature.

Huxley, C. J., Clarke, V., & Halliwell, E. (2014). A qualitative exploration of whether lesbian and bisexual women are 'protected' from sociocultural pressure to be thin. *Journal of Health Psychology, 19*, 273–294.

Kelly, L. (2007). Lesbian body image perceptions: The context of body silence. *Qualitative Health Research, 17*, 873–883.

Kyle, T. K., & Puhl, R. M. (2014). Putting people first in obesity. *Obesity, 22*, 1211–1211.

Lew, K. N., Dorsen, C., Melkus, G. D., & Maclean, M. (2018). Prevalence of obesity, prediabetes, and diabetes in sexual minority women of diverse races/ethnicities: Findings from the 2014–2015 BRFSS surveys. *Diabetes Education, 44*, 349–360.

Luis, K. N. (2012). Karma eaters: The politics of food and fat in women's land communities in the United States. *Journal of Lesbian Studies, 16*, 108–134.

Maor, M. (2012). The body that does not diminish itself: Fat acceptance in Israel's lesbian queer communities. *Journal of Lesbian Studies, 16*, 177–198.

Morrison, M. A., Morrison, T. G., & Sager, C.-L. (2004). Does body satisfaction differ between gay men and lesbian women and heterosexual men and women? A meta-analytic review? *Body Image, 1*, 127–138.

National Center for Health Statistics. (2020). *Public-use data file documentation, 2017–2019 National Survey of Family Growth, User's Guide, appendix 7C.* National Center for Health Statistics.

Palad, C. J., & Stanford, F. C. (2018). "Use of people-first language with regard to obesity" [letter to the editor]. *The American Journal of Clinical Nutrition, 108*, 201–203.

Peplau, L. A., Frederick, D. A., Yee, C., Maisel, N., Lever, J., & Ghavami, N. (2009). Body image satisfaction in heterosexual, gay, and lesbian adults. *Archives of Sexual Behavior, 38*, 713–725.

Poston, J., Dudley, L., & Baumle, A. K. (2010). Patterns of asexuality in the United States. *Demographic Research, 23*, 509–530.

Rao, J. N. K., & Scott, A. J. (1984). On chi-squared tests for multiway contingency tables with cell proportions estimated from survey data. *Annals of Statistics, 12*, 46–60.

Semlyen, J., Curtis, T. J., & Varney, J. (2019). Sexual orientation identity in relation to unhealthy body mass index: Individual participant data meta-analysis of 93429 individuals from 12 UK health surveys. *Journal of Public Health, 42*, 98–106.

Simenson, A. J., Core, S., Markovic, N., & Kinsky, S. (2020). Disparities in chronic health outcomes and health behaviors between lesbian and heterosexual adult women in Pittsburgh: A longitudinal study. *Journal of Women's Health, 29*, 1059–1067.

StataCorp. (2021). *Stata survey data reference manual, release 17*. StataCorp, LLC.

Struble, C. B., Lindley, L. L., Montgomery, K., Hardin, J., & Burcin, M. (2010). Overweight and obesity in lesbian and bisexual college women. *Journal of American College Health, 59*, 51–56.

Swami, V., Frederick, D. A., Aavik, T., Alcalay, L., Allik, J., Anderson, D., Andrianto, S., et al. (2010). The attractive female body weight and female body dissatisfaction in 26 countries across 10 world regions: Results of the international body project 1. *Personality and Social Psychology Bulletin, 36*, 309–325.

Tuthill, Z., Denney, J. T., & Gorman, B. (2020). Racial disparities in health and health behaviors among gay, lesbian, bisexual and heterosexual men and women in the BRFSS-SOP. *Ethnicity & Health, 25*, 177–188.

World Health Organization. (2021). *Obesity and overweight*. World Health Organization. Available at: https://www.who.int/news-room/fact-sheets/detail/obesity-and-overweight. Accessed 1 June 2022

Yost, M. R., & Chmielewski, J. F. (2011). Narrating rural lesbian lives: Body image and lesbian community in central Pennsylvania. *Journal of Lesbian Studies, 15*, 148–165.

Obesity and Bisexuality: Is Being 'Bi' an Issue?

Mary Ann Davis

Introduction

This chapter addresses, from a demographic perspective, whether bisexuals are more likely to be obese than others. A preface to such a demographic analysis should begin by addressing data limitations and information regarding the identity and accepted definitions of sexual orientation. Ghaziani (2017) posits that the identification of a person's sexual orientation is complicated as people may either intentionally hide their orientation or not want to be measured due to the stigma of sexual minority status. There is also the issue of what is being measured to determine sexual orientation. As Ghaziani (2017) states,

> (E)stimates about the size of the gay and lesbian population will vary depending on whether we ask about sexual attraction or arousal; sexual behavior and contact; or sexual identity. These three items are weakly correlated and poorly predictive (p. 72).

There is concern about whether those surveyed accept the identity in the offered categories, whether they will acknowledge their status, due to stigma, and whether they are consistent in sexual attraction, sexual behavior, and sexual identity.

Historical demographic information about bisexuals in the United States is limited due to inadequate identification in the U. S. Census and most national surveys. This had led to gaps in demographic data as sexual minority and gender variables were excluded from federal data and other large-scale research projects. We thus include the recommendations made by the working group, Sexual Orientation and Gender Identity in Federal Surveys (SOGI) (2016), to correct these problems regarding sexual minority inclusion in future data collection efforts.

Research involving sexual minorities is further complicated because the U.S. Census and other national survey data are primarily cross-sectional and address a single point of disclosure. This further reduces the chance of accurate identification. Sexual orientation is not a stable, static identity as the individual may self-identify their sexual orientation in varying ways at different times during the life course. Thus, a bisexual may identify as heterosexual, gay or lesbian, or bisexual at different times and may "come out" or identify their sexual orientation or gender identity to others at differing times. See the discussions of this and related issues in the asexuality chapter in this *Handbook*.

These data limitations should be considered as we explore some of the available demographic studies and data used to study bisexuality. As is noted in other chapters in this volume, obesity has multiple causes. Thus, the studies reviewed herein include issues of the intersection of bisexuality and obesity with other health-related behaviors and socio-economic factors. Following

M. A. Davis (✉)
Department of Sociology, University of New Orleans, New Orleans, LA, USA
e-mail: madavis9@uno.edu

G. Garcia-Alexander, D. L. Poston, Jr. (eds.), *International Handbook of the Demography of Obesity*, International Handbooks of Population 12, https://doi.org/10.1007/978-3-031-10936-2_18

a review of prior research, we use the Behavioral Risk Factor Surveillance System, Sexual Orientation and Gender Identity (BRFSS-SOGI) 2020 sample data to explore whether male and female bisexuals are more likely to be obese than their straight or Cis-gendered counterparts. We offer an analysis of the relationship between bisexuality and obesity and conclude with recommendations and suggestions for future research.

Background

Sexual Orientation

The research on sexual minorities has been lacking. Though not a demographer, Alfred Kinsey is often cited as an early sexuality researcher. Using an admittedly flawed, but very large, convenience sample of several thousand participants, Kinsey provided a scientific study of sexuality via detailed "sexual histories," which indicated a greater presence of homosexual behaviors and desires than previously assumed. Kinsey (1948) estimated that 10% of the male population had some same sex desire and about 4% classified themselves as gay. Furthermore, Kinsey's work revealed that the study of sexuality in the U.S. population was feasible (IOM, 2011). A later probability sample of U.S. adults, the National Health and Family Life Survey (Laumann et al., 1994), provided reliable estimates of sexual orientation groups with approximately 2.5% of males and 1.4% of females identifying as homosexual or bisexual. Recent estimates suggest that approximately 3.5% of U.S. adults self-identify as lesbian, gay, or bisexual; and slightly more than half of these individuals (1.8%) are bisexuals (Gates, 2011).

Demographic studies of sexual minorities have only recently become more common given the earlier lack of probability samples including data on sexual orientation. For example, in a review of the literature, Baumle et al. (2009) searched population journals looking for demographic articles relating to sexual orientation. Their findings revealed that 69 articles included the term "sexual orientation," 40 included the term "lesbian", 221 included the term "gay" and 181 included the term "homosexual." Baumle (2013) argues that from the 1950s till the 2000s the demography of sexuality was limited to behaviors that resulted in sexually transmitted disease, increasing after the HIV epidemic. Since the early 2000s, research has expanded to include "a number of issues that are fundamental to population study, including migration, fertility, morbidity, and other areas (Baumle, 2013)".

One reason demographic research has been limited is because sexual minorities have not been counted in federal surveys. The 2016 Federal Interagency Working Group on Improving Measurement of Sexual Orientation and Gender Identity in Federal Surveys (SOGI) is a research group designed to explore best practices in measurement of sexual and gender minorities (SGM). This group has identified a number of challenges to their accurate measurement and has made several recommendations to improve and coordinate data collection efforts. Their review of the information on sexual orientation identifies several key concepts including: sex, gender, transgender, and sexual orientation. Also, there are related terms: lesbian, gay, bisexual, and transgender (LGBT).

The working group first distinguishes between sex and gender, which they consider to be foundational concepts. Sex is defined as the physical, hormonal, biological and anatomical characteristics assigned at birth. Gender has a broader definition which incorporates socially constructed characteristics, norms, roles, and relationships of men and women (SOGI, 2016: 9). The term gender identity refers to a person's affiliation with a gender community. This can be measured with a one or two-part question. Thus, it is recommended that federal surveys include a measure for sex, e.g., What sex were you assigned at birth? Male or Female, and a measure for gender identity, e.g., Do you currently describe yourself as male, female, or transgender? Those whose sex assigned at birth and gender identity are consistent are referred to as "consistent in sex", or cis-gendered; while those whose gender differs from the sex assigned at birth are referred to as transgender (SOGI, 2016).

Sexual orientation may be measured based on self-identification, sexual behavior, and sexual attraction. However, these three dimensions are not consistently captured in all federal surveys. The results of the SOGI working group suggest that sexual identity is routinely captured in federal surveys with a single-item measure, e.g. Do you think of yourself as…heterosexual or straight (not gay), homosexual/gay/lesbian, bisexual, or something else? For this reason, they utilize sexual identity as the primary measure of sexual orientation. However, best practices do acknowledge that sexual behavior and sexual attraction are important components of sexual orientation, and they may not always match self-identification (Badgett et al., 2009; SOGI, 2016). A few of the federal surveys (NSFG, NHANES, NIS, YRBSS) capture behavior, e.g. In the past year, who have you had sex with? men only, women only, both men and women, and I have not had sex. Finally, a few (PATH, NSFG, NSDUH) include a measure of sexual attraction, e.g. Which best describes your feelings? Are you: only attracted to females, mostly attracted to females, equally attracted to males and females, mostly attracted to males, only attracted to males, not sure. Thus, the existing federal data do permit identification and analysis of sexual minorities, however they do not consistently capture this information across surveys. The availability of federal data on sexual orientation is reviewed in detail in the following section.

Availability of Demographic Data on Sexual Behavior

In the past decade demographic data on sexual orientation including bisexuality have been addressed by researchers through a Federal Committee on Statistical Methodology research group, the Sexual Orientation and Gender Identity (SOGI) working group. According to the SOGI (2016), of the Federal surveys, eleven surveys and one study collect data on sexual orientation, including identity, attraction, and behavior, as well as data on gender identity. These include: Health Center Patient Survey (HCPS), National Adult Tobacco Survey (NATS), National Health and Nutrition Examination Survey (NHANES), National Health Interview Survey (NHIS), National Inmate Survey (NIS), National Crime Victimization Survey (NCVS), National Survey of Family Growth (NSFG), Youth Risk Behavior Surveillance System (YRBSS), National Survey on Drug Use and Health (NSDUH), National Survey of Older Americans Act Participants (NSOAAP), Behavior Risk Factor Surveillance System (BRFSS), and the study the Population Assessment of Tobacco and Health (PATH). Six include gender identity questions: Population Assessment of Tobacco and Health (PATH), Behavior Risk Factor Surveillance System (BRFSS), National Adult Tobacco Survey (NATS), National Crime Victimization Survey (NCVS), National Inmate Survey (NIS), and the Health Center Patient Survey (HCPS).

The following is an overview of the measures of sexual identity available in these surveys. They have addressed sexual identity for the past 20 years but have updated their surveys in the past decade. We include the current specific questions to highlight the issues of compatibility and variations of the questions across instruments. As mentioned previously, all surveys include a question on sexual self-identification. For instance, the BRFSS (DHHS/CDC) has addressed sexual identity from 2014 to present with this question: Do you consider yourself to be: Straight, Lesbian/Gay, or Bisexual? But, only one study includes a measure for all three measures of sexual orientation (NSFG). Two surveys include both sexual identity and sexual attraction, NSDUH and PATH. Three surveys, NHANES, NIS, and YRBSS include both sexual identity and sexual behaviors.

Other federal data are lacking by not including sexual identity, attraction and behaviors. The U.S. census represents the gold standard for providing demographic data. The census household membership questions have been used by demographers in teasing out same-sex partners. The 2010 Census was the first decennial census to provide estimates of same-sex married couples (Lofquist, 2011). However, O'Connell and Feliz (2011) in comparing the 2010 American

Community Survey (ACS) to the Census, found the number of same-sex couple households in the Census was 52% higher than the ACS estimate. The census bureau revised the question and added an automatic check to ensure relationship status was accurate. This revision was tested in the 2013 American Housing Survey (AHS), the 2014 and 2015 Census Tests, and the 2015 National Content Test that was to be used in the 2020 census. Thus, more accurate same-sex partner data should be available in the 2020 census. However, these data do not address bisexuality.

Other surveys have expanded their measures of sexuality including bisexuality. For example, the National Longitudinal Study of Adolescent Health (Add Health), a nationally representative cohort study of young adults in the United States, includes a host of demographic, social, and psychosocial information, contextual data, and biological data. The newest waves, Wave IV-V of Add Health included measures of sexual orientation, a range of CVD biomarkers, and multiple potential factors addressing the relationships between sexual orientation and these biomarkers.

Review of Bisexual and Obesity Research

In spite of the efforts by the SOGI working group to standardize the collection of data about sexual minorities in federal surveys, the inclusion of bisexuals in obesity research is relatively new. Due to the general lack of data about sexual minorities, one of the techniques used by researchers is to pool surveys over several years. Another method is to use weighted data to compare with the population. Studies using these techniques are described below.

According to Newton Lew et al. (2018) there is a lack of studies addressing obesity in sexual minority women (SMW), and existing studies often vary from state to state. There may also be issues with a lack of disclosure of sexual minority status, due to discrimination against SMWs, especially racial and ethnic minorities. Studies that use state-based data are often inconsistent. The 2003–2006 Washington State Behavioral Risk Factor Surveillance Survey (BRFSS) found bisexual (29.7%) and lesbian (28.8%) women had significantly greater odds for overweight compared with straight (22.3%) women. Results from Cycle 6 of the National Survey of Family Growth found that lesbians had higher rates of being overweight (35.3%) and obesity (34.2%), but not bisexual women (29.6% overweight and 21.9%) obese compared to straight women (25.6% overweight and 24.7%) obese, respectively (349). Later, research using the 2013 National Health Interview Survey found bisexual women had higher rates of obesity (40.4%) compared with straight women (28.8%) (348). We now describe findings from research that uses federal or other large-scale surveys.

Youth Risk Behavior Survey (YRBS)

Beach et al. (2018) studied risk for diabetes, including obesity, using a sample of 350,673 students from YRBSS data pooled across 44 jurisdictions biennially from 2009 to 2015; "88.4% identified as heterosexual, 2.1% as gay or lesbian, 5.7% as bisexual, and 3.7% as unsure" (p. 1137). Lesbian, bisexual, and not sure female youth were 1.55–2.07 times more likely to be obese than heterosexual female students. No significant differences in overweight, or obesity were found among gay, bisexual, or unsure male youth compared to heterosexual male youth. However, full models suggested factors that were more predictive of obesity including having experienced school bullying, a lack of physical exercise, racial and ethnic minority status, mental health depression and stress issues (p. 1143).

Calzo and colleagues (2019) also pooled YRBS data from 2009 to 2015 across multiple jurisdictions to conduct an analysis of sexual minority youth. Though not the focus of their study, they observed higher rates of overweight/obesity in sexual minority female students. Formally, 23.4% of heterosexual females, 39.4% of lesbian females, and 34.5% of bisexual females were overweight or obese. Among male students, 31.2% of heterosexual males versus 38.2% of bisexual males were overweight or obese.

Behavior Risk Factor Surveillance System (BRFSS)

Caceres and colleagues (2019) combined 3 years of BRFSS data, from 2014 to 2016 for a total of 395,154 participants. Sexual minority women reported higher rates of several cardiovascular risk factors, including obesity. Compared to heterosexual females, lesbian's adjusted odds ratios (AOR) for obesity were 1.50. The odds of obesity was also higher for bisexual females (1.29) and bisexual males (1.03). Adjusted odds ratios were lower for gay males (0.82).

Newton Lew et al. (2018), mentioned earlier, used 2014–2015 pooled BRFSS data from the 28 states that completed both the optional prediabetes module and the optional module on sexual orientation and gender identity (SOGI) to study prediabetes and obtained a sample of 136,878. They reported on the odds ratios of obesity by sexual orientation, namely, lesbian, bisexual, and straight. Of these 133,546 (97.6%) identified as straight; 1387 (1.0%) identified as lesbian; and 1945 (1.4%) identified as bisexual. They also used race and ethnicity (Hispanic, non-Hispanic black, and non-Hispanic white) in their analyses. Findings were that both lesbians and bisexual females, compared with heterosexual women, had an increased likelihood of diabetes. However, bisexuals had reduced odds of diabetes when they controlled for other variables including age, income, education, depression, and access to health care.

Azagba et al. (2019) pooled BRFSS data from 2004 to 2017 (n = 716,609), to study sexual identity and obesity. They observed that bisexual females had significantly higher odds of being overweight (OR 1.21; 95% CI 1.10–1.34) and obese (OR 1.43; 95% CI 1.29–1.59); whereas bisexual males showed no significant difference.

Gorman et al. (2015) pooled BRFSS data across seven U.S. states, from 2005 to 2010, to obtain a sample of 10,128 sexual minority (gay, lesbian, and bisexual) and 405,145 heterosexual adults. Logistic regression models did not specifically address obesity or BMI. However, they revealed that bisexual men and women reported the highest rates of poor self-rated health…"partially attributable to their heightened economic, behavioral, and social disadvantages relative to other groups" (p. 1357). Other research completed by Gorman and Oyarvide (2018), concurred that socioeconomic variables are important factors in long term health and living free from disease. This disadvantages bisexual elders as "compared to heterosexual and gay or lesbian older adults, bisexual elders have the lowest rates of completed schooling and live in lower-income households, which strongly contributes to their poorer health reports" (p. 56).

National Survey of Family Growth (NSFG)

Boehmer et al. (2007) used the 2002 National Survey of Family Growth data to explore obesity in sexual minority women. After eliminating those who were pregnant and those who refused the sexual orientation question or answered "don't know," they had a sample of 5979 females aged 20–44 years of age. BMI was calculated using height and weight as the measure of obesity. They found that there was no significant difference in weight by sexual orientation even though bisexuals differed significantly by other factors including "age, parity, insurance status, place of residence and nativity" (p. 1135). Only lesbians were significantly more obese than heterosexuals with the odds of being obese almost three and one-half times those of heterosexual women.

National Longitudinal Study of Adolescent Health

Hatzenbuehler et al. (2013) used Wave IV of Add Health to study sexual orientation disparities in cardiovascular biomarkers, including obesity. Their sample included 13,789 persons who disclosed sexual identity; of those, 214 identified themselves as bisexual. The authors found that, with respect to CVD risk factors, gay/bisexual men had higher educational attainment than heterosexual men but had lower BMI. No sexual orientation differences in the other risk factors were observed for men. In contrast, lesbian/bisexual women reported more risk factors for CVD than heterosexual women, including lower SES (education and income); more unhealthy behaviors (smoking, greater alcohol consumption); and higher BMI.

Massachusetts Youth Risk Behavior Survey

Hadland and colleagues (2014) used 2003 and 2009 pooled data of 12,984 youth from the Massachusetts Youth Risk Behavior Survey, a statewide survey of 9th through 12th-grade students. Data included both weight and perceptions of weight. Compared with exclusively heterosexual males, heterosexual males with prior same-sex partners and bisexual males were more likely to self-perceive as overweight despite being of healthy weight or underweight (respectively, adjusted odds ratio [AOR], 2.61; and AOR, 2.56). Compared with exclusively heterosexual females, lesbians and bisexual females were more likely to self-perceive as being of healthy weight or underweight despite being overweight or obese (respectively, AOR, 3.17; and AOR, 2.00) (p. 296). Both bisexual males and females were more likely than heterosexual males and females to be overweight. However, lesbians, were not different than exclusively heterosexual females.

Washington State Behavioral Risk Factor Surveillance System (WA-BRFSS)

Fredriksen-Goldsen et al. (2010) used the Washington State Behavioral Risk Factor Surveillance System (WA-BRFSS), a population-based dataset pooled from 2003 to 2007. They obtained a sample of 110,174, of which 1496 self-identified as lesbians and bisexual women. Bisexual women, as compared with lesbians, reported greater sociodemographic risks including being younger, having less education, lower incomes, and more children. They also had less access to health care, were less likely to have health insurance, and reported more health risk behaviors (tobacco use and acute drinking). Bisexual women reported poorer general health and were more likely to experience mental distress. Both lesbians and bisexuals had significantly higher rates of obesity than heterosexuals.

Fredriksen-Goldsen et al. (2013) studied the health of sexual minorities by pooling Washington State Behavioral Risk Factor Surveillance System 2003–2010 data to obtain a sample of 96,992 respondents. They studied multiple health outcomes, including access to care and chronic conditions by gender and sexual orientation. Their results indicated that "lesbians and bisexual women had greater adjusted odds of obesity (OR = 1.42) relative to heterosexual women.... gay and bisexual men had significantly lower odds of obesity than did heterosexual men (OR = 0.72), after adjustment for sociodemographic factors" (p. 1804). They further suggested that stress may complicate health issues. While "coming out" as gay may be stressful, in the long run maintaining a stable identity is protective versus the continual shifting and renegotiation of sexual preference over a lifetime.

National Health Interview Surveys (NHIS)

Carpenter and Eppink (2017) pooled data from the 2013 to 2015 National Health Interview Surveys (NHIS) involving about 35,000 households in the United States. Lesbians had approximately 9% higher annual earnings than heterosexual women, if they had full-time work. However, bisexual women had slightly lower, but not significantly different annual earnings than heterosexual women. Although income levels were indicated in the path toward health in other research, this research did not include obesity data.

Longitudinal and Non-federal Studies

Katz-Wand and colleagues (2014) used nine waves of pooled data from the prospective *Growing Up Today* study. From 1996, when the participants (7960 females and 5992 males) were between ages 12 and 14, to 2009 when the participants were between ages 20 and 25, using self-reported height and weight to determine BMI, they found the following:

> Bisexual females had higher BMI at age 17 years (β = 1.59, 95% CI = 1.00–2.18) and displayed greater one-year increases in BMI (β = .09, 95% CI = .03–.14), compared with completely heterosexual females. Gay males displayed smaller 1-year increases in BMI (β = −.19, 95% CI = −.25 to −.12), compared with completely heterosexual males. No sexual orientation differences in BMI at age 17 years were observed for males, but gay males' BMI at age 25 was less than completely heterosexual males' BMI by 2 units (p. 730).

Guadamuz et al. (2011) used longitudinal data (n = 379) from 1999 to 2007 from the Pitt Men's Study (PMS). This study, designed to study HIV among gay and bisexual men, also included obesity data. The study recruited participants in 1984–1985, 1987–1991, and 2001–2003. They were followed every 6 months (through questionnaire-based interviews, physical examination, and medical history review) with a 75% retention rate (p. 386). This study did not distinguish between gay and bisexual males. Their findings indicated that over 50% of the participants were overweight or obese and retained this weight over the eight-year period.

Jun and colleagues (2012) studied obesity and sexual orientation of 90,713 U.S. women from the Nurses' Health Study II 1989 through 2005. They examined the participants BMI trajectories from ages 25 to 59 years. They found that bisexual women were "more likely to be in an obese-to-overweight group relative to heterosexual women" (p. 350). Just as with findings in other studies, they found that "bisexual women in the cohort were similar to lesbians in experiencing elevated risk of continual weight gain trajectories compared to heterosexual women" (p. 351) with weight-gain increasing with age.

Struble and colleagues (2010) used the Spring 2006 National College Health Assessment of 31,500 female college students (aged 18–25 years) to compare the BMIs of lesbian, bisexual and heterosexual college women. They found that although about 23% of all the respondents were overweight or obese, the odds of bisexuals being overweight were 1.9 times those of heterosexual women (p. 55). The authors suggested that since lesbians are not trying to meet male's expectations for thinness and beauty, for them obesity is not a major issue. However, they noted that women's "risk of obesity may change ... when their current sexual partner is male vs. when their partner is female" (p. 54).

Obesity in Bisexuals: Mechanisms and Explanations

Recent work suggests that bisexuals are in poorer health than heterosexual individuals (though their health is somewhat better than lesbians and homosexual males) (Compton et al., 2015). Echoing this, a consistent finding in the literature on obesity is that obesity is higher in lesbians and bisexual females compared to heterosexual females (Caceres et al., 2017; Eliason & Fogel, 2015), with a slightly elevated risk in lesbians compared to bisexual women (IOM, 2011). Such findings have led to the development of several theories that might explain elevated rates overweight and obesity in sexual minority women including minority stress, body image disturbances, differential health behaviors, and exposure to childhood sexual trauma.

Eliason and Fogel (2015) present an overview of the reasons that sexual minority women may have greater problems with overweight and obesity. They argue that an ecological framework is necessary to understand the complex web of factors that surrounds an individual and promotes poorer health in minority groups. They further describe the minority stress model, which identifies stigma as an important stressor that has profound impacts on health and wellbeing (Eliason & Fogel, 2015). However, their review of the literature suggests no real differences in physical activity or nutritional patterns in sexual minority women, and a lack of sufficient evidence to determine whether other individual-level factors might explain higher levels of overweight or obesity. In fact, across all levels, they document a lack of research that addresses the links between sexual minority status and body weight. Given higher rates of stress in sexual minority women and its connections to mental health, more research is needed to better understand why sexual minority women are at greater risk of overweight and obesity.

Lick et al. (2013) similarly link poorer health outcomes in sexual minorities to excess stress produced by victimization and bias. They point to higher rates of exposure to negative social environments, higher levels of victimization, and elevated rates of minority stress that have direct linkages to negative health and mental health outcomes. Accordingly, they propose a yet to be tested path model that connects minority stress to physical health disparities. They propose that sociocultural stressors including gender-based prejudice and discrimination (including institutional discrimination) lead to limited access to- and possibly lower quality of health care as well as higher incidence of stress. This in turn, promotes psychological stress responses, including anxiety and depression, that may promote poorer health behaviors (possible substance use along with diet and exercise beliefs). In addition, chronic stress leads to wear and tear on the body with measurable health implications. Thus, they offer a model for how stressors are linked systematically to influence the health of sexual gender minority populations.

Another factor that is potentially relevant to the health and wellbeing of sexual minority women is socioeconomic status. Low SES has been tied to greater incidence of overweight and obesity. Among women, rates of obesity increase as education and income decreases (Ogden et al., 2010). Sexual minorities are diverse in terms of socioeconomic status, but those with lower education and income levels experience more negative health outcomes (IOM, 2011). Thus, there is likely an important intersection between sexual minority status, SES, and risk of obesity. Similarly, race/ethnicity's intersection with sexual minority status and low-income may also be important for outcomes related to weight. For example, Mays and colleagues (2018) observed higher rates of obesity in black and Latino lesbians. In addition, rates of bisexuality appear to be on the rise, particularly in young black women (Bridges & Moore, 2018). Given the elevated rates of obesity in sexual minority women and its intersections with race and class, more work is needed to understand these associations.

In the following sections, we conduct an analysis of obesity in bisexuals using recent data from the Behavioral Risk Factor Surveillance System (BRFSS). These data offer information on sexual identity as well as body mass index. Accordingly, we are able to examine overweight and obesity risk in various sexual orientation subgroups. We provide interpretations of results and offer suggestions for future research.

Methodology

Data

We selected the most recent BRFSS data, 2020, to examine the relationship between bisexuality and obesity. This survey, the largest continuous global health survey, includes data on health behaviors, chronic conditions, and use of preventive measures. It has been conducted annually since 1984 and has expanded to collect data from all 50 states. In 2020 the states whose surveys included SOGI questions were Alaska, Arkansas, California, Colorado, Connecticut, Georgia, Guam, Hawaii, Idaho, Illinois, Indiana, Iowa, Kansas. Louisiana, Massachusetts, Michigan, Minnesota, Montana, New Jersey, New Mexico, New York, North Carolina, Ohio, Oklahoma, Rhode Island, South Carolina, Texas, Utah, Vermont, Virginia, Washington, West Virginia, and Wisconsin. The BRFSS conducts about 400,000 self- reported telephone interviews annually, obtained using random digit dialing.

Participants are noninstitutionalized individuals over the age of 18. To increase representation of special populations, variables such as age, gender, and race/ethnicity are weighted so as to more accurately represent the population. Other variables may be included in weighted analysis such as education attainment, marital status, tenure (property ownership), and telephone ownership. Including these new variables in the weighting process can reduce the potential for selection bias while increasing representation. Thus, the BRFSS uses a complex sampling design requiring software such as STATA, SAS and SPSS for analyses (CDC, 2014).

Measures

There are three parts to the survey core questions asked of all the respondents, and then optional modules that address specific issues that are only asked of a sample of the population. In our analysis we use only the optional sexual orientation module. Accordingly, we use the SOGI variables on sexual orientation. The sexual orientation questions are asked separately for males and females. Response categories include Gay, Straight, Bisexual, 'Something else', Don't know, and Refused., To measure overweight and obesity status, we utilize the BMI categories available in the data, namely, underweight (BMI of <18.5), normal weight (BMI of 18.5–24.9), overweight (BMI of 25–29.9), and obese (BMI of $\geq$30). We also include several demographic questions in order to explore the socioeconomic factors that are related to obesity in bisexuals. These include race (non-Hispanic white, non-Hispanic black, non-Hispanic Asian, non-Hispanic American Indian or Alaska Native, Hispanic, and non-Hispanic other); education (1 = college degree 0 = less than college degree); employment status (1 = employed, 0 = else); and general health status (1 = good or better, 0 = fair/poor). To account for the complex sampling design of the NSFG we used the "svy" suite of statistical sample adjustment methods available in the Stata statistical package that will adjust the analyses according to the various population and strata weights in the NSFG.

Results

We present the number, percent, and weighted percentages in our descriptive analyses. The 2020 BRFSS SOGI included a total of 110,039 males for whom there were valid gender identity data, and 1775 (1.85%) of these males identified as Bisexual. By comparison, 130,078 women were included in the analysis; of these 3889 (4.00%) identified as Bisexual. After restricting to those respondents with valid BMI data, our analytic sample included 103, 841 males and 112,842 females.

Table 18.1 presents the weight distributions of males and females separately. Here, it is observed that there are significant differences across sexual categories on the basis of BMI category. Notably, higher percentages of both bisexual males (3.59%) and bisexual females (3.88%) were underweight, compared to straight males (1.4%) and straight females (2.23%). About the same percentage of bisexual males was obese (32.3%) compared to straight males (33.11%). However, greater percentages of bisexual females were obese (35.93%) compared to straight females (32.65%). As has been noted in previous studies, women who identify as lesbian have a higher rate of obesity (39.61%) than those who self -identify as bisexual. In contrast, 27.98% of males who identify as gay are obese, compared to 32.30% of males who identify as Bisexual. Chi-squared analyses indicated that the BMI distributions were significantly different across the sexual orientation categories for both females and males.

We next examine the intersectionality of racial and ethnic minority status and sexual orientation. In Table 18.2 we show that about 62% of female bisexuals are non-Hispanic white. Similarly, about the same percentage of lesbians and heterosexual females are white (60.79% and 61.85%, respectively). Slightly fewer bisexual females (11.45%) are non-Hispanic black in comparison to lesbian (13.15%) or straight (12.33%) women. However, bisexual females are significantly more likely to be Hispanic or NH other than straight females. Chi-square analyses indicated that the racial/ethnic distributions were significantly different across the sexual orientation categories for both males and females.

Table 18.1 BMI categories by male and female sexual orientation, BRFSS SOGI Sample 2020 (number, percentage, and weighted percentage)

		Female sexual orientation						
BMI category		Lesbian	Straight	Bisexual	S. else	DK	Refused	Total
Underweight	n	31	2187	90	59	43	55	2465
	%	1.99	2.12	2.55	3.77	3.15	3.29	2.18
	Wt.%	2.33	2.23	3.88	4.39	4.39	2.80	2.37
Normal	n	509	36,787	1210	514	497	643	40,160
	%	32.69	35.66	34.31	32.89	36.38	38.41	35.59
	Wt.%	32.98	34.98	35.86	33.12	26.45	40.96	34.93
Overweight	n	444	31,611	904	443	441	541	34,384
	%	28.52	30.64	25.63	28.34	32.28	32.32	30.47
	Wt.%	25.07	30.14	24.34	26.92	31.48	33.77	29.84
Obese	n	573	32,570	1323	547	385	435	35,833
	%	36.80	31.57	37.51	35.00	28.18	25.99	31.76
	Wt.%	39.61	32.65	35.93	35.57	37.69	22.47	32.86
	Total	1557	103,155	3527	1563	1366	1674	112,842
	Pearson chi^2 164.55, p = 0.000							
		Male sexual orientation						
BMI category		Gay	Straight	Bisexual	S. else	DK	Refused	Total
Underweight	n	51	993	52	33	20	24	1173
	%	2.3	1.03	3.08	2.53	2.45	1.59	1.13
	Wt.%	3.57	1.38	3.59	2.24	3.53	1.99	1.51
Normal	n	742	23,955	539	367	258	430	26,291
	%	33.53	24.87	31.93	28.14	31.66	28.51	25.32
	Wt.%	31.52	25.50	31.68	29.72	32.47	27.55	25.91
Overweight	n	798	40,068	579	480	313	641	42,879
	%	36.06	41.60	34.3	36.81	38.4	42.51	41.29
	Wt.%	36.93	40.02	32.42	37.74	36.55	41.06	39.75
Obese	n	622	31,297	518	424	224	413	33,498
	%	28.11	32.50	30.69	32.52	27.48	27.39	32.26
	Wt.%	27.98	33.11	32.30	30.30	27.44	29.40	32.82
	Total	2213	96,313	1688	1304	815	1508	103,841
	Pearson chi^2 326.25, p = 0.000							

Notes: Sexual Orientation Categories: Gay or Lesbian, Straight, Bisexual, Something Else, Don't Know, Refused
Weighted values shown as Wt. %

We next examined how our sociodemographic variables are distributed by sexual orientation. The results in Table 18.3 indicate that the associations between employment and sexual orientation were significant for both males (χ^2 (5) = 187.37, p = 0.000) and females (χ^2 (5) = 678.38, p = 0.000). Most notable were the differences between bisexual males, with fewer (47.65%) employed compared with 50.38% of straight males, and 52.79% of gay males. Bisexual and lesbian females, however were more likely to be employed than straight females, with 48.48% and 48.36%, respectively employed for wages.

Significant differences in education (females: χ^2 (10) = 1300, p = 0.000; males: χ^2 (10) = 900.72, p = 0.000) are observed across the sexual orientation categories. Bisexual females compared to lesbian and heterosexual females are disadvantages in education. Approximately 34% of bisexual women are college graduates, while nearly 40% of straight women and nearly 50% of lesbians have graduated from college. Bisexual men are similarly disadvantaged in education. Here, it is observed that 22.68% of bisexual males have college degrees, compared to 28.32% of straight men, and 36.65% of gay men.

Table 18.2 Race/ethnicity by male and female sexual orientation, BRFSS SOGI Sample 2020 (number, percentage, and weighted percentage)

		Female sexual orientation						
Race/ethnicity		Lesbian	Straight	Bisexual	S. else	DK	Refused	Total
NH White	n	1167	78,886	2453	1009	686	1233	85,434
	%	74.95	76.47	69.55	64.56	50.22	73.66	75.71
	Wt.%	60.79	61.85	62.27	55.23	27.96	56.79	61.20
NH Black	n	112	7570	253	123	87	124	8269
	%	7.19	7.34	7.17	7.87	6.37	7.41	7.33
	Wt.%	13.15	12.33	11.45	13.54	8.85	12.00	12.27
NH Asian	n	33	3042	81	64	92	44	3356
	%	2.12	2.95	2.30	4.09	6.73	2.63	2.97
	Wt.%	3.56	6.14	3.32	6.70	5.47	8.28	6.02
NH AIAN	n	25	1687	65	32	43	24	1876
	%	1.61	1.64	1.84	2.05	3.15	1.43	1.66
	Wt.%	1.59	1.00	1.06	0.69	1.76	1.00	1.01
Hispanic	n	132	8027	424	231	386	170	9370
	%	8.48	7.78	12.02	14.78	28.26	10.16	8.3
	Wt.%	17.95	16.59	18.58	20.75	54.66	19.76	17.34
NH other	n	88	3943	251	104	72	79	4537
	%	5.65	3.82	7.12	6.65	5.27	4.72	4.02
	Wt.%	2.97	2.10	3.32	3.09	1.30	2.17	2.17
	Total	1557	103,155	3527	1563	1366	1674	112,842
	Pearson chi^2 1200, $p = 0.000$							
		Male sexual orientation						
Race/ethnicity		Gay	Straight	Bisexual	S. else	DK	Refused	Total
NH White	n	1597	74,280	1223	830	361	1158	79,449
	%	72.16	77.12	72.45	63.65	44.29	76.79	76.51
	Wt.%	57.36	62.32	61.21	50.94	19.67	62.43	61.58
NH Black	n	124	5607	98	90	48	71	6038
	%	5.6	5.82	5.81	6.90	5.89	4.71	5.81
	Wt.%	11.04	10.57	10.90	10.97	5.52	11.67	10.55
NH Asian	n	76	3126	48	42	69	49	3410
	%	3.43	3.25	2.84	3.22	8.47	3.25	3.28
	Wt.%	7.17	6.06	4.32	6.12	19.03	5.21	6.18
NH AIAN	n	31	1520	40	44	17	24	1676
	%	1.40	1.58	2.37	3.37	2.09	1.59	1.61
	Wt.%	0.97	0.95	2.00	1.38	0.64	1.21	0.98
Hispanic	n	267	7759	166	186	285	142	8805
	%	12.07	8.06	9.83	14.26	34.97	9.42	8.48
	Wt.%	21.20	17.91	17.81	25.47	53.67	17.57	18.46
NH other	n	118	4021	113	112	35	64	4463
	%	5.33	4.17	6.69	8.59	4.29	4.24	4.3
	Wt.%	2.27	2.19	3.76	5.11	1.48	1.92	2.25
	Total	2213	96,313	1688	1304	815	1508	103,841
	Pearson chi^2 1100, $p = 0.000$							

Notes: Sexual Orientation Categories: Gay or Lesbian, Straight, Bisexual, Something Else, Don't Know, Refused
Weighted values shown as Wt. %

Table 18.3 Selected characteristics by male and female sexual orientation, BRFSS SOGI Sample 2020 (number, percentage, and weighted percentage)

		Female sexual orientation						
Employment		Lesbian	Straight	Bisexual	S. else	DK	Refused	Total
Not employed	n	804	63,393	1817	1025	1165	1255	69,459
	%	51.64	61.45	51.52	65.58	85.29	74.97	61.55
	Wt.%	48.52	58.41	53.47	63.83	79.28	71.22	58.62
Employed	n	753	39,762	1710	538	201	419	43,383
	%	48.36	38.55	48.48	34.42	14.71	25.03	38.45
	Wt.%	51.48	41.59	46.53	36.17	20.72	28.78	41.38
Education								
No degree	n	801	61,810	2337	1074	1149	1127	68,298
	%	51.45	59.92	66.26	68.71	84.11	67.32	60.53
	Wt.%	66.99	69.86	77.32	76.01	91.29	75.28	70.61
College degree	n	755	41,225	1187	480	205	501	44,353
	%	48.49	39.96	33.65	30.71	15.01	29.93	39.31
	Wt.%	33.01	30.03	22.59	23.53	8.07	22.34	29.24
Missing	n	1	120	3	9	12	46	191
	%	0.06	0.12	0.09	0.58	0.88	2.75	0.17
	Wt.%	0	0.1	0.09	0.46	0.64	2.38	0.15
Health status								
Good or better	n	1288	86,919	2835	1211	957	1327	94,537
	%	82.72	84.26	80.38	77.48	70.06	79.27	83.78
	Wt.%	79.55	84.44	82.88	77.95	66.89	79.06	83.87
Fair/poor	n	268	16,063	690	349	397	336	18,103
	%	17.21	15.57	19.56	22.33	29.06	20.07	16.04
	Wt.%	20.16	15.42	16.97	22.02	32.34	20.29	15.97
Missing	n	1	173	2	3	12	11	202
	%	0.06	0.17	0.06	0.19	0.88	0.66	0.18
	Wt.%	0.03	0.14	0.15	0.00	0.77	0.66	0.16
	Total	1557	103,155	3527	1563	1366	1674	112,842
		Male sexual orientation						
Employment		Gay	Straight	Bisexual	S. else	DK	Refused	Total
Not employed	n	1128	52,336	869	839	568	948	56,688
	%	50.97	54.34	51.48	64.34	69.69	62.86	54.59
	Wt.%	47.21	49.62	52.35	57.99	62.38	61.74	50.02
Employed	n	1085	43,977	819	465	247	560	47,153
	%	49.03	45.66	48.52	35.66	30.31	37.14	45.41
	Wt.%	52.79	50.38	47.65	42.01	37.62	38.26	49.98
Education								
No degree	n	1140	58,312	1126	939	662	848	63,027
	%	51.51	60.54	66.71	72.01	81.23	56.23	60.7
	Wt.%	63.35	71.44	77.23	82.03	89.55	67.11	71.62
College degree	n	1072	37,784	557	360	143	609	40,525
	%	48.44	39.23	33.00	27.61	17.55	40.38	39.03
	Wt.%	36.65	28.32	22.68	17.25	8.12	28.33	28.06
Missing	n	1	217	5	5	10	51	289
	%	0.05	0.23	0.3	0.38	1.23	3.38	0.28
	Wt.%	0.00	0.24	0.09	0.72	2.34	4.56	0.32

(continued)

Table 18.3 (continued)

Health status								
Good or better	n	1865	82,759	1402	977	568	1233	88,804
	%	84.27	85.93	83.06	74.92	69.69	81.76	85.52
	Wt.%	83.29	86.31	86.3	79.58	62.86	82.03	85.84
Fair/poor	n	344	13,343	281	318	240	265	14,791
	%	15.54	13.85	16.65	24.39	29.45	17.57	14.24
	Wt.%	16.57	13.47	13.59	20.08	36.91	17.72	13.93
Missing	n	4	211	5	9	7	10	246
	%	0.18	0.22	0.30	0.69	0.86	0.66	0.24
	Wt.%	0.14	0.23	0.11	0.34	0.23	0.25	0.22
	Total	2213	96,313	1688	1304	815	1508	103,841

Notes: Sexual Orientation Categories: Gay or Lesbian, Straight, Bisexual, Something Else, Don't Know, Refused
Weighted values shown as Wt. %

Finally, the self-reported health status of sexual orientation categories is displayed in Table 18.3. As with the other variables, significant differences are observed for males (χ^2 (10) = 342.90, p = 0.000) and females (χ^2 (10) = 356.27, p = 0.000). In comparison to straight women, bisexual and lesbian females are more likely to report fair or poor health. Among men, gay males (16.57%) are more likely to report fair or poor health, while both bisexual (13.59%) and straight (13.47%) men are similarly less likely to do so.

Finally, we turn to a series of logistic regression analyses treating obesity as the outcome variable (see Table 18.4). Model 1 includes the sexual orientation categories only; Model 2 adds Black race and Hispanic Ethnicity; Model 3 adds levels of education; Model 4 adds employment status; and Model 5 adds general health. The outcomes are shown as odds ratios. In Model 1 (females) it is observed that bisexuals have 1.30 times the odds of obesity compared to straight women. Importantly, once all controls are added to the model (Model 5), bisexual women's odds of obesity are increased in comparison to straight women. Among men, the odds of obesity are lower for bisexual men. In the fully adjusted model, the odds of obesity are reduced by 11% for bisexual men in comparison to straight men.

Overall, our findings are consistent with those observed in other studies. Specifically, we observed that bisexual women (as well as lesbians) have a somewhat elevated risk of obesity compared to straight women. We found the opposite association for bisexual men. In other words, bisexual men (along with gay men) were found to be less likely to have obesity than straight men. These associations persisted despite the inclusion of several sociodemographic controls including education, race, and overall health status. Ongoing work is needed to fully understand why the risk of overweight and obesity is higher in sexual minority women.

Conclusion

In this chapter we examined the relationship between obesity and bisexual sexual orientation. We reviewed the issues that have prevented the reliable study of sexual minorities in the past, examined the availability of information on gender identity and sexual orientation in federal surveys, and reviewed articles that addressed bisexual orientation and obesity.

The consensus from the articles reviewed is that indeed, bisexuals, especially female bisexuals, are more likely to be obese (Caceres et al., 2017). Several theories have been posited which might account for these findings. These include minority stress, body image disturbances, differential health behaviors, and exposure to childhood sexual trauma. The intersectional nature of sexual orientation with socioeconomic status and race/ethnicity may also help to explain persistently high rates of obesity in sexual minority females.

Table 18.4 Adjusted odds ratios of obesity, BRFSS SOGI Sample 2020

	Model-1 OR (95% CI)	Model-2 OR (95% CI)	Model-3 OR (95% CI)	Model-4 OR (95% CI)	Model-5 OR (95% CI)
	Females (n = 112,842)				
Sexual orientation (ref = straight)					
Lesbian	1.26 (1.14, 1.40)***	1.26 (1.14, 1.40)***	1.31 (1.18, 1.46)***	1.29 (1.16, 1.44)***	1.28 (1.15, 1.42)***
Bisexual	1.30 (1.21, 1.39)***	1.29 (1.20, 1.38)***	1.26 (1.18, 1.35)***	1.24 (1.15, 1.33)***	1.22 (1.13, 1.30)***
Something else	1.17 (1.05, 1.30)**	1.14 (1.02, 1.27)*	1.11 (0.99, 1.23)	1.11 (1.00, 1.24)*	1.08 (0.98, 1.21)
Don't know	0.85 (0.76, 0.96)**	0.80 (0.71, 0.90)***	0.74 (0.65, 0.83)***	0.77 (0.68, 0.87)***	0.72 (0.64, 0.81)***
Refused	0.76 (0.68, 0.85)***	0.75 (0.67, 0.84)***	0.73 (0.66, 0.82)***	0.75 (0.67, 0.84)***	0.73 (0.65, 0.82)***
Black (yes =1)		2.16 (2.07, 2.26)***	2.10 (2.01, 2.20)***	2.09 (1.99, 2.19)***	2.03 (1.94, 2.12)***
Hispanic (yes = 1)		1.36 (1.30, 1.42)***	1.27 (1.21, 1.33)***	1.25 (1.19, 1.31)***	1.22 (1.17, 1.28)***
College educated			0.65 (0.63, 0.67)***	0.63 (0.61, 0.64)***	0.66 (0.64, 0.67)***
Employed				1.22 (1.19, 1.25)***	1.30 (1.27, 1.34)***
Good health					1.61 (1.56, 1.66)***
Constant	0.46 (0.46, 0.47)***	0.42 (0.42, 0.43)***	0.50 (0.49, 0.51)***	0.47 (0.46, 0.48)***	0.26 (0.25, 0.27)***
	Males (n = 103,841)				
Sexual orientation (ref = straight)					
Gay	0.81 (0.74, 0.89)***	0.81 (0.73, 0.89)***	0.83 (0.75, 0.91)***	0.83 (0.75, 0.91)***	0.82 (0.75, 0.90)***
Bisexual	0.92 (0.83, 1.02)	0.92 (0.83, 1.02)	0.90 (0.81, 1.00)	0.90 (0.81, 0.99)*	0.89 (0.80, 0.99)*
Something else	1.00 (0.89, 1.12)	0.99 (0.88, 1.11)	0.96 (0.85, 1.08)	0.98 (0.87, 1.10)	0.95 (0.84, 1.07)
Don't know	0.79 (0.67, 0.92)**	0.75 (0.64, 0.87)**	0.72 (0.61, 0.84)***	0.74 (0.63, 0.86)***	0.71 (0.60, 0.83)***
Refused	0.78 (0.70, 0.88)***	0.78 (0.70, 0.88)***	0.80 (0.71, 0.90)***	0.81 (0.72, 0.91)***	0.80 (0.71, 0.89)***
Black (yes = 1)		1.21 (1.15, 1.28)***	1.16 (1.10, 1.23)***	1.17 (1.11, 1.23)***	1.15 (1.09, 1.22)***
Hispanic (yes = 1)		1.20 (1.15, 1.26)***	1.14 (1.09, 1.19)***	1.12 (1.07, 1.17)***	1.11 (1.06, 1.16)***
College educated			0.75 (0.73, 0.77)***	0.73 (0.71, 0.75)***	0.75 (0.73, 0.77)***
Employed				1.19 (1.16, 1.23)***	1.24 (1.21, 1.27)***
Good health					1.28 (1.25, 1.32)***
Constant	0.48 (0.47, 0.49)**	0.47 (0.46, 0.48)***	0.53 (0.52, 0.54)***	0.49 (0.48, 0.50)***	0.36 (0.34, 0.37)***

$^{*}p \le .05$, $^{**}p \le .01$, $^{***}p \le .001$

Another rationale for obesity in bisexual females has been offered by Struble and colleagues (2010). They found that the odds of bisexuals being overweight were 1.9 times those of heterosexual women (p. 55). Accordingly, they suggested that bisexual obesity risk may be variable in relation to the gender of their partner, with male ideas of thinness being less salient for women who are with other women. However, these theoretical arguments remain largely untested.

In the last section of our chapter, we analyzed BRFSS 2020 SOGI data. We relied on SOGI modules, which now appear in a number of federal surveys as part of an effort to make gender identity as well as sexual orientation available for study by population researchers. Our findings are consistent with those of earlier research, especially the work of Eliason and Fogel (2015) and McPhail and Bombak (2015). Specifically, we found significant differences among sexual orientation categories in BMI category. We observed higher percentages of both bisexual males (3.59%) and bisexual females (3.88%) in the underweight category, compared to straight males (1.4%) and straight females (2.23%). About the same percentage of bisexual males was found to be obese (32.3%) compared to straight males (33.11%). A greater percentage of bisexual females were obese (35.93%) compared to straight females (32.65%). In our regression analyses, we observed a significant association between bisexual orientation and obesity in women. This association remained despite the inclusion of controls. Among men, we observed reduced odds of obesity. Given the lack of understanding of why these associations are present, ongoing work is needed to explain why sexual minority females are at greater risk and what may be protective for gay males.

There are several limitations to both the review of articles and our analysis of the likelihood of bisexuals to be obese that must be addressed. First, the use of BMI to categorize obesity has been questioned. Siervo and colleagues (2015) have argued that the use of BMI to study obesity does not address the complexities of obesity, especially the influence of female gender, age, and obesity. BMI alone does not discriminate between "fat mass (FM) and fat-free mass (FFM)" or "simultaneous presence of excess adiposity (obesity) and low skeletal muscle mass (sarcopenia)" (p. 1245). These factors may be more accurate indicators of cardiovascular issues and physical health or disability. They concluded that BMI categories are questionable because they were based on young normal-weight individuals and gender- and then applied to all ages instead of allowing for age related disease risks.

Second, there are caveats about using large scale surveys of the population to address sexual minority populations. Some of these issues include the following: the survey data are collected for reasons other than sexual minority research and thus may have limited applicability; the sub-populations are not specifically targeted so they may not be equally represented in the survey; and the categories used may not be understood by the survey participants.

Third, due to the recent inclusion in the research of sexual minorities, including bisexuals, there is a significant gap in longitudinal research. Some researchers have initiated smaller longitudinal studies including bisexuals, such as Katz-Wand and colleagues (2014) and Guadamuz and colleagues (2011). However, larger federal studies including those with SOGI modules only include cross sectional data, and they do not offer opportunities for longitudinal research. Even when longitudinal studies can be expanded to include SOGI categories, the longitudinal gap will be of concern.

In closing, further research into the relationship between bisexuality and obesity is needed. The current research using BMI alone does not address the nuances of the relationship of obesity to physical health, cardiovascular disease, and how these are mediated by gender and age. In addition, there is a distinct lack of clarity surrounding the reasons why obesity risk is elevated in sexual minority females. Future research should incorporate more extensive measures of psychosocial variables along with behavioral and contextual measures to better understand these associations. In addition, more research is needed on factors that might be protective with respect to obesity, cardiovascular diseases, and diabetes in the aging bisexual sub-population.

Finally, the use of high-quality data on sexual minorities will help to advance our understanding of a range of health issues that are salient to sexual minorities. Thus, we support the use of SOGI guidelines designed to be included in federal surveys in order to fully measure sex and gender. These include sex-assigned at birth: male or female or intersexed; gender identity: woman/man "consistent in sex" (CIS), transgender, or other; sexual orientation (self-identification); sexual behavior; and sexual attraction. As these measures become increasingly available, it will offer broadened opportunities for consistency, comparability, and quality in research on sexual minority populations.

References

Azagba, S., Shan, L., & Latham, K. (2019). Overweight and obesity among sexual minority adults in the United States. *International Journal of Environmental Research and Public Health, 16*(10), 1828. https://doi.org/10.3390/ijerph16101828

Badgett, M. V. L., Goldberg, N., Conron, K. J., & Gates, G. J. (2009). *Best practices for asking questions about sexual orientation on surveys (SMART)*. UCLA School of Law Williams Institute. Available at https://williamsinstitute.law.ucla.edu/publications/smart-so-survey/

Baumle, A. K. (2013). *International handbook on the demography of sexuality*. Springer. https://doi.org/10.1007/978-94-007-5512-3

Baumle, A. K., D'Lane, C., & Poston, D. L., Jr. (2009). *Same-sex partners: The social demography of sexual orientation*. SUNY Press.

Beach, L. B., Turner, B., Felt, D., Marro, R., & Phillips, G. L. (2018). Risk factors for diabetes are higher among non-heterosexual US high-school students. *Pediatric Diabetes, 19*(7), 1137–1146. https://doi.org/10.1111/pedi.12720

Boehmer, U., Bowen, D. J., & Bauer, G. R. (2007). Overweight and obesity in sexual minority women: Evidence from population-based data. *American Journal of Public Health, 97*(6), 1134–1140.

Bridges, T., & Moore, M. R. (2018). Young women of color and shifting sexual identities. *Contexts, 17*(1), 86–88. https://doi.org/10.1177/1536504218767125

Caceres, B., Brody, A., Luscombe, R., Primiano, J., Marusca, P., Sitts, E., & Chyun, D. (2017). A systematic review of cardiovascular disease in sexual minorities. *American Journal of Public Health, 107*, 570–570. https://doi.org/10.2105/AJPH.2016.303630a

Caceres, B. A., Makarem, N., Hickey, K. T., & Hughes, T. L. (2019). Cardiovascular disease disparities in sexual minority adults: An examination of the behavioral risk factor surveillance system (2014-2016). *American Journal of Health Promotion, 33*(4), 576–585. https://doi.org/10.1177/0890117118810246

Calzo, J. P., Turner, B. C., Marro, R., & Phillips, 2nd. (2019). Alcohol use and disordered eating in a US sample of heterosexual and sexual minority adolescents. *Journal of the American Academy of Child and Adolescent Psychiatry, 58*(2), 200–210. https://doi.org/10.1016/j.jaac.2018.09.437

Carpenter, C., & Eppink, S. (2017). Does it get better? Recent estimates of sexual orientation and earnings in the United States. *Southern Economic Journal, 84*(2), 426–441. https://doi.org/10.2307/26633351

Centers for Disease Control and Prevention. (2014). *Behavioral risk factor surveillance system overview: BRFSS 2013*. Retrieved July 19, 2022 from https://www.cdc.gov/brfss/annual_data/2013/pdf/Overview_2013.pdf

Compton, D., Farris, N., & Chang, Y. (2015). Patterns of bisexuality in America. *Journal of Bisexuality, 15*(4), 481–497. https://doi.org/10.1080/15299716.2015.1048919

Eliason, M. J., & Fogel, S. C. (2015). An ecological framework for sexual minority women's health: Factors associated with greater body mass. *Journal of Homosexuality, 62*(7), 845–882. https://doi.org/10.1080/00918369.2014.1003007

Federal Interagency Working Group on Improving Measurement of Sexual Orientation and Gender Identity in Federal Surveys/SOGI. (2016). *Current measures of sexual orientation and gender identity in federal surveys*. Retrieved from https://nces.ed.gov/FCSM/pdf/buda5.pdf

Fredriksen-Goldsen, K. I., Kim, H. J., Barkan, S. E., Balsam, K. F., & Mincer, S. L. (2010). Disparities in health-related quality of life: A comparison of lesbians and bisexual women. *American Journal of Public Health, 100*(11), 2255–2261. https://doi.org/10.2105/AJPH.2009.177329

Fredriksen-Goldsen, K. I., Kim, H.-J., Barkan, S. E., Muraco, A., & Hoy-Ellis, C. P. (2013). Health disparities among lesbian, gay, and bisexual older adults: Results from a population-based study. *American Journal of Public Health, 103*(10), 1802–1809. https://doi.org/10.2105/ajph.2012.301110

Gates, G. J. (2011). *How many people are lesbian, gay, bisexual, and transgender?* The Williams Institute, UCLA School of Law. Available at https://williamsinstitute.law.ucla.edu/publications/how-many-people-lgbt/

Ghaziani, A. (2017). The closet. *Contexts, 16*(3), 72–73. https://doi.org/10.1177/1536504217732060

Gorman, B., & Oyarvide, Z. (2018). Sexual orientation, socioeconomic status, and healthy aging. *Generations:*

Journal of the American Society on Aging, 42(2), 56–60. https://doi.org/10.2307/26556361

Gorman, B. K., Denney, J. T., Dowdy, H., & Medeiros, R. M. (2015). A new piece of the puzzle: Sexual orientation, gender, and physical health status. *Demography, 2015*(52), 1357–1382. https://doi.org/10.1007/s13524-015-0406-1

Guadamuz, T. E., Lim, S. H., Marshal, M. P., Friedman, M. S., Stall, R. D., & Silvestre, A. J. (2011). Sexual, behavioral, and quality of life characteristics of healthy weight, overweight, and obese gay and bisexual men: Findings from a prospective cohort study. *Archives of Sexual Behavior, 41*(2), 385–389. https://doi.org/10.1007/s10508-011-9859-5

Hadland, S. E., Austin, S. B., Goodenow, C. S., & Calzo, J. P. (2014). Weight misperception and unhealthy weight control behaviors among sexual minorities in the general adolescent population. *Journal of Adolescent Health, 54*(3), 296–303. https://doi.org/10.1016/j.jadohealth.2013.08.021

Hatzenbuehler, K., McLaughlin, A., & Slopen, N. (2013). Sexual orientation disparities in cardiovascular biomarkers among young adults. *American Journal of Preventive Medicine, 44*(6), 612–621.

IOM (Institute of Medicine). (2011). *The health of lesbian, gay, bisexual, and transgender people: Building a foundation for better understanding*. The National Academies Press.

Jun, H. J., Corliss, H. L., Nichols, L. P., Pazaris, M. J., Spiegelman, D., & Austin, S. B. (2012). Adult body mass index trajectories and sexual orientation: The Nurses' Health Study II. *American Journal of Preventive Medicine, 42*(4), 348–354. https://doi.org/10.1016/j.amepre.2011.11.011

Katz-Wise, S. L., Jun, H. J., Corliss, H. L., Jackson, B., Haines, J., & Austin, S. B. (2014). Child abuse as a predictor of gendered sexual orientation disparities in body mass index trajectories among U.S. youth from the Growing Up Today Study. *Journal of Adolescent Health, 54*(6), 730–738. https://doi.org/10.1016/j.jadohealth.2013.11.006

Kinsey, A. C., Pomeroy, W. B., & Martin, C. E. (1948). *The sexual behavior in the human male*. W. B. Sanders and Company.

Laumann, E. O., Gagnon, J. H., Michael, R. T., & Michaels, S. (1994). *The social organization of sexuality: Sexual practices in the United States*. University of Chicago Press.

Lick, D., Durso, L., & Johnson, K. (2013). Minority stress and physical health among sexual minorities. *Perspectives on Psychological Science, 8*(5), 521–548. Retrieved 12 Feb 2021 from http://www.jstor.org.ezproxy.lib.uh.edu/stable/44289924

Lofquist, D. (2011). *Same-sex couple households*. US Department of Commerce, Economics and Statistics Administration, US Census Bureau.

Mays, V., Juster, R., Williamson, T., Seeman, T., & Cochran, S. (2018). Chronic physiologic effects of stress among lesbian, gay, and bisexual adults: Results from the national health and nutrition examination survey. *Psychosomatic Medicine, 80*(6), 551–563. https://doi.org/10.1097/PSY.0000000000000600

McPhail, D., & Bombak, A. E. (2015). Fat, queer and sick? A critical analysis of 'lesbian obesity' in public health discourse. *Critical Public Health, 25*(5), 539–553. https://doi.org/10.1080/09581596.2014.992391

Newton Lew, K., Dorsen, C., Melkus, G. D., & Maclean, M. (2018). Prevalence of obesity, prediabetes, and diabetes in sexual minority women of diverse races/ethnicities: Findings from the 2014-2015 BRFSS Surveys. *Diabetes Education, 44*(4), 348–360. https://doi.org/10.1177/0145721718776599

O'Connell, M., & Feliz, S. (2011). Same-sex couple household statistics from the 2010 census. *US Bureau of the Census*.

Ogden, C. L., Lamb, M. M., Carroll, M. D., & Flegal, K. M. (2010). *Obesity and socioeconomic status in adults: United States 1988–1994 and 2005–2008* (NCHS data brief no 50). National Center for Health Statistics.

Siervo, M., Prado, C. M., Mire, E., Broyles, S., Wells, J. C., Heymsfield, S., & Katzmarzyk, P. T. (2015). Body composition indices of a load–capacity model: Gender- and BMI-specific reference curves. *Public Health Nutrition, 18*(7), 1245–1254. https://doi.org/10.1017/S1368980014001918

Struble, C. B., Lindley, L. L., Montgomery, K., Hardin, J., & Burcin, M. (2010). Overweight and obesity in lesbian and bisexual college women. *Journal of American College Health, 59*(1), 51–56. https://doi.org/10.1080/07448481.2010.483703

Prevalence and Trends in Obesity Across Gender Identities 19

Mary Ann Davis, D'Lane Compton, and Nicole Farris

To me gender is not physical at all but is altogether insubstantial. It is the essentialness of oneself, the psyche, the fragment of unity (Morris, 1974) *Conundrum*.

We agree with Harris (2015) that "(T)transgender issues and images have been increasingly present in popular media, literature, journalism, and the legal landscape of the United States" (p. 1). In spite of this popularity, data regarding transgender persons are largely absent in demographic research and federal census and surveys. To address this void, our chapter offers insights into the background of gendered research.

Our review[1] of the literature addressing body weight and its implications in the transgender community suggests several issues that are explored in this chapter. First, we present the history of transgender in large scale surveys in the U.S. Until recently, appropriate categories have not existed and need to be implemented in federal and large-scale research. Next, we identify federal, large-scale surveys that include measures of obesity and describe their questions addressing sex and gender. We explore and describe the process in which a two-stage measure of gender identity was added to an existing survey, e.g. Lagos et al.'s inclusions to the General Social Survey. We also discuss several smaller surveys addressing sexuality/gender and obesity. Next, we review the limited empirical research findings to date.

Following the above, we then present an examination of obesity in the transgendered using BRSS data from 2020. Several of the preceding chapters in this edited volume examine available demographic data to describe issues related to obesity in sexual minority populations. We too offer an analysis based on available data; however, we highlight the limitations of the data and focus on arguments supporting greater inclusion and integration of transgender identification in future federal censuses and other surveys. Finally, we use available data to review and outline needed efforts to increase access to data and feasibility of representative analysis regarding gender issues and related health implications.

[1] We conducted a JSTOR search in February 2021 using the terms "transgender" and "obesity." We found 231 articles with 175 written from 2010 to 2021. From these articles we reviewed those involving a demographic analysis of survey and administrative data to examine the relationships between transgender and obesity.

M. A. Davis (✉)
Department of Sociology, University of New Orleans, New Orleans, LA, USA
e-mail: madavis9@uno.edu

D. Compton
University of New Orleans, New Orleans, LA, USA

N. Farris
Department of Sociology and Criminal Justice, Texas A&M University-Commerce, Commerce, TX, USA

G. Garcia-Alexander, D. L. Poston, Jr. (eds.), *International Handbook of the Demography of Obesity*, International Handbooks of Population 12, https://doi.org/10.1007/978-3-031-10936-2_19

Background

The demographic analysis of the intersection of transgender identity and obesity must begin with a brief background regarding the identity and accepted definitions of transgender that are quantifiable with demographic data. Transgender identity may be challenging to define as it includes many aspects of gender identity and expression (Gates, 2011). Allowing for self-identification, e.g. transgender, is one way to identify this group. Two-part questions that identify sex assigned at birth and current gender identity is another approach. But, this information is largely absent from, or lacking in specificity in, existing data (as we describe below). The U.S. Census, the gold standard for demographic analysis, includes sex but not gender. For example, U.S Census data have been used to quantify the number of persons in same-sex partnerships. However, the U.-S. Census does not include gender or sexual orientation information needed to identify whether these persons are transgendered. Another example is the National Survey of Family Growth (NSFG), which has been widely used in sexual behavior research but does not include gender questions.

Until recently, the ability to identify transgendered persons has not been possible in large-scale surveys. The 2018 General Social Survey (GSS) was the first nationally representative survey in the U.S. to include separate questions on sex assigned at birth and current gender identity. The specific questions included were: "What sex were you assigned at birth, for example, on your birth certificate? (female, male, intersex, don't know, refused)"; and "What is your current gender? (woman, man, transgender, – a gender not listed here (please specify), don't know, refused)." The GSS also includes height and weight variables that can be used to identify obesity. Unfortunately, as noted by Lagos and Compton (2021), the 2018 GSS data are limited due to the small transgender representation in the U.S. population. The 2018 GSS data included only nine persons whose responses to the two variables of current gender identity and sex assigned at birth were incongruent.

This lack of transgender data is further hampered by three additional factors. First, the current census and national survey data are primarily cross-sectional, addressing a single point of disclosure, whereas trans people may identify or "come out" at differing times. As such, this type of survey format may not effectively capture all individuals who may be at various stages in the "coming out" process. Additionally, given the small size of sexual minority populations, recruitment efforts may be costly, time-, and labor-intensive (IOM, 2011). Second, as noted by Meier and Labuski (2013), there are few agreed upon measures or standard definitions of "transgendered." Third, researchers may encounter problems locating the population to study because they may be "marginalized by political, religious, legal, medical, and other cultural institutions; transgender persons encounter levels of discrimination that range from simple misapprehension and exclusion by an uneducated public, to explicit acts of sexual and physical violence" (Meier & Labuski, 2013, p. 208). This likely leads to an unwillingness to disclose gender identity and/or avoidance of individuals perceived to represent exclusionary institutions.

Alfred Kinsey (1894–1956) is often cited as one of the earliest and foremost sexuality researchers (Kinsey Institute, 2019). His work yielded important insights into the richness and variety of human sexuality. For example, in his landmark study of male sexuality, Kinsey and his colleagues (1948) provided estimates with respect to homosexuality prevalence; he estimated that 10% of the male population had some same-sex desire and about 4% classified themselves as gay. However, he made no mention of the trans population in this contribution.

An extensive review of his work and correspondence reveals that Kinsey had some interest in transsexuals. Meyerowitz (2001) reported that although Kinsey interviewed persons with transgender orientation and supported a behaviorist model of gender over the biological essentialist dichotomy of sex as either male or female, he did not include these findings in his written research. He also published the Heterosexual-Homosexual Rating Scale (1948, pp. 636–659), and appears to have included those with male to female transgender orientation. However, Kinsey followed the prevailing attitudes of the 1950s and disapproved of genital surgery for the transgender oriented, as it might interfere with having orgasms, which he argued was a necessary part of sexuality.

The research of Meyerowitz (2001) reveals that by 1947 Kinsey had interviewed nine persons who identified as transgender. Interestingly, one of his interviewees seems to have impacted his views on this subject by arguing against his exclusion of transvestites and transgender oriented in his reports. She encouraged him to study this population, arguing that it was larger than he believed. To encourage his research, she supplied him with contacts of 19 cross dressers in the San Francisco area and 152 nationally (Meyerowitz, 2001, p. 77). An emerging group supporting rights of those with transgender orientation noted that "Alfred Kinsey left us out of his book . . . He is now trying to make amends and is collecting all available information on transvestites" (Meyerowitz, 2001, p. 77). Kinsey conducted substantive interviews resulting in. . ."100 male-to-female transvestites, 11 female-to-male transvestites, and 10 postoperative male-to-female transgenders" (Meyerowitz, 2001, p. 80) but he never published the results of this research.

In the 1970s and later, sexual research began to expand to include "a number of issues that are fundamental to population study, including migration, fertility, morbidity, and other areas" (Baumle, 2013). However, most of the research involving sexual minorities has been limited to sexually transmitted infections. Notably, although transgendered individuals have played an active role in history, art, literature, and more recently political life (as of 2021, Wikipedia listed 43 elected officials in the U.S. who stated that they were trans gender) the inclusion of transgendered persons in demographic data and analyses are limited.

To correct this issue, the first step in transgender research is to properly quantify the extent of the transgendered population, given that there are different estimates of its size in the United States. One accepted way that researchers can identify gender is through public documents. Spade (2008) indicates that identity documents from various government agencies have allowed changes in gender over the last 40 years. The author states the following:

> Departments of health, DMVs, and the SSA, have created policies or practices allowing individuals to change the gender marker on their documents and records from "M" to "F" (male to female) or "F" to "M" (female to male). 11 These policies emerged from a growing awareness of the existence of a population of people, currently labeled "transgender," 12 who live their lives identifying as and expressing a different gender than the one assigned to them at birth. Recognizing the social and economic difficulties faced by those whose lived expression of gender does not match their identity documentation, state and federal agencies have over time created a variety of policies aimed at allowing gender marker change on documents commonly used to verify identity (Spade, 2008, pp. 743–4).

Another researcher utilized this form of data to compile estimates of likely transgender individuals. Accordingly, Harris (2015) examined the records of those who changed either or both their first names or their sex-coding in Social Security Administration records from 1936 to 2010. Next, these were linked to the 2010 census data to identify "135,367 individuals who are likely to be transgender. Of these, 89,667 were alive during the 2010 Census" (Harris, 2015, p. 20).

Others have applied broader conceptions of gender identity resulting in much larger estimates. For example, Doan (2016) "used a more broadly defined transgender subjectivity that includes transgenders and cross-dressers, as well as intersex, gender-flux, or gender-nonconforming individuals for a total of 9,318,597 individuals or nearly 3 percent (2.92) of the U.S. population" (Doan, 2016, p. 89). Doan (2016) further argues that it is difficult to identify the transgendered population as many take hormones to enhance female characteristics and may not identify as transgendered. Also complicating the measurement of this population is the social and cultural awareness of trans identity. Some researchers have noted that individuals may not identify as transgendered for these reasons. Doan (2016) noted that in interviews with older lesbians, they reported that in retrospect they dressed in male clothes and adopted other male styles that may have identified them as transgendered. However, they were not familiar with this identity. Other males and females who do not have the finances to access drugs or surgery may cross dress but not self-identify as transgender.

Few population-based estimates of people who identify as transgender are available (Gates, 2011). One state-level survey found that 0.5% of people ages 18–64 self-identified as such (Conron et al., 2012). Another study used multiple sources to construct estimates and found that 0.5% are transgendered when defined based on having taken some steps toward transition (Olyslager & Conway, 2007). More recent estimates suggest that the size of the adult population has been steady over time, but the number of transgender youth has doubled to approximately 1.4% (Williams Institute, 2022). However, data remain limited, and the transgendered population may be at increased risk of poor health due to social isolation, discrimination in healthcare settings, and/or lack of access to care. Therefore, it is important to have accurate data about the transgendered population so it can be counted, recognized, and receive protection under the law.

A lack of consistent means for identifying transgendered persons empirically raises practical issues with respect to the ability, or lack thereof, to study obesity and its health implications. Arthur et al. (2021) posit that we are only beginning to study the health issues of transgendered persons and the barriers to care that they may encounter. One reason for this is a lack of training in the needs and special issues of the LGBTQ population in medical professionals. In a study of 252 medical students in UK, it was found that "The majority of participants (n = 160; 69%) had not received specific training on LGBT health needs, and 85% (n = 197) wanted to receive more training" (p. 2).

In addition to the issues cited above, since the transgendered population faces heightened prejudice and discrimination it is important to recognize that this places them at a greater risk of stress-related diseases. This is an area where demographers can contribute to our understanding of the implications for obesity and other health outcomes. As an example, Jura and Kozak (2016) found that the aging transgender population has a heightened risk for health-related conditions, including obesity, as they have faced multiple years of social stigma.

Researchers Argue for Transgender Data

The lack of demographic transgender data has been addressed by researchers in several working groups, with recommendations for greater inclusion of the transgendered in research. These groups include the Center of Excellence for Transgender Health at the University of California at San Francisco (n.d.), The Gender Identity in U.S. Surveillance Group (2014), The National Resource Center on LGBT Aging (2014), The Sexual Minority Assessment Research Team (2009), Williams Institute (2014) and the 2016 Federal Interagency Working Group on Improving Measurement of Sexual Orientation and Gender Identity in Federal Surveys (SOGI). These researchers all agree on the need to both include transgender questions in surveys, and to have these data standardized for comparison. According to the SOGI working group (2016), there are essential concepts to its study, i.e. sex, gender, transgender, and sexual orientation with the related terms: lesbian, gay, bisexual, and transgender (LGBT). These concepts have more than one meaning based on their social context and are thus not clearly measured in federal surveys. The SOGI prefers to focus on the sexual and gender minority (SGM) population as it includes those genders not specified in the lesbian, gay, bisexual, and transgender (LGBT) populations.

The SOGI working group first distinguishes between sex and gender. Sex is defined as the physical, hormonal, biological and anatomical characteristic assigned at birth. Sex refers to "the genetic, hormonal, anatomical and physiological characteristics on whose basis one is labeled at birth as either male or female" (IOM, 2011, p. 25). Sex is labeled as male, female or intersexed.

Gender has a broader definition involving socially constructed characteristics, norms, roles, and relationships. Gender refers to:

> ...the socially constructed characteristics of women and men.... Gender includes psychological, social, cultural, and behavioral dimensions including gender identity and gender expressions. Gender labels include, but are not limited, to masculine, feminine, and trans gender (SOGI, 2016, p. 9).

Efforts to standardize transgender data have been successfully undertaken by researchers. For example, Lagos and Compton (2021) advocated for these measures to be included in the General Social Survey in 2018 and described their process as follows:

> In these proposals, we advocated for a two-step gender measure, which asks for respondent's sex as indicated on their birth certificate in one question, and then asks respondents to identify their gender identity in another question. ...These proposals for the two-step gender question were accepted after peer-review by the GSS and have now yielded the first nationally representative dataset that accounts for transgender identity (Lagos & Compton, 2021, p. 4).

Results from the self-administered questionnaire in the 2018 GSS found that "between 0.44% and 0.93% of the respondents who were surveyed either identified as transgender, identified with a gender that does not conventionally correspond to the sex they were assigned at birth, or identified the sex they were assigned at birth inconsistently with the interviewer's assessment of respondent sex" (Lagos & Compton, 2021, p. 4).

However, the availability of data for the study of obesity in sexual minorities and transgendered persons is even more scarce. The consensus, as stated by Austin and colleagues (2009), is that sexual minorities have weight related issues; however, the relationship among sex, gender and weight are understudied. Furthermore, much of the research is mixed with respect to the extent to which sexual minorities may be at risk of under- or overweight, or obesity. Researchers have studied sexual minority males and found that although they appeared to have higher levels of concern about body weight, they were less likely to report physical activity compared to heterosexuals (Calzo et al., 2013, 2015; Miller & Luk, 2018). Studies of sexual minority females by Austin et al. (2013) found although sexual minority females were more likely than heterosexual females to have obesity, their findings regarding body norms and body issues needed further examination. Additionally, several have questioned the validity of findings of higher BMIs in lesbians as a result of small sample sizes, lack of generalizability, and misidentification (Bowen et al., 2008). As such, ongoing work is needed to determine whether there is a genuinely increased risk of overweight or obesity in sexual minority females (see Chap. 17 of this *Handbook* for a review of the literature and an analysis of obesity in lesbians).

Few studies have examined body weight in transgendered populations. One study used a retrospective review of electronic medical records and found that 32.7% of transgender adults had BMIs in the obese range; 26.4% were identified as having overweight (Sackey et al., 2021). Another found that transgender college students, in comparison to non-transgender individuals, were more likely to have either underweight or obesity versus normal weight (VanKim et al., 2014). They further observed differences in physical activity and screen time with transgender college students reporting less physical activity and more screen time. A recent study of adolescents revealed that transgender and nonconforming students were more likely to have overweight or obesity and less likely to be physically active (Bishop et al., 2020).

Some research suggests that transgendered persons may be at greater risk of underweight (Suarez et al., 2021), which may be tied to body dissatisfaction (Bandini et al., 2013; Vocks et al., 2003) or the barriers they face. For example, results compiled by the Williams Institute using the Census Bureau Household Pulse Survey of July 21 to October 11, 2021 found that 25.3% of transgendered persons were food insecure compared to 8.3% of cis-gendered persons. Food insecurity was worsened for transgendered individuals who were racial minorities, with 35.8% compared to 6% of White cis-gendered respondents being food insecure. Education did not eliminate the disadvantage. They found 22.1% of transgendered individuals with a bachelor's degree experienced food insufficiency compared to 13.5% of cis-gendered individuals with a high school or education (Conron & O'Neill, 2021). However, research in this area is very limited and the nature of these associations as well as factors that might put individuals at risk of bodyweight disturbances remain largely unexplored.

Inclusion of Sexual Orientation and Gender in Federal Surveys

According to the SOGI working group (2016), eleven Federal surveys and one study collect data on issues relevant to sexual orientation, including identity, attraction, behavior, and gender identity. These include the Health Center Patient Survey (HCPS), the National Adult Tobacco Survey (NATS), the National Health and Nutrition Examination Survey (NHANES), the National Health Interview Survey (NHIS), the National Inmate Survey (NIS), the National Crime Victimization Survey (NCVS), the National Survey of Family Growth (NSFG), the Youth Risk Behavior Surveillance System (YRBSS), the National Survey on Drug Use and Health (NSDUH), the National Survey of Older Americans Act Participants (NSOAAP), the Behavior Risk Factor Surveillance System (BRFSS), and the study of the Population Assessment of Tobacco and Health (PATH).

We focus on the seven surveys that include gender identity questions, namely, the Population Assessment of Tobacco and Health (PATH), the Behavior Risk Factor Surveillance System (BRFSS), the National Adult Tobacco Survey (NATS), the National Crime Victimization Survey (NCVS), the National Inmate Survey (NIS), the Health Center Patient Survey (HCPS), and the General Social Survey (GSS) (Table 19.1).

PATH and BRFSS (2013-present) ask similar two-part gender questions.

> (R02_AM0061/R03_AM00) Some people describe themselves as transgender when they experience a different gender identity from their sex at birth. For example, a person born into a male body, but who feels female or lives as a woman would be transgender. Do you consider yourself to be transgender? Yes, No, Don't know, Refused, Not Sure.
>
> [If R answers yes to R02_AM0061/R03_AM0061] (R02_AM0062/R03_AM0062) Do you consider yourself to be male-to-female, female-to-male, or non-conforming? Yes, Transgender, male to female Yes, Transgender, female to male Yes, Transgender, gender nonconforming No Not sure, Don't know Refused, Not Sure (Centers for Disease Control and Prevention, 2014b, 2022).

The NIS includes gender and transgender in the question stem "(D2) Are you male, female, or transgender? Male, Female, Transgender" The NIS also includes obesity via an ICD-9 Code for obesity.

The HCPS uses a one question gender format, with a follow up for clarity.

> (INT3) What is your gender? Male Female
>
> [If age >13]: Female to male transgender; male/trans- male/female to male, Male to female transgender; female/trans woman/male to female; Gender queer OTHER, specify

Table 19.1 Federal surveys including gender identity and obesity

Survey	Height	Weight	Obesity	Gender
Population Assessment of Tobacco and Health (PATH)	X	X		X
Behavior Risk Factor Surveillance System (BRFSS)	X	X	BMI	X
National Adult Tobacco Survey (NATS)				X
National Crime Victimization Survey (NCVS)			ICD-9	X
National Inmate Survey (NIS)			Obesity	X
Health Center Patient Survey (HCPS)	X	X		X
General Social Survey (GSS)	X	X	X	X

Source: SOGI, PATH, BRFSS, NATS, NCVS, NIS, HCPS, GSS

(INT3_SPEC) We have entered your gender as [INT3 RESPONSE: Genderqueer OR INT3_OTH RESPONSE: FILL]. In this interview, questions will appear based on gender. For example, we only ask questions about mammograms to females of a specific age. Since this is a research study collecting medical-related data, could you tell us your biological sex at birth? Male Female (HCPS).

The HCPS also includes height and weight which can be used to examine BMI and obesity.

Although NATS (2012 and 2014–) (Centers for Disease Control and Prevention, 2014a) NCVS (2016-present) ask similar gender two-part questions, sex at birth and current gender, NCVS also includes a follow up question to confirm the answers were intended. However, neither include obesity or weight data. Transgender identity along with a range of health issues have been included since 2014 in the BRFSS.

An additional limitation to the study of transgender and health issues is related to the small numbers surveyed in general demographic research. For example, the two-part gender question was included in the GSS for the first time in 2018. Lagos and Compton (2021) and Suarez et al. (2019) used these data to examine the transgendered population. Lagos and Compton (2021) found that of the 1409 who were asked self-administered questions, 1397 replied to the question about their sex assigned at birth. Of the 1409, 1401 responded to the question about their current gender. A total of 7, or 0.50% of persons responded to both questions, reporting to be transgendered. In the examination of Suarez et al. (2019), they used the criterion of whether one's sex assigned at birth and one's current gender were incongruent. They found, using raw data, that of the 1026 surveyed who responded to the two questions, nine were deemed to be transgendered. After weighting the data appropriately, analyses showed that 0.60% of the population was transgendered. These percentages were similar to individuals who were found by Gates (2011) to be transgendered.

In a follow-up study, Suarez et al. (2021) explored the extent of the transgendered population using data from the 2018 BRFSS, with both raw and weighted data. They found that of the 234,210 who responded to the sexual orientation and gender identity questions: 387 (weighed to 0.0018) reported to be "Yes, Transgender, male-to-female"; 400 (weighed to .0021) reported to be "Yes, Transgender, female to male"; and 251 (weighed to .0013) reported to be "Yes, Transgender, gender nonconforming"; and 230,617 (weighed to .9948) reported to "No". They found that there were no significant differences in BMI categories between transgendered and males, whose current gender matched their gender at birth (CIS). However, they found that transgendered females were significantly underweight and fewer had normal weight, compared to CIS females.

There are three caveats about conducting demographic research on the transgendered population using survey data. First, it must be acknowledged that the secondary data analysis is using questions that were not collected for the purpose of their research, so they may not be fully reflective of desired information. Second, inclusion as participants does not mean that the special sub-population is equally represented. Third, the sub-populations may not have the same interpretation or understanding of the questions.

Administrative Records

As mentioned previously, an additional means through which transgender individuals may be identified is through administrative records. This approach may also be used by demographers to study persons who are transgender, as follows: individuals are identified via name change and sex-coding. Next, SSA records are linked to Census records. Some have found that transgender individuals were more likely to leave blank the Census question pertaining to sex or to check both "M" and "F" (Harris, 2015).

SSA records need to be combined with other federal information, for example Medicare health records or death certificates, to obtain obesity data. Since these data are highly confidential, they would require research at a regional data center. The Regional Data Centers (RDCs) are secure U. S. Census Bureau facilities coordinating data from federal statistical agencies and research institutions. These RDCs provide for a secure access to a restricted use of microdata which can be used by researchers for statistical purposes, while protecting the identity of the participants.

One example of the use of secure administrative data is the research of Proctor et al. (2016), which used Medicare claims records to identify transgender beneficiaries. Codes were used for diagnosis, procedure, prescription drug, and billing. Using claims information, they validated the classification of transgender in 87% of cases (Proctor et al., 2016).

An Analysis of Transgender Individuals, BRFSS 2020

Following Suarez et al.'s (2021) use of BRFSS data, we used the 2020 SOGI survey BRFSS data that included the optional sexual orientation module to examine the relationship between transgender and obesity.

Sample

We selected the BRFSS data in our examination because, according to CDC, the survey is the largest continuous health survey. The survey includes health behaviors, chronic conditions, and use of preventive measures. The BRFSS has been conducted annually since 1984 and has expanded to collect data from all 50 states. The BRFSS targets multiple survey categories.

The BRFSS surveys different states by question categories in subsequent years to limit geographic bias in sampling. In 2020 the states whose surveys included SOGI questions were Alaska, Arkansas, California, Colorado, Connecticut, Georgia, Guam, Hawaii, Idaho, Illinois, Indiana, Iowa, Kansas. Louisiana, Massachusetts, Michigan, Minnesota, Montana, New Jersey, New Mexico, New York, North Carolina, Ohio, Oklahoma, Rhode Island, South Carolina, Texas, Utah, Vermont, Virginia, Washington, West Virginia, and Wisconsin.

The BRFSS conducts about 400,000 self-reported telephone interviews annually, obtained using random digit dialing. In 2020 there were 401,958 participants included in the SOCI survey questions. Survey details are provided in earlier chapters of this *Handbook*.

Measures

There are three parts to the survey core questions posed to all along with optional modules. We use the optional sexual orientation module, SOGI. Variables examined were the gender question, the four BMI categories, and several demographic questions.

The gender question is the following: Do you consider yourself to be male-to-female, female-to-male, or non-conforming? Yes, Transgender, male to female Yes, Transgender, female to male Yes, Transgender, gender nonconforming No, Not sure, Don't know, Refused, Not Sure.

The four BMI categories are: underweight or a BMI of <18.5, normal weight or a BMI of 18.5–24.9, overweight a BMI of 25–29.9, and obese a BMI of $\geq$30.

To account for the complex sampling design of the BRFSS we used the "svy" suite of statistical sample adjustment methods available in the Stata statistical package that will adjust the analyses according to the various population and strata weights in the survey.

Findings

First, we look at the data showing that there are significant differences in overweight and obese status, using both raw numbers, percentages, and weighted percentages. The raw BRFSS 2020 SOGI data provide an overview of the total sample surveyed as well as the BRFSS sample who were asked the SOGI questions used in these analyses. In 2020, of the 216,597 surveyed 335 were Transgendered male to female and 324 were transgendered female to male, and an additional 255 self -described as "Yes, nonconforming," an increase of about 50 from

2019. It is worth noting that this survey has a larger population of transgendered respondents than the GSS.

As was recommended by the CDC, we present weighted data in analyses to examine whether there were significant differences in the populations. Table 19.2 presents the number, percentages and weighted percentages of weight categories by Transgender status. The three categories of transgender provided in the BRFSS include: Male to Female (M to F), Female to Male (F to M), and the category "Yes nonconforming"; the remaining respondents are classified as "other." These categories are used in all subsequent analyses.

Bivariate analysis revealed a significant association between weight and transgender (the $\chi 2$ statistic was significant at <0.01 level). The most notable difference is that more of the M to F were underweight, a larger percentage than the other categories with the exception of the "Yes, nonconforming." Notably, greater percentages of both transgender male to female and female to male were of normal weight compared to the "no" or CIS. However, slightly more of M to T, 33.5%, and fewer F to M, 30.21%, were obese compared to the "no" or CIS, 32.85%.

Next, in Table 19.3 we explored the intersection of race and ethnicity and gender. The BRFSS includes data on eight race and ethnicity categories: Non-Hispanic White, Non-Hispanic Black, Non-Hispanic Native American, Non-Hispanic Asian, Non-Hispanic Hawaiian and Pacific Islander, Non-Hispanic Other, Non-Hispanic Multi, and Hispanic. We used the above gender categories: Do you consider yourself to be transgendered: Yes-Male to Female, Yes-Female to Male, and Yes-nonconforming to "others".

The basic finding is that the distributions of the race and ethnic categories across each of the four gender identity categories (the three transgender categories and the cisgender category) are significantly different. That is, race/ethnicity differs significantly by gender identity.

Table 19.4 continues to explore the intersectionality of gender identity status and education categories. The BRFSS 2020 SOGI education categories are: Never/Kindergarten, Elementary school, Some High School, GED or High School Graduation, Some College or Technical School, College Graduate, and Refused. The $\chi 2$ analyses indicate significant educational differences by gender identity.

Table 19.2 Number and percentage of BMI categories by transgender categories BRFSS SOGI Sample 2020

		Transgender categories				
Body Mass Index		Male to female	Female to male	Yes nonconforming	Other	Total
Underweight (BMI ≤ 18)	n	13	11	16	3596	3636
	%	3.88	3.4	6.27	1.67	1.68
	Weighted	4.22%	1.96%	3.30%	1.94%	1.94%
Normal (BMI 18.5/25)	n	102	103	86	66,135	66,426
	%	30.45	31.79	33.73	30.66	30.67
	Weighted	34.68%	43.81%	41.66%	30.36%	30.41%
Overweight (BMI 25/30)	n	104	92	75	76,959	77,230
	%	31.04	28.4	29.41	35.68	35.66
	Weighted	27.51%	24.03%	21.98%	34.86%	34.80%
Obese (BMI ≥ 30)	n	116	118	78	68,993	69,305
	%	34.63	36.42	30.59	31.99	32
	Weighted	33.59%	30.21%	33.07%	32.85%	32.85%
	Total	335	324	255	215,683	216,597
		100	100	100	100	100

Source: BRFSS SOGI Sample 2020, STATA 11.1 Survey Weighted Analysis
χ^2 (9) = 61.0155, p = 0.000

Table 19.3 Number and percentage of race/ethnicity categories by transgender categories

Race/ethnicity		Transgender categories: Male to female	Female to male	Yes nonconforming	Other	Total
NH White	n	229	229	171	175,798	176,427
	%	61.56	62.4	61.51	73.55	73.5
	Weighted	55.56%	35.38%	53.87%	58.56%	58.50%
NH Black	n	23	22	13	15,810	15,868
	%	6.18	5.99	4.68	6.61	6.61
	Weighted	9.22%	7.92%	8.57%	11.28%	11.26%
NH Native American	n	8	7	7	3783	3805
	%	2.15	1.91	2.52	1.58	1.59
	Weighted	0.69%	0.51%	1.24%	0.93%	0.93%
NH Asian	n	14	23	10	7421	7468
	%	3.76	6.27	3.6	3.1	3.11
	Weighted	6.13%	23.38%	2.12%	6.17%	6.20%
NH Hawaiian/Pac Islander	n	7	11	3	1716	1737
	%	1.88	3	1.08	0.72	0.72
	Weighted	0.26%	0.81%	0.53%	0.20%	0.20%
NH other	n	5	2	3	2121	2131
	%	1.34	0.54	1.08	0.89	0.89
	Weighted	0.32%	0.45%	0.34%	0.61%	0.61%
NH multi	n	18	14	26	5699	5757
	%	4.84	3.81	9.35	2.38	2.4
	Weighted	1.78%	4.03%	7.60%	1.32%	1.33%
Hispanic	n	58	51	33	21,172	21,314
	%	15.59	13.9	11.87	8.86	8.88
	Weighted	24.25%	26.20%	20.73%	18.77%	18.79%
Refused	n	10	8	12	5485	5515
	%	2.69	2.18	4.32	2.29	2.3
	Weighted	1.79%	1.32%	4.99%	2.17%	2.17%
Total		372	367	278	239,005	240,022
		100	100	100	100	100

Source: BRFSS SOGI Sample 2020, STATA 11.1 Survey Weighted Analysis
$Chi^2(24) = 176.94$ $Pr = 0.000$

Table 19.5 continues to explore the intersectionality of gender status and employment categories. The BRFSS 2020 SOGI surveys the employment categories of Employed for wage, self-employed, not working for 1 year, not working for less than 1 year, homemaker, student, retired, unable to work and refused. Once again, we see differences. That is, the distribution of the employment categories differs significantly by gender identity.

Table 19.6 continues to explore the intersectionality of sexual orientation and general health status. Health categories include: Excellent, Very Good, Good, Fair, Poor, Don't Know, and Refused. While fewer of the transgendered report excellent health, or very good health, they begin to gain equity with respect to good health. Overall, as with the previous analyses, we see differences. That is, the distribution of the health status categories differs significantly by gender identity.

Table 19.7 concludes our analyses with multinomial logistic regression analyses, with coefficients and t-tests of the relationships between gender identity and the independent variables of Obesity (Yes/No), Black Race, Hispanic Ethnicity, Education levels, ranging from 1 (None/Kindergarten) to 6 (college graduate).

Table 19.4 Number and percentage of education categories by transgender categories

		Transgender categories				
Education		Male to female	Female to male	Yes nonconforming	Other	Total
Never/kinder	n	5	1	0	305	311
	%	1.34	0.27	0	0.13	0.13
	Weighted	3.87%	0.14%	0.00%	0.33%	0.34%
Elementary	n	23	18	17	4684	4742
	%	6.18	4.9	6.12	1.96	1.98
	Weighted	5.38%	27.47%	6.39%	4.42%	4.47%
Some high school	n	33	20	20	10,393	10,466
	%	8.87	5.45	7.19	4.35	4.36
	Weighted	10.61%	7.24%	9.67%	8.43%	8.44%
Ged/graduate	n	134	121	88	63,153	63,496
	%	36.02	32.97	31.65	26.42	26.45
	Weighted	30.50%	31.21%	29.67%	27.31%	27.33%
Some college/tech	n	99	101	78	66,477	66,755
	%	26.61	27.52	28.06	27.81	27.81
	Weighted	33.58%	17.90%	34.76%	30.69%	30.68%
College grad	n	74	102	74	92,974	93,224
	%	19.89	27.79	26.62	38.9	38.84
	Weighted	14.98%	15.17%	19.40%	28.36%	28.30%
Refused	n	4	4	1	1017	1026
	%	1.08	1.09	0.36	0.43	0.43
	Weighted	1.08%	0.86%	0.11%	0.45%	0.45%
Total	n	372	367	278	239,003	240,020
	%	100	100	100	100	100

Source: BRFSS SOGI Sample 2020, STATA 11.1 Survey Weighted Analysis
$\text{Chi}^2(18) = 226.792$, Pr = 0.000

Five Multinomial Logistic Regression equations are estimated with the results presented in Table 19.7. Each equation has three sub-equations, one for each of the three transgender groups (the cisgendered group is the reference group). Our major interest is with Model 1, and then with Model 5.

Model 1 has only one independent variable, obesity; Model 2 adds Black race and Hispanic Ethnicity; Model 3 adds Education level; Model 4 adds Employed for wages; and Model 5 adds General Health. Most notable is the lack of statistical significance and the direction of the relationships. In each of the three sub-equations reported in Model 1, obesity is not related to any of the three transgender identity groups. As noted, these equations only include the single independent variable of obesity.

This lack of an association between obesity and gender identity persists across the equations in Models 2, 3, 4 and 5. Adding other independent variables in these models does not result in any changes in the relationships between obesity and gender identity. All of the relationships between obesity and gender identity are not statistically significant.

Conclusion and Directions for Future Research

This chapter reviewed the limited demographic research addressing the transgendered populations and obesity. The consensus from current studies is that while sexual minorities may have weight related issues, the relationships among gender identity and weight are understudied. We support the inclusion of gender identity in federal and other large-scale surveys to address these research gaps. To provide some

Table 19.5 Number and percentage of employment status by transgender categories

		Transgender categories				
Employment status		Male to female	Female to male	Yes nonconforming	Other	Total
Employed	n	140	139	98	99,586	99,963
	%	37.63	38.08	35.64	41.89	41.87
	Weighted	39.79%	52.69%	39.42%	45.52%	45.52%
Self-employed	n	29	26	25	20,398	20,478
	%	7.8	7.12	9.09	8.58	8.58
	Weighted	7.35%	5.68%	8.74%	8.71%	8.70%
Not working (more than 1 year)	n	19	10	16	4349	4394
	%	5.11	2.74	5.82	1.83	1.84
	Weighted	4.25%	5.73%	7.29%	2.35%	2.37%
Not working (less than 1 year)	n	24	37	29	10,371	10,461
	%	6.45	10.14	10.55	4.36	4.38
	Weighted	5.04%	7.45%	14.12%	5.63%	5.64%
Homemaker	n	12	13	9	10,395	10,429
	%	3.23	3.56	3.27	4.37	4.37
	Weighted	4.18%	2.52%	1.96%	5.25%	5.24%
Student	n	21	28	29	6162	6240
	%	5.65	7.67	10.55	2.59	2.61
	Weighted	8.30%	7.49%	10.02%	5.02%	5.04%
Retired	n	70	64	43	68,982	69,159
	%	18.82	17.53	15.64	29.02	28.97
	Weighted	15.07%	6.47%	9.58%	19.78%	19.73%
Unable to work	n	50	45	25	15,096	15,216
	%	13.44	12.33	9.09	6.35	6.37
	Weighted	11.79%	11.35%	8.34%	6.53%	6.55%
Refused	n	7	3	1	2396	2407
	%	1.88	0.82	0.36	1.01	1.01
	Weighted	4.23%	0.63%	0.54%	1.21%	1.21%
Total	n	372	365	275	237,735	238,747
	%	100	100	100	100	100

Source: BRFSS SOGI Sample 2020, STATA 11.1 Survey Weighted Analysis
$Chi^2(24) = 330.4739$, $Pr = 0.0$

insight into the available datasets that may permit population-based research on transgendered persons, we first examined six surveys that include gender identity questions: Population Assessment of Tobacco and Health (PATH), Behavior Risk Factor Surveillance System (BRFSS), National Adult Tobacco Survey (NATS), National Crime Victimization Survey (NCVS), National Inmate Survey (NIS), and the Health Center Patient Survey (HCPS). These surveys are evidence of the growing acceptance of the necessity of including gender identification in large scale research.

Next, we addressed the initial findings from these surveys. Various researchers, namely, Lagos and Compton (2021), Suarez et al. (2019) using data from the 2018 GSS, and Gorman and Oyarvide (2018) and Suarez et al. (2021) using BRFSS, have begun to study the transgendered. Thus, the efforts of the SOGI working group's efforts to include the transgendered in population research are beginning to produce research about this underrepresented population. Our analyses of the BRFSS 2020 SOGI sample support this need.

We included an analysis of the BRFSS 2020 SOGI sample. We found few significant

Table 19.6 Number and percentage of general health status by transgender categories

General health		Transgender categories				
Status		Male to female	Female to male	Yes nonconforming	Other	Total
Excellent	n	59	60	39	48,394	48,552
	%	15.86	16.35	14.03	20.25	20.23
	Weighted	18.79%	13.41%	14.69%	21.51%	21.48%
Very good	n	104	111	76	82,590	82,881
	%	27.96	30.25	27.34	34.56	34.53
	Weighted	29.72%	18.52%	25.80%	32.82%	32.77%
Good	n	120	116	87	71,360	71,683
	%	32.26	31.61	31.29	29.86	29.87
	Weighted	34.53%	47.72%	33.44%	30.54%	30.59%
Fair	n	62	47	50	27,041	27,200
	%	16.67	12.81	17.99	11.31	11.33
	Weighted	8.46%	12.67%	18.48%	11.40%	11.41%
Poor	n	25	29	24	9045	9123
	%	6.72	7.9	8.63	3.78	3.8
	Weighted	7.98%	5.70%	7.01%	3.51%	3.53%
Don't know	n	2	4	2	380	388
	%	0.54	1.09	0.72	0.16	0.16
	Weighted	0.52%	1.99%	0.58%	0.14%	0.15%
Refused	n	0	0	0	192	192
	%	0	0	0	0.08	0.08
	Weighted	0.00%	0.00%	0.00%	0.07%	0.07%
Total	n	372	367	278	239,002	240,019
	%	100	100	100	100	100

Source: BRFSS SOGI Sample 2020, STATA 11.1 Survey Weighted Analysis
Chi2(18) = 115.5567, Pr. = 0.0

differences in obesity among the three Transgendered categories, although greater percentages of trans M to F are underweight. Of interest is that transgendered individuals reported lower general health, lower education levels, and less employment for wages as well as inability to work. This may suggest that both underweight status and obesity are related to the intersectionality of gender, socioeconomic, and status conditions than gender orientation alone. Ongoing work is needed to investigate further the extent to which transgender individuals experience weight-related issues and if so, what factors might account for this.

Conron and O'Neill (2021) found that the transgendered are more likely to be food insecure, and this seems to be intensified by the intersectionality of other socioeconomic conditions. Food insecurity is more pronounced in transgendered persons of color. Education does not appear to remove the disparities in food insecurity. These disparities suggest possible support for a model proposed by Lick et al. (2013) indicating that sociocultural factors predispose sexual minorities to have poorer physical health.

First and foremost, we agree with Emlet that "while the acronym LGBT may unintentionally signal a single population, these individuals are unique unto themselves, but also comprise a variety of sub-populations defined by sexual orientation, gender identity, and other factors" (Emlet, 2016, p. 20). Thus, it is vital to include the variety of these sub-populations in demographic research. The push for the inclusion of gender orientation by numerous agencies and working groups and the addition of gender to federal surveys indicates that we are on the cusp of greater availability of data for demographic analyses of the transgendered at a time when there is an increased social and political

Table 19.7 Multinomial logistic regression equation weighted coefficients and t-test values: trans identified male to female, female to male, and nonconforming (cisgendered as reference) regressed on independent variables of obesity (yes/no) and race, hispanic, education, employment, and health 2020 BRFSS Data

Independent	Model-1		Model-2		Model-3		Model-4		Model-5	
Variable	Coef	t	Coef	t	Coef	t	Coef	t	Coef	t
Trans male to female										
Obese (yes = 1)	0.04	0.13	0.03	0.12	0.00	0.01	0.01	0.02	−0.02	−0.06
Black (yes = 1)			−0.17	−0.48	−0.24	−0.65	−0.23	−0.64	−0.24	−0.66
Hispanic (yes = 1)			0.37	0.15	0.14	0.48	0.15	0.52	0.15	0.51
Education[a]					−0.25	−2.65	−0.24	−2.32	−0.23	−2.06
Employed for wage							−0.15	−0.66	−0.13	−0.58
General health[b]									−0.06	−0.56
Constant	−6.84	−60.7	−6.90	−61.3	−55.68	−12.3	−55.67	−12.4	−5.53	−12.5
Trans female to male										
Obese (yes = 1)	−0.07	−0.17	−0.06	−0.18	−0.12	−0.34	−0.13	−0.36	−0.18	−0.51
Black (yes = 1)			−0.31	−0.80	−0.45	−1.00	−0.45	−1.01	−0.46	−1.04
Hispanic (yes = 1)			−0.47	−0.40	−0.14	−0.18	−0.19	−0.23	−0.20	−0.24
Education[a]					−0.58	−1.76	−0.62	−1.68	−0.59	−1.61
Employed for wage							0.52	0.94	0.59	1.01
General health[b]									−0.16	−1.69
Constant	−6.65	−23.1	−6.70	−18.2	−4.04	−2.30	−4.11	−2.48	−3.69	−2.12
Trans nonconforming										
Obese (yes = 1)	0.12	0.48	0.13	0.52	0.11	0.43	0.11	0.65	0.01	0.05
Black (yes = 1)			−0.30	−0.90	−0.35	−0.95	−0.35	−0.94	−0.38	−1.01
Hispanic (yes = 1)			0.16	0.43	0.01	0.03	0.03	0.46	0.02	0.05
Education[a]					−0.16	−1.61	−0.14	−1.42	−0.09	−0.86
Employed for wage							−0.21	−0.23	−0.12	−0.47
General health[b]									−0.26	−2.66
Constant	−6.96	−54.6	−6.96	−53.7	−6.19	−11.6	−6.18	−1.63	−5.53	−10.6

[a] 1 = none to 6 college graduate
[b] 1 = poor to 5 = excellent

acceptance of gender fluidity. Yet, there is still much to be done.

As stated by Lim (2014) we need good quality data to be able to address the health needs of LGBTQ population. We also need good quality data to plan for the financial coverage of the medical needs of the transgendered. Relatedly, we need to be able to train medical and health professionals so that they can be effective in treating the variety of sub-populations.

One area of study that needs to be expanded focuses on the importance of family in transgender research. Specifically, there is an unmet need for specific studies of family relationships for bisexual and transgender people and how these may change over the life course. Family relationships may be significantly altered as transgendered individuals assume a new name, gender pronouns and status within the family. Family members may also experience the grief of the loss of their family member. This also involves building different relationships with their community and the communities of family members, their parents and siblings, their partners, children, etc. (Biblarz & Savci, 2010, p. 492). The health implications of these transitions should be explored in more depth.

Another area of needed work relates to the aging of the population. Several scholars have called for increased attention to the services needed by growing population of aging transgendered individuals (Fredriksen-Goldsen, 2016; Jura & Kozak, 2016; Witten, 2016). This population has likely faced multiple years of minority related issues of stress, limited health access, and lower income and these are likely linked to health consequences. Finally, Adams (2016, p. 94) has suggested that there is a severe scarcity of data pertaining to LGBT older adults including the intersectionality of race, gender, gender identity, and socioeconomic status. This is an additional area of needed research in the future.

References

Adams, M. (2016). An intersectional approach to services and care for LGBT elders. *Generations: Journal of the American Society on Aging, 40*(2), 94–100. https://doi.org/10.1230/26556217

Arthur, S., Jamieson, A., Cross, H., Nambiar, K., & Llewellyn, C. D. (2021). Medical students' awareness of health issues, attitudes, and confidence about caring for lesbian, gay, bisexual and transgender patients: A cross-sectional survey. *BMC Medical Education, 21*(1), 56–56. https://doi.org/10.1186/s12909-020-02409-6

Austin, S. B., Ziyadeh, N. J., Corliss, H. L., Haines, J., Rockett, H. R., Wypij, D., & Field, A. E. (2009). Sexual orientation disparities in weight status in adolescence: Findings from a prospective study. *Obesity (Silver Spring, Md.), 17*(9), 1776–1782. https://doi.org/10.1038/oby.2009.72

Austin, S. B., Nelson, L. A., Birkett, M. A., Calzo, J. P., & Everett, B. (2013). Eating disorder symptoms and obesity at the intersections of gender, ethnicity, and sexual orientation in US high school students. *American Journal of Public Health (1971), 103*(2), e16–e22. https://doi.org/10.2105/AJPH.2012.301150

Bandini, E., Fisher, A. D., Castellini, G., Lo Sauro, C., Lelli, L., Meriggiola, M. C., Casale, H., Benni, L., Ferruccio, N., Faravelli, C., Dettore, D., Maggi, M., & Ricca, V. (2013). Gender identity disorder and eating disorders: Similarities and differences in terms of body uneasiness. *The Journal of Sexual Medicine, 10*(4), 1012–1023. https://doi.org/10.1111/jsm.12062

Baumle, A. K. (2013). *International handbook on the demography of sexuality*. Springer. https://doi.org/10.1007/978-94-007-5512-3

Biblarz, T., & Savci, E. (2010). Lesbian, gay, bisexual, and transgender families. *Journal of Marriage and Family, 72*(3), 480–497. Retrieved 12 Feb 2021 from http://www.jstor.org.ezproxy.lib.uh.edu/stable/40732492

Bishop, A., Overcash, F., McGuire, J., & Reicks, M. (2020). Diet and physical activity behaviors among adolescent transgender students: School survey results. *Journal of Adolescent Health, 66*(4), 484–490.

Bowen, D. J., Balsam, K. F., & Ender, S. R. (2008). A review of obesity issues in sexual minority women. *Obesity, 16*, 221–228.

Calzo, J. P., Corliss, H. L., Blood, E. A., Field, A. E., & Austin, S. B. (2013). Development of muscularity and weight concerns in heterosexual and sexual minority males. *Health Psychology, 32*(1), 42–51. https://doi.org/10.1037/a0028964

Calzo, J. P., Masyn, K. E., Corliss, H. L., Scherer, E. A., Field, A. E., & Austin, S. B. (2015). Patterns of body image concerns and disordered weight- and shape-related behaviors in heterosexual and sexual minority adolescent males. *Developmental Psychology, 51*(9), 1216–1225. https://doi.org/10.1037/dev0000027

Centers for Disease Control and Prevention. (2014a). *NATS codebook*. Retrieved from https://www.cdc.gov/tobacco/data_statistics/surveys/nats/pdfs/2013-2014-code-book-tag508.pdf

Centers for Disease Control and Prevention. (2014b). *Behavioral risk factor surveillance system overview: BRFSS 2013*. Retrieved July 19, 2022 from https://www.cdc.gov/brfss/annual_data/2013/pdf/Overview_2013.pdf

Centers for Disease Control and Prevention. (2022). *Behavioral risk factor surveillance system: 2019 and 2020 data*. Retrieved from https://www.cdc.gov/brfss/index.html

Center of Excellence for Transgender Health at the University of California at San Francisco. *Policy recommendations for inclusive data collection of trans people in HIV prevention, care & services*. Retrieved from http://transhealth.ucsf.edu/trans?page=lib-data-collection

Conron, K. J., & O'Neill, K. K. (2021). *Food insufficiency among transgender adults during the COVID-19 pandemic*. Williams Institute. Retrieved from https://williamsinstitute.law.ucla.edu/publications/trans-food-insufficiency-covid/

Conron, K. J., Scott, G., Stowell, G. S., & Landers, S. J. (2012). Transgender health in Massachusetts: Results from a household probability sample of adults. *American Journal of Public Health, 102*, 118–122.

Doan, P. (2016). To count or not to count: Queering measurement and the transgender community. *Women's Studies Quarterly, 44*(3/4), 89–110. Retrieved from http://www.jstor.org.ezproxy.uno.edu/stable/44474064

Emlet, C. (2016). Social, economic, and health disparities among LGBT older adults. *Generations: Journal of the American Society on Aging, 40*(2), 16–22. https://doi.org/10.2307/26556193

Federal Interagency Working Group of Improving Measurement of Sexual Orientation and Gender Identity in Federal Surveys/SOGI. (2016). *Current measures of sexual orientation and gender identity in federal surveys*. Retrieved from https://nces.ed.gov/FCSM/pdf/buda5.pdf

Fredriksen-Goldsen, K. (2016). The future of LGBT aging: A blueprint for action in services, policies, and research. *Generations: Journal of the American Society on Aging, 40*(2), 6–15. https://doi.org/10.2307/26556192

Gates, G. J. (2011). *How many people are lesbian, gay, bisexual, and transgender?* The Williams Institute, UCLA School of Law.

General Social Survey. (2019). *GSS godebook*. Retrieved from https://gss.norc.org/documents/codebook/gss_codebook.pdf

Gorman, B., & Oyarvide, Z. (2018). Sexual orientation, socioeconomic status, and healthy aging. *Generations: Journal of the American Society on Aging, 42*(2), 56–60. https://doi.org/10.2307/26556361

Harris, B. C. (2015). *Likely transgender individuals in U.S. federal administrative records and the 2010 census*. Retrieved from https://www.census.gov/content/dam/Census/library/working-papers/2015/adrm/carra-wp-2015-03.pdf

IOM (Institute of Medicine). (2011). *The health of lesbian, gay, bisexual, and transgender people: Building a foundation for better understanding*. The National Academies Press.

Jura, M., & Kozak, L. P. (2016). Obesity and related consequences to ageing. *Age (Dordrecht, Netherlands), 38*(1), 23. https://doi.org/10.1007/s11357-016-9884-3

Kinsey Institute. (2019). *Diversity of sexual orientation*. Retrieved from https://kinseyinstitute.org/research/publications/historical-report-diversity-of-sexual-orientation.php

Kinsey, A. C., Pomeroy, W. B., & Martin, C. E. (1948). *The sexual behavior in the human male*. W. B. Sanders and Company.

Lagos, D., & Compton, D. L. (2021). Evaluating the use of a two-step gender identity measure in the 2018 general social survey. *Demography, 58*(2), 763–772. https://doi.org/10.1215/00703370-8976151

Lick, D., Durso, L., & Johnson, K. (2013). Minority stress and physical health among sexual minorities. *Perspectives on Psychological Science, 8*(5), 521–548. Retrieved 12 Feb 2021 from http://www.jstor.org.ezproxy.lib.uh.edu/stable/44289924

Lim, F., Brown, D., & Kim, S. (2014). Addressing health care disparities in the lesbian, gay, bisexual, and transgender population: A review of best practices. *The American Journal of Nursing, 114*(6), 24–35. Retrieved 10 Feb 2021 from http://www.jstor.org.ezproxy.lib.uh.edu/stable/24466535

Meier, S. C., & Labuski, C. M. (2013). The demographics of the transgender population. In A. K. Baumle (Ed.), *International handbook on the demography of sexuality*. New York.

Meyerowitz, J. (2001). Sex research at the borders of gender: Transvestites, transsexuals, and Alfred C. Kinsey. *Bulletin of the History of Medicine, 75*(1), 72–90. Retrieved 14 Jan 2021 from http://www.jstor.org/stable/44445556

Miller, J. M., & Luk, J. W. (2018). A systematic review of sexual orientation disparities in disordered eating and weight-related behaviors among adolescents and young adults: Toward a developmental model. *Adolescent Research Review, 4*(2), 187–208. https://doi.org/10.1007/s40894-018-0079-2

Morris, J. (1974). *Conundrum*. New York Review Books.

National Center for Transgender Equality. (n.d.). Retrieved from https://transequality.org/know-your-rights/social-security

National Resource Center on LGBT Aging. (2014). *Inclusive questions for older adults: A practical guide to collecting data on sexual orientation and gender identity*. Washington. http://issuu.com/lgbtagingcenter/docs/inclusivequestionsolder_adults_guidebook/1?e=0

National Survey of Family Growth. (2020). *About the National Survey of Family Growth*. Retrieved from https://www.cdc.gov/nchs/nsfg/about_nsfg.htm#cycles1

Olyslager, F., & Conway, L. (2007). *On the calculation of the prevalence of transsexualism*. Paper presented at the WPATH 20th International Symposium, Chicago, Illinois.

Proctor, K., Haffer, S. C., Ewald, E., Hodge, C., & James, C. V. (2016). Identifying the transgender population in the medicare program. *Transgender Health, 1*(1), 2016. https://doi.org/10.1089/trgh.2016.0031

Sackey, J., DallaPiazza, M., Bentsianov, S., & Finkel, D. (2021). Overweight and obesity among adults identifying on the transgender spectrum in Newark, NJ between 2018 and 2020: A retrospective chart review. *Current Developments in Nutrition, 5*(Suppl 2), 1244.

Sexual Minority Assessment Research Team (SMART). (2009). *Best practices for asking questions about sexual orientation on surveys*. Los Angeles, CA: The Williams Institute, UCLA School of Law. Available from: http://williamsinstitute.law.ucla.edu/wp-content/uploads/SMART-FINAL-Nov-2009.pdf

Social Security. (2013). *Program operations manual*. Retrieved from https://secure.ssa.gov/poms.nsf/lnx/0110212200

Spade, D. (2008). Documenting gender. *Hastings Law Journal, 59*, 731–842. Available from http://williamsinstitute.law.ucla.edu/wp-content/uploads/Spade-Documenting-Gender-Apr-2008.pdf

Suarez, M. I., Marquez-Velarde, G., & Poston, D. L. (2019). *Demographic and socioeconomic analyses of the transgender and cisgender populations*. Presented at the Southern Demographic Association Annual Meeting.

Suarez, M. I., Marquez-Velarde, G., & Poston, D. L. (2021). *Demographic and socioeconomic analyses of the transgender and cisgender populations*. Presented at the International Sociological Association Meeting.

The Gender Identity in U.S. Surveillance Group. (2014). *Best practices for asking questions to identify transgender and other gender minority respondents on population-based surveys*. Los Angeles. Retrieved from http://williamsinstitute.law.ucla.edu/wp-content/uploads/geniuss-reportsep-2014.pdf

U. S. Census. (n.d.). Research Data Center (RDC). Retrieved from https://www.cdc.gov/rdc/index.htm

VanKim, N. A., Erickson, D. J., Eisenberg, M. E., Lust, K., Rosser, B. R., & Laska, M. N. (2014). Weight-related disparities for transgender college students. *Health Behavior and Policy Review, 1*(2), 161–171.

Vocks, S., Stahn, C., Loenser, K., & Legenbauer, T. (2003). Eating and body image disturbances in male-to-female and female-to-male transsexuals. *Archives of Sexual Behavior, 38*(3), 364–377.

Westat. (2019). *PATH study public use user files.* Retrieved from https://www.icpsr.umich.edu/files/NAHDAP/documentation/ug36498-all.pdf

Williams Institute, et al. (2014). *Sexual and gender minority youth in foster care: Assessing disproportionality and disparities in Los Angeles.* Los Angeles. Retrieved from http://williamsinstitute.law.ucla.edu/wp-content/uploads/LAFYS_report_finalaug-2014.pdf

Williams Institute. (2022). *How many adults and youth identify as transgender in the United States?* Los Angeles. Retrieved from https://williamsinstitute.law.ucla.edu/publications/trans-adults-united-states/

Witten, T. (2016). The intersectional challenges of aging and of being a gender non- conforming adult. *Generations: Journal of the American Society on Aging, 40*(2), 63–70. https://doi.org/10.2307/26556204

20 Conclusions, Review, and Needed Research

Ginny Garcia-Alexander

The chapters in this *Handbook* have covered a number of topic areas within the range of research conducted by demographers on obesity. This is a lively area of study with notable empirical and theoretical contributions. For example, demographers have played a vital role in detailing trends and tracking the severity of obesity across the globe. Global surveillance efforts have intensified with the growing awareness of the extent of obesity at all levels of socioeconomic development. These efforts were described in reference to a number of key countries and regions in Chap. 2 of this volume. Vidra and colleagues (Chap. 4) extended this discussion with their focus on European countries. Gu and colleagues (Chap. 5) described the trends and implications of increasing obesity prevalence in China; their chapter offers much needed insights into the unique structures and institutions in Chinese society in order to provide a clearer accounting of the factors that promote rising obesity levels. Furthermore, their review underscores the fact that more work is needed to fully describe and understand these patterns, particularly with respect to the role of urbanization and marketization. More broadly, the chapters in this *Handbook* suggest an urgent need for ongoing surveillance of global obesity trends for decades to come.

Demographic studies linking obesity with excess morbidity and mortality have been especially relevant and important and continue to produce important advances in our understanding of the health implications associated with overweight and obesity. Notably, this area of study has convincingly linked obesity, especially severe obesity, with the increased risk of mortality. In Chap. 4, Vidra and colleagues offered an analysis of obesity's impacts to life expectancy in 26 European countries and the United States. Their results suggest that the share of all-cause mortality attributable to obesity has increased over time. Adding to the existing body of knowledge documenting the negative impacts of excess weight, they found that while life expectancy increased over the study period, these increases would have been greater if not for obesity. Indeed, they argued that the negative effects of obesity are akin to those of smoking and alcohol on mortality risk. In Chap. 6, Mehta reviewed the literature linking obesity and mortality. He too argued that the mortality risk associated with obesity is substantial. Importantly, the impacts of obesity on morbidity and mortality are expected to accelerate as a product of increasing obesity prevalence across the globe, increased severity, and longer exposure in younger generations. As such, demographers will continue to play an important role in understanding these impacts and associations.

Beyond the health implications associated with obesity, demographers have done a great

G. Garcia-Alexander (✉)
Department of Sociology, University of Texas at San Antonio, San Antonio, TX, USA
e-mail: ginny.garcia@utsa.edu

G. Garcia-Alexander, D. L. Poston, Jr. (eds.), *International Handbook of the Demography of Obesity*, International Handbooks of Population 12, https://doi.org/10.1007/978-3-031-10936-2_20

deal to characterize and understand its economic and social implications. In Chap. 3, Viinikainen and colleagues summarized the evidence on the indirect economic costs associated with obesity in European countries. Their review offers three key insights. First, excess weight is negatively associated with labor market outcomes. Second, this negative association is present across European countries despite substantial differences in labor markets and cultural contexts. Third, European women suffer fewer wage-related obesity penalties in comparison to American women. Overall, the authors offered convincing evidence of the negative effects of obesity that warrant ongoing study.

Much of the demographic research on obesity has been devoted to describing and identifying disparities in its prevalence. Accordingly, several chapters in this *Handbook* described disparate outcomes in obesity that are patterned by race, ethnicity, nativity, and socioeconomic status, among others. A large body of evidence has documented persistent disparities by race, sex, and socioeconomic status, and these are expected to worsen over time. Demographers have been vital to the development of this research and will need to expand their investigations in various ways. For example, Frisco and her colleagues (Chap. 8), as well as Krueger and his colleagues (Chap. 9), pointed to several needed expansions including a greater focus on understudied populations (e.g., American Indian and Alaska Native and Black women); increased attention to the structural factors that lead to greater exposure to risk in disadvantaged populations (e.g. segregation and uneven exposure to environmental risk); and investigations that utilize more advanced methodological tools to more accurately capture exposure to risk. Garcia-Alexander and Marroquin (Chap. 7) described important advancements made by demographers studying immigration and obesity, most notably pertaining to the role of acculturation and health selection. But, there is an ongoing need for studies that consider pre- and post-immigration contexts, how increasingly hostile social environments may negatively impact the health of immigrants, and how health advantages may erode over time.

Many of the contributions in this *Handbook* focused on areas of study that have received comparatively less attention in the literature. These chapters offered numerous insights into the mechanisms that are helpful for understanding increasing obesity prevalence. For example, Cuevas and his colleagues (Chap. 12) underscored the importance of psychosocial stressors (childhood adversity, discrimination, neighborhood stress) that are connected to obesity risk via multiple pathways. Lopez and Anderson (Chap. 13) considered the role of stress in addition to a number of other neighborhood characteristics that may increase or offset obesity risk. Falbo and Lin (Chap. 10) examined how family structures, i.e. sibling effects, may impact obesity. Their review concluded that children without siblings are at a greater risk of obesity, and this is largely a product of differential diet and activity patterns. They offered several suggestions for further investigation.

Hill and colleagues (Chap. 11) described the body of research on religion and body mass. Their review, which included both national and international studies, revealed mixed findings. Specifically, they found a number of studies documenting a lack of association, a relatively sizeable number of studies indicating that religion is associated with greater body mass, and a small minority of studies indicating religious individuals may be leaner. This is somewhat inconsistent with the larger body of research on health and religion, which has long documented a beneficial effect. The authors attributed these inconsistencies to underdeveloped and inconsistently applied measures of body mass and religion, and they called for both theoretical and methodological advancements in order to progress this area of study. Kennel and colleagues (Chap. 14) described how obesity may impact treatment outcomes in emergency medical services (EMS). Their review described the harmful role of weight bias; yet, their analysis suggests a potentially protective effect with respect to pain outcomes. They offered several suggestions for how these paradoxical findings might be explored in future work.

The contributions on obesity in sexual minorities in this *Handbook* (Chaps. 15 through 19) described recommendations and best practices for the accurate measurement of both gender identity and sexual orientation. Each chapter included a review of the existing research and an analysis of representative data to provide additional insights into the patterns of overweight across sexual minority groups. Taken together, these chapters underscore the need to organize and reconcile inconsistent findings surrounding the presence of overweight and obesity in sexual minority populations, and they highlight the need for ongoing studies by population researchers.

Future Research Directions

The body of demographic work on obesity to date is far-ranging and has yielded many important insights. Yet, obesity levels continue to rise, and the implications of these increases have yet to be fully understood. Much work is needed to continue to track the extent and severity of obesity across the globe, identify protective factors, reduce or stem rising rates, and to fully establish the importance of the structural factors that promote global obesity.

A number of the contributors to this *Handbook* highlighted needed improvements to global monitoring and surveillance. This is necessary to determine the extent of obesity in locations that have not previously experienced widespread obesity, and to more closely examine levels in groups that have not previously been well-studied. Accordingly, efforts to collect high-quality data should be expanded as much as possible. We agree with Bentham and Di Cesare's (Chap. 2) assessment that these efforts should include NGOs, government agencies, and technical experts to maximize efficacy and impact. In addition, enhanced monitoring of food policies and environments that will enable cross-country comparisons may help to direct attention upstream and increase accountability among global actors that contribute to increased obesity (Swinburn et al., 2019). Ongoing comparative studies across countries are also needed, both to underscore the role of inequity and to establish the importance of various risk factors.

Many contributors to this *Handbook* also noted the shortcomings of BMI as an indicator of obesity and called for broader availability of expanded measures. Several noted the importance of measures such as waist-to-hip-ratio (WHR), weight histories, and/or more objective measures obtained via tracking devices or clinical assessments. Another area that could be expanded is related to the measurement of physical activity patterns. Future work should consider using more refined measures of activity to distinguish between levels of physical activity, physical inactivity, and sedentary behavior (i.e. waking behavior characterized by energy expenditure ≤ 1.5 METs while sitting or reclining) (Sedentary Behaviour Research Network, 2012) because some of these may be more relevant to obesity risk than others. Various forms of sedentary activity have been found to pose greater health risks (Biddle et al., 2016); this too is an area worthy of future study.

Another challenge to existing studies is the relative lack of longitudinal data. Many authors pointed to a variety of reasons why longitudinal data are so vital to ongoing research. For example, as younger generations face earlier exposure to obesity, age related effects will be important to track with longitudinal studies (see Chap. 6). Krueger and his colleagues pointed out how cumulative exposure to obesity and stressors may help us to understand disparate patterns of obesity. Studies using longitudinal data will also help to address issues of causality in studies of obesity. To the extent possible, researchers should utilize longitudinal data in their studies. Furthermore, data collection efforts should incorporate multiple measures of obesity, along with individual and contextual-level data.

Yet, demographers have applied innovations to overcome the shortcomings of existing measures and data. For example, multiple years of cross-sectional data have been combined to simulate cohorts in the absence of longitudinal data. In Chap. 6, Mehta described how weight histories offer another way capture the effects of obesity. He went on to describe how concepts such as peak BMI may be especially useful to studies assessing the risks associated with obesity. As mentioned by Hill and his colleagues in Chap. 11, demographers could also expand their studies via the use of growth curve analyses of body mass trajectories and fixed-effects models. Demographers should continue to apply these and other innovations to advance the field.

As was noted in several chapters, investigations of morbidity and mortality impacts have resulted in ongoing debates about the impact of obesity. One area of study has focused on the association between obesity and disability. Scholars have argued that obesity-associated morbidity risks seem to be increasing (Peeters & Backholer, 2012). Others have suggested that the obese population has experienced a leveling off or even an improving trend in recent years (Chang et al., 2017). Demographic work in this area needs to continue to document and clarify how excess weight impacts quality of life; and to examine how these associations may vary in subpopulations. Furthermore, it is unclear how this association will be changed as a result of COVID-19. A growing body of evidence indicates that obesity increases risk of severe COVID illness (Gao et al., 2021). Ongoing research is needed to determine the long-term implications of this finding.

A related finding is that the COVID-19 pandemic may have increased rates of overweight and obesity (e.g. Akter et al., 2022; Shalitin et al., 2022; Wu et al., 2022). A recently documented trend toward a leveling off of obesity prevalence in developed countries (Garcia-Gonzalez & Martin-Criado, 2022; Rokholm et al., 2010) may be reversed going forward. Further, it remains unclear how COVID-19 may have worsened obesity prevalence at various levels of development. This necessitates further study.

Several of the chapters in this *Handbook* identified important areas of study that have yet to be fully developed. For example, Hill and his colleagues identified several ways to expand theoretical and methodological approaches to the study of religion and obesity. Accordingly, they call for further study of the linkages (or lack thereof) between various measures of religion and body mass; increased attention to the mediators and moderators of the association between bodyweight and religion; and increased attention to the "dark side of religion" and its potential to worsen obesity-related outcomes.

In addition, the section on obesity in sexual minority populations reveals a great deal of opportunity for future investigations. For example, very little is known about obesity in transgendered populations. As more representative data become available, it will be important for researchers to provide reliable estimates of the extent of overweight or obesity in this group, and to conduct intersectional research that provides greater insights into observed disparities. Also, very few studies have focused on an emerging pattern that suggests sexual minority youth may have higher rates of obesity compared to heterosexual youth (Austin et al., 2009). This represents an important area of future investigation. Finally, more longitudinal research is needed along with work that can shed light on the mechanisms that increase risk in sexual minorities.

Demographers are particularly well-attuned to the broader contexts that shape population health. Increasing recognition of the economic conditions, food environments, and policies that promote global obesity will be needed in future research efforts. For example, studies of the food environment should focus on food swamps, or those areas with an abundance of unhealthy food, as this appears to have a stronger linkage with obesity than other measures (Cooksey-Stowers et al., 2017). In addition, the literature on the role of the neighborhood environment among immigrants has yielded mixed findings that warrant further study. Ongoing work should investigate the role of structural racism that may manifest itself via segregation, exposure to obsesogenic environments, and policy efforts that result in the exclusion of immigrants. Finally, an interesting area mentioned by several contributors relates to the role of air pollution. Several studies have shown that it increases the risk of obesity (Deschenes et al., 2020; Jerrett et al., 2014; Zhang et al., 2020), but this area is understudied and more work is needed to determine its effects, especially in developing countries.

Obesity is a complex issue, and its prevalence is on the rise across the globe. Demographic contributions to its analysis have resulted in an increased awareness of its prevalence, how it has and might be expected to impact various population subgroups, and the knowledge of its specific implications for population health and mortality. However, scholars continue to debate the source of its dramatic rise, and we have yet to realize its full impacts. Population health researchers should increasingly focus their efforts on identifying and understanding the root, or structural, causes of overweight and obesity via the use of multinational data sources and modeling strategies that appropriately account for the longitudinal and multi-level nature of the weight gain process. Importantly, population researchers are uniquely positioned to leverage perspectives from multiple disciplines to conduct these studies and provide nuanced interpretations of the complex web of factors that surround obesity prevalence. As such, demographers will continue to play an integral role in this area of study.

References

Akter, T., Zeba, Z., Hosen, I., Al-Mamun, F., & Mamun, M. A. (2022). Impact of the COVID-19 pandemic on BMI: Its changes in relation to socio-demographic and physical activity patterns based on a short period. *PLoS One, 17*(3), e0266024. https://doi.org/10.1371/journal.pone.0266024

Austin, S. B., Ziyadeh, N. J., Corliss, H. L., Haines, J., Rockett, H. R., Wypij, D., & Field, A. E. (2009). Sexual orientation disparities in weight status in adolescence: Findings from a prospective study. *Obesity (Silver Spring), 17*(9), 1776–1782. https://doi.org/10.1038/oby.2009.72

Biddle, S. J. H., Bennie, J. A., Bauman, A. E., Chau, J. Y., Dunstan, D., Owen, N., Stamatakis, E., & van Uffelen, J. G. Z. (2016). Too much sitting and all-cause mortality: Is there a causal link? *BMC Public Health, 16*(1), 635–635. https://doi.org/10.1186/s12889-016-3307-3

Chang, V. W., Alley, D. E., & Dowd, J. B. (2017). Trends in the relationship between obesity and disability, 1988–2012. *American Journal of Epidemiology, 186*(6), 688–695. https://doi.org/10.1093/aje/kwx092

Cooksey-Stowers, K., Schwartz, M. B., & Brownell, K. D. (2017). Food swamps predict obesity rates better than food deserts in the United States. *International Journal of Environmental Research and Public Health, 14*(11), 1366. Retrieved from https://www.mdpi.com/1660-4601/14/11/1366

Deschenes, O., Wang, H., Wang, S., & Zhang, P. (2020). The effect of air pollution on body weight and obesity: Evidence from China. *Journal of Development Economics, 145*, 102461.

Gao, M., Piernas, C., Astbury, N. M., Hippisley-Cox, J., O'Rahilly, S., Aveyard, P., & Jebb, S. A. (2021). Associations between body-mass index and COVID-19 severity in 6.9 million people in England: A prospective, community-based, cohort study. *The Lancet Diabetes and Endocrinology, 9*(6), 350–359. https://doi.org/10.1016/S2213-8587(21)00089-9

Garcia-Gonzalez, J. M., & Martin-Criado, E. (2022). A reversal in the obesity epidemic? A quasi-cohort and gender-oriented analysis in Spain. *Demographic Research, 46*(10), 273–290. Retrieved from https://www.demographic-research.org/volumes/vol46/10/

Jerrett, M., McConnell, R., Wolch, J., Chang, R., Lam, C., Dunton, G., Gilliland, F., Lurmann, F., Islam, T., & Berhane, K. (2014). Traffic-related air pollution and obesity formation in children: A longitudinal, multilevel analysis. *Environmental Health, 13*(1), 49–49. https://doi.org/10.1186/1476-069X-13-49

Peeters, A., & Backholer, K. (2012). Is the health burden associated with obesity changing? *American Journal of Epidemiology, 176*(10), 840–845. https://doi.org/10.1093/aje/kws328

Rokholm, B., Baker, J. L., & Soerensen, T. (2010). The levelling off of the obesity epidemic since the year 1999 – A review of evidence and perspectives. *Obesity Reviews, 11*(12), 835–846. https://doi.org/10.1111/j.1467-789X.2010.00810.x

Sedentary Behaviour Research Network. (2012). Letter to the Editor: Standardized use of the terms "sedentary" and "sedentary behaviours". *Applied Physiology, Nutrition, and Metabolism, 37*(3), 540–542. https://doi.org/10.1139/h2012-024

Shalitin, S., Phillip, M., & Yackobovitch-Gavan, M. (2022). Changes in body mass index in children and adolescents in Israel during the COVID-19 pandemic. *International Journal of Obesity, 46*(6), 1160–1167. https://doi.org/10.1038/s41366-022-01092-5

Swinburn, B. A., Kraak, V. I., Allender, S., Atkins, V. J., Baker, P. I., Bogard, J. R., et al. (2019). The global syndemic of obesity, undernutrition, and climate change: The Lancet Commission report. *The Lancet, 393*(10173), 791–846. https://doi.org/10.1016/S0140-6736(18)32822-8

Wu, Aris, I. M., Hivert, M.-F., Rocchio, C., Cocoros, N. M., Klompas, M., & Taveras, E. M. (2022). Association of changes in obesity prevalence with the COVID-19 pandemic in youth in Massachusetts. *Archives of Pediatrics & Adolescent Medicine, 176*(2), 198–201. https://doi.org/10.1001/jamapediatrics.2021.5095

Zhang, X., Zhang, M., Zhao, Z., Huang, Z., Deng, Q., Li, Y., et al. (2020). Obesogenic environmental factors of adult obesity in China: A nationally representative cross-sectional study. *Environmental Research Letters, 15*(4), 044009.

Index

G. Garcia-Alexander, D. L. Poston, Jr. (eds.), *International Handbook of the Demography of Obesity*, International Handbooks of Population 12, https://doi.org/10.1007/978-3-031-10936-2